Twentieth-Century World

Third Edition

Carter Vaughn Findley
The Ohio State University

John Alexander Murray Rothney
The Ohio State University

HOUGHTON MIFFLIN COMPANY Boston Toronto

Geneva, Illinois Palo Alto Princeton, New Jersey

Cover designer: Judy Arisman
Cover image: Space Shots, Inc.

Printed in the U.S.A.

Library of Congress Catalog Card Number:
93-78646

ISBN: 0-395-66863-8

1 2 3 4 5 6 7 8 9-DH-97 96 95 94 93

Topographical and Political Maps of the World, 1993

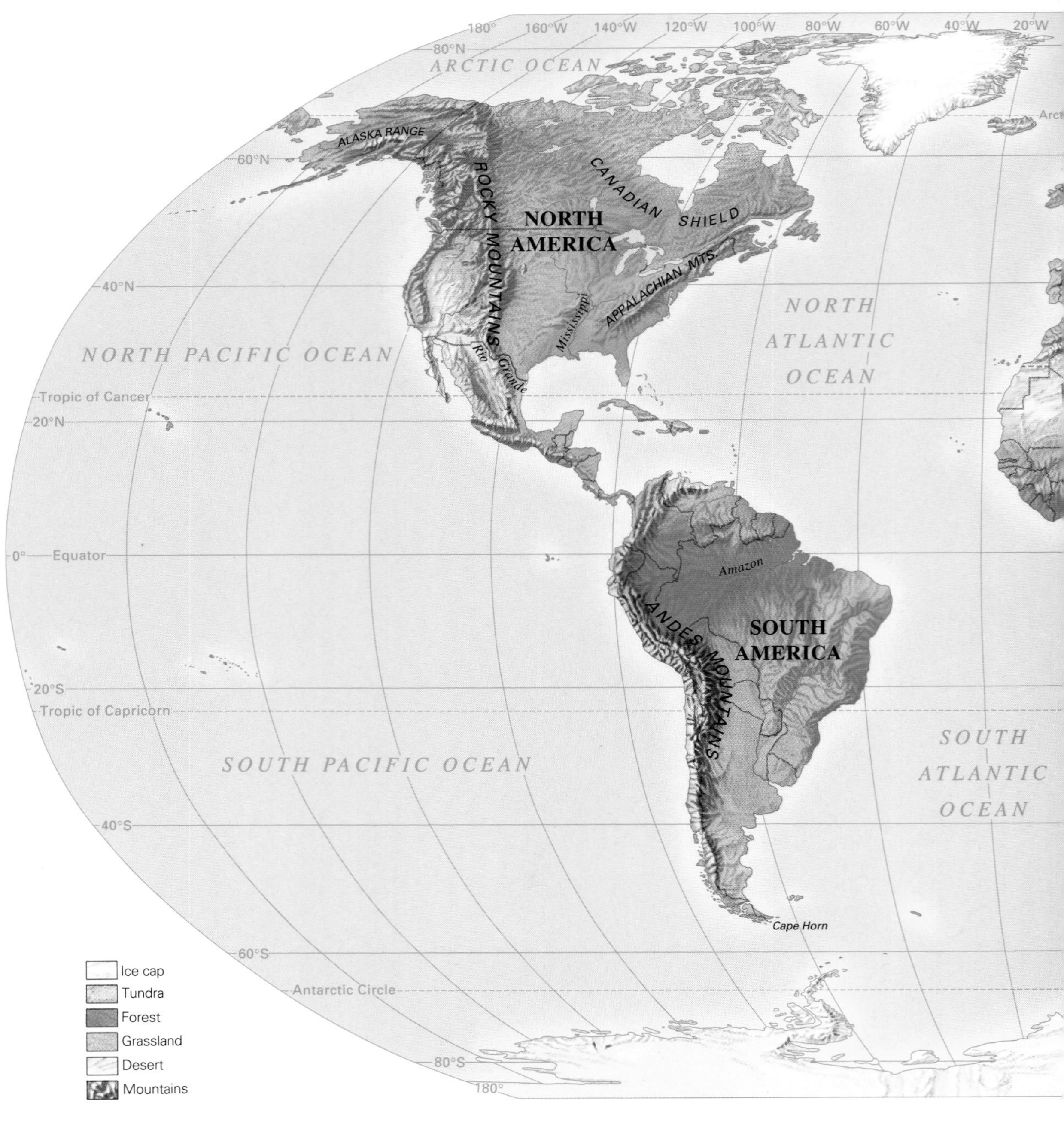

180°
160°W
140°W
120°W
100°W
80°W
60°W
40°W
20°W
80°N
ARCTIC OCEAN
ALASKA RANGE
60°N
ROCKY MOUNTAINS
CANADIAN SHIELD
NORTH AMERICA
APPALACHIAN MTS.
40°N
Mississippi
NORTH ATLANTIC OCEAN
NORTH PACIFIC OCEAN
Rio Grande
Tropic of Cancer
20°N
0° Equator
Amazon
ANDES MOUNTAINS
SOUTH AMERICA
20°S
Tropic of Capricorn
SOUTH PACIFIC OCEAN
SOUTH ATLANTIC OCEAN
40°S
Cape Horn
60°S
Antarctic Circle
80°S
180°
Ice cap
Tundra
Forest
Grassland
Desert
Mountains

20°E
40°E
60°E
80°E
100°E
120°E
140°E
160°E
180°
80°N
ARCTIC OCEAN
URAL MTS.
Ob
Volga
60°N
EUROPE
ALPS
GOBI DESERT
ASIA
40°N
HINDU KUSH
HIMALAYA MTS.
Indus
Ganges
Yangtze
SYRIAN DESERT
AHARA
Nile
Tropic of Cancer
20°N
DECCAN PLATEAU
AFRICA
PACIFIC OCEAN
Equator
0°
INDIAN OCEAN
GREAT SANDY DESERT
20°S
Tropic of Capricorn
AUSTRALIA
NAMIB DESERT
KALAHARI DESERT
Cape of Good Hope
0
1000
2000
3000 Km.
0
1000
2000
3000 Mi.
60°S
Antarctic Circle
ANTARCTICA
80°S
180°

GREENLAND
(DENMARK)
ICELAND
ALASKA
(U.S.)
CANADA
IRELAND
UNITED STATES
PORTUGAL
Azores
Bermuda
ATLANTIC OCEAN
Midway Is.
Hawaiian Is.
MEXICO
CUBA
BAHAMAS
DOMINICAN REP.
Virgin Is.
JAMAICA
HAITI
BELIZE
HONDURAS
Puerto Rico
ST. CHRISTOPHER AND NEVIS
ANTIGUA AND BARBUDA
DOMINICA
BARBADOS
ST. LUCIA
GRENADA
ST. VINCENT AND
THE GRENADINES
TRINIDAD AND TOBAGO
GUATEMALA
EL SALVADOR
NICARAGUA
COSTA RICA
PANAMA
PACIFIC OCEAN
VENEZUELA
GUYANA
FR. GUIANA
COLOMBIA
SURINAM
ECUADOR
Galapagos Is.
Equator
WESTERN
SAHARA
(MOROCCO)
MAURITAN
CAPE
VERDE
SENEGAL
GAMBIA
GUINEA-BISSAU
GUINEA
SIERRA
LEONE
LIBERIA
PERU
BRAZIL
WESTERN
SAMOA
TONGA
BOLIVIA
PARAGUAY
CHILE
Easter Is.
URUGUAY
ARGENTINA
Falkland Is.
80°N
60°N
40°N
20°N
0°
20°S
40°S
60°S
80°S
160°W
140°W
120°W
100°W
80°W
60°W
40°W
20°W

RUSSIA
FINLAND
SWEDEN
ESTONIA
LATVIA
LITHUANIA
BELARUS
POLAND
UKRAINE
MOLDOVA
ROMANIA
BULGARIA
ITALY
ALBANIA
GREECE
MALTA
TUNISIA
TURKEY
CYPRUS
GEORGIA
ARMENIA
AZERBAIJAN
SYRIA
LEBANON
ISRAEL
JORDAN
IRAQ
IRAN
KUWAIT
BAHRAIN
QATAR
SAUDI ARABIA
UNITED ARAB EMIRATES
OMAN
YEMEN
KAZAKHSTAN
UZBEKISTAN
TURKMENISTAN
KYRGYZSTAN
TAJIKISTAN
AFGHANISTAN
PAKISTAN
MONGOLIA
PEOPLE'S REPUBLIC OF CHINA
N. KOREA
S. KOREA
JAPAN
PACIFIC OCEAN
NEPAL
BHUTAN
BANGLADESH
INDIA
MYANMAR (BURMA)
LAOS
THAILAND
VIETNAM
CAMBODIA (KAMPUCHEA)
TAIWAN
PHILIPPINES
SRI LANKA
MALDIVES
BRUNEI
MALAYSIA
SINGAPORE
INDONESIA
INDIAN OCEAN
PAPUA NEW GUINEA
Mariana Islands
Guam
Wake I.
Marshall Islands
Belau
Caroline Islands
KIRIBATI
NAURU
SOLOMON IS.
TUVALU
VANUATU
FIJI
New Caledonia
AUSTRALIA
NEW ZEALAND
LIBYA
EGYPT
NIGER
CHAD
SUDAN
ERITREA
DJIBOUTI
ETHIOPIA
SOMALIA
CENTRAL AFRICAN REP.
CAMEROON
GABON
UGANDA
KENYA
RWANDA
ZAIRE
BURUNDI
TANZANIA
SEYCHELLES
COMOROS
MALAWI
ANGOLA
ZAMBIA
NAMIBIA
ZIMBABWE
BOTSWANA
MADAGASCAR
MAURITIUS
MOZAMBIQUE
SWAZILAND
SOUTH AFRICA
LESOTHO
20°E
40°E
60°E
80°E
100°E
120°E
140°E
160°E
ABBREVIATIONS
AUS. AUSTRIA
BEL. BELGIUM
B. H. BOSNIA AND HERZEGOVINA
CR. CROATIA
CZ. CZECH REPUBLIC
DEN. DENMARK
HUNG. HUNGARY
LUX. LUXEMBOURG
MAC. FORMER YUGOSLAV REPUBLIC OF MACEDONIA
NETH. NETHERLANDS
SLK. SLOVAKIA
SLN. SLOVENIA
SWITZ. SWITZERLAND
YU. YUGOSLAVIA

Thirty Most Populous Countries

Country	Population (millions)
China	1179
India	897
USA	258
Indonesia	188
Brazil	152
Russia	149
Japan	125
Pakistan	122
Bangladesh	114
Nigeria	95
Mexico	90
Germany	81
Vietnam	72
Philippines	65
Iran	63
Turkey	61
Egypt	58
United Kingdom	58
Italy	58
France	58
Thailand	57
Ethiopia	57
Ukraine	52
Korea, South	45
Myanmar (Burma)	44
Zaire	41
Spain	39
South Africa	39
Poland	39
Colombia	35

Source: Data from the World Population Reference Bureau, 1993 World Population data sheet.

Contents

Preface to the Third Edition

Although many features of *Twentieth-Century World* will be familiar to readers of earlier editions, this Third Edition also contains extensive revisions and additions. For the benefit of new readers, it may be useful to highlight first the basic principles of the book and then new features of the Third Edition.

Basic Principles of *Twentieth-Century World*

Global Integration. The goal of *Twentieth-Century World* is to help students understand how our world has evolved since World War I. No subject of such scale can be intelligible unless organized according to clear principles. The foremost of these principles is that the world is a tightly integrated whole. Today, responsible citizenship requires understanding global interrelationships. To explain these interrelationships, *Twentieth-Century World* emphasizes global patterns of integration and examines issues and events, not as unique occurrences, but in terms of their global impact. For example, Chapter 4 examines the Bolshevik Revolution not just as a turning point in Russian history but also as this century's most influential revolutionary experience.

Balanced and Selective Coverage. The authors reject an approach based on Europe or the United States. Instead, this book provides balanced coverage of both developed and developing societies. In keeping with their emphasis on global integration, the authors also reject the incremental method, which assumes that adding together national histories produces world history. Instead, this book takes a selective and thematic, not an encyclopedic, approach. The goal is to enable students to identify major themes, see them illustrated in selected cases, and thus perceive world history as more than a jumble of details. Selectivity permits meaningful discussion of examples taken up in the book and leaves instructors free to develop alternative examples in class.

A Multifaceted Conception of History. *Twentieth-Century World* discusses a broad range of subjects—economic, social, political, artistic, scientific, and military—to convey a fully rounded understanding of the contemporary world. Every chapter considers several of these subjects. Certain chapters perform special functions, however. Chapter 1 explains the book's themes. Chapters 2 and 18 illuminate these themes pictorially and through discussion of representative social environments of both the early and late twentieth century. Chapter 2 contrasts a European capital and a colonial village at the start of the century. Chapter 18 compares two present-day supermetropolises, one in an affluent country and one in a Third World country. The narrative chapters, beginning with Chapter 3, emphasize political, economic, and social developments. Chapter 7, however, explores the century's most influential intellectual and artistic innovations. Chapter 19 analyzes such vital future-oriented issues as population, environment and resources, and arms control. The Third Edition's new conclusion, Chapter 20 takes a forward look at what the world promises to be like as the twenty-first century opens.

Clearly Stated Themes. The authors have organized this book around four major themes defined in Chapter 1.

1. *Global interrelatedness* and its shifting patterns, from the 1914 world of great powers and colonies to today's world of interdependence amid scarcity.
2. *Disequilibrium among cultures in an era of accelerating change,* an imbalance that has repeatedly produced conflict between economically and technologically dominant societies, on the one hand, and weaker societies struggling for independence and development, on the other.
3. *The rise of the mass society,* sometimes in the form of pluralistic democracy, more often in the form of mass-based dictatorship.
4. *Technology versus nature,* the ambiguous triumph that has culminated in humankind's power to destroy the earth.

These four themes raise a final question: are the values that have shaped this century's dominant societies conducive to humanity's future welfare? Or do those values need critical re-examination if societies of the future are to provide equitably for their material needs without destroying the environment on which they all depend?

In addition to the clearly stated themes, other aids to understanding include division of the text into parts, chapters, sections, and subsections, as well as italicization of key terms. Maps, illustrations, and a timeline enhance the text, as do suggestions for further reading at the end of each chapter. These aids have been thoroughly revised for the Third Edition.

Accompanying the Third Edition is a new *Instructor's Resource Manual* by Thomas F. Arnold. In addition to chapter-by-chapter guides to the thematic elements contained in *Twentieth-Century World,* this useful manual also includes, for each chapter, a summary, possible lecture topics, suggested class activities, a list of teaching materials (including audio-visual aids), and approximately thirty multiple choice and five essay questions.

New Features of the Third Edition

The most momentous changes of the post-1945 era have occurred since the Second Edition went to press. Communism and the Soviet Union have collapsed; the Cold War has ended; and the 1993 peace accord between Israel and the PLO appears to have opened a new era of peacemaking for the Middle East. The end of the Cold War quickly produced repercussions all over the world, and rapid change will surely continue, as economic balances shift and global relationships evolve. Much of the Third Edition has consequently been rewritten to give a full account of these dramatic developments.

In Part 1, the presentation of the book's themes in Chapter 1 has been revised, and the number of themes has been reduced from five to four. The discussion of patterns of global integration has been revised to reflect the emerging trends of the post-Cold War era, and the discussion of technology has been updated and coordinated with the revisions in Chapter 19.

In Part 2, the discussion of the Mexican revolution in Chapter 4 has been fundamentally revised and the comparative discussion of the Soviet, Mexican, Indian and Chinese experiences has been rewritten to reflect this change. Chapter 6 now concludes with a brief consideration of the extent to which the end of the twentieth century portends a resurgence of fascism.

In Part 3, Chapter 8's discussion of social relations in Latin America has been revised. In Chapter 10, the discussion of Turkey, especially that of its economic development, has been brought into line with the most recent scholarship, and the discussion of India has been revised to shift the emphasis from the British to the Indians.

Parts 4 through 6 discuss the world since World War II. The authors have sought in Chapters 12 through 20 to carry their narrative and analysis as close to present-day events as the publication schedule of the Third Edition permitted.

Thus Chapter 12 not only describes the impact upon the global distribution of power of the collapse of the Soviet bloc, but also compares the respective strengths of the North American, European, and East Asian power centers that will contend for economic ascendancy in the new century. Chapter 13 now concludes with a consideration of how the economic crisis of the 1990s has undermined confidence in the welfare state and in conventional democratic politics and has strengthened movements seeking alternative governmental directions for the Western democracies. Chapter 14, after analyzing why Gorbachev's efforts at renovation could not prevent the collapse of the Soviet bloc, explores the post-Communist travails both of the former Soviet republics and of three former satellites: Hungary, Czechoslovakia, and Poland.

In Part 5, extensive updating begins with the data used to illustrate demographic, social, and economic issues. Chapter 15 now presents a fuller and more nuanced view of the socioeconomic variations among Latin American countries, updated information on the transition to civilian government and market-oriented economic policies, and a discussion of regional economic integration efforts (including the North American Free Trade Agreement as it relates to Mexico). The section on Nicaragua, found in earlier editions, has been dropped; that on Cuba has been expanded. In Chapter 16, Somalia has replaced Ethiopia as the illustration of the extremes of political and economic disintegration in Africa. The accounts of Nigeria and South Africa have been updated through late summer of 1993; careful attention has been paid to South Africa's transition toward majority rule. In Chapter 17, Egypt has been dropped from this edition's discussion of the Middle East for reasons of concision; Turkey, the most successful of Islamic Middle Eastern developing countries, and Iraq have been added. The entire chapter has been updated through the fall of the Liberal Democratic Party in Japan and the Israel-PLO Accord of September 1993.

In Part 6, Chapter 18's discussion of Los Angeles now includes an interpretation of the South Central riots of April-May 1992, and the discussion of Cairo analyzes recent trends in Islamic activism. Chapter 19 has been extensively rewritten. The most marked change is that the discussion of weapons of mass destruction no longer concentrates on Cold War issues and now includes an expanded analysis of arms control and proliferation worldwide. Chapter 20 adds an entirely new conclusion to the Third Edition by speculating what the twenty-first-century world may be like.

Sources and Statistics

The entire revision process has benefited from advances in electronic communications and information technology. The availability of computerized data bases, especially the Lexis Nexis service, has enhanced the speed and efficiency of retrieving current information. To avoid repetition, the "Suggestions for Further Reading" at the end of the chapters have not mentioned this resource or the major newspapers—particularly the *New York Times* and *Wall Street Journal*—which have been regularly consulted.

One important new source became available too late for systematic use throughout the Third Edition. The publication by the International Monetary Fund (IMF) of its *World Economic Outlook* of May 1993 attracted widespread attention to a debate that economists had carried on for some time about the best ways to calculate statistics on economic production and incomes. Heretofore, such statistics have normally been calculated in terms of monetary exchange rates, even though these are subject to distortion by political and other factors. In its May 1993 *World Economic Outlook,* the IMF shifted from the exchange rate method of calculation to the purchasing power parity (PPP) method, which attempts to eliminate exchange rate distortion. Chapter 17 introduces income statistics computed by the PPP method in discussing China, and Chapter 20 discusses the implications of calculating income statistics by these and other methods. Otherwise, the basic source for income statistics is the figures, calculated in exchange-rate terms, in data tables of the *World Development Report,* published annually by the World Bank.

Authorship and Acknowledgments

The writing of Twentieth-Century World has been a profoundly collaborative venture. The authors have sought, from their first days in team-teaching world history, to achieve a community of views about themes and interpretations. They have been their own most persistent critics, always with an eye to enhancing the thematic integrity of the book. Within this relationship, Carter Findley wrote Chapter 1 (with contributions from John Rothney), the section on Dinshawai in Chapter 2, Chapters 8 to 10 and 15 to 17, the section on Cairo in Chapter 18, and Chapter 19, and parts of Chapter 20. John Rothney wrote the section on Berlin in Chapter 2, Chapters 3 to 7 (with contributions from Carter Findley in Chapter 4), Chapters 11 to 14, and the section on Los Angeles in Chapter 18, and parts of Chapter 20. The authors are indebted to the following scholars for valuable comments:

Louis Haas, *Duquesne University*
T. H. Baughman, *Benedictine College*
Robert Patch, *University of California-Riverside*
Warren Lerner, *Duke University*
Dominick Letterese, *Kean College*
William Brazill, *Wayne State University*
Larry D. Wilcox, *University of Toledo*
Harry I. Stagmaier Jr., *Frostburg State University*
Philip J. Adler, *East Carolina University*

In addition to those named in earlier editions, the authors would like to acknowledge the assistance of the following scholars and colleagues: Engin Akarli, Kenneth Andrien, James Bartholomew, Robert Baum, Alan Beyerchen, Samuel Chu, Michael Curran, Jane Hathaway, John McLaren, Marjorie Murfin, Claire Robertson, Carole Rogel, Leila Rupp, James Scanlan, Gaddis Smith, Vladimir Steffel, Chris Taylor, Shibley Telhami, Warren Van Tine, and Robin Winks. The authors are greatly indebted to the Houghton Mifflin editorial staff. By what they understood, what they showed was not understandable, and what they contributed of their own, thousands of Ohio State students have contributed to the making of this book.

Carter Findley gratefully acknowledges the encouragement of four generations of family members: Inez Vaughn Oliver; Elizabeth and John Findley; Lucia Findley and Clay Findley; and Madeleine and Benjamin Findley. John Rothney is grateful for the enduring friendship of Malcolm and Dolores Baroway, Ronald E. Coons, Edward P. Hart, Sheila Porter, and Richard E. Rogers.

C.V.F.
J.A.M.R.

List of Maps

The Twentieth Century: A Time Chart

	Events and Issues of Global Significance	Scientific-Technical-Intellectual	North America
Pre-1900	Heyday of European world dominance	19th-century materialism, rationalism, and political liberalism increasingly challenged in the 1890s	Spanish-American War (1898) is first assertion of U.S. world power
1900		Freud's *On the Interpretation of Dreams,* 1900 Wright brothers make first powered aircraft flight, 1903 Einstein's "On the Electrodynamics of Moving Bodies," 1905 Picasso's *Demoiselles d'Avignon,* 1907	Presidency of Theodore Roosevelt, 1901–1909 Presidency of William Howard Taft, 1909–1913
1910	World War I, 1914–1918 Paris Peace Conference, 1919		Presidency of Woodrow Wilson, 1913–1921 U.S. declares war on Germany, 1917
1920	League of Nations founded, 1920 First Fascists in power with Mussolini's March on Rome, 1922 Great Depression, 1929	Franz Kafka's *The Trial,* 1924 First nonstop trans-Atlantic solo flight, 1925	Constitutional amendment gives women the vote, 1920 Presidency of Warren G. Harding, 1921–1923 Presidency of Calvin Coolidge, 1923–1929 Presidency of Herbert Hoover, 1929–1933 Wall Street crash, 1929
1930	Global population explosion since 1930 World War II, 1939–1945	Ortega y Gasset's *The Revolt of the Masses,* 1930	Smoot-Hawley Tariff, 1930 Presidency of Franklin D. Roosevelt, 1933–1945 Social Security Act, 1935

Europe	Latin America	Africa	Asia
Franco-Russian alliance, 1894, first step in forming a rival bloc to the Triple Alliance of Germany, Austro-Hungary, and Italy (1879)	Brazil's "Old Republic," 1889–1930	"Scramble" for Africa begins, 1880s Gandhi in South Africa, 1893–1914 Anglo-Boer War, 1899–1902	Meiji Restoration, Japan, 1868 British occupation of Egypt, 1882 Boxer Uprising, China, 1899–1901
Beginning of Anglo-German naval race, 1900 Anglo-French Entente, 1904 First Moroccan Crisis, 1905 Anglo-Russian Entente, 1907 Bosnian Crisis, 1908			Japanese-British alliance, 1902 Russo-Japanese War, 1904–1905
Second Moroccan Crisis, 1911 Italy enters World War I, 1915 Abdication of the Tsar and establishment of the Provisional Government in Russia, March 1917 Bolshevik Revolution, November 1917 Treaty of Brest-Litovsk, 1918 Establishment of the Weimar Republic in Germany, 1919	Mexico's "Great Rebellion," 1910–1920 Radical period in Argentina, 1916–1930	Creation of Union of South Africa, 1910 Unification of Nigeria under British Rule, 1914 French and British seize German colonies, 1914–1915; East Africa campaign, through 1918 France recruits African troops for Western Front	Revolution of 1911, China Gandhi returns to India, 1915 Japan participates in World War I and Paris Peace Conference, 1914–1919 Egyptian "revolution" of 1919 Amritsar Massacre, India, 1919 May Fourth Movement, China, 1919
Russian New Economic Policy, 1921 French occupation of the Ruhr, 1923 Runaway German inflation, 1923 First Labour Government in Britain, 1924 First Soviet Five-Year Plan, 1928 Second British Labour Government, 1929–1931	Growth of artistic interest in developing distinctly national culture in Brazil and Mexico	African National Congress founded, South Africa, 1923	Founding of Chinese Communist Party, 1921 Government of India Acts, 1921, 1935 Mandate system in Syria, Iraq, Palestine, 1922–1923 Turkish Republic founded, 1923 GMD gains control of all China, 1928
"National" government in Britain, 1931–1935 Adolf Hitler named German chancellor, 1933 Popular Front in France, 1936–1937 Munich Agreement, 1938	Getúlio Vargas in power, Brazil, 1930–1945 Presidency of Lázaro Cárdenas, Mexico, 1934–1940	Boom in South Africa, 1933–late 1970s Italy conquers Ethiopia, 1935–1936	Japanese aggres[illegible] China, 1931–[illegible] Japan and [illegible] 1937–[illegible]

The Twentieth Century: A Time Chart (continued)

	Events and Issues of Global Significance	Scientific-Technical-Intellectual	North America
1940	United Nations founded, 1945 Nuclear era begins with bombing of Hiroshima and Nagasaki, 1945	Germans launch first guided missile, the V-2, 1942	Presidency of Harry S Truman, 1945–1953 Truman Doctrine, 1947 Taft-Hartley Act, 1947
1950	Era of global economic growth, petroleum based, 1950–1973	Explosion of first U.S. hydrogen bomb, 1952 Explosion of first Soviet hydrogen bomb, 1953 Watson and Crick describe the double-helix structure of DNA, 1953 Soviets launch first orbiting satellite, Sputnik, 1957	Korean War, 1950–1953 Presidency of Dwight D. Eisenhower, 1953–1961 U.S. Supreme Court strikes down racial segregation in schools, 1953
1960	Population growth and superurbanization become major Third World issues. Cuban Missile Crisis, 1962 Global wave of protest by the young and disadvantaged, mid-1960s–early 1970s	United States lands first astronauts on the moon, 1969	Presidency of John F. Kennedy, 1961–1963 Presidency of Lyndon B. Johnson, 1963–1969 Tonkin Gulf Resolution, 1964 Assassination of Martin Luther King, Jr., 1968 Presidency of Richard M. Nixon, 1969–1974
1970	OPEC oil price increases (1973, 1979) symbolize opening of era of interdependence amid scarcity	SALT I Treaty, 1972 SALT II Treaty, 1979 (not ratified by U.S. Senate)	Watergate scandal, 1972–1974 U.S. Supreme Court strikes down anti-abortion laws, 1973 Presidency of Gerald R. Ford, 1974–1977 Presidency of Jimmy Carter, 1977–1981

Europe	**Latin America**	**Africa**	**Asia**
Winston Churchill, British prime minister, 1940–1945 Labour Government in Britain, 1945–1950 Fourth French Republic, 1946–1958 Marshall Plan, 1947 Berlin crisis, 1948 Foundation of German Federal Repbulic (West) and German Democratic Republic (East), 1949 NATO founded, 1949	Presidency of Juan Perón, Argentina, 1946–1955 Second Republic in Brazil, 1946–1964	North African Campaigns, 1941–1943 National Council of Nigeria and Cameroons, 1944 Apartheid becomes policy in South Africa, 1948	Japanese alliance with Germany and Italy, 1940 Japanese bomb Pearl Harbor, 1941 Muhammad Reza Shah, Iran, 1941–1979 U.S. occupation of Japan, 1945–1952 China's civil war, 1946–1949 India's independence, 1947; Jawaharlal Nehru, premier, 1947–1964 Israel's statehood, 1948
Hungarian Revolt, 1956 Khrushchev in sole leadership of the USSR, 1957–1964 Foundation of the European Common Market, 1958 Establishment of the Fifth French Republic, 1958	Fidel Castro's regime in Cuba, 1959–	Freedom Charter, South Africa, 1955	Iran's oil nationalization crisis, 1951–1954 Abdel Nasser's regime in Egypt, 1952–1970 Collectivization in China, 1955 Japan's GNP regains prewar levels, 1955 Suez Campaign, 1956 China's Great Leap Forward, 1958–1962 Multiparty democracy in Turkey; Democrat Party in power, 1950–1960 Overthrow of Iraqi Monarchy, 1958
Soviets crush Czech revolt, 1968 "Days of May" in France, 1968	Period of military authoritarianism and economic neocolonialism, mid-1960s–1980s Military rule in Brazil, 1964–1985 Military dominance of Argentine politics, 1966–1983	Decolonization, 1960s South Africa declared a republic, 1960 Sharpeville massacre, 1960 First Nigerian republic falls to military, 1966 Biafran civil war, 1967–1970	China acquires nuclear weapons, 1964 China's Cultural Revolution begins, 1965 Indira Gandhi, premier of India, 1966–1977, 1980–1984 Six-Day War, 1967 (third Arab-Israeli war) Turkey's Second Republic, 1961–1980 Ba'th Party takes power in Iraq, 1968
Nixon visits USSR, 1972 Helsinki Agreements, 1975, climax "Era of Detente"	Presidency of Salvador Allende, Chile, 1973 Presidency of Juan Perón, Argentina, 1973–1974 Major oil discoveries, Mexico, 1974 End of Brazil's economic "miracle," late 1970s Sandinista government in Nicaragua, 1979–	Nigeria becomes large oil exporter, 1970s Widespread drought and famine, early 1970s Ethiopian revolution, 1974 South Africa begins giving "independence" to homelands; Soweto incident, 1976 Nigeria returns to civilian government, 1979	Japanese-U.S. trade tensions, 1971–1980s October War, 1973 (fourth Arab-Israeli war) Indian nuclear explosion, 1974; self-sufficiency in gr [illegible] 1978 Death of Mao Zedo [illegible] Menachem Begin [illegible] in Israel, 1977– [illegible] Iranian revo [illegible] Saddam [illegible] Iraq, 1 [illegible]

The Twentieth Century: A Time Chart (continued)

	Events and Issues of Global Significance	Scientific-Technical-Intellectual	North America
1980	World population reaches 5 billion, 1986 Intermediate Nuclear Forces Treaty (INF), 1987 Montreal Protocol on Substances that Deplete the Ozone Layer, 1987	President Reagan calls for U.S. Strategic Defense Initiative ("Star Wars"), 1983 Chernobyl nuclear catastrophe, USSR, 1986 First patent of a genetically engineered animal, 1988	Presidency of Ronald Reagan, 1981–1989 U.S. foreign debt becomes world's largest "Black Monday," stock market crash, 1987 Presidency of George Bush, 1989–1993
1990	Conventional Forces in Europe treaty (CFE), 1990 Soviet Union collapses, 1992 Strategic Arms Reduction treaties (START I and II), 1991, 1993 UN Conference on Environment and Development (Rio de Janeiro), 1992 Chemical Weapons Convention (CWC), 1993	Revolution in global electronic communications technologies	Independent candidate Ross Perot wins 19 percent of U.S. presidential vote, 1992 Presidency of Bill Clinton, 1993– North American Free Trade Agreement signed, 1993; U.S. ratification still required

Europe	Latin America	Africa	Asia
Solidarity, independent Polish trade union movement, founded, 1980; forms government, 1989 Gorbachev becomes Soviet leader, 1985 East European countries end Communist dominance of governments, 1989	Argentina restores civilian rule, 1983 Brazil returns to civilian presidency, 1985 Mexican election, 1988, shows erosion of one-party system Chile elects civilian president, 1989	Widespread drought, famine, environmental degradation, c. 1982– Military coups, Nigeria, 1983, 1985 South African Constitution, 1984; black rebellion, 1984–	Deng Xiaoping in power in China, 1980– Israel invades Lebanon, 1982 (fifth Arab-Israeli war) Palestinian uprising in occupied territories, 1987– Chinese democracy movement, Tienanmen massacre, 1989 Death of Khomeini, 1989 Turkey's Third Republic, 1983–
Maastricht Treaty to complete West European unity, 1991 Elimination of most West European tariffs, 1992	Argentine economic growth resumes under civilian government, 1991–1992 Scandal topples President Collor, Brazil, 1992 North American Free Trade Agreement, 1992, and other economic integration plans Loss of Soviet subsidies provokes drastic economic decline in Cuba	Civil war and famine in Somalia; U.S. and UN intervention, 1992 Whites vote to end minority rule in South Africa, 1992 Nigeria's military government ignores results of election supposed to restore civilian rule, 1993	Iraq's annexation of Kuwait, 1990; Gulf War and Iraq's Defeat, 1991 Assassination of Rajiv Gandhi, 1991 Israel's 1992 election returns Labor Party to power China's rapid economic growth resumes under "market socialism" Hindu nationalists provoke crisis by destroying Ayodhya mosque (1992) Japan's Liberal Democratic Party defeated in election of July 1993; Hosokawa government takes power Tansu Çiller becomes prime minister of Turkey, June 1993, first woman to head government of an Islamic Middle Eastern country Israel-PLO Peace Accord (Sept. 1993)

Twentieth-Century World

Third Edition

PART 1

Introduction

CHAPTER 1

Twentieth-Century Themes

To understand the problems of the present and the foreseeable future, we must discern the historical processes at work in the world around us. All of us—but especially young people, who have the largest stake in the future—need this understanding, for the number of issues that affect our well-being seems to grow steadily. We encounter shifts in values that widen or narrow our freedom but leave us unsure what to expect from others. We confront problems that affect our environment, the supply of vital resources, and our economic security. Contemporary weapons and environmental hazards make us worry about the very survival of our species. Men and women of 1900 could scarcely have comprehended some of the challenges we face.

How can we understand something as vast as the world we live in? Can we recognize significant patterns in the mass of information before us? This chapter identifies four interrelated themes that run through twentieth-century world history. With these four themes in mind, we can work toward understanding the twentieth-century world selectively, without trying to survey every example of every issue:

1. *Global interrelatedness.* The world forms an interconnected whole. Its history is not simply the accumulated histories of the world's parts. There is, instead, a pattern of global interconnectedness, which changes over time. Understanding global history requires us first to define this pattern, which has changed in this century more than ever before.
2. *Disequilibrium among cultures in an era of accelerating change.* As global integration tightened over the centuries, the most influential nations extended their power

around the world, making inequalities in power among societies acutely visible. Although change seems to have accelerated for the whole world in modern times, today's power inequalities in part reflect different rates of change, and different attitudes toward change, in different societies. Given these differences, increased global integration, far from harmonious, has usually meant disequilibrium and conflict among societies.

3. *The rise of the mass society.* This phenomenon has been the greatest political consequence of accelerating change and cultural confrontation, which together have caused mass political mobilization and created demands for mass political participation everywhere. In different societies, mass politics assumes opposing forms: democratic or dictatorial. This difference in form, arising from each society's history, has been another of the century's great sources of conflict.
4. *Technology versus nature.* Accelerating scientific and technological change has largely reversed humanity's age-old vulnerability to the forces of nature, but this shift has posed grave new questions. First, has the technological triumph over nature reached the point where its destructive potentials threaten humankind's future? Second, can the benefits of technology, enjoyed disproportionately by the most powerful societies, be made to benefit the world's peoples more equitably?

These four themes raise a final question: Are the values that made the world what it is—largely those of the most powerful, competitive societies—conducive to future human survival? Or do the dangers that cloud the future signal that these values need critical re-examination? Many twentieth-century problems raise this question, and we shall consider it more carefully at the end of the book.

Chapter 2 begins this selective study by showing how two representative environments, one European and one colonial, illustrated these themes at the start of this century. In that chapter and others, the goal is not to amass facts but to reveal the large patterns that run through the history of this century, helping us to explain the specific cases discussed in these pages and suggesting explanations for many more. The remainder of this chapter defines the four themes more fully.

Global Interrelatedness and Its Shifting Patterns

Defining patterns of global interrelatedness requires classifying the world's societies into categories with common traits, then defining the relationships among the categories. Like any effort at simplification, this process risks some distortion. Yet the need for categorization often arises. Many classification schemes have been proposed in this century. We are all familiar with some of them: great powers and colonies; developed and underdeveloped (or developing) countries; East and West; First, Second, and Third Worlds (or, in 1950s terminology, the free world, the communist bloc, and the nonaligned countries); Affluent North and Hungry South; core and periphery. Different terms have seemed useful at different times.

The changing global pattern makes it hard to find one set of terms suitable for the entire twentieth century. Therefore, our usage will vary. The various sets of terms also present other problems. For example, the categories "developed" and "underdeveloped" divide the world into just two parts. But the world's societies have many differences that we need to recognize, even if sorting these societies into a few large categories defined by criteria such as wealth or power is useful for some purposes. While it is still often done, referring to the developing countries as the "Third World" became anachronistic after the collapse of communism in Eastern Europe in the late 1980s. Some classifications are also objectionable because they assume that the vantage point of some people should be that of all. This is especially true of the designations "East" and "West" and their derivatives "Middle East" or "Far East," which reflect a European viewpoint. Finding unobjectionable substitutes is not always easy. When we use debatable terms, we shall explain what we mean by them.

The realities that the terms symbolize are more important than the terms themselves. We shall, therefore, concentrate here on defining the pattern of global interrelatedness as it was in 1914 and as it is today. Also, we shall summarize the processes that governed the evolution of the global pattern.

The Global Pattern of 1914

Contemporaries saw the world pattern of 1914 as sharply defined in terms of great powers and colonies (Map 1.1). A few states also had an intermediate status.

A great power was a nation-state with an industrial economy and a colonial empire. We can define a *nation-state* as an independent political entity that rules over, and in a sense represents, a single nationality. A nationality normally consists of people who share the same language, culture, history, and sense of identity. Ideally, the territory the nationality inhabits is the territory of the state. Creating an independent nation-state meant fulfillment for the political *nationalism* (patriotic pride in one's own country) that was so strong in nineteenth-century Europe and has since appeared all over the world.

To Europeans of 1914, the great powers were Great Britain, France, Germany, Austria-Hungary, and Russia. Some of these were not nation-states at all, and none fulfilled the ideal perfectly. Austria-Hungary and Russia represented an older political form, the multinational empire, which the spread of nationalism threatened. Germany, unified only in 1871, did not include all speakers of German. The United Kingdom consisted officially of the "four kingdoms" of England, Wales, Scotland, and Ireland; the name Great Britain properly refers to the first three of these. There was a separatist nationalist movement in Ireland; in the twentieth century, local nationalisms have been an issue in Wales and Scotland also. France came closest to the nation-state ideal, though it too included unassimilated minorities, such as the Bretons.

Similarly, the great powers did not all possess industrial economies or colonial empires. Austria and Russia were late in industrialization and acquired no overseas colonies, though they continued to acquire adjacent territories. During the nineteenth century, for example, Russia acquired huge tracts in Asia, mostly peopled by Muslims. Germany was unified too late to acquire many colonies but had a few by 1914. It had certainly built up the military and industrial might of a great colonial power. France had long enjoyed national integration. It had a developed industrial economy and the second-largest colonial empire. Great Britain, the original homeland of the Industrial Revolution and still the leading maritime power, possessed the largest colonial empire, on which—the British proudly said—the sun never set.

The colonial lands included all of Latin America, Africa, and Asia, although most Latin American countries and a few in Africa and

Map 1.1 The World, 1914 

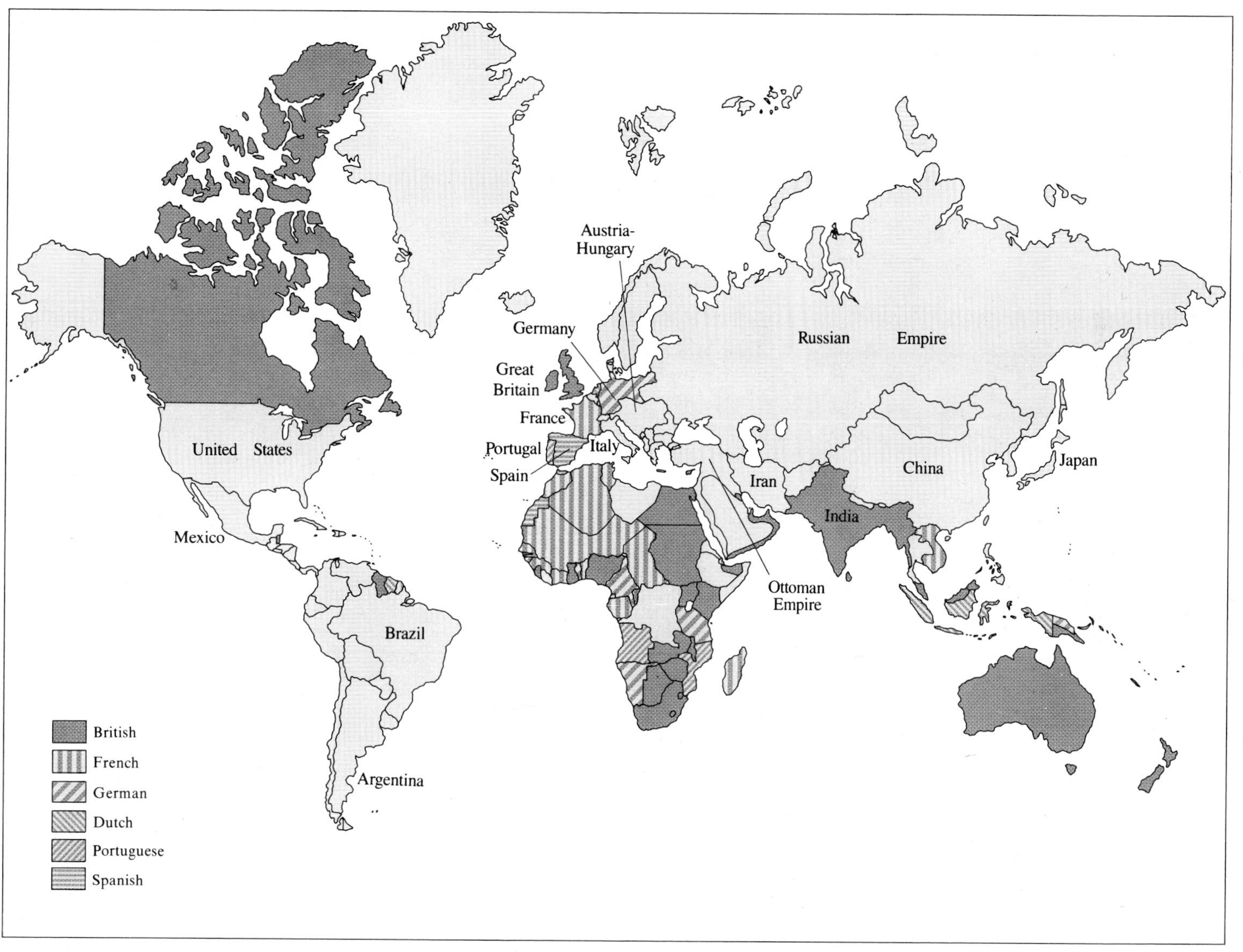
Austria-Hungary
Germany
Great Britain
France
Portugal
Spain
Italy
Russian Empire
Iran
India
China
Japan
Ottoman Empire
United States
Mexico
Brazil
Argentina
British
French
German
Dutch
Portuguese
Spanish

Asia were independent in name. Colonial dependence assumed many forms: economic, political, and cultural. Economically, it meant the colonial economy, in which the dependent country produced one or a few agricultural or mineral products for export to the dominant country, which processed these raw materials and exported industrial goods back to the dependent country. Many officially independent countries, especially in Latin America, were economically dependent.

Political dependency, too, assumed varied forms. Even supposedly independent countries, like Iran or the Ottoman Empire, suffered chronic interference by the great powers. Inside colonial countries that lacked nominal independence, political arrangements varied from direct military rule to what the British idealized as indirect rule, a system where a small European staff worked through survivors of the precolonial leadership.

Cultural dependence, too, was a fact of life for colonial countries. It could result from direct initiatives, especially those of missionaries in evangelization or education, or it might simply reflect local fascination with, and dread of, the European powers and a desire to understand them.

Some nations of 1914 fell into an intermediate group between the great powers and the colonies. The category includes some small European countries with overseas empires—Belgium, Holland, Italy—as well as the fallen leaders of the first age of European expansion, Portugal and Spain. Though regarded as great powers, Austria-Hungary and Russia really fit this category better. Japan, too, was beginning to command recognition as a power, as were the nations of the English-speaking world outside Europe. Of these, the United States had already become the world's most productive nation in both industry and agriculture and had begun to play an expansive role in the Caribbean and the Pacific.

The Rise of the West

The processes that created the European-dominated world of 1914 operated over long centuries. The result is what historians call "the rise of the West"—that is, Western Europe and its overseas extensions in the Americas and Australasia. The rise of the West illustrates that European societies possessed, from early times, a potential for self-transformation that was exceptional on a world scale. This potential no doubt derived from European civilization's uneasy blend of elements from two incompatible traditions: God-centered Judeo-Christian monotheism and human-oriented Greco-Roman philosophical culture. But other factors reinforced the readiness to change. When the ancient Roman Empire fell, for example, it was replaced not by another monolithic empire, as would have been normal in the other Old World centers of civilization, but by a multiplicity of power centers. This multiplicity, or pluralism, of authorities suggests a competitive dynamism that helped confirm the potential for change.

In the Middle Ages, European civilization also developed an outwardly expansive momentum. The militarism of this era of political decentralization and insecurity expressed itself in domination of outlying parts of Europe and in overseas expansion with the Crusades, campaigns that started at the end of the eleventh century and aimed to recapture Jerusalem from the Muslims. By the thirteenth century, competitive national monarchies with distinct languages and cultures were emerging. Significant innovations also occurred in economic life. These included the iron-pointed plow, which made it possible to cultivate the heavy soils of northern Europe, and the gradual clearing of the forests, which increased agricultural productivity. This productivity contributed to population growth, which reinforced the expansionist tendency and in fields such as metallurgy and navigation stimulated technological innovations that had direct applications in warfare and exploration.

Population growth stimulated the development of towns and trade in luxuries and in such basics as woolens, iron, and timber. Europe had good facilities for water transport of bulky commodities, and towns grew up to handle the trade. In the politically fragmented environment, townsmen united to press kings and feudal lords for privileges. Thus emerged autonomous municipalities, guilds, even leagues of commercial cities. European merchants acquired higher status and greater power than their counterparts elsewhere. New forms of business organization emerged along with new attitudes about practices such as lending money at interest. The evolution of Western capitalism, with its emphases on private ownership, individual initiative, and competitiveness, had begun.

Awareness of the world outside Europe drew capitalist interest toward overseas expansion. Europeans knew of other civilizations, starting with that of Islam, centered just across the Mediterranean in what is now commonly called the Middle East (Southwest Asia plus Egypt) and North Africa. Parts of Europe—Sicily and the Iberian Peninsula (Spain and Portugal)—had long been under Islamic rule. The Crusades exposed Europeans to the higher civilization of the Islamic world and spread tastes for luxury goods produced in the Middle East or brought there from farther east. Italians, especially Venetians, became rich from trade in these goods. The desire of other Europeans to undercut them helped open the age of exploration.

The key initiatives were launched from the Iberian Peninsula. The Portuguese, after inching down the African coast for years, reached the Cape of Good Hope at the continent's southern tip in 1488. Under Vasco da Gama, they reached India in 1498. Meanwhile, from Spain, Columbus set sail to the west, seeking the Indies of the east but finding his way to the Americas instead. His voyage of 1492 coincided with the fall of the last Muslim bastion in Spain, a fact suggesting that the Spanish drive against the Muslims led directly into the age of overseas expansion. In this way two of Europe's fledgling nation-states began tying the world into a European-dominated system.

Many more changes had to occur before that system assumed the form it had in 1914. Spain and Portugal were replaced as the dominant powers by countries with better-developed economies and with a larger population than Portugal's. The Netherlands contended for dominance in the seventeenth century, establishing its hold over the Dutch East Indies (now Indonesia). By the eighteenth century, France and Great Britain were the leading contenders.

Before the struggle could be decided, the combination of nation-state and capitalist economy had to develop into an efficient mechanism for ruling a world-embracing empire. Politically, the medieval decentralization of power gave way to centralized states with enhanced capabilities for administration, taxation, and warfare. Through the eighteenth century, the characteristic form of such states was the absolute monarchy, as illustrated by the France of Louis XIV. The two main exceptions were England, where Parliament emerged as the real center of power in the seventeenth century, and the Netherlands, which created a federal union in 1609. Other major changes included advances in navigation and in shipbuilding and new forms of commercial organization, such as the joint-stock company. European powers also sought to organize relations with one another by making alliances.

Meanwhile, Europe's *pluralism*—its pattern of multiple centers of power and authority—became even clearer with the Renaissance, which began in Italy in the fourteenth century and aimed to revive the culture of ancient Greece and Rome. The Renaissance overlapped with the Reformation, launched by Martin Luther in 1517 as an attempt to purify Christian faith and practice. Nothing better illustrates the exceptional European capacity for self-transformation than the simultaneous flourishing of these two movements, one attempting to revive a pagan culture, the other to revitalize Christianity. The Reformation produced a multiplicity of sects and religious authorities, thereby in- tensifying European pluralism. By challenging inherited practices and world views, the Renaissance and the Reformation both contributed to other changes that helped consolidate the emerging global pattern. In particular, the Scientific Revolution of the seventeenth century, by upsetting views of the universe that had enjoyed religious sanction, provided the basis for ongoing development in science and technology.

Among the greatest proofs of Europe's self-transformative potential, however, were the dual revolutions—industrial and democratic—of the late eighteenth and nineteenth centuries. The Industrial Revolution, beginning in England, opened a new phase in Europe's struggle to dominate the globe. The first breakthroughs in mechanization launched an unprecedented expansion in productivity. More important, technological breakthroughs continued not just for a time—as had happened in earlier cases—but indefinitely, in a self-compounding and accelerating way. With the advent of the modern factory, combining capital with machinery, raw materials, and labor, capitalism assumed its distinctive industrial form. Nineteenth-century European imperialism grew out of all that had preceded, since Columbus and da Gama. Yet its impact was raised to a new order, as the leading powers developed industrial economies with which nonindustrial economies could not compete.

Meanwhile, the Democratic Revolution, starting—as far as the Old World is concerned—with the French Revolution in 1789, began to transform the ideal political structure for the nation-state from absolute monarchy to some form of democracy, in which ultimate authority rests with the people. This shift gave a powerful push to the rise of nationalism or patriotism. To justify this political reorientation, a major political philosophy emerged: nineteenth-century *liberalism*. This aimed to free the individual politically and economically. Politically, liberalism demanded parliamentary-constitutional government with guaranteed individual rights. Such a political system might be either a constitutional monarchy, as in Great Britain, or a republic, as in France or the United States. Economically, nineteenth-century liberalism expressed the mentality of the Industrial Revolution. Government was not to interfere in business, and trade was to be free across international borders, with no tariff barriers. By 1914, industrial labor relations and international competition had created doubts about classical liberal economics. Doubt gave rise, in time, to a new liberalism demanding regulation of the economy to protect the disadvantaged. In contemporary U.S. terms, nineteenth-century liberalism has become the Republicans' conservatism; twentieth-century liberalism is the Democrats' ideology.

As industrial societies developed, some thinkers shifted emphasis from the rights that preoccupied affluent liberals to the economic relationships that made them affluent. The key figure here was Karl Marx (1818–1883). For him, politics depended on economic forces and class relationships. The middle class, with its liberalism, had destroyed absolutism in a few countries, but its ascendancy meant industrial capitalism and exploitation of the workers. Exploitation would become steadily worse, until the workers rose, destroyed liberalism and private property, and created a classless communist society. Moreover, since industrialization created the same problems everywhere, Marx believed that the revolution would not be limited to one country. The "workers of the world" would unite to throw off their chains.

Marx's revolutionary vision exerted vast influence, as evidenced by its importance for major twentieth-century revolutions, especially in Russia (1917) and China (1949). But it also gave rise to a reformist trend, aiming to achieve a more egalitarian order without revolution. This school of thought is usually referred to as socialist, rather than communist. Socialism is the background of the Social Democratic parties found in many countries' parliaments today; it is commonly no more "radical" than twentieth-century U.S. liberalism. Democratic socialism is perhaps the best name for nonrevolutionary socialism, because Marxists committed to revolution have also sometimes referred to themselves as socialists.

By 1914, then, processes of accelerating change had created a Europe-centered pattern of world domination. A few Western economies controlled an unprecedented share of the world's wealth. These were capitalist economies, oriented toward growth. Yet experience showed that growth could not continue indefinitely without crisis, in which much accumulated wealth would be lost. Added threats emerged from the fact that great, and would-be great, powers saw themselves in competition with one another. Each sought to protect itself by acquiring colonies and forming alliances, until the European powers became divided into two opposing alignments. A small crisis between these alignments could set off a chain reaction that might be felt all over the world.

From the Global Pattern of 1914 to That of the 1990s

The economic and political weaknesses of the Europe-centered global configuration produced a series of interlinked catastrophes—World Wars I and II and the Great Depression of 1929—that ultimately destroyed the pattern of 1914. As these crises undermined the old European powers' ability to maintain their position, new and more imposing powers emerged elsewhere. One was the United States, which by 1945 had become the world's leading model of democracy and capitalism, at least for the next quarter-century. The other was the Soviet Union, which emerged after revolutionaries acting on an adaptation of Marx's ideas had seized power in the Russian Empire in 1917, launching one of the century's most far-reaching experiments in social and economic change and, with it, another model for the world. After 1945, Western Europeans could not figure prominently among the world's power centers except by acting together.

From the late 1940s to the late 1980s, the most conspicuous pattern in international relations was the Cold War, the rivalry that followed the breakdown of the alliance of expediency between the U.S. and Soviet superpowers during World War II. In terms of the long-term evolution of global interrelationships, however, the collapse of communism in eastern Europe in the late 1980s suggests that the superpower bipolarity of the Cold War was only a passing phase in the transition to a different pattern of global interrelationships.

In debating the reasons for communist collapse, historians must not neglect the global level of analysis. There, a critical point is that the communists' economic experiment required isolating their countries from the world economy. Outside the communist bloc, global economic relationships remained capitalist in character, while—at the national level—market economies remained the world's most productive and innovative. In addition, the unprecedented explosion in the world's population, from 1.7 billion in 1900 to 5.4 billion in 1992, magnified the demands that ongoing change in technology and industry made on natural resources and the environment. With such rapidly growing human societies dependent on a natural resource base that could not grow

Crowds wait daily to apply for visas at the U.S. Consulate, Santo Domingo. *In search of opportunity, millions of the world's poor seek ways—legal or illegal—to migrate to wealthier countries.*
Michaele I. Cozzi/©1993 The New York Times.

proportionately, what ultimately proves critical is not *geostrategic* competition—the rivalry for political and military dominance on which the superpowers expended so much of their means during the Cold War. What becomes vital is rather *geoeconomic* issues—above all, human societies' struggle to satisfy their basic needs without destroying their resource base or their natural habitat (see Chapter 12). The Soviet command economy was able to concentrate vast resources on military or aerospace technology. Today, however, Eastern Europe's exceptionally befouled environments, its outmoded infrastructure, and its populations' declining life expectancy and abnormally high disease rates all measure different dimensions of the communists' failure in developing their natural and human resources. More than being a question of political and military power, as Cold War thinking had assumed, security proved to depend more on efficiency, equity, and long-term sustainability in the way a society uses its resources.

The end of the Cold War and the growing urgency of this new struggle for security, which now confronts all the world's peoples, reveal emerging outlines of the global configuration of the twenty-first century (discussed in Chapter 20). It will not have two superpowers, but rather a larger number of power centers distinguished more by sustainable economic productivity than military might. One of these will be located in North America. The European Economic Community will form another. East Asia will be home to a third, centered in Japan, but also including such rising stars as Taiwan, South Korea, Hong Kong, and Singapore. If China continues its rapid economic development and resolves the contradiction between its communist political system and its increasingly market-oriented economy, it may become the largest member of the East Asian group. Until its collapse, the Soviet Union seemed likely to be another of these economic power centers, even though it could only compete with major market economies in some sectors. Whether its successor states can perform even that well is an open question.

Because these centers of economic power lie in the Northern Hemisphere, some analysts have described the global economic pattern in terms of Affluent North and Hungry South—expressions used figuratively. China is geographically in the North but still a developing country, while Australia and New Zealand are affluent in the South.

Officially, the present-day world—North and South—has become more than ever one of independent nation-states. The European powers' loss of control over their former colonies following World War II and the Soviet Union's disintegration in 1991 has increased the number of independent states to over 180—four times as many as in 1914. Across the formerly colonial world, the spread of nationalism, new ideologies of resistance, and the wars of national liberation that grow out of them did much to produce this result. Most of the new nations are not fully viable as nation-states, however. The more successful developing countries, such as Taiwan and South Korea, are experiencing rapid economic development. However, the smallest and poorest, especially in sub-Saharan Africa, are losing ground economically and ecologically; these are often also plagued by corrupt governments and ethnic or religious strife. Large or small, formerly dependent countries have discovered, too, that the end of political control by outsiders is not the same as an end to economic control. Multinational corporations, some of which have larger budgets than most governments, perpetuate what critics call "neocolonialism"; the difficulties that economically weaker nations face in charting policies for economic development in their own interest will be a persistent concern of this book. Furthermore, in a world where economic and environmental issues now usually transcend national boundaries, where electronic messages and images can be transmitted around the globe in an instant, where intractable crises in countries like Somalia or the former Yugoslavia raise demands for new forms of international response, global integration steadily tightens at the expense of natural sovereignty.

Retaining formal political independence, the world's nation-states remain its premier political entities. Yet factors ranging from environmental degradation to the search for economic efficiency force national policy makers to recognize that their countries' destinies are increasingly intertwined. Nothing better symbolizes this trend than the European Economic Community's slow progress toward integration, or the many analogous plans for economic cooperation or integration—such as the North American Free Trade Agreement (NAFTA)—lately proposed in most other regions of the world.

Today less and less does political independence signify economic self-sufficiency for the world's nations. Economically, the opposite of colonial dependence is not independence but a relative ability to determine, or at least influence, the terms of a nation's integration into the thickening web of global interrelationships, which can now best be described in terms of an economically multicentered world of interdependence amid scarcity.

Disequilibrium Among Cultures in an Era of Accelerating Change

The European age of exploration tied the world together more closely than ever before and brought different civilizations into confrontation. By the late nineteenth century, the accelerated development of Europe's economic, technological, and military power had made this confrontation brutally disruptive.

Most Europeans of 1914 thought that they represented "civilization" and "progress" and the people they subjugated were "orientals" or "savages" whose cultures were "backward" or "primitive," the latter term having originally implied that those societies had not changed since earliest times. Today it is easy to see how such judgments combined racism, ignorance, and arrogance.

A more honest way to describe the interaction of cultures would have been in terms of a power disequilibrium, with the most powerful societies on one side and the less so on the other. Both groups were internally very diverse. The less powerful societies included everything from isolated kin groups living under Stone Age conditions to such great civilizations as the Chinese, which was as sophisticated as the European or more so. In 1914 the most powerful societies were Western, mostly European, although this had not always been true and would not necessarily be true in future. The power of the dominant societies derived from the West's historically exceptional potential for change, and responsiveness to change differentiated these two groups of societies as much as did disparity of power. In this sense, the two categories grouped societies with different rates of, and attitudes toward, change. Generalizing in terms of these attitudes, we may call the two groups "culturally conservative societies" and "in rapid transformation societies."

The global pattern of 1914 thus combined dominant societies, which were powerful and fast changing, and dependent societies, which were less powerful and normally slower to change—or would have been if the power disequilibrium between the two groups had not forced the West's accelerating rhythm of change on them, often with catastrophic results. This section examines characteristics common to societies on each side of this inequality in order to contrast the two categories. (Because actual societies of either group varied among themselves, Chapter 2 examines specific examples of both types.)

Although Europeans of 1914 may have thought in terms of superior and inferior, "white men" and "natives," all human societies really do form a continuum. What they share is far greater than their differences. Power disparities and rates of change themselves vary over time—thence changes in patterns of global integration. The differences considered here do not express dominance and inferiority in any terms other than the power-related ones that have created such sharp divisions in the modern world. Furthermore, a given society's dominance or dependence does not always last. In this century, Britain and Japan have shown, in opposite ways, what dramatic reversals of fortune can occur. For that reason, the last part of this section looks at what happens when societies of the two types confront each other and what conditions seem to govern movement from the dependent to the dominant camp.

Culturally Conservative Societies

Although Europeans of 1900 commonly valued change, this view was not the normal one in human history (not even in the Europe of early times). Outside the Western centers where rapid, self-compounding innovation had equated change with "progress," most societies emphasized not change but inherited patterns. Custom was an important sanction for these patterns. But most often the patterns were regarded as divinely instituted when God created the world or intervened in it—for example, through revelation to a prophet—to prescribe how people should live. An exception was ancient China, where Confucius took little interest in "spirits" yet created an ethical system that survived as the ancestral practice of millions of Chinese until this century.

Although Europeans used to dismiss non-Western societies as "primitive" or "changeless," no culture could remain unchanged over long periods of time. Members of some cultures thought that subsequent divine intervention altered earlier religious traditions. Thus Christianity emerged out of Judaism, and Islam emerged against a Judeo-Christian backdrop. Everywhere, the meaning of the central cultural tradition was elaborated through ongoing study. Members of each generation had to react to one another, to strangers, to ideas from other traditions, and to a changeable environment. These confrontations all meant change. Conservative cultures could also be extremely creative. In the eleventh century, for example, China came close to launching an industrial revolution. Different cultures also had their own accustomed concepts of change. Sometimes purists would advocate change to reassert ageold beliefs that they thought their contemporaries had ceased to honor; Islamic religious activists do this today. Sometimes innovators would try to mask change as the reassertion of old ways in their "original" form.

What culturally conservative world views did not appreciate, however, was change for its own sake. If anything, they identified change with decline. The historical fact that most such societies were agrarian, depended economically on the forces of nature, and had difficulty accumulating surplus resources to support experimentation reinforced this conservatism.

Cultural commitment to maintenance of inherited, sacrosanct patterns has far-reaching consequences for political, social, and economic life. Historically, the idea that authority and legitimacy came from on high through maintenance of a divinely appointed order encouraged authoritarian forms of rule. Small societies might run their affairs as participatory democracies, rely on councils of elders, or have chiefs who led by consensus or example. But in larger states the usual pattern was authoritarian monarchy. The ruler's authority blended political and religious functions. Such sovereigns have been said to rule by the grace of God (England), to be the shadow of God on earth (Islamic sultanates), or to be the son of heaven (China). In such a system, political authority flows from the top down. Participation in government means being a servant of the ruler. Commitment to established patterns restricts argument about policy. Court and bureaucracy monopolize politics, and the people usually have no part in it. The individual is not a citizen but a subject of the state. One compensation for this condition is that such states, despite the rulers' authoritarian claims, historically lacked the means to interfere in people's lives as extensively as even the freest present-day states can.

Socially, the most distinctive trait of conservative cultures has been the individual's submergence in larger groups. In some civilizations the most important social bond has been religious—that among Muslims or, in the Middle Ages, among Christians. But the group identification that affects individuals most intimately is membership in a kin group. War, disease, and hunger could keep kin groups from being large. Yet societies around the world idealized groups larger than the nuclear family (parents and children) as social entities—extended families, clans, tribes, even tribal confederations.

In such settings, kinship functions more as a way of talking about social organization than as a set of facts about genealogy. There are usually ways to add members to the kin group, and kin groups may split over conflicts they cannot resolve. Still, the idea that society should be organized around kinship and the genealogies that explain it provides an example of cultural conservatism in action. Everyone must know his or her place among the kin group and would be lost without its continuity. The kin group is normally the economically productive unit. The group plays a vital role in religious life and education. It polices morals. It perpetuates itself by arranging marriages, preferably within the extended kin group. It cares for the sick and old, arbitrates disputes, provides protection, and may function as a military unit. One or more senior members—elders, chief, or king—make major decisions. Historically, many kinship societies recognized no political authority above their own leaders and, without threat of force, few would.

For the individual, life in kinship society means limited personal freedom but few problems to face alone. Until its patterns come under question, members of the society are less likely to feel alienated or to protest than are individuals in freer or faster-changing environments. Arab children who grew up knowing they would marry a certain cousin seldom balked, until they learned that some other societies permitted young people to choose their own spouses.

Economically, members of culturally conservative societies mostly thought in local terms. Until recently, most countries had many local economies rather than a single national one. Rural people had to produce most of what they used, even clothing and housing. Before railroads and steamships, transport and communication problems limited large-scale economic integration. Exceptions to this rule included places—such as parts of Europe—where natural facilities for water transport lowered shipping costs, as well as goods—such as silks and spices—whose high value in relation to weight justified long-distance transport. Most people assumed that their local economy was fixed in size and could not grow, and therefore took stability and equity as their economic goals.

In the nineteenth century, even while such attitudes persisted, the growth of an integrated world economy with a few industrialized capitalist nations at its heart was forcing other types of economic systems into dependent roles in this global pattern. These subordinated economies fall into two general categories. The simplest type consisted of kinship groups that had not been integrated into strong states. Here the kin group itself served to mobilize the labor of its members and provide goods and services to them. Resources such as fields or flocks would more likely belong to the kin group collectively than to any individual. Economic inequalities might exist within the group, yet economic exchange emphasized reciprocity and redistribution among its members. In such settings the measure of wealth was not money or goods but having many kinfolk and resources to support them. Social status often depended on what one gave away, not on what one accumulated. However strange to Americans, this notion still prevails in settings as far apart as Bedouin tents in Arabia or native-American longhouses in British Columbia.

Among the dependent economies of the pre-1914 world, a second major category appeared wherever indigenous states existed, complicating economic life for their subjects by trying to extract resources from them. Historically, states, including great empires like the Ottoman or Chinese, collected taxes to support their governments, providing limited public services in return. Where large cities like Istanbul or Beijing existed and could become centers of revolt in times of scarcity, the rulers also sought to organize commerce so as to ensure the flow of goods toward the capital. In the marketplaces of towns and cities, the assumption of a no-growth economy might lead to the organization of craftsmen and shopkeepers into guilds, which distributed raw materials, controlled prices, and limited competition to ensure that every member made a living and no one made more than a fair share. Shops of a given type were likely to be located together, and a craftsman who had made his first sale of the day might be expected to pass the next customer to a neighbor who had not.

From the fifteenth century through the nineteenth, the global expansion of European power transformed economic systems elsewhere. As Europeans won control of trade in Asia's spices, Latin America's silver, Canada's furs, and Africa's human and commodity exports, local socioeconomic systems rose and fell the world over. Especially devastating was the impact of Europe's mass-produced industrial goods on hand producers. Where Europeans took direct control of territory, as the British did in India, their impact became particularly great. Many analysts used to argue that the end result of these changes would be to spread Western-style modernity around the world. More recently, others have argued that the very nature of the global pattern of interrelatedness has been to create and perpetuate inequalities between developed and underdeveloped. So viewed, "underdevelopment" is not the starting point of the poor countries' modern history but its result.

Societies in Rapid Transformation

By the 1800s, the West's most fundamental difference from other civilizations was its idealization of change, an idea that has since begun to spread around the world. As Europeans had come to identify change with progress, their readiness to experiment had increased. Whole new domains of endeavor had opened—through exploration or through creation of new branches of science, technology, or the arts—about which tradition had little to say. As experiment began to produce an ongoing stream of benefits, questions about the legitimacy of change decreased, and innovation became self-compounding.

So many of the West's innovations occurred in science and technology that modern Western civilization is often dismissed as "materialistic" in contrast to an ill-defined "spiritual East." Materialism is a problem in Western civilization and in others. However, the rise of the West brought nonmaterial benefits of immeasurable significance. The West has created the political systems that most effectively guarantee human rights, including religious freedom. The very idea of inalienable human rights is a product of European legal thought and is not found in the same terms in other traditions. The distinction of "material" and "spiritual" ultimately proves shallow, for many of the West's achievements are beneficial in both respects, as modern health-care systems illustrate. To dismiss Western civilization as materialistic is to underestimate its benefits.

But what happens to inherited beliefs as change accelerates? The question is important for both religion and politics. Secularization does occur as a society develops fields of thought not directly linked to religious tradition. Many people in the West lost interest in religion, and some scholars assumed as a result that future societies would be completely secular. Today this outcome seems unlikely. Religion no longer pervades all phases of life in the West, or in other parts of the world, as totally as it once did. Yet it endures. Religion offers believers a way to orient their lives to values that transcend the here and now. The moral questions that modern innovations raise heighten the appeal of such beliefs. What are the proper limits to the applications of genetic engineering or to the military uses of technology? Amid ceaseless change, people seek foci around which to integrate their lives.

If individuals have this need, societies also require basic principles with which to organize their political life. To be stable, political systems must be able to accommodate demands for change; yet their basic constitutional principles must be beyond controversy. Policies and politicians come and go. But if basic principles such as the definition of national identity or the rules for exercising power are matters of much controversy, then the nation risks falling into the chaos seen in the former Yugoslavia. The needed consensus about constitutional principles seems to depend in some measure on how long they have been in effect and how much they are rooted in long-held values. The strongest constitutional symbols tend to be old ones, such as the "self-evident truths" fundamental to the U.S. political system. Just as rapidly developing societies do not become fully secular, their political life needs unquestioned foundations, as well as the capacity to generate new policies.

The rise of a positive attitude toward innovation profoundly affects many realms of endeavor. Politically, the idealization of change has had revolutionary implications. The idea that people could achieve progress by using their powers of reason to analyze inherited ways of doing things undermined the sanctity of custom and of divine-right monarchy. No political order can both pursue innovative policies based on reason and maintain a divinely appointed pattern tracing back to the origins of the tradition on which the state is based. Before long, the innovations that reason demands disrupt the patterns that tradition decrees. How, too, can one determine which of many possible innovations to pursue? When a political system moves beyond maintaining patterns sanctioned by custom, or by the will of God as historically understood, the range of policy choices begins to assume the breadth familiar today. Political ideologies—general philosophies, such as liberalism or Marxism, about what kinds of policies are best—emerge. New concepts promising greater freedom or efficiency undermine the old order. Movements grow up to promote the new ideas and compete for popular support. Usually a coup or revolution occurs before the new demands for ongoing policy change become predominant. The danger of violence is greatest where change begins latest, as in Russia or China. Then revolution may transform not only political but also social, economic, and even cultural life.

Once the political transformation starts, the only satisfactory way to legitimate new policies is to seek approval from the people they affect. The old idea that *sovereignty* (ultimate authority in government) belongs to God, or to the ruler as God's representative, must give way to the characteristically modern idea that sovereignty belongs to the people, or to their elected representatives—hence nationalism and revolution. So far, Iran is the only revolutionary regime to affirm that sovereignty belongs to God; but even Iran's constitution tries to combine this idea with popular sovereignty.

Even the most democratic of revolutionaries have often understood popular sovereignty in a limited sense, however. The United States required lengthy struggles to expand the politically participatory "people" from propertied white males to all adults. Not all political systems in which sovereignty "belongs to the people" turn out to be democratic in any profound sense. We shall return to the problem of authoritarianism in mass politics in the next section. In one sense or another, however, the acceleration of change has meant a shift to mass-oriented political systems.

The social changes that accompany the shift to mass politics have put increasing emphasis on the individual and on his or her freedom of action. In the West, where individual liberation has gone furthest, even the nuclear family has seemed threatened. By the 1980s almost a quarter of all U.S. households contained only one person. To a degree, individuals so freed have been mobilized into

Bomb blast in London's financial district, April 1993. *Opposed to British control of Northern Ireland, Irish Republican Army is suspected. Terrorism and frustrated nationalism at work in western Europe. Reuters photo/©1993 UPI/Bettmann Archive.*

other social groups, often larger than the old kin groups. Such groupings include voluntary associations, interest groups, business firms, the citizenry of the modern nation, or the army.

Membership in these groups differs significantly from membership in a kinship society. Increasingly, social relations are with nonrelatives and strangers, and the old personalization of relationships gives way to impersonality. In contrast to total obligation to the kin group, an individual's obligations become segmented. The types of service and loyalty due to nuclear family, employer, club, church, and nation all differ. If these obligations are important enough, they may be defined in a written contract, enforceable by the impersonal procedures of the law. Even the freest modern states have greater means of controlling their citizens—as in tax collection and military conscription—than had the authoritarian monarchies of old. Finding our own societies complex, bureaucratic, and bewildering, many of us respond with alienation and protest.

No field has expressed the acceleration of change more than the economic. The inventions that mechanized Britain's cotton textile industry extended into a self-compounding process of innovation that has never stopped, so launching modern industrial capitalism. Its demands for raw materials, labor, and markets went on to transform the world: they enriched successful capitalists, drew peasants from Europe's villages into the labor market of the factory towns, drove older forms of production out of business, and turned peoples around the world into suppliers of raw materials and consumers of European exports. This integration of the whole world into an economic network dominated by Western capitalism then caused some of the most wrenching conflicts of modern times, as represented in struggles over labor organization, the emergence of communism, the rise of first one nation and then another to industrial leadership, and the efforts of non-Western nations to escape subordination and achieve meaningful industrial development. These issues will demand repeated comment in later chapters, and Chapter 19 will offer a comparative evaluation of development strategies.

Cultures in Confrontation

The societies that European imperialists encountered on other continents—far from "primitive" or changeless—were all products of their own historic developmental processes, which the arrival of powerful outsiders disrupted. The technological superiority that Europeans had acquired by the nineteenth century worsened the disruption, assuring integration into the European-dominated world economy as its sequel. This was a threatening process that created new conflicts among the world's peoples and aggravated old ones. Sometimes, societies were destroyed and peoples exterminated. At the least, the world's peoples confronted new ways of life introduced by aliens who sought to profit from them on unequal terms. Those who felt the impact of this confrontation reacted with varying mixtures of repulsion and attraction as they sought both to defend their cultures and to identify and appropriate the sources of European strength.

At the beginning of this century, the tensions implied in this complex reaction existed in raw form. Two world wars and the Depression had not yet dissipated Europe's advantage, and non-Western peoples had only begun to acquire the resources—ranging from better firearms to ideologies of resistance—that would better enable them to assert themselves in the twentieth century.

Several dimensions of future struggles were becoming clear, however. The future of non-Western societies did in some measure depend on mastering secrets of Western strength and productivity, especially in science and technology. The magnitude of the cultural gap between a non-Western society and the West would affect this learning process. For example, India or China, whose cultures included highly developed scientific traditions, would have an advantage over cultures that lacked such traditions. Further, the extent to which each society's culture inclined it to accept, rather than resist, borrowings from other cultures would make a positive difference in the appropriation process. The fact that Japan, for example, had an exceptional history of cultural borrowing long before Westerners reached it helped to make its modern development uniquely rapid. Yet no one-sided, global "westernization" has occurred. The more modern innovations and attitudes toward change have spread, the more people in other parts of the world have sought to integrate them into a way of life based on their own values. In this sense, the insecurities of the imperialist age have been replaced with more confident outlooks. Islamic activists, whose forebears feared that borrowing from the West would undermine Islam, today seem confident that they can choose what they want, certainly in such fields as communications or health care, and blend the imports into a securely Islamic way of life.

Indian villagers watch an educational television program. *A mass medium like television—here being used as an educational tool—can serve to mobilize public opinion.* *Raghu Rai/Magnum*

However, the Japanese remain the masters of cultural synthesis. It is no longer mere borrowing: the Japan of kimonos and tea ceremonies remains as alive as that of cameras and computers, partly because the Japanese have used their own approaches to entrepreneurship and learning to become leaders in many fields of science and technology.

Some observers have said that the world would become a "global village." Today's Japan is effectively a modern "Western" nation, but it is also Japanese. It is not clear how many developing countries can achieve as much. But even if the world becomes as intimately interconnected as a village, it will not become culturally homogenized.

The Rise of the Mass Society

How is it that popular sovereignty leads in some cases to democratic, libertarian political systems and in others to authoritarian, repressive systems? We have noted that accelerating change not only undermines political orders based on tradition but also leads to a shift—at least in symbolism—from authoritarian rule to popular sovereignty. The idea that ultimate authority in government belongs to the people implies that the people should participate somehow in political life.

Such political participation is but one kind of *mobilization* that occurs, drawing men and women into new forms of interaction, as change accelerates. For example, the clash between cultural conservatism and emerging demands for change tends to break down old social structures, "freeing" individuals for mobilization into new organizations such as labor unions and political parties. Population growth furthers mobilization, for more people in a given space are likely to interact and communicate more intensively. Compulsory education draws the young into the national culture and trains them for citizenship. National economic integration requires the mobilization of labor, as when emerging industries draw workers out of agriculture. Advances in transport and communication activate the populace by expanding people's range of movement and awareness of events outside their local communities. The rise of mass media stimulates development of public opinion and political awareness. As political controversy intensifies, activist movements mobilize the populace by competing for support. Revolution or war leads to military mobilization—the original use of the term. Old-fashioned monarchies, in which the individual was a passive subject, seldom attempted mass conscription. But mass politics means citizen obligation, at least for males, to join in the national defense. The sovereign people are their own defenders.

Pluralistic Mass Societies

The results of political mobilization depend, however, on the underlying concept of "the people." Some societies combine mass mobilization with political pluralism. There, people are seen as individuals, entitled to differences and possessing natural rights that society must protect. Not surprisingly, the clearest examples of such political systems have emerged in the pluralistic societies of Western Europe and their overseas extensions.

The concern for rights and freedoms has grown slowly in these societies, but on the world scale their accomplishments are unexcelled. For example, proclamations of basic rights began with the English Bill of Rights (1688), the French Declaration of the Rights of Man and the Citizen (1789), and the U.S. Bill of Rights (1791). The British abolished slavery in their colonies in 1833; the United States abolished it in the 1860s. In the United States, all adult males (except slaves) had the vote by the 1830s, in France by 1848, in Britain (with some exceptions) by 1884, in Germany by 1871. By the mid-1800s, movements had emerged to demand the vote for women in Britain and the United States. The kind of competitive political party system found in the United States today emerged in Britain in the first half of the nineteenth century. Of key importance in making it possible to change leaders and policies without revolution—and so reduce the political violence that still prevails in much of the world—such a system embodies political pluralism.

In time the pluralistic political systems concerned themselves with more than political rights. Legislation to protect workers began in England in the 1840s. Social insurance legislation emerged in the authoritarian Germany of the 1880s. England passed a national insurance act in 1911. To pay for social benefits, among other things, every major power had begun to collect an income tax by 1918. Great economic inequity still existed in the more democratic societies. In 1914 the wealthiest 5 percent of the U.S. population received about a quarter of the national income; in Britain the same percentage received almost half. Yet such countries were committed to pluralistic democratic principles that later achieved fuller realization, combining individual freedom with social justice in a way unmatched elsewhere.

Authoritarian Mass Societies

Unlike pluralistic systems, other twentieth-century mass societies treat the masses as an undifferentiated totality not entitled to individual rights and differences but required to maintain unity under its leaders. Most such nations lack Western Europe's pluralistic heritage and have authoritarian traditions of rule. Examples include the Soviet Union, China, and Iran, as discussed in Chapters 4, 14, and 17. Some European states had great difficulty in achieving unity or independence and so, for a time, emphasized the nation at the expense of its members. The obvious examples are Fascist Italy and Nazi Germany (see Chapter 6). Among developing countries, finally, authoritarian states predominate. In historic state centers, such as Iran or China, tradition contributes to this. Many other cases are "weak" or "soft" states, that is, states whose institutions—and even the idea of their existence as nations—began as byproducts of European imperialism that survived and "hardened" after independence. Because national identity and governing principles are not matters of consensus, weak states tend to have repressive regimes. The most repressive try to reverse the century's global trend toward mass mobilization, an effort doomed to ultimate failure.

Even authoritarian states must respond to the forces that shaped modern ideas of popular sovereignty. Many such states emerged out of revolutions that destroyed authoritarian monarchies and advanced seemingly democratic ideologies. "Democracy" and "the people" loom large in such regimes' political symbolism. Yet even if the new regimes represent government "for the people," it is not government "by the people." Under totalitarian regimes, elections typically present but a single candidate for an office. There is normally only one political party, which is more the government's way to regiment the people than the people's way to express their demands. Individual rights have no protection. And no one is at greater risk than those who do not or—like Jews in Nazi Germany—cannot conform to official expectations.

No one can justify such injustice. But we must acknowledge that the most effective authoritarian mass-oriented regimes have used their vast power to realize "social," though not "political," rights. They have improved living conditions for the masses—not counting dissenters and vulnerable minorities, to be sure. In the former Soviet Union and the People's Republic of China, this has been possible partly because earlier living conditions were so bad and partly because the new regimes did not hesitate to carry through programs with enormous human costs. Much as ancient emperors used slaves to build temples, their successors use inhumane methods to build dams and steel mills for the masses—and for the consolidation of state power.

A terrible twentieth-century irony lies in the ability of authoritarian politics to survive the collapse of old regimes and the transition to the mass society. Later chapters will show how much authoritarian mass mobilization has cost the world and how it continues to divide societies today.

Technology Versus Nature

The modern love of change springs in great measure from the technical achievements that made possible the Industrial Revolution and today's high technology. Such achievements have drastically altered societies and their relationship to their natural environment. Before the rise of modern science, most humans lived close to nature, having little control over it and taking little from it in the way of nonrenewable resources. People were extremely vulnerable to natural forces. Disease and famine carried off vast numbers and kept population within narrow limits. Over time, people caused environmental damage through deforestation or overexploitation of the land, probably without realizing what they were doing. But the integration of human and natural worlds was deeply imprinted on people's thinking. Chapter 2 shows how turn-of-the-century Egyptian villagers experienced this integration.

The twentieth century has altered this symbiotic relationship in unprecedented ways. Humankind has triumphed over many of the natural forces that used to threaten it, but not without creating the potential for its own destruction. The two world wars—especially the Holocaust (the Nazis' destruction of 6 million Jews, plus other minorities) and the nuclear bombing of Hiroshima and Nagasaki—illustrate our ability to mass-produce death and destruction. By the 1980s, enough nuclear weapons had been stockpiled to destroy the earth many times over. The Soviet Union's nuclear power plant disaster at Chernobyl (1986) exemplified the hazards that seem to accompany many advanced technologies. Today, growing evidence for global warming and stratospheric ozone depletion show, too, that individual decisions about use of energy or other resources have consequences of global scope. The anxieties about science and technology that such facts provoke scarcely existed in 1900.

Modern technology, moreover, is unevenly distributed over the world, a fact that has fueled the determination of disadvantaged peoples to gain access to its benefits at whatever cost. By the time evidence for human-induced climate change had begun to mount up in the 1980s, technologically advanced countries had begun to make significant progress in energy conservation and pollution control. In developing countries, in contrast, unprecedented population growth—a product of modern gains in public health—was multiplying the impact of both natural resource exploitation and technologies that were often less energy-efficient and more polluting than those demanded by affluent societies. Some multinational corporations exploited both the poorer countries' depressed wage rates and their less strict environmental standards by relocating labor-intensive or polluting operations from affluent to poor countries. With the collapse of its communist regimes, however, it became clear that many of the most degraded environments were in eastern Europe—grim legacies of decades of struggle to overtake the capitalist world in heavy industry and armaments (see Chapters 14 and 19). The human impact of this legacy helps explain why environmentalist "green" movements emerged all over eastern Europe by the 1980s and quickly became forces for political change.

The negative side of the balance sheet must not obscure the fact that twentieth-century science and technology have produced unprecedented benefits, as well as dangers. Medical advances have repeatedly added to the duration and quality of life. Advanced technologies for communication and information processing—particularly when available in forms accessible to many individuals, such as photocopiers, personal computers, or fax machines—have in their way become democratizing forces. While they can also serve oppressive purposes, they clearly magnified the impact of the underground opposition press in eastern Europe and eroded the governments' ability to control what people thought and knew. Together with satellite television transmissions, the same devices have prompted greater openness in many developing countries, as well as greater global awareness everywhere. Environmentalists now note an emerging trend, too, for industry—if prompted by consumer demand and appropriate government policy—to move beyond cynical reactions to environmentalist issues and provide leadership for gains in recycling, energy conservation, and the transition to renewable, nonpolluting energy sources.

The critical issue about modern science and technology is not whether it is inherently good or bad, but how people use the unprecedented power it gives them. Fields like nuclear energy or genetic engineering have potentials that are difficult to understand in early stages of development and can be extremely difficult to control once understood. Recent developments in arms control, while highly encouraging, are far from having eliminated danger from nuclear and other dangerous weapons systems, whose proliferation around the world has not at all been stopped by the end of the Cold War.

Today, our ability to dominate nature has become so great that we are at risk of overdoing it, especially considering how twentieth-century population growth magnifies technology's impact on natural habitats. Unless population growth is checked, and unless our use of technology and resources is reorganized so as neither to deplete essential natural resources nor degrade the earthly environment on which human life depends, then accustomed ways of life will become unsustainable, and mere survival will ultimately become an issue. Never before the second half of the twentieth century have human beings held such power, or such responsibility for its use. When the fate of the earth and the survival of humankind are at stake, will we use this power wisely?

Conclusion: Values for Survival

The fascinating but frightening questions at the heart of contemporary world history have implications extending far beyond the technological realm. Ultimately, they raise still more questions, about the values that have guided the development of the societies that are now most influential and about how those values will affect humanity's future.

In considering these value questions, we have to ask, Is there a need to redirect the development of contemporary societies? Many people now think there is such a need. The acceleration of change has created a world so complex and fragmented that many people feel isolated and bewildered. In the world of knowledge, the multiplication of fields and specialties has created serious problems of communication. The result is a great need for efforts at reintegration—including the study of world history. It may be that the push for economic growth, so central to the dynamics of Western society, cannot continue unrestrained in a world so tightly integrated yet so plagued by inequality. Processes of secularization could not go much further without aggravating an already serious sense of moral drift. Finally, considering the waning of superpower conflict and the steady mounting of demographic and environmental problems discussed in Chapter 19, the very meaning of security no longer seems as clear as it once did.

In many respects, we live at a turning point in history. If we negotiate it successfully, a reformulation of values seems likely to be a major part of our future. The values at the heart of many of the societies that lost out in the age of European expansion may have much to contribute to this reformulation. This is obviously true for the modern successors to those societies, for Egyptians and Koreans, and it may be true for Europeans and North Americans as well. Many of us already feel a desire for greater emphasis on social solidarity, on the symbiosis of human beings and nature, on social and cultural reintegration, and on traditional values. We sense that these ancient ideals should perhaps moderate the search for individual profit and fulfillment, the thrust for mastery of nature, the emphasis on growth and profit, and the competitiveness in commerce and international relations. One of the great challenges facing us, individually and collectively, is to respond to these concerns in productive and socially beneficial ways.

We cannot simply return to the past, but it may help us face the future. People who grew up in the optimistic atmosphere of the late nineteenth century were caught unawares by the horrors of World War I. Today, people oppressed by their consciousness of the world's problems may turn their awareness to good account. The philosopher George Santayana warned that those who will not learn from history are condemned to repeat it. In today's world, as the discussion of critical contemporary problems in Part 6 will illustrate, we could be condemned to something far worse.

Guided by the four themes discussed in this chapter—global integration, disequilibrium among cultures in an era of accelerating change, the rise of the mass society, and technology versus nature—we now set out to learn from the history of the twentieth-century world. Some readers of the chapters that follow will ask what difference they as individuals can make in face of the unprecedented problems of this century. In fact, the twentieth century has given proof that ordinary individuals can make a difference against odds that may appear hopeless. Examples include struggles for national independence all around the world, the women's movement, the U.S. civil rights movement, the antinuclear movement, and the collapse of the Soviet empire. In the face of danger, excessive pessimism leads to self-defeat.

Suggestions for Further Reading

Braudel, Fernand. *Civilization and Capitalism, 15th–18th Centuries*. Translated by Siân Reynolds. 3 vols. (1981–1984).

Crosby, Alfred W. *Ecological Imperialism: The Biological Expansion of Europe, 900–1900* (1986).

Kennedy, Paul. *The Rise and Fall of the Great Powers: Economic Change and Military Conflict from 1500 to 2000* (1987).

McNeill, William H. *A History of the Human Community*. 2 vols. (1992).

———. *The Pursuit of Power: Technology, Armed Force and Society, Since A.D. 1000* (1982).

———. *The Rise of the West: A History of the Human Community* (1991).

Stearns, Peter N., Michael Adas, and Stuart B. Schwartz. *World Civilizations: The Global Experience*. 2 vols. (1992).

Stavrianos, L. S. *Global Rift: The Third World Comes of Age* (1981).

Viola, Herman J., and Carolyn Margolis. *Seeds of Change: A Quincentennial Commemoration* (1991).

Wallerstein, Immanuel. *The Modern World-System*. 3 vols. (1976, 1980, 1989).

Wolf, Eric R. *Europe and the People Without History* (1982).

CHAPTER 2

European and Colonial Horizons of the Early Twentieth Century: A Photographic Essay

The world of 1914 was an integrated whole dominated by the rapidly changing societies of Europe and North America. Many members of dominant societies saw this global pattern in terms of sharp opposites: great powers and colonies, superior and inferior, "white men" and "natives." Such views were biased and wrong. However different they were in power or rates of change, the societies of the world were connected to one another like points along a spectrum. In 1914, most of humanity found itself at the wrong end of the power spectrum. But even "white men" and women were "natives" somewhere. Nothing assured them everlasting dominance, and the wisest knew that their civilization did not have all the answers.

In many respects, then, differences among societies in 1914 were matters of gradation. What had made Europe dominant was not any inherent superiority but the accumulated effects of Europe's exceptional potential for self-transformation: its pluralism of political and other authorities, the economic and political competitiveness that its liberal ideology idealized, its external expansiveness, and its generation of ongoing, self-compounding innovation. Compared to all that, many non-European societies were slow to change—and were probably content to be so. Usually, too, the development that they might have generated on their own was thwarted by the European impact, which made itself felt even in remote villages. However, the Europeans' image of their homelands as great powers misled them if it caused them to see such peoples as different in kind or inferior.

To illustrate the nature of the 1914 world and the range of possible contrasts between dominant and dependent societies, it helps to look at representative environments of both types: a European capital and a colonial village. Each city and village was unique in many ways, but the two examples presented here illustrate both the general traits discussed in Chapter 1 and the linkages between dominant and dependent societies.

Imperial Berlin: European Metropolis

To understand Europe's world dominance in 1914, we must visit one of its great metropolises, for the economic and intellectual creativity of its urban population was what made European dominance possible. Berlin may seem an obvious choice, because it was the capital of the newest and most powerful of the continental great powers, the German Empire, or Reich. But a more important reason for choosing Berlin over London, Paris, or Vienna is that it had only recently achieved worldwide prominence. Until the unification of Germany in 1871, Berlin was merely the capital of Prussia, the largest of thirty-nine German states. Berlin's rapid growth in size and influence came in the half-century before 1914, coinciding with the consolidation of European world dominance. Thus the characteristics of the new century can be seen particularly clearly in Berlin (Map 2.1).

Capital of the German Nation

An American visitor of 1914 might have felt more at home in Berlin than in the older European capitals. Europeans were invariably struck by Berlin's stark newness. To meet the demand for housing, the city was expanding into the open countryside; streets and apartment buildings were being constructed practically overnight. "You would think yourself in America at the moment a new city was being founded," wrote one astonished French visitor. "In twenty years Berlin will have four million inhabitants and it will be Chicago."

Both Berlin and Chicago had grown to giant size at unprecedented speed. Chicago had doubled its population within fifteen years and by 1914 was the world's fourth-largest city. Its development reflected the tremendous growth of the American economy after the Civil War. In 1914, however, the United States was only beginning to assert a worldwide influence corresponding to its economic power. Otherwise we might have chosen Chicago as our representative Western urban environment.

Berlin's growth also reflected the consolidation of a national state through war. Many of its monuments commemorated the battles of the Franco-Prussian War of 1870, in which Prussia had defeated France and created a united Germany under Prussian leadership. Glittering cavalry and goose-stepping infantry were on parade everywhere. Berlin's monuments were intended not only to impress the foreign visitor but also to enhance the German people's own identification with their nation. Half a century after German unification, many non-Prussian Germans still identified with their local state or city. But as accelerating economic and social change uprooted more and more people from local backgrounds, Germans, like other Europeans, inevitably came to think of themselves as belonging above all to a national state.

From identification with a unique national group, it was only a step to the belief that the

Map 2.1 Berlin, 1911, and Population Growth Since 1800 (in millions). *After 1945, Berlin became two cities: East Berlin and West Berlin. It was reunited in 1989.*

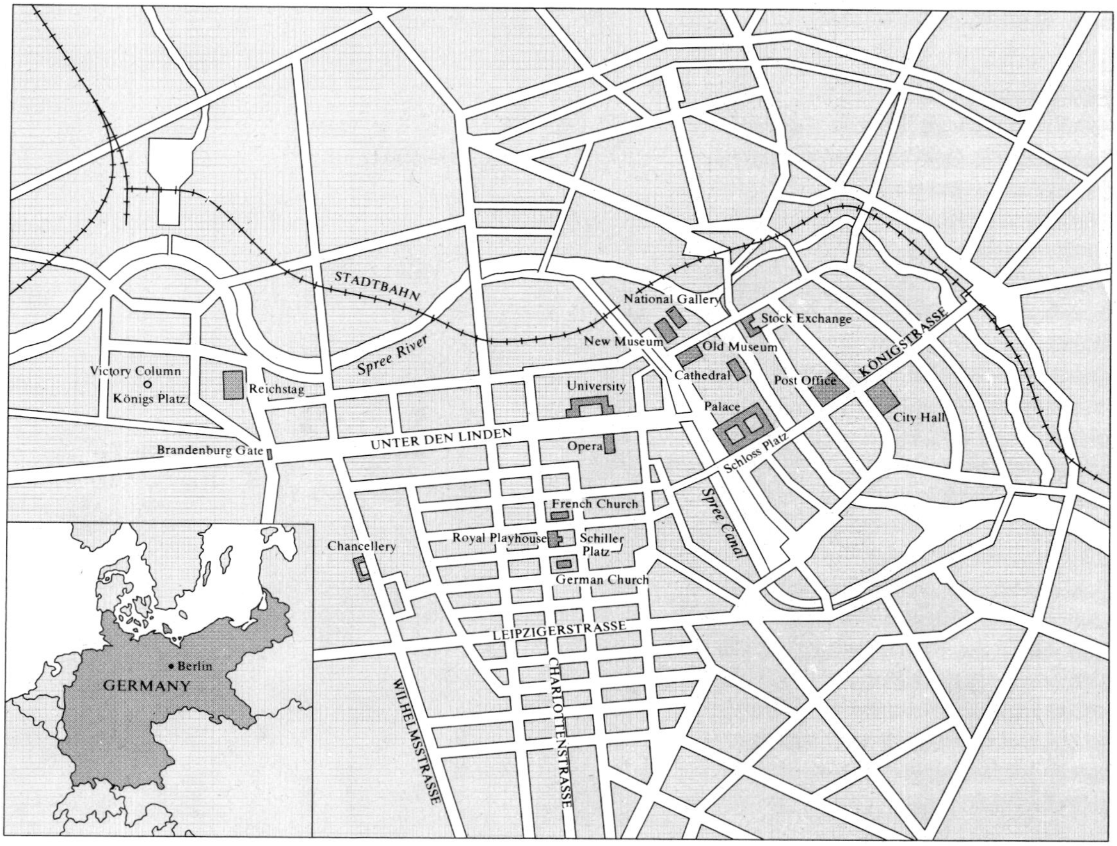

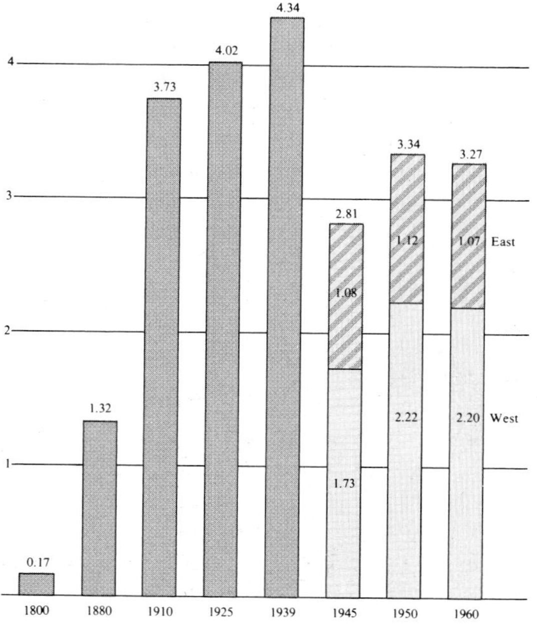

Map 2.1 Berlin 1911, and Population Growth Since 1800 (in millions). After 1945, Berlin became two cities: East Berlin and West Berlin. Only late in 1989 did the Wall between them begin to come down.

Guards cavalry returning to their Berlin barracks. *The elite Guards regiments, officered for generations by the same landowning aristocratic families, were a reminder of Prussia's warlike past. Album von Berlin (Berlin, Parnassus, c. 1900)*

world was divided among biologically differing races. In the United States in 1914, there was much talk of the virtues of the "Anglo-Saxon race." Many Germans believed themselves to be especially valuable members of the white "race" that had so easily seized domination of the world. Latecomers to the colonial contest, the Germans had only a tiny empire in tropical Africa and the South Pacific, far smaller than the holdings of their British or French rivals. Most Germans took tremendous pride in ruling over some 15 million "natives." It seemed unimportant that their colonies attracted few settlers and cost the German government more than they benefited the German economy. By conquering Africans, Germans felt, they were giving savages the opportunity to benefit from a superior civilization—such was the European perception of global interrelatedness. Africans were exhibited at carnivals

Four levels of traffic in Berlin. *The different economic activities of a modern metropolis required varied transport: the canal with barges and boats; the street traffic; the freight railway above these; and the electric passenger train taking the fastest route, through a building.* *Album von Berlin (Berlin, Parnassus, c. 1900)*

like sideshow freaks, with no recognition that their civilization was as old and in subtle ways as complex as any in Europe. Indeed, African resistance to colonization was regarded as perverse, and the German army had punished such resistance by systematic massacres.

German militarism was not focused on the colonial lands, however. Instead, Berlin's monuments and parades advertised Germany's preparedness for the "real" war, the one among the great powers. Berliners disagreed as to whether such a war was coming, but all were confident that if it did, Germany would win it.

The City as Crucible of Change

Their role in preparing for war sustained the prestige of the Prussian aristocracy, the top 1 percent of Berlin's society. Titled landowners continued to dominate the army officer corps, in prestige if not in numbers. Observing their arrogant demeanor on the sidewalks of Berlin, foreigners might have wondered why these relics of Prussia's past remained influential in a giant modern city. In culturally conservative societies the caste of warriors has often been pre-eminent. But Berlin by 1914 was far more than the garrison city for the Prussian Guards. It had become a laboratory and workplace for an innovative society, like the other great cities of Europe and North America. Titled officers might still elbow civilians aside, but it was bankers, chemists, and lathe operators, not generals and colonels, that had made Berlin a world city.

The transformation had taken only two generations. Germany had not joined the world's headlong rush to urbanization and industrialization until after the unification of 1871. As late as 1870, almost half of Germany's people were still employed, as most human beings have been throughout history, in farming. By the early 1900s, that proportion had dropped to a third. During roughly the same period, the number of German cities with a population over 100,000 rose from eight to forty-eight. Berlin's population doubled.

Today we take for granted the near-miracles of technology and hygiene that enabled people to find a better life in the city. In the late twentieth century we expect pure drinking water, adequate sanitation and fire protection, safe and dependable transportation systems. In 1914, however, these triumphs of human organization were so new that they seemed remarkable. Electric trains swept into their stations in quick succession, each disgorging hundreds of hurrying passengers, who might push a visitor aside without even a glance of apology. Each morning the streets were washed by a disciplined brigade of boys.

Perhaps half of 1914's Berliners had come from the very different environment of villages and farms. Urban life offered in one day a greater variety of new experiences than their former homes could provide in a lifetime. Even a poor Berliner could see the world's great art in a museum, borrow a book on any subject from a library, and marvel at the world's most exotic animals collected in the zoo. At a store on the corner one could buy the inventions of faraway countries, such as the Kodak camera George Eastman had first produced in Rochester, New York, in 1888.

In many ways, Berliners' lives were far freer than those of their rural ancestors. But paradoxically, the complexity of urban life also required the authorities to maintain more control over the individual. The law compelled every child in Berlin to attend school, for example, and hygiene demanded an annual physical examination for each schoolchild. By 1914 such measures had largely eliminated the danger of epidemics in the closely packed population. Detailed records were kept for every child—and for the investigations of meat inspectors, factory inspectors, and building inspectors. More and more government officials were employed in maintaining these records. Watching them at work, a visitor might have admired their efficiency but worried about the potential for bureaucratic interference in individual lives.

The space and time of Berlin were quite unlike those of the village and the farm. Berliners might commute twenty miles to work. To catch their trains, they had to know the time exactly, and so they carried watches. As they rode, most commuters glanced through one of Berlin's cheap newspapers, whose numbers had grown even faster than the city's population.

The large metropolitan newspaper was the first of the twentieth-century mass media. Telegraph and radio enabled it to involve its readers in events on the other side of the world and encourage them to hold opinions, informed or not, about distant happenings. Not that Berliners lingered long over their newspapers. Like Americans, they were usually in a hurry, often munching a quick lunch standing up at one of

Friedrichstrasse and Unter den Linden. *The Victoria Hotel at this busy Berlin crossroads honors Kaiser Wilhelm's mother, oldest daughter of Britain's Queen Victoria and her namesake. This close relationship between the two royal families did not prevent war in 1914.* *Album von Berlin (Berlin, Parnassus, c. 1900)*

a chain of identical restaurants. Berliners' rapid-fire slang, in which words were often abbreviated to initials, was regarded as very "American" by other Germans.

Like Chicagoans, Berliners in 1914 lived in a highly organized, fast-moving world of strangers. Their horizons extended around the world. Their entirely man-made environment—an "ocean of buildings"—could hardly have been more different from the environment of village and farm, where people still walked most places, recognized most of the people they saw, and told time by watching the sun move across the sky.

Its pace made Berlin exciting. The city welcomed four times as many tourists in 1914 as it had two generations earlier. Some thoughtful people, however, were worried by the growth of the giant twentieth-century metropolis. The German philosopher Oswald Spengler, for example, lamented that urban populations would soon outnumber rural people bound to traditions—"live people born of and grown in the soil." To Spengler, "the parasitical city dweller" was "traditionless, utterly matter of fact, religionless, clever, unfruitful, deeply contemptuous of rural people."

Conservatives in Germany and elsewhere have continued to criticize the great metropolis, the most visible symbol of twentieth-century change. But the very qualities of the metropolis that Spengler disliked—the impersonal crowding together of millions, each person responsible for the speedy performance of a specialized job—made possible rapid development and with it European global dominance.

A city such as Berlin or Chicago was a great human beehive. What might seem a confused swarm of people was actually the intricate interaction of millions of individuals. Together, their efforts yielded the city's products. Berlin was a world leader in such modern industries as electrical equipment, chemicals, and machine tools. Their profits helped supply capital to the city's big banks, which invested around the world from Turkey to Argentina to China.

Berliners' collective efforts also created innovation: an intangible product just as real as machinery and capital. Many of Berlin's huge factories had begun as small workshops where entrepreneurs perfected their discovery of an industrial process such as the making of a synthetic dyestuff. More recently the Kaiser (the emperor) had supported creation of research institutes, backed by both industry and government, to institutionalize the business of discovery. Scientists working in Berlin laboratories had discovered both the bacillus that causes tuberculosis and the x-ray that could detect the deadly disease. A government-sponsored researcher won a Nobel Prize for discovering a cure for syphilis. Such discoveries had made Germany the world leader in science and medicine. Emerging U.S. research universities were designed to follow German models.

Berlin provided the human critical mass for an explosion of creativity felt around the world. The contribution of its millions of workers was as essential as that of the industrialists and scientists.

The Social Classes

Not every contribution received equal reward. Berlin in 1914 was a society of layers. Each social class differed sharply from those above and below it in income, lifestyle, and even appearance.

Far outnumbering the aristocrats, who represented the top 1 percent of this social pyramid, the middle classes may have represented almost 40 percent of the population. Wealth varied widely within this group. The richest members of the middle class included many of the three hundred or so powerful company directors who controlled most of German industry. Such men would have been among the few Berliners who could afford a Mercedes or another early automobile. They lived in mansions rivaling those of the imperial family.

Hardly less comfortable were the homes of doctors, senior civil servants, and university professors: ten- or twelve-room apartments overlooking fashionable streets and squares. Guests could confirm their invitation by telephone, ride up in an elevator, announce themselves to a uniformed maid, and await their hosts in a room lit by electricity and warmed by central heating. The lower middle class did not enjoy all these comforts, but even a young journalist could find a comfortable apartment by following the building boom out into the suburbs.

Jews occupied a special place in Berlin society. The Jewish community numbered nearly 160,000, four times more than in 1871. Because of their successful careers in banking, journalism, manufacturing, and entertainment, most Jews would have qualified as middle

Bayrischerplatz, Berlin. *Nursemaids and children from nearby apartment buildings crowd this square in an upper-middle-class neighborhood. Album von Berlin (Berlin, Parnassus, c. 1900)*

class. Yet partly because their success coincided with accelerating change in Germany, they met hostility from many who regretted change and wished to blame it on someone. Prejudice excluded Jews from much of high society and from government employment down to the level of postman. Though its strength seemed to be waning by 1914, an anti-Semitic party had elected members to parliament on a platform of expelling Jews from Germany. But few Berlin Jews doubted that their future lay in that city or sympathized with the Zionist movement's aspiration to found a Jewish state in Palestine.

At the base of Berlin's social pyramid were the working classes, about 60 percent of the population. They lived much as American workers did. Though Berlin was too new to have extensive slums, the typical working-class couple inhabited a one- or two-room walkup apartment in a cheaply constructed tenement. Often the family took in a lodger,

Moving day. *Even in the prosperous metropolis of Berlin, a majority of working-class people like these had few possessions. Still their standard of living was much higher than that of most people in the non-Western world.* *Heinrich Zille/Schirmer/Mosel Verlag, Munich*

who would occupy a bed in one corner of the kitchen. Landlords were harsh, and evictions were frequent. Moving was relatively easy, for most of a couple's possessions could be loaded onto a small cart. Most workers spent long hours on the job six days a week. Significantly, workingmen's cut- rate streetcar tickets were good only before 7 A.M. and after 5 P.M.

The life of a Berlin worker was far from desperate, however. Most ate meat—only recently a rare luxury—once a day, with perhaps even a roast goose on Sunday. The family might spend Sunday at the shore of some suburban lake or working in their garden. To attract workers away from the bars, the city rented them suburban garden plots.

German and American workingmen in 1914 differed in two important respects. Berlin's workers were protected by the world's first comprehensive welfare state, and they were virtually all committed Socialists. Beginning in the 1880s, the German government had insured workingmen against the risks of sickness, accidents, and disability. Government benefits also provided "social security" in old age. These benefit plans, which required contributions from both employer and employee, violated the basic principles of nineteenth-century liberal economics, which held that the government should not tamper with the operation of a free-market economy by interfering with employment conditions. Germany's welfare state had actually been constructed in defiance of these liberal ideas by conservative politicians, who hoped to wean Germany's workers from Marxism.

Germany in the Age of Mass Politics

By 1914 this conservative hope appeared to have been disappointed. Five of "Red Berlin's" six representatives to the German parliament, or Reichstag, were members of the Socialist party, the nation's largest. In the 1912 elections, a third of the electorate had voted for this party, which still officially followed Marx in advocating revolution to overthrow the middle class, give power to the workers, and abolish private property. The rise of the mass society thus seemed to threaten social revolution.

The typical Berlin Socialist voter, however, was probably not wholly committed to his party's official program. Workingmen wanted to eliminate some relics of Prussia's oppressive past, such as systematic brutalizing of army recruits, and sought such economic benefits as the eight-hour day. They were not so sure that abolishing private property was a good idea or that Marx's idea of class warfare still made sense in a modern society where trade unions were becoming stronger and workingmen had the right to vote.

Some workers undoubtedly felt that if the Kaiser and his regime continued to obstruct reform, the working class would simply sweep them away. Under the German constitution of 1871, the Kaiser continued to play a political role that seemed strangely out of date. He still claimed authority as God's delegate on earth. His "divine right" to rule was derived not from the consent of the people but from heaven itself. Just as in the Middle Ages, crowds of petitioners gathered daily outside the royal castle, significantly near the cathedral, hoping to win a moment's attention from the monarch. Thus Berlin retained a medieval model of kingship that other Western European nations had abandoned for a limited constitutional monarchy. Kaiser Wilhelm II boasted that he had never read the constitution. But it was he, not the Reichstag, who appointed and dismissed the cabinet members who formed Germany's executive branch of government.

Despite universal manhood suffrage, Germany was not a real democracy in 1914. The Reichstag had little power. Because its proceedings were not decisive, they were dominated by the petty quarrels and cynical deals of special-interest parties and well-organized lobbies. Germany's first experience with the rise of the mass society was one of corruption and frustration, rather than a lesson in self-government.

Berlin and the Coming Century

Even in a European society accustomed to welcoming change as progress, tradition died hard. In Germany, the global power of a modern urban and industrial economy was entrusted to a backward political system that left power in the hands of one man, the Kaiser, who was known to be unstable. Most Berliners, however, were optimistic about their city's future. Berlin spent a quarter of its budget to provide an elementary education for every child. Like most other Europeans and North Americans, Berliners believed that common schooling would break down whatever cultural differences lingered among the young and would inspire continuing innovation to improve the quality of life.

A newspaper poll showed that the two historical figures Berliners most admired early in the twentieth century were Joseph Lister, discoverer of antiseptics, and James Watt, in-

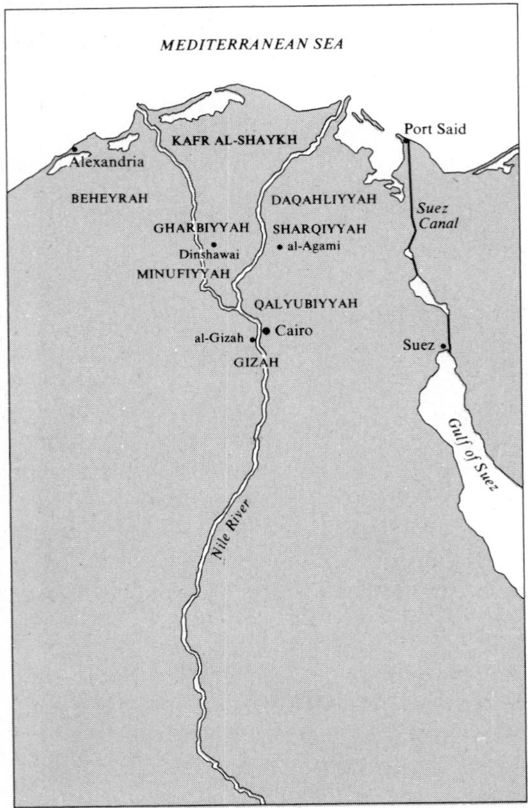

Map 2.2 Egypt, 1911, Showing the Location of Dinshawai and al-Agami. *(Province names are fully capitalized.)*

ventor of the steam engine (both Englishmen). The control of disease had raised German life expectancy from thirty-five to forty-seven years within a few decades, and the new source of energy had revolutionized the German economy. It seemed likely that the talent and energy of Berliners would produce equally miraculous triumphs of technology in the next half-century. In such an era of change, how long could traditional ideas and practices survive? Already the practice of religion was dwindling, so that only a quarter of the babies born in Berlin in 1914 were baptized. Now that science was unraveling the secrets of the universe, many Berliners thought, the values of the superstitious past could be discarded.

A mere thirty years later, devastated by the bombing of World War II, Berlin would lie in ruins. But in 1914 only the most pessimistic of people recognized the dangers that lurked in the very characteristics that had enabled European civilization to conquer the world. The rivalries of national pride would prove disastrous when Europeans in two world wars turned on one another the ferocity they had already shown against Africans and Asians. The advances of science, reinforced by the methods of administrative control that had made Berlin so efficient, would make those wars far more deadly. War's unequal stress on social classes would bring revolution in 1918. The domination of the masses in politics would help give power to leaders such as Adolf Hitler with ideas far more dangerous than the Kaiser's vague dream of extending German influence everywhere.

In twenty years, these developments would fatally undermine the global pattern of European domination. In 1914, however, it still stood triumphant. To see that system from the perspective of non-Europeans is our next task.

Dinshawai: An Egyptian Village

The characteristic setting for life in the colonial world in 1914 was the village. No single village can typify the colonial countries as well as Berlin did the Western powers. But Dinshawai, in Egypt, illustrates not only how villagers lived but also how European power made itself felt in far parts of the world (Map 2.2). An ugly incident that occurred in Dinshawai in 1906 provides a good starting point for a discussion of village life in the Nile Delta at the beginning

Pigeon tower, said to be atop the house of Zahran, one of the heroes of Dinshawai, Minufiyyah Province, 1983. *C. V. Findley*

of this century. Many features of the village's physical appearance, its social composition, and its political, economic, and spiritual life are specific to the Nile Delta. But in important respects Dinshawai resembled villages all over the colonial world of the early twentieth century.

The Dinshawai Incident of 1906

Egypt had passed under European domination in an unusual way. Politically, Egypt was still a province of the Ottoman Empire, which was ruled by the sultan at Istanbul and included part of southeastern Europe, together with Turkey, the Arab countries of southwestern Asia (including what later became Israel), and Libya. Yet Egypt was no ordinary province. Members of the same family had governed it since 1805, as they would until 1952, and they had acquired powers that made them little less than independent. When the British occupied Egypt in 1882, they did not bother to remove the family of hereditary governors, then known as *khedives,* or to deny—until World War I—the sovereignty of the Ottoman sultan.

Prisoner No. 48—perhaps Muhammad Zahran himself—leaves the court at Dinshawai after being condemned to death. *The British press denounced the condemned men as murderers.* Illustrated London News, *July 14, 1906*

The British left outward forms unchanged, but they took charge.

What happened at Dinshawai has never been entirely clear. People of different cultures perceived the incident differently. It began when British officers, on march through Minufiyyah Province, northwest of Cairo, went pigeon shooting. Western accounts of the incident usually fail to mention that pigeons in Egypt are not wild birds. The peasants raise them for food and build towerlike houses, atop their own houses, for pigeons to nest in. At Dinshawai, a British shot apparently started a fire in some grain on the threshing grounds at the edge of the village. Another shot hit a woman. The villagers sought vengeance, as their code demanded. In the ensuing fracas, several officers and villagers died, and more troops were called in.

The annals of imperialism include many similar episodes. In a sense, they were part of the costs of the game, and it was not always possible for the dominant power to avoid losing. But this time, Lord Cromer, the highest British official in Egypt from 1883 to 1907, decided to exact punishment. He had fifty-two

Skyline of al-Agami Village, Sharqiyyah Province, 1983. *The painted domed building is the shrine of a local saint. Al-Agami is a Delta village with many resemblances to Dinshawai.* C. V. Findley

villagers arrested and tried under a regulation against attacks on British army personnel. In keeping with the pretense that the khedive ruled Egypt, prominent officials from Cairo were sent out to serve as judge and lawyers. Thus Egyptians prosecuted Egyptians for attacking foreigners who had inflicted the first injury. Four men were sentenced to death, others to hard labor, others to public flogging. The hangings and floggings were carried out on the threshing grounds at the village edge, while the victims' families looked on helplessly.

Egyptians have never forgotten these events. Village bards immortalized them in folk ballads. As a boy, Anwar al-Sadat, president of Egypt from 1970 to 1981, heard his grandmother sing about Zahran, the villagers' hero and one of those hanged. Sadat and others grew up wanting to overthrow those responsible for what had happened—a dream that the 1952 revolution fulfilled.[1] In the Cairo of 1906, intellectuals poured forth their outrage in verse and newspaper articles. As an example of political mobilization, this was a great moment: the first time educated Egyptians supported peasant violence. Critics of British policy as far away as France and England wrote about the incident. Cromer had to retire a year later, and his successor arranged for the

Brickyard at al-Agami Village, Sharqiyyah Province, 1983. *Villagers mix mud and straw (foreground) to make unbaked mud brick, the traditional building material of the village. Newer building techniques are also now in use.* *C. V. Findley*

pardon and release of the villagers still in prison.

The Village as Setting of the Rustic Drama

Passing by a village in the Nile Delta in 1906, one ordinarily saw little sign of events as dramatic as those that led to the trials. From afar, the village looked like an indistinct mass of low houses, with a few trees, surrounded by fields. In the United States, farmhouses were normally isolated. In contrast, in the Middle East and in most other parts of the world, those who tilled the soil lived together in a village and went out each day to their fields. Very likely, the only structure in the village that differed noticeably from others was the domed and painted shrine of the local saint. The village might have a small mosque or simply an open space at the edge of the fields to use for prayers. If some villagers belonged to Egypt's Coptic Christian community, there was a church. The village displayed few signs of occupational specialization. There might be one or two religious functionaries, a barber who also served the villagers' medical needs, and a grocer selling sugar, tea, soap, oil, kerosene, tobacco, and matches. To find other shops or to market their own surplus produce, villagers went to a larger market town down the road.

Many villages lacked streets. Often, there were only one or two lanes, muddy and littered with wastes, because Egyptian villagers had none of the amenities that enabled Berliners to live at close quarters in cleanliness and comfort. Often, the lanes penetrated only part way through the mass of buildings, far enough to give access to the various quarters, where the households of each kinship group were clustered together. In such a case, the main thoroughfare was a circular route around the village. Threshing grounds and open spaces for prayers or festivals lay near this route.

Within the village, the crowded, flat-roofed houses were much like those of ancient times. The villagers still built with the same kind of unbaked mud-and-straw bricks mentioned in the Bible. They still lit their houses with Roman-style oil lamps and heated them with braziers. Houses and furnishings thus expressed cultural conservatism. Yet a visitor from Berlin or Chicago would have been wrong to think the villagers primitive. Mud bricks are not only low in cost and free to those who make their own but also durable in a hot, dry climate and more efficient insulators than many modern materials. Villagers may have had little access to modern technologies, but their traditional ones were sophisticated adaptations to their environment and resources.

Inside the houses, one might find chickens or cows, as well as people. On the rooftop, one might see a pigeon tower, drying crops, or dung cakes for use as fuel. The human and natural worlds were intimately associated. The French sociologist Jacques Berque studied a village near Dinshawai and likened its life to a rustic drama with earth, water, plants, animals, and people as its heroes.[2] Someone habituated to Berlin's frenzied pace might think that drama was hardly the word for village life. But a sensitive observer could perceive that much action did occur, sometimes violently.

Village Society

The greatest difference between social life in the village and in the United States or Europe lay in the role of the individual. In the village, the extended kin group was all-important; the individual counted for much less. Death claimed more than a quarter of all infants within their first year, and partly for that reason, average life expectancy for the entire population barely exceeded twenty years. Most people had little time to make a mark of their own. While life lasted, its quality was not good. Tuberculosis and hereditary syphilis were endemic, as were such parasitic diseases as bilharziasis, hookworm, and malaria. Almost all men of the village contracted parasitic diseases from long work in water and mud.

Social roles also limited the individual. They were highly standardized and little differentiated except in terms of sex and age. The normal routine for the men was fieldwork, including irrigation. Women were in charge of housework, child care, and the milking and feeding of livestock. They also helped in the fields and took produce to sell in the market town. Men had a very limited range of occupational choices. After their years at the village Qur'an school, a few bright boys would go elsewhere for advanced study and become religious scholars. Some would take up barbering, building, or singing in addition to their fieldwork. Choice was almost nonexistent for the women. Uncontrolled fertility dominated their lives. Their standard dress, the long black *gallabiyah* (the same term used for the nightshirt-like outfit of the men) was always full enough to accommodate pregnancy and had two slits at the side of either breast for nursing.

Villagers often married during their teens. A young couple normally remained in the groom's father's household and shared in its work. Even after they had children, the young couple acquired little autonomy as long as the older generation lived. The closest thing to independence came with age, when males became heads of extended-family households and their wives thus acquired charge of their daughters-in-law and grandchildren.

To the extent that the short average life expectancy allowed the pattern to be maintained, a villager lived much of his or her life in an extended household that included not only parents and children but also grandparents, uncles, aunts, and cousins. This three-generation household was the meaningful social unit for some purposes, such as farming its own land. But in many respects, even more extended kin groups were the fundamental social units. A village like Dinshawai might have had only five or six such kin groups, but each kin group might have had one or two thousand members at the start of this century and today would have several times that many.

The feelings of solidarity associated with common descent were the strongest loyalties that village society knew. Often the founder of the kin group was regarded as a saint. Nothing, except the claim to descent from the Prophet Muhammad, could enhance family prestige more than for one of the domed shrines that dominated the village skyline to be the tomb of the family founder. The kin group preserved its integrity by arranging marriages, usually within its own circle. The group had a male head, whose functions included dispensing hospitality, solving disputes within the group, and handling relations with the outside world, especially the government. The elders who traditionally ran the village were kin-group heads. When the government created the office of village headman (*'umdah*), it was usually filled by the leading kin-group head, with the others grouped around him as elders. The unofficial institutions of kin-group leadership thus became the first link in an official chain that extended to Cairo and on to London.

Sabiha, a woman in Dinshawai, with a child from the village, 1983. *C. V. Findley*

The kin group expressed its solidarity through several physical institutions. The most important was the "big house" (*duwwar*), which served as headquarters for the kin-group head, guesthouse, meeting place for the leading members of the kin group, and scene for the celebration of marriages, circumcisions, healings, or returns from journevs, especially the pilgrimage to Mecca. So frequent were the meetings, and the shared meals that accompanied them, that the big house played a major economic role in redistributing goods within the kin group. One of the many burdens on the women was the requirement to help with the chores there.

The legendary image of Middle Eastern hospitality was formed in settings like the big house. A visitor with an introduction to a village kin group could rely on this hospitality for accommodation. As the village elders' meeting place, the big house also had an official function. In the Dinshawai trials of 1906, a big house served as courthouse. It still stood eighty years later, with an empty weapons rack in a corner to symbolize the importance of defense among the common concerns of the kinsmen who used to meet there.

Other physical expressions of kin-group solidarity included the family tombs, which were vaults built, maintained, and used by the group. Grain for all its members was ground in a cooperative mill. Collectively maintained waterwheels required the group to make joint decisions on their repair and use. Even religious structures expressed the solidarity of the kinspeople who had joined forces to build them.

Common activities also reaffirmed kin-group solidarity. The men met to decide issues, such as the sharing of irrigation water. The kin group gathered at the big house for family occasions. Today one still sees parties of children in the fields pulling weevils off the cotton plants. Some religious observances had family significance, particularly if a family member was claimed as a saint. Finally, there was the common defense.

Normally only a few constables, under the control of the village headman, represented the forces of law and order in the village. Disputes over irrigation water, or over injuries to the persons or to the honor of kinspeople, could give rise to feuds that went on for generations, marked by destruction of crops and other acts of violence, including murder. Every kin group included some men ready to sleep in the fields to protect the crops or ready to defend the family against other families or against agents of the government. Some of these valiants became village heroes, like Zahran.

The Kinship Society and the World Outside

Because the kin group meant so much, village society de-emphasized not only the individual but also larger social groupings. The sole exception was the common religious bond among all Muslims.* Countless features of Islam emphasize the equality and solidarity of all believers. But a spiritual message, even one so often repeated, can be difficult to apply in everyday life. In the village, few occasions brought together different kin groups. The most important were the nativity festivals for the saints of the village and for the Prophet Muhammad.

Apart from economic links, the village was relatively isolated from the outside world. Some of the boys went to study at the higher religious schools of the major towns or at the Al-Azhar Mosque University in Cairo; many such scholars never returned. Pious villagers of sufficient means would make the Islamic pilgrimage to Mecca. Their social system was so

*A Muslim is a believer in Islam. Islam is a form of monotheism (faith in one God) and is based on scripture, the Qur'an (Koran), revealed to the Prophet Muhammad. Islam is related to Judaism and Christianity and resembles them in many ways. Islam was founded in the seventh century.

Villagers tilling the soil with a wooden plow, al-Agami Village, Sharqiyyah Province, 1983. *C. V. Findley*

self-contained, however, that villagers still had little sense of political integration into any entity larger than the kin group. The "politics" that meant most to them concerned matters such as marriage and irrigation or feuds among kin groups.

Villagers knew about the khedive in Cairo and the sultan in Istanbul, and they had some notion of the British. But they also had the apathy of people whose opinion was never asked. Agents of the central government usually came to the village to collect taxes, conscript soldiers, or exact forced labor. In their dealings with officials, villagers tended to be submissive but evasive. The officials generally responded by treating the peasants like brutes.

Among Egypt's urban elites, nationalist movements had been working for political mobilization at least since the 1870s, but the villagers knew little of these. The Dinshawai incident of 1906 helped set the stage for political mobilization of the villagers by causing the urban elites to take a greater interest in them. The villagers themselves had little concern about national politics until the revolution of 1919, Egypt's response to the pressures of World War I.

Economic Life of the Village

In the economic life of the village, agriculture reigned supreme. Tilling one's own land was virtually the only occupation that had prestige among villagers, who were aptly known as *fellahin* ("cultivators"). Many things about Egyptian agriculture seemed timeless, yet European interference had fundamentally changed the rustic drama during the the nineteenth century.

If the villagers had been left to themselves, their economic life in 1906 would have resembled that of many other culturally conservative societies. Villagers would have spent their time cultivating and irrigating their fields, divided into many small plots by the provisions of Islamic inheritance law. Villagers would have consumed some of their produce, used some for hospitality, bartered some, sold some, and yielded up a good part for rents or taxes. They would have given little thought to saving or investment, except to buy more land. Wealth, in their view, would have consisted in having many kinsmen—and land to support them. The delta villager's economic world would have been radically different from the European capitalist's. Instead of profit and growth for the individual, the village would have emphasized the kin group's common interests and the equitable distribution of resources within it.

A woman using canal water to wash, al-Agami Village, Sharqiyyah Province, 1983. *C. V. Findley*

But delta villagers had not been left to themselves. A new economic order had come into existence, one closer to European capitalist norms than to kin-group communalism. Until the rapid population growth of this century, Egypt produced agricultural surpluses. Since the early nineteenth century, the family that governed Egypt had sought to take advantage of this productivity. The rulers introduced changes in land tenure that led to the formation of huge estates owned by individuals associated with the government; they undertook large-scale public works to extend irrigation, with permanent irrigation in the delta. Thus delta agriculture no longer depended on the annual Nile flood, and cultivators could work year-round, producing several crops.

Together with other factors, expensive public works led to tax increases that strained the resources of peasant families. Aiming to maximize agricultural exports, the government introduced new crops—especially long-staple cotton. But cotton cultivation required more investment than did cultivation of other crops, further straining villagers' resources. And increased emphasis on production for export compounded a problem common to all colonial economies: vulnerability to unforeseen price shifts in world commodity markets. During the U.S. Civil War, for example, when the South could not export its cotton, the price of Egyptian cotton more than tripled. But between 1865 and 1866, when U.S. cotton reappeared on the world market, cotton prices fell by more than half. The collapse of cotton brought ruin to Egyptians and helped push the khedive's government toward bankruptcy, preparing the way for the British occupation in 1882.

More and more village families sank into debt as their taxes and operating costs grew; finally they lost their lands. By 1906, less than a quarter of the rural work force consisted of landowners cultivating their own land. The rest were sharecroppers, tenants, or wage laborers, many of whom had formerly owned land. Some villages now consisted entirely of landless fellahin, often working for absentee landlords. Peasants who had once cultivated their own fields of wheat, vegetables, and clover spent most of their time growing cotton for the landowners. In the remaining hours, they worked small plots to produce the crops, especially beans and onions, that formed their meager diet.

Agricultural Egypt was being integrated into the world economy under conditions of colonial subordination. Egypt was also becoming a market for goods that its colonial masters had to sell, although villagers were too poor to buy much. Shifting tastes in beverages illustrate this point. Historically, the villagers preferred coffee, consumed in the Middle East long before it became known in Europe. But in 1906 a visitor would probably have been offered tea, for Egypt was then ruled by the British, who dominated the world's tea trade. Today, a visitor is just as likely to be offered a soft drink, such as Coca-Cola.

Although they made no headlines, the changes in village economic life were as drastic as the violence of 1906 at Dinshawai.

The Life of the Spirit

The aspect of village life that the appearance of monotony most misrepresented was the life of the spirit. Egyptian villagers' religious life was a rich mixture of elements ranging from formal Islam, through a variety of popular religious practices sanctioned only by custom, to superstition and magic. Although the people were Muslims, or sometimes Coptic Christians, their religious life included traces of beliefs that had prevailed in Egypt in pre-Islamic or even pre-Christian times.

Formal Islam was based directly on the Qur'an and the Islamic religious legal system (*shari'ah*). Formal Islam included the profession of faith, the five daily prayers, almsgiving, the fast during the month of Ramadan, and—for those who could afford to do so once in a lifetime—the pilgrimage to Mecca. Annual observance of the two major religious festivals and of the Prophet's birthday was another part of formal Islam, and Islamic law regulated countless features of daily life, from concepts of cleanliness to inheritance. The Islamic world view also expressed itself in many pious forms of speech. For example, one never expressed any intention about the future without saying *In sha'a 'llah* ("if God wills"): "If God wills, I'll help you pick cotton tomorrow."

Popular Islam included practices that did not grow directly out of the Qur'an and religious law but had been established by custom. Eventually, religious reformers began to attack these practices precisely because they had no justification except custom, but this change was not felt in delta villages until the 1930s. The two main expressions of popular Islam in the village were mystical societies and the local saint's nativity festivals.

The mystical societies, branches of orders (*tariqah*) found in many parts of the Islamic world, met periodically to engage in special religious exercises, ranging from repetitive prayer to music and dance, in an effort to deepen their religious experience. These societies combined religious fulfillment with social interaction in an environment that offered few leisure activities. They might also appeal to kin-group loyalty, for society members often belonged to a single kin group. One of the village saints might be remembered as founder of both kin group and mystical society.

The saints' tombs, which were thought to radiate grace, were places for prayer and visitation at all times. Once a year, a nativity festival (*mawlid*) was held at the tomb. A pole was erected on an open space near the tomb, and village families set up tents at the site. The pious and the mystical societies passed in procession. Litanies were recited. Supplicants circulated around the saint's tomb, seeking intercession. But the mawlid also included an earthier component. Merchants came from far and wide to set up booths. Musicians and snake charmers delighted the crowd. Boys circulated in hopes of catching a glimpse of pretty girls. The nativity festivals were fairs, communal celebrations, and religious events, all in one. The nativity of the Prophet produced a similar celebration on a grander scale. Then and now, these festivities were the high points of the villagers' year.

Modern scholars believe that some local saints' shrines were shrines of Christian saints in pre-Islamic times and of ancient Egyptian gods in pre-Christian times. If so, the shrines are among many links with pre-Islamic types of religious consciousness. Such links are especially abundant in the realm of superstitious and magical practices.

Generally, these practices can be grouped under the heading *animism*: the belief that the natural world is inhabited by spirits. Egyptian villagers believed in many spirits. A magic serpent haunted houses. A barren woman could conceive if she went inside an abandoned tomb. Certain practices could help ward off the evil eye. Physical and mental disturbances were also attributed to spirits. Against these afflictions, villagers relied on the folk remedies of the barber or wore amulets. A cult called the *zar*, especially frequented by women, used rituals—music, dance, song, and sacrifice—as means of exorcism.

By identifying the spirit world with that of nature, animism fosters an intense spiritual involvement in the processes of nature. Many beliefs and practices of delta villagers expressed this involvement. The fellahin loved the land, and their ideas of what was good for them were dominated by their concept of what was good for land, crops, and livestock. For example, muddy canal water was not only good for irrigating fields, it was also better than clear water to drink. Canal water was best for washing clothes. To improve an inadequate milk flow, a nursing mother would wade into the canal up to her breasts and express a few drops of her milk into the water. The same practice was used to increase a buffalo's milk. To Berliners of the age of Lister, such beliefs would have been unthinkable. The assumed fusion of human, natural, and spiritual realms, however, was one of the dominant notes of village life.

Conclusion: Berlin and Dinshawai

Berlin, with its explosion of creativity, and Dinshawai, with its rustic drama, give an idea of the range of variation between the great powers and the colonial world as of 1914. The two contrast in terms of virtually all the twentieth-century themes defined in Chapter 1. Berlin flourished as capital of one great power;

Dinshawai suffered as victim of another. Berlin was a crucible of change; Dinshawai was a living example of cultural conservatism. In the Berlin of 1914, the age of national integration and mass politics had begun, despite such anachronisms as the Kaiser and aristocracy. In Dinshawai, the incident of 1906 marked a first step in the villagers' political mobilization. Berlin led in developing modern technology; Dinshawai relied on time-tested technologies adapted to its environment and resource-endowment. Berlin represented many of the values that would shape the twentieth century; Dinshawai embodied those that had molded human experience through the ages.

In 1914 the world's Berlins and Dinshawais looked radically different. Yet the global economic relationships that had brought cotton cultivation to the Nile Delta linked them. So did the political domination that brought death to Dinshawai in 1906. Most Europeans and Americans of 1914 would have thought the comparison between Berlin and Dinshawai was all to Berlin's favor. The crises that destroyed the global pattern of great powers and colonies left Berlin ruined and divided a generation later, however, while the mudbrick houses of Dinshawai stood intact. Today, in a world where European dominance is a memory and global interdependence increasingly a reality, the values that made places like Dinshawai work command our interest in a way that bids us recognize the shared humanity of men and women everywhere.

Since 1914, global integration has tightened. The disparity between representative living environments in affluent and poor countries has diminished, as we shall argue in Chapter 18. Most important, the power inequalities that fostered Europe's imperialist arrogance have diminished, however vast and threatening the inequalities that persist among nations.

Notes

1. Anwar El-Sadat [sic; for al-Sadat], *In Search of Identity: An Autobiography* (New York: Harper & Row, 1978), pp. 16–17.
2. Jacques Berque, *Histoire sociale d'un village égyptien au XXe siècle* (Paris: Mouton, 1957), p. 9.

Suggestions for Further Reading

Berlin

Kollmann, Wolfgang. "The Process of Urbanization in Germany at the Height of the Industrialization Period." In *The Urbanization of European Society in the Nineteenth Century,* edited by Andrew Lees and Lynn Lees (1976).

Liang, Hsi-Huey. "Lower-Class Immigrants in Wilhelmine Berlin." In *The Urbanization of European Society in the Nineteenth Century,* edited by Andrew Lees and Lynn Lees (1976).

Masur, Gerhard. *Imperial Berlin* (1970).

Dinshawai

Ayrout, Henry Habib. *The Egyptian Peasant.* Translated by John Alden Williams (1963).

Berque, Jacques. *Histoire sociale d'un village égyptien au XXe siècle* (1957).

Fakhouri, Hani. *Kafr el-Elow: An Egyptian Village in Transition* (1972).

Goldschmidt, Arthur. *Modern Egypt: The Formation of a Nation-State* (1988).

Richards, Alan. *Egypt's Agricultural Development, 1800–1980: Technical and Social Change* (1982).

PART 2

Crisis in the European-dominated World Order

CHAPTER 3

World War I: The Turning Point of European Ascendancy

The collapse of Europe's world dominance began with an assassination. It took place on June 28, 1914, in Sarajevo, the capital of Bosnia, then under Austro-Hungarian rule but today the scene of savage ethnic strife after the disintegration of Yugoslavia. A nineteen-year-old terrorist, Gavrilo Princip, stepped up to the car in which Archduke Franz Ferdinand, heir to the Austrian throne, was making an official visit to the city. With a shaking hand he pumped bullets into the archduke and his wife, fatally wounding them both.

Because the Austrian government correctly suspected that Princip's terrorist organization, the Black Hand, had the covert backing of the head of intelligence of the neighboring kingdom of Serbia, Austria-Hungary retaliated by threatening and then declaring war on Serbia. The hostilities soon expanded. One after another, honoring commitments made in treaties with their allies, the major powers of Europe entered the most costly war the world had yet witnessed.

In the end, some 10 million young men were killed and another 20 million crippled. In France, more than 1.3 million died, a quarter of all the men of draft age (between twenty and thirty-eight) in 1914; in addition, half the draft-age population had been wounded by 1918. Death reaped a rich harvest among civilians as well. Millions died from malnutrition in Germany, as the British blockade cut off food supplies, and in Russia, where the still-developing economy could not cope with both total war and normal requirements.

Other consequences of World War I had even longer-lasting significance. To mobilize manpower and material, governments extended their control over the lives of citizens, creating a precedent for later government management of society to meet crises. To meet the gigantic costs of World War I, governments resorted to methods of financing that continued to strain the world's economy for generations. The stresses of the war gave communism its first opportunity when V. I. Lenin and the Bolsheviks seized control of the 1917 revolution that had toppled Russia's tsarist government. Thus began the formation of the hostile blocs that divided the world until communism finally collapsed. Above all, the impact of the war and its aftermath helped Adolf Hitler take power in Germany in 1933. The rise of a man dedicated to reversing the outcome of World War I by force probably made a second world war inevitable. From that conflict, Europe would emerge in ruins in 1945, too feeble ever to re-establish control over the rest of the world.

Causes of World War I

The shots fired by Princip at Sarajevo in 1914 killed not only the heir to the Hapsburg throne but eventually the European-dominated world system. They marked one of the great turning points of history. When the slaughter stopped in 1918, people groped for an explanation of its origins. How could a political assassination, in a town unknown to most Europeans of 1914, have led to such a disaster?

Aggression or Accident?

In the peace treaty they wrote at Versailles, the "winners" of World War I (France, Britain, and the United States) naturally held the "losers," especially Germany, responsible—though it makes little sense to speak of winners and losers after a conflict that mortally weakened every country involved, except the United States. Article 231 of the Versailles treaty placed the blame on decisions made by German leaders between the shooting of the archduke on June 28 and the outbreak of general war in early August.

If we could believe, as the victors claimed at Versailles, that World War I was caused by the deliberate aggression of evil leaders, we would have the key to preventing future wars. Peace could be maintained by preventing people with such intentions from obtaining power, or by constantly resisting them if they already held power. In fact, however, most historians believe that well-meaning, unimaginative leaders in every capital stumbled into World War I. By doing what most people believed was normal for defense, they produced a result none had ever intended.

Ideas cause wars: ideas of how the world is divided and how to resolve conflicts within it. Ideas of nationalism and of alliances underlay World War I. The idea of South Slav nationalism inspired Princip to fire his fatal shot. The local conflict between South Slav nationalism, represented by Serbia, and the Austro-Hungarian Empire escalated into a world war because of European leaders' notion that their nations' safety depended on maintaining credible alliances. These two ideas were reflections of some more basic characteristics of the European-dominated world of 1914. We cannot explain why South Slav nationalists like Princip wanted to destroy the Austro-Hungarian Empire, and why Europe was tangled into alliances that pulled everyone into the conflict, without understanding the nature of international relations in 1914, the assumptions that Europeans made about their obligations to their national communities, and even the general mood. A full appreciation of these factors makes it much easier to understand the link between the shots at Sarajevo and a war of 30 million casualties. If that assassination had not triggered a world war, some similar event elsewhere might have done so.

The Multinational Empire

The shots at Sarajevo might never have been fired had multinational Austria-Hungary not survived into the twentieth century. A state that included people of a dozen ethnic groups seemed out of date to a nationalistic age that believed every ethnic group should have a nation of its own. Austria-Hungary was a mosaic of ethnically diverse provinces collected over a thousand years of wars and dynastic marriages (Map 3.1). Some of these ethnic groups felt they were unfairly treated by the dominant Austrians and Hungarians, and by the twentieth century their rebelliousness had been encouraged by developments on the empire's borders. Nations such as Italy had emerged as independent homelands for some of the ethnic groups that felt oppressed under Hapsburg rule.

In the capital, Vienna, it was feared that a rebellion by another ethnic minority would mean the end of the empire. The nightmare was that the independent kingdom of Serbia would do for the empire's South Slavs what Italy had done for its Italians. Since a palace revolt in Serbia had replaced rulers sympathetic to Austria-Hungary with fanatical nationalists, discontented South Slavs within the empire could look across the border for arms and encouragement. Through the assassination of the archduke, Princip and his fellow terrorists, Austrian subjects who sought a nation of their own, aimed to provoke a war that would destroy the Austro-Hungarian Empire.

They succeeded. In Vienna, the Austro-Hungarian government took the assassination as a historic opportunity to eliminate the Serbian menace. On July 23, Austria-Hungary dispatched to the Serbs an insulting set of demands that no independent nation could have been expected to accept.

Alliances and Mobilization

The ultimatum to the Serbs set off a chain reaction that within ten days involved almost all the major powers in war. Government leaders believed that in a showdown the loser would be the first country that did not stand with its allies. A power that proved a weak or disloyal ally would soon have no allies left.

In 1914 Europe was divided into two combinations of great powers: the Triple Alliance of Germany, Austria, and Italy and the Triple Entente of France, Russia, and Britain. Ironically, these alliances had originally been formed for defensive purposes. In a clash over European or colonial issues, diplomats had felt their countries would face less risk of attack or defeat if backed by a strong ally.

The events that led to the outbreak of World War I suggest that the leaders had miscalculated. Alliances made it easier, not more difficult, to go to war. The more aggressive partners tended to recklessness because they were counting on allied help. The less aggressive partners were afraid to restrain their ally, lest they appear unreliable and thus find themselves alone in the next crisis. Had the rulers of Austria-Hungary not been sure of German support, they might not have risked war with the greatest Slavic nation, Russia, by attacking Serbia. But the German government essentially gave the Austro-Hungarian government a blank check to solve the Serbian problem as it chose. Because of their own blundering foreign policy of the past quarter-century, the Germans felt encircled by unfriendly nations. Ringed by France, Britain, and Russia, the Germans felt they could not let down their one reliable ally.

In the Bosnian crisis of 1908–1909, Russia had challenged Austria-Hungary's annexation of Bosnia but eventually had backed down. In 1914, however, the Russians were determined to stand by their South Slavic kinfolk. When Austria-Hungary declared war on Serbia on

The capture of the assassin of Archduke Franz Ferdinand and his wife in Sarajevo, June 28, 1914. *The Granger Collection*

July 28 (despite Serbian acceptance of all but one of the demands), the Russians began mobilization. Tsar Nicholas II, who had recently sponsored two international disarmament conferences, would have preferred war against Austria-Hungary alone. Russian military experts, however, explained that their mobilization plan did not permit that kind of flexible response. The tsar had only two choices, they said. He could remain at peace, or he could launch total war on all fronts.

When the tsar chose the latter course on July 30, the events that followed were almost automatic. Though some German leaders began to think of drawing back, it was too late. With the Russian army mobilizing on their borders, they felt forced to launch full-scale war. Germany expected to fight both France and Russia; its only hope of success would be to finish off France quickly before the slow-moving Russians posed too great a threat. Thus German mobilization meant a direct threat to France. The French, outnumbered almost two to one by Germany, believed that their national survival depended on the Russian alliance. Having done little to restrain Russian belligerence, the French responded to the German threat by mobilizing.

Although Britain and France had long been enemies, British rivalry with Germany had recently drawn Britain into a loose alliance, involving some joint military planning, with France. Thus British leaders felt a commitment to help the French. The new friendship of Britain and France, and the cooling of once-friendly British-German relations, resulted above all from the German decision at the turn of the century to build a high-seas fleet. The ensuing arms race convinced the British that the new German battleships were a direct threat to the Royal Navy. Even so, the British public probably accepted the need for war in 1914 only when the Germans invaded neutral Belgium. German military planners, guided by strategic rather than diplomatic priorities, thought the quickest way to defeat France was to attack through Belgium. The British government could now lead its people to war for the moral cause of defending a violated neutral country. Thus, by August 4, all the major European powers but Italy had toppled over the brink into war.

The immediate blame for this catastrophe falls on the monarchs and ministers who made crucial decisions with the aim of either bluffing their opponents into backing down or entering a war with maximum allied help. All considered the preservation of their national interests more important than the vaguer general European interest in maintaining peace. The vital interests of Serbs, Austrians, and Russians justified waging a local war even if it might spread. The Germans and French believed they served their own interests by backing even aggressive allies, because the loss of an ally seemed more dangerous than the risk of war.

In one sense, then, World War I was the result of a series of apparently reasonable calculations, as national leaders decided that each new step toward war was preferable to a backward step that implied national humiliation or isolation. Thus the confrontation was played out to the point of collision.

Nationalism and Interdependence

To avoid the trap into which they fell, Europe's leaders would have had to go against people's perceptions of the nature of the world and against values derived from those perceptions. In a general sense, World War I was caused by the fact that people were nationalists, feeling themselves to be not Europeans but Frenchmen, Germans, Russians, or South Slavs. Although growing global interdependence was making this vision of an ethnically divided continent obsolete, most Europeans knew no higher goal than national self-preservation.

The decade before the war had seen a few steps toward internationalism. An International Office of Public Health and a World Missionary Congress had been created; these institutions recognized that neither disease nor the word of God was restrained by borders. Over half of Europe's trade union members belonged to internationally affiliated unions, united by the idea that workers of all countries had more in common with each other than with their employers. A growing peace movement placed its hopes in the permanent International Court of Arbitration recently established in The Hague. But such expressions of internationalism counted for little against the prevailing nationalism, which exalted individual countries. Many people interpreted international politics the way Charles Darwin had interpreted the world of nature: in the struggle for survival, the weak perished and the strong dominated.

To many people the major European powers seemed already locked in economic struggle for raw materials and markets. Germans resented the fact that their belated achievement of national unity had denied them a colonial "place in the sun" like the empires of Britain and France. By creating a navy to assert its aspirations to world power, Germany came

Map 3.1 Ethnic Groups in Germany, the Austro-Hungarian Empire, and the Balkans Before World War I 

ESTONIANS
North Sea
Baltic Sea
LETTS
GREAT RUSSIANS
LITHUANIANS
WHITE RUSSIANS
GERMANS
GERMANS
POLES
UKRAINIANS
CZECHS
RUTHENIANS
KALMYKS
SLOVAKS
SWISS.
MAGYARS
SLOVENES
AZERBAIJANIS
CROATS
RUMANIANS
BOSNIANS
Black Sea
GEORGIANS
SERBS
ITALIANS
Adriatic Sea
BULGARIANS
GREEKS
ALBANIANS
ARMENIANS
Dardanelles
TURKS
KURDS
Aegean Sea
Mediterranean Sea
GREEKS
Political boundaries, 1914

into confrontation with Britain, even though each country was the other's best export customer. Substantial sectors of both economies would have collapsed without the markets provided by the "enemy."

The perception of the world as an arena of conflict rather than interdependence weighed heavily on the calculations of statesmen in 1914. Most people everywhere had learned in school to accept this view. Even Russia was fumbling toward making elementary education compulsory by the time of the war. In parts of Germany all young children had been educated since the early nineteenth century. Britain and France had made their educational systems universal in the 1880s. After school came miliary service. All the major powers except Britain had universal conscription—the draft.

The patriotism young men learned from their schoolmaster and the drill sergeant was reinforced by what they read in the newspapers. Now that most of the population could read and write, mass journalism entered its golden age. The number of European newspapers, the first of the twentieth-century mass media, doubled in twenty years. And patriotism sold papers. The international conference held at Algeciras in 1906 to deal with a colonial confrontation between Germany and France was the first to be covered by a pack of reporters. Although nations continued to keep their treaties secret, diplomats would henceforth have to negotiate their way out of international showdowns with patriotic public opinion looking over their shoulders.

An Age of Militarism

Hemmed in by public opinion, statesmen struggling to resolve international issues also had to reckon with increasing military influence on decision making. Europe in 1914 was in the grip of *militarism:* the dominance of a military outlook and of the men who embodied it. Of the major heads of state, only the president of the French Republic never appeared in uniform. The German Kaiser, the Austrian emperor, and the Russian tsar always wore uniforms. This custom suggests the supreme prestige of soldiers, especially the generals who commanded the vast armies the draft made possible.

Europe's generals and their allies in industry, finance, and journalism formed a kind of military-industrial complex. The creation of the German fleet, for example, was facilitated by a publicity campaign financed and managed by admirals and shipbuilders. Lucrative contracts were their reward. Such military spending did not mean that a country's leaders were planning aggression. Armaments were amassed in the name of defense, to provide a "deterrent" against attack. These buildups did not prevent war in 1914, however. Indeed they had the opposite effect. Measuring their armaments against those of a potential enemy, some commanders became convinced that they had the upper hand and could risk war. Others feared that they were about to lose their advantage and argued that if a war was to be fought, it should be soon. Estimations of this kind were particularly dangerous because military men were specialists trained to think almost entirely in military terms. Such were the advisers who persuaded Nicholas II that partial mobilization was impractical in 1914. And General Alfred von Schlieffen's strategic masterstroke of launching the German attack on France through Belgium brought Great Britain into the war, thus leading to the German defeat.

Against this background of intense national rivalry and expanding militarism, the decisions statesmen made in 1914 are understandable. None of them had any idea of how long and devastating a war between countries armed with twentieth-century technology would be. Neither did the public. Cheering crowds filled the streets of every European capital in the summer of 1914, greeting declarations of war with delirious enthusiasm.

Europeans had been taught that war was the real test of a nation's toughness. Only those past middle age could remember a war between major powers in Europe. For the young, war meant a short-lived colonial contest that occurred far away, involving someone else, and brought profit and prestige to the victor. For the last ten years, tension had been mounting domestically and internationally. Within each of the major powers, social conflicts had produced strikes and violence. Europe had gone from one diplomatic crisis to another, all ended unheroically through negotiation. Now a crisis had come along that diplomats could not solve, and many people felt relief. The whole society could unite against a common enemy.

As they rushed off to fight that enemy, the soldiers of 1914 could not know that they were embarking on the first of two European civil wars that would end Europe's domination of the world.

Battlefronts, 1914–1918

The war that began in 1914 led to fighting in almost every part of the globe. In Africa south of the Sahara, invasions from British and French colonies quickly captured most of Germany's holdings, though in East Africa a German force continued the battle against a British Indian army until 1918. In the South Pacific, British imperial troops from Australia and New Zealand seized German outposts. Britain's ally Japan snapped up other German possessions and appropriated the German slice of China.

Closer to Europe, the long-decaying Ottoman Empire entered the conflict on the side of the Central Powers (Germany and Austria-Hungary). This move threatened not only Russia's southern flank but also Britain's link to India through the Suez Canal. The British not only fought the Ottomans but also encouraged revolt among the Ottomans' Arab vassals, while making a conflicting promise—the Balfour Declaration—that Ottoman Palestine would become a national homeland for Jews. As a result, the war provoked by the frustrated aspirations of the Serbs, once Ottoman subjects, helped unleash the turmoil of conflicting national aspirations that still torments the Middle East.

All these conflicts were extensions of the European battle lines. Only in 1917 did the war become a world war in the sense that whole continents were pitted against one another. Then the weight of the United States, dominant in North and South America, had to be thrown into the scales to match a Germany that had overrun much of continental Europe, penetrated deeply into Russia, and fought Britain and France and their worldwide empires to a standstill.

The Entente Versus the Central Powers

Though hardly anyone in 1914 foresaw the bloody stalemate of the European war, calculation might have predicted such an outcome. The Central Powers and the Entente Powers were rather an even match. Britain's naval might gave the Entente the advantage on the seas. Though the construction of the German fleet had made Britain an enemy, the two nations had only one significant naval encounter, at Jutland in 1916. There the Germans sank more British ships than they lost but did not risk a second confrontation. Too precious a weapon to be hazarded, the German battleships rusted in port while the British blockade cut Germany off from the overseas world. Against blockade, Germany could muster only its submarines, the weapon that would eventually make the United States another German enemy.

On land the two alliances were more equally matched, despite the Entente Powers' two-to-one advantage in population. Russia's millions of peasants in uniform were so inadequately equipped that some were sent into battle unarmed and expected to find the weapons of dead or wounded comrades. France and Britain could do little to help, for their prewar lines of communication to Russia were blocked by the Central Powers and their Turkish ally. Indeed, Germany's enemies never successfully coordinated their strategies. The war effort of the Central Powers, by contrast, was effectively directed from Berlin.

Since the citizens of each nation were convinced that they were defending their homeland against unprovoked attack, neither alliance had an edge in morale. Both were sufficiently determined to fight the land war to a draw. Thus victory could be achieved only by mobilizing overseas manpower and material, either by squeezing resources from the colonial empires or by drawing the world's most powerful neutral nation, the United States, into the conflict. Since British control of the sea lanes gave the Entente Powers better prospects of developing these advantages in a long war, the Germans felt they had to score a quick victory.

Stalemate in the West

The campaign of 1914 failed to produce the hoped-for victory. Germany's initial rush through Belgium carried its advance guard up to the Marne River, scarcely twenty miles from Paris (Map 3.2). The French victory on the Marne was a very close brush with destruction, but it was a victory.

The Battle of the Marne may have decided the war. By Christmas 1914 the armies' rapid advances and retreats had given way to stationary front lines. Both sides dug into the soil of a corner of Belgium and northeastern France. The French drive against Germany failed, and the Germans reversed the Russian advance on their eastern border. But these successes could not compensate for the loss of German momentum in the west. Germany found itself in the very situation its prewar strategy had tried to avoid: a protracted war on two fronts. Though few sensed it at the time, Germany had perhaps already lost the war. Many million lives were to be sacrificed, however, before that loss was driven home.

During 1915 and 1916 the war was dominated by the futile efforts of both sides to punch a hole in the enemy front. Launched against elaborately fortified lines of trenches, these offensives became massacres. The German attack on the French fortress at Verdun in 1916 cost each side a third of a million men. In the same year the British attack on the Somme River won a few square miles of shell-torn ground at the cost of over a half-million lives. The defending Germans lost nearly as many.

Numbers like these do not convey what life in the trenches was like. Probably no earlier war, and perhaps no later one, imposed such strains on fighting men. Soldiers spent months in a filthy hole in the ground, their boredom interrupted only by the occasional crack of a sniper's rifle or a dogfight between airplanes. (Both sides had quickly learned to put this new technology to military use.) Sometimes the clang of the gas alarm warned the men to put on their masks as a poisonous cloud drifted toward them. When the rumble of artillery fire in the background had risen for a few days or weeks to a roar, they knew they would soon have to go "over the top," out of their trenches and across no man's land toward the enemy's barbed wire, under a hail of machine gun and heavy weapons fire. The result of these offensives was always the same—failure to break through.

Both sides tried but failed to break through on other fronts. The Entente Powers attracted neutral Italy into the war by promising it a share of the spoils. The Italian challenge to the Austrians soon bogged down, however, giving the Entente's leaders another stalemated front to worry about. They also tried, half-heartedly, to establish a closer link with the Russians by sending an expedition to seize the Ottoman-controlled straits that connect the Mediterranean to Russia's Black Sea ports. Ottoman forces, led by the future creator of modern Turkey, Mustafa Kemal, offered effective resistance. The expedition to Gallipoli proved another fiasco.

The Central Powers also tried to break the deadlock by expanding the conflict. Bulgaria was encouraged to join the German side and successfully invaded Serbia. By 1917 Germany and its satellites controlled most of southeastern Europe, but this success was no more decisive than the continuing German victories against the Russians.

The German submarine effort to cut Britain's ocean lifelines had to be suspended after a U-boat torpedoed the British liner *Lusitania* off the Irish coast in May 1915. Though it was rightly suspected that the ship carried a secret cargo of munitions, most Americans did not believe that excused the drowning of more than twelve hundred people, among them over one hundred Americans. American outrage compelled the Germans to abandon the practice of torpedoing without warning.

The two sides staggered into 1917 with no hope of victory in sight. By now the enthusiasm of 1914 had evaporated, and the mood everywhere was one, at best, of determination to survive. Some people, particularly socialists, urged that the war be stopped by declaring it a draw. But leaders everywhere shrank from such a solution. Without a victory, the previous butchery would seem pointless. And there would be rich prizes for winning.

German industrialists and military men expected to annex Belgium and parts of northeastern France, as well as a hugh swath of Russia. For France, defeat of the Central Powers would mean recovery of the northeastern provinces of Alsace and Lorraine. Victory would enable Italy to incorporate within its borders the remaining Italian-speaking regions of Austria. For Britain it would mean ending the German challenge to its commercial and naval pre-eminence. Hard-liners were now in control in almost every capital, and they used their wartime powers of censorship and arrest to silence doubters. Because technology seemed to have made defensive positions impregnable and offensives unbearable, the weary armies of Europe faced the prospect of apparently endless struggle.

1917: The Turning Point

Two events made 1917 the decisive year of the war. Russia withdrew from the conflict, and the United States declared war against the Central Powers. The net result was an advantage to the Entente side.

Why did the United States enter the war? Idealists point to a U.S. feeling of kinship with the Western democracies. Cynics note that an Entente defeat would have cost the U.S. industrial and financial communities a great deal in contracts and loans. In any case, U.S. entry probably became inevitable when the Germans decided, in January 1917, to resume unrestricted submarine warfare. This was a calculated risk. The German high command expected that renewed Atlantic sinkings would bring the United States into the war but hoped to starve Britain into submission before American intervention could become decisive. The Germans also tried to incite Mexico to reclaim vast territories lost to the United States in the nineteenth century. The disclosure of this plan by British intelligence showed Americans just how far the Germans were prepared to go.

Triple Entente and its Allies
Central Powers
Neutral nations
Farthest German-Austrian advance
Major battle
ICELAND
NORWAY
SWEDEN
FINLAND
Helsinki
St. Petersburg
British
blockade line
NORTH SEA
BALTIC SEA
DENMARK
IRELAND
GREAT BRITAIN
London
NETH.
BELG.
LUX.
ATLANTIC OCEAN
Paris
FRANCE
SWITZ.
Rhine R.
Danube R.
GERMANY
Berlin
Tannenberg 1914
Warsaw
POLAND
Brest-Litovsk
Riga
Moscow
RUSSIA
Kiev
Treaty of Brest-Litovsk, March 1918
Armistice line, Dec. 1917
GALICIA
Vienna
AUSTRIA-HUNGARY
Caporetto 1917
Sarajevo
SERBIA
MONTENEGRO
ALBANIA
RUMANIA
Bucharest
BLACK SEA
BULGARIA
Constantinople
Dardanelles
Gallipoli 1915
GREECE
OTTOMAN EMPIRE
ITALY
Rome
SPAIN
PORTUGAL
MEDITERRANEAN SEA
NETHERLANDS
Ostend
Antwerp
Dover
Calais
FLANDERS
Passchendaele
Ypres
Brussels
BELGIUM
Liège
Cologne
English Channel
Somme R.
Amiens
Meuse R.
Ardennes
Sedan
Moselle R.
Rhine R.
LUXEMBOURG
Aisne R.
Argonne Forest
Reims
Saar R.
Seine R.
Marne R.
Verdun
LORRAINE
Nancy
Strasbourg
ALSACE
Germany, 1914
German offensive, 1914
Farthest German advance, Sept. 1914
Front at beginning of 1915
German offensive, Summer 1918
Armistice line, November 1918

The entry of the United States marked the turning point of World War I. But it took time for the Entente's new advantages in manpower and material to become apparent. Meanwhile, the emergence in Russia of a revolutionary government determined to make peace at any price seemed a devastating blow to Entente hopes. The Bolsheviks believed the war had given them a historic opportunity to make a revolution by fulfilling the yearning of the Russian masses for peace. Even so, they hesitated for a time to pay the price the Germans demanded. The Treaty of Brest-Litovsk (March 1918) required them to hand over a quarter of Russia's prewar European territory, a third of its population, and half of its industrial plant. When Lenin signed, he ratified a decision many Russian peasant soldiers had already made by starting home from the battlefield.

The final phase of the war, from the spring to the autumn of 1918, amounted to a race between trains carrying German troops west to France from the Russian front and ships transporting U.S. soldiers eastward to France. Reinforced from the east, the German spring offensive did break through. Once again the Germans were at the gates of Paris. This second Battle of the Marne, however, was Germany's last gasp. In August the German army's chief strategist, General Erich Ludendorff, admitted to the Kaiser that he had no hope of victory. Germany's enemies were counterattacking its collapsing allies. As the Austro-Hungarian Empire disintegrated, its subject peoples declared their independence.

The Hapsburg crown was the oldest but not the greatest to fall in 1918. In Germany, sailors mutinied rather than sail on a final suicide mission. This spark of rebellion set the whole country alight. Deserted even by the generals who had once been his staunchest supporters, the Kaiser fled. Democratic and socialist politicians proclaimed Germany a republic.

It was their representatives who met the supreme commander of the Entente and American armies, French general Ferdinand Foch, aboard his command train. The terms he demanded were stiff. Germany must withdraw its armies, which were still fighting deep in their enemies' territory, behind the Rhine River. It must renounce the Treaty of Brest-Litovsk and hand over much of its railway rolling stock and shipping to the victors. With the British blockade threatening their country with starvation, Germany's representatives had no real choice. Protesting bitterly, they signed an armistice. Thus at 11 A.M. on November 11, 1918, the guns at last fell silent in ruined northeastern France.

Since 1918, there have been other wars, and we now celebrate Veterans Day, not Armistice Day. We do not always recall that the occasion commemorates men who died fighting what they believed was a war to end war. The generation that first observed November 11, however, was vividly aware that it had survived an experience unparalleled in history, not only for the men in the trenches but even for those who remained at home.

◆ ***Map 3.2 World War I in Europe, 1914–1918***

Home Fronts, 1914–1918

World War I was fought on the "home front" as well as on the battlefield. Everyone in each country, not just the men in uniform, was in the battle and had to make his or her contribution to the national effort.

Though the air blitz and guided missile attacks of World War II were foreshadowed thirty years earlier by German bombing raids on London, the technology of 1914–1918 was

Indian soldiers under British command fire at enemy aircraft during the Mesopotamian campaign, 1918. *The British mobilized almost 1.5 million Indians to fight for them during World War I. Imperial War Museum, London*

inadequate to make every citizen a target of enemy attack. In a sense, however, Europe's shops, factories, and farms became another fighting front. As it became clear that neither side was going to win a quick victory, leaders realized that it was essential to harness the efforts of every individual. Unprecedented coordination and coercion would be required. No aspect of people's lives could be left unmanaged.

In this way, World War I had a revolutionary impact on the societies of all the major powers. The new controls imposed on citizens were justified as wartime expedients, and many were relaxed when the war was over. Even so, they established precedents that made the postwar world a very different place. Many of the basic trends in twentieth-century government, politics, economics, and thought can be traced back to the experience of total war in 1914–1918.

War and Government

The war gave a new dimension to the role of government. Before 1914, Western governments had gradually made themselves more and more responsible for the welfare of their citizens, insuring them against old age or disability, limiting their hours of work, forbidding unhealthy workplaces. Germany was the most protective; France and the United States were the least. Every new measure met vigorous opposition, however, for political thought was still dominated by the basic nineteenth-century liberal conviction that the best government is the one that governs least. Government today is the largest and most powerful organization in society. But in most major European nations in 1914 the "government" was a committee of legislators who exercised limited functions as long as they enjoyed the confidence of a parliamentary majority (or, in Germany and Russia, the confidence of the monarch).

A committee, or cabinet, of ministers oversaw bureaucracies whose numbers and powers varied from one nation to another. Nowhere, however, were bureaucrats very numerous, nor did their responsibilities extend much beyond providing the basic services for which governments had long been responsible. They maintained law and order and raised the modest taxes needed to balance the budget every year, while providing defense and the few other essentials not left to private initiative.

All this changed radically after 1914. Prolonged war demanded a more effective mechanism for planning and decision making than could be provided by the prewar parliamentary system, in which government was essentially a debating tournament. Even in countries with long-established parliamentary traditions, prime ministers emerged who personally exercised wide emergency executive power, tolerating little parliamentary interference: David Lloyd George in Britain and Georges Clemenceau in France. World War I pushed aside even venerable traditions "for the duration." The British Defense of the Realm Act, for example, allowed the government to censor or even silence newspapers, violating one of the most cherished British freedoms.

The number of government employees increased enormously. Twenty clerks had handled the purchase of munitions for the prewar British army. But by 1918, when the draft had put 3 million in uniform, the procurement of arms was the work of a Ministry of Munitions employing 65,000 civil servants. The wartime concentration of power into a few hands and the extension of that power into every sphere of life were most marked in Germany, where the tradition of parliamentary government was weaker and political tradition had long subordinated the citizen to the state.

In Germany, as in the rest of the modern Western world, private economic power had become concentrated in trusts and *cartels** before 1914. Nevertheless, the belief remained strong that the best economy was one of free competition, with a minimum of government interference. Now, cut off by the British blockade from many essential supplies, the German government began to make all the economic decisions. Scarce commodities were rationed, and skilled workers were directed by government order to the jobs where they were needed. The government mobilized the scientific community in such fields as industrial chemistry to develop synthetic substitutes for unavailable imports such as rubber. A government bureaucracy headed by Walter Rathenau, the prewar head of the giant German General Electric Company, oversaw the distribution of available raw materials to the most efficient producers, usually the largest. In the process the prewar economy was altered beyond any hope of restoration.

By the war's end, the German government managed so much of the economy that the system was described as "war socialism." It was operated, ironically, by the conservative military men and industrialists who had been most hostile to socialism before the war. Individual Germans had become cogs in the military machine: every man between the ages of seventeen and sixty was mobilized under mili-

*Cartels are associations of private producers who agree to share markets and fix prices, thus limiting competition.

tary discipline. And the German case is only the most extreme example. In each of the countries involved in the war, government authority was concentrated and expanded.

War, Economics, and Society

In addition to changing ideas about the proper functions of government, the war altered conventional notions of how governments should get and spend money. Traditional methods could not produce the vast sums needed. The British and French governments liquidated between a quarter and a third of their citizens' foreign investments to pay for essential goods purchased overseas, but they still emerged from the war owing enormous debts. In every belligerent country, new taxes were introduced and old ones raised. Nowhere was the resulting income more than a fraction of what governments were spending. They made up the difference by borrowing from their citizens, harnessing the new art of advertising to exhort savers to invest in the war effort. The supply of money was further enlarged by the easiest and most dangerous means of all: printing more of it.

The result was staggering inflation, though its full impact was not felt until after wartime price and wage controls were abolished. Only then did people realize what a new and terrifying financial world they lived in. The budget of the French government, for example, was forty times larger in 1918 than at the beginning of the war. The sum the French treasury had to pay out in interest alone was more than its entire annual budget before the war. The financial legacy of the war made the years 1918–1939 a period of almost constant economic strain.

Such economic changes inevitably produced profound social changes. For some social groups the war meant new opportunities. For example, as U.S. factories tooled up to produce the munitions the Entente demanded, industrialists took labor wherever they could find it. Thus began the migration of blacks from the rural South to the industrial North, a trend that continued into the post–World War II years, profoundly transforming American life. In the increasingly interconnected world of the twentieth century, sharecroppers from Georgia found jobs in steel mills in Pittsburgh because farm boys from Bavaria were finding death in northeastern France.

European societies that had drafted a large proportion of their male populations, exempting only workers with critical skills, also recruited a "reserve army" of labor by hiring women for jobs monopolized before the war by men. Thereafter it was more difficult to argue that women's place was in the home. In fact, wartime necessity may have done as much as prewar agitation to break down the distinctions between the roles of men and women.

In 1903 a bill giving British women the vote had been laughed down in the House of Commons. The next decade saw continuing lobbying and occasional violence by Emmeline Pankhurst's Women's Social and Protective Union, whose suffragettes threatened ministers with horsewhips and burned the slogan "Votes for Women" into golf course greens with acid. But not until after the war, in 1919, did British women get the vote. American and German women obtained the vote a year later. Only France, among the major democracies, restricted suffrage to men until after World War II.

World War I created new opportunities for some groups but ruined others. Governments obsessed with maintaining production proved readier than prewar private employers to engage in collective bargaining. Trade unions thus won greater recognition. But workers felt they had not received just compensation for their contribution to the war effort, and a wave of strikes swept around the world with the coming of peace. In fact, workers' gains were vastly exceeded by the fortunes of profiteers who borrowed to build armaments factories, then paid their debts in a currency depreciated by inflation. Those hit hardest by the war, however, were the people who had lived comfortably before 1914 on a fixed income provided by a pension or on the interest from government bonds. In 1919 an income in British pounds (not by any means the most inflated currency) bought only a third of what it could purchase in 1914.

These economic distortions deepened prewar social divisions. When people had to accept a decline in their standard of living because of inflation, they naturally assumed that others must have gained at their expense. Wartime social upheaval laid the groundwork for the success of postwar political movements based, like those founded by Mussolini and Hitler, on hatred and an appeal to vengeance.

War's Psychological Impact

The postwar years were marked by a mood of cynicism and disillusionment, an inevitable reaction against the war enthusiasm every government had tried to drum into the heads of its citizens. World War I prompted the first systematic efforts by governments to manage information and manipulate mass emotions. Such efforts were inevitable in twentieth-century society. All the major powers except Russia were approaching universal literacy and universal male suffrage by 1914. People who could read and felt they had a right to vote could not be commanded to blind obedience; they would have to be shown reasons for making the sacrifices the national cause demanded.

Thus each government in World War I mounted a vast propaganda campaign to persuade its public, and potential allies, of the justice of its motives and the wickedness of the enemy. British propagandists convinced a generation that Germany had ordered its soldiers to chop off the hands of Belgian children. But even more damage was done by the *positive* slogans of the propagandists: that soldiers were fighting for the defense of civilization against barbarism, or for democracy against militarism, or for the abolition of war.

The postwar world quickly revealed that these slogans had been hollow half-truths. Postwar cynicism was a direct reaction to wartime campaigns that had played on pride, shame, and fear to mobilize opinion. When the Bolsheviks published the secret Entente treaties, showing that neither side's motives had been pure, when none of the lofty goals for which the war had supposedly been fought materialized even for the "winners," public opinion turned on the leaders whose official news turned out to be lies. The very values that had supposedly motivated the war were discredited. Wartime idealism, deliberately overheated, turned sour in the postwar world.

The postwar mood also reflected a more basic change in the human outlook. No generation since 1914–1918 has ever matched the nineteenth century's confidence in progress. The world had gone through an orgy of destructiveness that seemed to prove false everything the prewar world had believed in. In the words of the soldier in Erich Maria Remarque's classic novel *All Quiet on the Western Front,* "It must be all lies and of no account when the culture of a thousand years could not prevent this stream of blood being poured out." No wonder the postwar Dadaist movement of artistic rebels mocked the pretensions of the past by exhibiting a copy of the *Mona Lisa* wearing a moustache or suggesting that poetry should henceforth be written by cutting a newspaper into scraps and shaking them at random out of a bag. Such painting and poems might make no sense, but, as the war had just proved, neither did anything else. This was a dangerous discovery, for, as the great Russian novelist Feodor Dostoevski had warned, "If nothing is true, then everything is permitted." Today, when human beings permit themselves cruel-

Women munitions workers during World War I. *The Trustees of the Imperial War Museum, London*

ties on a scale that earlier ages could not have imagined, we know what he meant.

In every sphere of modern life World War I accelerated trends already visible before 1914 and still powerful today. Politically it stimulated the growth of executive authority and government power. Economically it spurred the concentration of economic power in large corporations increasingly interlocked with government, while destroying forever the comforting idea that money retains a constant value. The war leveled social distinctions between groups and destroyed some groups altogether. In every country, for example, the sons of Europe's landed aristocracies became the second lieutenants of elite regiments and were killed out of all proportion to their numbers. At the same time the war gave greater status to working men and women. By lessening the distances between social classes, however, the war may have heightened tensions, for now hostile classes were in closer contact.

Spiritually, too, World War I marked a turning point. Before 1914, only a minority doubted the nineteenth century's faith in the future. The skeptical mood became general after 1919, as the world began to guess how unsatisfactory a peace had been made.

Peacemaking, 1919 and After

No international meeting ever aroused such anticipation as the conference that convened in Paris in January 1919 to write the peace treaties. Surely, people thought, so great a war would result in an equally great peace.

The Wilsonian Agenda

Many hopes focused on U.S. president Woodrow Wilson. He arrived in Europe to a welcome greater than any other American leader has ever received. Wilson seemed to embody a new kind of international politics based on moral principles, rather than on selfish interests.

Early in 1918, Wilson had outlined American objectives in the war. Some of his Fourteen Points simply called for a return to prewar conditions. Germany must evacuate Belgium and restore its freedom, for example. But other points seemed to promise change in the whole international order. Wilson called for an end to the alliances that had dragged all the major powers into World War I. He advocated the removal of tariff barriers between nations and a general reduction of armaments. In settling the European powers' disputes over colonies, he declared, the interest of the colonized must be taken into account. The implication was that all peoples had an eventual right to choose their own government. This indeed was what Wilson promised to the subject peoples of the Austro-Hungarian and Ottoman empires. To the Poles, too, Wilson promised a restoration of the country they had lost when Austria, Russia, and Prussia had carved up Poland during the eighteenth century.

For many critics of prewar power politics, the most hopeful of Wilson' s Fourteen Points was the last, which proposed to reconstruct the framework of international relations. The countries of the world should form an association—a League of Nations—whose members would pledge to preserve one another's independence and territorial integrity. In this way, the system that keeps the peace in a smaller human community—willingness to obey the law and condemnation of those who defy it—would replace the international anarchy that had brought disaster in 1914.

Wilson had not consulted his allies about any of his proposals. The United States entered the war in 1917 with no obligation, Americans believed, to support the objectives of earlier entrants. The Fourteen Points seemed to promise Europe a just peace and to recognize the national aspirations of colonial peoples. Unfortunately the Paris Peace Conference produced no such results. To the rights of the non-Western peoples it gave little more than lip service. To Europeans it gave a postwar settlement—the Treaty of Versailles—so riddled with injustices that it soon had few defenders.

Colonial Issues in 1919

Four years of world war had undermined European rule over non-Western peoples. In their frantic search for essential war materials, European powers increasingly treated their colonies as extensions of their home fronts. The non-Western peoples were thus subjected to many of the same strains that eventually broke the morale of European populations. In fact, European governments used much greater coercion on their non-Western subjects than they dared try at home. The British, for example, used methods of drafting labor and requisitioning materials that would have been enough in themselves to explain the postwar explosion of Egyptian nationalism. Colonies were also a reservoir of manpower. Almost 1.5 million Indians, for example, fought for Britain, and 62,000 of them were killed in the Middle East, Africa, and the trenches of France. The French recruited in their colonies in Sub-Saharan Africa, as well as among the Arab population of Algeria.

To dress a man in your own country's uniform is implicitly to admit that he is not your inferior. The French recognized this by opening French citizenship to Algerians who had fought under the French flag. But many Algerians had greater ambitions than becoming honorary Europeans. Their pride demanded an Algerian nation of their own. The image of European superiority had been drastically undercut by World War I. Hearing the propaganda Europeans published against each other, non-Western people could conclude that the real savages were their colonial masters. As fighting spread around the world, some non-Western peoples actually saw their European conquerors beaten and driven out. A successful defense often depended on the help of the non-Western population. These developments—economic, military, and psychological—undermined the prewar colonial order and launched a wave of postwar restiveness from Africa to China.

Trusting Wilson's rhetoric of self-determination, some non-Western nationalists journeyed to Paris in 1919 to argue their case. But the peacemakers hardly acknowledged them.

They handed over to Britain and France the territories in Africa and the Middle East that had belonged to Germany or the Ottoman Empire. The only concession to Wilsonian rhetoric was that these territories became "mandates" rather than colonies. This new term implied that Britain and France did not own these lands but held them in trust for the League of Nations. The European country was responsible for preparing the territory for eventual self-rule. In practice, however, there might be little difference from prewar colonial rule. The French, for example, responded to Syrian complaints with tanks and bombers.

Ultimately, the statesmen in Paris not only refused to redefine the power relationship between the world's whites and nonwhites but rejected the principle of racial equality proposed by Japan, the nonwhite great power that could claim a place among the victors. The Latin Americans, the Italians, and the French supported the Japanese. The British, speaking for Australia—a thinly settled white outpost that greatly feared its neighbors on the Asian mainland—opposed the proposal. Without U.S. support, the Japanese initiative came to nothing. It was clear that the peacemakers intended, despite all the noble rhetoric, to re-create the European-dominated world of 1914.

This outcome had a tremendous impact on a whole generation of ambitious young Africans and Asians. Western ideas of democracy were shown to be reserved for Europeans. As the Wilsonian promise faded, some future Asian and African leaders turned instead to the country the Paris peacemakers had outlawed from the international community: revolutionary Russia. Only Lenin and his regime seemed inclined to offer sympathy and support to the wave of protest that swept the colonial world after World War I.

Whatever the intent of the Paris peacemakers, European colonial rule could never again be as secure as it had been in 1914. In Egypt, something close to full-scale revolution broke out against the British. In India, a local British commander in the Punjab demonstrated the firmness of British authority by ordering his soldiers to fire on an unarmed crowd. Brigadier Reginald Dyer's troops killed nearly four hundred people and wounded more than a thousand. A century earlier, this massacre at Amritsar would hardly have been news. In 1919, however, the world reacted with horror. General Dyer was reprimanded by his military superiors and censured by the House of Commons.

Times had changed. Colonialism had acquired a bad conscience, perhaps in part because of all the wartime talk about democracy. By the early 1920s, Britain had launched both Egypt and India on the road to self-government. Indeed the colonial powers had little choice. Bled by four years of war, no European country could devote the same level of resources to colonial pacification as it had spent before 1914. But it took many years and another world war to persuade the British, and even longer to persuade the French, that their empires were too costly to maintain.

The Peace Treaties

The fate of the colonial peoples was a side issue for the peacemakers of Paris, whose real task was to draft the treaties ending the war with the Central Powers and their allies. They produced five such treaties. The Treaty of Sèvres imposed on the Ottoman Empire is discussed in Chapter 10. The three treaties that dealt with southeastern Europe essentially ratified what had happened in 1918. Out of the wreckage of the Austro-Hungarian Empire new nations emerged: Czechoslovakia for Czechs and Slovaks, Yugoslavia for the South Slavic peoples. Balkan nationalists like Gavrilo Princip got what they wanted. Whether their desires were wise remains a question. Most of these new countries remained economically little developed. Their ethnic animosities made cooperation among them unlikely. Miniature versions of the Hapsburg Empire they had replaced, most of them contained dissatisfied minorities within their borders. Even so, most of these countries felt they had been cheated of the borders they deserved.

These states suffered a dismal fate. They were dominated after Hitler's rise by Germany and after his fall by the Soviet Union almost until its collapse. As separate victims of Hitler and Stalin, these countries suffered much more than when they all belonged to the Hapsburg emperor. But there was no hope of resurrecting his regime in 1919, even if the peacemakers had wanted to. Even today, almost every ethnic group insists on having its own nation: in the 1990s, both Czechoslovakia and Yugoslavia, multinational creations of 1919, disintegrated.

The hardest task in Paris was to decide what to do about Germany. To justify the loss of millions of lives, the statesmen had to ensure that future generations would not have to fight another German war. One approach that appealed to much of European public opinion and to military minds, notably in France, was to destroy Germany's military capability and economic strength. Now that Germany had surrendered, it should be broken up, so that there would be several weak Germanies, as there had been through most of European history.

The emotions that prompted demands for such a drastic solution are easy to understand. Would it have worked? After Russia's collapse, the Entente Powers had not been able to defeat Germany without the help of the United States. Was it likely that this wartime alliance could be maintained indefinitely in the postwar period to hold down an embittered German population? Moreover, in a world of economic interdependence, a country's former enemies are its future trading partners. A bankrupt and broken Germany might drag the whole world's economy down.

Considering such dangers, some concluded that a harsh peace was not the answer. The Kaiser and his regime, who bore responsibility for the war, had been driven from power. Germany was now in the hands of democratic leaders. Why not let it return on relatively moderate terms to membership in a world community ruled by law?

Not surprisingly, this point of view was far more widely held in Britain and the United States than in France, on whose soil the war had been fought and whose richest farming and industrial regions the Germans had devastated. It would be difficult to convince the French to give up their guns. In 1919 the prevention of aggression by the League of Nations was only the dream of idealists.

The peacemakers of Paris failed because of this conflict of views between the wartime allies. It is just possible that World War II might have been avoided if one of these approaches to the German problem had been fully applied. The Treaty of Versailles, however, was a compromise that combined the disadvantages of both approaches. Despite some Wilsonian language, it imposed on Germany a peace no patriotic German could accept. But it did not cripple Germany enough to prevent it from eventually challenging the verdict of 1919 by force.

This outcome may have been inevitable. Wartime alliances usually come apart as soon as the common objective has been attained. Though all twenty-seven countries that had declared war on the Central Powers sent delegations to Paris, most of them, notably the Latin Americans, had made insignificant contributions to the war. The major powers shunted them into the background. Though Italy was considered a major power, it fared little better.

Believing that their country had been denied its fair share in the spoils of victory, the Italian delegates left the conference for a time. Neither their departure nor their return could win them a larger share of the remains of the Austro-Hungarian Empire or any of Germany's former colonies.

The important decisions of the Paris Peace Conference were the work of the Big Three: President Wilson, French Prime Minister Clemenceau, and British Prime Minister Lloyd George. Lloyd George was caught in the middle. He could foresee the dangers of a harsh peace, but he represented an exhausted, bankrupt country, some of whose newspapers had mounted a campaign to "hang the Kaiser." The worst clashes were between Wilson and Clemenceau, who were temperamentally far apart.

Clemenceau Versus Wilson

Clemenceau's determination had made an unmeasurable but real contribution to France's victory. Cynical and sarcastic, he cared for nothing but his martyred country. France had suffered, he believed, as a result of incurable German aggressiveness; in time the Germans could be expected to attack again, and only force would stop them. All the talk about new principles in international affairs left him cold. "Fourteen Points!" he snorted. "Even the Good Lord only had ten points." Yet Clemenceau knew that France's safety depended on British

Paul Nash,* The Menin Road, *1918. *The painting reveals the artist's horror at the landscape of modern war: trees stripped bare by gunfire, earth cratered by shells, soldiers dwarfed by destruction.* *Imperial War Museum, London*

and American support, especially since Russia had disappeared into a dark cloud of communist revolution.

Wilson, the sublimely self-confident former professor, believed that his country had no selfish motives—a position easier to maintain in relation to the United States' role in Europe than to its role in Latin America. He thus spoke from a position of moral superiority that Clemenceau, and others who did not believe that morality ruled international affairs, found hard to endure. Wilson spoke with the zeal of a missionary from the idealistic New World to the corrupt Old World. But he may not have spoken for U.S. public opinion. The congressional elections of 1918 had gone against his party, and a reversal of wartime enthusiasm would soon lead the United States back to its traditional isolation from European affairs.

Only the necessity of producing some conclusion enabled two such different men to hammer out a treaty both could sign. When its terms were published, both were bitterly attacked by their countrymen. French hard-liners condemned Clemenceau for not insisting on the territorial demands they thought essential to French security. Many of Wilson's advisers thought he had too often given in to European-style power politics, sacrificing the principle of a people's right to choose its own government.

Wilson's supreme goal was the creation of the new international organization, the League of Nations. Clemenceau could hardly take the idea seriously, for Wilson could not promise that membership would require any nation, least of all the United States, to help a future victim of aggression. The same difficulty arose when the United Nations was created in 1945. Sovereign nations proved unwilling to subject their freedom of action to international authority.

In return for French agreement to the establishment of the League, Wilson allowed Clemenceau to impose severe penalties on Germany. The German army was to be limited to a hundred thousand men. Germany could have neither submarines nor an air force. Characteristic of the compromise nature of the treaty, this virtual disarmament of Germany was described as the first step toward the general disarmament called for in the Fourteen Points. The Treaty of Versailles was full of provisions intended by Clemenceau to weaken Germany. The new Republic of Austria, the German-speaking remnant of the former Hapsburg state, was forbidden to merge with Germany, though a national vote made it clear this was the solution preferred by most Austrians.

With the Russian alliance gone, Clemenceau intended to surround Germany with strong French allies to the east. The new state of Czechoslovakia was given a defensible mountainous border that put millions of Germans under Czech rule. The Poland the Paris peacemakers resurrected included a "Polish corridor" cutting through German territory to the Baltic Sea. Such terms made sense if the aim was to cripple Germany. But they flouted Wilsonian principles, and the Germans complained that the principle of self-determination had been honored only when it worked against them.

The Paris peacemakers also demanded that Germany should pay reparations. The word implies that Germany was to repair the damage its war had caused—not an unreasonable demand. But the bill drawn up by the victors was so astronomical—132 billion gold marks—that the Germans would still be making huge payments today if anybody were still trying to collect them.

The old idea of collecting large sums from a defeated enemy may be outdated in the twentieth century, when national economies are so interdependent. If the Germans had to turn over everything they earned, they would be unable to buy the goods the victorious nations wanted to export. The economists who raised such questions were drowned out by the insistence that "the Germans will pay." Indeed when the Germans did not pay enough, soon enough, French and Belgian armies reoccupied German territory to collect what was due. Germans then concluded that reparations were not a bill for damages but an excuse for Germany's enslavement.

To prevent another German invasion like those of 1870 and 1914, many Frenchmen felt German territory should be amputated in the west as well as the east. In particular, they wanted to detach the Rhineland—the region between the French-German border and the Rhine—and place it under reliable French control. (Map 3.3 makes clear why the French would have liked to control this territory.) Even as the conference was meeting in Paris, renegade Germans working for the French tried to establish a separate Rhineland Republic, though the effort soon collapsed. The Rhineland issue provoked the bitterest of the many quarrels of the Paris conference. Wilson, backed by Lloyd George, warned that taking the Rhineland from Germany would create a permanent German grievance, comparable to Germany's taking of Alsace-Lorraine from France in 1871. Speaking for a country that had suffered casualties at thirty-six times the American rate, Clemenceau insisted that French control of the Rhineland was essential for French security. But he finally agreed to a compromise. The Treaty of Versailles stipulated only that the Rhineland be demilitarized. The Germans would keep it but could not fortify it or station troops there. In return for this concession, Wilson and Lloyd George signed a separate treaty committing their countries to help France if it was again attacked by Germany.

After months of argument, the Treaty of Versailles was complete. The victors handed it to the Germans to sign—or else. Germany's representatives were horrified. Their contacts with Wilson before the armistice had led them to expect a compromise peace. Now they were told to confess that Germany alone had caused the war, as Article 231 of the treaty proclaimed, and to pay a criminal's penalty.

By accepting the Treaty of Versailles, Germany's new postwar democracy, the Weimar Republic, probably signed its own death warrant. But its critics, like Adolf Hitler, never explained how the republic's representatives could have avoided the "dictated peace" of Versailles. Germany had lost the war. Because the fighting ended before Germany had been invaded, many Germans did not recognize this harsh reality. They saw the Treaty of Versailles as a humiliation to be repudiated as soon as possible. The treaty's reputation among the victors was hardly better. French hard-liners charged that Clemenceau had conceded too much and thrown France's victory away. "This is not a peace," said Marshal Foch, "but an armistice for twenty years."

The pessimism of these critics was confirmed within six months as the United States repudiated the agreements its president had negotiated. In November 1919 the Senate refused to ratify the Treaty of Versailles or the treaty promising American help to France. Americans were increasingly impatient with Europe's messy, faraway problems. The Old World, which had seemed so close in 1917–1918, again became remote: another world, a week away by the fastest ship. The 1920 presidential election was won by a likable, small-town newspaper publisher from the Midwest, Warren G. Harding. The choice reflected Americans' longing for a return to what Harding called "normalcy"—the way things had been before the United States became involved in a European war.

This American return to isolationism suggests the fatal weakness in Wilson's vision of a new world order. As an international organization, the League of Nations could keep the peace only if its members committed themselves to use force against any country determined to be an aggressor. Yet Wilson himself could offer no such commitment on behalf of the United States. The Senate's rejection of the Treaty of Versailles showed that Americans, like other people, still insisted on judging international conflicts in terms of their national interests. With no power of its own, the League of Nations proved pathetically inadequate to the task of keeping the peace when international tensions mounted again in the 1930s.

The limitations of the League were particularly serious because the balance of power in Europe had been destroyed. The collapse of Austria-Hungary had left a vacuum of power in central and southeastern Europe. Russia was in the hands of revolutionaries who encouraged the overthrow of all other governments; no one could form an alliance with such an outlaw regime. Indeed the new states the peacemakers had created in Eastern Europe were intended to contain not only Germany but the Russian communist threat. Britain, like the United States, now decided that the costs of getting involved in Europe outweighed the likely benefits. Using as their excuse the American failure to honor Wilson's commitment, the British also repudiated their pledge to defend France. This left an exhausted France alone (except for resentful Italy) on the Continent with Germany. And Germany, though disarmed and diminished, was still the same nation that had held off the British Empire and two other major powers for most of the war. Its fundamental strengths—its numbers and its highly developed economy—could be mobilized by some future regime less willing than the Weimar Republic to accept the Versailles verdict.

World War I did not end until U.S. troops became combatants, along with many from the British overseas empire. If peace were to be maintained by some renewed balance of power, that balance had to be global. But many people in all countries were unable to draw this conclusion. Americans tended to see their intervention in international politics as a choice rather than as a necessity of the twentieth-century world. Over the next decades, they continued to come and go as they pleased on the world stage. Similarly, the British Empire soon became the British "Commonwealth of Nations," whose members did not automatically follow where Britain led. It would take a second world war to persuade all these peoples that they had a permanent stake in the global contest for power.

Conclusion

Although it is sometimes said that wars do not settle anything, World War I resolved several prewar questions, though hardly ever in the way the people who started the war had hoped. It settled the fate of the ramshackle Austrian, Russian, and Ottoman Empires. It showed that Europe, the smallest though the most developed of the continents, could not indefinitely dominate the globe. The war also settled prewar uncertainties about the possible limits of government power over individuals. The disciplined fashion in which millions had marched to their deaths showed that power was virtually unbounded. At the same time, the war settled some questions about inequalities of civil rights based on birth or sex. Distinctions among citizens had given way to the demands of total mobilization (though discrimination had certainly not disappeared in 1918). And certainly the war gave a shocking answer to the prewar question of whether progress was inevitable. The art of surgery, for example, had advanced significantly during the war—prompted by improvements in the design of high explosives to blow people apart. It was hard to see this as "progress."

World War I also created a whole new set of postwar questions. If the fall of the Austro-Hungarian Empire proved that multinational

Demilitarized Zone
Areas lost by Austro-Hungarian Empire
Areas lost by Russia
Areas lost by Germany
Areas lost by Bulgaria
Boundaries of 1926
FINLAND
Leningrad (St. Petersburg)
NORWAY
Stockholm
SWEDEN
ESTONIA
LATVIA
LITHUANIA
NORTH SEA
BALTIC SEA
DENMARK
SOVIET UNION
IRELAND
Danzig
EAST PRUSSIA
Kiel
GREAT BRITAIN
POLISH CORRIDOR
Elbe R.
Berlin
Vistula R.
POLAND
Warsaw
Amsterdam
NETH.
Kiev
RUHR
GERMANY
Brussels
Cologne
BELG.
Weimar
Prague
LUX.
Frankfurt
GALICIA
Paris
CZECHOSLOVAKIA
Dniester R.
BESSARABIA
ATLANTIC OCEAN
Versailles
LORRAINE
Strasbourg
Rhine R.
ALSACE
Vienna
Budapest
AUSTRIA
HUNGARY
FRANCE
SWITZ.
RUMANIA
S. TYROL
Geneva
Trieste
Zagreb
Belgrade
Bucharest
BLACK SEA
Milan
Venice
Fiume
CROATIA
YUGOSLAVIA
SERBIA
BULGARIA
MONTENEGRO (To Yugoslavia. 1921)
ITALY
Sofia
Istanbul (Constantinople)
PORTUGAL
SPAIN
Rome
ALBANIA
Naples
TURKEY
GREECE
MEDITERRANEAN SEA
Athens
CRETE

states could not survive and that each people must have its own country, how could nations be established for all the hundreds of peoples around the world? And what would happen in places such as Ireland, Palestine, and South Africa, where more than one people claimed the same territory as their home? What would happen if government expansion continued? If the mobilization effort had created a greater social equality, would that eventually mean equal rights for everyone or an equal loss of freedoms? Would the mechanization of human life, so dramatically accelerated by the war, result in greater comforts or greater dangers?

By the mid-1920s some optimists thought they could see hopeful answers to all these questions. They found them in a country that was seeking to replace the European-dominated world system with a new system based on worldwide revolution. There, in Russia, an experiment in unlimited government power was taking shape. The country's goal was said to be the creation of a society based on literal equality. Its officially anointed heroes were its steelworkers and tractor drivers, whose machines would modernize a peasant land and make it the model for the twentieth century. Like those optimists of the 1920s from the West, but with a more analytical eye, we shall look at the Union of Soviet Socialist Republics (USSR)—the country that emerged, after the Bolshevik Revolution of 1917, under Lenin and Stalin.

Suggestions for Further Reading

Bruun, Geoffrey. *Clemenceau* (1943).

Eksteins, Modris. *Rites of Spring: The Great War and the Birth of the Modern Age* (1990).

Falls, Cyril. *The Great War* (1959).

Feldman, Gerald D. *Arms, Industry, and Labor in Germany* (1966).

Fussell, Paul. *The Great War and Modern Memory* (1975).

Horne, Alistair. *The Price of Glory* (1979).

Joll, James. *The Origins of the First World War* (1984).

Kaiser, David. "Germany and the Origins of World War I." *Journal of Modern History,* 55 (September 1983).

Lafore, Laurence. *The Long Fuse* (1965).

Mayer, Arno J. *The Politics and Diplomacy of Peacemaking* (1968)

Mee, Charles. *The End of Order: Versailles 1919* (1980).

Nicolson, Harold. *Peacemaking, 1919* (1984).

Remarque, Erich Maria. *All Quiet on the Western Front* (1929).

Tuchman, Barbara. *The Guns of August* (1988).

Williamson, Samuel R., Jr. *The Origins of a Tragedy, July 1914* (1981).

◂ ***Map 3.3 Post–World War I Boundary Changes***

CHAPTER 4

Restructuring the Social and Political Order: The Bolshevik Revolution in World Perspective

World War I not only began the decline of European world dominance. This "European civil war" also opened the way for the triumph of a revolutionary movement in Russia: Bolshevism, committed in principle to destroying the social and economic bases of the European-dominated system worldwide. The Bolshevik Revolution of 1917 therefore influenced world history, as well as Russian history. This chapter explains why Russia's prewar tsarist regime was vulnerable to revolution, how Lenin and the Bolsheviks seized power, and how Stalin in the 1930s began to transform the Soviet Union into an industrial superpower.

This chapter also has a comparative goal. Russia's revolution was the early twentieth century's most important revolution but not its only one. By 1917, revolutions had also occurred in Iran (1905), the Ottoman Empire (1908), Mexico (1910), and China (1911), challenging the dominance of Europe's great powers or (in Mexico) of the United States. The question that arises is, why did Russia's revolution prove the most influential?

We shall argue that the Bolsheviks defeated internal and external enemies and established their independence, while none of the earlier revolutions proved as decisive either in winning independence from great-power dominance or in restructuring society. The earlier revolutions fell short partly because they lacked leadership or organization comparable to Lenin's but more importantly because they had essentially nationalist goals. Aiming to free one country, they offered no model for transforming the world. Mexico's revolution illustrates this problem (see also Chapter 8).

The Bolshevik Revolution, by contrast, claimed to liberate Russians by implementing a set of relatively simple ideas about history and politics—Marxism-Leninism—that were equally applicable everywhere. Economic forces determined the course of history, in Marx's view. Capitalist industrial societies emerged when middle-class interests overthrew feudal societies dominated by monarchs and aristocrats. The middle-class capitalists then created the means of their own eventual destruction by exploiting industrial workers (the proletariat). Eventually, Marx said, workers would rebel and overthrow capitalism in a revolution inaugurating the communist dictatorship of the proletariat. As imperialistic capitalism spread its control over the world, the revolutionary potential would become an international, ultimately a global, one.

Lenin modified Marxism for a country where industrial workers made up only about 1 percent of the population. His innovation was to insist that the proletariat be guided in establishing its dictatorship by a tightly organized and disciplined party in which power flowed from the top down, a system he called "democratic centralism."

After 1917, people in the colonial world inevitably asked themselves whether Marxism-Leninism was an effective way to shake off European domination. Although the situation of colonial peoples differed fundamentally from that of workers in industrial societies, the global dominance of capitalist societies had created a powerful connection between the two groups. In Russia, Marxism-Leninism had provided a way to topple despotism in one of its European homelands. Could it do as much in colonial lands? Could other ideas produce such results?

Non-Western leaders' answers to these questions varied widely. At one extreme, in India Mohandas Gandhi produced an ideology of mass-mobilization that rejected both colonialism and violent revolution. His career illustrates what could be accomplished through a reformist, not a revolutionary, approach to national independence and regeneration. His ideas could be borrowed and used successfully in other countries. Could his movement have succeeded, however, if European dominance had not been weakened by the shocks of world war and depression?

At the other end of the spectrum from Gandhi, Mao Zedong (Mao Tse-tung) was perhaps the most important non-Western political leader of the twentieth century (see Chapter 10). His early career shows how much Marxism-Leninism could do, compared with the less radical ideology of Sun Yat-sen and the Chinese Nationalists, to revive the world's most populous nation. But first Mao had to adapt Marxism-Leninism to the Chinese setting by formulating the ideas that later became known as Mao Zedong thought. Mao's ideas provide the best example of the influence of the Bolshevik Revolution on the wider world, and of the limits and ambiguities of that influence.

The End of Tsarist Russia

Russia has always loomed menacingly over Central and Western Europe. In the nineteenth century, however, Russia was dreaded by Europeans not as the homeland of revolutions but as the crusher of revolutions. Russian troops repeatedly snuffed out the Poles' hopes for independence. Russia's tsar saw himself as Europe's policeman and played an equally autocratic role at home. Even as it had expanded five thousand miles across a continent, subjecting a hundred nationalities to its rule, the Russian Empire never departed from its inherited political system. Its law was the will of the tsar, whose secret police still curbed freedoms taken for granted in Western Europe or North America—freedom of speech, press, association, and self-expression.

Wandering beggars traveled the muddy roads of prerevolutionary rural Russia, subsisting on the charity of peasants.
Hoover Institution, Stanford, CA

Society and Politics

At the beginning of the twentieth century, Russia was still socially and economically backward. Nine out of ten Russians were still peasants. Until 1861 their grandparents had been serfs, literally the property of the aristocrat or the state whose land they worked. Even now the peasants were Russia's "dark people," largely illiterate, often lacking sufficient land to feed themselves. Their tradition was one of endurance, interrupted periodically by violence, as in the six hundred separate serf rebellions of the first half of the nineteenth century. Between the peasants at the bottom of Russian society and the wealthy, untaxed aristocracy at the top was a small middle class. The economic functions of a middle class—commerce and industry—had developed slowly in nineteenth-century Russia. Until 1830 there had not even been a paved road connecting Moscow and St. Petersburg, the empire's two principal cities.

In the early twentieth century, middle-class political liberals hoped to convert the tsarist autocracy into a Western-style constitutional monarchy. But by 1900, many intellectuals had despaired of any peaceful evolution of Russia's government. So grim was the tsarist record of repression and resistance to change that Social Democrats believed Marxist revolution offered the only hope. Other revolutionaries favored the distinctively Russian politics of assassination that had killed one tsar and dozens of high officials since the mid-nineteenth century. Many revolutionaries paid for their political beliefs with their lives or with long terms in Siberian prisons. Others fled Russia to await the coming of revolution. The tsarist regime was happy to see them go. There was no room for people influenced by Western notions of freedom and tolerance in a society that used the state-dominated Orthodox church to control popular opinion, that imposed rule by Russians on the many ethnic minorities, and that systematically persecuted Jews. To official Russia, Western ideas were alien and dangerous.

The Western Challenge

Russia could not do without Western ideas, however. If it was to remain a great power as its rivals modernized, Russia must modernize too. This lesson had been painfully driven home in the mid-nineteenth century when Britain and France defeated Russia in the Crimean War. One of the war's consequences was the tsar's decision to emancipate the serfs in 1861—a decision inspired less by humanitarian concern than by economic calculation. A modernized agricultural system no longer based on serfdom might produce more grain for export, and grain was what Russia had to exchange for the products of Western ingenuity. By the turn of the century, Russia had become a large exporter of grain, even in years, such as 1891–1892, when famine killed millions of peasants.

Apart from the large loans it received from Western Europe and particularly from France, Russia could finance its industrialization only by exporting food even while its own people went hungry. Although it claimed to be a great power, preindustrial Russia stood in almost the same colonial economic relationship to Western and Central Europe as the dependent peoples of Africa and Asia. By the 1890s progressive ministers had persuaded the tsar that Russia must undertake a crash program of industrialization.

The program produced impressive economic results. Russian industry doubled its output from 1900 to 1913, raising the nation from near insignificance among industrial powers to fifth rank. Russia still had a long way to go, however. Its per capita income was one-sixth that of the United States, one-third that of Germany.

The social consequences of rapid industrialization were explosive. The capital needed for development was literally wrung out of the peasantry, already burdened by the debt they owed their former masters for emancipation. Their taxes increased 50 percent in a decade. A more immediate danger to the government was the condition of Russia's rapidly growing cities. As in almost every other country, the first phase of industrialization was a grim era for workers. The Russian factory worker often returned home after an eleven-and-a-half-hour day under relentless supervision to a hovel he shared with ten other people. He could not protest such conditions to anyone, for strikes, like unions, were illegal. Many Russian factories were huge places where the worker had no human contact with his employer, only with his fellow employees. In such settings, though propaganda could circulate only secretly, the Marxism of the Social Democratic party gained ground among the urban working class.

The massacre of hundreds of working people on Bloody Sunday (January 22) triggered the Revolution of 1905. Their peaceful attempt to petition the tsar—the "Little Father," Nicholas II (r. 1894–1917)—by gathering outside his palace in St. Petersburg ended in a hail of bullets. The uprising that followed was inconclusive, a dress rehearsal for the Revolution of 1917. Nevertheless, it revealed the deep disaffection of almost all of Russian society.

Military defeat had already exposed the regime's weaknesses. The tsar's advisers had led him confidently to war with Japan in 1904, expecting to defeat the "little monkeys" easily and end their interference with Russian expansion in East Asia. The Russo-Japanese War turned out instead to be the first major defeat of a European great power by a non-Western people. Admiral Heihachiro Togo's battleships sank much of the Russian fleet in a single battle. It was just one in a seemingly endless series of revelations of the tsarist government's incompetence. By the time Russia sued for peace, the government had been wholly discredited.

After Bloody Sunday, Russia's cities became the scene of continuous strikes and demonstrations until the army could be moved back from the front to restore order. Reinforced by violence in the countryside, this wave of revolt compelled the tsar to yield concessions, including a constitution. He even promised that the new parliament, or Duma, would have real power. But the tsar's heart was never in such promises; he had come to the throne denouncing petitions for reform as "senseless dreams." He intended to rule Russia exactly as his forefathers had ruled. As his government gradually regained control of cities and countryside, he took back most of the concessions he had made.

Thus Russia was still an autocracy as it entered World War I. The electoral system had been rigged to give the Duma, which was virtually powerless, a conservative majority. The parliament consequently provided no real outlet for the grievances of the middle class, workers, or peasants. Despite the failure of the 1905 revolution, the tsarist system seemed doomed to fall before long.

Lenin's Russia, 1917–1924

Revolutions seldom begin among people who have no hope. Like many others, the one that occurred in 1905 was a "revolution of rising expectations." Rapid modernization had showed Russians the possibility of change. It also increased their frustration with a government that seemed both incompetent and oppressive. People seem able to endure a harsh, efficient government or an inept government that is not harsh. But they will rebel against a government that combines harshness and ineptitude if its defenders lose confidence. That is what happened to the tsarist government in March 1917.

World War I proved disastrous for Russia. As German armies drove deep into Russian territory, the government showed itself incapable of mobilizing society for total war. It was so frightened of losing control that it prohibited the patriotic efforts of citizens to organize to help the war effort. In 1915 the tsar took personal command of his armies, asserting his autocratic responsibility. But his bureaucracy could not organize Russia's industrial and transport systems to supply those armies. The home front was no better managed. Shortages of food and fuel led to ceaseless protests. The prestige of the imperial family vanished as it became known that a sinister monk, Grigori Rasputin, had acquired such a psychological hold on the tsar and his wife that he virtually dominated the government.

By the spring of 1917 the only support remaining to the autocracy was its forces of law and order, and they were wavering. When the troops disobeyed orders to fire on food rioters in Petrograd (formerly St. Petersburg), joining the rioters instead, Nicholas II could do nothing but give up his throne. Four years would elapse before it became clear to whom power had passed.

The Provisional Government

As often happens in revolutions, the people who first came into power could not hold on to it. The Provisional Government of Duma liberals that proclaimed itself the tsar's successor immediately enacted reforms. It prepared to convene a democratically chosen Constituent Assembly to give Russia a real constitution. Nevertheless, the government quickly became almost as unpopular with the masses as the tsar had been. It could not bring order out of the chaos into which Russia had fallen. As honorable men, its leaders insisted on continuing the war to fulfill the commitments the tsar's government had made to Russia's allies, even as millions of peasant soldiers declared *their* war over by simply starting to walk home from the front. Moreover, an explosion of grassroots democracy challenged the Provisional Government. Workers and soldiers everywhere elected Soviets (councils) to govern each factory and regiment. These Soviets in turn elected a hierarchy of Councils of Workers' and Soldiers' Deputies that amounted to a rival governmental authority.

Lenin addresses Red Army troops in Moscow, 1920. *The uniformed officer to the right of the rostrum is Trotsky. After he became an "unperson" under Stalin's dictatorship, Soviet propagandists painted him out of this famous picture.* *David King Collection, London*

In this confused situation one of the most formidable figures of modern times saw his opportunity to change the course of history. Vladimir Ilyich Ulyanov, better known by his revolutionary name of Lenin, was forty-seven in 1917. Child of a middle-class family of academics, he had been a revolutionary at seventeen, when his older brother was hanged for conspiring to assassinate the tsar. In exile since 1900, he had taken a leading role among Russian Social Democrats abroad.

Lenin combined tactical brilliance and ruthlessness. He was certain that he knew how to make a revolution that would change the world, and he was prepared to use any means and to destroy any opposition. Thus in April 1917 he accepted the offer of the Kaiser's generals to send him from Switzerland through the German battle lines into Russia. Their intent was that Lenin should undermine the Provisional Government's continuation of the war, and he did not disappoint them. As soon as he arrived in Russia, he announced that the revolution should provide "peace, land, and bread." The Provisional Government, having failed to produce these, should be overthrown and replaced by giving "All power to the Soviets."

Lenin believed that his faction of the Social Democratic party, the Bolsheviks, with its base in the Soviets, could now seize power and make Russia's revolution real. The rival Menshevik faction believed that Russia must industrialize further before it could have the proletarian revolution Marx envisioned. But Lenin saw the possibility of capturing power now by giving Russia's masses what they demanded: End the war, even by accepting defeat. Give the peasants the land many were already beginning to seize. Feed the starving cities, imposing whatever controls were necessary.

Second Revolution, 1917

So exactly did Lenin's program correspond to the aspirations of war-weary Russians that Bolshevik representation in the Soviets continued to climb through 1917. In vain the Provisional Government tried to fight back. Ineffective, torn by dissension, threatened both by tsarist generals and by Bolsheviks, it could not endure. Hardly a shot was fired in its defense during the second (November) revolution of 1917. When Bolshevik soldiers occupied government headquarters, it was all over. Lenin had been right, and everyone else wrong. The Bolsheviks, a tiny minority of Russian society, could capture the power the tsar had let fall.

As often happens in revolutions, power had passed from the moderates to a small band of dedicated extremists with a vision of an entirely changed society. Only after four more years of civil war, however, did the Communist party (as the Bolsheviks renamed themselves early in 1918) secure its victory. Lenin swiftly implemented changes that inevitably turned much of his country and the world against him. He made peace on Germany's terms in the Treaty of Brest-Litovsk in March 1918, surrendering Russia's most fertile and industrialized regions and a third of its population. He abolished private ownership of land.

It was more difficult to meet the goal of providing bread from Russia's war-ravaged economy, though he sent the army to seize food from recalcitrant peasants. But Lenin did not hesitate to decree complete economic reorganization. In the name of "War Communism," he nationalized Russia's banks. He confiscated industries and merged them into giant government-controlled trusts. He repudiated Russia's foreign debts. Private property was not the Communists' only target, however. They attacked the patriarchal family by establishing legal equality of women with men, easing conditions for divorce and abortion, and providing for universal compulsory education.

Lenin did not seek popular consent to these changes. He knew that many of them would not have commanded majority support. Indeed, the Bolsheviks won only about 25 percent of the votes cast for the Constituent Assembly, which the Provisional Government had ordained. Lenin's solution to this problem was simply to dissolve the Assembly on the first day it met. So vanished the only democratic parliament Russia had ever known, unmourned by most Russians.

Parliamentary democracy was not part of the Russian tradition. Since the 1905 revolution Soviets *had* been part of the Russian tradition, and in theory the Council of People's Commissars, dominated by Lenin, now governed as the delegates of the All-Russian Congress of Soviets. In reality, the Soviets had served their purpose, and Lenin had no intention of letting them continue their disorderly experiments in direct democracy. He quickly brought them under control of the Communist party.

Invasion, Civil War, and New Economic Policy

In concentrating power in the hands of a few, Lenin was following his deepest instincts. He had always believed that a revolution was made by a small elite—a party "like a clenched fist"—that directed the masses. In 1918 to 1921, moreover, his regime was fighting for its life against enemies within and without. Russia's former allies sent in 100,000 troops (British, French, Japanese, and 7,000 Americans) to occupy strategic points in Russian territory. The goal was first to bring Russia back into the war and later, as Winston Churchill put it, "to strangle Bolshevism in its cradle." Most of the troops were withdrawn by 1919, but their presence symbolized the world's refusal to recognize the Communists as Russia's masters. This refusal encouraged some non-Russian nationalities within the former tsarist empire to rebel, and raised the hopes of several high-ranking tsarist officers, who mobilized "White" armies to march against the new "Red" regime. Against these multiple enemies the Red Army, led by the brilliant Leon Trotsky as commissar for war, fought at one time on two dozen fronts.

The White counterrevolution failed. The mutual suspicions of the White leaders made cooperation impossible. Moreover, fighting to restore the old tsarist order, they could not win the support of the majority of Russians. However disillusioned they might become with Communist rule, the people had gained from the revolution.

There was soon much reason for disillusionment. In his fight for survival Lenin had not hesitated at any step. He re-established the secret police, for example, and demanded the shooting of hostages. He ordered the murder of the captive tsar and his family. In protest against the iron rule of his party dictatorship the sailors at the Kronstadt naval base rebelled in March 1921. Though they had once been ardent Bolsheviks, Lenin crushed their uprising without mercy. Within four years, "heroes" of the revolution had become "traitors."

Many of the world's revolutions have followed a similar path from enthusiasm to disillusionment. In the resulting atmosphere of cynicism, the extremist leadership has often been overthrown by leaders less bent on total change. Lenin's pragmatism, however, told him that he must temporarily slow the pace of revolution to consolidate Communist rule. The revolution's enemies had been beaten, but the economy was a shambles. Thus in 1921 his New Economic Policy (NEP) ended War Communism by re-establishing the free-enterprise system in agriculture and retail trade, though not in heavy industry.

There was no corresponding relaxation of political control from the top. In 1922, the Communist state became, ostensibly, a federal state, the Union of Soviet Socialist Republics, a concession to the nationalist demands of the former tsarist empire's many non-Russian minorities. In fact, however, Moscow ruled everywhere through the All-Union Communist Party. After 1921, disagreement with the party line meant expulsion from the party. To the distress of some old Bolsheviks, by the time Lenin died in 1924 the party was becoming the privileged, conformist bureaucratic machine that governed the Soviet Union until the 1990s.

At the end of his life Lenin seemed clearly to regret that he had created a party dictatorship rather than a truly egalitarian society. For this reason, his defenders try to dissociate him from the later totalitarian regime of Joseph Stalin. It was Lenin, though, who laid the foundations for the one-party police state that Stalin built. Lenin could hardly have done otherwise. His genius had been to see how his party could capitalize on war-weariness, land hunger, and economic chaos to take power. But only for that brief interlude did the Bolshevik vision of the future coincide with the ideas of most Russians. Once in power, the Bolsheviks had to use force to turn their vision into reality. To do that required re-creating the kind of authoritarian rule the revolution had just overthrown. The only means to the Communist end were means that mocked that end—a paradox that partly explains why communism eventually failed.

Stalin's Soviet Union, 1924–1939

The realities of the Soviet Union (USSR) were never anticipated by Marxist theory. Communism had won its first great victory not by a worldwide workers' revolution but by imposing a party dictatorship on a largely peasant country. There was no clear Marxist prescription for what to do next. After Lenin died, leaving no clear successor, the question of the USSR's future direction divided the Communist party leadership.

In this debate, which became a power struggle, the advantage lay with the man who dominated the bureaucratic machine. This was General Secretary of the Communist party Joseph Stalin (1879–1953). Though a Bolshevik since his youth, Stalin came from a background very different from that of most of the men who surrounded Lenin. Son of a cobbler and grandson of serfs, Stalin had emerged from among the "dark people." Like them, he had little to say. When he did speak, it was often in the peasant's earthy proverbial language. He had never lived in the West and had none of the old Bolsheviks' fluency in Marxist theory. By 1927, however, Stalin's ruthless ambition allowed him to gain control of the Communist party and Soviet state. The party congress of that year forbade any deviation from the party line as Stalin defined it. This final blow to party discussion drove many old Bolsheviks into retirement or exile. Some of them concluded that the Russian Revolution, like earlier revolutions, had convulsed an entire society only to end up in the dictatorship of a tyrant.

Socialism in One Country

Because the world had not yet followed Russia into revolution, Stalin was convinced, the task of Marxists was to strengthen "socialism in one country." This could only be done by making the Soviet Union a mighty industrial power. As he declared in 1931, "We are fifty or one hundred years behind the advanced countries. We must make good this lag in ten years. Either we will accomplish this or we will be crushed."[1]

The USSR's first Five-Year Plan, launched in 1928, made it clear that Stalin intended to squeeze capital for industrialization out of agriculture, just as the last tsars had done. To make agriculture more productive, Stalin believed, required smashing the rural society that had developed under the NEP. Wealthy peasants (kulaks) were to be "liquidated" and the millions of family farms abolished. Surviving rural Russians were to be massed on collective farms a thousand times bigger than the typical peasant holding, better suited for efficient mechanized agriculture. The immediate results of this agricultural revolution were catastrophic. Peasant resistance to collectivization reduced agricultural productivity to nothing, and Russia endured mass starvation during 1931–1933, only the first of the Stalinist horrors of the 1930s.

Meanwhile the industrial sector grew enormously—by a factor of three during the 1930s, according to one evaluation. Production rose at an annual rate of 14 percent. The Soviet Union rose from fifteenth to third rank worldwide in production of electricity, fulfilling Lenin's definition of communism as "socialism plus electricity."

The contrast between this frenzied Soviet development and the stagnation of the Western economies during the Depression was striking. Soviet propaganda attributed the nation's accomplishments not only to Stalin's genius but to the heroism of Soviet workers like the miner Stakhanov, who supposedly exceeded his production quota by 1,400 percent in 1935. Some Western visitors came away marveling at such achievements. But shrewder observers could guess at some of the human costs.

Soviet workers, who had no right to strike, were not spurred to produce by any hope that their low earnings would purchase consumer goods. Hardly any were available. Soviet workers were goaded to productivity by all the managerial tricks of early industrial capitalism, including piecework rather than hourly pay. They could not change jobs. Any protest meant arrest and deportation to one of the large projects being built with slave labor. Under Stalin, some twelve million Russians were prisoners on such sites, or in Siberian camps, or in jails—far more than the tsars had ever incarcerated.

Soviet "crash industrialization." *Under the gaze of a giant portrait of Stalin, the Molotov plant in Gorky turned out two hundred cars daily in the 1930s.* *Sovfoto/Eastfoto*

Assessing the Soviet Experience Under Lenin and Stalin

On the eve of World War II, the Soviet Union projected two sharply contrasting images to the world. The image of progress emphasized the great dams, factories, even whole new industrial cities sprouting across the land. But there was also the image of terror, particularly during the great purge of 1936–1938, when Stalin got rid of most of the surviving old Bolsheviks. Courtroom cameras filmed them confessing to improbable crimes against the state before disappearing forever.

Defenders of Stalin's historic role explain that these contrasting images are inseparable. The factories, they maintain, could not have been created so quickly without the threat of the prison camps. By forcing the discipline of modernity on Russian society, Stalin transformed a largely peasant nation into an industrial superpower in just two decades. Because we cannot rerun history to see the results of alternative approaches, we cannot know whether the Soviet Union could have industrialized quickly without Stalin's inhumanity.

For world history, the important consideration is the import of what Lenin and Stalin did. They showed that it was possible to break away from the European-dominated world system. The Soviets did so both politically, by rejecting Western liberal democracy, and economically, by undertaking their own industrial development. Western capitalist societies had industrialized over several generations, as their citizens slowly adjusted their lives to the rhythms of the machine age. The Soviet Union seemed to provide a model for accelerating this process and overcoming economic dependency rapidly. In the Bolshevik model, modernization was imposed from above by force. But for the vast majority of the world's people, who had never known Western-style liberal democracy, authoritarian modernization was not necessarily unattractive. Comparing the results of the Russian Revolution with those of less radical revolutions and independence movements elsewhere, the aspiring revolutionary might well find the Bolshevik model more attractive.

Contrasts in Revolution and Mass Mobilization

To understand why the Russian Revolution has been the most influential twentieth-century revolution, we need to compare it with other revolutions and measure its impact on revolutionary movements elsewhere. The Mexican Revolution provides a contrast because it brought less fundamental change. Lacking a consistent ideology, significant party organization, or leaders comparable to Lenin or Stalin, Mexico's revolution neither restructured society radically nor ended dependence on the United States.

In contrast to Mexico's violent but incomplete revolution, in India a movement based on Gandhi's ideas of nonviolence ultimately ended British rule without a revolution. Like Lenin but more enduringly, Gandhi succeeded in mobilizing the masses behind a powerful ideology and a charismatic leader. Unlike Marxism-Leninism, however, Gandhi's principle of nonviolent resistance did not aim to restructure Indian society thoroughly. India's transformation can thus be contrasted with the Chinese revolution of Mao Zedong. By adapting Marxism-Leninism to Chinese conditions, Mao launched a convulsive social upheaval far closer to the Russian than to the Mexican or Indian models.

The Mexican Revolution

The Mexican revolutionaries of 1910 faced a daunting task. Like Latin America in general, Mexico was an agricultural country, still poorly integrated after a century of independence. Regimes in Mexico City faced conflicting regional interests. The divergent interests of different social classes complicated the picture further. Three-fourths of Mexicans tilled the land, but only 2 percent of them owned the land they tilled, the proportion of owners long having been in decline. The vast majority of the rural population was illiterate; perhaps a third of them were native Americans who spoke no Spanish. Landlessness, mining, and the beginnings of industrialization had created a working class, still small but badly exploited and responsive to radical ideas. Middling landowners (*rancheros*), business and professional interests in the towns, and intellectuals provided elements of a "middle class." Though not highly coherent as a social class, these elements performed key roles in running the economy, articulating ideas, and providing revolutionary leadership. At the top stood the wealthy few, typically owners of plantations (*haciendas*) with huge interests in export-oriented agriculture and mining.

In 1910, Mexico had been ruled for three decades by Porfirio Díaz (1830–1915) and a clique of wealthy associates. Díaz had started out as one local boss among many and had come to the top backed by U.S. interests. In some ways, Mexico developed spectacularly under him. Railroad mileage increased more than fortyfold. National income also doubled in the decade preceding the international financial crisis of 1907.

By then, however, Díaz had become a classic example of the conservative ruler who undermines himself by encouraging change without equitable distribution of its benefits. As he and his cronies grew old in office, younger Mexicans saw their ambitions frustrated. Export-oriented estate agriculture spread to such an extent that some traditional native American communities lost all their land except the ground beneath their houses. Mexico's ability to feed itself declined, and enterprises set up only to export raw materials could not create enough jobs to employ displaced Mexicans. Most provocative to Mexicans was the regime's subservience to foreign, especially U.S., interests. By 1900, half of all U.S. foreign investment was in Mexico. Mexico's railroads had been laid out to transport goods to the ports or to the U.S. border and did little to bring Mexicans closer together. Eventually, inflation and devaluation of the peso hindered all Mexicans' efforts to defend their interests against foreigners. By 1910, 130 of Mexico's 170 largest enterprises were foreign controlled. U.S. investors had bought over 100 million acres (22 percent of Mexico's surface) and had resold some of this to fifteen thousand American settlers, who expelled any Mexicans found living on "their" land. Díaz once sighed, "Poor Mexico! So far from God, so near the United States!" Other Mexicans reacted more militantly: "Mexico for the Mexicans!"

Francisco "Pancho" Villa (left) and Emiliano Zapata. *Heading movements of the common people, both opposed elite politicians. Yet differences in their geographical bases and interests limited their contacts and kept them from uniting.* *Special Collections, University of Texas, El Paso*

Mexicans' clear-cut nationalist grievances eventually united the nation against Díaz. The result was a decade-long firestorm of violence that no leader or movement controlled. Before the violence ended, the revolution would pass through phases of mass mobilization against Díaz, class conflict among the revolutionary forces (and U.S. military intervention), and resolution. Leading the challenge to Díaz in 1910, and forcing him into exile in 1911, were wealthy landowners whose interests had been hurt by government policy. These moderate "constitutionalists" soon found themselves surrounded by forces of other kinds. Central authority broke down; regional and class interests came to the fore; and Mexico lapsed into violence and anarchy, as leaders from different parts of the country mobilized to seize the capital and the presidency.

A few examples of revolutionary leaders and movements will give an idea of the differences among them. Francisco Madero, the wealthy northerner who raised the call to arms against Díaz, was a nineteenth-century liberal who saw the cure to Mexico's ills in political democracy. As president (1911–1913), he had time, before being murdered, to discover that not all those who had answered his call could be so easily satisfied. Popular imagination has been more captured by leaders like Francisco "Pancho" Villa, from the northern state of Chihuahua. Viewed by U.S. authorities as a "bandit," he was more exactly the leader of peasants and workers from a region of landlessness and foreign-owned agro-mineral export enterprises. Emiliano Zapata came from Morelos, just south of Mexico City, where the spread of export-oriented estate agriculture had destroyed the native American communities within living memory. (Zapata spoke the native American language Nahuatl as well as Spanish.) His peasant movement aimed to restore communal balance by giving a third of the haciendas to landless peasants, with compensation to the owners. This was hardly a radical demand, compared to the Bolsheviks' abolition of private property in 1918, but it made Zapata a rebel against the constitutionalist politicians, who had him killed in 1919. The man whose presidency (1920–1924) opened Mexico's postrevolutionary history—Álvaro Obregón—was different. He ran on a platform that mentioned both security of foreign investments and agrarian reform. From the northwest, he had kept ties to U.S. financial interests even during the revolution, and U.S. interests took his election as the signal to seek accommodation with the new Mexico.

With such disparate goals and leaders, what did the revolution accomplish for Mexico? The revolution had winners and losers, and Mexico did change appreciably from what it had been under Díaz (see Chapter 8). The losers were the peasants, industrial workers, the big landowners, and capitalists. Forced to choose between lower-class revolutionaries and nationalist moderates, foreign interests made concessions, too, particularly by acquiescing in the 1917 constitution's insistence that subsoil rights belonged to the nation. (Obregón later conceded that mines and oil wells owned by foreigners before 1917 would not be nationalized.) The winners were the middle-class who gained from the revolution a government open to their interests and ambitions. The 1917 constitution reflected their liberal, nationalist, and inclusive approach to creating a new order. Even the defeated received some recognition, The constitution promised rural Mexicans agrarian reform and the breakup of large estates. It granted workers the eight-hour day, overtime pay, and restrictions on child labor. In fact, major progress in land reform would not occur for decades, and the labor laws would never be enforced, partly because industrialists found it easier to make peace with the middle-class winners than with their workers. Such, at any rate, are the bases of the political order that has developed in Mexico since the revolution.

Mexico's was the first Third World uprising against U.S. interference. It improved conditions in Mexican society without totally restructuring it, and it renegotiated Mexico's dependence on the United States without severing it. Mexico's revolution did not put forward a model that the world could follow.

Gandhi's Nonviolence: An Alternative to Revolution?

Before World War I, only a small minority of Indian intellectuals and politicians actively challenged British rule in their country. Then a charismatic personality, inspired by a unique mixture of Indian and Western ideas, made the drive for Indian independence a mass movement. The philosophy of Mohandas K. Gandhi (1869–1948) proved a powerful force for change, though its methods and effects differed greatly from those of Marxism.

Gandhi was the son of the prime minister—we might say secretary—to the Hindu ruler of one of the tiny native states that the British permitted to survive within their Indian empire. Earlier the family had been grocers. In fact, the surname Gandhi was a term for the subcaste of grocers in the larger Banya subcaste of shopkeepers that belonged in turn to the *Vaisya* caste of traders and farmers. This was one of the hereditary castes into which tradition divided all Hindus, except the casteless Untouchables, at birth. The other castes were those of priests and scholars (*Brahman*), warriors and nobles (*Kshatriya*), and manual laborers (*Sudra*). Only members of the top three castes were entitled to an education, and the mere shadow of an Untouchable was spiritually polluting to a caste Hindu. Gandhi's early life reflected the force of tradition in these and other details, such as the extended family household into which he was born and his arranged marriage. His parents found a bride for him when he was about twelve.

To assure his future, however, Gandhi's family decided he must complete his education in England. He had to leave his wife and newborn son behind. His mother—a strict vegetarian Hindu—made him take a vow not to touch meat, liquor, or women while away. Because he had crossed the "black waters," the elders of his subcaste pronounced Gandhi an outcaste.

Gandhi arrived in England in 1888, aged nineteen. He had been an indifferent student, but over the next three years he completed his legal studies and qualified as a barrister. More important, he discovered a new world of ideas. At first, Gandhi identified with English society in superficial ways, paying much attention to dress and taking dancing lessons. Then realizing that he could never become English, he began to seek out people with whom his own way of life gave him something in common: first vegetarians, then enthusiasts of various religions and cults. These contacts led Gandhi to wide reading in religious texts, ranging from Christ's Sermon on the Mount to the great Hindu scripture, the Bhagavad Gita, or "Celestial Song," which he read first in English translation. In both, God summons human beings to a life of selfless dedication to the welfare of others. This, not the law, became Gandhi's lasting lesson from his years in England.

Returning to India at twenty-one, Gandhi had trouble readjusting to life with his uneducated wife, Kasturbai, and lacked the self-confidence needed to succeed in legal practice. Within two years, he was so frustrated that he leapt at a chance to go to South Africa to represent an Indian merchant in a legal case there. Though he had gone through religious rites to be received back into his caste, Gandhi again set out across the "black waters." He was to remain in South Africa most of the time from 1893 to 1914. There he developed the methods he later applied in India.

Gandhi had not been in South Africa long before he discovered the racial discrimination to which all non-Europeans were subject. One of his earliest experiences there was being thrown off a train, although he had the proper ticket, because a European objected to his presence in a first-class compartment. This humiliation led him to mobilize the Indian community in a campaign against the laws that made such discrimination possible. Although he had planned to stay only a year, he remained in South Africa to work on behalf of his fellow Indians.

Over the next twenty years, Gandhi worked out a distinctive way of life and political action. He read widely, studying the scriptures of Hinduism and Islam, India's two most widespread religions; the works of Henry David Thoreau, the U.S. apostle of civil disobedience; and the later writings of the Russian novelist Leo Tolstoy. In his personal life, Gandhi became noted for his ascetic emphasis on diet, fasting, and nature cures. From 1906 on, he formulated his principles as *brahmacharya,* the ancient Hindu vow of celibacy (within marriage in his case); *ahimsa,* or nonviolence; and *satyagraha,* the force of truth and love. Gandhi himself developed the last concept, which he equated with passive resistance. His ability to express partly new concepts in terms drawn from Hindu tradition enhanced Gandhi's appeal, as did his selflessness in living according to those principles. Gandhi would clean latrines as a spiritual discipline, and he led ambulance units in hazardous service during the Boer War.

Gandhi was no solitary ascetic. He organized his family and followers into communal settlements that became models for the *ashrams* (a Hindu term for a religious retreat) he later created in India. In these settlements, he propagated a life of egalitarian self-reliance. He also became a mass mobilizer, championing the interests of women and Untouchables. In fact his emphasis on latrine cleaning and self-reliance was part of his attempt to persuade Indians to forget differences of religion and caste, which condemned Untouchables to do jobs that Hindus classed as unclean. Finally, Gandhi became a political organizer and leader. He staged his first great passive-resistance campaigns against laws that required Asians to carry special registration certificates and that made only Christian marriages valid in South Africa. By the time Gandhi left South Africa, he and his followers had won some concessions from the government.

Returning to India in 1915, Gandhi soon took up the cause of Indian independence, as we shall discuss in more detail in Chapter 10. In the communal settlements he founded in India, Gandhi elaborated his ideas of self-reliance into a Constructive Program. His goal was to revitalize village India by getting villagers to breed cattle, learn elementary hygiene, take up useful crafts such as beekeeping or pottery, spin and weave their own cloth, form cooperatives and village assemblies, overturn hereditary obstacles to learning, learn Hindi so that India could have one national language, and eliminate religious hatred and discrimination against Untouchables, whom Gandhi called *harijans,* or children of God. He also advocated equality for women, prompting the Indian National Congress party to adopt a bill of rights (1931) that called for equality without regard to religion, caste, or sex. Politically he worked through the Congress party and organized a number of passive-resistance campaigns. Above all, Gandhi identified with the poor by traveling among them and living in the style of a Hindu holy man. India's poor responded with enthusiasm. Gandhi could command the attention of a crowd with a gesture. His fasts, which he used not just to discipline himself but also to pressure others, could halt widespread intercommunal violence. Indians hailed him as a *mahatma* ("great soul"), or even as a manifestation of divinity.

Compared to other revolutionaries and nationalist leaders, Gandhi had an unusual combination of strengths and limitations. The most important limitation was that he was ultimately not a revolutionary. True, Gandhi, like others, used nonviolence as a powerful instrument for change, but his goals for social change were limited. Although he wanted independence from the British, his aspirations for Hindu society did not go beyond ending discrimination against Untouchables and women. Gandhi never took a consistent stand against the caste system, the heart of the Indian problem of inequality. Although he favored unity among members of India's religions, he never seemed to realize how much the Hindu character of his ideas and style irritated some non-Hindus. Finally, though his Constructive Program anticipated later rural development concepts, it represented a move more toward the past than toward the future. Gandhi rightly saw that Indians could hurt Britain by refusing to use British textiles and by making their cottons by hand instead. He was correct, too, in seeing the dehumanizing effects of industrial labor. But Gandhi was almost unique in the non-Western world of his day in not calling for economic independence *through* industrialization—the path India ultimately took.

Gandhi's strength was his ability to bridge the gap between Hindu and Western ideas and to combine new elements with old in a form of political action that was probably the only realistic alternative for an India faced with British power. Forty years after his death, many of his disciples thought that the rulers of independent India had more in common with the British than with Gandhi. But his ideas have not been forgotten. They have influenced people all over the world, many of whom compare Gandhi to the greatest figures of all time.

Marxism as a Challenge to Imperialism: Mao Zedong

To find another twentieth-century revolutionary or nationalist leader comparable to Lenin or Gandhi in impact on his nation and the world, we must look to China and Mao Zedong (Mao Tse-tung, 1893–1976).*

For most of Mao's life, however, his later importance was far from obvious. In 1911 a revolution toppled the entire combination of traditional institutions and Confucian ideology that had dominated China for two millennia. The underlying causes of the revolution were European imperialism, which had undermined the traditional Chinese imperial system without establishing direct foreign rule (except in some enclaves), and the nationalism that developed among Chinese as a result. But the revolution of 1911 merely started China down the road to mass mobilization and popular sovereignty. The change was not complete before 1949.

Meanwhile, the greatest question facing China's leaders was how to organize a regime that could re-establish China's independence and survive the stresses of mass politics in a rapidly changing world. For years the Chinese Communists were not the most successful contenders in the struggle (see Chapter 10). Their eventual triumph was in great measure the work of Mao Zedong. An examination of his early career will show how Marxism came to the non-Western world, changing in the process.

Unlike many Chinese leaders, even Communists such as Zhou Enlai (Chou Enlai, 1898–1976), long-time premier of the People's Republic, Mao came from a peasant family. Mao's father, an authoritarian with whom he often clashed, eventually became a "rich" peas-

---

*Following current usage, we will use the Pinyin, rather than the Wade-Giles, system for the rendering of Chinese names and terms. At the first appearance of each name or term, however, the Wade-Giles version will be shown in parentheses following the Pinyin. The only exceptions will be cases where the two forms are identical or cases in which the identity of individuals who are well known by the Wade-Giles spelling would be obscured by the Pinyin form. Two such individuals mentioned in this book are Sun Yat-sen and Chiang Kai-shek; the Pinyin forms of their names are Sun Yixuan and Jiang Jieshi.

ant, owning a bit over three acres, on which the family produced five or six tons of rice a year. In addition he traded in grain.

The family's relative affluence enabled Mao to go to school. His education began with memorization of Confucian classics in the local primary school. But China's changing politics also was changing education; new types of schools were coming into existence. By his mid-twenties, Mao had been in and out of a number of schools and had studied for a time on his own. He acquired enough Confucian culture to be able to write essays and poems in traditional style. He also absorbed China's traditional popular literature; from some of its Robin Hood–like heroes, he learned military strategies that he later applied. He began to write for newspapers, and he read some of the most influential works of Western literature in translation. At a time when many Chinese took an unprecedented interest in the army as a way to throw off imperialism, he was briefly a soldier.

When other future leaders, including Zhou, went to France to study during World War I, Mao stayed behind, perhaps because he was not good at languages. Mao remained close to China's common people, read foreign books only in translation, never left the country in his early years, and dealt with foreign ideas only in Chinese. These factors may explain why it was he who naturalized Marxism into the Chinese setting.

Ultimately, Marxism was the intellectual influence that affected Mao most. In 1918, when the Bolshevik Revolution was beginning to attract attention in China, Mao spent a half-year in Beijing (Peking) as assistant to the university librarian, Li Dazhao (Li Tachao), who organized a Marxist study group. Like other Chinese, Li and Mao did not then understand Marxist theory and had not committed themselves fully to it. What appealed to them, following the conflict of 1914–1918 among the Western imperialist nations, was the idea that the Bolshevik model offered an alternate way to reorganize China and improve its place in the world.

On May 4, 1919, a massive student demonstration broke out in Beijing to protest Japanese encroachment on China and the decision of the Paris Peace Conference to support Japanese claims. The demonstration created a lasting excitement, the May Fourth Movement, that favored the spread of new ideas. In his native Hunan Province, Mao took an active role in political organization and helped found the Chinese Communist party (CCP) in 1921.

Mao and his colleagues, still not proficient in Marxist theory, were uncertain how to launch revolution in China. The country hardly had the urban working class that Marx assumed. Mao's work in the countryside convinced him of the peasants' revolutionary potential. But party leaders of the 1920s thought peasants wanted only land and would lose interest in revolution once they got it.

The CCP sought help from the Soviet Union through the Communist International, or Comintern, founded in 1919 to serve as a "general headquarters" for world revolution. But neither the Comintern advisers in China nor the Soviet leadership understood Chinese conditions. Under Stalin, whose real goal was socialism in one country, the Comintern became a mere tool of Soviet foreign policy. Soviet advice to the CCP generally ranged from bad to disastrous. Because Marxist theory held that the overthrow of feudalism (the imperial system in China) should lead to a period of bourgeois capitalism (like the liberal capitalist societies of Western Europe) before the proletarian revolution, the Soviets called on the CCP to ally with the larger Nationalist party, the Guomindang (GMD, Kuomintang).

The GMD was based in the port cities and among the landlord class. Its leader, Sun Yatsen (1866–1925), agreed that Communists

Mao Zedong with peasants of Shensi Province during the war against Japan. *According to the official caption supplied for this picture, "Chairman Mao cherishes the masses most ardently."* *Sovfoto/Eastfoto*

could join the GMD and work within it as individuals. Mao and others did so. But as the GMD sought to consolidate its control throughout China, Sun's successor, Chiang Kai-shek, turned violently against the CCP in 1927, killing many of its supporters. Nevertheless, Stalin continued for months to advocate GMD-CCP cooperation, and the influence of Moscow-trained leaders in the CCP remained a problem into the early 1930s.

Among those who survived the GMD terror, Mao again went south to Hunan Province. After an unsuccessful uprising, he joined other Communists in the mountains on the border of neighboring Jiangxi (Kiangsi) Province, becoming chairman of their Jiangxi Soviet. Isolated from the CCP Central Committee and Comintern representatives in Shanghai, Mao developed his own ideas of organization and tactics, emphasizing rural base areas, agrarian revolution, and development of the Red Army.

In 1930, Chiang Kai-shek began a series of campaigns against the Jiangxi Soviet that eventually forced the Communists to strike out on the Long March. During this six-thousand-mile trek, which led from Jiangxi to a new base in the northwest, Mao emerged as the leader of the CCP. Of the hundred thousand people who began the Long March, only a fraction lived to complete it. At Yan'an (Yenan), the CCP base from 1935 to 1947, Mao finally came to grips with Marxist theory and began evaluating the Chinese experience in its light.

With this effort began the modification of Marxism-Leninism that later became known as Mao Zedong thought.[2] The main themes of

Mao's thought underscore its potential for conflict with Soviet Marxism-Leninism. One theme was Mao's emphasis on will. He had become a Marxist out of excitement over the 1917 revolution, without knowing Marx's ideas about the stages of history. For Mao, revolution emerged from will and activism, not from predetermined levels of economic development. From this idea followed the emphasis on thought reform as a way of bringing people into conformity with the party line. From this also followed a concept of class struggle that made class identification more a matter of how one thought than of how one earned a living. If Mao's ideas made a muddle of Marx's stages of revolution, so be it: China would have permanent revolution. For a society in which cultural conservatism had reigned supreme, change would become permanent.

A second Maoist theme was nationalism—anathema to Marx but a powerful force in the minds of most Chinese. Mao's nationalism expressed itself in his closeness to China's traditional culture and his hostility to the Comintern and the Soviet Union. Some reasons for the Sino-Soviet split in the late 1950s went back more than thirty years. Mao's nationalism also appeared in his tendency to see the real enemy of the revolution as foreign imperialism, to identify class struggle with national struggle, and so to allow willing Chinese of any class background to join the revolution.

Perhaps the most important Maoist theme stemmed from his origins: *populism,* or emphasis on the common people. Mao's radicalism showed itself most clearly in his romantic faith in the peasants' revolutionary potential. Since this faith conflicted with strict Marxist theory, Mao became distrustful of theorists and experts in general. Differing not only from Marx but also from Lenin, who thought that the vanguard party could impose revolutionary consciousness on the workers, Mao came to believe in a "mass line," a revolutionary consciousness among the peasant masses, which the party must understand before it could guide them. From this view followed a commitment to mass mobilization that enabled the CCP, unlike the GMD, to succeed in dealing with peasants, who might not have responded to communism otherwise.

Like most Chinese of his time, Mao also thought an effective military was necessary for overcoming imperialism. He believed his cause required a military force that could survive among the people, as it did during the Long March, without alienating them. That meant treating peasants like human beings, paying for supplies, and doing a host of other things not done in the past.

Mao's ideas enabled the CCP to survive through World War II, during which it again cooperated with the GMD against the Japanese. His ideas enabled the CCP to win support while the GMD crumbled, setting the stage for the civil war (1946–1949) that gave the Communists control of the country. Chapter 17 will show how Mao's thought left its mark on the People's Republic of China.

Conclusion: Revolutions Compared

Revolutions vary widely in scope. Some affect only the domestic political order. Some restructure underlying social and economic relationships. Others transform the society's culture as well. Internationally, revolutions may or may not transform a society's place in the global configuration.

The examples in this chapter suggest that for a country with a domestic history of exploitative social and economic relationships, the only real revolution is a social one that not only changes political institutions but also redistributes wealth and power. The Bolshevik leaders did this in Russia, and so did the

Maoists when they gained control of China. Mexico's elite revolutionaries made such concessions half-heartedly; China's Nationalists (GMD) made practically none. As such cases show, a revolution needs a coherent ideology that provides a program for action, as Marxism-Leninism did in Russia and as Mao's adaptation of those ideas did in China. The contrast between successful and unsuccessful revolutions also underscores the importance of effective leadership and a well-organized movement or party.

In addition, for a country in a subordinate position in the global pattern of power relationships, a revolution does not triumph until it transforms these external relationships. Mexico made limited gains in this respect. The Bolsheviks succeeded by breaking links of debt and investment that had made the tsarist regime, though supposedly a great power, dependent on Western Europe. Both the GMD and the CCP contributed to ridding China of imperialist encroachment.

The Soviet experience with revolution has been so influential in the twentieth century that it is difficult to discuss the requirements of successful revolution in terms that do not seem to refer to this example. Gandhi's significance lies in his showing the possibility of other ways. Although his movement did not produce revolution, it included the aspiration to socio-economic and cultural change, the ideology to chart a course for change, the charismatic leader, organized movement, and mass mobilization. Clearly, too, Gandhi aimed to transform India's place in global power relationships. The main limiting factors were that Gandhi sought to reform Indian society but not systematically to eliminate the bases of inequality in the caste system, and that Gandhi's method perhaps also assumed a certain type of adversary, one accessible to moral arguments. The method worked against the British and in some other settings, especially the U.S. civil rights movement. Could it have worked against a more ruthless adversary, like some of the other leaders discussed in these pages?

Notes

1. Quoted in Theodore H. Von Laue, *Why Lenin? Why Stalin? A Reappraisal of the Russian Revolution, 1900–1930* (Philadelphia: Lippincott, 1964), p. 212.
2. This summary of Mao's ideas follows Maurice Meisner, "Yenan Communism and the Rise of the Chinese People's Republic," in James B. Crowley, ed., *Modern East Asia: Essays in Interpretation* (New York: Harcourt, Brace & World, 1970), pp. 283–296.

Suggestions for Further Reading

Carr, E. H. *The Meaning of the Russian Revolution* (1979).

Crowley, James B., ed. *Modern East Asia: Essays in Interpretation* (1970).

Green, Martin. *The Origins of Nonviolence: Tolstoy and Gandhi in Their Historical Settings* (1986).

Hart, John Mason. *Revolutionary Mexico: The Coming and Process of the Mexican Revolution* (1987).

Knight, Alan. *The Mexican Revolution*. 2 vols. (1986).

Mehta, Ved. *Mahatma Gandhi and His Apostles* (1976).

Schram, Stuart. *Mao Tse-Tung* (1966).

———. *The Thought of Mao Tse-Tung* (1989).

Snow, Edgar. *Red Star over China*. Rev. ed. (1968).

Stavrianos, L. S. *Global Rift: The Third World Comes of Age* (1981).

Von Laue, Theodore H. *Why Lenin? Why Stalin? A Reappraisal of the Russian Revolution, 1900–1930* (1964).

CHAPTER 5

Global Economic Crisis and the Restructuring of the Social and Political Order

The triumph of communism in Russia challenged the European-dominated global pattern of 1914 in three ways. It offered an alternative to the liberal capitalist model for the organization of an economy, society, and government. It severed the links that had subordinated Russia economically to Western Europe. It encouraged revolutionaries everywhere who dreamed of restructuring their own societies and freeing them from foreign domination.

This challenge to the pre-1914 order produced panic that the communist "disease" might spread. Politicians blamed communists for the 1919 wave of strikes in which workers protested their loss of purchasing power under wartime wage controls. In the United States, the postwar "Red Scare" led to the so-called Palmer raids, in which Wilson's attorney general rounded up and deported foreigners without regard to their rights. In France, the right-wing parties won a landslide victory in the elections of 1919 partly by playing on voters' fear of "the man with a knife between his teeth"—a hairy and terrifying Communist depicted on conservative election posters.

The Deceptive "Normalcy" of the 1920s

By the mid-1920s, however, it seemed clear that the Russian Revolution was not going to spread. Conservative forces overturned the communist regime established in Hungary after the Hapsburg collapse. The new German republic crushed communist attempts to seize power in 1919 and 1923. Arguing that communist subversion was still a threat probably helped British Conservatives defeat the first Labour cabinet in 1924. But by then Europeans and Americans were beginning to see communism as a Russian abnormality.

People could more easily believe that the Russian Revolution had not changed the course of world history because some semblance of prewar politics and economies seemed re-established by the late 1920s. In the great democracies, politicians whose very ordinariness reassured people that nothing had changed replaced dynamic wartime leaders like Wilson and Clemenceau. Humorist Will Rogers said of Calvin Coolidge, who became the U.S. president after Harding's death in 1923, that "Silent Cal" did exactly what Americans wanted: nothing. His administration was reminiscent of the nineteenth century, when U.S. presidents had been relatively inconspicuous. In Britain and France, too, conservative prime ministers—Stanley Baldwin and Raymond Poincaré—held power for much of the 1920s. They also were committed to the pre-1914 view that the government's role in a free society should be minimal.

After the mid-1920s, some nations' economies seemed to have regained or exceeded their prewar levels. By 1929, for example, U.S. industrial production was 75 percent greater than in 1913. British factories in 1929, however, were producing only 10 percent more than they had before the war. The war had seriously weakened the British economy, around which the world economy had pivoted throughout the nineteenth century. Nevertheless, Britain took the controversial step of returning to the gold standard in 1925—that is, the British government again offered to sell gold for an established price in pounds. As a result, the pound became overvalued, making British exports too expensive for many countries to buy. But deeply felt psychological need, rather than economic calculation, motivated the return to the gold standard. By the mid-1920s, people wanted to see World War I as a short and accidental interruption of "normalcy"—President Harding's word—rather than as the beginning of a grim new era of change. So Britain declared that the pound would once again be "as good as gold."

Because people wanted so much to believe that World War I had not fundamentally changed the world, they ignored the ominous structural faults that were the war's legacy to the global economy. Wartime demand had everywhere expanded both agricultural and industrial capacity beyond peacetime needs. By the late 1920s prices were beginning to fall and unsold goods and crops to pile up. The prewar pattern of international finance was replaced by an absurd system of overextended international credits that reflected political pressures rather than economic good sense. For example, in order to pay their huge war debts to the United States, Germany's other former enemies insisted that the Germans pay them reparations. When the Germans insisted they could not afford to pay, American bankers lent them the money, as they also lent other Europeans money to pay their debts. This was all very well as long as the lenders felt sure they would get their money back, but it would prove calamitous when that confidence was lost, dragging the whole developed world into economic ruin.

Thus the prosperity of the late 1920s rested on fragile foundations. Because the economies of the developed world were so interdependent, a catastrophe in any one of them would quickly spread to the rest. When prices on the New York Stock Exchange collapsed in October 1929—the biggest loss stocks have ever experienced—the eventual result was a worldwide Great Depression far worse than any earlier downturn.

In economic terms, a *depression* is a time when curves on all the graphs—prices, wages, employment, investment, international trade—head persistently downward. After 1929 all these variables dropped to, and stayed at, unprecedentedly low levels.

The Great Depression wrecked more than the global economy. By 1932, with one American in four and two Germans in five unable to find jobs, much of the world was living in psychological depression. Economists, business leaders, and politicians admitted they could not find a cure. No experience from the pre-1914 world was relevant to an economic disaster so big and long lasting.

Gravely eroded by World War I, the foundations of the European-dominated global pattern were further undermined by the Depression. The dependent peoples of the world had already seen their European masters locked in a death struggle that left none unscathed. After 1929, Asians, Africans, and Latin Americans saw that the technological dynamism of Western civilization had not averted an economic calamity that engulfed them, too. The Depression of the 1930s cruelly drove home to the dependent peoples the extent of their economic subordination and further discredited the Western claim to rule the globe by right of cultural superiority. Though most colonial peoples would win political independence only after the second "European civil war" (World War II), 1929 like 1914 was a fateful date on the way to the post-1945 "end of empire."

In the developed Western nations, despair and rage led people to reject many of the economic and political ideas taken for granted until the crash, and stimulated frantic demands for new ideas that could put people to work again. Now interest in the communist alternative truly began to develop. When European and American coal mines were closed for lack of sales while unemployed people froze to death for lack of coal, the Soviet idea of a government-planned and -managed economy suddenly seemed to make more sense.

In Western Europe, political parties had emerged since 1917 that accepted the need for socialism but argued that it was not necessary to destroy parliamentary democracy in order to institute government ownership and management of the economy. In Britain and France, the Great Depression would provide a first test of this idea of achieving socialism through democracy.

Still found today in Europe and much of the rest of the world, democratic socialism was never a strong movement in the United States. Its most successful presidential candidate, Eugene Debs, won no more than 6 percent of the vote in 1912. Yet many critics of President Franklin D. Roosevelt, elected in 1932, attacked his New Deal programs as "socialistic." Though incorrect, the label reflected the deep controversy the New Deal provoked among Americans. All agreed that it profoundly changed the bases of American life—but was it for better or for worse?

What role the federal government should play in controlling the U.S. economy is still a matter of hot controversy. Americans tend to debate that issue without placing it in historical context or drawing comparisons with the experiences of other nations. But, as we shall see, in the light of world history the New Deal is best understood as the U.S. answer to a worldwide problem revealed after the Wall Street crash.

From Wall Street Crash to World Depression

In the summer of 1929, American ingenuity seemed to have produced an economy invulnerable to the ups and downs of economic history. The new president, Herbert Hoover, an engineer and self-made millionaire, proclaimed, "We in America today are nearer to the final triumph over poverty than ever before in the history of any land . . . we shall soon with the help of God be in sight of the day when poverty will be banished from this nation."[1] Such confidence seemed justified when all but 3 percent of the work force had jobs and manufacturing output had risen by 50 percent in a decade.

At the New York Stock Exchange on Wall Street, the mood was euphoric—and why not? Stock prices were climbing with unprecedented speed, as much in June and July alone as in all of 1928. After Labor Day the rise slowed, but few of the million or so Americans speculating in stocks were disturbed. They trusted authorities like the president of the National City Bank, who declared, "Nothing can arrest the upward movement of the United States."

In October, however, the bottom fell out. October 29 was the worst day in the history of the exchange. As panic-stricken investors tried to sell, an unheard-of 16.5 million shares were dumped. Some found no buyer at any price. Within two months American stocks lost half their value. Paper millionaires in August were bankrupt by Christmas.

The impact of this disaster was not limited to investors or even to Americans. As business leaders' confidence sagged, they reduced production, throwing employees out of work. As the unemployed stopped buying anything but necessities, reduced demand put more people out of work. As the unemployed failed to pay what they owed to banks, the bankers called in the loans they could collect. Because U.S. banks had made huge loans to Europe, panic spread there. After one of Vienna's leading banks, the Credit-Anstalt, failed in the spring of 1931, the cycle of fear and economic paralysis spread quickly into neighboring Germany and from there to the rest of the Continent.

By 1932 the Depression was everywhere. In the United States its symptoms were padlocked factories, vacant stores, deserted transportation terminals, and empty freight yards. City streets were relatively empty, for many people now had no place to go. On the sidewalks were unemployed people attempting to sell apples for a nickel or simply seeking a handout. The fortunate were those who were still working, though at reduced wages, and those who still had their homes, though they might have lost their savings. Others, homeless, huddled in improvised shantytowns bitterly called Hoovervilles or rode the rails in empty freight cars, crisscrossing the country in a hopeless search for work.

Such were the human realities behind the grim statistics. In the United States, gross national product had fallen by nearly a half, and the number of suicides had increased by a third. Things were as bad in Düsseldorf as in Detroit. Worldwide industrial production in 1932 stood at only two-thirds of its 1929 level. World trade had fallen by more than half.

Nothing better illustrated the twentieth-century global pattern than the Depression's impact on parts of the world whose peoples knew nothing of stock markets and little of industrial development. Because natural rubber prices fell 75 percent from 1929 to 1932, for example, fewer jobs were available on the rubber plantations of Ceylon (now Sri Lanka). Because Western manufacturers were ordering less rubber for automobiles and appliances, half the Indian laborers who had worked on the Ceylonese rubber plantations had to return jobless to their homeland.

The Depression stretched to the ends of the earth. What was worse, it seemed to go on forever. The world's earlier economic crises had often been short and sharp, followed quickly by recovery. But despite politicians' assurances that prosperity was "just around the corner," the current economic decline seemed beyond remedy. How had this disaster of unprecedented size and duration occurred?

Origins of the Crisis

Economics is not an exact science. Moreover, the history of an economic crisis cannot be

Homeless in New York City. *Except for the "home" in the background, one of the Depression's unemployed workers tries to sell apples.* *Culver Pictures*

discussed without evaluating opposing economic policies. For these reasons, explanation of the Depression is controversial. Although historians generally agree on why the stock market crashed, they differ as to what the crash implies about the structure of the U.S. economy. Still more controversy surrounds the relation of the crash to the worldwide slump. In attempting to explain the crisis, we shall move from the surest ground to the most contested: from Wall Street to the U.S. economy and finally to the world scene.

Stock Market Collapse

The Wall Street crash that triggered the Depression was the collapse of a house of cards. It ended a decade of speculation that involved dangerous though hidden risks for the speculators, the bankers who lent them money, and the brokers who sold them shares. During the 1920s all three groups began to assume that financial paper like shares of stock had a value of its own that could only increase. Buyers bought stock "on margin," paying only 10 percent of the price and borrowing the rest from the broker; they expected to stock's value to increase fast enough to allow them to pay off the loan. Often the initial 10 percent was lent by bankers who accepted the stock itself as collateral while investing their depositors' money in similar shares. Shady financiers created glittering opportunities for these eager investors by launching holding companies whose only assets were paper ones: shares of other companies. They also bribed financial advisers and newspaper columnists to circulate tips that would stimulate a rush to buy shares in these paper creations.

The stock market's climb owed as much to psychology as to economics. For example, people borrowed money at high rates of interest to purchase the stock of Radio Corporation of America (RCA), not because they expected to collect dividends—RCA had never paid any—but because they were sure its price would continue to soar. And while the optimism lasted, its price quintupled in a single year.

Once the mood changed, and people became convinced that the market could only go down rather than up, the plunge was as steep as the climb had been. As prices fell, brokers demanded a larger margin. When speculators could not pay, their shares were dumped onto the market, further depressing prices. Meanwhile the holding companies melted away as their paper assets became worthless.

In one sense, the 1929 crash was the inevitable end of a financial boom generated within the small world of Wall Street. But it had a devastating impact on the entire U.S. economy. It wiped out much investment capital and made investors cautious about risking what they still had. The resulting damage to individual purchasing power, to international lending, and to trade would not be repaired in the next ten years.

Mass Production and Underconsumption: Basic U.S. Economic Flaws

Many economic historians believe the Wall Street crash was only a symptom of basic flaws in the U.S. economy that would inevitably have produced a depression at some point. These flaws were not apparent at the time. Throughout the 1920s, U.S. industry continued the rapid growth stimulated by the war. By 1929 there were 26.5 million automobiles on American roads, compared to 1.3 million in 1914. Once a curiosity, radio became an industry of mass entertainment. Americans in the Far West and the Deep South listened to identical network programs. In 1929, expenditures on radios were forty times the level of 1920, when they were first mass-produced. The apparent affluence represented by American ownership of automobiles, radios, and other gadgets did not surprise visiting Europeans. They knew that World War I had transformed the United States from a debtor nation to the principal creditor of the rest of the world. With industry booming and the rest of the world owing them money, Americans thought nothing could be wrong with their economy.

But the distribution of wealth in U.S. society may have been too unequal in the 1920s to create demand for all the goods that industry was pouring forth. Some domestic markets were becoming glutted with unsold goods as early as 1926. The productivity of American factory workers rose by almost 50 percent in the 1920s, as mergers created firms large enough to afford more efficient machinery. But firms' cost savings were channeled primarily into corporate profits, which tripled during the decade. Prices were not substantially reduced, and even in unionized plants, wages rose less than profits.

Thus the purchasing power of the U.S. labor force was not greatly increased. Nor was the boom creating jobs. The number of Americans employed remained fairly constant through the 1920s. In some industries mechanization actually reduced the number of jobs steeply while increasing output. The problem of *technological unemployment*—of human workers displaced by machines—dates back to the beginning of mass production.

In human terms, these trends meant that the average American might be able to maintain a car in the 1920s but not to trade it in for a new one. Industrial expansion proceeded on the assumption that consumers could afford to keep buying indefinitely, though the 20 percent of Americans who worked in agriculture did not realize even the modest gains of industrial workers.

World War I had been a bonanza for American farmers, who vastly expanded their acreage to provide the food once grown on European battlefields. When European production revived after the war, the world's markets were soon glutted with agricultural produce. Long before the Wall Street crash, world farm prices had collapsed to about half their level of 1919. When the Depression began, the wages of American farm and factory workers were farther apart than they had been in 1910.

While some of the poor were getting poorer, the rich were getting richer. The proportion of total U.S. income earned by the wealthiest 5 percent of the population had grown since 1910 from a fourth to a third. In 1929, almost a fifth of American income was collected by the top 1 percent. Wealthy people's purchases of yachts and jewelry could not sustain a boom.

The United States had developed an economy of mass production without a corresponding society of mass consumption. The concentration of wealth had been less important during the nineteenth century, when Americans had been building and equipping a nation of continental dimensions. Now, however, the railroads the tycoons had built were all finished. Stringent postwar laws restricted immigration, which had increased the American population by as much as a million people a year before World War I. With nation building complete and population growth greatly reduced, the possibilities for constructive investment were less obvious. There was no guarantee that the wealth increasingly concentrated in fewer hands would be invested in ways that benefited the economy as a whole. The stock market boom, like an earlier craze for buying Florida land, showed that too much money was at the discretion of people who could afford to spend it foolishly. The purchasing power of most consumers was far more limited. The shrewdest investors recognized these warning signs. In 1928, when they noticed that company profits were not increasing nearly as rapidly as stock prices, they began the trickle of selling that became an avalanche in October 1929.

Maldistribution of income also helps explain why the Depression persisted so long. Although the economy would remain stagnant without investment, the wealthy few who could afford to invest were afraid to do so. The vast majority of Americans confined their expenses to necessities. Thus a vicious circle developed. With no hope of sales, there was no inclination to invest. With no investment, there were no jobs, no income, and consequently no sales.

The Spread of the Depression

If the Depression resulted from weaknesses in the U.S. economy and society, how did it spread to the rest of the world? Historians disagree on this question. But it is clear that the

U.S. crash and U.S. government policies in reaction to it were the final blows to a world economic order already mortally weakened by World War I.

The European-dominated global pattern of 1914 was centered on Great Britain. Because the British were committed to free trade, many goods could enter their country tariff-free, even when British industry and agriculture were suffering from an economic downturn. British wealth had been so great that the bankers of the City of London continued to make long-term loans to the rest of the world regardless of the fluctuations of the British economy. When investment opportunities at home were limited by an industrial slump, British investment abroad actually increased. Whenever a banking crisis threatened anywhere in the world, bankers turned to the London banks for prompt help. After the Wall Street crash, however, it became clear that Britain could no longer play the central role in the global pattern and that the United States, Britain's logical successor, would not do so.

Britain had been the first nation to industrialize. In 1914 its industrial plant was already outmoded in comparison with those of its later-starting competitors. During World War I, Britain sold many of its overseas assets to buy arms but nevertheless amassed huge debts to the United States. The war enabled nations like Japan to invade British markets. Whereas over three-fifths of India's imports in 1914 came from Britain, by 1929 fewer than half did.

Britain's weakness became obvious when the Depression struck. After nearly a century of free trade, it adopted protective tariffs in 1932. A year earlier, the drain on British gold reserves had forced Britain to stop paying gold for pounds. Once again off the gold standard, and with a depreciating currency, Britain itself was in too much trouble to help reinflate the world economy with new investment. A large British loan might have saved Vienna's Credit-Anstalt after the recall of American loans and might have forestalled the economic collapse of Central Europe. But the Bank of England would offer only a comparatively small loan, to be repaid in weekly installments: hardly the terms of a long-term offer of salvation.

Britain could no longer be the world's financier, and the United States declined to take on any such responsibility. Throughout the 1920s the U.S. government rejected European arguments that war debts and reparations destabilized international payment balances and should be canceled. Not until 1932 were these economic reminders of wartime hatreds abandoned. The German economy increasingly relied on short-term American loans to make its reparations payments—which in turn were needed by Britain and France to pay their American debts. Germany was already in trouble before October 1929, as U.S. bankers reclaimed their money to invest it on Wall Street. After the crash, demands for immediate repayment completed the damage.

In 1930, Congress passed the Hawley-Smoot Tariff Act, imposing the highest import duties in history. Ignoring protests from thirty countries, President Hoover signed it into law. Now foreign countries could no longer sell their goods in the American marketplace to earn dollars to buy American products. Nor could they borrow dollars, for after the crash American banks became much more cautious lenders. Meanwhile, U.S. producers found they sold less abroad, for many countries retaliated by shutting their doors to U.S. products.

Because the United States produced nearly half the world's goods, it was the obvious candidate to assume Britain's former role of financial leadership. But instead of providing a market and loans in a crisis, the U.S. government signaled that in a world depression, it was every nation for itself. In such an atmosphere, what were the weak to do?

The Depression in the Developing World

The peoples of the developing world, whether living in colonies or in technically independent countries such as those of Latin America, were even less able to combat the Depression than were Europeans and North Americans. The more a developing country's economy had been integrated into the European-dominated global pattern, the more it suffered after 1929.

Those who fared best were the new nations whose principal economic activity was still subsistence agriculture—growing food to feed themselves. By 1929, however, many countries of Latin America, Africa, and Asia were economically dependent on their sales of agricultural or mineral products to Europeans or Americans. In many cases a single crop or mineral constituted most of a country or colony's exports.

The world agricultural glut had cut into export earnings well before 1929. To many crop-exporting countries the Depression was the final blow. The price of rice, the principal export of Siam (today Thailand), fell by half within a year. As the factories of Europe and the United States shut down, the bottom fell out of the market for industrial raw materials like copper and tin. The value of Chile's exports fell by 80 percent, and that of other Latin American exports by at least half. Despite international efforts to restore prices by agreeing to limit production, the countries that had earned their living by selling such goods as tea, rubber, and copper remained in deep trouble throughout the 1930s. Unable to sell, they could not buy what their trading partners might offer, nor were they credible risks for loans. Their wealth of natural resources was now worthless. In two years, for example, Brazil burned or shoveled into the ocean enough coffee to fill the cups of the whole world for a year. Although Brazil had been ostensibly independent since the 1820s, the Depression showed that its economic well-being was at the mercy of prices set in markets it did not control.

The experience of India, still a British colony, suggests that colonies beginning to develop economies less dependent on a few commodities might actually benefit from the Depression's impact on their masters. After World War I, British industry never regained its prewar dominance of Indian markets. When Britain in response to postwar unrest granted its colony power to manage its own economic affairs, India promptly erected tariff barriers to protect its infant industry from foreign competition. In the twenty-five years after India opened its first large steel mill in 1913, Indian steel production grew more than eightfold. Though raw cotton remained India's principal export, its own cotton-spinning industry grew rapidly, encouraged both by protective tariffs and, after 1930, by Gandhi's campaign to boycott British goods. In 1939 modern textile mills—largely owned by Indians, not Englishmen—produced almost three times as much cotton cloth as the primitive hand looms Gandhi's campaign had encouraged.

India did not escape the Depression entirely. In 1939, total steel consumption, including imports, was still less than in 1929. Agricultural exports fell, partly because of a 15 percent growth in population in the 1930s. (The population explosion began in much of Asia during this period, as these countries' rates of population growth overtook those of Europe and North America.) The need to feed many more people encouraged the overcultivation and exhaustion of Indian soil. Already one could foresee the question that became critical for India during the 1980s: Could industrialization raise the standard of living among so many hungry mouths? Even so, India came through the Depression far more easily than countries wholly dependent on raw-material exports.

Indian boycott of British products, 1931. *Preparing to burn an effigy of the British cotton cloth industry, these followers of Gandhi were protesting colonial dependency.* Popperfoto

Britain, France, and the Dilemma of Democratic Socialism

An astute observer in the 1930s might have realized that if the rest of the dependent world followed the Indian example and made its own cloth and steel, the global pattern of European and North American dominance would eventually collapse. Today, in fact, the American steel industry has shrunk as steel imports have increased—some from countries like Brazil and India. Few foresaw this development in the 1930s, however. Europe and North America still made the economic decisions. If a remedy for the Depression was to be found, it was up to them to find it.

The Failure of Economic Liberalism

As the Depression deepened, it became clear that the old remedies were not working. According to the liberal school that dominated economic thinking throughout the nineteenth century, governments could do little about a depression. They could no more legislate their way out of a depression, President Hoover declared, than they could "exorcise a Caribbean hurricane." What governments could do was *deflate.* If people were not buying, the remedy was to push prices down to a level low enough to stimulate demand. This also meant driving down the price of labor: wages. If people lacked confidence in the future of their money, the way to restore it was to balance the government's budget. Since a depressed economy produced fewer tax receipts, government would have to reduce its expenditures and raise taxes.

Most economic historians agree that these measures actually made the Depression worse. Higher taxes further reduced the public's purchasing power. With government spending also limited, there was no stimulus to boost confidence and revive the economy.

As the 1930s dragged on, the failure of traditional politics and economics drove more and more Europeans into a search for alternatives. The longest-established alternative was Marxism, which had always warned that capitalism was ultimately doomed by its failure to pay workers enough to buy the things they made. Now that the warning seemed to have come true, the Marxist alternative had much appeal. In a society where income was evenly distributed and the government planned and controlled production, Marxists argued, a disaster like the Depression could not have happened. Nor would government be indifferent to the sufferings of the jobless. But although many Europeans were attracted to a vision of a fairer social system, they shrank from the Soviet model of violent revolution and totalitarian government, preferring instead the nonrevolutionary socialist path.

The Socialist Alternative

To combine a socialist economy with political democracy was the central hope of the Social Democrats, or Socialists. In the 1930s, as today, they constituted the principal opposition to conservative or liberal parties in many countries with a democratic political tradition.

The Bolshevik Revolution had caused a split in all pre–World War I Marxist movements. To be allowed to affiliate with the Comintern, non-Russian Socialist parties had to accept the Soviet model of change. Many Socialists, however, were already sick of Bolshevik methods. At the 1920 annual convention of the French Socialist party, for example, a minority led by Léon Blum, a future prime minister, walked out rather than accept Moscow's control. The majority accepted Moscow's terms and became the French Communist party. Blum and his followers refounded the Socialist party. Germany's Social Democratic party broke apart during the war, and in the chaotic first years of the postwar republic, the German Socialist party (SPD) and the German Communist party (KPD) fought each other in the streets.

Deep differences of principle divided socialists and communists. To communists, it was a dangerous illusion to believe that it would be possible to create a socialistic society by winning an election. Why, communists asked, would capitalism yield to anything but force? Socialists, in contrast, believed that Lenin had made an unacceptable sacrifice of political freedom to achieve the socialist goal of a society based on economic equality.

Who was right? The Depression provided several tests of the idea that a socialistic society could be created through democratic politics. In Scandinavia the formula proved partially successful. After socialist electoral victories, Denmark, Norway, and Sweden developed a kind of "mixed" economy. Although most businesses were still privately owned, the mixed economy made government responsible for protecting all citizens' welfare "from the cradle to the grave." The high taxes needed to sustain the welfare state have recently prompted protests. Nevertheless, Scandinavian Socialists and their political opponents have seemed until recently to agree on the necessity for this "middle way" between capitalism and socialism.

The record of democratic socialism during the Depression was much more disappointing in larger countries such as Britain and France. The failures of the British Labour party and the French Popular Front were not entirely their own fault. But their experience shows some of the obstacles to establishing socialism within a democratic system.

Britain

When leaders of the British Labour party formed the first "socialist" cabinet in European history in 1924, middle- and upper-class Englishmen were filled with anxiety. Supported chiefly by working-class voters organized by Britain's increasingly powerful trade union movement, Labour had made an official commitment to socialism in 1918. The party's prime minister, Ramsay MacDonald, was the illegitimate son of a Scottish tenant farmer—a very different kind of person from the aristocrats and conservative businessmen who had previously occupied his office. But the fears of the well-to-do were soon allayed, as they saw that Labour was not going to make many changes. MacDonald's government, which lasted less than a year, made no attempt to convert Britain to a socialistic economy. Its most radical measure was to construct public housing with controlled rents, a measure continued by the Conservative government that replaced it.

To the second Labour government, formed after elections in 1929, fell the task of finding a remedy for the Depression. By 1931, one Englishman in four was unemployed. Unemployment benefits—"the dole"—were meager. Nevertheless, conventional economic wisdom demanded that this burden on the budget be reduced. A majority of the Labour cabinet resigned in 1931 rather than accept such a cut, which they saw as a betrayal of Labour's responsibility to the poor. MacDonald formed a new cabinet, composed largely of Conservatives but called a "National" government because all parties were represented in it. The Labour party expelled MacDonald as a traitor but remained crippled by its internal divisions. Labour did not get another chance to govern until after World War II. Meanwhile, under the governments of MacDonald and his Conservative successor Stanley Baldwin, the country muddled through the Depression without imagination. There would be no experiment in democratic socialism until after 1945.

In 1929 as in 1924, most Labourites wanted to preserve the political consensus that had enabled English men and women of all classes to live together in democracy. Then as now, the party was an uneasy alliance of trade unionists (the majority) and middle-class intellectuals. However much they hated Britain's class society, the trade unionists were not sure it could be replaced by a socialist alternative within the existing democratic framework of Crown and Parliament, which most of them cherished. MacDonald's cautious policies corresponded to their views, not those of Marxist intellectuals. Even the Labour ministers who broke with MacDonald when he agreed to inflict deflation on the unemployed in 1931 did not urge the socialist alternative. If the British Labour party was an example of a democratic socialist movement, it clearly reflected the basic dilemma of democratic socialism: If a majority of society, or even of a social democratic party, is mistrustful of the profound change associated with socialism, then how can the goal of a socialist society be attained under a system respectful of majority rule?

France

In France the question of creating socialism within democracy presented itself somewhat differently. Here the ideas of Karl Marx had more influence than in Britain. While bitterly opposing each other until the mid-1930s, both French Socialists and French Communists proclaimed their allegiance to his ideas. Dividing the votes of France's Left,* they allowed the conservative Right repeated victories. Those French who wanted a different society, particularly members of the urban working class, became deeply frustrated.

In 1935, however, faced with the threat posed to the USSR by Germany after the arch anti-communist Adolf Hitler became German dictator, Stalin imposed a complete reversal of policy upon the Comintern and the Communist parties of Europe. Instead of reviling Socialists, Communists henceforth were to ally with them and other democratic parties in a Popular Front against the fascist threat. In France, after the formation of the Popular Front, Communists and Socialists united with the middle-of-the-road, nonsocialist Radical party to back a single candidate in each electoral district in the general election of 1936.

The victory of the Popular Front aroused tremendous hope in the French working class. At last, it seemed, a reunited Left could impose a socialist alternative to the capitalistic economy that had collapsed. But the Socialist party leader, Léon Blum, faced the same dilemma as British Labour when he became France's prime minister. Some of those who had voted for the Popular Front wanted it to make France a socialist country. But the majority, including supporters of the Radicals, did not want a socialist France. If Blum did not implement a socialist program, he would be undercut by his Communist allies. But if he did, he would lose the support of Radicals, whose votes he also needed to maintain a majority coalition in parliament. Both groups would turn on him unless he found a way to relieve the Depression.

Blum hoped to escape from this dilemma by improving the conditions of the French working class enough so that its rising productivity and purchasing power would stimulate recovery. Thus, when a wave of strikes followed the victory of the Popular Front, he pressured French employers into making such concessions as the forty-hour workweek, annual paid vacations, and workers' rights to bargain collectively. Although he encouraged working-class demands, Blum moved very slowly toward actual socialism. He took over from private ownership only the railways, munitions factories, and the Bank of France.

Blum's efforts to conciliate all groups in French society ended by satisfying none. Productivity fell with the establishment of a shorter workweek. Meanwhile, fearing a socialist tax collector, the wealthy sent their money abroad for safekeeping. Reluctant to aggravate their fears, Blum did not impose strict controls to keep money from crossing the border. Many poor voters concluded he was not really committed to socialism.

With productivity declining and investors frightened, France remained mired in depression while Blum's coalition of Communists, Socialists, and Radicals quarreled over the direction he should take. One year after coming to power, Blum, no longer able to muster a parliamentary majority, resigned.

---

*The use of the terms *Right* and *Left* to designate opposing political beliefs dates back to the parliament of the French Revolution of 1789. Supporters of the king and of the existing society happened to sit on the right side of the hall, supporters of the revolution and of change on the left. Ever since, opponents of change—conservatives—have been described as the Right, and proponents of change—from progressives to radicals—have been the Left.

A "stay-in" strike at a French factory during the Popular Front period. *The workers have occupied the plant and locked management out. Similar U.S. strikes were called sit-down strikes.* *Popperfoto*

France's experiment with democratic socialism ended on an ambiguous note. Some Popular Front legislation had a lasting effect on French society. Annual paid vacations brought the first working-class families to France's beaches, for example, shocking the middle-class people who had always had these resorts to themselves. Yet Blum's inability, after winning a majority in democratic elections, even to begin to create a socialistic society, raises questions about the possibility of democratic socialism. It may seem that his failure resulted from the particular French circumstances of 1936, notably the need to satisfy a coalition of groups with very different aspirations. Yet this was a problem likely to confront all democratic socialists in power. To give a genuinely socialistic direction to the French economy, Blum would have had to defy the rules of the democratic game, which require a parliamentary majority. Using undemocratic means, however, would have violated his convictions. Moreover, it would have confirmed the communist view that social change can be imposed only by revolution.

Conventional economic thinking had proved to be of little use in countering the Depression. But Europe had not found an effective democratic alternative. How much more successful was the United States?

The New Deal in Global Perspective

President Franklin D. Roosevelt promised Americans a New Deal after his election in 1932. Despite the charges of Roosevelt's critics, the New Deal was not socialistic in any sense that European socialists would have understood. Nevertheless, the measures Roosevelt adopted to combat the Depression fundamentally altered the role of government in American life, setting a pattern that persisted without real challenge until the inauguration of President Ronald Reagan in 1981. Today most Americans seem to resent and distrust the role of the federal government in their lives. Relatively few recall how that federal role developed in response to the worst economic collapse the country had known. Americans turned in desperation to government in 1933 because all other sources of leadership were helpless.

Roosevelt was inaugurated in March 1933, almost four years after the Wall Street crash. A quarter of the work force was unemployed. Farmers were threatening to hang bankers who tried to repossess their farms. Bankers had just closed the doors of all U.S. banks after a wave of failures created panic among depositors. Public opinion, the business community, and even Congress were ready to follow wherever Roosevelt led. He had already made it clear that he would seek "broad executive power to wage a war against the emergency, as great as the power that would be given to me if we were in fact invaded by a foreign foe."

During the first "Hundred Days" of the New Deal, Congress passed whatever legislation the administration proposed. The banks were reopened, with depositors' savings guaranteed by a Federal Deposit Insurance Corporation (FDIC). A Federal Emergency Relief Act replenished the funds used by states and cities to relieve the distress of one out of seven Americans.

The "Roosevelt Revolution"

Beyond such rescue measures, Roosevelt tried to attack the basic problems of the American economy. The descendant of generations of aristocratic Hudson River Valley landowners, he was not committed to any particular doctrine. He was as skeptical of the theories of economics professors as of the platitudes of businessmen. Launched helter-skelter, the New Deal's programs were usually vote-catching, often ineffective, and sometimes inconsistent. Nevertheless, the whirlwind of activity rekindled hope. Skillfully projecting his cheerful optimism in radio "fireside chats," FDR became a hero to a majority of Americans.

The New Deal's congressional supporters attacked the farm problem by legislating limits on production. The Agricultural Adjustment Act (AAA) paid farmers not to contribute to the glut. Thus began the federal administration of farm markets that continues today.

To combat mass unemployment, the federal government became an employer of last resort. The Civilian Conservation Corps (CCC), for example, hired idle young men and set them to work on improving the American environment.

To promote industrial recovery, the New Deal allowed business to escape some of the stress of free-market competition. In 1931 the president of General Electric had called for the establishment of government-enforced cartels to fix prices and regulate competition in every industry. The National Recovery Administration (NRA) met this demand by establishing "codes of fair competition" in some eight hundred industries. These rules were designed to limit competition so that all businesses might survive. When the Supreme Court struck the NRA down as unconstitutional, the New Dealers retorted by creating a series of "little NRAs" in separate industries.

Such legislation, and loans from the Reconstruction Finance Corporation (RFC), helped to keep many businesses afloat. Nevertheless, most business leaders came to hate Roosevelt and the New Deal, perhaps because the Roosevelt administration also supported labor, especially in the so-called second New Deal after 1935. The Wagner Act endorsed trade unions and collective bargaining, prohibited employers from opposing unionization, and set up a National Labor Relations Board

(NLRB). The Fair Labor Standards Act of 1938 established a forty-hour week and a forty-cent minimum hourly wage.

Even this summary list of New Deal legislation suggests how much the role of the federal government, and its impact on the individual, had grown. A host of new agencies was created—like the SEC (Securities and Exchange Commission), intended to prevent the kind of Wall Street malpractices that had led to the crash. How effective were these laws and agencies?

Evaluating the New Deal

The New Deal did not end the Depression. Unemployment still stood at 17 percent in 1939. Only the need to make weapons for a new world war provided jobs for virtually every American man who wanted one, and for some women too.

Today, as in the 1930s, the New Deal remains controversial. Conservatives think its basic mistake was to attempt, vainly, to alter the normal operations of a free-market economy. Spending more money than the government had collected, Roosevelt began the system of federal budget deficits that have become so enormous today. Deficit-financed government investment to restart the economy had been recommended as a depression remedy by the most innovative economist of the day, the Englishman John Maynard Keynes. But conservatives argued that deficit spending was a double mistake. It proved ineffective, and it taught Americans to rely on an overgrown federal government rather than on their own efforts.

Such criticism is rejected by liberals, the New Deal's most ardent supporters. Their support has given a special American twist to the word *liberalism*. Unlike their nineteenth-century European predecessors, New Deal liberals favored an active role for government in social and economic life. Liberals see in the New Deal a sensible progressive adjustment of American institutions to the new reality of a world depression. In this view, by humanizing and democratizing the economy, and above all by restoring people's hope, the New Deal became one more chapter in the continuous success story of American history.

This interpretation was challenged, especially in the 1960s, by the historians of the New Left. Looking back from the decade of the Vietnam War and ghetto riots, they wondered whether American history really was a success story. In their view, far from undermining American capitalism, as conservatives charged, the New Deal had given it a new lease on life by alleviating its worst abuses. Liberals were equally mistaken, according to the New Left, when they applauded the New Deal for its concern for the common people. Ordinary people actually benefited little. It was the big farmers, the future founders of agribusiness, who were helped by government management of the marketplace.

Organized labor tripled its membership between 1933 and 1941, unionizing one of four American workers, but organized labor was almost entirely white and male. Unorganized labor—like blacks and women—did not fare so well. Moreover, the New Deal did not eliminate "unjust concentrations of wealth and economic power," the professed goal of one piece of legislation. In 1941 the poorest 20 percent of American families collected 4.1 percent of American personal income, compared with 3.5 percent in 1929. The richest 20 percent were still collecting 49 percent of national income in 1941, a small decline from the 54 percent they earned in 1929 and a very long way from the equal shares prescribed by socialism.

There is some truth in each of these conflicting assessments of the New Deal. The federal government did grow: it had 50 percent more employees in 1937 than in 1933. Federal spending rose from 3 percent of the gross national product in 1929 to 14 percent a decade later. The deficits required to pay these employees and fund this spending were unprecedented—though minuscule compared with the deficits of today. The rich did pay more taxes: the rate in the highest income bracket went up from 20 to 79 percent. Nevertheless, the New Deal was far from a social revolution. At the end of the 1930s, Roosevelt admitted, one-third of Americans remained "ill housed, ill fed, ill clad."

Those same words can be cited as evidence that the New Deal had created a norm of government responsibility for the economic well-being of its citizens. Though he was probably more hated than any other twentieth-century American president, Franklin Roosevelt was also more loved. He was re-elected to an unprecedented four terms. Above all, his popularity was inspired by his willingness to mobilize the forces of government against economic disaster (though the New Left historians are correct in asserting that New Deal benefits were unequally distributed).

After the New Deal, the federal government became a "guarantor state."[2] Before 1933 the American government had guaranteed its citizens practically nothing. Thereafter, at least until the 1970s, the federal government sought to guarantee more and more to all citizens: an education for the young; a safe and adequately paid job for adults, with compensation if the job was lost; an adequate standard of living; and medical care for the elderly.

Such guarantees of the quality of life were evidence of the new social role the New Deal assigned to the federal government. It also set a precedent for an enhanced governmental economic role. Government was henceforth held responsible for guaranteeing that there was sufficient demand for the economy's products to avert a return to Depression conditions, even if this meant spending more than its income in tax revenues. So widely accepted did this Keynesian idea of the creative possibilities of government deficit financing become that by the 1970s even the conservative Republican president Richard Nixon could declare, "We are all Keynesians now."

Moreover, government henceforth was expected, by taxing some and spending on others, to effect a degree of redistribution of the wealth of society, guaranteeing that the rich did not become too rich or the poor too poor. Some observers believe that only these enlargements of the role of government as social and economic guarantor—enlargements sooner or later matched everywhere in the developed world—rescued Western capitalism from the doubt and discredit into which it fell during the harsh years of the Depression.

Conclusion: The Global Trend Toward the Guarantor State

The New Deal was the American example of a worldwide trend toward enlarging governments' responsibility for their people. Perhaps the emergence of the guarantor state was inevitable in democratic societies, once World War I had shown that a government could coordinate an entire society and the Depression had reduced whole peoples to despair. Though democratic socialism failed in Britain and France during the 1930s, both countries eventually established welfare states more elaborate than the one the New Deal created. So did other developed industrial nations and even some Third World countries.

Despite the current disenchantment with big government, the guarantor state may have become indispensable in the complex, mobile, urban societies of the late twentieth century. Who else today will take care of young and old as the extended family did before 1914 in villages of the non-Western world like Dinshawai?

The growth of government power can pose grave risks, however. Democratic socialism and New Deal democracy were not the only possible answers to the Depression. President Roosevelt once declared: "My desire is to obviate revolution. . . . I work in a contrary sense to Rome and Moscow." If he could not make the New Deal work, in other words, the American people might turn from democracy to another model of government and society. We already know the Moscow model. We must now examine the model that began in Mussolini's Rome: fascism, which seemed on its way to conquering the world in the 1930s.

Notes

1. Quoted in Robert L. Heilbroner, *The Making of Economic Society,* 6th ed. (Englewood Cliffs, N.J.: Prentice-Hall, 1980), p. 140.
2. The term *guarantor state* is taken from Carl N. Degler's essay "The Establishment of the Guarantor State," in Richard S. Kirkendall, ed., *The New Deal: The Historical Debate* (New York: Wiley, 1973).

Suggestions for Further Reading

Books

Childs, Marquis. *Sweden: The Middle Way* (1936).

———. *Sweden: The Middle Way on Trial* (1984).

Colton, Joel. *Léon Blum: Humanist in Politics* (1987).

Galbraith, John Kenneth. *The Great Crash* (1988).

Heilbroner, Robert L. *The Making of Economic Society.* 7th ed. (1985).

Johnson, Paul. *Modern Times: The World from the Twenties to the Eighties* (1983).

Kent, Bruce. *The Spoils of War: The Politics, Economics, and Diplomacy of Reparations, 1918–1932* (1990).

Kindleberger, Charles P. *The World in Depression, 1929–1939.* 2d ed. (1986).

Kirkendall, Richard S., ed. *The New Deal: The Historical Debate* (1973).

Latham, A. J. H. *The Depression and the Developing World, 1914–1939* (1981).

Orwell, George. *The Road to Wigan Pier* (1937).

Taylor, A. J. P. *English History, 1914–1945* (1985).

CHAPTER 6

Restructuring the Social and Political Order: Fascism

The word *fascism* derives from the Italian *fascio (di combattimento)* and originally referred to the street-fighting combat groups of an Italian political movement. But in the 1920s and 1930s the fascist label was applied indiscriminately to virtually every government in the world that was clearly neither democratic nor socialist. As a term of abuse, the word is still carelessly used to refer to almost anybody politically to the right of center. To deal precisely with such an ambiguous concept, this chapter begins by defining fascism. It then discusses the two most important fascist regimes, those of Mussolini in Italy and Hitler in Germany, and shows how Hitler's rise prepared the way for World War II. Like other models of social and political organization that developed in Europe, fascism influenced political movements in other parts of the world. As strictly defined, fascism may seem to have perished in World War II. But the stresses that produced European fascism can lead to a similar phenomenon anywhere.

The Varieties of Authoritarianism After 1918

The years between the world wars were not healthy ones for democratic government. Initially the new states of eastern and southeastern Europe created from the ruins of the German, Austrian, and Russian empires all had democratic constitutions. Within a few years, however, most of those governments were forcibly replaced by some form of authoritarian or dictatorial rule. Poland became a dictatorship in 1926. After years of chronic political chaos, the kings of Yugoslavia and Romania abrogated their countries' constitutions and became dictators in 1929 and 1938, respectively. In the other least-developed corner of Europe, a 1926 military coup in Portugal paved the way for the dictatorship of Dr. Oliveira Salazar, an austere economics professor. His regime lasted from 1930 to 1968—long enough to become an accredited part of the "free world" through its membership in the North Atlantic Treaty Organization. In Spain, General Francisco Franco led the army in rebellion against the Popular Front government of the Republic in 1936. After a three-year civil war, Franco established a dictatorship that endured almost as long as Salazar's until Franco's death in 1975.

All these governments were sometimes called fascist. But their appearances were deceiving. Though most borrowed language from fascism and occasionally mimicked fascist rituals, fundamentally these regimes were simply dictatorships by conservatives. Challenged by real or imagined threats of democracy or socialism, the long-established elites of these little-developed countries—landowners, the church hierarchy, the army officer corps—abolished politics and began to govern by force. Their goal was to restore or perpetuate their own rule by forestalling all change. Once they had consolidated their power, they usually domesticated and sometimes annihilated the fascist movements whose slogans and cooperation they had borrowed.

Borrowings from Left and Right

The old elites feared fascism's revolutionary potential. Authentic fascism—the fascism preached by Mussolini and Hitler and their imitators around the world—did not fit into the usual political categories of Left and Right. It borrowed some of the ideas of both. Like the right-wing regimes established in places like Portugal, fascism was ferociously hostile to liberal democracy and Marxist socialism. Like most conservatives, fascists were intransigent nationalists. Moreover, fascists proclaimed their determination to restore law and order in society, using whatever force was needed—another favorite conservative theme.

Yet much about fascism should have alarmed a genuine conservative. Like movements of the Left, fascism was avowedly revolutionary. Fascists said they intended to smash the existing order of things, including much that conservatives held dear. Fascists often declared that their mission was to replace capitalism with a "national" socialism, although this bore little resemblance to the Marxist variety, which stressed international worker solidarity.

Fascism's leaders were young men, drawn not from the old elites but from the middle and lower strata of society. They sought power by mobilizing mass movements whose disciplined readiness for violence was symbolized by their uniforms. Italian Fascist Black Shirts and German Nazi Brown Shirts had counterparts around the world, from the tan shirts of the Lebanese *Phalange* to the green shirts of the Brazilian *Integralistas*.

Once in power, many fascists aspired to a new kind of unified society, ruled by an all-powerful state that would mold every individual's life. None of these themes is conservative, and some were clearly borrowed from the Left, indeed from the far Left.

Faced with this basic ambiguity in fascism's nature, historians and political scientists have long argued about how to interpret it. Most would probably agree, however, that fascism is a revolutionary movement whose mass appeal is achieved by invoking largely conservative values. Fascism triumphant was a revolution from the Right.

Economic and Social Change and the Growth of Fascism

Why did people on the Right, who usually oppose change, flock to join fascist movements that promised to change everything? Some powerful trends that underlay fascism's success were already apparent in European society and culture before World War I. The war, its aftermath, and the Great Depression accentuated these trends, bringing Mussolini to power in 1922 and Hitler in 1933.

One such prewar trend was the impact of social and economic change on the groups in every society least able to defend themselves. These groups included small businessmen, small farmers, and self-employed craftsmen. Before 1914 they saw themselves as being crushed between big business and big labor. Chain stores belonging to anonymous corporations reduced the sales of the corner shopkeeper. The exchanges of a worldwide economy meant that the small dairy farmer in northwest Germany had to compete with New Zealand butter brought halfway around the world in refrigerated ships. Ingenious machines designed for high-speed mass production threatened the livelihood and status of handworkers everywhere.

Parliamentary politics, which often seemed a mysterious and corrupt game benefiting only the politicians, offered no protection against these looming dangers. Nor could these people turn to Marxist socialism, for they were proudly respectable citizens who looked down on proletarian factory workers, who voted Marxist. These middle-class groups and low-level office workers—the fastest-growing component of society in much of Europe in 1914—derived their sense of security from identification with such apparently solid institutions as the German monarchy. When World War I swept these institutions away and the following decade of uncertainty led into the Depression, these groups stampeded into fascist movements that promised to restore order and security.

Paradoxically, however, fascism also drew support from groups that had found the complacency of pre-1914 European society unbearably confining. In 1914, Europe had not had a major war for fifty years. The younger generation found itself in a world without prospect of the glorious conflict that patriotism taught it to value. Moreover, for the first time in history, medicine was beginning to cure as many patients as it killed. As the older generation lived longer and longer, young people's wait for opportunity was indefinitely prolonged. Fascist ideas reflected the impatience and quest for adventure of this prewar younger generation.

This generation was inspired by an intellectual revolt against many of the dominant ideas of the nineteenth century, such as scientific materialism and parliamentary democracy. The prophets of this revolt saw in the civilization of imperial Berlin a symbol of decay rather than progress. The routine of technological society had produced, they complained, a contemptible kind of human being: selfish, complacent, weak, irreligious. Parliamentary democracy had given political authority to the clever people who knew how to manipulate these gullible masses. They had tamed even the threat of revolutionary socialism. The time was coming to sweep all this away, to replace what one fascist derided as "the politics of ink, saliva, and ideology" with a real politics of "soil, flesh, and blood."

This contrast between the artificial and the real sums up fascism's revolt against modernity. While capitalists and socialists argued about what should become of "economic man," fascists held up the ideal of "heroic man," strong and cruel, joyful believer in the destiny of his nation or race. Fascists, Mussolini declared, were "against the easy life," because only a life of continuous hardship and struggle, like that of peasants of earlier centuries, could retrieve modern human beings from the decay of a world grown too comfortable. Only a movement dedicated to such a life of primitive virtues could reunite nations divided by the strife between social classes of the twentieth century.

Without World War I, such ideas might have remained confined to the fringe of European society. It was the war and its aftermath that made them meaningful to millions and decisively encouraged the growth of fascism. Their experiences in the trenches of World War I deeply affected the first fascists, those who joined up in the hard days before their movement won power. The more thoughtful of them found in the war's horrors a reason to condemn the whole prewar way of life. At the same time, the anguish of life on the front line produced a camaraderie among young men who in peacetime Europe would have been kept apart by sharp class distinctions. As veterans, many of these men tried to prolong this wartime sense of classless camaraderie by joining paramilitary street-fighting movements dedicated to smashing the prewar social order that had condemned them to the battlefronts. In its place they wanted to install the kind of government World War I had brought to the home front of every belligerent: one that would use centralized authority to impose a united society and a controlled economy.

Such movements emerged in all the countries that fought in World War I. Only in Italy and Germany, however, did they win control of the government. Why did those two societies prove especially vulnerable to the fascist temptation?

Both Italy and Germany were new nations, united only in the second half of the nineteenth century. Defeat—or, for Italy, a victory that seemed like defeat—in World War I revealed their internal fragility and external helplessness. Both Italy and Germany were rocked by near civil war at the very moment they were humiliated by the Versailles settlement. Frustrated nationalism and widespread fear of a Bolshevik-style social revolution thus reinforced the appeal of fascism.

Neither Italy nor Germany had the kind of long-established liberal or democratic institutions that gave some confidence to Englishmen and Frenchmen. Faced with social chaos or economic disaster, the Italian and German middle classes preferred to abandon their feeble newborn democracies for the strong government the fascists promised. They acquiesced in a revolution that they hoped would end the disturbing changes brought by the war—a revolution from the Right.

We now turn to an examination of the fascist experience in particular cases, first Italy, then Germany. Six years after Adolf Hitler came to power, his Nationalist Socialist regime had drawn the nations into a new world war. By then, as we shall see, fascism's apparent success had spawned a host of imitations throughout Europe and beyond.

The Original Fascism: The Italian Model

Italy had gained little from its alliance with the winners of World War I. This disappointment was the last in a series of frustrations since the unification of the nation in 1870. Italy's status as the sixth great power was a fiction. The country remained desperately poor. The Italian south was notorious for the backwardness of its huge landed estates. Recent industrialization in the North had added urban social tensions to the age-old clash between peasants and landowners.

Nor could Italians take much pride in their constitutional monarchy. The nation's parliamentary system, long based on corrupt bargains and rigged elections, faced paralysis after every Italian male became eligible to vote in

1912. This mass electorate did not provide support to the traditional liberals and conservatives, but divided it between two mass parties, Socialists and Catholics. Each was strong enough to prevent the other (or anyone else) from governing, but they were separated by differences too deep for compromise.

The Versailles settlement gave Italy far less of the disputed territories on its borders than Italians felt their country deserved. Only nine thousand square miles compensated for the loss of 600,000 young men. Moreover, this "mutilated" victory brought Italy the same economic dislocations and social unrest that other nations faced. Cabinets based on parliamentary coalitions that typically collapsed after a few months did little to combat the fourfold increase in the postwar cost of living, the sevenfold increase in the public debt, and the rising rate of unemployment. When discontented workers seized control of factories in the fall of 1920, the contagion of revolution seemed to have spread from Russia to northern Italy.

Benito Mussolini (1883–1945) skillfully mobilized his compatriots' anxiety and disgust. Since his adolescence he had been a rebel against Italian society, though originally, like almost all rebels, on the Left. At the outbreak of World War I, he was a leading Socialist journalist. But he disagreed with the Socialist party's position that Italy should stay out of the war, and broke with the Left permanently over that issue. For Mussolini the violence of war was a promise of revolution. In war, a proletarian nation like Italy might throw off its dependence on the more developed industrial nations. When Italy entered the war on the Anglo-French side in 1915, partly as a result of Mussolini's agitation, he promptly joined the army.

The war won as little for him as for his country. As a demobilized veteran, Mussolini became a spokesman for his comrades' rage for something better. On March 23, 1919, with about 145 friends, including former *arditi* (shock troops) whose black uniform he adopted, Mussolini founded the first *Fascio di Combattimento.*

The Rise of Fascism

During its first year, Mussolini's Fascism, championing such radical causes as votes for women and the eight-hour day, attracted little attention. Its real growth began when frightened conservatives recognized its potential to suppress social disorder. Industrialists, landowners, and the army rushed to bankroll the movement, whose brutal *squadristi* beat up strikers and other troublemakers, often forcing them to drink near-fatal doses of castor oil. By late 1922, growing as fast as the unemployment lines, Fascism had a membership of over 300,000. Its leaders loudly demanded at least a share in the government. With Fascist thugs controlling the streets of many major Italian cities, their threat of a march on Rome, the capital, seemed plausible.

Yet Mussolini did not take power by violence. Power was handed to him. Rather than challenge so formidable an enemy of their own enemies—Socialists and Communists—the king and his conservative advisers decided to name Mussolini prime minister. In October 1922, Mussolini "marched" comfortably on Rome in a railroad sleeping car, with a royal invitation to head a fourteen-member cabinet including only three Fascists.

For a time he appeared content with this role, although many of his followers called for a "second wave" of revolution to transform Italy's society and political system. Behind his bluster, Mussolini was a hesitant adventurer—a "roaring rabbit," as he was once called. It took a major threat to his new position to force him into the final steps to dictatorship. Fascists close to Mussolini kidnapped and murdered a Socialist member of parliament, Giacomo Matteotti, who had exposed Fascist misdeeds. In

Mussolini harangues the crowd. *In a characteristic pose on a visit to a provincial city in 1930, the Duce promises Italians a return to the greatness of ancient Rome. The photographer captures the essence of authoritarian mass mobilization.* *UPI/Bettmann Archives*

reaction to this scandal, Catholic and some liberal politicians began to boycott parliament, hoping to force Mussolini to resign. Instead, this show of opposition apparently pushed him, after months of wavering, to establish a dictatorship.

By 1926, after dissolving opposition parties and independent unions, establishing strict press censorship, and reducing parliament to subjection, Mussolini appeared to be Italy's only master. Whenever he appeared on the balcony of his Roman palace, frenzied crowds saluted him as leader with cries of *"Duce! Duce!"* A similar, if more restrained, enthusiasm was expressed by many foreign visitors. Fascism, it appeared, had taught the formerly "undisciplined" Italians to "make their trains run on time." Mussolini's propaganda machine proclaimed that his genius had created a successful alternative to both capitalist democracy and Soviet communism. A closer examination of the regime's record and its relationships with various groups in Italian society, however, suggests that this was a gross exaggeration.

Fascist Myth Versus Fascist Reality

Fascism's remedy for social conflict was the corporatist society. This concept derived from

Catholic social thought, which had always been troubled by the ruthless individualism of the free-enterprise system and took models for social organization from the precapitalist past, notably from the guilds of the Middle Ages. Fascist *corporatism* sought to unite members of the same economic calling, both employers and employees, by abolishing political parties and geographical election districts. In place of these divisive institutions, "corporations" were to be established for each sector of the economy. In these institutions representatives of bosses and workers could resolve their differences in an atmosphere of mutual understanding.

Mussolini eventually created twenty-two such corporate bodies and in 1938 replaced his rubber-stamp parliament with a Chamber of Fasces and Corporations. Far from fulfilling Catholic hopes of social reconciliation, the system was a façade disguising the repression of Italian labor. The leaders of big business effectively controlled the corporate bodies. Italian workers, forbidden to strike, had little voice in them. By 1939, workers' real wages—the purchasing power of what they had earned—had fallen below the level of 1922.

Workers, who tended to be Socialists, had never been Fascism's best supporters. Small businessmen were generally much more enthusiastic, but even they got little help from the Mussolini regime when the Depression struck. Government planning consistently favored big businesses. Small ones were allowed to fail while their larger competitors got loans from the Agency for Industrial Reconstruction. The effort to build an efficient industry took precedence over Fascist rhetoric about preserving the little man. Perhaps the best rewarded of Fascism's early supporters were the students and white-collar workers who found jobs in the expanding party and government bureaucracies.

Fascist propaganda declared that these bureaucracies gave new unity and direction to Italian life. In reality Mussolini's movement never began to achieve his totalitarian dream of integrating every individual into society. Long accustomed to political cynicism, many Italians simply went through the Fascist motions. In Sicily, for example, members of the Mafia put on black shirts and continued business as usual.

Nor was the Mafia the only group beyond Mussolini's control. In 1929 he tried to placate the Catholic church by signing a treaty that ended the long quarrel over Italy's seizure of Rome, the pope's city, as the national capital. But the Church objected to Mussolini's efforts to enroll children and young people into Fascist youth movements that rivaled the Catholic ones. Though much overshadowed, king and court also remained a potential rival power center. And despite all the talk about a new social order, the leaders of industry continued to direct the economy much as before, in cozy consultation with the higher bureaucracy. The Duce had not fully realized his boastful slogan: "Everything for the state, nothing against the state, no one outside the state."

The original Fascist regime in Italy bore some striking resemblances to systems like Franco's and Salazar's because such conservative groups as the church, the court, and big business remained influential. By the mid-1930s, Fascism appeared to be a gigantic bluff even to some of its original supporters. It did not save Italy from the Depression. After 1929 Italians who had emigrated to the United States sent less money home—a heavy blow to the Italian budget. Despite Mussolini's emphasis on public works projects, all his construction sites could not provide jobs for the many who fled the poverty-stricken countryside for the cities.

Mussolini's policies were crippled by contradictions. It made little sense, for example, to try to keep people on the overpopulated farms while encouraging Italians to have more children. But Fascist ideology insisted on both agricultural self-sufficiency and an ever-growing population to make Italy strong. Similarly, the goal of an "autarkic" economy, independent of foreign suppliers, had patriotic appeal. But in practice the Fascist regime restricted the purchasing power of the working-class majority without planning systematically for investment—hardly a recipe for economic growth.

Mussolini raged as he became entangled in the contradictions between Fascist myths and hard reality. In 1935 he turned again to violence, launching an invasion of Ethiopia to avenge Italy's humiliating defeat there in 1896 (Map 6.1), a rare victory of Africans over Europeans. Instead of establishing an Italian empire, however, this adventure began the undoing of Fascism. For a country as underindustrialized and poor in raw materials as Italy, war would eventually mean dependence on a more powerful ally. Hating (and spurned by) the domineering democracies, Britain and France, Mussolini eventually turned to his fascist neighbor, Nazi Germany. Its leader had come to power much as Mussolini had. But Hitler had created a far more terrifying regime. In the end, he would drag Mussolini with him to destruction.

From Weimar Republic to Third Reich

In Germany as in Italy, fascism owed its success to a masterful demagogue who mobilized popular anger against a feeble democracy during a period of upheaval. In Germany too, the conservative establishment handed the fascist leader supreme power in the expectation of exploiting his movement. Hitler had a far greater impact on world history than did Mussolini, however. From the moment a leader determined to reverse the humiliation of Versailles took power in Germany, another European "civil" war became likely. That conflict brought the final collapse of European domination of the world.

Weakness of the Weimar Republic

Like Fascism's, the story of Nazism's triumph begins with the end of World War I. The conditions imposed on Germany by the Versailles settlement were an enormous liability for the new Weimar Republic. Right-wing propaganda implanted in the minds of many the lie that the war would not have been lost if the German army had not been "stabbed in the back" by Republican "November criminals," who had allegedly preferred revolution to victory. The Weimar Republic's first five years were a constant struggle for survival against attacks from both Left and Right. In 1919 the Socialist-dominated government mastered Communist uprisings only by using both the old imperial army and private armies of right-wing veterans (*Freikorps*). The old army remained unsympathetic to the republic, however. When several of the Freikorps backed the attempt of a right-wing bureaucrat, Wolfgang Kapp, to overthrow the government in 1920, the army refused to move against them. The republic defeated Kapp only by calling out its worker supporters in a general strike.

This sequence of events already revealed the Weimar Republic's fatal weakness. On paper it was a model of democracy. Its bill of rights guaranteed freedoms never before recognized in Germany, including the vote for women. But in reality the republic was aptly described as a "candle burning at both ends." It faced a continuous Communist threat on its Left and also had to contend with a hostile Right that included many of its own officials, as the Kapp putsch proved. In truth the German revolution of 1918 had hardly been a revolution at all. Far from stabbing the army in the back, the Republicans had merely occu-

ICELAND
Germany and Italy
Italian possessions in Africa before 1935
German expansion, 1935–1939
Italian aggression, 1935–1939
NORWAY
SWEDEN
FINLAND
ESTONIA
LATVIA
LITHUANIA
BALTIC SEA
Moscow
NORTH SEA
DENMARK
Memel
IRELAND
NETHERLANDS
GREAT BRITAIN
London
Danzig
EAST PRUSSIA
SOVIET UNION
Berlin
POLISH CORRIDOR
Warsaw
POLAND
Brussels
BELGIUM
GERMANY
RHINELAND 1936
SUDETENLAND 1938
Weimar
Prague
ATLANTIC OCEAN
Paris
LUXEMBOURG
CZECHOSLOVAKIA 1939
Nuremberg
Munich
Vienna
AUSTRIA 1938
FRANCE
SWITZERLAND
HUNGARY
RUMANIA
BLACK SEA
YUGOSLAVIA
BULGARIA
ITALY
PORTUGAL
Madrid
SPAIN
(Civil War, 1936-1939)
Barcelona
Rome
ALBANIA 1939
GREECE
TURKEY
MEDITERRANEAN SEA
LIBYA
ERITREA
AFRICA
ETHIOPIA 1935-1936
IT. SOMALILAND
A F R I C A

pied the political vacuum temporarily created by its collapse. They did not shatter the old power structure, for they needed the empire's bureaucrats and officers. Many of these, though ostensibly serving the new government, remained as contemptuous of democracy as they had been before 1914.

The republic might have endured if it had won the support of the German middle classes. But this group lost its savings when a terrifying wave of hyperinflation—the worst ever recorded anywhere—destroyed the value of the German currency overnight in 1923. Soon a billion marks were worth only about twenty-five cents, and many people blamed the republic. Few recalled that the imperial government had begun the inflation by printing floods of money to fight the war. Meanwhile, to force the payment of reparations, France occupied the Ruhr, Germany's industrial heartland, thus compounding the financial crisis.

To many, the Weimar Republic appeared to be on the point of collapse in 1923. Communists threatened a rising in Saxony. In Bavaria, Adolf Hitler led his Nazi storm troopers from a Munich beer hall in an attempt to overthrow the Bavarian state as a prelude to destroying the central government. The Beer Hall putsch was a fiasco. The police fired on the advancing Nazis, killing several, and arrested Hitler, who was sentenced to a five-year prison term. This apparent failure marked a turning point in the career of one of the most sinister figures of modern history.

Born in Austria, the son of a minor customs official, Hitler (1889–1945) left his provincial birthplace for Vienna at the age of eighteen. Failing to get into art school, he drifted, like many unsuccessful migrants to the great metropolis, into a lonely and marginal life. From his observations of Viennese society and politics, he developed two basic beliefs. The German nationalists there, who despised the multiethnic Hapsburg monarchy, taught him the necessity of uniting the Germans of Europe into one nation. Viennese anti-Semitism persuaded him that Jews were Germans' worst enemies in the worldwide struggle for survival. Though Hitler exploited these themes to move the masses, these were also his deeply held beliefs. World war and genocide would later prove how sincerely he meant them.

When World War I broke out, Hitler chose to fight not for the Hapsburgs but for Germany. Though he did not advance beyond the rank of corporal, he thrived in the army as he never had done in civilian life, winning decorations and commendations. The worst day in his life was the one in November 1918 when, lying wounded in a hospital, he heard the news of Germany's defeat. Later, drifting in bewilderment like so many demobilized veterans, he came to Munich, where army intelligence hired him as a political agent. His job was to infiltrate an obscure group called the National Socialist German Workers Party—Nazi for short. Hitler soon took it over from its founder, a locksmith whose aim was to combine German nationalism with a socialism dedicated not to Marx's proletarian revolution but to the protection of respectable little men in the middle—like locksmiths.

German society included millions of people to whom such a mixture would appeal. Hitler had exceptional gifts for reaching such an audience. Films of his speeches show that he had an uncanny ability to rouse crowds to frenzy by expressing their rage and frustration. He articulated the grievances of the many Germans who believed their nation was destined by racial superiority to rule Europe but was now disarmed and held captive by a

◀ ***Map 6.1 German and Italian Expansion, 1935–1939***

conspiracy of alien forces: Jews above all but also Communists, Socialists, Catholics, and democratic politicians. It was wholly irrational to attribute Germany's misfortunes to the co-operation of such ill-assorted groups or even to any one of them alone. But Hitler knew that emotion, not reason, wins political commitment.

For a time Hitler's message of hate went unheeded as a renewed currency and a reviving economy gave the Weimar Republic a respite after 1924. Hitler served only eight months of his prison sentence, an indication of the Weimar judges' leniency toward right-wing revolutionaries. He emerged from prison to find Nazism largely forgotten. In the 1928 elections, his party won only twelve seats in the Reichstag, with only 3 percent of the popular vote. It remained largely a refuge for a hard core of veterans unable to readjust to civilian life. They reveled in the brown-shirted uniforms of the Nazi storm trooper brigade, or SA (for *Sturm-Abteilung*).

From Hindenburg to Hitler

It was the Depression that finally doomed the Weimar Republic and gave German fascism its opportunity. As in Britain, parliamentary factions became deadlocked over the issue of reducing government spending by cutting unemployment benefits. A government based on a Reichstag majority became impossible. After 1930 the president of the republic, the aged Field Marshal Paul von Hindenburg, governed with the emergency powers given him by Article 48 of the constitution. Thereafter the political battle was fought in two places: between the SA and the uniformed brawlers of the other parties in the streets, and among rival factions in the circle of conservative intriguers who surrounded Hindenburg.

Desperate economic circumstances intensified political violence in the streets. By 1932, two of five trade union members were unemployed, and another was working short hours. Meanwhile, trying to break the political deadlock, the government held one election after another. In this atmosphere of economic despair and political frenzy, the extremes gained at the expense of the middle-of-the-road parties. The Communist vote rose dramatically but not nearly as fast as the Nazi totals. The Nazis had 12 seats in the 550-member Reichstag in 1929, 107 in 1930, and 230 in the summer of 1932.

Sensing that momentum was with them, some Nazis urged Hitler to overthrow the republic. But he had learned from Mussolini's experience and his own failure in 1923. As leader of the largest party, he could simply wait for the conservatives around Hindenburg to offer him a deal that would enable them to end emergency government under Article 48. On January 30, 1933, an agreement was reached: Adolf Hitler became chancellor of Germany as head of a coalition government whose eleven members included only three Nazis.

Many groups share the blame for this development. Conservative German politicians sneered at Hitler's "gutter" following but still tried to use his mass movement for their own purposes. Convinced that the Socialists were their real enemies, the Communists joined the Nazis in attacking the republic. Yet it should not be forgotten that Hitler could claim power because so many Germans backed him. Careful comparison of election results shows that the Nazis had relatively little success among working-class Socialist voters or the Catholic voters of the Center party. Many Nazi votes came at the expense of the conservative middle-class parties, which were virtually wiped out. Others were cast by new voters, especially the young. A third of the Nazi party's membership was made up of young people between eighteen and thirty.

Disgusted with the floundering of the Weimar government, which could not restore sanity to an economy gone crazy for the second time in ten years, these voters saw a striking contrast in Nazi dynamism. They also expected Nazi force to restore law and order to a turbulent political scene. Eighty-two people had been killed and hundreds wounded in six weeks of street fighting in one German state alone. If the price of an end to chaos was the establishment of a dictatorship, many were prepared to pay it—indeed looked forward to it.

The Nazi State

Dictatorship was not slow in coming. When a fire devastated the Reichstag building less than a month after Hitler's inauguration, the Nazis proclaimed that Germany was faced with a Communist plot. As a "defensive measure against Communist acts of violence," they "suspended" constitutional guarantees of personal freedom—never to be restored. As the first concentration camps opened to hold Communists and other Nazi enemies, the Reichstag convened to consider an Enabling Act that empowered Hitler to make laws, even unconstitutional ones, on his own authority for the next four years. With Communist members of parliament under arrest, only the Socialists were there to vote against the proposal. Combining his Nazis' votes with those of the Catholic Center party and what remained of the other parties of the Right, Hitler won an easy victory.

Now invested with unlimited authority, Hitler swiftly destroyed most of the institutions of a free society. He outlawed rival political parties or prodded them to dissolve themselves. He abolished the federal system, making Germany a country with an all-powerful central government for the first time in its history. When Hindenburg died early in 1934, Hitler simply absorbed the president's office into his own. Never was the Weimar constitution modified. The "constitution" of the new Third Reich was simply whatever the Nazi *Führer* (Leader) commanded.

He gave a fearful demonstration of the extent of his power in the summer of 1934. By then, many Nazis, especially in the SA, were complaining that the political revolution had not gone far enough. Taking the socialism of National Socialism seriously, they were impatient to see Germany's old elites displaced. The SA's leaders dreamed of replacing the old officer corps, dominated by aristocrats, with their own street brawlers. Their demands forced Hitler to choose between some of his earliest supporters and the conservative and army leaders who had just given him power. He favored his most recent benefactors, ordering his black-uniformed SS bodyguards to massacre his most troublesome SA followers. When this Night of the Long Knives (June 30, 1934) was over, Hitler bluntly warned the Reischstag that if anyone "raises his hand to strike the State, then certain death is his lot."

Nazi Society and Economy

The Nazis overhauled German life and institutions through a process of "coordination" (*Gleichschaltung*) designed to compel obedience by peer pressure. To prevent individuals from combining to oppose the regime, Hitler ordered the Nazification of every organized activity in Germany, right down to clubs of stamp collectors and beekeepers. He dissolved the labor unions and made every German worker a member of the Nazi Labor Front—without, of course, any right to strike. He ordered the consolidation of the Protestant denominations into a single church under Nazi domination. In addition to bringing these older institutions under control, the Nazis also created new ones, such as the Hitler Youth, to enroll whole categories of the population.

All these groups were organized according to the *Führerprinzip*, the idea that authority comes from the top down and must be obeyed without question. Nazi society thus became an example of mass mobilization carried to its most extreme and authoritarian form. Until 1938 the army high command seemed exempt from "coordination." But in that year Hitler took advantage of trumped-up scandals involving the most senior officers to retire them and take the supreme command into his own hands. Unlike Mussolini's Italy, Nazi Germany seemed to have fulfilled the fascist revolution; the prefascist power structure was forced into obedience.

Joseph Goebbels, Hitler's propaganda minister, described the Third Reich as "one great movement of obeying, belonging, and believing." Historians have shown that this image was only partially accurate. Behind the façade of totalitarian efficiency was a bureaucratic nightmare of confusion and rivalry. Hitler was bored by the routine of government and ignored it, while deliberately encouraging organizational enmities that only he could resolve. Nevertheless, the accomplishments of his regime, particularly its economic achievements, were enough to make it genuinely popular with a majority, at least until war came in 1939.

Six million Germans were out of work in 1932. By 1938, the figure had dropped to 164,000 and was still declining. Three factors contributed to this success. First, the Nazis—unwitting Keynesians—used government spending, even at a deficit, to restart the economy. These appropriations went originally for public works—the Nazis built the world's first network of superhighways—and later almost exclusively for rearmament. By 1938 the Nazis were committing at least half the budget—far more than any other country—to an arms buildup. Second, they brought the economy under tight government control. The government fixed prices, established production quotas, and allocated raw materials according to a Four Year Plan, practically abolishing the forces of the marketplace. The third anti-Depression tactic was an effort—called for by the Plan—to make Germany's economy self-sufficient. The chemical industry, for example, was stimulated to develop synthetic substitutes to replace imported oil and rubber.

Together these policies produced a full-employment economy that contrasted sharply with the stagnation of the democracies. Not that all Germans fared equally well. Industrial workers, who had never been enthusiastic Nazis, were the least rewarded. The fate of farmers and small businessmen was only marginally better, though they had provided much of Nazism's voting strength. Their earnings increased faster than those of factory workers but not nearly as fast as industrial corporate profits, which grew fourfold in the 1930s. Nazi promises to safeguard the little man proved hollow. The flight from the farm continued, and the number of small businesses actually declined faster than in the 1920s.

Like Fascism, Nazism proved a disappointment to those who had supported it as a conservative revolution against change. In practice, Nazism proved to be a means of forcing rapid modernization by mobilizing the German masses under totalitarian control. Under the Third Reich, change actually accelerated, further eroding German small-town and rural society. The reason is quite simple. Hitler's goal was a powerful Germany. That meant a Germany equipped for war by the latest technology, which only large corporations could supply. The little people who had flocked to Hitler in fear of change could contribute little to that goal. He sacrificed them ruthlessly to the needs of war.

The Road to War

Compared to the causes of World War I, the causes of the European part of World War II have provoked little debate. The story of European international relations between 1933 and 1939 is the story of how Hitler dismantled the Versailles treaty piece by piece, unresisted by the democracies, until they finally went reluctantly to war in defense of Poland. Although one might conclude that Hitler was the cause of World War II, the leaders of the democracies are often also blamed for giving in to him. Even today, this interpretation remains an important historical model in the minds of foreign policy planners. The lesson American leaders felt they had learned from the sorry outcome of the 1930s was surely one reason for the prolonged U.S. involvement in Southeast Asia in the 1960s and 1970s. The lesson appeared to be that any failure to resist an aggressor nation, even in the remotest and most unimportant-seeming place, simply emboldens it to further aggression. Today, too, the world situation is often analyzed by analogy to the 1930s, for example, in justifying U.S. intervention in the Persian Gulf war in 1991. We need to know precisely what happened then if we are to judge the aptness of these analogies.

Design for Aggression

Sometimes the suggestion is made that the democracies' failure to resist Hitler in the 1930s was the more inexcusable because his book, *Mein Kampf,* made no secret of his objectives. This rambling, unreadable work, written during his short stay in prison, clearly revealed his basic beliefs. Hitler was a "social Darwinist," who applied to human life the evolutionary vision of nature as a struggle among species for the survival of the fittest. For Hitler, history was a struggle for survival among biologically distinct races. The German race would not be able to compete effectively unless all Germans were brought within one country—a program that implied the destruction of independent Austria, Czechoslovakia, and Poland, where many "racial Germans" lived. Because France had consistently blocked German unity, another French war was probably essential. Yet Hitler's ambitions for the Germans did not stop with their unification, for he believed that all the lands they inhabited were overcrowded. They must conquer additional *Lebensraum*—living space—in the east, taking land from the racially inferior Slavs, particularly of the Soviet Union.

Mein Kampf thus does contain a kind of "design for aggression." Moreover, we know that Hitler vaguely contemplated still further struggles—ultimately, perhaps, a war with the United States for mastery of the world. Yet we cannot really blame democratic statesmen for not taking the message of the book seriously. Many politicians out of power have made promises that they later failed to keep. *Mein Kampf* was dismissed as this kind of propaganda.

Hitler's Destruction of the Versailles System

As chancellor, Hitler at first proceeded very cautiously in foreign policy. He had no predetermined timetable for destroying the Europe of the Versailles treaty, though this remained his goal. Instead he took advantage of opportunities as they arose, avoiding risks and accepting whatever successes circumstances gave him. His speeches stressed his own experiences of the horrors of war and his determination to prevent a new one. He was always careful to stress that the changes Germany sought in the Versailles settlement were only what was "fair." Hitler's rhetoric appealed to the guilty consciences of many people in the democracies. They had forgotten that the Versailles treaty had been intended not to be fair to Germany but to weaken and control it.

Arguing that the Versailles treaty had called for all countries to disarm but only Germany had been forced to do so, Hitler withdrew Germany from international disar-

Chamberlain at Munich, September 29, 1938. *The British prime minister (third from left) reviews a Nazi SS honor guard before his return flight to London.* *Popperfoto*

mament talks and the League of Nations in the fall of 1933. He used a similar justification in 1935 when he announced the creation of a German air force, or *Luftwaffe*, forbidden by the Versailles treaty, and the expansion of the German army to five times its permitted size.

Perhaps encouraged by the failure of Britain and France to counter these challenges, Hitler began moving troops in the spring of 1936. In violation of the Versailles treaty and later agreements, he "remilitarized" the German Rhineland. This strengthening of Germany's western defenses would make it much harder for the French to move into Germany—the only action they could take to help Germany's eastern neighbors if Hitler threatened them. But the French confined themselves to an ineffectual protest. On the eve of their Popular Front experiment, they were divided domestically and dreaded a new war after the fearful toll the last one had taken of their youth. They surrendered European leadership to Britain. The British could see nothing wrong with Hitler moving German troops into German territory. So Hitler got away with it.

Hitler tours the Sudetenland after the Munich pact removed it from Czech rule. *If there were Sudeten Germans who did not welcome going "home to the Reich," they are not in this photograph.* Keystone Collection, London

It is sometimes suggested that the Rhineland crisis of 1936 was the one time when Hitler could have been stopped without much bloodshed. Armed resistance to remilitarization might have forced him to retreat, destroyed his prestige, and perhaps prompted the German generals to overthrow him. But it is not clear that the German generals would have had the courage to mount a coup. Moreover, Hitler's ambitions were not his alone. Most Germans wanted to reverse the Versailles treaty. Their country had territorial ambitions long before Hitler came to power, as illustrated by the peace Germany imposed on the Russians in 1917. A rebuff in the Rhineland might not have toppled Hitler. Even if it had, he might have been followed by a German government no more peacefully inclined.

In 1937, Hitler directed his generals to be ready for war in connection with his next move. This precaution proved unnecessary, for the democracies did not oppose his annexation (*Anschluss*) of Austria in the spring in 1938. After he marched in, Hitler arranged a plebiscite in which a majority of Austrians approved the annexation. This result eased the consciences of people in the democracies, who thought in terms of national self-determination rather than strategic realities.

The annexation of Austria left Czechoslovakia in the position of a man with his head in the lion's mouth. By September 1938, Hitler was preparing to devour the Czechs. The complaints of the more than 3 million Sudeten Germans whom the Versailles settlement had placed under Czech rule served as his justification this time.

The Czech situation brought the most severe of the prewar crises, for France and the Soviet Union were committed by treaty to protect the Czechs. At every Czech concession Hitler escalated his demands and threatened a solution by force. He was not bluffing. In May he had issued secret orders stating his "unalterable intention to smash Czechoslovakia by military action in the near future."[1] But he was also willing, grudgingly, to let the democracies deliver Czechoslovakia to him without war.

The British prime minister, Neville Chamberlain, obliged him. Chamberlain made three frantic trips to Germany to negotiate a settlement. In Munich, with Mussolini's encouragement and France's acquiescence, Chamberlain and Hitler made terms. The Czechs, who were not represented, lost their defensible mountain frontier regions, where the Sudeten Germans (and nearly a million Czechs) lived.

The Munich agreement made *appeasement* a dirty word and Chamberlain's umbrella a symbol of surrender. But in 1938, most Europeans were relieved by this settlement. They were not eager to go to war again. It is in hindsight that Chamberlain's sacrifice of the only remaining democracy in Eastern Europe has been condemned.

Often such condemnation has been made without any understanding of Chamberlain's position. He was no admirer of Hitler, whom he regarded as half-crazed. Nor was he simply yielding to threats. He was pursuing a deliberate policy of peacefully eliminating sources of conflict. He foresaw correctly that another bloodbath like World War I would mean the end of the European-dominated world order. He had little faith in help from the Soviet Union, whose communism seemed to conservatives a greater menace than Germany's anticommunist Nazism, or from the United States, whose citizens clearly wanted to avoid further involvement in Europe. In this perspective, the sacrifice of a small remote country seemed a lesser evil than a new war.

Chamberlain's error was to believe that Hitler, like most people, would prefer peace to war, especially if his grievances were satisfied. In fact, Hitler was glad to get what he demanded without war. But if Chamberlain had not appeased him, the war that began in September 1939 would probably have begun in September 1938, and the British would have been even less well prepared than they were a year later.

When Chamberlain returned to Britain, he announced that the Munich agreement heralded "peace in our time." But in the spring of 1939, Hitler seized what was left of Czechoslovakia. In retaliation, the British government promised support to Poland, clearly destined to be his next victim. Even so, Hitler probably did not expect his invasion of Poland to produce full-scale war, which German planning anticipated would come only in 1943 or 1945.

In August 1939, preparing to attack Poland, Hitler cynically signed an agreement with the Soviet Union that ensured Germany would not have to fight on two fronts. In return, this

Nazi-Soviet Pact guaranteed Stalin a share of the Polish spoils and at least temporary immunity from German attack. Hitler probably calculated that such odds would prove daunting to Britain and France, and indeed those countries hesitated to respond for almost two days after German troops crossed the Polish border on September 1. But the Poles refused to have a surrender negotiated over their heads, as had happened to the Czechs. And so, with the British and French declarations of war on September 3, Europe's second world war began.

The Record of the 1930s and the Lessons of History

What "lessons of history" are to be learned from the story of the 1930s? Winston Churchill, soon to become Britain's prime minister, had systematically condemned each successive failure to curb Hitler. The prestige of his wartime leadership has lent much weight to the lesson he preached: the need for timely resistance to dictators. Yet it cannot be proved that following Churchill's policy would have allowed Europe to avoid war or even to fight on terms more advantageous to the democracies. We cannot know what would have happened if Hitler had been forced to back down in 1936. And by 1938 he was eager to fight. In historical perspective, Churchill's lessons no longer seem so certain.

Ironically, Neville Chamberlain in 1938 was convinced that *he* had learned the lessons of history. How incredible it was, he said during the Munich crisis, that the British government should be issuing gas masks to its civilians and digging trenches in London "because of a quarrel in a faraway country between people of whom we know nothing." Clearly he was remembering the origins of World War I. The lesson Chamberlain had learned from 1914 was that great wars began when great powers were dragged into them by alliances with quarrelsome small powers like Serbia. Hence his determination to defuse a similar crisis, as he saw it, by opening a dialogue.

Perhaps there was no way to stop German expansion except by war. Hitler was in a hurry, believing that destiny called him to realize Germany's ambitions and that his own days were numbered. It may be that the fascist revitalization of Germany, always potentially the strongest power on the European continent, forced the democracies to choose between war and submission. As we shall see, Germany's power was finally destroyed only when the country was invaded and dismembered, as French hard-liners had wanted to do in 1919. Chamberlain at Munich may have been wrong to believe that negotiation allowed the democracies to avoid both war and surrender. But no one can be certain that earlier resistance to Hitler would have offered a way out of the dilemma.

War or submission? Our views of what should have been done to stop Hitler in the 1930s are influenced by hindsight—by knowledge of World War II and the ghastly sufferings the Nazis inflicted. We find it difficult to imagine how Chamberlain could have believed it wise to accommodate Germany in hope of avoiding a conflict that seemed to him the greater evil. Perhaps the greatest wisdom is to realize that the lessons of history do not repeat themselves exactly. Chamberlain correctly recognized that World War I resulted from the great powers' failure to manage a peripheral crisis effectively. The origins of World War II, however, lay rather in the limitless ambitions of a revived Germany. Before applying the lessons of history to the present and future, we need to examine carefully the validity of the analogy linking our own situation with the past.

Despite the rapidity of twentieth-century change, 1914, 1939, and our own times do have one thing in common. Now as then the world is divided among sovereign nations that acknowledge no law except that of self-preservation, by force if necessary. In such a world, fascism, with its glorification of patriotism and violence, found imitators almost everywhere.

Fascism Around the World

As Hitler systematically overturned the obstacles to German power set up by the Versailles system, the momentum of fascism seemed irresistible. In imitation of this success, fascist or fascist-inspired movements appeared all over the world—testimony to the power of the European-dominated global configuration in shaping the ideologies of other countries as well as their economies.

Other European Fascist Movements

Few of these fascist movements succeeded in capturing power, and some did not even command much attention. In developed northwestern Europe, British, Dutch, and Scandinavian fascists were insignificant political forces. In linguistically divided Belgium, ethnic tension produced two fascisms, one speaking Flemish and the other French, that together captured 20 percent of the vote in 1936. Militant right-wing leagues rioted in Paris in 1934, arousing fears of a fascist coup in France. But they were conservative rather than revolutionary, tamely submitting to dissolution by Léon Blum's government.

In southeastern Europe, by contrast, substantial fascist movements included the Hungarian Arrow Cross and the Romanian Iron Guard. In both Hungary and Romania, however, the conservative dictatorships were at least as ruthless as the fascists. Corneliu Codreanu, leader of the Iron Guard, was "shot while attempting to escape" after King Carol II suspended the Romanian constitution and threw him into jail. When the Iron Guard attempted to regain control, the army crushed it.

In Spain, the fascist *Falange* was not nearly so powerful a force as the Iron Guard was in Romania. It failed to win a single parliamentary seat in the fateful election of 1936 won by the leftist coalition, the Popular Front. Among the groups who backed General Franco's Nationalist revolt against the Popular Front government of the Spanish Republic, the Falange was far less numerous than traditional conservatives: monarchists and Catholics. For many people, it was the intervention of Mussolini and Hitler on the Nationalist side in the ensuing savage three-year Spanish Civil War (1936–1939) that turned resistance to Franco into a crusade against the international march of fascism. As the fascist dictators poured in arms and reinforcements for Franco, idealistic volunteers from many countries formed "international brigades"—among them the American Abraham Lincoln Brigade—to defend the Spanish Republic. Many became disillusioned as the Republic, abandoned by the governments of the democracies, became more and more reliant on Soviet aid and thus fell increasingly under Communist control. When Stalin left the Republic to its fate and Franco won the civil war, he soon made it clear, now that he no longer needed Italian or German aid, that he was no more inclined to a revolution from the Right than to one from the Left. Though his regime had adopted some of the slogans and trappings of fascism, Franco relegated the Falange to political insignificance. His ultimate legacy to Spain was not fascism but, oddly in the 1970s, the restoration of the monarchy.

The Brazilian Integralistas

An even harsher fate than the Falange's befell the most interesting of the Latin American fascist movements, the Brazilian Integralistas. After borrowing many of their slogans, dictator

Getúlio Vargas prudently outlawed his fascist allies.

The Depression caused a collapse of Brazilian coffee prices. The resulting crisis dealt the final blow to Brazil's republican government, which had been run by a tiny minority of the wealthy. In 1930 it was overthrown by Vargas, an ambitious provincial governor. This coup marked the beginning, not the end, of political uncertainty. The new constitution of 1934 extended the right to vote, launching Brazil on the perilous new course of democratic politics in a time of growing social unrest. An abortive Communist coup in 1935 expressed the discontent of urban and rural workers.

Amid similar anxieties, the middle classes of Italy and Germany had turned to fascism. In Brazil the urban lower middle class and small landowners made up three-quarters of the Integralista movement founded by Plinio Salgado in 1932. The movement copied many aspects of European fascism, from its emphasis on centralized and authoritarian government and a corporatist economy to the stiff-armed salutes exchanged by its green-shirted militia. But it also reflected Brazil's particular circumstances. In this fervently Catholic country, the fascist motto was "God, Country, and Family." Moreover, Salgado explicitly condemned the racism of some European fascisms as inappropriate for a country with Brazil's mixed racial heritage.

As Brazil's first truly national political party, the Integralistas initially expected to take power by legal means, the only ones Salgado admitted. They were also encouraged by the tacit support they received from President Vargas, whose speeches stressed themes similar to theirs. But Vargas refused Salgado's offer of Green Shirt help against the Communists. He would tolerate no armed power to rival his own. The Integralistas would not, he explained, "Hindenburg" him. In 1937 he carried out a new coup d'état and established a more authoritarian political system, the Estado Novo (New State). To their horror, the Integralistas discovered that the new system's press censorship and prohibition of political parties applied to them, too. When some of them attempted a coup against Vargas in 1938, the ensuing shootout marked the end of the movement.

The Integralistas failed partly because of their own political naiveté. Trusting in Vargas and nonviolence, Salgado had none of Hitler's cunning. But the parallel failures of fascist movements in Mexico and Chile suggest that Latin American societies still lacked some of the essential ingredients for successful fascism. None of these countries had experienced the mass mobilization and disruptive horror of World War I. Indeed, Latin American armies rarely fought wars. They devoted their time to politics instead, providing their own brand of authoritarian rule. Moreover, despite some industrialization, most of Latin America in the 1930s had not yet developed mass movements of the proletarian Left, such as those that had made fascism attractive to the European middle classes. For all these reasons, fascism failed in Latin America in the 1930s.

The Lebanese Phalange

The 1930s produced short-lived proto-fascist movements in the Middle East: Blue Shirts and Green Shirts in Egypt, Gray Shirts and White Shirts in Syria, Khaki Shirts in Iraq. Arabs under British and French rule had reason to copy the political style of Germany and Italy, the enemies of their enemies. But in the Middle East, the social groups that constituted the core of European fascism were too small or too strictly controlled to permit Arab fascism to develop fully. Nonetheless, at least one such movement founded in the 1930s survives today, a reminder of the permanent temptation of fascism for people who feel that history has wronged or is threatening them.

Five young Western-educated Christian Arabs founded *Al Kata'ib*, otherwise known as the Lebanese *Phalange,* on November 21, 1936. Their leader was pharmacist Pierre Gemayel, captain of the Lebanese soccer team at the 1936 Berlin Olympic Games. Gemayel had been struck by German discipline, which contrasted sharply with the bitter division of his homeland.

Historically, the name Lebanon referred not to a state but to a region within Syria. Mountainous Lebanon had long been a refuge for religious minorities. When the League of Nations gave France control of the region after World War I, France created the Republic of Lebanon, which contained some seventeen religious sects. Maronite Christians, like Gemayel, who had important historic links to the Papacy and France, were the largest sect, though they represented less than a third of the population. Most of the rest were Muslims. Most Muslims resented Maronite dominance, which they believed rested on foreign support. Then and now, many Muslims even resented the French-imposed idea that Lebanon should be a country separate from Syria and the rest of the Arab world.

In such a situation, the task of Gemayel's Phalange was obvious. It recruited Maronite students, apprentices, shopkeepers, and minor bureaucrats into a militia that could defend their community and the Maronite-dominated Lebanese order. Their slogan was "God, Country, and Family"—the same as that of the Brazilian Integralistas. Members between the ages of eighteen and thirty-five were organized into 600-man "phalanxes," which carried out military drills in their tan shirts. The motto, the military trappings, and the early insistence of the Phalangists that they were not a political party, all link this movement with fascistic movements elsewhere. After Lebanon became independent from France in 1943, the Phalange gradually evolved into a political party. Yet it never lost its military dimension and still had seventy thousand men under arms a generation after Pierre Gemayel's visit to Berlin. In the Lebanese civil war that began in 1975, the Phalange played a leading role in defending the Maronite position.

Conclusion: The Permanent Temptation of Fascism

To what extent has fascism survived into our own time? For decades after World War II, it appeared that fascism had arisen in response to a specific set of conditions in the aftermath of World War I and had ended with the destruction of the regimes of Hitler and Mussolini in 1945. Their defeat, it was supposed, had discredited most of the ideals and symbols associated with them. Thus the survival into our own time of the Lebanese Phalange, which may never have fully met our definition of fascism, could seem to be merely a historical curiosity.

Yet postwar appearances have proved deceiving, for fascism is really best understood as a response to the central themes of the twentieth century defined in this book. Fascism's nationalism appeals to the resentment of peoples who feel oppressed or cheated by history. Its revolutionary conservatism is a violent protest against the erosion of culturally conservative societies by the acceleration of change. Fascists boast that they can succeed where democracy always fails, in combining the politics of a mass society with effective government. Ideologically, fascism curiously mingles the twentieth century's mania for futuristic technology with its uneasy suspicion that human beings are losing touch with their natural environment. Above all, fascism offers its adherents a set of values—belief in the nation and the leader—that can prove comforting in an age when, as we shall see in the next chapter, most values have come into question.

Since fascism claims to have answers to central problems of modern life, we should not be surprised that movements resembling interwar fascism continue to appear. As we shall see in Chapter 17, the Iranian revolution of 1979 can be interpreted as a revolution from the Right in an Islamic society. The most pessimistic observers of the Soviet Union's collapse fear that the eventual successor of communism will be not today's fragile democracy but various blends of nationalism and fascism. Most disturbing, the 1990s have seen a resurgent neo-Nazism in newly reunified Germany. The mobs of young Germans who brandish swastika-like symbols and persecute ethnic minorities were born long after Hitler's death. But like his followers in the 1930s, they are driven by economic despair and frustration with ineffectual government. Their numbers remind us that in times of trouble, fascism remains for many a tempting alternative to democracy.

Note

1. Quoted in Alan Bullock, *Hitler: A Study in Tyranny,* rev. ed. (New York: Harper & Row, 1964), p. 408.

Suggestions for Further Reading

Adamthwaite, Anthony. *The Making of the Second World War* (1979).

Aycoberry, Pierre. *The Nazi Question: An Essay on the Interpretations of National Socialism* (1981).

Bullock, Alan. *Hitler: A Study in Tyranny.* Rev. ed. (1971).

Cassells, Alan. *Fascism* (1975).

De Grazia, Victoria. *How Fascism Ruled Women: Italy, 1922–1945* (1992).

Hiden, John, and John Farquharson. *Explaining Hitler's Germany: Historians and the Third Reich,* 2nd ed. (1989).

Hilton, S. "*Ação Integralista Brasileira:* Fascism in Brazil, 1932–1938," *Luso-Brazilian Review,* 9 (December 1972).

Laqueur, Walter, ed. *Fascism: A Reader's Guide* (1976).

Smith, Denis Mack. *Mussolini: A Biography* (1982).

Taylor, Alan. *The Origins of the Second World War* (1983).

Weber, Eugen. *Varieties of Fascism* (1982).

CHAPTER 7

Western Intellectual and Artistic Life

At the beginning of the twentieth century, Western societies still took a largely optimistic view of the world and human nature. This confident perspective had almost been destroyed by the end of the 1930s. The slaughters of World War I, the degeneration of the Bolshevik Revolution into Stalinist dictatorship, and the success of fascist movements that glorified violence and scorned liberal values made nonsense of the idea that the future would be a story of progress. The twentieth century had become, in the words of poet W. H. Auden, the "age of anxiety."

Early in the twentieth century, new discoveries had undercut confident nineteenth-century assumptions about the nature of the universe and human beings. These new ideas, reinforced by postwar disillusionment, eventually colored social scientists' assumptions, artists' forms of expression, and political philosophers' analysis of that characteristic form of twentieth-century life, the mass society.

The Optimistic Vision Shattered

The Nineteenth-Century World of Certainty and Uniformity

Throughout history, the sciences, the arts, and political analysis have evolved to reflect each era's understanding of the universe and of human personality. The liberalism that dominated the Western world at the end of the nineteenth century, for example, took for granted a model of the universe that any informed person could comprehend. Two hundred years earlier, Isaac Newton had worked out physical laws describing the motions of the planets and of the particles that made up matter. This "majestic clockwork" universe ticked along as the result of invariable interactions between forces and masses. Energy was assumed to impart motion to matter in a uniform manner regardless of the place in space and time of the person observing their interaction. On this Newtonian model of a uniform nature, all the scientific and technical triumphs of modern Western civilization had been based. At the end of the nineteenth century, though new instruments and experiments were revealing some unaccountable deviations from Newton's laws, they had not yet been fundamentally challenged.

Human beings held a privileged place in this regular universe. By the end of the nineteenth century most educated people probably accepted the Darwinian view that human beings were a species of animal that had evolved from "lower" species over millions of years. Many scientists and philosophers argued that human actions and thoughts were determined by the same chemical and physical reactions that governed the rest of nature. They hoped eventually to work out laws of behavior that would make human beings as predictable as the physical phenomena of the Newtonian universe.

Still, people's ability to comprehend their own nature and that of the world around them set them apart from the rest of the animal world, at the top of the evolutionary ladder. And Westerners felt that their particular capacity to understand the workings of the universe and of the mind set them above people of other cultures. Europeans and Americans tended to regard the customs and ideas of the African or Asian societies they had subjected to Western dominance as primitive or savage, characteristics of people less "evolved" than Westerners.

Until late in the nineteenth century, the mainstream of Western literature and art also embodied these basic assumptions about the nature of the world and of humanity. Graphic artists since the Renaissance had seen their task in much the same way. They devoted their skill to re-creating the beauties of a natural world that everyone could see and understand. Or they illustrated traditional themes—from the Greek and Roman classics, for example—taken from the long story of the human struggle with nature, including human nature.

Nineteenth-century Western artists differed in their choice of means to achieve their goal. Academic painters emphasized formal draftsmanship, whereas the Impressionists valued vivid colors more. But all believed that their paintings instructed their audience in the nature of visible reality. Some artists insisted that art existed for itself alone and required no social or intellectual justification, but even they regarded themselves as educators.

Education was the cherished priority of late-nineteenth-century Western liberalism. Belief in the possibility of educating humanity is what linked the nineteenth century's understanding of physical and human nature with its faith in liberalism and even democracy. If human intelligence already understood the physical universe and might one day discover laws of human behavior, then governments must eliminate all obstacles to the development and use of the mind. Democracy was mobilizing great masses of people for participation in the political process. Universal education could raise even these mass societies to the level of rational decision making that the nineteenth century's small middle-class elites believed they had already achieved.

The Discovery of Relativity and the Unconscious

Even before 1914, this optimistic vision of the world and humanity had been undermined—ironically, by thinkers who themselves believed in an unvarying universe and in the rational powers of the human mind. Albert Einstein's equations depicted a universe of unknowable size whose operations flouted conventional notions of cause and effect. (Later scientists, better able to look out into space and within the atom, confirmed Einstein's theories experimentally.) At almost the same time, Sigmund Freud asserted that conscious reasoning is only one facet of the human mind, and not the basic one. Much human behavior, Freud said, springs from feelings of which the individual remains unconscious. This revelation proved as devastating to nineteenth-century certainties as did Einstein's equations. Among their other effects, Freud's discoveries undermined the assumption of Western cultural superiority by showing that "primitive" drives are common to all human beings.

Though both Einstein and Freud had completed their most important work before the end of World War I, they became famous only after 1918. In the disillusionment that followed the war, people were more receptive to their conclusions, which helped discredit the sometimes smug certainties of 1914. Similarly, authors and painters after 1918 used experimental techniques developed before the war as weapons against prewar society's basic assumptions.

The events of the 1920s and 1930s did little to restore prewar certainties. It was discouraging to find that large numbers of democracy's new mass electorate freely voted for fascist dictators. Insensible to liberal politics, mass humanity sometimes also seemed indifferent or hostile to modern literature, art, and architecture. People's readiness to consume mass-produced entertainment led some intellectuals to despair of the future of both democracy and traditional high culture.

On the eve of World War II, not much was left of the optimistic synthesis of Newtonian physics, rationalist psychology, objective literature and painting, and political and economic liberalism. The foundations of nineteenth-century certainty had been so undermined that there could be no going back. Everywhere one looked, uncertainty reigned. To discuss the Einsteinian natural world of astromechanics and atomic physics, for example, one had to use terms that only "relatively" approximated what they attempted to describe, rather than corresponding to the bedrock reality earlier centuries had taken for granted.

Einstein's Universe: Curved Space and Subatomic Particles

In the history of scientific understanding, occasional revolutions have interrupted long periods in which investigators accumulated experimental detail to confirm preexisting assumptions. A scientific revolution occurs when new data cannot be fitted into the old framework of understanding. Scientists are then forced to abandon their old assumptions and propose new explanations. This new framework of basic explanations in turn stimulates experiments to develop new data to confirm it.

Such a revolution transformed physics, the science of matter and motion, between 1900 and 1950. Today we are accustomed to the practical consequences of its discoveries, from nuclear weapons to space vehicles. Early in the century, however, the men and women who provided the vision and the data for this physics revolution were so few that they could meet annually in quite a small room.

Well before 1900, some of these scientists had noted experimental results that were hard to reconcile with the Newtonian model. In the Newtonian world of matter bounded by an absolute space and an absolute time, the same causes invariably produced the same results. In 1900 the German physicist Max Planck demonstrated that energy on the atomic scale proceeded not in a continuous flow but by periodic emissions, which he called *quanta*. Attempts to reconcile such internal phenomena of atoms with the Newtonian model of matter and motion proved unsatisfying.

At that moment in its history, physics needed not more observations but a revolution. It was Albert Einstein (1879–1955) who provided a new insight into the nature of the universe that was as all-encompassing as Newton's had been.

Although it is impossible to explain genius, certain of Einstein's youthful traits help to explain how, at the age of twenty-six, he was able to "rebuild the universe in his head."[1] He grew up in the Jewish community of Munich, a mediocre student who dropped out of school at fifteen. By then, however, he had educated himself by wide reading, especially in the works of critical philosophers. This reading made him skeptical of the most widely accepted ideas, including the tenets of formal religions. But Einstein had a special faith: though God might be unknowable, He would not have created a world unintelligible to humankind. The idea of such a world offended the young Einstein's sense of beauty as well as his faith.

Einstein's aesthetic sense of the necessary unity and order of the world, reinforced by a remarkable self-confidence, enabled him to set aside the accepted formulas of physics and to conceive new ones that better explained recent experimental findings.

The Theory of Special Relativity and $E = mc^2$

When Einstein finally completed his education in Switzerland, the only job he could find was as a patent examiner, evaluating the work of Swiss inventors. On the backs of discarded patent applications, he scribbled the equations that would make the twentieth century the age of atomic energy, the laser, and space flight. In 1905, within a few months, he published three papers that began a basic redefinition of space and time, matter and energy. The first paper, for which Einstein was awarded the Nobel Prize in 1921, demonstrated mathematically that light is composed of particles whose energy can be characterized by the quanta Planck had described.

A greater leap of the imagination was involved in Einstein's famous paper "On the Electrodynamics of Moving Bodies." As a boy he had wondered, "What would the world look like if I rode on a beam of light?" Sitting up in bed one morning, he suddenly found the answer to this question. To someone traveling at the constant speed of light, time on the earth would appear not to pass. What we observe of the passage of distance and time is "relative" to our own motion within the universe. Absolute distances and times do not exist.

This theory of special relativity had no practical consequences in 1905. (Today it explains why an astronaut in orbit sees the earth tumbling rapidly through space, while we on the earth's surface are unconscious of any such motion.) But in space and in the invisible world of subatomic particles, the theory had revolutionary implications. Einstein used it to arrive at a conclusion developed in his third 1905 paper and later expressed in the momentous equation $E = mc^2$. This meant essentially that energy and mass were equivalent (so that, for example, the sun must lose mass as it dispenses the energy of sunlight). This equation proved fundamental to the future of both astronomy and atomic physics.

These papers established Einstein's reputation, and in 1914 he won a prestigious appointment at the Kaiser Wilhelm Institute in Berlin. There, a year later, he published his theory of general relativity, which argued that because light has mass, it is subject to the force of gravity. He suggested that the theory be tested by measuring how the light from a distant star was deflected as it passed through the sun's gravitational field. In 1919, two British expeditions traveled to the coasts of Africa and of South America to take the prescribed measurements. When their results confirmed his prediction almost exactly, Einstein, to his amazement, suddenly found himself world-famous. The *London Times* proclaimed "Revolution in Science: Newtonian Ideas Overthrown."[2]

For the rest of his life, Einstein was the world's most prominent scientist. For almost four decades he continued to elaborate his mathematical idea of a curved universe with both space and time as dimensions. Forced to flee Germany in 1933, he found refuge in the United States, becoming a professor at Princeton's Institute for Advanced Study. He worked there until his death in 1955.

From Atomic Physics to Atomic Weapons

So rapidly did the physics revolution advance that by the time Einstein died, he had become a figure out of the past to younger physicists. He found it difficult to accept some of their new theories about the atom. A significant example was Werner Heisenberg's "principle of uncertainty" (1927), which held that the motion of subatomic particles (which we cannot directly observe) cannot be predicted except within a range of statistical probabilities. "God does not throw dice," declared Einstein. Though his discoveries had overthrown the predictable regularities of Newtonian physics, Einstein always hoped to construct a new general framework for the universe that would not have to allow for such uncertainty.

Einstein was also unsympathetic to those who charged that in the relativistic world he had revealed, there could no longer be any absolute rules, even of moral conduct. He did not hesitate to condemn on ethical grounds the development of nuclear weapons, a stand that cost him some of his popularity in the Cold War years.

Nuclear weapons were the most spectacular consequence of the revolutions in astronomy and nuclear physics that followed on Einstein's demonstration that energy has mass and mass has energy. In the 1920s American astronomers, measuring the distances of stars by spectrographic analysis of their light emissions, confirmed the vision of an infinite universe of countless billions of stars. Another German refugee physicist, Hans Bethe, working at Cornell University in 1939, dramatically illustrated that Einsteinian principles could be simultaneously applied to both astrophysics and nuclear physics. Bethe showed precisely how the sun's loss of mass produces the energy of sunlight by transforming hydrogen into helium. In this way, he traced the origins of the matter that composes us and our world to the energy of stars that disintegrated several billion years before the sun and earth existed.

In 1905, Einstein had proposed testing his theory of special relativity by experimenting with the newly revealed phenomenon of radioactivity. By 1939 much more was known of the subatomic components of matter. Experiments at Cambridge University in England in 1932 confirmed Einstein's formulation of the relationship of energy to mass and revealed that the nucleus of the atom was not the basic unit of matter. Nuclei were composed of protons and neutrons. Within two years, at the University of Rome, Enrico Fermi applied this discovery by bombarding the nuclei of various atoms, including that of the heaviest element, uranium, with neutrons.

Fortunately for Nazism's future opponents in World War II, Fascist racism diverted the unfolding of scientific inquiry. Fermi, whose wife was Jewish, had to flee Rome in 1938, when Mussolini imposed anti-Semitic laws similar to Hitler's. By then, nuclear scientists everywhere had learned of the tremendous energy that could be released in a chain-reaction splitting of uranium atoms. Politicians reacted slowly to this revelation. Hitler gave the potential weapon a low priority. Not until late in 1941 did the U.S. government decide to go all out to make a bomb. By then most of the physicists with the knowledge to undertake the task were refugees, like Einstein, in North America. Fermi led the team that achieved the first self-sustaining chain reaction releasing nuclear energy, at the University of Chicago on December 2, 1942. This date marked the dawning of the atomic age and the first step toward the atomic bombs that would be exploded over Japanese cities in 1945.

When Einstein learned of the first test of an atomic weapon, he groaned aloud. The equations he had developed in the Swiss patent office had led indirectly to the most destructive weapon yet devised. The advent of nuclear weapons heightened the uncertainty of the twentieth century. Nor in the long run were the implications of relativity theory and probabilistic quantum mechanics reassuring. Scientific popularizers interpreted those implications in the best light for the societies they addressed. The British astrophysicist Sir Arthur Eddington, a Quaker, firmly denied that the Einsteinian view of the world in any way invalidated the Christian view. At the same time, Soviet physicists contended that Einsteinian physics affirmed the material reality underlying Marxist dialectical materialism.

Historically, people have reassured themselves of their grasp on reality by citing scientific discoveries to bolster their basic beliefs. Still, the world view of Albert Einstein revealed that human perceptions of the realities of both space and matter are imperfect: subjective, not objective. The psychological doctrines of Freud reinforced this humbling evaluation of human capabilities.

Einstein at Princeton. *In later life, the gentle, unworldly physicist became a popular celebrity, the image of the scientist for millions unacquainted with his theories.* Bettmann Newsphotos

Freud: The Path into the Unconscious

Sigmund Freud (1856–1939) launched another intellectual revolution. Freud was guided by a nineteenth-century faith that reason can ascertain regular causes for all behavior. Like Einstein, he was tough-minded enough to persevere in his explanations even when they led him to conclusions that contradicted his initial assumptions. But Freud's investigations of the human personality had a far more direct influence on intellectuals and the public than did Einstein's theories of the cosmos. Freud's conclusions were far more controversial. Although he emphasized dimensions of human nature that many people would prefer not to discuss, his ideas have been assimilated into the foundations of twentieth-century Western culture.

Freud 1921. *In his mid sixties, Freud was at the height of his powers, and the psychoanalytic movement was winning new disciples in Berlin, Budapest, London, and New York. FPG International*

The Founding of Psychoanalysis

Though he had won some earlier international recognition among psychologists, Freud's work became popularly known only in the disillusioned aftermath of World War I. His emphasis on the irrational elements of human motivation appealed to a generation outraged by a pointless war. Ironically, however, it was Freud's nineteenth-century faith in the ability of the reasoning mind to discover the causes of phenomena that led him into the realm of the unconscious. He based his model of the mind's workings on an analogy with the nineteenth-century concept of energy. To the end of his life, he regarded himself as an experimental scientist. Although some people felt his discoveries revealed the hypocrisy of conventional Western standards of behavior, Freud remained a moralist.

All these traits can be traced to his youth in Vienna, where he spent almost all his life. The son of a Jewish merchant, he was a voracious reader, like Einstein. Freud felt strong artistic inclinations but decided he must discipline this side of his personality by pursuing a scientific career. He wrote a postgraduate thesis on the reproductive system of the eel. Ultimately he became a doctor of medicine, specializing in neurology.

By the late nineteenth century, physicians had begun to try to treat the victims of mental disorder, rather than simply locking them up as earlier ages had done. Their working assumption was that mental illness arose from organic causes—for example, damaged brain cells. This was a natural assumption in an age that was discovering the bacterial causes of most infectious diseases. But there was evidence that an organic explanation did not always apply.

An older friend and colleague, Josef Breuer, described to Freud his treatment of a patient, "Anna O.," whose hysterical symptoms included occasional paralysis, inability to drink water, and trances. Breuer had experimented with the novel technique of hypnosis. When hypnotized, Anna O. recalled memories of which she had been unconscious, and recalling them relieved her symptoms. Such evidence made Freud doubt that the workings of the mind were determined wholly by physical causes. Mistrustful of hypnotism, he began asking his patients to relax and concentrate on their symptoms while he questioned them to evoke related memories. Bringing such memories to the surface often relieved the symptoms. Clearly, then, some symptoms of mental illness had a "functional" cause: the mind itself, under the pressure of unconscious memories, generated painful symptoms.

Freud's next advance along the path into the unconscious came when a patient told him not to interrupt the stream of her recollections with questioning. Freud started to encourage his patients to "free-associate": to tell him whatever came into their consciousness, however shameful or absurd it might seem. He found that patients who talked in this way repeatedly brought up suppressed memories of a childhood sexual seduction by a parent. Freud soon decided that not all these parental sexual assaults could actually have occurred. The origins of such "recollections" were as mysterious as the strange events of his patients' dreams. Yet Freud had been schooled in the nineteenth-century conviction that all phenomena have definite causes. To find the cause of his patients' fantasies and dreams, Freud began to look within his own personality, following his own free associations wherever they led, regardless of pain. This self-analysis took him over the threshold of the unconscious mind. He did not "discover" that world, which had long haunted artists. Freud's achievement was to demonstrate the influence of the unconscious on human behavior and to develop a therapeutic method for dealing with that influence.

The model Freud developed for explaining the workings of the human mind is already visible in his book *The Interpretation of Dreams* (1899). His fundamental metaphor derived from pre-Einsteinian physics. Like physical energy, Freud believed, psychic energy—thoughts and emotions—might be transformed but not eliminated altogether. Dreams, for example, offered a harmless way to express feelings forbidden to daytime consciousness. Neurotic behavior and hysterical symptoms such as paralysis were other forms of transformation. The unconscious found a variety of outlets for the pressure of unthinkable thoughts.

Freud gave the name *id* to the dynamo within the human personality that produces all this emotional energy. The id's power comes from primitive drives toward physical, essentially sexual, pleasure. But human societies could not function if the only outlet for emotional energy were the satisfaction of animal instincts. Therefore, Freud held, another element of the mind, the *ego,* redirects psychic energy into socially acceptable channels. These are defined by the *superego,* which enforces parental and social standards of behavior. Freud thus saw the human personality as a system of emotional energies in constant tension. The ego faces a continuous challenge to transform the animal impulses of the id, which are always present in the unconscious, into behavior acceptable to the strict superego. Sometimes this transformation is successful, as when the sexual impulse that Freud called *libido* are "sublimated" into the creative artistic impulse. Sometimes it is not: unconscious drives then become neurotic behavior or even disabling mental illness. The treatment Freud developed for such conditions is called *psychoanalysis.*

In his later years, Freud increasingly turned from the specifics of psychoanalysis to wider concerns. Like Einstein, he aspired to a comprehensive explanation of the phenomena he studied—all human behavior. Comparing the myths and taboos of "primitive" peoples with those of the West, he concluded that the tension between instinct and repression affects human societies as well as individual personalities. The price human beings paid for social organization was an immense burden of guilt over repressed instincts (incestual ones, Freud believed). Because guilt found its outlet in violence, civilization was a fragile creation in which people's instinct to love was perpetually counterbalanced by their impulses to destroy one another.

Because Freud had studied the human aggressive impulse, the destructiveness of World War I was far less surprising to him than it was to most people. Nor was the postwar emergence of political movements such as Nazism unpredictable. When Hitler annexed Austria in 1938, Freud had to flee the city that had been his home for over eighty years. While the Nazis gleefully burned his books, he died a refugee in London in 1939.

Freud's Influence

An attempt to assess Freud's impact on the twentieth-century world yields a complicated verdict. Even psychologists who acknowledge their debt to his inspiration have modified his ideas by stressing nonsexual motivations and the effects of social as well as instinctual drives, and adult as well as childhood experiences, on personality development.

Since 1973, a new organic interpretation of behavior has arisen from the dramatic development of "molecular psychology." Scientists have identified chemical reactions in the brain corresponding to such mental states as depression or aggressiveness. As one leader of this school explained, "People who act crazy are acting that way because they have too much or too little of some chemicals . . . in their brains. It's just physical illness! The brain is a physical thing!"[3] If this molecular approach eventually revolutionizes psychology's basic framework of assumptions, we may conclude that science has come full circle since Freud abandoned purely organic explanations for mental illness before 1900. Indeed, critics are now arguing that many of the human characteristics Freud believed universal were merely the peculiarities of his middle-class, turn-of-the-century Viennese patients. For example, Freud asserted that women think of themselves as incomplete men. But feminists have rightly pointed out that Freud's view reflects the male dominance in Viennese society of his day, not a universal truth.

None of these developments means that Freud has lost his importance for the twentieth-century world. On a nontechnical level, his model of human psychology has been so widely diffused through Western culture that we are almost unaware of its influence. Such terms as "Freudian slip," the slip of the tongue that betrays our unconscious feelings, or the concept of "wish fulfillment," the process by which we fantasize about what we cannot have, have become part of the everyday vocabulary of educated people. Everyone from advertising copywriters to political campaign managers assumes that decision making reflects subconscious as well as conscious motivations.

In the 1920s, popular oversimplification led many people, especially in the United States, to conclude that the chief lesson of Freud's teachings was that human beings should not feel guilty about their sexual impulses. Freud himself was no advocate of unbridled permissiveness, but he recognized the intensity of the conflict between the dictates of instinct and the rules of society. In the long run, his work has probably led to greater tolerance of those who fail to resolve that conflict—not only the officially mentally ill and the socially deviant, but the many "normal" people who suffer breakdowns or violate the moral standards set up by some authority. Such tolerance has proved to have narrow limits, however, and twentieth-century societies are periodically confronted by demands for a return to punitive standards. Freud's demonstration that every society develops its own repressive codes to control the universal impulses of the unconscious was another example of the twentieth-century collapse of certainty. It implied that far from being absolute, ethical standards, like the physical observations of the Einsteinian universe are "relative" to whoever pronounces them.

Cultural Relativism: Non-Western Societies and European Global Dominance

The years after World War I also produced a relativist revolution in the study of human societies and cultures. A new kind of anthropology significantly altered Western intellectuals' perspective on the many other peoples of the twentieth-century world.

The methods and assumptions of Western study of non-Western peoples remained ethnocentric well into the twentieth century. Information about non-Western customs and beliefs was typically collected as the quaint behavior of peoples who had not yet reached the "higher" levels of civilization prevailing in the West.

If any single individual was responsible for rejecting this approach and founding modern cultural anthropology, it was Bronislaw Malinowski (1884–1942), professor of anthropology at the University of London and later at Yale. Born a Polish subject of the Austro-Hungarian Empire, he studied in Germany, did research in the Southwest Pacific, and taught in Britain and the United States. His career is an illustration of the shrinking of the twentieth-century world. Its turning point came when he accompanied a team of British anthropologists to study Australian aborigines. When the outbreak of World War I made him an enemy alien, the Australian authorities consented to intern him in the Trobriand Islands of eastern New Guinea. His first book about the islanders, *Argonauts of the Western Pacific* (1922), marked an anthropological revolution. In the next thirteen years he wrote six more books about every aspect of Trobriand life, from sexual behavior to methods of cultivation.

Like Einstein and Freud, Malinowski began with a conviction that careful observation would yield universal laws—in this case, of societal organization. A man of cosmopolitan background, he was shocked by the ignorance of white people who had lived in places like the Trobriands for years but had learned nothing of a "native" culture they scorned. A Westerner could not understand such a culture by looking at it from outside. Intensive fieldwork, such as Malinowski had used to study the Trobrianders, was necessary. That meant living among the people, speaking their language fluently, learning "to grasp the native's point of view, his relation to life . . . *his* vision of *his* world."[4]

To Malinowski, a culture was a totality. Every part of a people's system of customs and beliefs, however odd it might appear, served an essential social function, sometimes better than the corresponding Western ones did. Although a Westerner might dismiss the Trobrianders' magic as superstition, for example, it served the essential function of relieving human anxiety about the unknown. Every culture was a complex structure functioning to meet basic human needs. Descriptions like "savage" or "primitive" were all relative, and every culture had its own value.

This "functionalist" revolution in anthropology challenged the easy assumption of Western cultural superiority. The principle of cultural relativism, though now taken for granted by social scientists, was not immediately accepted by everyone. European colonial administrators joked scornfully about the mythical anthropologist who would tolerate headhunting if it was an authentic tribal custom. For many other people in the West, Hollywood's stereotype of the prancing, grunting, simple-minded "native" probably remained intact.

Ironically, as revolutionary movements aimed at throwing off Western dominance developed in the non-Western world, especially after World War II, some of their leaders denounced anthropological interest in traditional ways of life. They saw it as a neocolonial attempt to keep Africans and Asians dependent by isolating them from Western progress. Nevertheless, in the years after World War I, Western cultural superiority was seriously questioned—in part because of the advent of cultural relativism but also because of the war's revelation that Western peoples, too, lived by myths. It was myth, for example, that mobilized men in the trenches of 1914. Malinowski wrote:

> We cannot possibly reach the final . . . wisdom of knowing ourselves if we never leave the normal confinement of the customs, beliefs, and prejudices into which every man is born. Nothing can teach us a better lesson . . . than the habit of mind which allows us to treat the beliefs and values of another man from his point of view. Nor has civilized humanity ever needed such tolerance more than now, when prejudice, ill will, and vindictiveness are dividing each . . . nation from another.[5]

For many Western intellectuals who thought as Malinowski did, twentieth-century standards of culture and social organization, like observations of physical phenomena and moral norms, revealed not an absolute but only a relative truth.

Modern Art and Architecture: Mind Versus Eye

Twentieth-century art underwent a transformation as dramatic as the revolutions in physics and psychology. Artists came to believe that their quest for absolute truth demanded more than faithfulness to the appearances of nature and to traditional themes. Even before 1914, an "advance guard" of painters and architects was experimenting with radically new forms. World War I reinforced these artistic revolutionaries by discrediting the prewar order of things. As modern physics penetrated behind appearances to a subatomic reality it could describe only by abstractions, and as modern psychology probed the human unconscious, avant-garde modern art tried to express these new aspects of experience through continued experimentation with new forms. Some of these artists portrayed a world whose reality was so relative to their own perceptions that it appeared absurd. Most, however, still believed that the function of art was to explain experience, though they now used new idioms to express the new realities. Within the first generation of the twentieth century, a cultured minority of Western art lovers accepted these radical new forms of modern art as standard. But their abstract quality opened a gap between artistic standards and popular tastes wider than Western civilization had yet known.

Probably the most popular school of painting in the history of art, and one that still delights gallery-goers, was French Impression-

Pablo Picasso,* Les Demoiselles d'Avignon, *1907. *In this work, Picasso painted faces like African masks; he admired what he saw as the imaginative distortion of African art. Picasso did not know about the symbolic and ceremonial function of masks in African culture (see example on page 182). Oil on canvas. 8′ × 7′8″. Collection, The Museum of Modern Art, New York. Acquired through the Lillie P. Bliss Bequest*

ism. The Impressionists were the advance guard of the 1870s, who attempted to convey a genuine "impression" of nature by using color to depict the play of light over objects. By 1900, however, their appeal to the eye had become routine. Some of the greatest Impressionists by then were experimenting with new forms, which were avidly taken up by a younger generation. Monet practically dissolved nature into an indistinct shimmer of light. Cézanne tried to get beneath the impressions of the eye to an underlying reality that was almost geometric. Landscape painting, he declared, "is not copying the object, it is realizing one's sensations."[6]

Around 1905, the same goal inspired the painting of the Fauve (Wild Beast) group. This short-lived school was given its name by a critic startled by the contrast between the painters' distorted lines and violent colors

Edvard Munch,* The Scream, *1893. *The Norwegian artist depicted in broad brush strokes of lurid color a nightmare world from which the lonely figure flees, shrieking.* *Courtesy, National Gallery, Oslo*

and the cool moderation of the classical tradition.

It was the Cubist movement that most dramatically signaled twentieth-century artists' new idiom. In one painting (*Les Demoiselles d'Avignon,* 1907) the young Pablo Picasso (1881–1973) summed up the revolutionary currents that combined to launch the modern art of the twentieth century. Like many artists before him, Picasso portrayed a group of standing female nudes—but in a manner that has been called "the first radically new proposition about the way we see that painting had made in almost five hundred years."[7] The faces are those of African masks. (Picasso, a Spaniard then living in Paris, had seen such masks at a colonial exhibition.) The jutting, distorted angles and planes seek to capture the underlying geometric essence of being, not its superficial appearances. "I paint forms," Picasso explained, "as I think them, not as I see them." Addressed to the mind rather than to the eye, *Les Demoiselles* still shocks by its boldness. So does another classic of modern art, Marcel Duchamp's *Nude Descending a Staircase.* Derided as "an explosion in a shingle factory" when it was exhibited in New York in 1913, *Nude* had to be carefully guarded against vandals. Its effort to portray muscular motion seemed as outlandish as Einstein's vision of a universe in which space-time was a dimension.

Twentieth-century physicists' discovery of an ultimate reality that we cannot actually see—the subatomic particle—helped to inspire another revolutionary prewar artistic school, Abstract Expressionism. *Expressionism* simply meant that artists' task was to tell the truth as they perceived it. For the Russian Vasili Kandinski (1866–1944) the truth of this invisible subatomic world was God's presence everywhere. An artist who sought to convey spiritual reality therefore had to teach his or her audience to disregard what they saw in favor of symbols of what they could only sense. In this way, Kandinski's expression of truth became an art of pure abstraction, representing no recognizable object at all.

Although Kandinski's abstractions expressed a joyful, personal truth, many Expressionists' truth was a lonely, fear-ridden existence in the twentieth-century metropolis. A forerunner of Expressionism, Norwegian Edvard Munch (1863–1944) anticipated the world of Freudian psychology, in which human reason was torn between instinctual needs and society's constraints. The terrified face in *The Scream* (1893) is modeled on that of an Inca mummy that Munch had seen in a Paris anthropological museum. The picture itself became one of the twentieth century's most frightening

Max Beckmann,* The Night, *1918–1919. *The painting reflects the artist's horror at the cruelty and chaos of both World War I and the postwar German revolution. The sinister figure in the cloth cap at far right is clearly modeled on Lenin.* *Kunstsammlung Nordrhein-Westfalen, Düsseldorf*

images of the human experience: a cry of personal, subjective horror to a merciless sky and indifferent passers-by. Munch wrote on the canvas, "Can only have been painted by a madman." Before 1914 his vision was an isolated one. World War I, however, made the madman's nightmare real.

The Night (1918–1919) is the work of Max Beckmann (1884–1950), a German stretcher-bearer who became so depressed at what he saw on the front lines that he was given a medical discharge. The obscene and senseless violence on this grisly canvas shows a truth of war very different from the heroic images projected by the parades and monuments of prewar Berlin.

Not all artists shared Beckmann's dark vision of the human future. Most of the brilliant Russian painters who had made Moscow a center of the avant-garde before 1914 enlisted their art in the service of the Bolshevik Revolution. They were encouraged by Lenin's commissar of education, Anatoli Lunacharski, who believed as they did that art could reach the masses and inspire political commitment. Thus modern art became part of the effort to mobilize Russia's peasant masses for the revolution through agitation and propaganda. "Agitprop"

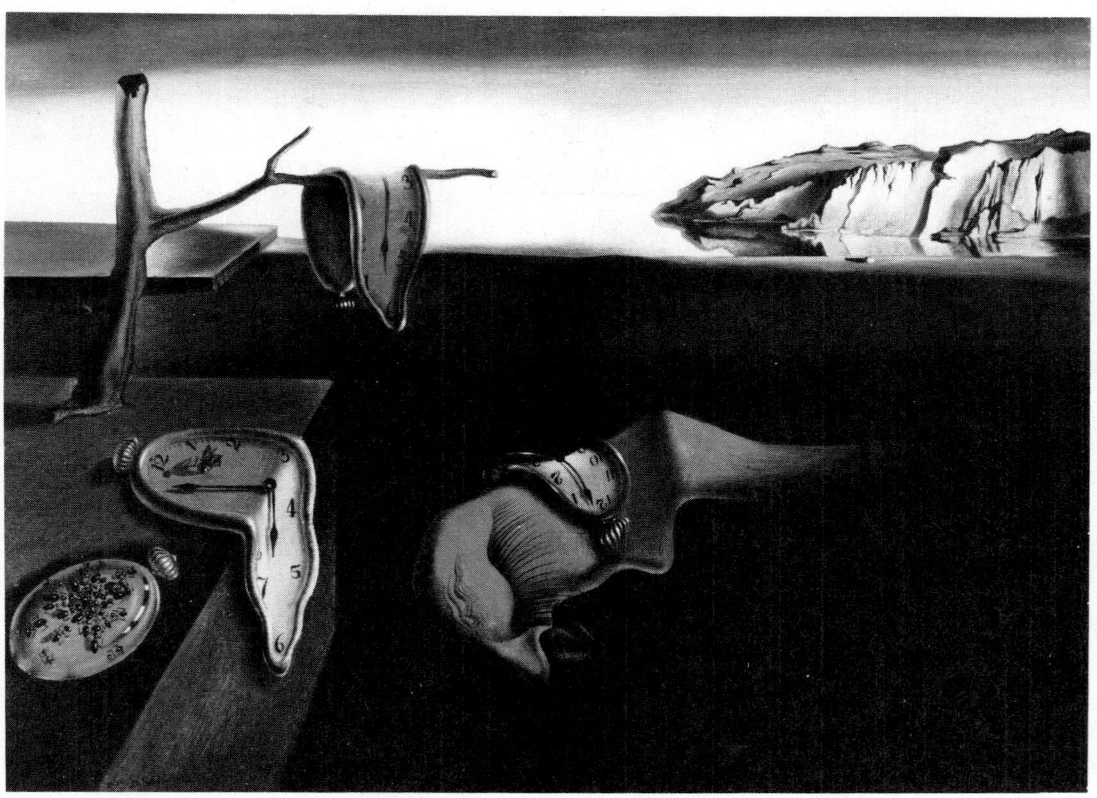

Salvador Dali,* The Persistence of Memory, *1931. *In this Surrealist lesson in the unreliability of the senses, the objects are real, but the whole landscape is madly unreal. Oil on canvas, $9^1/_2$" × 13". Collection. The Museum of Modern Art, New York. Given anonymously.*

artists decorated railroad cars to become rolling billboards for the Bolshevik cause: a modernization of the long Russian tradition of painting icons—religious images—to inspire the faith of the illiterate.

The association of modern art with Soviet communism ended with Lenin's death. Stalin rejected the forms of modern art as pretentiously middle class, demanding instead "socialist realism": portraits of smiling, heroic, muscle-bulging tractor drivers, for example. By the 1930s, as modern-minded artists such as Marc Chagall fled Stalinist censorship, official Soviet art sank into mediocrity. For the Russian school of modern art, revolutionary hope ended in cruel disappointment.

In most of the rest of Europe, where there was no revolution to inspire the postwar artistic generation, the most important school during the 1920s was the Surrealists. They took their inspiration not from politics but from their radical break with the Western tradition of perceiving reality. They saw the destructiveness of World War I as disastrous proof of the Western error of detaching human beings, as supposedly independent observers, from their own natural surroundings. Westerners' tendency to attribute reality to only certain objects

Pablo Picasso,* Guernica *(1937, May–early June). *The Cubist images, in black, white, and gray, of this famous twentieth-century painting, portray modern warfare's shattering of civilian lives. Oil on canvas. © SPADEM, Paris/VAGA, New York, 1982. Giraudon/Art Resource, N.Y.*

of their imperfect sense perceptions was leading them to eventual annihilation. The French poet André Breton, spiritual leader of Surrealism, remarked after 1945, "The atomic bomb had its origin in Descartes' brain." He meant that Western civilization had been on the wrong track ever since the seventeenth-century philosopher had declared that human existence was defined by the capacity for rational thought—a capacity that enabled people in the twentieth century to design a weapon of total destruction.

Challenging the stubborn Western insistence that things must be what perception says they are, the Surrealists sought artistic truth as far from reason as possible. They found it in the unconscious, as it emerged from the perceptions of children and madmen, from the "primitive" art of non-Western peoples, and from dreams. The young, the mad, the savage, and the dreamer were more in touch with the real world, Surrealists believed, because their thought remained unfocused, unlike the specialist thinking of Westerners. The goal of art was to free the mind from reason's constraints, enabling it to break through to the surreal—the "more than real"—these nonreasoners could perceive. Surrealist painting extended the forms of World War I Dadaism, which had tried to shock people into rethinking their assumptions by offering the familiar in a jarringly unfamiliar way. Salvador Dali's limp watches outrage our sense of reality but remind us that in the Einsteinian universe time is relative to the observer and can be told as well by a melting watch as by a normal one. The message of modern art, like the message of twentieth-century physics and psychology, was that things are not as they appear to the eye but as they appear to the mind.

The principal idea of the dominant twentieth-century school of architecture was that if decoration were stripped away, buildings could reveal their underlying essence, appearing to the eye what they were to the mind. Form should reflect function: a railroad terminal should look like just that, not like a Roman bath. Improvements in building materials and methods in the late nineteenth century prepared the way for this architectural revolution. A steel framework, rather than the walls, now could carry the load of a structure. The structure itself could be built of lighter materials like reinforced concrete and glass. The Bauhaus architects (who took their name from the famous school of design that flourished briefly in Weimar Germany) used these materials to build the severely unornamented buildings they felt realism required. The most famous example is New York's Seagram Building, built in the 1950s according to a design by Ludwig Mies van der Rohe. By then, Bauhaus architecture had become the so-called international style, spreading its undecorated glass boxes around the world.

By the 1950s, this avant-garde style had become standard. What had once been revolutionary became ordinary. The same fate befell modern art. Its institutionalization began as early as 1929, with the establishment in New York of the Museum of Modern Art. Collection in a museum was a sign of acceptance for modern styles like Cubism and Abstract Expressionism. A late Cubist painting like Picasso's *Guernica* (1937), his protest against the Nazi bombing of a Spanish republican town and by extension against all inhumanity, quickly became an anti-fascist symbol recognized far beyond the circle of artistic connoisseurs.

Acceptance did not come without a struggle. For many people, modern art expressed everything that was new and disturbing about the twentieth century: the crumbling of a comprehensible universe, the exposure of once unmentionable human drives, the suggestion that "primitive" cultures had something to teach the West, the growth of uncertainty about everything. Stalin was not the only dictator to reject it. In 1937 Hitler ordered the staging of two contrasting exhibitions, one of "degenerate" modern art, the other of "German" art depicting the blond and muscular "Master Race" at work and play. His goal was to demonstrate how politically motivated art could restore the certainty undermined by modernism and its questions.

The Emergence of "Mass" Culture

Hitler had at least one thing in common with many modern artists: a belief that art's function was to instruct and inspire as many people as possible. In the 1920s and 1930s, however, it became clear that a great many people, "the masses," were not much interested in art-gallery art of any kind. To the dismay of many intellectuals, a new kind of popular culture was emerging. It was very different from either the high culture of the nineteenth-century middle-class elite or traditional folk cultures.

Sociological and technological change fostered this new popular culture in the twentieth century. As improved transportation and universal schooling broke down rural isolation and people migrated from the countryside to the cities, the old peasant folk cultures—the regional costumes, dances, dialects, and legends—began to disappear even before the end of the nineteenth century. Increasingly they were replaced by a commercial, standardized culture. By the late 1930s, most households in Western Europe and in the United States had radios, for example. The movies had become an international industry. The products of these mass media—radio soap operas and quiz shows, movie serials and Westerns—helped to fill the urban masses' new leisure time, made possible by shortened workweeks. To intellectual critics, such entertainment amounted to little more than escapism, empty diversions from reality. Moreover, they were increasingly the same the world over. Jazz, for example, once the special music of New Orleans, spread in the 1920s over the airwaves of the world.

Many critics were profoundly disappointed by people's uncritical enthusiasm for the trite and trivial. A basic assumption behind the nineteenth-century drive for a democratic political system was that a majority would decide intelligently when offered a choice. After World War I, the revelation of the level of popular taste reinforced many intellectuals' doubts about the practicability of the democratic ideal in a mass society.

Even before 1914 the conservative Italian political philosophers Vilfredo Pareto and Robert Michels had argued that every government or political movement, even a democracy, really expresses the power of an elite, which legitimizes its rule with slogans calculated to win mass support. Max Weber, the leading German figure in the new twentieth-century science of sociology, suggested that in modern Western societies the growth of democratic participation was a less significant trend than the expansion of bureaucracies' power to control whole populations by subjecting them to standardized rules. He also warned that as other forms of government broke down, the masses would follow with religious zeal leaders who had the magical attribute of *charisma*—a prediction soon borne out when Mussolini and Hitler came to power.

It was a Spanish philosopher, José Ortega y Gasset, who offered the most sweeping indictment of mass society. His *Revolt of the Masses* (1930) predicted that Western societies would be overwhelmed by masses too numerous to educate in the art of critical thinking essential to freedom. Swamping the cultured minority, they would impose their low standards on everything from art to politics, ultimately destroying the fragile foundations of a civilization whose material benefits they took for granted. "The world is a civilized one," he wrote; "its inhabitant is not":

> . . . he does not see the civilization of the world around him, but he uses it as if it were a natural force. The new man wants his motor-car, and enjoys it, but he believes it is the spontaneous fruit of an Edenic tree. In the depths of his soul he is unaware of the artificial, almost incredible character of civilization, and does not extend his enthusiasm for the instruments to the principles which make them possible.[8]

We may dismiss criticisms such as this as the laments of an educated minority that had lost its political dominance. Nevertheless, they reflected still another twentieth-century uncertainty. Just as Newtonian physics, rationalist psychology, and the assumption of Western cultural superiority had been undermined, late-nineteenth-century faith in the future of liberal democracy was profoundly shaken.

Conclusion: The Quest for Something to Believe in

An Age of Uncertainty

Developments in physics, psychology, social science, and art together amounted to a cultural revolution. In fact, the twentieth century produced or reinforced breaks with the past in almost every field. The twelve-tone compositions of Arnold Schönberg, for example, designed to appeal to the mind more than to the ear, marked a radical departure from classical music's harmony and melody. In philosophy, the publication in 1921 of Ludwig Wittgenstein's *Tractatus Logico-Philosophicus* was a fundamental turning point. Wittgenstein contemptuously dismissed centuries of philo-

René Magritte, Belgium,* La Trahison des Images *(1928–1929). *The painting stresses the surrealist theme that images are treacherous clues to reality. "This," says the inscription in French, "is not a pipe." Instead, it is an image of something that people agree to* call *a pipe. H: 23⅝" (60 cm.) W: 37" (81.3 cm.). Oil on Canvas. The Los Angeles County Museum of Art. Purchased with funds provided by the Mr. and Mrs. William Preston Harrison Collection*

sophical speculation about ethics and the causes of things as mere superstition. Henceforth, he declared, philosophy should consider only propositions that could be expressed mathematically.

From these multiple breaks with the past emerged the Western intellectual and cultural world we know today. One of its most noteworthy features is its unintelligibility as a whole. In the nineteenth century, it was still possible for an individual to grasp the basic principles of most categories of human knowledge. In the twentieth century, knowledge has become increasingly fragmented. No one thinker any longer claims to provide an interpretation of the whole of experience. Scientists, psychologists, authors, artists, and philosophers all specialize in providing particular sorts of difficult abstractions from reality, ranging from the language of astrophysics to that of molecular biology. Less and less are the discoveries of each set of specialists understandable to others, let alone to the vast majority of nonspecialists.

To the extent that ordinary people associated scientific discoveries with the advent of bountiful new technologies, they welcomed them. Mass media made Einstein and Freud popular celebrities. But like the masters of modern literature and art, these scientists also encountered a great deal of hostility, for the uncertainties they revealed tended to undermine some valued human convictions. Though Einstein was deeply religious in his own way, it was difficult to see his infinite, only "relatively" comprehensible universe as the work of a Creator. Freud's model of unconscious motivations threatened the foundations of traditional morality, which assumed that people could readily distinguish right from wrong. Anthropologists' comparisons of non-Western and Western societies, not always to Western advantage, implied to many people an insulting disregard of Western civilization's achievements. The incomprehensible quality of much modern literature and art offended people accustomed to more conventional images, reminding them again that everything once apparently solid and unassailable had become fluid and problematical. Instead of providing reassurance, novels and paintings strained the understanding in an effort to prove that all human judgments were subjective and all human statements about reality merely relative.

The twentieth century's vision at its bleakest was embodied in Franz Kafka's famous novel *The Trial* (1925). Its hero is matter-of-factly tried and executed, amid the bustle of a great city, for some crime of which he knows nothing and which is never explained to him by his bland judges. The novel is a powerful metaphorical statement of the human predicament as it appeared to many twentieth-century thinkers. The individual seemed a lonely, uncomprehending speck in a universe where nothing was as it appeared and nothing meaningful could be said. For many thoughtful Europeans in the 1930s, this anguish of uncertainty was heightened by consciousness that European global dominance was waning and another war was approaching.

Recent Intellectual Trends

Though science and technology have advanced more rapidly in the decades since World War II than at any other time in human history, it is still early to assess which advances of this period will prove of greatest significance. None of these advances, however, has yielded any system of thought—an ideology, a faith, a sense of certainty—to replace the confidence and optimism of 1900. In the postcolonial era, moreover, the unease provoked by uncertainty has become common to cultures around the world.

Chapter 13 will examine the impact of two of the Western world's most controversial technological triumphs, television and the computer. Among the sciences, today's physicists and astronomers continue Einstein's quest for a general theory of matter that will encompass and explain the phenomena of both the subatomic world and the universe as a whole. Meanwhile, as we have noted, psychology has increasingly turned from Freud's "functional" to a "molecular"—that is, biochemical—explanation of behavior. This change reflects the fact that the years before 1914 marked a scientific revolution in physics while the years since 1945 have witnessed a similar revolution in biochemistry.

The most significant breakthrough of this revolution came in 1953, when a British and an American biochemist together described the double-helix structure of deoxyribonucleic acid (DNA), the chemical component of living cells that transmits inherited characteristics from one generation to the next. So rapidly have researchers advanced from this breakthrough that by 1988 the U.S. Patent Office actually granted its first patent of a living creature: a mouse "designed" by genetic engineers manipulating the matter of life itself.

It is significant of the changes in the nature of scientific research that the names of those two pioneers of biochemistry of 1953, Francis Crick and James Watson, though they shared a Nobel Prize in 1960, are not nearly so widely known as those of Einstein and Freud. Science since World War II has become far less the work of solitary pioneers. Breakthroughs today are much more likely to be achieved by teams of researchers. So complex and costly is present-day scientific research, moreover, that whereas research teams may include members from all over the world, only the wealthiest nations can afford to maintain extensive laboratory facilities.

In art and literature, as in science, little remains today of the late nineteenth century's optimism. Perhaps this is because world history since 1939 has afforded relatively few grounds for optimism. World War II's concentration camps and nuclear weapons more than confirmed the human propensity for destructiveness revealed in World War I. As later chapters will indicate, postwar events have tended to reinforce trends that had already made this century the "age of anxiety"—for example, the growth of vast bureaucracies, ranging from governments to universities, that dwarf the individual, and the mounting sense that reality is too complex for any individual to grasp.

It is too soon to know which recent artistic and literary achievements will ultimately prove most memorable. The earlier confidence of artists—that they could teach us to find reality by looking behind appearances—has come to seem overly optimistic, even naive. Before a public saturated with images from the mass media and largely indifferent to fine art, today's artists seem unsure what they have to communicate and to whom. Once a popular medium capable of producing a broad cultural impact, painting seems to have become a commodity for collectors to buy and sell. The modern movement that began with Picasso's *Les Demoiselles d'Avignon* has run its course, without any particular wave of comparable impact rising in its wake. Instead, divergent trends have proliferated, from the abstractions dripped from Jackson Pollock's brush to the playful treatments of familiar faces and everyday objects derived by Andy Warhol from the media imagery that surrounds us.

Perhaps because of the manifold uncertainties of the age, the most influential authors since World War II have often been those who set their characters adrift in a Kafka-esque world of total absurdity. The title of Joseph Heller's novel *Catch-22* (1961), widely read on college campuses, has become a common term for a situation in which nothing makes sense. In fact, the Western world's most influential philosophical school since World War II took as its starting point the idea that we live in an absurd world. All we can truly be sure of, said Existentialist philosophers such as Jean-Paul Sartre, is that we exist. There is no God, no prescribed moral law, no reliable human reason to tell us, in this "silent" world, *how* we are to exist. We are all in the same situation as the hero of Albert Camus's 1947 novel *The Plague,* a doctor living in a city suddenly struck by an inexplicable and incurable pestilence. The best the individual can do, alone in a world where incomprehensible evil lurks, is to accept that loneliness allows one to choose to live *as if* what he or she does really matters. Camus's doctor freely chooses to remain in the stricken city to help its victims, knowing full well that what he does will in no way alter the course of the disease or prevent it from recurring.

Thus the consolation the Existentialists held out for a world of absurdity was that it left the individual free to choose what to make of his or her life. This was cold comfort indeed, the most extreme statement of the Western human-centered view of the world that reached a climax in the twentieth century. It is not surprising that many people today have found it unacceptable and have turned elsewhere for an interpretation of reality that would somehow reconnect human beings to an intelligible world and a hopeful destiny.

As the twentieth century draws to a close, this search for reintegration and meaning is becoming one of its most pervasive themes. Evangelical Christianity, now the fastest-growing religious movement in the United States and Europe, responds to this search through its emphasis on personal salvation and religious experience. The upsurge of evangelicalism, however, is only one example of a global phenomenon. In the Soviet Union, for example, the 1988 millennium of Russian Christianity provided the occasion for relaxation of governmental restrictions on the Orthodox church and for widespread outpouring of religious feeling. In Latin America, Roman Catholic activists have rebelled against the church's historic identification with privilege by formulating a liberation theology intended to transform the lives of the poor. In Islamic lands from West Africa to the Philippines, religious activists have renewed their appeals, sometimes backed by violence, for reassertion of strict Islamic norms in all phases of life. As Islamic radicalism illustrates, religious reassertion can express a Third World society's yearning to reject the alien ideologies and world views that imperialism left behind and so begin to reorder all thought and action according to the society's own belief system.

One of the great ironies of twentieth-century history is that such a sense of cultural integrity has been lost, not only to history's victims in the poor countries, but even to its beneficiaries in affluent lands. If Latin America's liberation theologists, or the Islamic world's religious radicals, can reach their goals of cultural reintegration, they will have attained a sense of coherence and meaning that the twentieth-century West has not yet been able to regain. If they fail to attain those goals, the "age of anxiety" will prove to have been not a Western but a global phenomenon.

Notes

1. Nigel Calder, *Einstein's Universe* (New York: Penguin Books, 1979), p. 12.
2. Raymond V. Sontag, *A Broken World* (New York: Harper & Row, 1971), p. 181.
3. Dr. Candace Pert of the National Institutes of Health, quoted in the *Baltimore Evening Sun*, July 23, 1984.
4. Bronislaw Malinowski, *Argonauts of the Western Pacific* (New York: Dutton, 1922), p. 25.
5. Malinowski, *Argonauts*, p. 518.
6. Quoted in Robert Hughes, *The Shock of the New: Art and the Century of Change* (New York: Knopf, 1981), on which this section is largely drawn, p. 125.
7. Hughes, *Shock of the New*, p. 15.
8. José Ortega y Gasset, *The Revolt of the Masses* (New York: Norton, 1957), p. 82.

Suggestions for Further Reading

Bronowski, Jacob. *The Ascent of Man* (1974).

Calder, Nigel. *Einstein's Universe* (1979).

Ellenberger, Henri F. *The Discovery of the Unconscious* (1981).

Graham, Loren R. *Between Science and Values* (1981).

Hall, Calvin S. *A Primer of Freudian Psychology*. New ed. (1983).

Hoffman, Banesh. *Albert Einstein: Creator and Rebel* (1972).

Hughes, H. Stuart. *Consciousness and Society: The Reorientation of European Social Thought, 1890–1930* (1958).

———, and James Wilkerson. *Contemporary Europe: A History*. 6th ed. (1987).

Hughes, Robert. *The Shock of the New: Art and the Century of Change* (1981).

Jones, Ernest. *The Life and Work of Sigmund Freud.* 3 vols. (1953–1957).

Kafka, Franz. *The Trial.* Rev. ed. 1937 (reprint, 1988).

Kuhn, Thomas S. *Structure of Scientific Revolutions.* 2d ed. (1970).

Kuper, Adam. *Anthropology and Anthropologists: The Modern British School.* Rev ed. (1983).

Malinowski, Bronislaw. *Argonauts of the Western Pacific* (1922).

Ortega y Gasset, José. T*he Revolt of the Masses* (1930).

Paxton, Robert O. *Europe in the Twentieth Century.* 2d ed. (1985).

Sontag, Raymond V. *A Broken World* (1971).

Watson, Robert I. *The Great Psychologists.* 4th ed. (1978)

PART 3

Latin America, Africa, and Asia: The Struggle Against Colonialism

CHAPTER 8

Latin America's Struggle for Development

Some readers may wonder why a chapter on Latin America appears in the same part of this book as chapters on Africa and Asia. Whereas settler colonies were the exception in Asia and Africa, the Latin American countries began as European colonies of settlement. In this way, Portuguese became the national language of Brazil, and Spanish became the national language almost everywhere else, though native American languages are still spoken in many parts of the continent. Most Latin American nations have been politically independent since the early nineteenth century, whereas in Asia and Africa, only a handful of countries were independent in 1914. Yet in the Latin America of 1914, as in the few Asian and African countries that were formally independent then, the impact of imperialism was so great as to make independence virtually a sham. The struggle to change this situation had begun, but progress before World War II was slight.

This chapter begins with an overview of how Latin America was integrated into the global configuration of 1914. In this context we shall speak of a Western-dominated, not European-dominated, global pattern, for the United States was the dominant outside power in this region. The chapter then illustrates the themes of the continental overview more concretely by examining the development of three of the most important Latin American nations—Argentina, Brazil, and Mexico—through World War II.

Continental Overview: The Illusion of Independence

Whatever their differences, the Latin American countries have much in common. They share many social, economic, and political traits, and they show common patterns in their relations with the outside world.

Latin American Societies

To a large extent, the Latin American nations' similarities and problems stem from the way their populations developed. Compared to English-speaking North America, what stands out historically is the much greater number of native Americans and blacks compared to people of European origin. When the Spanish reached the mainland following Columbus's voyages of 1492–1504, some 60 million native Americans inhabited the region, mostly in present-day Mexico, Guatemala, and Peru. By the nineteenth century, probably over 10 million Africans had been imported as slaves. In contrast, fewer than 1 million Europeans immigrated to Latin America in the colonial era.

Spread by the sudden mixing of peoples, disease became a major factor in shaping Latin America's population. Perhaps 90 percent of the native Americans died from the newly introduced diseases of smallpox and measles in the sixteenth century. Malaria and yellow fever afflicted nonnatives, too. By 1800, South America's population may have fallen as low as 20 million.

Another factor shaping Latin American peoples was the mixing of races. In some countries, most people—in Brazil virtually all—are of mixed ancestry. Over time, the human blend changed. The importation of Africans ended with slavery. European immigration increased thereafter, confirming Argentina's comparatively European aspect, in particular. Still, the racial mix of colonial times prevailed over most of the continent.

Latin American societies did not become integrated, however. Spanish and Portuguese settlers had a capitalist outlook, but one wedded to ideas of class and privilege developed in Europe in earlier centuries. They did not come to work the land with their hands. They came as conquerors who would exploit the resources of the New World by commanding the labor of others. Rather than pushing aside native Americans, as North American settlers did, Spaniards and Portuguese settled where they could exploit the indigenous peoples in greatest numbers. Alternatively, they brought in African slaves. The Spanish and Portuguese crowns supported settlers' aspirations by issuing land grants, thereby laying the foundation for the huge estates that continue to exist. The melding of races began with sexual exploitation of the conquered.

Meanwhile, the conquerors elaborated their ideas about social relations into a virtual caste system. At the top stood Europeans, followed by mixed-bloods of all types. Last came black slaves and native Americans. At independence, Latin American countries proclaimed legal equality, and some nonwhites rose into the elites. But discrimination persisted, and those who were, or could pass for, white still dominated the rest.

Latin American Economies

Because Latin American economies remained primarily agricultural, the most important expression of white dominance lay in the great estates—known as *fazendas* in Brazil, *estancias* in Argentina, and *haciendas* in other Spanish-speaking countries. Some estates were unimaginably vast. The Díaz d'Avila fazenda in colonial Brazil was bigger than some European kingdoms. Around 1900, the Terrazas-Creel clan of the state of Chihuahua, Mexico, owned fifty estates having 7 million acres. By 1914, urban middle and working classes were forming and assuming important roles. But Latin American society still consisted mostly of small landowning elites and huge peasant masses.

The gulf between the elite and the masses was wide in every respect. Members of the elite were well dressed, well fed, relatively well educated, European in culture as well as origin, and keen to preserve a way of life that assured them power, wealth, and leisure. The poor were ill fed, ill clad, largely illiterate, and attuned to folk cultures in which native American and African elements and older communal ways played a major role. Among elite and mass alike, women were repressed by factors ranging from the elites' refined etiquette to the crude cult of male dominance (*machismo*) in all classes.

The rural population was generally poor and subordinated to the owners of the great estates. Most rural folk were either small subsistence farmers or free peasants who lived in independent villages but worked part-time for hacienda owners to make ends meet. In Brazil and Cuba, many of the rural poor were slaves until slavery was abolished in the late 1800s. In the highlands of Spanish America, many people were debt peons working full-time on the haciendas. The difference between slave and peon was often slight, thanks to the debt servitude promoted through the hacienda store. Many hacienda owners paid their peons with scrip or tokens usable only at the store, which charged inflated prices to force the peasants into permanent indebtedness. By law, peasants could not leave the hacienda as long as they owed money. They responded with passivity and occasional rebellion, a combination that led the elites to regard them with a mixture of paternalism and fear. No wonder hacienda agriculture was inefficient. Critics have labeled the hacienda world one of "internal colonization."

In Latin America's economic history internal colonization went with external dependency. Europeans first came to South and Central America seeking new routes to Asia. They stayed to exploit the mineral, agricultural, and human resources of the New World "Indies." Following the then-widespread economic philosophy of mercantilism, Spain and Portugal each set out to monopolize its colonial trade so as to assure the mother country a positive trade balance. The trade restrictions never fully succeeded, but they implanted on Latin American economies a pattern they have never completely shaken off: supplying raw materials to more powerful economies abroad and importing finished goods.

Latin American elites profited from this arrangement and have done much to perpetuate it. One legacy of economic colonialism was that imitation of highly developed economies occurred more in consumption than in production. Consuming European products was easier than mastering advanced production techniques. Such behavior increased demand for imports and deepened dependency but did not jeopardize the elites' positions as middlemen.

In the long run, Spain and Portugal were too weak to remain the dominant outside powers in the region. When Latin American countries won independence in the early nineteenth century, they opened their ports to world trade—that is, to a flood of British industrial goods. The British had aided Latin American independence movements with this end in view. Great Britain was then the greatest naval and commercial power and the only industrial power.

Free trade set in motion a sequence of events that became familiar around the colonial world: the ruin of local merchants and manufacturers (in the old sense of production by hand), a drain of precious metals toward the countries from which industrial imports came, accumulation of foreign debts by the local governments, and eventual bankruptcy or near-bankruptcy, with the risk of intervention by foreign governments to protect their citizens' investments. Such events did not fail to provoke conflict over economic policy, but supporters of free trade won in the long run. Major steps toward industrialization occurred in Latin America in the late nineteenth century, but they were often the work of foreign capital and tied the local economies more tightly into

Slaves raking coffee beans, Brazil, 1880. *Brazil was the last country in the Western Hemisphere to abolish slavery (1888). From H. L. Hoffenberg,* Nineteenth-Century South America in Photographs. *Reproduced by permission*

the global economy. The railroad networks, for example, developed in typical colonial style. They were designed to drain products of the interior toward the ports, rather than to link regions and countries to serve Latin American needs.

Over time, Latin America's focus of dependency shifted toward the United States. In 1823, President James Monroe had announced the policy that became famous as the Monroe Doctrine: the United States would regard any European attempt at colonization of the independent Americas as a threat to its own peace and safety. At that time, the United States lacked the strength or the interest to protect Latin America. The dominant outside influence remained that of Great Britain, which sought economic domination rather than outright colonization. In the early twentieth century, however, U.S. interest and investment began to outstrip the British, especially in the Caribbean. The Panama Canal (completed in 1914) symbolizes this growth. The United States was prepared to use military force to protect such investments, as it did in Cuba during the Spanish-American War (1898).

By 1914 it was clear that the Latin American states' independence was limited, whether politically or economically. The powerful industrial nations had indeed established colonial economic relations the world over. The fact that a country could achieve political independence but remain economically dependent was simply a variation, often called *neocolonialism,* on the theme.

Economic dependency has many disadvantages for countries that suffer from it. In Brazil, for example, a long series of export products—dyewood, sugar, gold, diamonds, tobacco, cotton, cacao, coffee, rubber—have succeeded one another as the major determinants of prosperity. There were several reasons for these changes. Mineral resources do not last forever, nor does demand for a given country's production of a crop. Cheaper sources may be found elsewhere. New processes or products, such as synthetics, may wipe out demand entirely. Even when such changes do not occur, the colonial economy remains at risk because it has little or no influence over the price of its exports, which is determined far away in international trade centers. During the Great Depression, for example, the value of Latin American exports fell about two-thirds between 1929 and 1932.

Because Latin America's ties to the outside world were economic far more than they were political, the 1929 Depression marked a clearer turning point in the region's history than either world war. Industrialization efforts had begun earlier and been stimulated by import shortages during World War I. After 1929, however, the virtual stoppage of international trade created an opening for a major push to escape economic colonialism. The larger Latin American countries intensified their efforts to industrialize, first through *import substitution* (local production of previously imported goods), then through *development* of heavy industry. High tariffs and other measures were used to protect the budding industries from competition. These policies produced unexpected consequences, and the relation between agricultural and industrial development was not well thought out, as we shall see. But a new era in Latin America's economic history had begun.

Politics and International Relations

Nineteenth-century revolutions freed most of Latin America from European rule, but the new states did not fit local reality. By 1914 the independent Latin American countries were officially all republics (Map 8.1). But political reality was determined not so much by fashionable ideas like republicanism and liberalism as by Iberian traditions of absolutism and Catholicism and by local conditions. The absolutist heritage made it seem natural for presidents to dominate the legislative and judicial branches and interfere in local government in ways unheard of in the United States. Catholic social thought supported executive dominance in the sense of favoring strong states as a means of asserting moral values and harmonizing social relations.

Translated into Latin America's poorly integrated societies, the result of these ideas fell short of the ideal. Power generally belonged to elite factions and military strongmen (*caudillos*), usually representing regional more than national interests. The caudillos rigged elections. They told legislators what laws to pass and judges what decisions to render. They kept administration inefficient and corrupt. Their military forces did little but interfere in politics. To preserve the elites' wealth, the caudillos

Map 8.1 Latin America, 1910 

UNITED STATES
ATLANTIC OCEAN
PACIFIC OCEAN
MEXICO
Mexico City
Veracruz
Havana
CUBA
DOMINICAN REP.
PUERTO RICO
JAMAICA
HAITI
BR. HONDURAS
CARIBBEAN SEA
Guatemala
GUATEMALA
HONDURAS
NICARAGUA
COSTA RICA
PANAMA
Caracas
VENEZUELA
BR. GUIANA
DUTCH GUIANA
FR. GUIANA
Bogota
COLOMBIA
Quito
ECUADOR
Amazon
PERU
Lima
BRAZIL
Bahia
La Paz
BOLIVIA
MINAS GERAIS
SÃO PAULO
São Paulo
RIO DE JANEIRO
Rio de Janeiro
PARAGUAY
Parana
RIO GRANDE DO SUL
Valparaiso
Santiago
CHILE
URUGUAY
Buenos Aires
Montevideo
ARGENTINA
Bahia Blanca
PATAGONIA
FALKLAND/MALVINAS ISLANDS
Independent nations
0
1000 Km.
0
1000 Mi.

kept direct taxes very low. Well into this century, import and export duties provided half of the revenues of many governments. With such narrow resource bases, governments could do little for the masses.

In time, new leaders won power by attempting broader political mobilization. The decades preceding the Depression of 1929 produced a wave of nineteenth-century-style liberal leaders such as revolutionary Mexico's elite politicians (see Chapter 4), who demanded political rights and freer elections but not fundamental social change. In Latin America as elsewhere, the Depression exposed these liberals' incapacity to cope with economic crisis. Power then began to pass to a new type of authoritarian mass mobilizer, such as Lázaro Cárdenas in Mexico, Getúlio Vargas in Brazil, and Juan Perón in Argentina, all of whom applied corporatist policies.

Under *corporatism* (as noted in Chapter 6), the state organizes or "incorporates" interest groups defined by occupation—combining owners and workers without regard to class differences—and bases representation on these occupational groups, rather than on constituencies defined in terms of geography or population. Sometimes confused with fascism, corporatism differs in being authoritarian but not totalitarian. In theory, corporatism allows the occupational groups their own spheres of action; it also stops short of the ideological elaboration and militarism of fascism. Rooted in precapitalist social structure and traditional Catholic social thought, corporatism aims to use the state to protect individuals from excessive competition and to harmonize, not deny, different class interests. Corporatism thus contrasts with liberal individualism, Marxist collectivism, and fascist totalitarianism. Fascism perverted the benevolent intentions of corporatism—not that Latin American corporatists have always done much better. Yet through World War II, corporatism provided a way to mobilize, from the top, workers and peasants who had previously had little political voice. By combining corporatism and *populism* (commitment to the common people), Cárdenas, Vargas, and Perón became their respective countries' most popular leaders and still remain so.

These developments strengthened the Latin American states' power domestically, but international politics still reflected their historical dependency. Their most important economic relations were always with countries outside the region. Partly to compensate for their poorly developed relations with one another, Latin American states joined in international agreements and organizations, such as the Pan American Union (1889)—although U.S. sponsorship made it an object of suspicion—and later the League of Nations.

Latin America's biggest international problem was U.S. aggressiveness. Size and distance helped protect countries like Argentina and Brazil from this danger, but Caribbean countries, especially the smallest of them, lay fully exposed to it. For example, while Woodrow Wilson argued for national self-determination at the Paris Peace Conference, five Caribbean nations—Cuba, the Dominican Republic, Haiti, Nicaragua, and Panama—were under U.S. rule, a policy that Washington deemed vital to protect U.S. interests. Later, under the Good Neighbor Policy (1933), the United States backed away from interventionism. But the corollary of this policy was reliance on pro-U.S. regimes, often brutal dictatorships such as Nicaragua's Somoza regime (1936–1979).

The Latin American states eventually entered World War II on the U.S. side, though they provided primarily bases, supplies, or intelligence, rather than combat troops. The war illustrated that U.S. interests were global in scope, rather than hemispheric like those of most Latin American states. Tensions have

Gauchos branding cattle on the Argentine pampas, 1880. *These cowboys' costumes and customs helped give Argentine culture a distinctive stamp. From H. L. Hoffenberg,* Nineteenth-Century South America in Photographs. *Reproduced with permission*

continued to arise from this disparity, as well as from further U.S. interventions, especially in Caribbean countries such as the Dominican Republic, Guatemala, Nicaragua, and El Salvador.

Context of the Struggle for Independence and Development

Lack of social integration, agrarian inequity, caudillo politics, corporatist-populist mass mobilization, external economic dependency—these common traits provide the background against which Latin American states evolved in the interwar years. As we look more closely at Argentina, Brazil, and Mexico, we shall see that they shared not only these traits but also developmental patterns reflecting the major themes of twentieth-century world history. All three nations experienced both major growth in demand for political participation and widespread mobilization from the slow-paced village world into the swifter currents of national life. Eventually, each country produced a charismatic leader responsive to these changes. The main economic theme, especially after 1929, was the attempt to break out of dependency through a strategy of industrialization aimed at import substitution followed by development of heavy industry. This development strategy proved as problematic as Latin American political life. Still, the progress made and the limits encountered, both political and economic, essentially defined the basis for Latin American development in the post–World War II era.

The Amazing Argentine

Argentina's economy and political system have historically developed in parallel stages. In the colonial period, economic interest centered on the Andean region, which supplied agricultural and manufactured products to the nearby silver-mining centers of what is now Bolivia. By the late eighteenth century, with the decline of the silver mines, the economic center began to shift to the pampas, grassy plains near the coast, lying inland and southward from Buenos Aires and containing some of the world's richest soil. The agricultural system that developed on the pampas spread to the windy plateaus of Patagonia in the south and to the northern lowlands, tying the country into a unit dominated by the port-capital, Buenos Aires.

The foundations for agricultural prosperity were created by accident in the sixteenth century, when Europeans introduced horses and cattle to the New World. Some animals escaped and flourished on the pampas. By the eighteenth century, people had begun to hunt these animals for their hides. The hunters began to form herds and stake claims to vast, inefficiently managed landholdings. Gradually, people learned to exploit Argentina's natural resources more intensively, always with political results. In the 1780s the introduction of meat-salting plants made it possible to export meat, as well as hides. This development increased the commerce of Buenos Aires, heightened resentments of Spanish commercial restrictions, and led to the proclamation of independence—at Buenos Aires in 1810, in the interior in 1816. Politically, independence brought regionalism and caudillo politics.

In the mid-nineteenth century, the rise of sheep raising and wool exports opened a new chapter. Since a given amount of grazing land could support four or five times as many sheep as cattle, sheep raising led to more intensive use of established grazing lands near Buenos Aires, and cattle raising shifted to new lands to the south and west. The growth of the sheep economy attracted European immigrants, and the extension of the frontier climaxed with a military campaign against the Araucanian people of Patagonia in 1879–1880.

This campaign, which added 100 million acres of new grazing land, coincided with the development of techniques for transoceanic shipment of frozen meat. These two events touched off a major boom in the 1880s. Over the next fifty years, "the amazing Argentine" became a leading export economy. But the exports were mostly agricultural, the trade was largely foreign controlled, and Argentina's profits were poorly distributed among the populace. Argentina experienced growth but not balanced development.

The boom of the 1880s made Buenos Aires one of the first New World super-metropolises. Henceforth the city dominated the nation politically and economically. By 1914, Buenos Aires had a population of 1 million, and the province of Buenos Aires contained 46 percent of Argentina's population. The rail network converged on the city, which was by far the most important port.

Radiating out from Buenos Aires, land-use patterns assumed a distinctive form. This emphasized livestock and grain production on huge estates with small numbers of laborers, often immigrants who lacked the rights of citizens. This pattern of development distinguished Argentina from other Latin American countries in an important way: Argentina never acquired a large peasant class, and land reform never became a key issue, as it often did elsewhere.

Politically, the period after 1880 was one of oligarchical domination by the National Autonomist party (later known as the Conservatives), whose corrupt politicians ruled in the interest of large landowners and foreign capitalists. In 1889–1890 as the boom collapsed, a protest movement emerged from the growing middle class, itself a byproduct of urbanization. With this movement, Argentina's twentieth-century political history began.

The Radical Period

By 1892, the protest movement had taken form as the Radical Civic Union and found a charismatic leader in Hipólito Yrigoyen. Not really radical, the party did not attack economic inequity. Yrigoyen and other Radicals were middle-class reformers with economic interests in the export sector. Both self-interest and nineteenth-century liberal ideas limited their grasp of socioeconomic issues. Yet their demands for honest elections and broader power sharing amounted to calls for further political mobilization. In 1912, seeing that genuinely leftist forces were forming, the Conservatives tried to steal the Radicals' thunder by granting their demands—votes for all adult males and the secret ballot.

The Radicals profited from these reforms by winning the election of 1916. Yrigoyen assumed the presidency, and the Radicals remained in power until 1930. Under the gaze of political opponents of the Right and Left, foreigners with economic interests in the country, and their own middle-class supporters, who were eager for power and patronage, the Radical leaders proved unprepared to solve the social and economic problems that emerged, especially in times of crisis, from the inequities of Argentina's export economy. For example, when the economic pressures of World War I led to strikes, Yrigoyen first supported the strikers but then yielded to Conservative and British pressure and used force against them. In 1930, the Great Depression again spotlighted the Radicals' inability to cope with economic crisis, and a military coup toppled them. The Radicals had tried to broaden political life. But their vision was not yet broad enough to meet the needs of most Argentines in times of hardship.

The Depression and the "Infamous Decade"

Just as economic changes had been associated with earlier political milestones in Argentina, the same correlation occurred in the 1930s. Until the Depression, its agriculture-based export economy had made "the amazing Argentine" Latin America's most dynamic economy. Thereafter, the emphasis was increasingly on industrialization. World War I had already stimulated industry by creating needs for import substitution and even opportunities to supply the Allies' wartime needs. The Depression made expanding domestic production still more important because the price of Argentina's exports fell faster than the prices of the goods it had been importing. The Conservative politicians who succeeded the Radicals in 1930 restricted imports to protect Argentine industry and fought to defend their share of the British market for agricultural goods. One development with future implications was that U.S. manufacturers reacted to discriminatory import restrictions by establishing plants in Argentina.

Such changes essentially ended the Depression for Argentina by 1936. World War II provided another economic stimulus. An inflationary export boom ensued, and the war left Argentina with $1.7 billion in foreign exchange reserves. Argentina was now an industrial, as well as an agricultural, country. Because industry was concentrated around Buenos Aires, industrialization further heightened the dominance of the country's one great city.

The period known as the Infamous Decade (1930–1943) marked a move away from democracy but ended with a further step toward authoritarian mass mobilization. The Depression ended the agrarian elite's control of government, fragmented the upper class politically, and allowed the state to assume greater autonomy and dominance over society. Politically, the period featured a Radical-Conservative coalition, with the military in the background. In a 1943 coup, however, generals took over the government, thus completing the trend toward a dominant state uncontrolled by any broad sector of society.

The army officers of this period were mostly middle class, keenly nationalistic, and eager for industrialization and technology, which they saw as the means to end neocolonialism. (As so often in the colonial world, their pro-German feeling was largely an expression of anti-British and anti-U.S. sentiment.) The officers wanted to industrialize; but they reacted to recent events in Spain and Italy, from which so many of Argentina's immigrant workers had come, with exaggerated fear of worker politicization. The military therefore tried to control labor by force. When this approach threatened to wreck industrialization, the military had the good fortune to produce from its ranks one of the most effective political mobilizers of Latin American history: Colonel Juan Perón (1895–1974), a man with ideas about the workers' social and economic needs.

The Rise of Perón

Perón took charge of the Department of Labor in 1943, upgrading it into the Ministry of Labor and Welfare. Taking a corporatist-populist approach to preventing working-class revolution, which many officers groundlessly feared, he encouraged workers to organize under state control and supported them in negotiations. Wages increased, expanding demand for goods and stimulating industrialization. Perón also created a system of pensions and health benefits. In return for these gains, the unions became part of a corporatist apparatus that Perón controlled. All the while, his power (and conservative resentment of it) grew.

Perón was an impressive figure, and his readiness during speeches to pull off the jacket that Argentine politicians had always worn and identify with the shirtless workers (*descamisados*) won him their loyalty. His opponents overthrew and jailed him in 1945 but, bewildered by the massive labor demonstrations that followed, released him. He then retired from his government and military posts, organized his followers as the Labor party, and campaigned for the presidency in 1946. In one of Argentina's most honest elections, Perón won with 56 percent of the popular vote.

The story of what followed belongs to the postwar era (see Chapter 15). Yet Perón's rise to power, and the charisma that surrounded both him and his politically active wife, Eva Duarte Perón, decisively advanced the trend, observable ever since the Radicals' heyday, toward broadened political participation. Events would show that this was still mass politics in the authoritarian mode.

Brazil from Empire to New State

Brazil has such great natural promise that it has been known for centuries as the "land of the future." Unfortunately, the struggle to fulfill this promise has encountered most of the difficulties found elsewhere in the continent, together with some distinctive problems.

Colonial Brazil presented the spectacle of a huge colony—now the world's fifth-largest nation in population—dependent on a tiny mother country, Portugal, which itself slipped into dependency on the most powerful economy of the day, Britain. During the Napoleonic wars, which shaped the European background for Latin American independence, the Portuguese government responded to its danger in a unique way: fleeing to its most important colony. Rio de Janeiro became the imperial capital from 1807 to 1821. This episode led to a political consolidation that enabled Brazil to weather the transition to independence, and later crises, without loss of unity or much political violence. Another consequence was that the Portuguese court, which fled to Brazil in British ships, opened Brazil to free trade and so to British economic domination.

When the king returned to Portugal in 1821, he left his son, Pedro, as regent in Brazil. Frictions soon developed between colony and mother country, and Pedro declared independence in 1822. In what amounted to a bloodless coup, he assumed the title emperor of Brazil.

For most of the nineteenth century, the emperor ruled in alliance with slave-owning coffee planters concentrated in the three adjoining states of Rio de Janeiro, Minas Gerais, and São Paulo. The alliance was so close that when Brazil abolished slavery in 1888 (the latest emancipation date in the Western Hemisphere), the emperor fell in a bloodless coup a year later. Emancipation had alienated the slave owners, who got no compensation for losing their "property." Other groups were already estranged from the regime of crown and coffee. Especially so was the urban populace, from which a commercial-professional middle class and an industrial proletariat would soon emerge.

The Old Republic

The period from 1889 to 1930 is known as the Old Republic. At first it resembled Argentina's Radical period, in that the urban elites replaced the coffee interests as the politically dominant group. By 1893, however, the new government's clumsy efforts to stimulate the economy and promote industrialization, coupled with shifts in coffee prices, had produced economic crisis and revolts. The government could cope with these only by striking a deal with the coffee planters of São Paulo, who controlled a well-trained militia: support against the rebels in return for the presidency at the next election. Thus in 1894 the political emergence of the urban middle class, which came only later in other Latin American countries, ended for the time being, and the coffee interests regained the ascendancy.

After 1894 the Old Republic turned regressive. With no political parties in existence, the two richest coffee states, São Paulo and Minas Gerais, made a deal to monopolize the presidency. Such a deal was possible in part because the electorate was small and geographically concentrated. Illiterates could not vote, so the electorate never exceeded 5 percent of the adult population before World War I. Since education and wealth went together, over half of the electorate lived in just four of twenty states: São Paulo, Minas Gerais, Rio de Janeiro, and Rio Grande do Sul.

Securely in power, the coffee interests abandoned the industrialization efforts of 1889–1894. Economic policy concentrated on the agrarian interests of the leading export-producing states. One of the government's chief concerns was coping with the oversupply that resulted from the spread of coffee production. In 1906 the government set up a system of valorization: large government coffee purchases to drive prices up. This helped Brazil's growers, although no measure taken by a single producing country could overcome the uncertainties of the global commodities markets. Another problem was lack of diversification in agricultural exports. Brazil's second most important export of this period—rubber, which rose from 10 percent of exports in 1890 to 39 percent in 1910—was not cultivated but collected from trees growing wild in Amazonian jungles. When the British began to cultivate rubber in Asia, they destroyed Brazil's position in the world market in a few years.

Between 1910 and 1930, the Old Republic's dominant political alignment fell apart. When the president unexpectedly died in office in 1909, Brazil's first hotly contested presidential race developed. Neither candidate was from one of the big states, and new demands for democratization were heard. After the election, the country faced revolts fed by resentment of oligarchical rule. World War I relieved tension by touching off an agricultural export boom and boosting industrial production. But the boom collapsed soon after the war.

Politicians from São Paulo and Minas Gerais continued to occupy the presidency by turns, but scattered events in the 1920s showed that discontent was spreading. In February 1922 a Modern Art Week was organized in São Paulo to celebrate the centennial of independence. Young artists used the occasion to express rebellion against European forms and determination to develop a Brazilian culture. Here, as later in Mexico, cultural nationalism had political significance, for it meant a growth of interest in the common people. The year 1922 also saw the formation of the Brazilian Communist party. Perhaps more important, army officers began to join the opposition. A handful of junior officers revolted at a fort on Copacabana Beach at Rio de Janeiro and fought to the death for their ill-defined cause. Their seemingly foolish heroics started a series of revolts that lasted until 1930, culminating in the overthrow of the regime. The ideas of the "lieutenants' movement" gradually became widely held demands for revolution, modernization, national integration, and expanded political participation. Soon even the Catholic church was taking an active concern in the plight of workers.

The Depression Destroys the Old Republic

When coffee prices were high, the government could contain such pressures, but a drop in prices threatened the status quo. When the Depression drove coffee from 22.5 cents a pound in 1929 to 8 cents in 1931, making valorization unworkable, things fell apart. The 1930 presidential election destroyed the Old Republic.

The trouble began when the outgoing president selected another man from his state, São Paulo, to run instead of allowing Minas Gerais its turn at the presidency. The Minas Gerais politicians then joined opposition groups all over the country in a Liberal Alliance, which selected Getúlio Vargas, from the southernmost state of Rio Grande do Sul, as its presidential candidate. As always, the incumbent president's candidate won. But when the congress refused to seat some Liberal Alliance deputies, and when Vargas's vice-presidential candidate was assassinated, the Liberal Alliance overthrew the government, bringing Vargas to power. He was to dominate Brazil from 1930 to 1945 and again from 1951 to 1954.

Vargas and the New State

Vargas's rise was a new victory for the urban elites and set the stage for important social and economic changes. Since he came to power backed by a diverse coalition and faced urgent needs to deal with the problems of the Depression, Vargas acted cautiously at first. He tried to raise coffee prices by limiting production. He promoted agricultural diversification—for example, into cotton. He encouraged industrialization to supply goods Brazil could no longer afford to import. His policies included increased import duties, tax exemptions for industry, low-interest loans, and government operation or ownership of certain enterprises. These efforts paid off in a doubling of industrial production between 1931 and 1936.

Gradually, too, Vargas laid the bases for a new political order. Maneuvering among the interests he had to consider, he won the support of important groups—business, labor, the military, some landowners, nationalists—and gave his regime a character of authoritarian populism. Political reforms began with an electoral code of 1932 that granted the secret ballot, lowered the voting age to eighteen, and enfranchised working women but not illiterates. Under the new constitution of 1934, which strengthened the presidency but set a limit of one four-year term, the Chamber of Deputies dutifully elected Vargas president. The constitution also asserted government responsibility for economic development, provided for gradual nationalization of minerals and energy resources, and granted benefits to workers under Labor Ministry control. There were still no national political parties, except the small Communist party and a fascist movement, the *Integralistas*. Repressing the Communists, Vargas moved to the right. Because he could not legally be a candidate in the scheduled 1938 presidential election, he prepared a coup.

Vargas announced over the radio on November 10, 1937, that he had canceled the elections, dissolved the legislature, and assumed dictatorial powers under a new constitution. So began the New State (*Estado Novo*), a corporatist restructuring with resemblances to European fascism. Vargas abolished political parties and violated many rights. He used fascistic language to expound his mass-mobilizing authoritarianism. Attacking democracy as decadent, he said, "The New State does not recognize the rights of the individual against the collective. Individuals do not have rights; they have duties. Rights belong to the collective."[1] But in 1938, Vargas used his troops to put down a challenge from Brazil's true fascists, the Integralistas (see Chapter 6). In fact, his regime had few opponents, for it represented the regimented approach to modernization called for by the lieutenants' movement.

Vargas's real priority was not fascism but Brazil's development. His economic policy made this clear. An economic nationalist, Vargas expanded trade with Germany and Italy primarily as an alternative to trading with the United States. The New State reaffirmed restrictions on foreign exploitation of natural resources and adopted policies of centralized economic planning and government initiative to develop major industries in energy, metallurgy, and chemicals. Brazil began its first five-year plan in 1940. By then, industry employed 944,000 workers, belonging to hundreds of state-controlled unions, and could satisfy domestic demand in many fields. At last, the economy no longer depended solely on agricultural and mineral exports.

Brazil's active support for the Allied side in World War II—another indication that Vargas was not a fascist—further accelerated industrial development. Wartime shortages made it possible to begin exporting manufactures, especially textiles. Because the Allies had little to sell back at the time, this export boom enabled Brazil to accumulate over $600 million in foreign exchange during the war. Brazil's industrial development also moved beyond import substitution into heavy industry, a fact symbolized by the accomplishment of one of Vargas's most cherished goals, the opening of the Volta Redonda steel mill in 1946.

Development did not benefit Brazil's 40 million citizens equally. Industrialization would surely have proceeded faster if Vargas had reformed the agricultural sector to increase the purchasing power of the impoverished rural masses. Yet Vargas, born into the landowning class, could not afford to antagonize it. Even to visit the interior of the country was an innovation, and he was the first Brazilian head of state ever to do so. Those who benefited most from Vargas's policies were in the cities, to which he shifted the center of power. Under Vargas, the growing urban populace became divided into a middle class of business and professional people and an industrial working class. Vargas's concern for workers' welfare is clear from the labor code of 1942, then one of the world's most advanced, though not systematically enforced.

Toward the end of World War II, Brazilians who had fought fascism in Europe while living under authoritarian rule at home began to demand change. Calls for an end to the New State prompted Vargas to readjust his policies and announce presidential and congressional elections. When it appeared that he might manipulate the elections and mount another coup, the military struck first and forced him to resign. In the election, one of the generals who had led the coup emerged as president, and a new constitution was drawn up. Vargas was elected senator from two states and congressman from a half-dozen others. There would be more to hear from him politically. But the part of his career most significant for Brazil's political and economic development was over.

Mexico and Its Revolutionary Legacy

The revolution of 1910 overshadowed Mexican history throughout the first half of the twentieth century. Chapter 4 has already raised the question of how Mexico's compares with other revolutions. We must reconsider some aspects of the crisis to understand its significance for Mexico through World War II.

Mexico's Revolutionary Experience

The main problem about Mexico's revolution was that it expressed in politics the Latin American societies' lack of integration. Like the Berkeley-educated Francisco Madero, who called for the republic to "rise in arms" in 1910, many of the revolutionary leaders came from the elite class. Their ideas, like those of the Argentine Radicals, seldom went beyond political liberalism. Any thought of social and economic change that would upset their interests, which were largely tied to the export sector, was enough to turn most of them into defenders of law and order. Leaders from other classes did identify with the masses, and their appeals roused passions that could not be ignored. Yet the only prominent leader with a consistent social program was the southern caudillo Emiliano Zapata, who was radical only by comparison with his northern colleagues. His call for partial redistribution of hacienda lands, with compensation to the owners, was not the stuff of which social revolution is made.

Although radical hopes were doomed to disappointment, the rising against the regime of Porfirio Díaz plunged Mexico into a decade of brutal violence. More than anything else, it is this impact on the populace, and the vast military and political mobilization that accompanied it, that justified Mexicans in remembering what they went through as an epic struggle. Within a few years, the army numbered a quarter-million, twelve times its size at the fall of Díaz. Vast forces also mobilized in different regions to fight against government troops. Those drawn into the struggle found their lives transformed, and not necessarily for the worse. Hacienda peons and mineworkers escaped into a life of adventure as revolutionary soldiers or, in the case of women, as camp-following *soldaderas,* many of whom also fought. By their testimony, these men and women found these experiences far preferable to their former lives.

At the top, the rebellion pursued a zigzag course as different leaders occupied the presidency. First came Madero, elected in 1911. As president, he predictably showed his faith in political democracy but never developed a program for social or economic reform; he also appointed many conservative relatives to high office. Madero was murdered in 1913 by one of his generals, Victoriano Huerta. Assuming the presidency himself, Huerta faced revolts by all the regional leaders. U.S. president Woodrow Wilson was determined to undermine him. In 1914, U.S. Marines occupied Veracruz. Huerta recognized that he could not regain control and resigned. A chaotic period followed, from which Venustiano Carranza emerged as president, partly because Woodrow Wilson gave U.S. recognition to him as the most conservative contender. Angry that he was not the one recognized, Pancho Villa led a raid into U.S. territory, provoking the punitive expedition sent into Mexico under General John Pershing in 1916–1917.

As these events unfolded, the revolution progressed through three phases, noted in Chapter 4. The initial mass mobilization to overthrow Díaz (1910–1914) extended into widespread conflict among revolutionary forces and the destruction of U.S. interests. The second phase (1914–1916)—that of class conflict, U.S. intervention, and worker defeat—included the U.S. occupation of Veracruz in 1914, which set up a vast flow of weapons to the Constitutionalist forces led by Carranza and ended with the urban workers' defeat by middle-class interests. The final phase of synthesis and reorganization included the adoption of the 1917 constitution, pacification of most of the countryside, and the coup that brought Álvaro Obregón to the presidency in 1920. With its concessions to workers and peasants in matters such as land reform and labor relations, the 1917 constitution provided a charter for reconstruction—at least on paper.

Reconstruction and Depression

Two presidents, Álvaro Obregón and Plutarco Calles, dominated the reconstruction period, which lasted until 1934. Taking only limited steps toward fulfilling the constitution, they distributed some 11 million acres of land in the 1920s, mostly as communal lands (*ejidos*) for native American villages. This was enough to worry hacienda owners but not to satisfy radicals. In education, there were significant efforts to develop rural primary schools to teach native Americans Spanish and draw them into national life. The new interest in rural Mexico also had a profound effect on the arts. Artists such as Diego Rivera (1886–1957) and David Alfaro Siqueiros (1896–1974) were commissioned to paint murals in public buildings. Inspired by indigenous cultures and meant for the people, their works also won international acclaim.

Calles in particular enacted important measures for business and industry. Road building, electrification, and the founding of the Bank of Mexico all assisted economic development. Government subsidies and high tariffs on imports also stimulated the growth of consumer-goods industries. But U.S. interests still found ways to flourish inside Mexico's tariff walls, as in 1925 when Ford opened an automobile assembly plant organized on terms highly favorable to the parent company. And frictions continued with U.S. oil companies, which feared that the constitutional restrictions on foreign control of natural resources might yet be applied to them.

In the later 1920s, just as Argentine Radicals and Brazilian coffee oligarchs seemed to

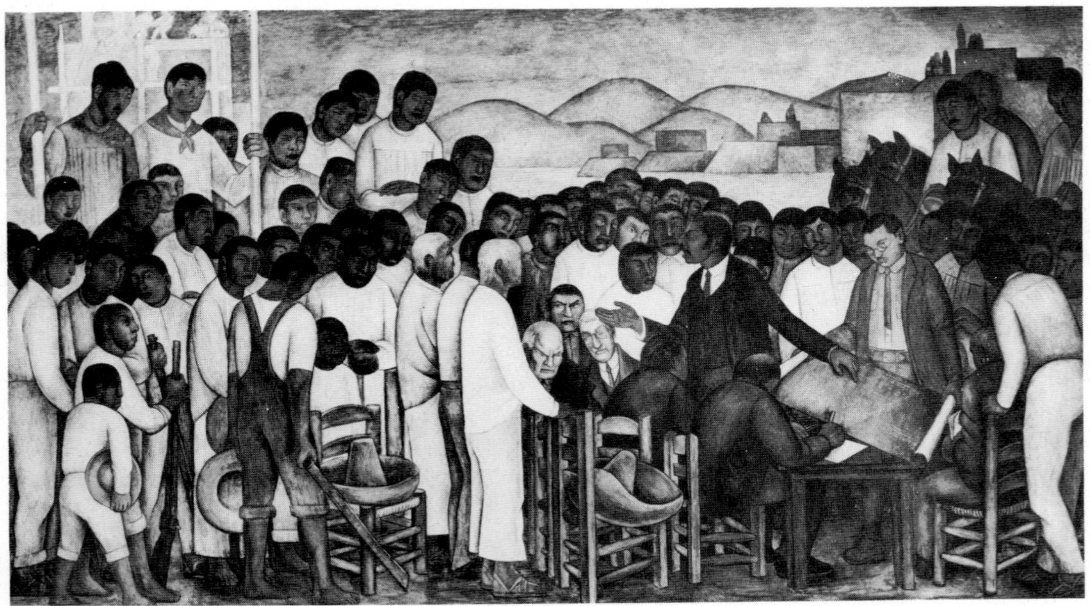

Diego Rivera, Distribution of the Land to the Peasants. *This Indian-inspired work illustrates one of the most important issues raised by Mexico's revolution. Instituto Nacional de Bellas Artes de Mexico/Art Resource*

run out of ideas, Mexico's reconstruction lost momentum. Aggravated during the revolution, church-state conflict gave rise to a unique church "strike"—all religious services were suspended throughout Mexico for three years—and a guerrilla war between militant Catholic *Cristeros* and government forces. Other problems emerged when the presidential election of 1928 degenerated into violence. Two candidates were executed for starting rebellions before the election, and the winner, Obregón, was assassinated by a Cristero before taking office.

Only Calles had enough influence to run the government but a constitutional amendment prevented any president from succeeding himself. He arranged for puppets to serve Obregón's term while he pulled the strings. Calles also organized the National Revolutionary party (PNR in Spanish), which, with changes of name, has dominated Mexican politics ever since. The creation from the top of a single mass party in support of the regime suggests the influence of corporatism, if not also European fascism. The virtual suspension of land reform and other social programs in the later Calles years also indicates a shift to the right, which the Depression confirmed. Fortunately for those who still believed in the revolution, a progressive wing was forming in the PNR.

Cárdenas and the Revolutionary Legacy

The PNR nominated Lázaro Cárdenas, former party chairman and progressive leader, for the presidency in 1934, and he was duly elected. Calles proved unable to control the new president. Democratic in style, Cárdenas made himself accessible to peasants and workers. When Calles made threats, Cárdenas deported him.

Cárdenas proved himself the most committed reformer so far. He distributed 49 million acres of land, roughly twice as much as all his predecessors. By 1940, about a third of the population had received land, much of it through the communal *ejidos*. The historical patterns of the hacienda system and peasant servitude had been broken. The government also provided other facilities—roads, credit, electrification, medical care. A six-year plan for economic development had gone into effect shortly before Cárdenas came to power. He added new credit facilities and further tariff protection to benefit industry, which under his regime grew even more than agriculture.

In 1938, Cárdenas scored his most dramatic foreign policy success. When controversy with U.S. oil companies flared after a strike by Mexican workers, Cárdenas went on the air to announce nationalization of the companies' holdings. This assertion of economic independence created a sensation all over Latin America. The oil companies were outraged; but because the administration of Franklin D. Roosevelt had decided on a policy of nonintervention in Latin America, they had to settle for monetary compensation.

A few days after the oil nationalization, Cárdenas moved to consolidate his domestic support by reorganizing the official party, with agrarian, labor, military, and "popular" (essentially middle-class) sectors. One reason for the continued dominance of Mexico's single party, known since 1945 as the Institutional Revolutionary party (PRI in Spanish), may be that Cárdenas's corporatist-populist approach to mass mobilization kept workers and peasants separate, in competing sectors.

The events of 1938 marked a high point for Cárdenas and his effort to fulfill the revolutionary ideal. Conservative fears over his policies prompted a flight of Mexican capital abroad and a scaling back of reform during his last two years in office. World War II opened a long period of rapid economic growth but confirmed the rightward political shift. Since Cárdenas, the "revolution," supposedly institutionalized in the PRI, has been increasingly a conservative force.

Conclusion: Charismatic Leaders and Their Policies Compared

By World War II, three of Latin America's most important countries had produced memorable charismatic leaders: Perón, Vargas, and Cárdenas. We can sum up the significance of the first half of this century for their countries by comparing these men and their policies.

Each came to power only after demands for wider political participation had already produced changes in his country. The Argentine Radicals' electoral victory in 1910, the urban elites' brief ascendancy in the early years (1889–1894) of Brazil's Old Republic, and Mexico's revolution of 1910 all signified such a broadening. Yet then and later, most politicians had but limited concern for the common people. Neither Madero in Mexico nor Yrigoyen in Argentina had clear policies for attacking socioeconomic, rather than political, problems. Even Zapata made only limited demands.

More than anything else, the Depression exposed such leaders' inadequacies and called forth a new approach. The collapse of the markets for Latin American exports toppled both the Argentine Radicals and the coffee oligarchs of Brazil's Old Republic. Coming after the church-state crisis of the 1920s and the 1928 election violence, the Depression also heightened the confusion of the later Calles years in Mexico.

Out of this disruption, Perón, Vargas, and Cárdenas emerged to carry political mobilization into a new phase. In doing so, they displayed important common characteristics and policies. They all took an authoritarian, corporatist-populist approach to mass mobilization. In Argentina, Perón's followers, drawn largely from the state-controlled labor movement, became the largest party, though not the only one. Vargas's New State monopolized political life, allowing no parties. Cárdenas contributed to the development of Mexico's corporatist single party.

Pursuing nationalist developmental goals, Perón, Cárdenas, and Vargas expanded the state's economic role and pushed for industrialization so as to overcome the effects of the Depression and economic dependency. Assuming power with Argentina's drive for industrialization already well launched, Perón championed the working class, thus creating for himself a wider base of support than earlier politicians had enjoyed. Vargas ended the coffee interests' political dominance, introduced central planning for economic development, carried Brazil into the age of heavy industry, and shifted power to the cities, where both the middle class and workers benefited from his authoritarian paternalism. In Mexico, which also undertook centralized economic planning, Cárdenas transformed land tenure, promoted significant industrialization, and nationalized petroleum.

To break out of economic dependency, Latin American leaders of the Perón-Vargas-Cárdenas era typically pursued a state-led industrialization strategy aimed first at import substitution behind high tariff barriers and then at heavy industry, without necessarily reforming the agricultural sector. How sound was this strategy?

Adopted when high tariffs prevailed almost everywhere, the protectionist import-substitution strategy produced some positive results. Yet neglect of the agricultural sector was unwise. An agricultural policy aimed at reducing inequality in the countryside would have enlarged the market for industrial products by increasing the majority's income. A development policy that increased the efficiency of estate agriculture could also have helped to provide both capital for industrial investment and food for a population who increasingly worked in factories rather than fields. Finally, rural mass education would have produced a more skilled and productive labor force.

A sound approach to industrialization would have required starting with agriculture and fundamentally changing Latin America's historical pattern of internal colonization. Argentina was a partial exception because it lacked the large peasant class found in other Latin American nations. Mexico was also exceptional because its reforms, especially under Cárdenas, met some of this approach's requirements. But Argentina and Mexico were only local variations in an agrarian problem of continental scope, still unsolved today.

The high import duties typical of the Depression posed another danger to the import-substitution strategy: the protected industries might not acquire the ability to compete in an international market. Until domestic need for basic consumer goods had been met, only Mexicans, or Brazilians, or Argentines had to put up with the inferior goods. But a time would come—in the 1960s for these countries—when domestic demand for light industrial goods had been met and industrialization could proceed only by mastering more advanced technologies or by facing the competition of international markets. By then, too, U.S. manufacturers' response to the creation of protective barriers (setting up subsidiary firms in Latin America) would show that protectionism offered no sure way to overcome subordination to foreign economic interests.

In time, the state's expanded role in the economy also produced troubling consequences. During the Depression, state initiative may have looked like the only way to advance Latin America's struggle against economic dependency. Then or later, many developing countries made the same choice. By 1970, however, the state sectors had grown so much that they accounted for 30 percent or more of all goods and services produced in some Latin American countries, compared to 2 percent in Japan or 4 percent in the United States. This growth vastly expanded government payrolls, injected bureaucratic inefficiencies into the economy, and raised the stakes—and bitterness—of political struggle. Like the consequences of authoritarian mass mobilization, those of state-led industrialization remained key issues after World War II.

Because most Latin American nations enjoyed political, if not economic, independence when most of Africa and Asia was still struggling against European rule, the problem of choosing effective economic development strategies arose earlier for Latin America than for most other parts of the colonial world. The Depression similarly highlighted questions of economic strategy for the powerful nations of Europe and North America, as noted in Chapter 5. With the collapse of European colonialism after 1945, an increasingly populous and interdependent world would find its attention fixed more and more on problems of resources and productivity such as those discussed here. Many developing nations would repeat Latin America's economic mistakes. Few would do better.

Notes

1. Quoted in E. Bradford Burns, *A History of Brazil,* 2d ed. (New York: Columbia University Press, 1980), p. 410.

Suggestions for Further Reading

Burns, E. Bradford. *A History of Brazil.* 2d ed. (1980).

Hart, John Mason. *Revolutionary Mexico: The Coming and Process of the Mexican Revolution* (1987).

Keen, Benjamin, and Mark Wasserman. *A History of Latin America* (1988).

Knight, Alan. *The Mexican Revolution.* 2 vols. (1986).

Loveman, Brian. *Chile: The Legacy of Hispanic Capitalism.* 2d ed. (1988).

Meyer, Michael C., and William L. Sherman. *The Course of Mexican History.* 4th ed. (1991).

Skidmore, Thomas E., and Peter H. Smith. *Modern Latin America.* 3d ed. (1992).

Stepan, Alfred. *The State and Society: Peru in Comparative Perspective* (1978).

Viola, Herman J., and Carolyn Margolis. *Seeds of Change: A Quincentennial Commemoration* (1991).

CHAPTER 9

Sub-Saharan Africa Under European Sway

Over three times the size of the United States, Africa includes the sites in Kenya where the oldest human fossil remains have been found, as well as the monumental remains in Egypt of one of the first great civilizations. Ancient African cultures left behind a rich "triple heritage,"[1] combining indigenous, Semitic, and Greco-Roman elements; in modern times, this triple heritage expresses itself in terms of indigenous, Islamic, and Western influences. Africa's past includes much to glorify. Sub-Saharan examples of monumental scale include the remains of Great Zimbabwe and the empires of Ghana and Mali; all three names have been reused to designate modern republics. Subtler expressions of African creativity range from masterpieces in sculpture to widely influential musical styles, the consensual democracy of village Africa, and some African peoples' success at living together without creating states.

African societies have also historically had strong ties to the outside world—to the Mediterranean, to the Islamic lands to the east, and to the Americas. Yet understanding the last five hundred years of Africa's history requires recognizing not only its vastness and creativity but also the painful fact that its integration into the modern world has occurred, unfortunately for its peoples, at the price of drastic exploitation and dependency—keynotes of the Western part of Africa's triple heritage today.

This history of exploitation contains a major paradox, for compared to the Americas and Asia, most of Africa was late in becoming integrated into the European-dominated global pattern. The European voyages of exploration began decades before Columbus, as Portuguese navigators inched their way down Africa's coast. Asia was the principal source of the silks and spices the explorers sought, but Africa also produced precious goods such as gold and ivory. How could Africa remain long outside the sphere of European control?

Disease and topography hindered Europeans in Africa, as did the presence of strong African kingdoms controlling trade to the interior. In most of the non-Western world, diseases that Europeans brought with them, especially smallpox, helped to ensure European triumph over local populations lacking immunity. Until the advent of modern tropical medicine, however, Europeans could not resist the diseases endemic to Africa. Yellow fever and malaria caused high death rates among newly arrived Europeans. Diseases spread by the tsetse fly made animal transport impracticable in many places. Topography, too, slowed European penetration of the continent; the rivers mostly had high cataracts near the coast, and existing paths were not suitable for wheeled vehicles. Much of direct European trade with Africa had to connect with established networks controlled by Africans and Arabs. Europeans consequently knew so little of Africa's interior that they had to leave it blank on maps.

In the late nineteenth century, however, advances in tropical medicine, combined with superior military technology, made possible an unstoppable European advance into the African interior. To study this epoch-making change, this chapter begins with an overview of Africa and its recent history up to World War II. Later sections will look more closely at two of the largest African colonies: Nigeria, where few Europeans went, and South Africa, where many settled. The comparison of these two countries sheds light on the conditions in which the processes of social and political mobilization characteristic of the twentieth century proceeded where Africans did, or did not, have to contend with large numbers of Europeans.

Continental Overview: African Diversity, European Domination

Africa comprises a vast array of environments and societies. We need to consider some key dimensions of the continent's diversity—topography, modes of adapting to the environment, language, forms of social organization—and some common traits, before examining Europe's impact and African responses to it.

African Diversity

Among many indicators of African diversity, the most basic are ecological differences that divide the continent into zones running across it roughly east and west. Northernmost, Algeria and Morocco have a small coastal zone with a Mediterranean climate like that of Spain and Italy. Below this zone, the Sahara Desert extends from the Atlantic Ocean to the Red Sea. Below the Sahara, the desert grades into savanna, a zone of grassland and scattered trees, running from Senegal in the west to the southern Sudan, from which the same environment also extends to the southeast. Next comes the tropical forest, found in a coastal strip running from Senegal through Nigeria, then widening to the east and south to cover the Zaire (Congo) River valley. Pockets of rain forest recur farther south and east. South of the Zaire River valley, much the same zones as in the north appear in reverse order: a zone of woodland and shrub; a savanna zone; an arid zone including the Kalahari Desert to the west and grassy steppes in eastern South Africa; finally,

Sixteenth-century ivory mask from the Bini people of Nigeria. *Such masterpieces of African artistic achievement exerted a major international influence in the twentieth century. The Metropolitan Museum of Art; The Michael C. Rockefeller Memorial Collection. Gift of Nelson A. Rockefeller, 1972*

a small zone of Mediterranean climate at the Cape of Good Hope. These regions produce many products that Europe lacks: rubber, cacao, palm oil, ivory, gold, and diamonds.

One way to classify African peoples is according to how they adapt to their environments, how they survive and obtain food. We can distinguish four adaptations, all of which also exist in other parts of the world. The two more common are agriculture and pastoralism; the two less common are fishing, and hunting and gathering. Most societies have combined various of these activities and have also traded.

In the most ancient way of life, hunting and gathering, people subsist on wild plants and animals, without either agriculture or animal husbandry. This way of life survives for a few Africans: the Mbuti of the rain forest and the San of South Africa's open grassland. Hunting and gathering communities must remain small and migratory in order to find subsistence year-round. In such communities, which never exceed a few hundred members, the need for chiefship has never been felt. Decision making and control of conflict are communal tasks. Communal egalitarianism and highly developed skills for taking advantage of difficult landscapes are notable features of this way of life.

The first communities to settle permanently in one place were probably fisherfolk, located along rivers, lakes, or the ocean, which provided an adequate food supply year-round. A permanent food supply permitted the formation of larger communities, specialization of roles, and the emergence of chiefs. Few fisher communities survive, but they probably provided the setting for the development of a sedentary (as opposed to migratory) lifestyle, such as later became known in agricultural communities.

Agriculture has long been the most widespread of the environmental adaptations. By cultivating plants and domesticating animals, agriculturists could use the environment more intensively than hunter-gatherers and could spread over a much larger part of the landscape than fisherfolk. Agricultural productivity permitted formation of larger societies in which people's roles and statuses became more differentiated, trade began, and the institution of chiefship evolved into kingship as the societies grew.

Where conditions were, or became, too dry for agriculture, as in the Sahara, pastoralism appeared. This way of life depends on herding livestock, such as sheep or camels, in arid zones where there is too little water to support year-round grazing. Pastoralism is a migratory or nomadic way of life, requiring intimate knowledge of the environment because the community's survival depends on knowing how to find grass and water year-round. Chiefship is sometimes an important institution in the pastoralist community, which is normally an extended kin group. But some pastoralist groups have stateless societies in which elders keep order with no formal government.

However African societies adapt to the environment, another factor differentiating them is language. The continent has over eight hundred languages and many more dialects. Virtually all of them belong to five language families with common structural traits that indicate a common origin. The Afro-Asiatic family includes the Arabic and Berber languages of North Africa, various languages of Somalia and Ethiopia, and Hausa, widely spoken in West Africa. In western South Africa and adjacent territories are the speakers of the Khoisan languages. The Nilo-Saharan family is found in a zone running from Chad, through the southern Sudan, to the eastern side of Lake Victoria. The fourth language family, the Austronesian,

A Nigerian carver's view of a local ruler encountering his first British official, 1890s. *A masterpiece of African artistry, these doors suggest a wide gap between the way European imperialists saw themselves and the way Africans saw them.* Werner Forman Archive

is of Southeast Asian origin. This family is found on the island of Madagascar, whose people migrated from Indonesia long ago, bringing a language closely related to Malayo-Polynesian. Sub-Saharan Africa's most widely dispersed language family is the Congo-Kordofanian. These languages are spoken across much of the savanna belt of West Africa, the forest zone, and most of the southern part of the continent. Widely spoken in East Africa, Swahili is structurally part of this family, but it also contains many words borrowed from Arabic. Finally, several European languages—English, French, Portuguese, Dutch-derived Afrikaans—remain in use. European languages provide common media of communication in regions that might otherwise not have one. But these languages also served as one more European tool for dividing and ruling Africa.

Variations in concepts of kinship provide yet another way to classify African societies. Historically, some societies were patrilineal, organizing themselves in terms of descent relationships among males; some were matrilineal; and some recognized bilateral kinship. Some societies preferred marriage among kin (endogamy); some preferred marriage among nonkin (exogamy). African societies differed vastly in scale, from bands of a few hunter-gatherers to huge kingdoms ruling many kin groups. Some societies developed complex variations on the kinship theme. For example, the Lunda people of Central Africa practiced *perpetual succession* (each successor to an office took the name, as well as the title, of the original incumbent) and *positional kinship* (later occupants of the offices assumed the same kin relationships to one another as the original incumbents had had). If originally several chiefs were brothers, generations later the chiefs bore the same names and were still considered brothers. For many societies, in Africa as elsewhere, nonkin relationships could serve as extensions to the range of kinship ties. Slavery especially served as a way to expand the master's household. The contrast with the plantation slavery of the New World could be radical. The Ijo people of the Niger Delta, for example, developed an organizational form known as the *canoe house,* which began as an extended family plus the family head's slaves. The slaves were treated as full members of the household and might succeed to its headship.

Kinship and its extensions, such as slavery or blood brotherhood, were certainly not the only meaningful social relationships. Shared religious orientation could be extremely important. The Sokoto caliphate of northern Nigeria was one of many African states to grow out of an Islamic reform movement. Groups defined in terms of age and sex were also sometimes important. The Zulu regiments of nineteenth-century South Africa consisted of contemporaries who went through initiation rites together as youths. A Zulu ruler bent on military expansion could use these age-grade societies to separate young fighters from their kin and form them into units dependent on himself alone. The women of Aba, in Nigeria, used their age-grade societies and trading contacts to organize a revolt in 1929.

Yet these examples remain exceptions to the rule that African societies—like most others historically—were basically kinship societies. Their structural variations were largely variations on the kinship theme. Because differences among kinship groups often coincided with differences in language and culture, and because kinship groups often acknowledged no allegiance to any larger body, the kinship groups were Africa's key social entities.

One approach to the study of Africa is to classify its societies along the dimensions just discussed—the different environments, environmental adaptations, languages, and kinship structures. Other criteria could also be added, especially the triple religious heritage of Christianity, Islam, and traditional African religions. Such an approach can lead to very extended discussion. Cultural borrowings can also complicate the picture by creating close relationships in certain respects—religion, artistic styles, ideas of kingship—among societies that are otherwise different.

Common Traits

Amid their diversity, African societies also shared common traits. Two of them held especially important implications for the twentieth century: the effects of ethnic and kinship divisions on efforts at large-scale political integration, and the problems created by Africa's relative insulation from the impact of European expansionism until the late nineteenth century.

Especially because they so often coincided with linguistic, cultural, and political differences, the distinctions among kinship groups and the rivalries among African states of the precolonial period made it easier for Europeans to take power in Africa. As Europeans consolidated their control in the late nineteenth century, most African societies proved too underdeveloped technologically to resist effectively. Africa then had some states that were relatively large and powerful, many microstates of village size, and stateless societies. The larger monarchies were often easiest for Europeans to master, since if they could defeat the ruler, his subjects then became theirs. Stateless societies were hardest to subdue, because practically the only way to gain control was to make each member of the society submit. This fact supports anthropologists' view that the ability to live in a stateless society is a great African achievement.

By the end of the nineteenth century, Ethiopia and Liberia were the only African countries that remained independent. Elsewhere, as Europeans established control, they consolidated African societies into larger entities. The arbitrary boundaries European imperialists drew still survive, with relatively few changes, as those of Africa's independent nations (Map 9.1). Because these boundaries reflected the Europeans' interests, ignoring and cutting across those of Africans, the European-defined colonies and the states that emerged out of them after independence had an artificial quality in African eyes. In any given colony, Africans of different ethnic backgrounds would unite to oppose European rule, but most Africans had difficulty shifting their primary loyalty from their own kin and ethnic groups to the larger colony and later to the nation. Splits in independence movements sometimes resulted, as did the subordination of postindependence national politics to ethnic and regional interests. Not unique to Africa, such problems in state building have also appeared in the Middle East and in Europe's formerly socialist countries. No European state fully lived up to the nation-state ideal, and the nations that colonialism created did so far less.

African societies also suffered from the lateness and abruptness with which the European impact hit much of the continent. It may seem strange to argue that Africa suffered by being insulated from the full impact of imperialism until the late nineteenth century. Yet European civilization had begun to develop so rapidly, in its technologies of production and destruction, that insulation from European expansionism tended to make its impact more destructive when it could no longer be averted. As noted, advances in tropical medicine and the widening gap in military technology ultimately enabled Europeans to establish control over the continent with a suddenness unmatched elsewhere.

Integration into the Europe-centered Global Pattern

Africa's integration into the European-dominated world progressed in several stages. The transatlantic slave trade dominated the first. Africans were already trading in slaves when the Europeans appeared off their coasts. The

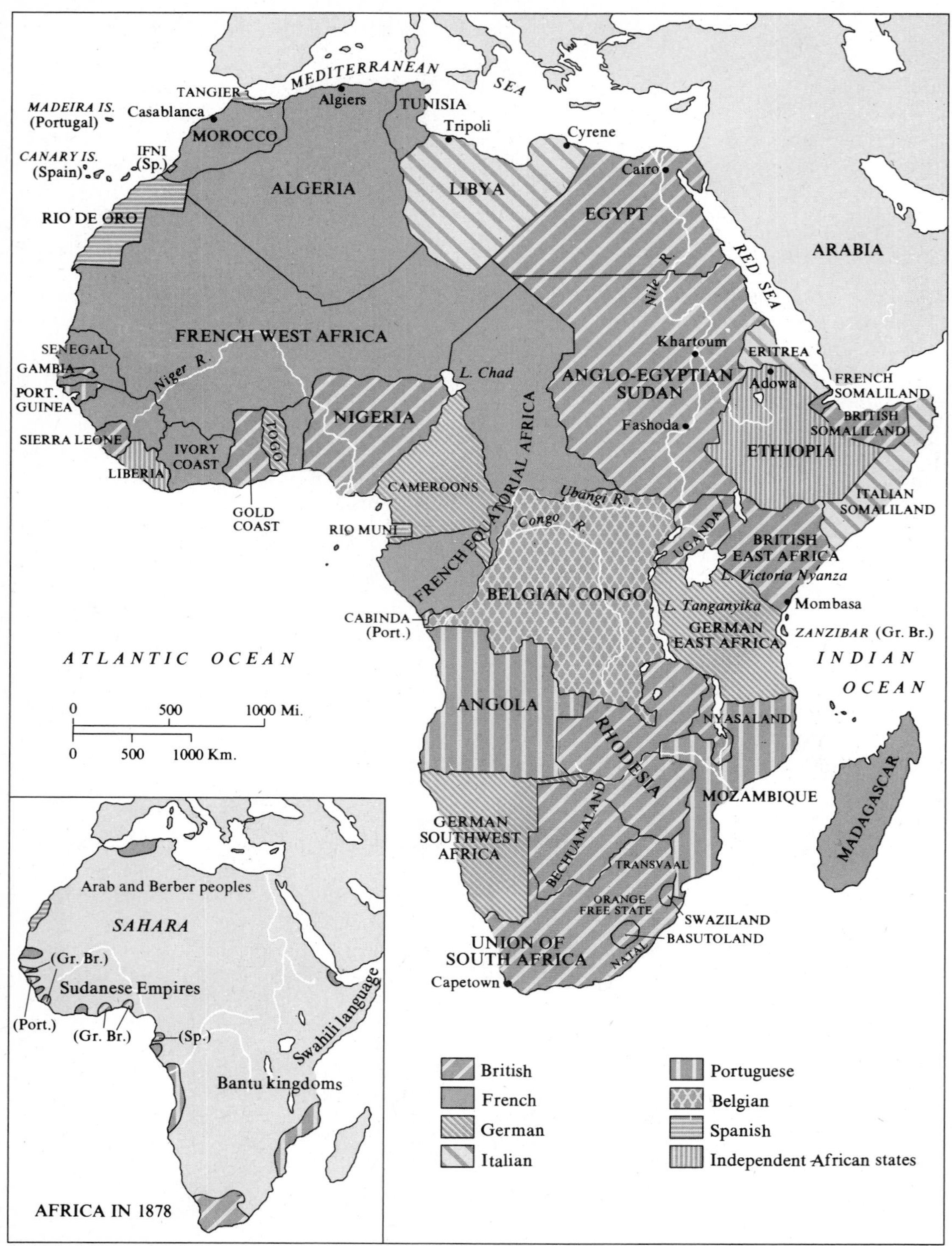

MEDITERRANEAN SEA
TANGIER
MADEIRA IS. (Portugal)
Casablanca
Algiers
TUNISIA
Tripoli
Cyrene
MOROCCO
CANARY IS. (Spain)
IFNI (Sp.)
Cairo
ALGERIA
LIBYA
RIO DE ORO
EGYPT
RED SEA
ARABIA
Nile R.
FRENCH WEST AFRICA
Khartoum
SENEGAL
GAMBIA
ERITREA
Niger R.
L. Chad
ANGLO-EGYPTIAN SUDAN
Adowa
FRENCH SOMALILAND
PORT. GUINEA
BRITISH SOMALILAND
NIGERIA
Fashoda
SIERRA LEONE
IVORY COAST
TOGO
FRENCH EQUATORIAL AFRICA
ETHIOPIA
LIBERIA
CAMEROONS
Ubangi R.
ITALIAN SOMALILAND
GOLD COAST
Congo R.
RIO MUNI
UGANDA
BRITISH EAST AFRICA
L. Victoria Nyanza
BELGIAN CONGO
CABINDA (Port.)
L. Tanganyika
Mombasa
GERMAN EAST AFRICA
ZANZIBAR (Gr. Br.)
ATLANTIC OCEAN
INDIAN OCEAN
0 500 1000 Mi.
0 500 1000 Km.
ANGOLA
RHODESIA
NYASALAND
MOZAMBIQUE
MADAGASCAR
GERMAN SOUTHWEST AFRICA
BECHUANALAND
TRANSVAAL
ORANGE FREE STATE
SWAZILAND
BASUTOLAND
UNION OF SOUTH AFRICA
NATAL
Capetown
Arab and Berber peoples
SAHARA
(Gr. Br.)
Sudanese Empires
(Port.)
(Gr. Br.)
(Sp.)
Swahili language
Bantu kingdoms
AFRICA IN 1878
British
French
German
Italian
Portuguese
Belgian
Spanish
Independent African states

European export of African slaves quickly began and grew as Europeans spread the plantation system of agriculture in the Americas. In the end, some 12 million slaves were exported, mostly from West and Central Africa. Not all survived the crossing. An older pattern of slave exportation across the Sahara and the Red Sea also continued, accounting for perhaps 3 million people during the period of the transatlantic trade. Africans thus became the second most widely distributed of the world's races.

Though Europeans were long unable to enter Africa's interior, the slave trade produced profound changes there too. In the Niger Delta, the rise of the Ijo canoe houses, which used their manpower to staff large canoes for slave trading and war, was one example of how African societies adjusted to their new economic opportunities. Accustomed to trading in prisoners of war and criminals and knowing little of the nature of slavery across the Atlantic, many Africans were little more shocked by the trade than were Europeans.

In the nineteenth century, "legitimate" trade in industrial, agricultural, and mineral products replaced slaving as Africa's principal link to the world economy. This transformation owed more to economics than to abolitionism. Britain's abolition of the slave trade (1807) coincided not only with growth of interest in human rights but also with the early phases of the Industrial Revolution. British ships had new products to take to Africa, and British demand for raw materials began to exert a stronger pull on African exports than did American demand for slaves.

African societies had to reorient themselves as trade shifted in character and grew in volume. In the Niger Delta, which had been the most prolific source of slaves for export, the volume of legitimate trade increased 87 percent between 1830 and 1850. At the same time, Europeans began to extend the influence of their coastal representatives: consuls, explorers, missionaries, and merchants. There were also efforts to resettle freed blacks in Africa—the British settlement at Sierra Leone (1787) and the U.S. settlement in Liberia (1822). The pace of European involvement was quickening.

The 1880s marked the critical phase in consolidation of European control. Several factors combined to touch off what Europeans called the "scramble for Africa." In Europe, the unification of Italy and Germany (1870–1871) had intensified international rivalry and increased the number of would-be colonial powers. Advances in European industry increased demand for goods such as vegetable oils and rubber. Military applications of new technologies widened the gap in military capabilities, especially after European nations agreed by treaty not to sell guns in Africa. That agreement left Africans with breechloaders to face Europeans with maxim guns, an early form of machine gun. In South Africa, fabulous mineral discoveries—the Kimberley diamond finds of 1867 and the Witwatersrand gold finds of 1886—whetted European greed. In the north, France, which had controlled Algeria since 1830, set up a protectorate over Tunisia in 1881, and Britain occupied Egypt in 1882. But the "scramble" was most intense in the tropical forest of the Niger and Congo basins, once medical advances—starting with the use of quinine against malaria—gave Europeans access to that region. To deal with competition there, the European nations convened a congress at Berlin in 1884–1885. The conference agreed on an easy way for Europeans to gain international recognition of their African claims, a procedure summed up as "notify and occupy." European powers had only to notify one another of their claims, then stake them.

◀ ***Map 9.1 Africa, 1914***

Over the next three decades, Europeans staked claims until only Liberia and Ethiopia remained independent. In a continent where precise linear boundaries were scarcely heard of, Europeans carved out colonies as they pleased. The resulting territorial divisions reflected the perspective of someone entering from the coast. Togo was just a thin strip running in from the sea. The Belgian Congo, in contrast, was a vast interior expanse, but it too had an outlet to the sea. Capital cities grew up on the coast as beachheads of imperialism. Everywhere, boundaries cut across patterns of settlement and economic life that mattered to Africans. European imperalists did not care. Their aim was to plant the flag and claim their place in the sun.

By World War I, virtually all of Africa was divided into dependencies of seven European states. France and Britain were the winners. In addition to Morocco, Algeria, and Tunisia, France held vast sub-Saharan tracts grouped into two federations: French West Africa and French Equatorial Africa. The British held Gambia, Sierra Leone, the Gold Coast (now Ghana), and Nigeria in West Africa. They also held a strip that ran from north to south, from Egypt to South Africa, broken only by German East Africa (the Tanganyika of the interwar period, now the mainland part of Tanzania). In 1898 war almost broke out between Britain and France when both tried to claim the Sudan. If the French had succeeded, they would have emerged with a strip of territories running across the continent from east to west. Instead, they backed down, allowing the British almost to fulfill their dream of controlling territory from "Cape to Cairo."

After Britain and France, Belgium and Germany probably won most in the scramble. Belgium acquired the Belgian Congo (now Zaire). King Leopold, acting on his own account, had begun to establish claims there in the 1870s. His personal regime exploited the country scandalously, through forced labor backed by brutal discipline, until the Belgian government took it over in 1908. Germany acquired Togo, Cameroon, South-West Africa, and German East Africa. The government tried, with little success, to persuade Germans to settle in those territories rather than emigrate to America.

Although World War I weakened the European powers, and Woodrow Wilson's principle of self-determination attracted attention around the world, European dominance of Africa appeared to become even stronger during the interwar years. Defeated Germany lost its colonies, but they were entrusted to Belgium, France, South Africa, and Britain under mandates from the League of Nations. Mandates theoretically differed from colonies, for the powers that held the mandates were supposedly accountable to the League of Nations. Because the League was not a strong organization, not all mandatory powers lived up to their obligations. Not until 1988 did South Africa consent to give up control of Namibia (the former German colony of South-West Africa), which it had continued to administer despite United Nations resolutions revoking its mandate (see Chapter 16). One consequence of the transformation of German East Africa into the British-mandated Tanganyika was that Britain briefly acquired its band of territory running the length of the continent. European empire building in Africa did not stop, even with the mandates. In 1935, Mussolini's Italy invaded Ethiopia—the last campaign in the conquest of Africa and the first for Africa in World War II. Italy held Ethiopia only until 1941. During those few years, Liberia was the only independent African nation, and even it was virtually a colony of the Firestone Rubber Company, which owned millions of acres of plantations.

The Impact of Colonial Rule

Inside the colonies and mandates, political and economic conditions varied. The biggest difference was whether or not a colony attracted white settlers. Settler colonies developed regimes that allowed political participation to whites but few rights to Africans. In other colonies, Europeans regarded government as a matter of administration, not politics, and scarcely allowed questions of political participation to come up. There were also differences of national style in colonial administration. For example, as compared to the British, French administration was more centralized, allowing local chiefs no real power and their people no political rights. Yet conditions everywhere had enough in common to permit generalizations.

The foremost common trait was Europeans' limited understanding of Africans. Even in the best-run colonies, the African populations were likely to be dismissed as savages. Those who acquired a Western-style education were still viewed as "trousered natives." They also risked becoming alienated from their own peoples. The French and Portuguese encouraged this alienation by offering full rights of citizenship to members of their colonial populations who met certain cultural standards. The Portuguese called such people *assimilados* (assimilated). The French used the patronizing term *évolués* (ones who have evolved or developed).

All forms of colonial rule were disruptive. Where white settlers were not present to contend for power, the organization of colonial rule ranged from military despotism to the British ideal of "indirect rule." *Indirect rule* meant taking local chiefs and kings under "protectorate" and giving them places in a colonial hierarchy with only a few Europeans at the top. Some African rulers were removed. Others found their powers and their relations with their people changed as Europeans tried to turn them into cogs in the colonial machine.

In stateless societies, Europeans sometimes arbitrarily appointed "warrant chiefs," on the presumption that chiefship was the African way to rule. The European impact also extended "below" the chiefs to Africans at the grassroots level. Key figures here were the interpreters and messengers who worked for the Europeans. Because Europeans usually lacked the concern or language skills to check on them, interpreters and messengers had a way of becoming corrupt petty tyrants—the imperialists' much-hated lackeys.

Colonial administrators cared little for political mobilization or social needs. The administrators at first relied on missionaries to meet such needs as education or public health and only slowly broadened the range of government functions. Some imperialists acknowledged a responsibility to prepare the people of their colonies for self-government in the remote future, but they felt no responsibility to develop the colonies' resources for the benefit of the populace. They exploited those resources for the world market.

In Africa the colonial economic pattern assumed even starker contours than in Latin America, and no country except South Africa came close to throwing off economic dependency prior to World War II. African prosperity, too, rested on exports of raw materials produced by mining or single-crop agriculture. Working conditions were scandalous and highly unequal for Africans and whites. In 1939, black South Africans in mining or industry received one-eighth the wages of whites in the same jobs. Export agriculture centered on such crops as palm kernels and palm oil, peanuts, cotton, rubber, and cocoa. Plantations did not totally dominate the agricultural scene, especially in West Africa. Yet even independent peasant households suffered indirect exploitation by the complex of interests—trading companies, local middlemen, banks, shippers, insurance companies—that stood between African producers and the faraway markets for colonial goods. The governments had intimate links to these interests and aided them by such means as requiring forced labor or imposing taxes that could be paid only in money, thus forcing Africans to produce new crops for export or to hire out as wage laborers.

One principle of colonial administration was that each colony should be financially self-sufficient. In the Belgian Congo, this policy degenerated into an "economy of pillage." Everywhere, colonial economies were at the mercy of fluctuating commodity prices. The Depression of 1929 underscored this fact so strongly that Britain and France began to consider economic diversification and improvements in public welfare for their colonies. But few practical improvements emerged before World War II. Economically, far from preparing Africa for independence, colonial rule led to what radical critics call "the development of underdevelopment."

African Responses to Imperialism

African responses to Europeans have a long history. Even before the late nineteenth century, many African social and economic systems, such as the Ijo canoe houses, had developed as responses to European-created changes. Some religious movements, too, expressed African reactions against Europeans. Whereas many Africans adopted Christianity in European forms, others joined anti-European movements that grew out of African traditional religion, Islam, or Christianity itself. One such movement began when Nongqause, a Xhosa girl in South Africa, saw in a vision in 1856 that if her people would destroy their cattle, their ancient heroes would be reborn and the Europeans would be driven into the sea (instead, starvation resulted). Opposition to Europeans also took the form of Islamic holy war (*jihad*) movements—notably that of Muhammad Ahmad, who claimed to be the *Mahdi* (the leader who would restore justice to Muslims at the end of time) and who successfully fought off the British in the Sudan of the 1880s—and Africanized churches like the one founded in the Belgian Congo by Simon Kimbangu (d. 1951), a black prophet for a black people. One hallmark of the movements based on Christianity or African religions is the prominent role women often took as leaders, even founders, such as Kimbangu's precursor in Africanizing Christianity in the Congo, Donna Beatrice (martyred 1706).

To respond to European inroads, African rulers had a range of choices, from armed resistance to accommodation. By defeating the Italian attempt of 1896, Ethiopia became the only African country to defend itself successfully against imperialism, until it fell to Mussolini in 1935. But other nineteenth-century kingdoms, such as the Zulu of southern Africa and the Ashanti of what is now Ghana, managed to resist colonial occupation for decades. Some ethnic groups—the Maures of Mauritania and the Nuer of the Sudan—for example—managed to resist the Europeans until the 1930s. Faced with European encroachment, Africans responded with an outburst of creativity and leadership, organizing resistance movements based on ideas and symbols drawn from indigenous belief systems, Islam, or even European ideologies.

Even where armed resistance was not totally successful, it was seldom entirely futile, for it forced the thinly staffed European administrations to realize the limits of their power. Accommodation, too, had advantages, for it sometimes enabled Africans to influence the terms of colonial rule.

After colonization, Africans created new institutions to pursue their interests. In Senegal, public letter writers helped develop a communications network linking the French-educated urban leaders to the rural populace. In South Africa, efforts to form broadly based African political organizations began during the 1880s.

World War I also affected Africa in important ways. Thousands of Africans from the French colonies served on the Western front, as noted in Chapter 3. Because African territories under German and Allied control shared borders, there was some fighting in Africa. The

World War II begins for Africa. *Ethiopia mobilizes to resist the Italian invasion, 1935.* Bettmann Newsphotos

Allied seizure of Togo, Cameroon, and South-West Africa presented little difficulty, but the campaign for German East Africa lasted for most of the war and involved many African troops. For Africans as for other colonial peoples, the spectacle of a brutal war among their colonial masters shattered the myth of European supremacy.

Consequently, Africans grew more assertive after World War I. In West Africa, for example, wartime pressures provoked widespread rioting in Sierra Leone, and a political association, the National Congress of British West Africa, was formed in 1920. In the towns, recent migrants from the countryside began to form voluntary associations, alumni groups, dance societies, sports clubs, and religious or ethnic associations. Such groups provided needed support for people who were not yet at home in town. The societies served, too, as communication channels between town and hinterland. In time, the societies became channels for political mobilization, as overtly political organizations grew out of them. One sign of Africans' limited adjustment to the new colonial boundaries was that nationalism focused at first on larger entities: unity for English- or French-speaking West Africa, even unity for all Africa (Pan-Africanism).

World War II precipitated the end of colonial rule. In 1935 Italy's attack on Ethiopia—the ancient Christian kingdom whose culture and independence symbolized for blacks everywhere all that colonialism denied them—started a trend of radicalization. From 1941 to 1943, North Africa provided the stage for major campaigns. All Africans felt the impact of wartime shortages and restrictions. Far more than in World War I, Africans were drawn into forces fighting in far parts of the world, where they saw that Europeans were not all governors and generals: many were peasants and privates who fought and died as they did. Broadened awareness and increased confidence compounded existing pressures for political mobilization. For nonsettler colonies such as Nigeria, the age of independence was coming, although it did not open for most until the 1960s. For settler colonies such as South Africa, the struggle would be longer and more difficult.

Nigeria Under the British

Nigeria today is Africa's most populous state and one of its most important. Like most African nations, it is a colonial creation and shares the diversity of the continent as a whole. Nigeria's many peoples speak several hundred languages or dialects from various language families. Four peoples have been especially prominent in Nigeria's modern history, however. The Hausa and Fulani live in the semiarid northern savanna, where Muslims form a majority. In the forest near the coast, where traditional religions historically prevailed, are the Yoruba in the west and the Ibo (Igbo) in the east.

Unification Under British Rule

Nigerian history had unifying factors even before Europeans arrived. Yet their coming reoriented the economy toward the sea, rather than toward the old trans-Saharan trade routes, and tied Nigeria's regions together. Through the early nineteenth century, the main theme in the reorientation was the slave trade, which drew many of its victims from the Ibo lands of the southeast and the Yoruba lands of the southwest.

For a long time, Europeans had little effect on northern Nigeria, which still responded more to stimuli coming from other Islamic lands across the Sahara. The most important event of the century preceding British rule was one of the Islamic revival movements then sweeping Africa's savanna region and the rest of the Islamic world. The movement began among Fulani townsmen, turning them against the Hausa rulers under whom they lived. Led by the religious activist Usman dan Fodio, the movement erupted in 1804, toppled the Hausa kings, and established a caliphate—the term implies a state organized strictly according to early Islamic practice—centered at Sokoto. When the British eventually took control in northern Nigeria, they did so by defeating the Sokoto caliphate.

First, the British had to take the coastal zone. This occurred as slaving gave way to legitimate trade. Not all parts of Africa had commodities, other than slaves, that Europeans valued. But the Niger Delta had several. The most important was palm oil, used for soap making (hence the name "Palmolive") and as an industrial lubricant in the prepetroleum era. By midcentury, British naval and consular personnel had become assertive in regulating trade. In 1861, the British annexed Lagos on the western coast and soon after appointed a governor. Lagos later became the capital of all Nigeria, a fact that gave the

Yoruba people of the vicinity exceptional prominence in Nigerian politics.

European interest also extended into the interior. In 1854 an exploration mission, using quinine against malaria, penetrated nine hundred miles inland without the fearful loss of life that had accompanied earlier attempts. Missionaries and merchants then enlarged their efforts. By 1900 the confrontation of cultures had assumed the starkly destructive form depicted in Chinua Achebe's aptly named novel about what happened when the first whites arrived in an Ibo village: *Things Fall Apart* (1959).

It was traders who put Nigeria together economically and politically. In the 1870s the companies trading on the Niger River combined into the United African Company. The British government gave it the right to make treaties with local chiefs. After the Berlin African Congress of 1884–1885, the British claimed the territory around the Niger. By 1900 they had established several protectorates in what is now Nigeria and created a military force, the West African Frontier Force, to operate in the interior under command of Frederick Lugard. He more than anyone consolidated British rule in Nigeria.

In 1900, rivalry with the French to the west and desire for greater coordination inside Nigeria led the British government to take over the functions of the trading company, then known as the Royal Niger Company. The country was reorganized into the Lagos Colony and separate Northern and Southern Protectorates, with Lugard as governor in the north. In the south, British control was a reality. In the north, Lugard's mission was to make it so.

Lugard had only a small force with which to conquer the Sokoto caliphate, which, though in decline, presented a huge target. This situation suggested to Lugard what became known as *indirect rule,* a policy that he is often credited with creating, though the British had long used it in India. The strategy was to defeat the rulers of the caliphate, then take over their government apparatus and dominate their former subjects through it. By skillful use of superior technology, Lugard achieved military success by 1903 and then went on to consolidate indirect rule in the north. In 1912 he was appointed governor-general of Nigeria with the task of amalgamating the entire country under a single administration, a task formally completed on January 1, 1914.

Development Under the British

Between 1900 and 1914 the consolidation of British rule quickly broke down accustomed ways of life. Economic development was extensive, although starting from levels so low that the results were impressive only on a colonial scale. Political amalgamation created a huge free-trade area. Local rulers were deprived of trade tolls they had collected; but trade grew, and the distribution of wealth and power changed substantially. A major integrating factor was the extension of the railway. When it reached Kano, a key city of the Sokoto caliphate, in 1911, peanut shipments from that town rose to 19,288 tons, up from 1,179 tons in the preceding year. Amalgamation also gave Nigeria its first uniform monetary system.

Cultural and administrative change accompanied economic development. Missionaries challenged traditional beliefs but offered the country its first common system of literacy. Initial suspicion of missionary education waned as people realized that it offered opportunities in economic life and in the central administration. Western-educated Nigerian men who moved into low-level central administrative jobs became the first Africans oriented to thinking of Nigeria as a whole. In the north, where the Sokoto caliphate survived under British protection, indirect rule made government less flexible and more autocratic. More serious consequences followed Lugard's attempt to introduce his pet policy to the south. For example, the "warrant chiefs" whom Lugard appointed among the historically stateless Ibo proved highly unpopular.

Change slowed during the interwar years. The administrative system, introduced abruptly on the eve of World War I, evolved only gradually after 1918. Economic change slowed as well, especially during the Depression. Nigeria still had only 1,903 miles of railroad track in 1945. Foreign trade grew in value from 0.2 British pounds for each Nigerian in 1900 to 1.3 pounds in 1945—a substantial rate of increase, yet at low levels that clearly indicated limited purchasing power. By World War II, industrialization had barely begun, outside of mining. Low per capita incomes limited the internal market for industrial products and made it difficult for the governor to raise revenue to support development projects. As in all colonial economies, severe fluctuations in export prices posed a major obstacle to development. During the Depression, the value of Nigerian exports fell by about half and did not recover before World War II. After a vigorous beginning from 1900 to 1914, colonialism did little for Nigeria's development.

The Rise of Nigerian Nationalism

Nigerian political activism emerged as a demand for participation, not independence. The National Congress of British West Africa, a political association founded in 1920, included

Delegation from the National Congress of British West Africa, 1920. *This delegation included delegates from Gambia, Sierra Leone, Gold Coast (now Ghana), and Nigeria.* *Courtesy, Royal Commonwealth Society, London*

representatives of four British colonies: Gambia, Sierra Leone, Gold Coast (now Ghana), and Nigeria. Its demands included an end to racial discrimination in civil service appointments, control of specific administrative functions, and the founding of a university in West Africa.

In 1920, Europeans still felt they could reject such demands outright. Yet small concessions occurred. The Lagos town council became elective in 1920. More important, under the constitution of 1922, elected African representatives joined the colony's legislative council, though they were outnumbered there by the governor and his staff. Comparable provisions appeared in the constitutions of Sierra Leone (1924) and the Gold Coast (1927). Political parties quickly formed at Lagos to contest the seats, and newspapers sprang up to support the parties.

At first this political activity remained largely localized at Lagos, among the Yoruba people. In other regions nationalist politics emerged only later, or in different forms. In the north, as in the princely states of India, indirect rule fossilized the political forms of a bygone era. In the southeast the main problem was resentment of warrant chiefs. Here, after a census that counted women as well as men, a crisis developed over a rumor that women were to be taxed. In 1929 the women of Aba and Owerri responded to this threat, and to the Depression, in an uprising known as the Aba Women's War. Organizing through their age-grade societies and market associations, they attacked unpopular chiefs and institutions, causing enough damage to provoke armed police retaliation. The British then recognized the failure of indirect rule in this region and began efforts to devise a policy better suited to it.

In the 1930s the Depression, the growing integration of the country, and the spread of education stimulated the emergence of new forms of political activity. One of the first new organizations, the West African Students' Union formed in London, exerted a major influence on nationalist leaders of later decades. The Nigerian Youth Movement, in turn, formed at Lagos in 1936. It became an organization of national importance under leadership of Dr. Nnamdi ("Zik") Azikiwe, a U.S.-educated Ibo, the first prominent non-Yoruba politician. The Nigerian Youth Movement suffered because of quarrels among its leaders, and the fact that different leaders came from different peoples injected ethnic rivalries into the national movement.

As the 1930s wore on, Nigerian nationalists pressed for economic and social, as well as political, concessions. World War II, which stimulated growth in the economy and the labor movement, heightened these demands. In 1944, after virtual disintegration of the Nigerian Youth Movement, Azikiwe founded the National Council of Nigeria and the Cameroons (NCNC), a confederation of trade unions, small parties, ethnic associations, and other groups, to pursue these goals. When the British introduced a new constitution in 1947 without consulting Nigerians on its terms, virtually all the nationalists attacked it. With political mobilization now well advanced, Nigeria began to move—not toward participation but toward independence.

As concerned British-Nigerian relations, the transition to independence would prove relatively easy. The greater challenge was to divide power among Nigeria's peoples and regions so as to ensure peace and unity.

South Africa: A History of Two Struggles

Today's South Africa is the product of two struggles. One was between two white communities—the British and the Afrikaners, who are largely of Dutch origin—for political control. The other was between Europeans, of either community, and Africans for control of the land.

White settlement in South Africa began almost accidentally. In the seventeenth century, the Dutch East India Company set up a station at the Cape of Good Hope on the way to its possessions in what is now Indonesia. In 1657 the company allowed colonization of the countryside. Gradually, a Dutch-speaking, slave-owning agricultural community developed, favored by the moderate climate near the Cape. Over generations, the Boers (Dutch for *peasant* or *farmer*) spread out, coming into conflict with African peoples. As Europeans expanded from the sparsely settled territories in the west into the more thickly settled territories of the Bantu speakers in the east, these conflicts became serious. Adapting their Calvinist faith to justify their intentions, the Dutch identified white dominance with the will of God. Enough racial mixing occurred to form a "colored" population—the South African term for people of mixed ancestry—but racial mixing remained less extensive than in Latin America.

Dutch expansion to the east worsened existing competition for land among the Bantu-speaking chiefdoms there. By the early nineteenth century, a people that needed more land for its cattle could expand only at the expense of its neighbors. One people, the Zulus, did this with dramatic results, referred to in Zulu as the *mfecane* (crushing) of the peoples.

The Zulus' rise to military power was the work of a chief named Shaka (1787–1828). Becoming chief in 1816, he reformed an existing system of military organization based on age-regiments. He tightened discipline over his regiments and improved their tactics and weapons. In addition, he expanded the powers of Zulu kingship and enlarged the customary scope of war into a total effort to wipe out his enemies' resistance and incorporate the survivors into his own kingdom. In 1818, Shaka embarked on a career of conquest. The effects were felt far and wide. Some peoples fled his forces, clashing with one another. Some fled toward Cape Colony, worsening conflict with the Dutch. Some started their own campaigns of conquest, extending as far as Lake Victoria. The mfecane became one of the most widely felt upheavals of nineteenth-century Africa. The Zulus remained a small independent nation on the Indian Ocean coast of Natal into the late 1870s, and a Zulu rising occurred as late as 1906.

Meanwhile, conflict had developed within South Africa's white population. The democratic ideas that swept Europe and the Americas in the late eighteenth century also influenced the Dutch at the Cape of Good Hope, awakening a concern for individual rights (their own, at least) and republicanism. Then, as a consequence of the Napoleonic wars in Europe, Cape Colony came under British control, permanently so in 1806. The ideas of Dutch rights and republicanism became ways to express anti-British feeling.

British settlers, who began to arrive in 1820, disapproved of much the Dutch said and did. British missionaries were shocked at the way the Dutch treated Africans. The British soon abolished slavery and enacted other reforms. In 1853 they granted the Cape Colony a constitution that allowed for parliamentary government and a nonracial franchise for males, although a property qualification limited black registration. Ultimately, British-Dutch differences gave rise to Afrikaner nationalism and spurred the development of Afrikaans, derived from Dutch, into a language in its own right.

Many Dutch had had too much of British policy long before 1853. By the 1830s, some had decided on migration (*trek* in Dutch) beyond the frontiers of Cape Colony. They would create a republic, their ideal political form, where they could assure "proper relations" between blacks and whites. Their frustrations and the mfecane interacted, for the Dutch learned that lands to the east of Cape Colony had been depopulated and turned into grazing land by the Zulus. By 1839, Dutch migrants had defeated the Zulus and set up a republic in Natal. Unwilling to accept this arrangement, the British annexed Natal in 1845. But the Dutch migrated again and created the republics of the Transvaal and the Orange Free State to the north. The British recognized these states in 1852 and 1854. At that point, the area now covered by South Africa consisted of two British colonies (Cape Colony and Natal), the two Dutch republics, and numerous African chiefdoms and kingdoms.

In the late nineteenth century, both the black-white struggle for land and the Afrikaner-British struggle for political dominance intensified. The land struggle proved tragically unequal, as it did in many other cases where capitalistic and communalistic economic outlooks confronted each other in the age of European expansion. Whites took much land by conquest and much by other means. They entered the struggle for land armed with tools and ideas unfamiliar to Africans: surveying instruments, title deeds, and the very ideas of individual ownership and a market for land sales. Conquest gave the whites power to create a legal environment that enforced their ideas. In some cases, unwary Africans traded land rights for guns or liquor or, where formerly communal lands had been divided into individual holdings, lost their land through inability to adjust their way of life quickly to the new conditions. In a few cases, African rulers avoided annexation by getting their kingdoms made protectorates of the British crown. By this means, Swaziland, Bechuanaland (now Botswana), and Basutoland (Lesotho) remained separate as High Commission Territories when the Union of South Africa was formed in 1910. They acquired formal independence in the 1960s.

Competition for the land and its resources was also a major factor in the Afrikaner-British struggle. In 1867, diamonds were discovered near the junction of the Orange and Vaal rivers, just outside the western edge of the Orange Free State. That discovery began a race between the British—who won—and the Orange Free State to annex the diamond territory. Then, in 1886, gold was discovered in the Transvaal at Witwatersrand, near Johannesburg. An influx of gold-hungry outlanders (*uitlanders*) ensued, and the building of railway lines toward the mining centers accelerated. South Africa had four thousand miles of track by 1899. The Afrikaners felt threatened, for most of the great entrepreneurs were British. The outstanding example was Cecil Rhodes (1853–1902), who acquired vast wealth from gold and diamonds, served as prime minister of Cape Colony in the early 1890s, and directed British expansion into the regions that became Northern and Southern Rhodesia (now Zambia and Zimbabwe), thus blocking Afrikaner dreams of expansion to the north.

In the 1890s, Anglo-Afrikaner tensions built toward a climax. Rhodes tried to destabilize the Transvaal government by encouraging the outlander gold seekers to revolt. In 1895 a raid led by a Rhodes agent, Leander Starr Jameson, tried to raise a revolt but failed. Reactions to this episode finished Rhodes's political career. But because the monetary systems of most major nations were based on gold, the British government took over the struggle for control of South Africa and provoked a showdown. War broke out in 1899 and lasted until 1902.

Compared to other colonial wars, the Boer War proved trying indeed. Afrikaner commandos used their accustomed guerrilla tactics deep in British territory. Not prepared for that kind of war, the British responded brutally, burning farms and moving civilians into concentration camps, where over 25,000 died of disease. The war turned into one of attrition, which the Afrikaners could not win. The British got peace on their terms in 1902, after a bitter foretaste of twentieth-century conflicts.

The Union of South Africa: Politics and Economy

The Boer War set the stage for South Africa's unification. Having bullied the Afrikaners, the British now yielded to many of their demands. The Afrikaners found, too, that they could get more through conciliatory tactics—for example, by soft-pedaling their wish for a republic. In 1910, after long negotiation between the two white communities but no consultation of nonwhites, the four colonies became the Union of South Africa under a constitution that recognized the union as a dominion (a term used for former colonies that acquired autonomy within the British Empire). A governor-general, representing the British monarch, headed the government, which had a two-chamber parliament. Dutch and English were both official languages. Because the British feared that extending the colorblind franchise of the Cape Colony to the entire country would wreck the union, voting rights were left as they had been in each of the colonies before union. As a result, nonwhites remained permanently disenfranchised in Transvaal and the Orange Free State. Peace with fellow whites mattered more to the British than votes for Africans, whose cheap labor mattered most of all.

So began the Union of South Africa, as the country was known until it became a republic and broke with the British Commonwealth in 1961. Three trends dominated the country's development through World War II. The Afrikaners, the majority among whites (about 60 percent in the 1970s), gained political control. The rights of nonwhites—the real majority—were steadily reduced. Finally, thanks to mineral wealth and exploited black labor, the country grew from an economy based on mining to one combining mineral exports with industrial self-sufficiency. South Africa's success in industrialization was a rare achievement in the colonial world, but one produced at grim social and political cost.

The Union's political life began auspiciously. The first two prime ministers, Louis Botha (1910–1919) and Jan Smuts (1919–1924), belonged to the South African party. Boer generals who had fought the British, they now tried to unite the white communities. They also participated in the Paris Peace Conference and influenced the emerging concept of the British Commonwealth. Smuts suggested the mandate concept that the League of Nations adopted, and South Africa acquired South-West Africa (Namibia) as a mandate. Smuts gained a reputation as a world-class statesman.

The untroubled mood of 1910 did not last long. In 1913 the National party formed under the leadership of J. B. M. Hertzog, with an Afrikaner nationalist platform. The Hertzog movement opposed the government's participation in World War I, for many Afrikaners sympathized with the Germans to the point of open rebellion. In race relations, though Botha and Smuts were moderate compared to later prime ministers, passage of restrictive laws soon began. The Native Land Act of 1913, for example, confined African landownership to Native Reserves, based on former chiefdoms. The reserves then contained only 7 percent of the land for 78 percent of the population. Africans were supposed to be in other parts of the country only as temporarily resident workers. A system of passes controlled their movements, and the Native Urban Areas Act of 1923 imposed residential segregation.

South Africa's economic growth nonetheless caused thousands of African laborers to migrate to urban centers. Development thus produced racial interdependence, not separation. Conflict was bound to result. When gold prices fell after World War I, for example, mine owners attempted to cut costs by admitting blacks to jobs previously held by whites. White workers responded with the Rand Rebellion of 1922, taking as their slogan "Workers of the World, Unite for a White South Africa." When Smuts used troops to put down the protest, his popularity waned, and Hertzog's Nationalists came to power in alliance with the Labour party in 1924.

The policies of the Hertzog government from 1924 to 1933 were those of Afrikaner nationalists opposed to the British Empire and insistent on white dominance. Hertzog played a key role in hardening segregation and launching South Africa's drive for industrial self-sufficiency. Politically, he pushed for recruitment of Afrikaners into government service, formerly dominated by English speakers. He made Afrikaans (as well as Dutch) an official language, required it to be taught in public schools, and campaigned for all civil officials to be bilingual in Afrikaans and English. Hertzog also moved toward greater independence from Britain, a process favored by the British Statute of Westminster (1931), which transformed the empire into a Commonwealth of Nations and gave the dominions complete independence to make laws and conduct foreign relations.

Hertzog's economic policies aimed to advance Afrikaner interests. Since British capitalists dominated the economy, he pursued this goal largely through state intervention in it. In 1927 the government set up the South African Iron and Steel Corporation as a public enterprise intended to create jobs for Afrikaners and use the country's abundant coal and iron ore to achieve economic independence. Other state enterprises followed, for electric power, radio, and air transport. South Africa was industrializing and growing into a regional economic power. From 1933 on, the country entered a sustained boom that lasted into the late 1970s. The majority could not enjoy this boom, for it depended on a black underclass working for minimal wages to pay taxes enacted to force them into wage labor. At the same time, the government passed laws to reduce white unemployment by barring nonwhites from many better jobs (the "color bar").

Gold exports made the impact of the Depression on South Africa relatively slight and brief. Hertzog's popularity suffered nevertheless, and he merged his Nationalist party with Smuts's South African party in 1934 to try to stave off electoral defeat. Extremist Afrikaners resented this compromise, and Daniel Malan formed a Purified National party. Meanwhile, the Smuts-Hertzog fusion government (1933–1939) pushed through further segregationist laws. The Native Representation Act of 1936 effectively eliminated Africans in the Cape Province from the common voter rolls. Thereafter, Africans of the various provinces were to vote separately to select whites who would represent them in parliament. Another law of the same year enlarged the native reserves, but only to 13 percent of the country's land surface, while extending segregation elsewhere.

Segregation was hardening. The influence of European fascism compounded South African racism in these years, a fact illustrated by Malan's Purified Nationalist party and many hard-line Afrikaner organizations. With Afrikaner opinion moving in this direction, the Smuts-Hertzog United party had difficulty holding together.

On September 2, 1939, the government split over the question of war with Germany. The British governor-general asked Smuts to form a new government without Hertzog. Committing itself primarily to the war, the Smuts government (1939–1948) showed some moderation in racial policy. War made it necessary to set aside some of Hertzog's segregation policies, for labor needs could be met only by hiring blacks without regard to the color bar (though at wages lower than those paid to whites). Smuts, whose ideas on racial policy were more moderate than Hertzog's, also created a "Native Laws" Commission, whose report of 1948 urged concessions. Since blacks were already incorporated in the economy, the report urged that they be included in the country's political life too.

Most whites saw the report as a bombshell. Hertzog's Nationalists and Malan's Purified Nationalists had by then reunited, and the more extreme Malan had captured party leadership. In the 1948 election, Malan's Nationalists won. The Nationalists then unveiled their doctrine of apartheid, which elaborated Hertzog's policies into a program of strict racial separation.

Nonwhite Responses to the Consolidation of White Supremacy

For nonwhites, political developments between 1910 and 1948 meant a steady erosion of rights, against which protest proved less and less effective. Part of the problem was disunity, for the nonwhite category included three types of people, all referred to in South Africa as "black." These three types are racially mixed coloreds, Asians (mostly Indians, who originally came to South Africa as migrant workers), and Africans, who belong to many different ethnic groups. White governments reinforced this fragmentation by legally defining the status of different groups in different ways and by setting up separate "native reserves" for specific African ethnic groups. In the preunion period, nonwhites' rights also differed from one colony to another.

Political activity among nonwhites developed first in the relatively free atmosphere of Cape Colony. There, in 1884, John Jabavu founded the first African political newspaper. An Aborigines Association was founded in 1882 to encourage cooperation among religious denominations, an effort motivated in part by the proliferation of separatist churches. In 1902 the colored population of the Cape established the African Political Organization, which had branches outside Cape Colony and was reportedly the first political organization for nonwhites from all parts of South Africa.

Natal was the original center for the Indian population, and laws discriminating against them were passed there in the 1890s. Chapter 4 noted the importance of Gandhi's South African years (1893–1914) for his development and his contributions to the South African Indian community. Gandhi formed the Natal Indian Congress in 1894, patterned after the Indian nationalist movement. His passive-resistance campaigns also won concessions from the Union government in the Indian Relief Bill of 1914.

The fact that the Union of South Africa was created without consulting nonwhites gave new impetus to political mobilization and cooperation among nonwhite communities. In 1909 a South African Native Convention met to protest the terms of union. In 1912 the South African Native National Congress was formed. Its name was shortened in 1923 to African National Congress (ANC), and it is still the most influential political organization among South African blacks. Influenced by Gandhi, the ANC long remained a small organization dominated by moderates. Its goal was not revolution but political participation and equal rights. It remained committed to nonviolence for almost half a century. Gradually, however, the deteriorating political situation of South African blacks led to radicalization and broader efforts at political mobilization. The Native Representation Act of 1936 was a special shock that helped to bring forth new leadership. Alfred Xuma, a U.S.-educated physician, became president of the ANC in 1940 and broadened it into a mass movement of national scope. During World War II, a still more radical generation formed the Congress Youth League and toppled Xuma from ANC leadership in 1949.

The ANC and the many other political organizations that emerged during the interwar years all faced common problems. One was agreeing on how to respond to government policy changes. Even a measure as drastic as the Native Representation Act of 1936 divided nonwhites. Some thought it was to their interest to cooperate in the procedures of indirect representation provided by the law. Others opposed cooperation. The question of political methods was also difficult. Some have asserted that Gandhi's nonviolence and passive resistance are ideal methods for a people confronting oppressors who use superior force to impose morally indefensible policies. Yet, when South African blacks tried the same methods, whites responded with violence, not concessions. Smuts, the scholar-statesman, was personally impressed by Gandhi. Hertzog candidly admitted that white settlers' fears of being deluged by the African majority lay behind his segregationist policies. One of the greatest dangers to nonwhite unity lay in exclusive African nationalism, opposed to other nonwhites as well as to whites. In fact, a movement of this type, the Pan-Africanist Congress, eventually broke off from the ANC.

In the years just after World War II, a new era was clearly beginning. The racial gulf was widening inside South Africa, and its racial policy was also beginning to attract criticism abroad. A sign of the change was the leadership of newly independent India (1947) in attacking South African racism at the United Nations.

By then the Afrikaners had won political control from the British, and the whites together had wrested control of the land from the Africans. South Africa had diversified economically and embarked on a sustained period of economic growth. But these accomplishments rested on a radical denial of majority rights, an injustice that had begun to isolate South Africa in world opinion.

Conclusion: Imperialism as Preparation for Independence?

Before the late nineteenth century, Europeans knew little of Africa's interior. If they had been able to penetrate it, ignorance and bias would have kept them from appreciating Africa's "triple heritage," dynamically expressed in the rise of the Zulu kingdom, in Islamic movements like the Sokoto caliphate, and in the proliferation of Africanized Christian churches. Yet the slave trade, which crystallized white attitudes of superiority, as well as later "legitimate" trade, had long since tied Africa into a Europe-dominated network of economic relations. Once Europeans could enter the interior, they quickly dominated Africa, imposing a map of their own making, with boundaries that have survived as added Western components of the triple heritage.

In the early twentieth century, apologists for imperialism tried to justify it as preparation for independence. Applied to Belgian or Portuguese colonies, any such idea was a grim mockery. French colonies were better run, although they, too, denied their African subjects basic rights. The British probably came closest to the supposed ideal. But the Nigerian and South African cases show this was not very close.

In Nigeria, unification produced a burst of development on the eve of World War I, but gradually the pace slowed, especially during the Depression. British attempts to generalize the system of indirect rule by appointing "warrant chiefs" in the south, and the abandonment of this program after the Aba Women's War, illustrated British uncertainty about how to prepare Nigeria for self-government. Meanwhile, limited economic development showed that the real goal of colonialism was to exploit the country's economic resources. Under the circumstances, mobilization of the nationalist opposition proved surprisingly gradual, although here as elsewhere European ideas and forms of political action in time also became Western elements of the triple heritage.

South Africa's history illustrates the differences that large numbers of European settlers could create. Competition among the two white communities clearly compounded the problem. English-Afrikaner competition for political control and European-African competition for the land thus form the distinctive themes of the country's history. Between the formation of the Union of South Africa in 1910 and the end of World War II, the Afrikaners gained political control, black rights were steadily eroded as the foundations of apartheid were laid, and the economy developed from reliance on mineral exports to reliance on mining plus industry. The nature of white rule makes it even more surprising here than in Nigeria that the nonwhites' political goals remained so moderate throughout this period. The influence of Gandhi's nonviolent philosophy, not just on the Asian community but also on the African National Congress, is especially significant.

Perhaps the most exceptional thing about South Africa, in comparative world perspective, is its attempted denial of the processes of political mobilization that have made the twentieth century into the age of the mass society. Complicated by British-Afrikaner competition, however, the whites' struggle to dispossess and dominate the Africans made it impossible to mobilize the masses, producing polarization instead. The polarization appeared first among whites as they rallied behind steadily more uncompromising leaders, from Smuts to Hertzog to Malan. The African majority's radicalization in the opposite sense was only beginning by World War II. The intricacy of South Africa's discriminatory legislation, and the fact that the majority would have to face not a few colonial troops and administrators, as in Nigeria, but rather all the political and military institutions of a sovereign state, would make the inevitable struggle more painful. Still, elsewhere in Africa, white settler regimes proved unable to survive for long after the collapse of European global domination in World War II. The ultimate fate of white South Africa might be postponed, but could it be different?

Note

1. Ali Mazrui, *The Africans: A Triple Heritage* (Boston: Little, Brown, 1986), pp. 44, 81.

Suggestions for Further Reading

Abrahams, Peter. *Mine Boy* (1976).

Achebe, Chinua. *Arrow of God* (1969).

———. *Things Fall Apart* (1959).

Afigbo, A. E., et al. *The Making of Modern Africa*. 2 vols. (1986).

Crowder, Michael. *The Story of Nigeria* (1978).

———, ed. *West African Resistance: The Military Response to Colonial Occupation*. rev. ed. (1978).

Curtin, Philip, Steven Feierman, Leonard Thompson, and Jan Vansina. *African History* (1978).

Hafkin, Nancy, and Edna Bay, eds. *Women in Africa* (1976).

Mazrui, Ali. *The Africans: A Triple Heritage* (1986).

Oliver, Roland, and Anthony Atmore. *Africa Since 1800*. 3d ed. (1981).

Paton, Alan. *Cry, the Beloved Country* (1948).

Rodney, Walter. *How Europe Underdeveloped Africa* (1974).

Shostak, Marjorie. *Nisa: The Life and Words of a !Kung Woman* (1983).

Thompson, Leonard. *A History of South Africa* (1990).

Wilson, Monica, and Leonard Thompson, eds. *The Oxford History of South Africa*. 2 vols. (1969–1971).

CHAPTER 10

Asian Struggles for Independence and Development

Generally defined as extending from the eastern Mediterranean coast and Russia's Ural Mountains to the Pacific, Asia is in many ways not a distinct or coherent unit. In one sense, it is part of a larger entity, the Afro-Eurasian landmass. Asia is the largest, most populous continent and by many criteria—ecological, ethnic, cultural, and linguistic—is the most diverse. Asia's diversity is highly important historically, for Asia contains three of the four zones in which the world's most influential civilizations have emerged: the Middle East, India, and East Asia, the fourth being Europe. Asia also has zones, Central and Southeast Asia, that have usually been peripheral to the major civilizations but at times have assumed very large importance in world history.

This chapter begins with an overview defining the major Asian zones and their relations with one another and with the rest of the world. The overview presents a flashback to eras preceding the rise of the West, times when Asia's civilizations were the world's most influential. As Chapter 1 noted, the lure of Asia's riches launched Europeans on the voyages that helped establish Western dominance. By 1914, parts of Asia—the Ottoman Empire, Iran, Afghanistan, Siam, China, and Japan—remained free of formal European domination, but European influence had become so great that real self-determination was nonexistent. Asians of the twentieth century have had to struggle to escape this dominance and recover their earlier standing in the world.

The overview provides the setting for closer examination of the three major Asian zones as we focus in on early twentieth-century Asia, highlighting India, China, Turkey, and Japan. Asia's most populous countries, India and China, failed to regain meaningful independence before 1945, although both did shortly after, as Chapter 17 shows. Between the world wars, Turkey became Asia's second most successful country in reasserting its independence. Uniquely successful in escaping the common Asian fate of subordination to the West, Japan had already accomplished the most important part of its modern transformation before 1914. Between the world wars, it continued its ascent before falling to dire—but temporary—defeat by 1945.

The comparison of India, China, Turkey, and Japan reveals factors that governed each country's success in adapting to twentieth-century conditions. The conclusion of this chapter identifies these factors as four: responsiveness to foreign ideas, consensus about the definition of national identity and the organization of political life, basic social change to support the drive for independence, and ability to devise an economic strategy that could overcome the effects of colonialism. Chapter 17 will show that these factors, assuming some new dimensions after 1945, remained critical into the 1990s.

Asian Centers of Civilization

The most fruitful way to study Asia's history is to compare its major civilizations. This overview first examines their growth and interaction chronologically, then highlights key topics for the twentieth century.

Stages in the Development of Major Asian Civilizations

Africa has the oldest known human remains, but the earliest cities grew up in Asia, about 3500 B.C. on the Tigris and Euphrates rivers in what is now Iraq. The next urban centers emerged about 3000 B.C. in Egypt, an African land linked in its later history to southwest Asia. Cities appeared in India about 2500 B.C., in China about 1500 B.C., and in Central America about 200 B.C. "City" and "civilization" are related concepts: the word *civilization* derives from the Latin *civis* (citizen of a city). The rise of cities became possible once ancient societies had domesticated plants and animals and farmers had begun to settle in permanent villages. Some villages produced enough food to support craftworkers or religious leaders. Specialization of roles and production processes continued; some settlements kept growing in size and complexity, and gradually cities and civilizations emerged. As such growth occurred, craftworkers' need for raw materials and markets gave rise to trade and efforts to expand the city's zone of control. Organized governmental institutions took form, with their military forces and tax collection systems. Village shrines grew into temples staffed by religious functionaries who exerted wide influence. Merchants, rulers, and priests needed ways to keep track of information. The solution was the development of writing, which gradually began to be used also for "less practical" purposes, such as philosophy and literature. Technical innovation—in this period inventions like irrigation canals, sails, and wheeled vehicles—proved basic to civilization's advance. The cities generated most of the ferment that creates great civilizations, but their development required the extension of control over a wider area—not just a city but a kingdom or an empire.

Not all civilizations had all these traits. For example, Andean civilizations lacked writing. Specific cases varied, but the traits described above generally appeared as civilizations emerged.

The earliest civilizations developed along river valleys. Beyond them lived peoples whom the "civilized" saw as "barbarians." Such peoples had their own cultures but lacked some of the urban centers' refinements. In time, however, the pattern of civilizations isolated like islands in a sea of "barbarism" began to change.

Between about 1000 B.C. and A.D. 500, larger-scaled civilizations arose, extending their influence outward over local cultures and gradually coming into contact with one another. This process created an *ecumene* stretching from the British Isles to the China Sea. From a Greek word for the "inhabited part of the world," *ecumene* refers in present-day usage to parts of the world whose peoples knew about and interacted with one another. The civilizations of this period also proved "classic" in the sense that they created philosophical or religious systems that have retained normative force until the present. In this period emerged Greek philosophy, Christianity, Hinduism, Buddhism, and Confucianism. In each civilization, one language, sometimes more, acquired special prestige as the medium for transmission of such belief systems; such "classic" languages include Greek and Latin in the West, Sanskrit in India, and Chinese in East Asia. Several belief systems extended their influence beyond their regions of origin: ancient Greek culture as far as Spain and India; Christianity from the Middle East to Europe and eventually throughout the world; and Buddhism from India through most of South and East Asia.

In the period between 1000 B.C. and A.D. 500, technical advances again furthered the growth of civilization. Iron smelting, developed earlier in Asia Minor, spread from there and led to major improvements in tools and weapons. Growing trade created a need for new media of exchange—hence the invention of coinage in Asia Minor and Greece. Useful plants and animals also became more widely known: India's chickens and cotton, China's oranges and peaches. The first waterwheels were placed in use. In Iraq and China, for example, governments built extensive irrigation canals, which doubled as communication networks for expanding trade and consolidating political control over larger areas. More common were the road networks created by the major empires. The Roman roads are the best known in the West, but similar systems ran, with interconnections, all across the ecumene. The "Silk Routes" crossing Central Asia from Iran to China were the most important routes for intercivilizational trade and communication until the European voyages of exploration shifted world trade to the sea. The Silk Routes also illustrate the importance that a peripheral zone lying outside the major centers of civilization—in this case Central Asia—could assume.

From about A.D. 500 through 1500, the Eurasian ecumene became yet more tightly interlinked. The spread of technical improvements, such as paper, printing from movable type, gunpowder, and the compass—apparently all originating from China—facilitated communication and transport. One sign of tighter Eurasian integration was the rise of empires larger than any yet known, such as the Islamic Empire, which stretched, by the eighth century, from Spain to the borders of China; or the thirteenth-century Mongol Empire, which arose in Central Asia but included much of East Asia, Russia, and the Middle East. Emerging at a time when weakness and disunity created exceptional opportunities for Central Asia's mounted horsemen to deploy their much-feared military skills against the major civilizations, the Mongol Empire became the only one ever to rule across Eurasia, from the Baltic Sea to the Pacific.

Between 500 and 1500, the civilizations that emerged in the preceding period survived or were transformed to varying degrees, despite invasions by such "barbarian" outsiders as the Germans in northern Europe or the Mongols farther east. While absorbing extensive Buddhist influence in this period, China became the outstanding example of cultural continuity. No other culture has retained such consistency among so many people across such vast stretches of time. From the sixth century, too, dates the massive transmission of Chinese cultural influence to Japan, Korea, and Vietnam. In India, cultural continuity was less strong but still significant. Buddhism went into decline from the sixth century on in India, and Hinduism regained ground, partly by absorbing Buddhist ideas. Conquerors from the Middle East introduced Islam into India, as well. The rise of Islam in the seventh century caused sharper discontinuity in the Middle East than in either China or India. Islam forms a single monotheistic tradition with Judaism and Christianity, and Islamic civilization also absorbed many elements from earlier Middle Eastern and Greek cultures. Yet the rise of Islam marked a break: it abruptly changed the religious map of the Middle East and far beyond, and it established Arabic as the "classic" language of a major new civilization, in place of other languages formerly used in the region. The greatest discontinuities occurred, however, in Europe. There the Roman Empire's collapse cleared the ground for a substantially different civilization. Largely from this break stems the exceptional self-transformative dynamic that propelled the West's rise to global dominance after 1500, as noted in Chapter 1.

In 1500, if there had been observers equally well informed about all major civilizations, probably only the most perceptive could have predicted that Western civilization would eventually become the world's most powerful. China would have impressed all observers by its size, productivity, and brilliance. The Islamic world would have impressed them by both its brilliance and its extent, from West Africa far up into Central Asia and, in a different line of advance extending across India, all the way to what we now call the Philippines. Moreover, a series of great regional Islamic empires was developing, centered in the Middle East and South Asia. Europe, in contrast, would have appeared small, poor, and divided. In 1500 it would have taken a discerning observer indeed to see in Europe's early voyages of exploration, so different from the great Asian empires' patterns of landwise expansion, the prospect of enlarging the ecumene into a global one under European sway.

Today, generations that have grown complacent about Western pre-eminence do well to learn about Asia's civilizations and about how hard Asians have striven to regain their historic prominence.

Political and Economic Themes in Asian History

Comparative study of major Asian civilizations suggests political and economic themes that have retained their importance in the twentieth century. The most salient political theme was the persistent drive to integrate each of the great Asian centers into one or a few large states. Western Europe's pattern of division into multiple states, following the Romans' collapse, formed the exception, not the rule, by comparative Eurasian standards. Asian centers had periods of political disunity, even anarchy; but in each the push for integration would in time reassert itself. Moreover, the periods remembered as the greatest were those when the large Asian empires flourished. The Chinese were perhaps most successful in maintaining this unity, despite foreign invasions and chaotic periods between dynasties. India's history was less consistent but includes a number of periods when large empires integrated much of the Indian subcontinent. The Maurya Empire included all but India's southern tip in the third century A.D., and the Mughal Empire controlled most of northern and central India in the seventeenth century. The unity and power of the Islamic Middle East was greatest under the Abbasid rulers, who flourished in the ninth century, and the Ottomans, who flourished in the sixteenth. In Islam, the drive for unity became an article of faith: the community of Muslims (*ummah*) should be not only a spiritual but also a political unit. Even the episodes during which peoples from outside the major civilizational centers most influenced Asian history underscore the theme of political unity. These peoples either invaded the major civilizational centers and created large states in them, as the Turks did in the Middle East; or—in the unique case of the Mongols—they created an empire combining parts of several major civilizational zones with the Mongols' Central Asian homeland.

We can sense why the drive for large-scale integration has been so important in Asia's great centers of civilization if we consider what disunity could mean for them, or if we look at zones outside the major civilizational centers. In a vast region where so many peoples and cultures interacted and competed, fragmentation meant vulnerability. The breakup of the Islamic Empire after the ninth century, or the chaos that preceded the rise of China's Ming dynasty in the fourteenth, reinforced the assumption that a large, centralized state was needed to maintain the order required for civilization to flourish. Only in exceptional circumstances, it seems, could a society combine relative security with politcal decentralization. Western Europe, isolated at the far end of the ecumene and too primitive for much of its history to attract covetous eyes, illustrates this point in a general way. Perhaps the best examples, however, are two island nations at the extreme ends of Eurasia: England, which idealized political decentralization to a unique degree; and Japan, where reverence for the state was much stronger but where political fragmentation under the Tokugawa shogunate (1600–1867) could easily have opened the way to conquest if it had not been for the surrounding sea. If, as Chapter 1 argues, the most democratic societies are those in which multiple power centers historically coexisted, then it is not hard to see why Asia has few real democracies or why Japan became the most democratic Asian nation.

If the necessities of survival over much of Eurasia indicated that the individual's best interest lay in subjection to a great ruler, at least the Asian civilizations' material and intellectual achievements remained unmatched over most of human history. We have noted some of the many innovations that came to Europe from Asia. China, with its vast production of tea and luxury goods, especially silk and porcelain (which we call "china" because Europeans were unable to produce it until the eighteenth century), was surely the most productive and creative Asian country of all. Yet most of Asia historically produced goods that Europeans coveted, and the original thrust of Europe's overseas expansion was to gain direct access to and control of these markets.

Eventually succeeding in this effort, Europeans shifted the economic equilibrium between themselves and Asia. Previously in Asia's favor, from the sixteenth century on, this balance favored Europe and eventually also North America. Yet the West's intrusion proved but an episode in Asia's long history. The twentieth-century breakup of European dominance implied that the economic balance might shift back toward Asia. Recent decades have offered signs that such an economic shift is indeed occurring. If confirmed, these signs will prove the durability of the Asian civilizations' vigor and will mark the greatest change in five hundred years in the history of Asia's economic relations with the outside world. Taking up the three major Asian civilizational zones in the order of their passing under European sway, this chapter examines Asia's modern history through 1945.

India Under the British

Colonialism hit India first and hardest. After the Portuguese arrived in 1498, a series of European peoples vied for control of India's trade. By the eighteenth century, the leading contenders were the officially chartered British and French trading companies. The British company won against the French and began consolidating its control, a formidable task. The country was large, about half the size of the continental United States today. India's peoples spoke hundreds of languages and dialects, including some fifteen major languages. Among the half-dozen religions, the Hindus were by far the most numerous, although the Muslims had long been dominant politically. And the political situation was chaotic. The Mughal Empire, the last independent state to rule most of India, had fallen apart in the eighteenth century. In the 1790s the British directly controlled only a little territory, mostly in the northeast, but the East India Company repeatedly extended its zones of direct control. Elsewhere, it sought alliances with local rulers, cultivating cooperative ones as supporters of British rule.

From Company Rule to Crown Rule

Company rule lasted until 1858. By then, nearly all of India lay under direct or indirect British rule. With unification, company rule brought many changes. The British abolished *sati,* the ritual suicide of Hindu widows on the cremation pyres of their husbands, and promoted English-style education. They introduced the ideas of nineteenth-century liberalism—for example, through the Charter Act of 1833. Politically, the act promised equal rights for all Indians, including the right to employment under the East India Company. Economically, the act abolished the company's monopoly over most branches of trade and opened India to unrestricted British immigration and enterprise. Although the political provisions of the act were not fully enforced, the economic ones were. Free trade had come to India.

These measures had mixed effects. Intervention in matters of Hindu or Muslim religious belief provoked the Sepoy Mutiny of 1857–1858. This Anglo-Indian war, the bloodiest conflict ever fought in India, created lasting distrust of the "natives" and prompted the British government to take control away from the East India Company. In the long run, because Britain was the only industrialized state at the time, free trade was more devastating than the mutiny. For an unindustrialized country like India, free trade meant the collapse of production by hand, massive unemployment, and economic subordination.

When crown rule replaced company rule in 1858, India assumed the status in the British Empire that it retained until independence in 1947. With its huge markets and large production of spices, tea, and other exotic goods, India was the "jewel of empire." Queen Victoria became sovereign over the country and assumed the title empress of India in 1877. A viceroy represented her there. In London, where the Colonial Office managed most of Britain's overseas dependencies, another ministry, the India Office, managed India alone. Its head, the secretary of state for India, was a member of the prime minister's cabinet.

In India, crown rule had a conservative impact in some ways. British control over the Indian army was tightened. Many local princes were left in place (indirect rule). But technological modernization continued, as steamships, telegraphs, and railroads tied India more tightly into the imperial system. As usual, colonial administration siphoned off much of the country's wealth. By 1892, about a fourth of the Indian government's annual expenditures went for overseas expenses. Indians had little to say about this. The governance of India remained mostly in the hands of British bureaucrats.

Gradual Progress Toward Self-Rule

From 1858 to 1947, Indian participation in public affairs expanded but slowly. Indians became eligible for certain appointments in the civil service in 1854. But until 1921, the examinations required for appointment occurred only in England, not in India. The first steps toward giving Indians some control of local affairs, and representation on the councils of the viceroy and the governors of Bombay and Madras, also took place during the first half-century of crown rule. But not until 1907 were the first Indian members appointed to the council of the secretary of state for India in London.

Far-reaching change began only after World War I. In 1917, Secretary of State for India Edwin Samuel Montagu promised gradual steps toward "association of Indians in every branch of the administration," "development of self-governing institutions," and "responsible government." Delivery on these promises came with two acts of the British Parliament, the Government of India acts of 1921 and 1935. These acts broadened the franchise and transferred nearly all government responsibilities at the provincial level, as well as some at the central-government level, into Indian hands. In 1935 some 35 million men and women, one-sixth of the adult population, were eligible to vote. Although the 1935 act at first dissatisfied nationalists, large sections of it were included in independent India's constitution of 1950.

The British did not make such concessions before Indians had invested years of effort in political organization and action. India's major nationalist party, the Indian National Congress, was founded in 1885, very early by colonial standards. Hindus dominated the Congress party from the start, and tensions with Muslims and other communities soon arose. The Hindu majority, however, had certain qualities that enabled it to respond effectively to India's political situation. The Hindus had not been sorry to see the British end the earlier Muslim domination. Hinduism also lacked the doctrinal definition or closedness of some other religions. Hindus could absorb Western ideas into their outlook with less sense of conflict than could Muslims. Finally, there was charismatic leadership, furnished by Muhammad Ali Jinnah (1876–1949) to the Muslims and, even more, by Mahatma Gandhi (1869–1948) to the Hindus. In the long run, the British had to make concessions. Among the many who contributed to this outcome, Gandhi holds a unique place.

Gandhi and Nonviolence

Chapter 4 has examined Gandhi's background and ideas. When he returned to India in 1915, he was already known for his work in South Africa and his writings. He soon began applying his nonviolent techniques on behalf of the poor and dispossessed. When the British prolonged the wartime suspension of civil liberties into the postwar years, after having promised reforms that eventually became policy in the Government of India Act of 1921, Gandhi called for a nationwide campaign of civil disobedience. The ensuing tensions climaxed in 1919 at Amritsar, where the British commander, who had forbidden gatherings, led the massacre of a crowd that had peaceably assembled to celebrate a Hindu festival. Outraged, the Congress party then abandoned cooperation with the British and brought Gandhi to leadership of the movement.

In 1920 Gandhi opened a major campaign of noncooperation—refusal to work for the British, pay taxes, use British products, associate with the British at all. He predicted that this strategy would produce self-rule by the end of 1921. When it did not, disillusionment spread, and violence broke out. The British imprisoned Gandhi in 1922. By the time of his release in 1924, enthusiasm for noncooperation had waned, and Hindu-Muslim tensions had increased dangerously.

It was time for a different approach. Later Gandhi mounted two more large civil disobedience campaigns: in 1930–1932 against the

Mahatma Gandhi and his wife, Kasturbai, on their return to India, 1915. *D. G. Tendulkar*

British salt monopoly and salt tax (salt was a major dietary requirement for poor workers in this hot country) and in 1940–1942 in protest against the fact that Indians were forced to fight in World War II as British subjects. But for most of the 1920s and 1930s, he devoted himself to his Constructive Program, symbolized by his spinning wheel and the homespun cloth he wore and tried to popularize. With this program went further reformist efforts to improve the lot of women, whom Gandhi regarded as having greater capacity for nonviolence than men, and Untouchables. Meanwhile, India's industrialists—including wealthy Gandhi disciples who bankrolled his experiments in communal poverty—pursued goals of import substitution and heavy industrial development. In a sense, Gandhi and the industrialists pursued the same goal: self-sufficiency. The industrialists took the same developmental path that most developing countries chose, but Gandhi knew better how to capture the people's imagination.

Gandhi was politically astute. For example, fearing a split in the Congress party in 1928, he worked to elect Jawaharlal Nehru as its president, even though the younger man's reformist socialism placed him well to Gandhi's left. Later, though he disliked certain features of the Government of India Act of 1935, Gandhi decided that Congress members should participate in elections and take office. Congress leaders had waited so long for power that many misused it. Muslims protested, but they had fared poorly at the polls while the Congress won a smashing victory. Soon Jinnah and many other Muslims shifted to demanding a separate state. Meanwhile, officeholding unquestionably helped prepare the Congress leadership for independence.

With time, especially under the stress of World War II, Gandhi's hold over the masses seemed to weaken, but it never vanished. As British rule approached its end and preparations were made to divide the country into separate Hindu and Muslim states, Gandhi sought to restrain violence and maintain goodwill among religious communities. He had always opposed the "vivisection" of India. But on August 15, 1947, India and Pakistan became independent as separate states (Map 10.1). The Muslim state, Pakistan, combined two widely separated territories under a single national government. The mood of India had shifted away from Gandhi's vision. In January 1948 he was assassinated by a member of an extremist Hindu movement.

Even in his own country, Gandhi's methods have not been the ones most used to solve

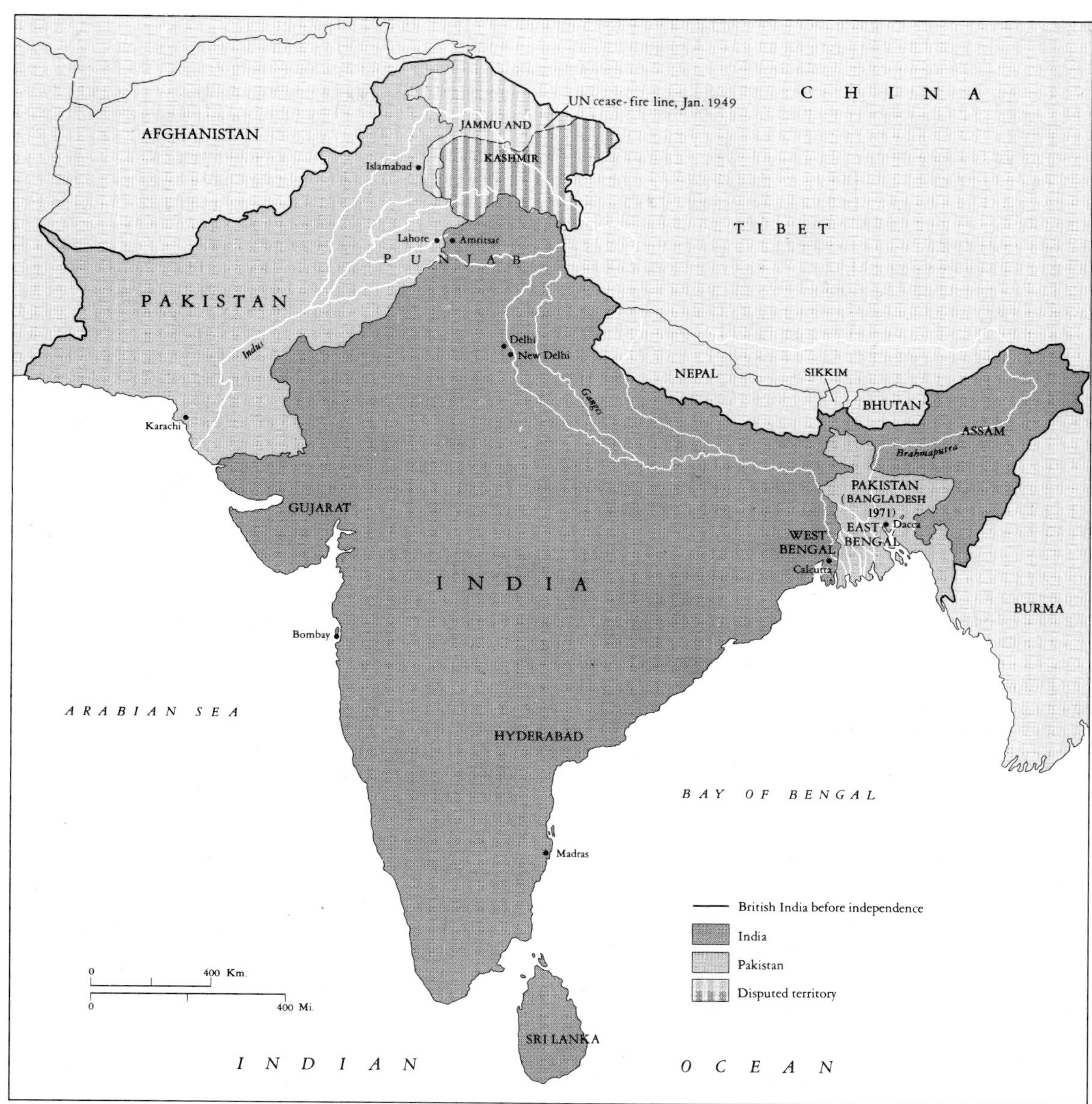

Map 10.1 *The Partition of British India, 1947*

the political and economic problems of peoples trying to escape from colonialism. Yet his memory lives on. His nonviolent principles have exerted a far-reaching influence, from the African National Congress in South Africa, to Martin Luther King and the U.S. civil rights movement, the European antinuclear movement of the 1980s, and popular movements working for development in South Asia today.

The Middle East and North Africa in the Era of European Expansionism

Unlike India, most of the Middle East survived to World War I without being brought formally under European rule.* But this region had special significance for European colonialism from the beginning. Earlier, Europe's prime source of exotic goods had long been the Islamic ports of the eastern Mediterranean. Knowing that many of those goods were produced farther east, Europeans began to seek direct access to their sources, thus opening the age of oceanic exploration that brought Columbus to the Americas and the Portuguese to India.

Dimensions of European Dominance

Europeans first undermined the economy of the Middle East. The sea route they established around Africa diverted the trade that had enriched the Middle East, slowly choking off its economic vitality. Then, although they did not take control, Europeans intervened in the internal affairs of Middle Eastern countries. By continuing to allow foreign trade to be organized along traditional lines, Islamic rulers opened the way for this intervention.

For centuries, when Europe still had few goods to entice Muslim merchants, Islamic rulers had granted Europeans the right to trade in their countries in return for the payment of certain duties. Traditional Islamic states were officially committed to maintaining Islamic religious law, but they typically allowed European traders in the Middle East to be governed by their own law in dealings among themselves. Islamic rulers applied the same legal policy to the non-Muslim communities among their subjects. The term *extraterritoriality* is often used to refer to the foreigners' legal privileges. The word does not mean that Europeans acquired control of territory in the Islamic lands. It means the opposite: they were allowed to operate under the law of their homelands, even though they were in an independent country that gave them this privilege only as a convenience.

As long as European civilization remained less developed, extraterritoriality did not harm Islamic interests. When the balance shifted, Islamic rulers were slow to recognize the change. Gradually, Europeans acquired a technological lead and began to import into the

*The expression *Middle East* is objectionable because it defines the region's location from a European viewpoint (the fact that the same region is sometimes called the *Near East* adds further confusion). Yet we shall use *Middle East* for want of a concise alternative. The Middle East consists of Turkey, Iran, the Arab lands of southwest Asia (including what is now Israel), and Egypt; some authorities also include the Sudan and Afghanistan. We could call the region *southwest Asia,* except that Egypt, one of its most important countries, is in Africa. North Africa (Libya, Tunisia, Algeria, Morocco) is an extension of the Middle East, sharing both Islamic faith and Arab culture with Egypt and with the Arab countries of southwest Asia. The Middle East is the historic heartland of the Islamic world, which includes much of Africa and Asia. *Islamic* is an adjective referring to the religion of Islam, the civilization that grew up around Islam, or the people who believe in Islam. *Muslim* is the Arabic term for a person who accepts this faith. *Arab* refers not to religion but to language and ethnic identity. Most Arabs are Muslim, some Arabs are Christian, and a few Jews still live in Arab countries. Among Middle Eastern Muslims, the major non-Arab linguistic groups are Turks and Iranians.

Middle East goods they had once exported from it: staples like sugar and coffee, as well as manufactures. Because of the Europeans' commercial privileges Islamic rulers could not raise import duties to protect local producers and merchants. Europeans also kept up constant pressure for enlargement of their privileges.

The process reached the point in 1838 where the Ottoman Empire—which then included all of the Middle East except Iran, as well as much of southeastern Europe and part of North Africa—had to accept a treaty with Britain that introduced free trade. In the Middle East the British thus obtained by treaty what they had obtained in India by the Charter Act of 1833. The economic effects were predictable. Trade balances shifted strongly in Europe's favor. Local manufactures and monetary systems fell into disarray. By the 1870s, Middle Eastern governments were going bankrupt, and Europeans were seizing control of their revenues to repay European creditors.

European powers also pressed to enlarge their noncommercial privileges. In the Ottoman Empire, these included the right to enroll a few locals, serving on consular staffs, as subjects of European governments. This privilege gradually extended into virtual sale of passports. Merchants who were subjects of the Ottoman sultan were eager buyers, since acquiring foreign nationality was the only way for them to enjoy as many advantages in their own country as their foreign competitors did. Local merchants' ability to acquire foreign nationality further weakened the Ottoman economy and the government's ability to raise revenue. Because many merchants who took foreign nationality were non-Muslims, the passport trade also worsened relations among religious communities. In time, European states extended their protection beyond individuals to whole religious communities. The French protected churches that acknowledged papal authority. The Russians protected Orthodox Christians. So it went, until almost all religious communities had foreign protectors—except the Muslims.

By the nineteenth century, both the Ottoman Empire and Iran had been so undermined that they probably had less real independence than the Latin American republics. The Ottoman Empire made vigorous efforts at reform, which created the basis for more successful twentieth-century reforms. At times, Europeans recognized Ottoman efforts. During the Crimean War (1854–1856), several European states allied with the Ottomans against Russia, symbolically accepting the Ottoman Empire as an equal in military alliance (1854) and as a member of the European family of nations in the Treaty of Paris (1856). More often, the great powers regarded this partly European empire to the east as the "sick man of Europe." When they wished, they took outlying provinces. France helped itself to Algeria (1830) and Tunisia (1881). England took Cyprus (1878) and occupied Egypt (1882). When not grabbing territory, the European powers cooperated to preserve the Ottoman Empire, whose condition so favored their interests. Iran was in sorrier shape, chiefly because the government was weaker even after the revolution of 1905–1911 introduced a supposedly constitutional monarchy. In Iran the dominant outside powers were Russia and Britain.

Political Fragmentation and the Drive for National Independence

After World War I, European control seemed to grow stronger, as Europeans divided the territories of the Ottoman Empire and asserted political dominance over much of the Middle East. This region, which until recently had known only two states of consequence, the Ottoman Empire and Iran, now suffered a new degree of political fragmentation, which maps still reflect (Map 10.2). Uncomfortable with this innovation, many Middle Easterners have since sought to re-create unities of larger scale, such as historically prevailed in the Middle East and in other great Asian centers of civilization. For the short run, however, a more immediate problem was to recover independence at what appeared on the region's redrawn map as the "national" level. As this struggle began, European control proved less solid in some places than at first appeared. For illustrations, we shall look first at Iran, then at Ottoman successor states.

Iran Although Iran declared neutrality during World War I, it still suffered from fighting and foreign occupation. Afterward, while the Bolsheviks took the Soviet Union temporarily out of the imperialist game, the British tried to fill the gap. In 1919, they prepared a treaty that would have made Iran a virtual British protectorate. When Iranian and foreign opposition forced abandonment of this idea, the British withdrew.

Shortly afterward, a military officer, Reza Khan, emerged as shah (1925–1941), founding the Pahlevi dynasty. Iran's first effective modernizing ruler, Reza Shah founded the nation's army, its modern educational system, and its railway network—all long overdue reforms. But he also set the example of despotism and greed that ended in revolution against his son, Muhammad Reza Shah (1941–1979). Reza had to abdicate in 1941, when the British and Soviets occupied Iran—a measure he patriotically opposed—to use it as a conduit for war aid to the Soviet Union. Becoming shah under such circumstances, young Muhammad Reza only slowly regained his father's power (see Chapter 17).

The Succession to the Ottoman Empire

The consequences of World War I were more serious for the Ottoman Empire, which had entered the war on the German side. During the war, Britain and its allies began planning to liquidate the empire. Ultimately, they made too many plans. To start an anti-Ottoman revolt in the Arabian peninsula, the British encouraged Arab aspirations to independence in certain territories. To smooth relations with France, Britain agreed to divide some of those territories into zones that the two powers would control directly or indirectly. Then, in 1917, Britain aligned itself with the Zionist movement by issuing the Balfour Declaration, which declared that Britain favored establishment of a "national home for the Jewish people" in Palestine and would support efforts to realize this goal on certain conditions. Many Zionists, and many of their opponents, interpreted the declaration to mean British support for the creation of a Jewish state or even a British promise of such a state.

At the peace conference, it proved impossible to reconcile all these commitments. British and French interests won out in the Treaty of Sèvres. The Zionists managed to get their goals recognized. The Arabs were not so lucky. Nor were the Turks at first.

The treaty disposed of every part of the former empire. Istanbul and the straits that flowed past it, connecting the Black Sea with the Aegean, were to form an international zone. Other regions on the edges of what is now the Republic of Turkey were to go to various foreign powers or to local non-Turkish peoples (the Kurds and the Armenians). The Turks were to have only what remained. Mandates from the League of Nations assigned Syria, including what is now Lebanon, to France and Iraq to Britain. A special mandate, including many Zionist goals, gave Britain control of the territory that is now Israel and Jordan. Other provisions of the treaty recognized the British position in Egypt and Cyprus. Thus direct European domination came to parts of the world that had not previously known it.

The struggle for political independence consequently became the main theme of the interwar years in the former Ottoman territories. As examples, we shall consider the cases of Egypt, Palestine, and the Turkish Republic.

Egypt In Egypt, a nationalist movement predated the British occupation of 1882. Nationalism re-emerged in anti-British form in the 1890s and erupted in what Egyptians remember as the revolution of 1919. Unable to suppress this uprising, and unwilling to negotiate with the nationalists, the British unilaterally declared the country independent under a constitutional monarchy (1922–1923). But they attached conditions that required negotiations. Not until 1936 could the British and the Egyptian nationalists agree on these conditions. Abolition of extraterritoriality followed in 1937. Although Egypt was supposedly fully independent after 1936, the British retained a "preferential alliance," giving them special rights in wartime. During World War II they exercised these rights with such force as to nullify Egypt's independence and discredit the Egyptians who had negotiated the 1936 treaty.

This experience showed just how elusive independence could be for a colonial country. A new push for independence required the emergence of a new leader, Gamal Abdel Nasser, in 1952.

Palestine How the League of Nations mandates worked out depended on local conditions and the policies of the European power in charge. One familiar theme was that boundaries drawn—in some cases—by Europeans had little relation to local social and economic realities. The British adhered to the mandate ideal fairly successfully in Iraq. The French did not try to in Syria and Lebanon. In Palestine, even the British failed.

The mandate concept required preparation for self-government. But Palestine included two communities with incompatible goals: the Zionists, mostly immigrants from Europe, and the local Arabs. The Arabs' goals were at first less clear-cut: Palestinian nationalism emerged only gradually. But an international Zionist movement had been active even before World War I. Its goal was to redevelop Palestine as a Jewish homeland with a Jewish culture and all the social and economic institutions needed for self-sufficiency. The idea of a Jewish state had been current in the movement at least since one of its founders, Theodor Herzl, had published a book called *The Jewish State* in 1896. But for a long time, an independent Jewish state seemed a remote goal. Not until May 1942 did the Zionist movement in general formally commit itself to the demand for a sovereign "Jewish commonwealth" after the war.

After World War I, Palestinian Arabs began to realize what extensive Jewish immigration could mean for them. Outbreaks of violence began in 1920 and culminated in the Arab Revolt of 1936–1939. The British struggled to satisfy both sides. The mandate permitted them to specify that the terms of the Balfour Declaration would apply only to part of the mandated territory. In 1922 they exercised this option, setting aside the territory east of the Jordan River to be an Arab state, now known as the Kingdom of Jordan. West of the river, British difficulties in bridging the Arab-Zionist gap continued. They grew worse after the rise of Nazism in Europe increased the demand for unlimited Jewish immigration. Ultimately, the British could not devise immigration and land policies that satisfied both Zionists and Palestinian Arabs, who feared that they would become a minority in their homeland.

By the time World War II broke out, the Zionists bitterly resented the British. They hated the Nazis still more, however, and backed Britain in the war. But resentment of British policy played a major role in prompting the Zionist demand of May 1942 for a sovereign state. Later, as the horrors inflicted on European Jewry became known more fully, Zionist feeling grew even stronger. By the time the war ended, the British could no longer

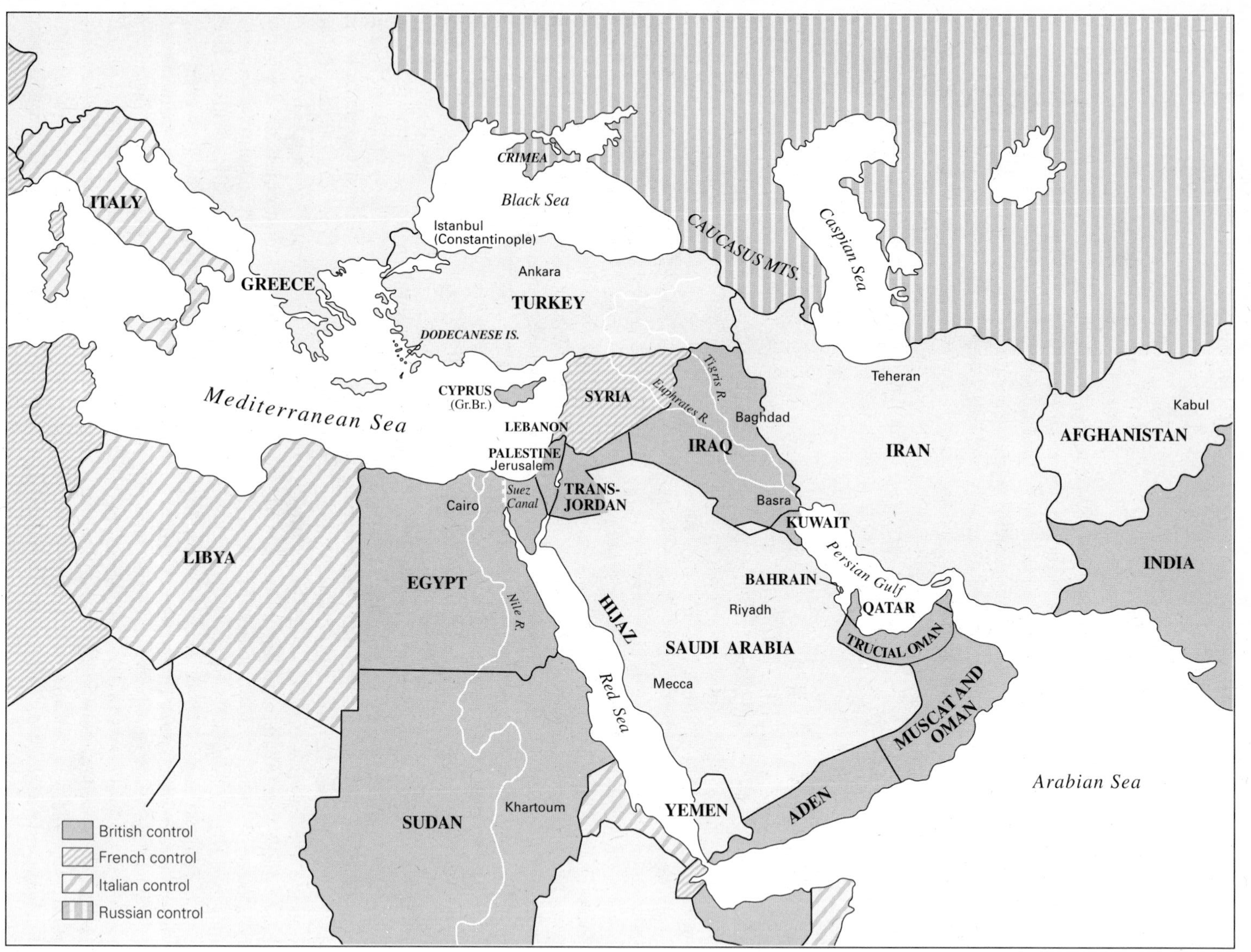
CRIMEA
Black Sea
ITALY
Istanbul (Constantinople)
CAUCASUS MTS.
Caspian Sea
Ankara
GREECE
TURKEY
DODECANESE IS.
Teheran
CYPRUS (Gr.Br.)
SYRIA
Euphrates R.
Tigris R.
Kabul
Mediterranean Sea
Baghdad
LEBANON
AFGHANISTAN
IRAQ
IRAN
PALESTINE
Jerusalem
TRANS-JORDAN
Suez Canal
Cairo
Basra
KUWAIT
LIBYA
Persian Gulf
INDIA
BAHRAIN
EGYPT
Nile R.
HIJAZ
Riyadh
QATAR
TRUCIAL OMAN
SAUDI ARABIA
Mecca
Red Sea
MUSCAT AND OMAN
Arabian Sea
ADEN
Khartoum
YEMEN
SUDAN
British control
French control
Italian control
Russian control

manage Palestine. They decided to turn it over to the United Nations (UN), as successor to the League of Nations, and withdraw.

In the ensuing melee, Zionist organization and will proved decisive, even after five Arab countries sent in forces to support the Palestinians against the new state of Israel, which declared its independence on May 14, 1948. The story of this remarkable state will merit fuller attention in Chapter 17.

Turkey Among Middle Eastern countries, Turkey came closest to defying the apparent postwar strengthening of European power. Sure that the multinational Ottoman Empire was finished, the Paris peacemakers did their work as if the Turkish people, among whom the empire had arisen, were also finished. Yet a mass-based Turkish nationalist movement, led by a charismatic general named Mustafa Kemal, emerged from the collapse of the empire and took up arms in 1919. Its goal was to create a nation-state and prevent the carving up of what is now Turkish territory.

By 1922 the military effort had succeeded so well that attempts to divide the territory were abandoned. The nationalists then destroyed what was left of the imperial government and declared a republic, with Ankara as capital. The Western powers convened a conference to negotiate a new peace, in which they renounced their extraterritorial privileges (1923). Through its nationalist revolution, Turkey had become the only defeated power of World War I to force revision of the peace terms.

But the "national struggle" of 1919–1922 was only the beginning of revolutionary change in Turkey. With Mustafa Kemal as president, the republic went on from political to social and cultural changes that were revolutionary in many respects. After a century of agony over the clash of Western and Islamic civilizations, the new state sought to overcome the conflict by turning its back on the heritage of Islamic empire. Instead, while keeping many late Ottoman reforms, it became a pro-Western, secular, nationalist republic—an Asian democracy emerging from a historic center of empire.

In the twentieth century, at least one other Asian country, Japan, has been more successful than Turkey in learning from the West, but no other has remade its own culture so completely in the process. Geography gave Turkey a unique potential for such reorientation, for it lies immediately next to Europe. In fact, part of its territory is in Europe. This potential gave a distinct stamp to the Turkish effort at state formation, the most successful such effort in the Islamic world of the interwar period.

Turkey's westernizing reforms began in 1924 with abolition of the institutions that had made Islam an official part of the imperial political system. Henceforth, as in the West, religion was to be a matter of private conscience. The old religious bureaucracy, religious courts, and religious schools were abolished or drastically modified. The legal system was almost completely secularized through adoption of Western-style codes.

Social and cultural reforms of other types followed. Western dress was prescribed for men. For women, veiling was discouraged. Polygamy was abolished, and civil marriage became mandatory. Major efforts were made to improve education for women and bring them into professional and public life. Mustafa Kemal, as political mobilizer, played an important role in the advancement of Turkish women, who became eligible to vote in local elections in 1930 and in national ones in 1934—exceptionally early dates by Asian

◀ ***Map 10.2 The Middle East, 1920s–1930s***

standards. Another important social reform was the adoption of Western-style family names, which became compulsory in 1935. It was then that Mustafa Kemal acquired the surname Atatürk, "father Turk." Among other things, the family names aided government efforts to implement modern systems of census registration, taxation, and military recruitment.

To strengthen the national character of its culture, Turkey adopted the Latin alphabet and launched a language revolution to purify Turkish by removing many borrowings from other Islamic languages. Simultaneously, the spread of education doubled the literacy rate, from 11 percent of the population in 1927 to 22 percent in 1940. The cultural inheritance of the Ottoman Empire became inaccessible to generations schooled only in the new language.

By Atatürk's death (1938), Turkey had experienced a cultural revolution and much social reform, but no social revolution. Turks had experienced extensive political mobilization, but no radical redistribution of wealth and power. Several factors contributed to this outcome. One was that Turkey had extensive uncultivated lands and distributed these in small holdings to the rural poor. Through the 1950s, expansion of the cultivated area was as important a factor in Turkish economic growth as was industrialization. Except in the southeast, landholding remained much less concentrated than in many other countries. A substantial minority of rural households owned no land or had to supplement what they owned by renting or sharecropping other fields; yet land reform never became a burning issue in Turkey.

In a different sense, the replacement of the multinational empire by a Turkish nationalist state also compensated for the lack of a fundamental restructuring of Turkish society. Yet this substitution left some important problems unsolved. The collapse of the empire had turned once-internal nationalist antagonisms into international problems. Despite the peace of the Atatürk years, lingering tensions between Turks and Greeks or Armenians illustrated this fact.

While not revolutionary, economic policy under Atatürk featured one major innovation. In 1932, Turkey became the first developing state (Mexico being the second) to adopt central planning for economic development. Inspired partly by Soviet practice, Turkey differed in that the state took responsibility only for key sectors of the economy, while leaving others in private hands. As in Latin America, the industrial drive aimed first at import substitution, then at heavy industry. The first five-year plan accomplished its goals in a number of fields, and the second produced an iron and steel mill, if an inefficient one. In the 1930s, industry's share of gross national product almost doubled, reaching 18 percent. A Turkish managerial class also began to develop; it would play a major economic and political role after World War II.

Not all of Atatürk's reforms were equally successful, but together they created a new concept of a Turkish nation and helped mobilize the populace into citizenship. This intent is clear from the organization of Atatürk's followers into the Republican People's party (1923) and from the nationwide creation of "people's houses" (*halkevi*) and "people's rooms" (*halkodasi*) as political and cultural centers.

Democratic values played a key role in the moblization process. Like other major Asian cultures, Turkey had no heritage of political pluralism. Under Atatürk it was a one-party state. But he and many others believed Turkey should be democratic. Atatürk encouraged experiments with opposition parties. After World War II, his successor, Ismet Inönü, authorized the formation of a second party. When this Democrat party won national elections in 1950, the Republican People's party stepped aside, opening an era of two-party—soon multiparty—politics. Turkey's democratization

Heroes of Turkish Independence, 1922. *Mustafa Kemal (left), first president of Turkey (1923–1938), with his deputy Ismet (president, 1938–1950). In 1935, under Turkey's surname law, they become Mustafa Kemal Atatürk and Ismet Inönü.* *The Mansell Collection*

has since faced many obstacles, but it remains an outstanding chapter in the non-Western world's political history.

Comparison with Japan shows a wide developmental gap between the two countries. The causes of this gap must include Turkey's low starting levels in development of its economy and human resources (witness the low literacy levels). Yet Turkish success in creating a new order was impressive. It is little wonder that Atatürk became an inspiration to Middle Eastern leaders of his own and later generations, from Reza Shah in Iran to Nasser and Sadat in Egypt.

China and Japan: Contrasts in Development

The easternmost of the great Asian centers of civilization did not feel substantial effects of European expansion until much later than either India or the Middle East. Although the Portuguese reached China and Japan in the sixteenth century, those countries were long able to manage their contacts with the faraway West. Japan chose to isolate itself almost entirely from 1639 on, confining contact with both Europeans and Chinese to the single port of Nagasaki. In the eighteenth century, China almost entirely limited its Western contacts to trading posts at Guangzhou (Canton).

Both traditional values and geography insulated Japan and China from European expansionism. Much as Muslims long rejected the idea that a non-Muslim culture could be on a par with their own, the Chinese traditionally saw other people as inferior. China was the "middle kingdom," and other peoples had to acknowledge its cultural and political superiority. Though China's relations with the outside world were more complex, the Chinese view was that envoys from other peoples could present themselves at the Son of Heaven's court only as payers of tribute. The Chinese entered the nineteenth century thinking of Europeans—when they thought of them at all—in such terms and saw nothing to learn from the West. Having borrowed from the Chinese and others in the past, the Japanese were more ready to learn. Their decision to exclude foreigners reflected a desire to avoid foreign domination and escape acknowledging Chinese superiority on Chinese terms.

In the mid-nineteenth century, isolation ended as Westerners forcibly "opened" China and then Japan. British merchants first went to China from India. At first, the trade was profitable to the Chinese. The only way the British could achieve a positive trade balance with China was to import Indian opium, thus fostering drug addiction in China. When the Qing (Ch'ing) ruling house tried to stop the drug traffic, the British responded with high-sounding rhetoric about free trade and with force. The First Opium War (1839–1842) was a sordid affair. Europeans had the means to exert force and goods to sell but no intention of accepting the status of "barbarians" owing tribute to the Chinese emperor.

The British used their victory to create the unequal treaty system, which completely turned the tables on China. This system, which remained in force until 1943, reduced a formally independent country to colonial status. The unequal treaties were patterned after the extraterritoriality of the Ottoman Empire but eventually went further. By the late nineteenth century, China had made many treaties, and the number of Chinese ports open to foreign trade had grown to about fifty. In China, extraterritoriality meant that foreign law covered foreigners anywhere in the country and everyone—including Chinese—who resided in the treaty ports. Opium was legalized. Restrictions on missionary activity were eliminated. Tariff rates were set low by treaty, so that the government lost part of its power to raise revenues. As the government slipped into debt to foreign interests, its revenues were placed under foreign control as security for the loans. At the end of the century, as doubts about the Qing dynasty's survival increased, emphasis shifted from extraterritoriality to the creation of spheres of influence—zones where a given power's interests took precedence.

At midcentury, Japan had seemed headed for a fate no better than China's. The United States took the lead in "opening" Japan. Naval missions commanded by Commodore Matthew Perry visited the country in 1853 and 1854 to press U.S. demands. Over the next few years, the unequal treaty system was established in Japan, too.

The process of "opening" was similar in both countries, but later events differed greatly. China's development remained among the least successful in Asia. Japan's quickly became the most successful.

China's Crisis of Authority

China was slow to respond to outside challenge for many reasons. One was the country's vast size and its population of 300 to 400 million people by the early nineteenth century. Even after many ports had been opened to foreign trade, most Chinese lived far in the interior, isolated from foreigners. Culturally, China was more homogeneous than other large empires. A monolith with tremendous inertia is extremely difficult to move. The rich intellectual tradition and self-centered worldview of the Chinese gave them many ways to explain external challenges. They had done this many times before. More than other Asian cultural centers, China first reacted to the West with a reinterpretation of its own traditionally dominant value tradition, Confucianism. Only at the end of the nineteenth century did China begin significant borrowing from Western cultures.

The Qing Dynasty and the Western Challenge The decline of the Qing ruling house (1644–1912) complicated China's reaction to the Western challenge. The Qing were not Chinese but Manchu, a tiny minority trying to rule the world's most populous country. Partly in reaction against European pressures, a series of provincial rebellions broke out in the second half of the nineteenth century, complicating the dynasty's problems. The Taiping Rebellion (1850–1864), the most serious, probably caused 20 million deaths, more than World War I. Unable to quell such disturbances with its own forces, the Qing government had to rely on forces led by the local gentry. Thereafter the central government progressively lost control of the provinces, and local affairs became militarized. At the turn of the twentieth century, the empress-mother, who hated Europeans, backed the anti-foreign Boxer Uprising. Her policy backfired when foreigners intervened. They put down the Boxers and imposed disastrous terms that inflamed nationalist resentments, thus undermining the dynasty more than ever.

Under the circumstances, serious reform efforts began slowly. Once under way, they further weakened the regime. In the 1860s, as part of a larger effort to reassert the Confucian ideal of government, the Chinese had made their first experiments in defensive westernization. They tried to obtain modern military technology and organized something like a foreign ministry and a system to train interpreters. Japan's victory in the Sino-Japanese War of 1894 revealed how much more rapidly Japan had changed; this triggered a new seriousness in Chinese reform efforts. A burst of reform ensued in 1898, soon frustrated by the empress-mother's opposition. But the catastrophic end of the Boxer Uprising left her and her supporters no choice but to carry through many of the reforms thwarted only a few years earlier.

The last decade of Qing rule thus brought major reforms. The examination system that had capped traditional education was replaced by new schools with a mixed Chinese-Western curriculum. Efforts were made to create new military schools and forces. Changes in administration included the creation of ministries and attempts at legal and budgetary reform. Under a plan to create a constitutional system, elective provincial and national assemblies came into being. Meanwhile, widespread demand to nationalize China's developing railways helped politicize the populace.

Revolution was on the way. Sun Yat-sen, China's first professional revolutionary, and others were at work by the 1890s. In 1905 Sun helped found a United League, intended to bring together all opposition elements. When revolution broke out in 1911, however, it was not entirely the work of this organization. The elective provincial and national assemblies played a critical role, becoming rallying points for opponents of the dynasty. Another essential factor was a government plan for nationalizing the railways on terms favorable to foreigners. When the assemblies' protests against the plan went unheeded, fifteen provinces proclaimed their independence in the fall of 1911. The provincial military forces that had grown up since the mid-nineteenth century then assumed a leading role in overthrowing the Qing regime. Sun, who was outside the country, returned to assume the provisional presidency of the Chinese Republic. The three-year-old emperor, bowing to the "mandate of Heaven . . . manifested through the wish of the people," abdicated in February 1912.

Nationalists Versus Communists Recent emperors had been weak, but their office had remained the focus of authority. With the fall of the dynasty, the entire Confucian system of ideas that had supported it came into question. What could hold China together? The revolutionary leadership set out to expand the United League into a National People's party (Guomindang, GMD) and made an attempt at parliamentary government. But the GMD had great difficulty gaining control of the country. Sun relinquished the provisional presidency of the republic to General Yuan Shikai (Yuan Shih-k'ai) after the general forced the emperor to abdicate. But Yuan turned into a dictator and would have made himself emperor if he

Student demonstration, Peking, November 29, 1919. *China's May Fourth Movement opened a new phase in mass politicization. Its memory helped provoke the student-led Tienanmen Square demonstrations of 1989. From the exhibition "China Between Revolutions." Photographs by Sidney D. Gamble, 1917–1927. Copyright 1989, the Sidney D. Gamble Foundation for China Studies*

had not died in 1916. After 1912, real control of much of China passed to local "warlords," military men with their own armies. The GMD did not regain control of China until 1928. Even then, GMD control proved only an episode in China's authority crisis, which continued through the civil war of 1946–1949.

Japanese expansionism worsened China's problems. During World War I, Japan tried to exploit China's weakness by occupying the German positions on the Shandong (Shantung) Peninsula and presenting twenty-one demands, which would have given Japan far-reaching control over China's government. China resisted some of the demands but had to accept a treaty recognizing Japan's claims in Shandong, southern Manchuria, and eastern Inner Mongolia. After the war the Paris Peace Conference failed to restore Chinese interests; this failure provoked the May Fourth Movement, a patriotic outburst that marked a new phase in the growth of Chinese nationalism (see Chapter 4).

Students, male and female, were prominent in the movement, for the new schools had done much to promote political mobilization. New political ideas were also spreading, including Marxism. The GMD tried to keep abreast of the changes and absorb the newly politicized elements of the population. Still, in 1921, the Chinese Communist party (CCP) was founded. The GMD and the CCP became leading forces in the struggle to create a new order.

At first, in line with Soviet thinking on Asian national revolutions, the CCP worked with the larger and stronger GMD in hopes of gaining power through it. Sun Yat-sen himself became interested in the Soviet model, tried to reorganize the GMD along Soviet party lines, and was eager for Comintern aid. Believing he could control the Communists, he accepted them as members of the GMD. One example of this collaboration occurred at the Huangpu (Whampoa) Military Academy. There, Chiang Kai-shek, who later succeeded Sun as head of the GMD, was superintendent, and Zhou Enlai (Chou En-lai), later premier of the People's Republic of China (1949–1976), had charge of political education.

In the 1920s, during the struggle against the warlords, the GMD-CCP relationship degenerated. A year after Chiang succeeded to GMD leadership in 1925, he launched his Northern Expedition to reunify China. By 1928, this campaign had been so successful that foreign powers recognized the Nationalist regime and began to give up some privileges of the unequal treaty system. Meanwhile, GMD-CCP tension worsened to the point of civil war in 1927, and the Communists were defeated—for the time being. Many Communists were killed, and many were forced underground or into exile.

For the next several years the Communists struggled to survive. In time they would emerge as China's most effective mass mobilizers. The key to their success was the idea, discussed in Chapter 4, that the revolution could be based on the peasantry, rather than on the proletariat, which scarcely existed in China. Mao did not invent this idea, but it came to dominate CCP policy as he became leader of the party during the Long March (1934–1935), which led the Communists to their new northwestern base at Yan'an in Shaanxi Province (Yenan, Shensi). Mao expressed his understanding of the relationship between mass mobilization and the military struggle in memorable terms: "such a gigantic national revolutionary war as ours cannot succeed without universal . . . mobilization. . . . The popular masses are like water, and the army is like a fish. How . . . can it be said that when there is water, a fish will have difficulty preserving its existence?"[1]

Meanwhile, the GMD faced huge problems in governing China. Chiang spent much of his time manipulating GMD factions. In a country with no tradition of political pluralism, he tried to turn his party into a political machine that would include everyone important. "Generalissimo" Chiang also had only limited control over the GMD military and the countryside. Limited administrative control meant a weak fiscal system. In the 1930s the government still got about half of its revenue from customs duties—a familiar indicator of fiscal underdevelopment—compared with about 1 percent in the United States at the time. Based on Sun's Three People's Principles—nationalism, democracy, and "people's livelihood" (a classical concept sometimes later equated with socialism)—the GMD ideology also lacked the clarity of communist thought. Largely urban oriented, the GMD regime failed to work effectively among the peasantry. The GMD's economic development efforts, too, almost exclusively benefited the modern sector of the economy, centered in the coastal cities. Agriculture, in which some 80 percent of the popu-

Japanese invasion of Manchuria. *The rail line built by the Japanese replaces one that the Chinese blew up in 1939. Control of the railroads was a key strategic issue during both the Japanese invasion of China and the later conflict between the Chinese Nationalists and the Communists.* *Pepperfoto*

lace worked amid serious problems of landlessness and exploitation, remained nearly untouched—except where the Communists gained control.

Japanese Aggression The GMD also had to contend with Japanese aggression in Manchuria. Manchuria's population was almost entirely Chinese, but the Japanese felt they had acquired interests there through the Russo-Japanese War of 1904–1905. Most foreign investment in Manchuria was Japanese, too. In warlord days, Japan wielded considerable power in Manchuria behind a front of Chinese sovereignty. But the spread of Chinese nationalism challenged that. In 1931, Japanese officers in Manchuria responded by attacking the Chinese at Mukden, going on to create

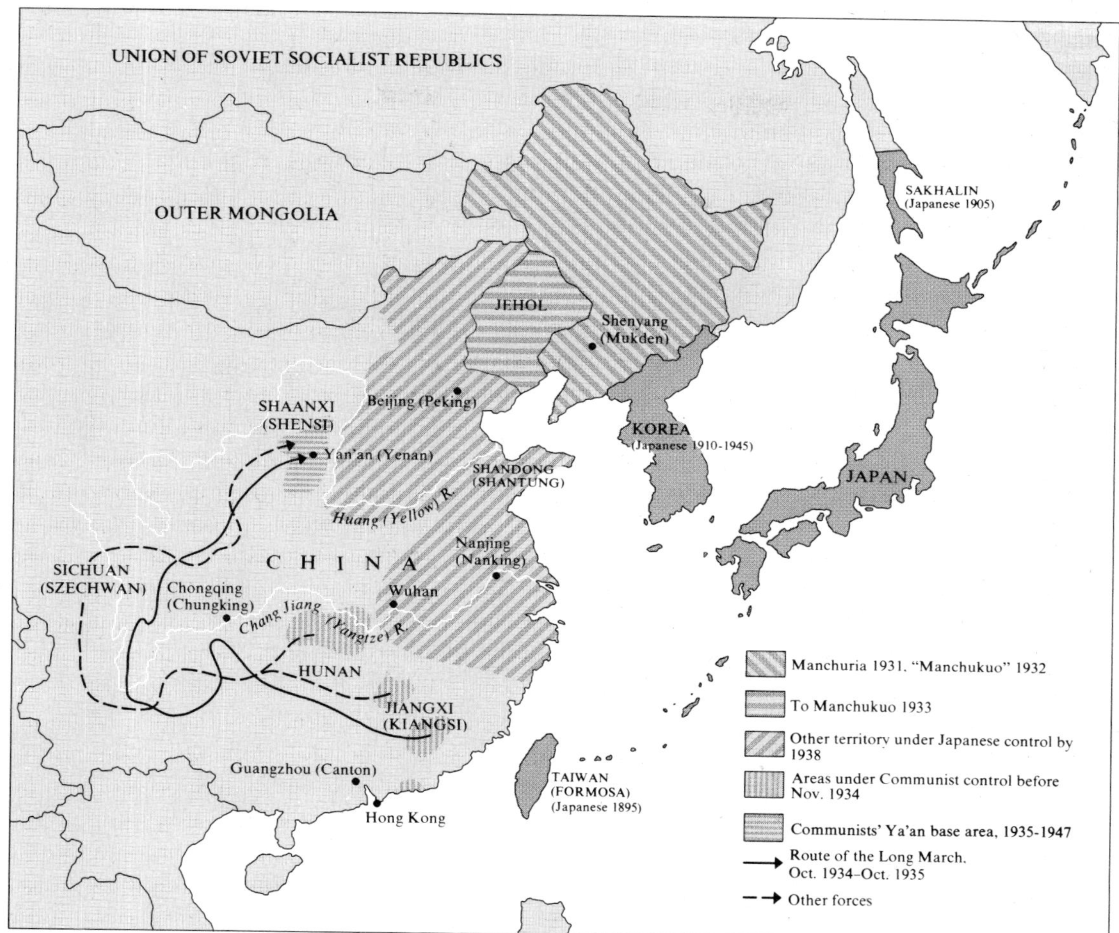

Map 10.3 China and Japan in the 1930s

the Japanese-dominated puppet state of Manchukuo (Map 10.3). Interfering farther south, the Japanese combined five Chinese provinces into a Japanese-influenced North China-land in 1935.

As in 1918, Japanese aggression inflamed Chinese nationalism. Chiang knew he was not strong enough to take on Japan. The Communists posed a more direct threat to his government. But his strategy of military campaigns against the Communists, rather than against the foreign invader, roused Chinese resentment until Chiang found himself forced to form a second common front between GMD and CCP in 1937. By then, a full-scale war between China and Japan had begun. For China, it was the beginning of World War II.

As in the Russia of 1917, war became the midwife of revolution. Japanese attacks forced the Nationalists into the interior, cutting them off from the major cities, their main bases of support. The landlord class, which had supported them in the countryside, either had to flee with them or remain helpless behind. The Japanese, in turn, had enough manpower to occupy the cities but not to control rural areas. That left the Communists to extend their bases, undermine the landlord gentry's two-thousand-year-old domination, and apply their skills in guerrilla warfare. With the Nationalists unable to defend the nation, the Communists began to seem like the real nationalists. Anti-Japanese feeling led thousands to slip out of the cities to join the Communists and also helped rally the peasantry to them. By war's end, Nationalist government authority had declined seriously, and the economy was near collapse. The stage was set for Communist triumph in the civil war of 1946–1949.

Japan's First Rise to Great-Power Status

U.S. commodore Matthew Perry's visits to Japan in 1853 and 1854 sparked a crisis that illustrates basic differences between Japan and China. Those differences explain why Japan's response to the West differed so from China's.

Whereas in China the emperor remained the central political figure despite dynastic decline, real power in Japan had for centuries belonged to a leading member of the warrior class, the *shogun,* though the emperor retained legitimacy and prestige. In China, the leading social class was that of scholar-officials, who served the emperor; in Japan, it was the warrior class of the *samurai*. All samurai felt themselves superior to commoners and jealously guarded their monopoly of warlike skills and privileges. But they differed vastly in wealth and power. After the shogun, the most important samurai were the lords (*daimyo*) of large and supposedly autonomous domains. There were 260 such domains in the nineteenth century. Each daimyo had many samurai retainers. It took a strong shogun to maintain authority over this system, and by the 1850s the shogunate was in decline. The need to respond to U.S. demands touched off its final crisis.

Japan needed consensus about such a controversial question. Most Japanese wanted the foreigners repelled, but the nation lacked the strength to do so. The shogun found himself forced to make treaties with the United States and with other powers, granting extraterritorial privileges of the sort that foreigners enjoyed in China. The shogun's inability to apply the policy that most Japanese wanted, and economic disruption following the country's sudden opening, brought the shogunate into question. Samurai discipline began to collapse. The emperor's prestige remained intact, however, and in 1868 a rebellion broke out under the slogan of "restoring" the rule of the emperor. The shogunate fell.

Revolution by Way of Restoration This event is called the Meiji Restoration, after the emperor. The Meiji emperor (1867–1912) did not wield real power, which the men who made the rebellion retained. The changes they introduced mark the beginning of modern Japan and deserve the name of revolution.

Major changes began with the organization of the central government system. In 1868 a Council of State was created, with various ministries under it. The revolutionary leaders soon assumed control of these ministries. In the same year, the imperial capital was moved from Kyoto to Tokyo, which—under its old name of Edo—had been the shogun's center. The next priority was to reassert the central government's authority over the autonomous domains; otherwise, Japan could produce no coordinated response to the Western challenge. The new leaders persuaded the daimyo to return their holdings voluntarily to the emperor. At first the daimyo were allowed to stay on as governors. But soon the domains disappeared entirely as the country was redivided into prefectures, the basis of the centrally controlled system of local government that still exists. The next step was to create a modern army and navy. The leaders of the revolution came from daimyo domains in which experiments in military modernization predated the revolution. The new leaders made such experimentation a national policy. They also undermined the status of the lower samurai by requiring universal military service for men (1873). Thus the new government eliminated Japan's old social class distinctions almost entirely.

A key problem for the new regime was finance. Existing revenue had been inadequate for the shogun. Because the new regime did not have good enough credit to borrow abroad and did not want to, Japan escaped the slide into bankruptcy and foreign financial control that other Asian countries experienced in this period. The new government limited its borrowing to the internal market and worked to improve its finances by reforming its monetary, banking, and taxation systems. Land tax reform gave landownership in the countryside to the peasant cultivators who actually paid the tax. Its effect was to stimulate growth in agricultural output and provide much of the capital for the first phase of Japan's modern economic development.

At first, economic growth was fastest in traditional sectors—agriculture, commerce, and handicrafts. Stimulants to growth included domestic security, expansion of foreign trade, unification of the national economy, and improvements such as modern shipping, telegraphs, and railways. A distinctive combination of government leadership and private enterprise also developed in this period. The government took the initiative in certain fields of industry, later selling many of the enterprises it founded to private investors. Even in the Meiji period, however, the individual initiative of Japan's businessmen probably contributed more to industrialization than did the government.

In fact, the readiness of the Japanese to respond to opportunities for economic growth was extraordinary by any standard. Even before the Meiji Restoration, Japan may have had an adult literacy rate of 40 percent, Asia's highest. Because of the country's isolation and ethnic homogeneity, its commerce remained essentially in the hands of Japanese, as opposed to foreigners or unassimilated minorities. Japan was also unusual among Asian cultures in not associating low prestige with commerce. Outside the samurai class, the Japanese had a long history as eager businessmen. With the eclipse of the warrior class after the Meiji Restoration, even former samurai assumed important roles in business. In time, Japanese business and industry developed a dual character, with both huge conglomerates (*zaibatsu,* "financial cliques") and small enterprises. By the early twentieth century, Japan's industry was diversified and strong, and the economy had enjoyed a quarter-century of significant growth.

By 1900, then, Japan had responded to the Western challenge more successfully than any other non-Western country, including ones that had faced serious challenge far earlier. The contrast with China reflected major differences between the two. Japan lacked China's size and inertia but was at least as uniform in culture and more so in population. Japan had no vast interior isolated from contact with foreigners, and Japan had much more of a history of cultural borrowing. Once Japan was "opened," revolution quickly followed, provoking rapid change in many fields. For example, Japanese writers produced popular books about the West, introduced journalism, and translated Western literary successes. Japanese were popularizing Western ideas on a large scale by the 1860s and 1870s, much before the Chinese and almost as early as the Ottomans, whose contacts with Europe went back centuries earlier. Japan's government fostered these cultural developments by becoming Asia's first to develop a Western-style, national, secular school system, from compulsory elementary schools through universities.

Japan as a Great Power Its leaders wanted Japan to gain acceptance from the major powers as an equal. This concern had important implications for internal politics. Japanese leaders, like other non-Western leaders of the time, assumed that representative government had something to do with the success of the great powers. They also had to contend with demands from former samurai for political participation. As a result, the Meiji regime introduced representative bodies at the prefectural level in 1878. Political parties emerged in the 1880s. In 1889 the country received a constitution, drafted along German lines.

The constitution of 1889 vested supreme authority in the emperor, who held vast executive, legislative, and military powers. Ministers were responsible to him, rather than to parliament. As in Germany, the chief of staff remained independent in matters of command from the army minister. Thus the military was not under civilian control. There was a parliament, known in English as the Diet, with two houses. The budget and all permanent laws required approval of both houses, although the government could continue to operate under the budget of the preceding year if the Diet failed to pass the new one. For the people, the constitution guaranteed a number of rights, usually with restrictions.

Compared to the Japan of a quarter-century before, the constitution was a remarkable change. But it contained problems. It did not say who would exercise the many powers formally vested in the emperor. In practical terms, the top civil and military officials would have to do so. The constitution also did not clearly regulate relations among the various power centers. What if the Diet tried to assert control over the cabinet, as is normal in parliamentary systems? What if military commanders used their independence of command to launch operations that the cabinet opposed? Both these things eventually happened, and the latter produced tragic results.

Their wish for recognition as a great power required Japan's leaders to pay particular attention to foreign policy. Their method, typical of the time, was imperialist expansion. By 1895, Japan had seized the Ryukyu Islands and made war against China, winning Taiwan and other concessions. These gains were economically significant, for Japan was losing self-sufficiency in rice. From then on, it could supply its needs with cheap rice from its dependencies.

Japan's diplomatic gains were more important. Impressed by Japan's rise, the Western powers began to conclude new pacts surrendering the unequal treaty privileges. In 1902, Britain entered into an alliance with Japan on a footing of formal equality; this was the first peacetime military alliance between an Asian and a European power. Most astonishing was Japan's victory in the Russo-Japanese War of 1904–1905, triggered by Russian expansion in Manchuria. This was the most dramatic case in which a non-Western people defeated a great power before World War I. The victory was also memorable as a step in the development of Japan's interests in Manchuria.

By 1914, Japan had risen from semicolonialism to nominal equality with the great powers and had acquired its own overseas dependencies. Siding with the British in World War I, it did little militarily but used the occasion to pick up German possessions in China and the Pacific. Japan was the only non-Western power to sit with the victors at the peace conference. There the great powers showed that they still did not accept Japan fully as an equal, for when it tried to get a clause on racial equality inserted into the Versailles peace treaty, U.S. and British opposition thwarted the effort. But the conference did aggravate Chinese nationalist grievances by leaving Japan the territories it had acquired in China.

Democratization or Militarism?

Between the world wars, Japan's development into a great power continued. From 1914 on, the economy enjoyed spectacular growth that lasted into World War II. The record was marred by unimpressive performance from 1920 to 1932. But Japan was already recovering from the Depression by 1932, earlier than any other major power. By 1940, less than half of Japanese workers were employed in agriculture, and some zaibatsu firms had grown into the largest financial empires in the world. In the economy, as in other spheres, Japan no longer simply imitated the West. By the 1930s, for example, the Japanese designed and produced the biggest battleships ever built.

Political parties grew in influence during this period. At first, this development seemed likely to answer the question of how much influence the parliament would exert over the cabinet. Although it never became a principle that the majority leader in the Diet would become prime minister, from 1924 to 1932 the prime minister was always the head of one of the two major parties. Suffrage was broadened in 1925 to include all men of twenty-five and older (women did not get the vote until 1947). Through 1937, the popular vote showed public support for democratization.

Japan did not consolidate its democracy during the interwar period, however. The main reason was lack of civilian control of the military. Various developments—the Depression, conflict with China over Manchuria, the rise of fascism—prompted the military to assert its independence in ways that upset the liberal trend.

The Depression contributed by calling down blame for economic distress on the parties and the big firms. Rightists and militarists asked whether Japan could afford to depend on world markets or should expand its empire. By 1931 the army was also concerned that Chinese Nationalist progress threatened its position in Manchuria. Two Japanese colonels organized a plot, not without high-level complicity. A Japanese-staged railway bombing at Mukden became the pretext to attack Chinese troops in Manchuria, and the conflict spread. The Manchurian episode seriously affected the Japanese government's credibility. Repeatedly, the government announced it had limited the scope of conflict, only to have further military initiatives follow. By 1932, Japan had been condemned by the League of Nations, had withdrawn from it, and had moved beyond Manchuria to occupy parts of Inner Mongolia. Inside Japan, extreme rightist groups went into action, using violence against first the Left, then the liberals. By 1937, when the war with China began, militarists had essentially captured control of the cabinet. For all their electoral support, the parties were reduced to an oppositional role. Japan's naval commanders, meanwhile, resented treaty limits on Japan's and other states' sea power. By 1937, Japan had withdrawn from the disarmament system and begun a naval buildup.

Japan never acquired the charismatic dictator, mass movement, or clear-cut ideology of a fascist regime. But it moved toward authoritarianism and militarism. Japan's aggression in China and its naval expansion upset relations with the United States and Britain, and many of the Japanese responsible for these developments preferred Fascist Italy and Nazi Germany. In September 1940, impressed by German victories, Japan signed an alliance with Germany and Italy. The alliance bound each country to go to war against any nation attacking any one of them. Japan had committed itself to the Axis, a decision that would bring it to virtual destruction in World War II.

Conclusion: China, India, Turkey, and Japan Compared

With the integration of Asia into the European-dominated world order, no Asian country entirely escaped the effects of European expansion. In reaction, independence movements emerged everywhere. A comparison of Asia's two most populous countries, China and India, and of its two most successful independent nations of the interwar period, Turkey and Japan, suggests several prerequisites for the success of these efforts at independence. These are openness to new ideas, consensus about the definition of constitutional principles and national identity, effective social change to support the drive for independence, and formulation of an economic development strategy that could overcome economic colonialism. A comparison of the four countries will illustrate the significance of these points.

During the interwar period, China was the least successful of these countries. It had to survive not only a change of dynasty but the collapse of both the imperial regime and the Confucian value system, which had formed its core for two thousand years. China's traditional resistance to foreign ideas magnified its problems. Despite the ideological efforts of the GMD, only the Communists would finally overcome this resistance. Meanwhile, consensus about the definition of national identity was not a major issue for the hundreds of millions who were ethnically and culturally Chinese, despite their differences of dialect. Achieving consensus on how to organize a new political order proved extremely hard, however. The effort produced two rival nationalist movements and, after 1949, two regimes—the People's Republic on the mainland and the Republic of China on Taiwan—each professing to be the real China. The prolonged political struggle showed how hard it was to mobilize China's huge population. In this, the GMD failed, and the CCP under Mao succeeded. CCP membership rose from 40,000 in 1937 to over 1.2 million in 1945. For the GMD, social and economic failure went together in this period. After 1949, revitalization of the economy remained one of the greatest challenges for the Communists.

India, in contrast, proved unable to forge a broad enough consensus about national identity to prevent partition into separate Hindu and Muslim states in 1947. In other respects, India's record through 1947 was at least partly positive. Gandhi epitomized the Hindus' openness to foreign ideas. The need for principles that could appeal to all religious communities helped to forge a constitutional consensus that has made independent India the world's largest democracy. India has experienced no radical revolution in social structure, and some of India's major problems still reflect this lack. But some of the social reforms undertaken before 1947—the Gandhian mobilization of women and Untouchables or the extension of the vote to both sexes—were major social gains. India's record was perhaps most unusual in the economic sphere. Perhaps fortunately for India's later development, the less publicized efforts of others to achieve industrialization counterbalanced Gandhi's call to regain self-sufficiency through hand production. Gandhi's methods remained a moral inspiration, however, and they proved highly successful in a situation where an outside power, responsive to moral arguments, dominated a huge population that it could not control indefinitely.

In Turkey, the resistance of Islamic tradition to alien ideas was such that, as in China, really reorienting the country required the drastic means of cultural revolution. Geography made Turkey unique among all non-Western countries in its potential for the reorientation toward the West that Atatürk carried out. Because of the Ottoman Empire's collapse and the success of the Turkish independence movement (1919–1922), Atatürk's Turkey came through this readjustment with relatively high levels of consensus about national identity and democratic government. Change stopped short of revolution in Turkey's social structure, however. For most Turks, the shift from polyglot empire to Turkish republic and the many social and cultural reforms of the Atatürk years probably seemed revolutionary enough. The availability of uncultivated land and its distribution to smallholders also spared Turkey the acute agrarian problems found in India or parts of Latin America. Turkey's policy of state initiative in developing key industries set an example that most other developing countries emulated through the 1960s. Yet in the long run this policy could not match the productivity of Japan's distinctive approach.

Japan, indeed, performed superlatively along all four dimensions considered here. Its openness to foreign ideas was exceptional. By the interwar period, Japan's use of modern ideas and techniques, as in industrial production, had gone beyond cultural borrowing to a synthesis between Japanese tradition and Western—or now international—ways. This uniquely homogeneous Asian country had no need to redefine national identity concepts. A redefinition of constitutional principles did occur with the Meiji Restoration, a change of revolutionary significance. But the fact that the Japanese could conceptualize the shogunate's elimination as a re-emphasis on another institution of ancient and unimpaired legitimacy, the imperial throne, greatly eased their transition. The Japanese emperor, though powerless, thus illustrates the power of long-established symbols to legitimate the political order in a rapidly changing society. Socially, Meiji Japan experienced significant structural change with the destruction of the samurai, the elimination of the old class distinctions, and the land tax reform, which gave landownership to the peasant cultivators. Thereafter, the ethnocultural homogeneity, high literacy, and business spirit of the Japanese contributed to an extraordinary transformation of the economy. By the interwar period, Japan could supply many agricultural needs from its colonies and had become internationally competitive in industry.

A nation-state with a powerful industrial economy and a colonial empire, Japan had truly become a great power. Some problems remained unresolved, especially the lack of civilian control over the military. These flaws would bring Japan to defeat in World War II—the final crisis of the European great powers it had come to resemble—before its extraordinary rise resumed.

Note

1. Quoted in Michael Gasster, *China's Struggle to Modernize,* 2d ed. (New York: Knopf, 1983), p. 78.

Suggestions for Further Reading

India

Chaudhuri, K. N. *Asia before Europe: Economy and Civilization of the Indian Ocean from the Rise of Islam to 1750* (1990).

Fischer, Louis. *The Life of Mahatma Gandhi* (1950).

Lal, Deepak. *The Hindu Equilibrium.* vol. I of *Cultural Stability and Economic Stagnation: India, c. 1500 BC–AD 1980* (1988).

Mehta, Ved. *Mahatma Gandhi and His Apostles* (1983).

Wolpert, Stanley. *A New History of India.* 4th ed. (1993).

The Middle East

Goldschmidt, Arthur, Jr. *A Concise History of the Middle East*. 4th ed. (1991).

Lewis, Bernard. *The Emergence of Modern Turkey*. 2d ed. (1968).

Richards, Alan, and John Waterbury. *A Political Economy of the Middle East: State, Class, and Economic Development* (1990).

Shaw, Stanford J., and Ezel K. Shaw. *History of the Ottoman Empire and Modern Turkey*. Vol. 2 (1977).

Yapp, M. E. *The Making of the Modern Near East, 1792–1923* (1987).

———. *The Near East Since the First World War* (1991).

China and Japan

Fairbank, John K. *The United States and China*. 4th ed. (1983).

Fairbank, John K., Edwin O. Reischauer, and Albert M. Craig. *East Asia: Tradition and Transformation* (1978).

Gasster, Michael. *China's Struggle to Modernize*. 2d ed. (1983).

Reischauer, Edwin O. *Japan: The Story of a Nation*. 4th ed. (1989).

Schram, Stuart. *The Thought of Mao Tse-Tung* (1989).

PART 4

World War II and the Period of Superpower Rivalry

CHAPTER 11

World War II: The Final Crisis of European Global Dominance

The habit of looking at the twentieth-century world from the perspective of European dominance is hard to shake. Even now, a half-century after that dominance collapsed at the end of World War II, Western historians often date the war from Hitler's invasion of Poland in 1939. Americans often date the war from the Japanese attack on the U.S. fleet at Pearl Harbor on December 7, 1941. By then Britain had been fighting Germany for a year alone, while German armies overran most of Europe. Britain found an ally against Hitler only when he invaded the Soviet Union on June 22, 1941, the day the war begins in Russian history books.

For many non-Europeans, however, World War II dates from well before 1939. For the Chinese, it began in 1931 against the Japanese in Manchuria. For the Ethiopians, virtually the only Africans not under European rule, it began with the Italian invasion in 1935.

The significance of these differing dates is that what we call "World War II" was the convergence of originally separate drives for empire into one conflict. One drive began with Hitler's war with Britain and France over Poland, one of the last two surviving creations of the Versailles system. This last of Europe's "civil wars" became a German campaign for "living space," which culminated in a Hitlerian empire stretching across Europe.

Another drive for empire began with Japan's penetration of China in the 1930s. Profiting from Hitler's attack on the European colonial powers, the Japanese extended their control over a large part of the East Asian mainland and the islands of the southwest

Pacific, including the Dutch East Indies and the Philippines.

By the end of 1941, the German and Japanese drives for empire had converged to make World War II a conflict of continents. It pitted Europe, under Hitler's rule, against the worldwide British Empire, which also had to face much of Asia, under the dominance of Japan. Had Germany not attacked the Soviet Union, and had Japan not attacked the United States, those other two continent-sized powers might not have been drawn into the struggle. Until Hitler attacked, Stalin had adhered to the Nazi-Soviet Pact of August 1939. A clear majority of U.S. citizens favored neutrality in the war until the Japanese attacked them.

Russian and American participation brought World War II to a turning point by mid-to-late 1942. Until then, the so-called Axis Powers (Germany, Japan, and Italy) had achieved an unbroken series of victories. German armies surged to the northern tip of Norway, to the shores of the Greek peninsula and the Black Sea, and over much of the North African desert. The Japanese swept to the eastern frontiers of India and to the arctic fringes of North America in the Aleutian Islands.

Even in this early period, however, the Axis leaders made fateful mistakes. Hitler failed to defeat Britain. He neither invaded it nor cut its lifelines across the Atlantic and through the Mediterranean. Meanwhile, he repeated Napoleon's fatal blunder of invading Russia while Britain remained unconquered. The Japanese leaders did not join in this attack on their enemy of the war of 1904–1905 but tried to avert U.S. interference with their empire building by destroying the U.S. Pacific fleet. After the attack on Pearl Harbor, it was Hitler who declared war on the United States, not the United States on Hitler.

It was these uncoordinated Axis attacks that forced together what Churchill called the Grand Alliance of Britain, the Soviet Union, and the United States. Together, these dissimilar Allies were too strong for the Axis. Consistently victorious through most of 1942, the Axis encountered nothing but defeat thereafter. Germany and subjugated Europe had been a match for Britain, despite the troops sent by British Dominions, such as Canada, Australia, and New Zealand. But the Russian war destroyed Hitler's armies, and the U.S. agreement to give priority to Germany's defeat made it certain. After mid-1942, the Americans, the British, and their allies also steadily pushed the Japanese back. When the Soviet Union, after Hitler's defeat, joined Japan's enemies in 1945, Japanese prospects became hopeless, even without the awful warning of two American nuclear attacks—the first in history and the last, so far.

Throughout the war, the Axis Powers failed to cooperate effectively. They also did not mobilize their home fronts as effectively as the Allies. Despite German rhetoric about uniting the peoples of Europe and Japanese claims to be leading an Asian crusade against imperialism, neither Germany nor Japan was able to mobilize the enthusiasm of a majority in the lands they overran. Instead their treatment of conquered peoples was marked by cruelty and greed, which inspired even civilians to abandon passivity for active resistance.

After World War I, people quickly concluded that most of the slogans for which they had fought were hollow. After World War II, the revelations of Japanese and Nazi brutality kept alive the sense that this second global conflict had been fought for a just cause. But although the war defeated evil regimes, this struggle of continents also destroyed the power of Europe as a whole and the European-dominated global system. Within a generation after 1945, even Britain, bankrupt and exhausted in victory, would grant independence to most of its Asian and African colonies. From this "end of empire" would soon emerge the Third World of countries reluctant to subordinate themselves to either the United States or the Soviet Union, the only great powers left after 1945.

Not only in the already threatening conflict of these two superpowers does the world of 1945 foreshadow our own era. Even more intensively than in 1914–1918, the pressures of total war expanded the powers of governments, transformed societies, and revolutionized the economies of the world. Moreover, with official encouragement, scientists produced a weapon so incomparably deadly that thoughtful people wondered whether human beings still had a future. We still live with that unprecedented uncertainty of 1945. In this respect as in most, World War II marks the turning point of the twentieth-century world, though few people foresaw this transformation when Hitler's armies crossed the Polish border on September 1, 1939.

From Phony War to Operation Barbarossa, 1939–1941

The German attack on Poland revealed the revolutionary impact of the internal combustion engine on warfare. *Blitzkrieg* (lightning war) used fast-moving masses of tanks, closely supported by aircraft, to shatter opposition. The gallant charges of Polish cavalry could not stop them. Within a month Poland ceased to exist. Russian troops moved in to occupy the eastern half of the country, where a majority of the population were not Poles but Ukrainians. The Russians deported over a million Poles eastward, most to their deaths. Stalin now had a common border with his German ally, some two hundred miles west of the former Soviet-Polish frontier. He also regained control of the strategic Baltic seacoast by annexing the three small nations of Latvia, Lithuania, and Estonia, former provinces of the tsarist empire that had declared their independence after the 1917 revolution.

The Phony War and the Fall of France

Meanwhile the British and French did nothing, though they had declared war on Poland's behalf. The French army and a small British contingent moved into defensive positions and bombarded the Germans with propaganda leaflets. For the moment, they were unwilling to attack, and Hitler was unready. The resulting "phony war" profoundly damaged the morale of Germany's enemies, especially the French. Governments that had gone reluctantly to war now debated where to fight it. Defeatists who had argued it was crazy to go to war for Poland now declared it was even crazier to fight after Poland had been destroyed. Communist propaganda explained the war as a conflict between equally greedy imperialist powers. Meanwhile Hitler conquered Norway, whose location was strategically essential in an Anglo-German naval and air struggle (Map 11.1). The Norwegian king and his ministers fled to London, the first of many governments-in-exile to find sanctuary there. Hitler established a puppet government headed by Vidkun Quisling, a Norwegian fascist. His name has became a generic term for traitors who do a conqueror's dirty work.

The lull ended when Hitler launched the Blitzkrieg westward on May 10, 1940. Horrified by the destruction of Rotterdam—the first European use of aerial bombardment to terror-

Map 11.1 World War II: The European Theater

Hitler's Greater Germany
Allied with Germany
Occupied by Germany and its allies
Advances by Allied forces
Major battle
NORTH SEA
NORTHERN IRELAND
IRELAND
GREAT BRITAIN
Battle of Britain (Fall 1940)
London
Dunkirk
English Channel
Invasion of Normandy (June 6, 1944)
NORMANDY
NETHERLANDS
Rotterdam
Antwerp
BELGIUM
Bastogne
Sedan
Battle of the Bulge (Dec. 1944)
Paris
Western front, Feb. 1945
ATLANTIC OCEAN
FRANCE
Vichy
VICHY FRANCE (Occupied Nov. 1942)
SWITZERLAND
Rhine R.
NORWAY
Oslo
SWEDEN
Stockholm
BALTIC SEA
DENMARK
Copenhagen
Elbe R.
Berlin
GERMANY
CZECHOSLOVAKIA
Vienna
AUSTRIA
FINLAND
Helsinki
L. Ladoga
Leningrad
Moscow
Riga
Smolensk
Tula
SOVIET UNION
Russian front, Spring 1944
Russian front, Dec. 1941
Russian front, Feb. 1945
Posen
Warsaw
POLAND
Krakow
Pinsk
Kiev
UKRAINE
Stalingrad
Volga R.
Don R.
CASPIAN SEA
Russian front, Nov. 1942
SLOVAKIA
HUNGARY
Budapest
Yalta
RUMANIA
Bucharest
BLACK SEA
Bologna
Italian front, Feb. 1945
YUGOSLAVIA
Sofia
BULGARIA
ITALY
Rome
Anzio
Monte Casino (May 1944)
ALBANIA
Salerno (Sept. 1943)
GREECE
Athens
Ankara
TURKEY
SYRIA
Lisbon
PORTUGAL
Madrid
SPAIN
Gibraltar (Gr. Br.)
SP. MOROCCO
Casablanca (Nov.1942)
FRENCH MOROCCO
Algiers
ALGERIA (Vichy France)
SICILY (July 1943)
Tunis
MALTA (Gr. Br.)
Rommel defeated in Tunisia (May 1943)
TUNISIA
MEDITERRANEAN SEA
CRETE
CYPRUS
LEBANON
PALESTINE (Br. Mandate)
TRANS-JORDAN (Br. Mandate)
Alexandria
El Alamein (Summer 1942)
Suez Canal
Nile R.
Cairo
EGYPT
LIBYA

ize the population of a large city—the Dutch soon surrendered. Belgium held out little longer. No one had expected these small countries to withstand Hitler. The great shock of 1940 was the fall of France.

The country that had held off Germany for almost five years in 1914–1918 now collapsed within six weeks, suffering over a quarter-million casualties. Such losses are proof that despite the prewar quarrels that had continued through the phony war, many of the French still believed in their country's cause. What they lacked was not courage but the weapons and especially the leadership needed for mechanized war. France's elderly generals had ignored the warnings of the soldier-scholar Charles de Gaulle that the machine had revolutionized warfare. Unable to hold a line as they had in 1914–1918, they could only surrender.

Hitler savored his revenge for Versailles, forcing the French to capitulate in the very railroad car where Foch had accepted the German surrender in 1918. Hoping to make the French reliable satellites, he allowed them to keep their fleet and colonies. There would still be a French government in the southern two-fifths of the country, where German columns had not penetrated. Thus the little resort of Vichy replaced Paris as the capital, and Marshal Philippe Pétain, a hero of World War I, set up an authoritarian regime to replace the fallen democratic republic. Stunned by defeat, most Frenchmen at first accepted this dictatorship. Few heeded the radio appeal of General de Gaulle, who had fled to London, for Frenchmen to join him in continuing the battle overseas.

"Their Finest Hour"

Within a few weeks of Hitler's attack, the British found themselves all alone against him. Hitler publicly proposed peace. He had never really wanted a war with the British Empire. His onslaught, coming after the British failure to keep the Germans out of Norway, had discredited Neville Chamberlain's government. The new prime minister, Winston Churchill, replied that Britain would make peace if Hitler gave up all his conquests.

Churchill combined apparently contradictory traits into a remarkable personality—the last great figure of the age of European global dominance. Child of an old, aristocratic family, he had been a political maverick throughout his forty years in the House of Commons. As First Lord of the Admiralty at the beginning of both world wars, he had been at the center of the British military establishment, yet he remained a consistent champion of military innovations. Excluded from government through the 1930s because he opposed appeasing Hitler, he became Britain's leader chiefly because the policies he had criticized had failed. But the vision, energy, and determination that had made him a loner were now the qualities Britain needed.

Steeped in history, Churchill did not always see the future clearly. He had opposed concessions to Gandhi as resolutely as he opposed them to Hitler. Churchill's understanding of the past, however, gifted him with words to unite Britain's class-ridden society in old-fashioned patriotism. The battle of France was over, he declared on June 18:

> I expect that the Battle of Britain is about to begin . . . Hitler knows that he will have to break us in this island or lose the war . . . [If] we fail, then the whole world . . . will sink into the abyss of a new Dark Age. . . . Let us therefore brace ourselves to our duties, and so bear ourselves that if the British Empire and its Commonwealth last for a thousand years, men will say "This was their finest hour."[1]

Since Churchill ignored Hitler's prophetic warning that the British Empire would not long survive another world war, the Nazi leader reluctantly ordered his staff to plan an invasion. As his generals and admirals wrangled over how to carry the Blitzkrieg across twenty miles of the English Channel, the *Luftwaffe* (air force) offered the alternative of bombing Britain into submission.

Through the summer of 1940 the Battle of Britain raged in the English skies. Just as it was devastating British air bases, the Luftwaffe made the mistake of switching its target to London. Thus Londoners became the first to prove, as the citizens of Tokyo and Berlin later confirmed, that people can continue to live and work under the stresses of nightly air raids. Meanwhile the Royal Air Force, aided by a radar early-warning system in operation only since 1939, shot down two Germans for every plane it lost. Unable to establish air superiority, Hitler "postponed" his invasion of Britain—a delay that proved to be permanent.

The Battle of Britain may have determined the entire future course of the war. Hitler now faced the prospect of a long war, requiring a level of preparedness he had told his planners to expect only in 1944 or 1945. Moreover, though Britain was as incapable of attacking Germany as Germany was of attacking Britain, Britain might find an ally. Striving, while half-prepared, to eliminate such potential allies, Hitler was drawn into an ever-widening, eventually global, war he could not win.

Mediterranean Campaigns

The failures of Mussolini provoked the first dispersions of German strength. Having remained neutral, except for a belated attack on defeated France, the Duce decided that Italy would risk less by joining the general war than it would by failing to profit from Germany's victories. In September 1940, he struck from Libya, Italy's North African colony, at the British in Egypt. A month later, he invaded Greece. Both attacks were fiascos. The British pushed the Italians out of Egypt; the Greeks pushed them out of Greece. Hitler had had little notice of the Italian plans—only one example of the general Axis failure to coordinate strategies. But he had to retrieve Mussolini's failures. If he did not, the British might overrun North Africa and return to the European mainland by way of the Balkans. In the spring of 1941, German troops arrived in North Africa to stiffen the Italians. Hitler thus involved himself in a seesaw desert battle that would end in an Axis defeat two years later. Almost simultaneously, he invaded Greece and Yugoslavia, quickly defeating them.

Neither of these campaigns proved decisive. Hitler never really accepted the idea that the way to defeat Britain was to cut its Mediterranean link to the Empire at both ends—at Gibraltar and at the Suez Canal. Though the Spanish dictator Franco coveted Gibraltar, he was too wily to let Hitler draw him into the war. Hitler never gave the *Afrika Korps* sufficient means to dislodge the British from Egypt. Most of the Balkan countries had already become economically dependent on Germany before the war began. The campaign to reinforce this dependency militarily delayed for five critical weeks the blow Hitler thought would decide the war: invasion of the Soviet Union.

Operation Barbarossa

In December 1940, Hitler decided to "crush Soviet Russia in a quick campaign even before the end of the war against England."[2] The failure to defeat Britain had reinforced his long-standing purpose of expanding German "living space" at Russian expense. Though Stalin had lived up to the Nazi-Soviet Pact, to "crush" him was the only sure way to prevent him from changing sides.

Because the Soviet Union and the West became antagonists after World War II, few Westerners realize the size of the Russian contribution to the conflict Russians call "the Great Patriotic War." On June 22, 1941, 4 million German and allied troops began crossing the Soviet frontier in Operation Barbarossa. They constituted the biggest invading army in history. Within three weeks they had advanced two-thirds of the way to Moscow, taking a million prisoners. Surprised by the attack, despite ample warnings, Stalin could only trade space for time, retreating deeper and deeper into the vastness of Russia. Hitler's optimism—he had neglected to equip his armies with warm clothing or antifreeze—seemed justified. But in December 1941, "General Winter" took command, halting the German advance only twenty miles from Moscow. The Blitzkrieg had stalled, and Barbarossa proved to be no quick campaign.

Stalin counterattacked, in weather of thirty degrees below zero, with troops transferred from Siberia, where they had been guarding against a Japanese attack. His spies in Tokyo had reassured him that the Japanese would honor their nonaggression pact with the Soviet Union. A coordinated Axis strategy would have forced Stalin to fight on both fronts. But to the extent they listened to Hitler at all, the Japanese agreed with him that their interest lay in attacking the United States.

Meanwhile, on the other side, Churchill, a lifelong anti-communist, pledged all-out British help to the Soviets when they were invaded. "If Hitler invaded Hell," he explained, "I would at least make a favorable reference to the Devil in the House of Commons."[3] He understood that mutual interests dictated Allied cooperation. No such commitment bound the Axis Powers together. The attack on Pearl Harbor on December 7, 1941, surprised Japan's allies as much as its victims.

The Japanese Bid for Empire and the U.S. Reaction, 1941–1942

By the 1930s Japan had produced the most successful non-Western response to European global dominance. Both the ancient and the modern elements of that response inclined the Japanese toward empire building. Aloof from democratic politics, the Japanese officer corps still lived by the code of *Bushido,* the way of the warrior, whose fate was to die for the emperor. Many leaders of big business saw more practical reasons for war. Japan was an overcrowded set of islands practically devoid of essential raw materials and dependent on exports for survival. The impact of the Great Depression had confirmed these harsh realities. Economic motives inspired the Japanese thrust into China in 1931. When the League of Nations condemned this act, the feeling grew within military-industrial circles that Japan was besieged.

This feeling was heightened by the constant rebukes of the United States, whose traditional insistence on an "open door" for American trade in East Asia clashed directly with Japanese ambitions. In 1940 President Roosevelt reinforced his moral condemnations with an embargo on scrap iron and weapons for Japan. In July 1941, after the Japanese took advantage of the fall of France to seize French Indochina, he extended the ban to include oil and steel. In the ensuing negotiations, the United States made it clear that the U.S. condition for lifting the ban was Japanese withdrawal from China. Thus the Japanese were faced with the choice of giving up the imperial ambitions upon which they had staked their future or overcoming U.S. opposition by diplomacy or by force.

Pearl Harbor

As negotiations failed to resolve the embargo issue to Japan's satisfaction, power within the Japanese government shifted to the military-industrial advocates of war against the United States and the European colonial powers. Japan's decision to enter the war was not prompted by any sense of solidarity with the fascist powers. Hitler had not warned the Japa-

Escorting an army recruit to barracks, Tokyo, 1938. *Being drafted was an occasion for great public ceremony. Accompanied by a procession including bugles, banners, and his family, the young Japanese marched off to fulfill his supreme duty—to the divine Emperor.* Life *Pictures*

nese he would invade Russia, despite the German-Japanese pact signed in 1940, nor did the Japanese consult him before Pearl Harbor. Rather, the war they planned had three objectives: to break the stranglehold of embargo, to end interference with their conquest of China, and to build an overseas empire that would give Japan the supplies and markets it lacked.

Early on a Sunday morning, December 7, 1941, Honolulu awoke to the roar of explosions. The surprise Japanese air attack sank or damaged much of the U.S. Pacific fleet at its moorings in Pearl Harbor. Having disabled their most-feared enemy, the Japanese quickly overran Hong Kong, the Dutch East Indies, Burma, and Malaya. The surrender of the great base at Singapore dealt a lasting blow to the prestige of the British Empire in East Asia. By May 1942, American and Filipino resistance in the Philippines had also ended in surrender (Map 11.2).

At the time of Pearl Harbor, U.S. intelligence had cracked the Japanese codes and was expecting an attack someplace. Why then was the Pacific fleet so unprepared? No credible evidence supports the allegation that Roosevelt deliberately allowed the attack so that outraged public opinion would accept war. Several factors contributed to the disaster: the secrecy that shrouded the Japanese strike force, the racist overconfidence of commanders who believed the "little yellow men" would not dare attack Hawaii, and the habits of peacetime routine. The Federal Bureau of

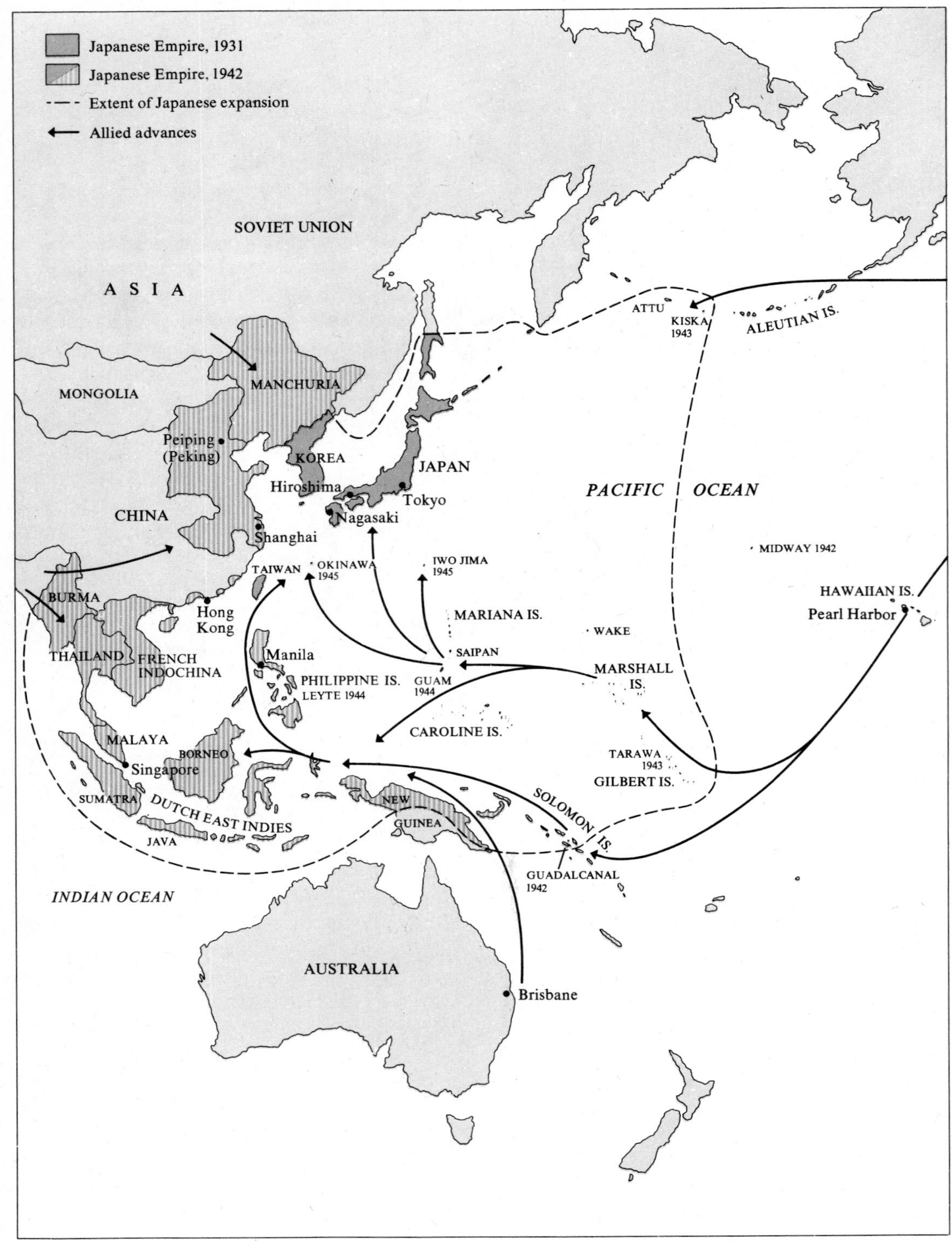

Japanese Empire, 1931
Japanese Empire, 1942
Extent of Japanese expansion
Allied advances
SOVIET UNION
ASIA
MONGOLIA
MANCHURIA
Peiping (Peking)
KOREA
JAPAN
Hiroshima
Tokyo
Nagasaki
CHINA
Shanghai
TAIWAN
OKINAWA 1945
IWO JIMA 1945
BURMA
Hong Kong
THAILAND
FRENCH INDOCHINA
Manila
PHILIPPINE IS.
LEYTE 1944
GUAM 1944
MARIANA IS.
SAIPAN
WAKE
MARSHALL IS.
CAROLINE IS.
MALAYA
BORNEO
Singapore
SUMATRA
DUTCH EAST INDIES
JAVA
NEW GUINEA
SOLOMON IS.
GUADALCANAL 1942
TARAWA 1943
GILBERT IS.
ATTU
KISKA 1943
ALEUTIAN IS.
PACIFIC OCEAN
MIDWAY 1942
HAWAIIAN IS.
Pearl Harbor
INDIAN OCEAN
AUSTRALIA
Brisbane

Investigation, for example, failed to alert Roosevelt that it had intercepted a German spy whose mission was to assemble detailed information about Pearl harbor, to be passed on, undoubtedly, to the Japanese.

The End of U.S. Isolation

Pearl Harbor unquestionably simplified Roosevelt's foreign policy problem, which arose from the clash between two enduring characteristics of American thinking about foreign relations. Protected by oceans and bordered by far weaker neighbors, Americans, unlike Europeans, had little experience of adjusting foreign policy to the necessities of the balance of power. The threat to Britain of a Europe dominated by Germany, for example, spurred Churchill's opposition to Hitler far more than his distaste for Nazi politics. Americans, with their strong Puritan heritage, were more likely to judge others in moral terms. This view implied that the United States should help "good" countries and oppose "bad" ones. By the late 1930s most Americans probably judged Nazism and Japanese imperialism to be bad. But an equally powerful American tradition urged against any "entangling alliance" abroad. The widespread feeling that the United States had been led into World War I under false pretenses had reinforced this tradition. To prevent its happening again, Congress had passed a series of neutrality acts aimed at preventing any peripheral involvement in foreign wars that could be used to justify U.S. intervention.

In keeping with this isolationist sentiment, Roosevelt had proclaimed U.S. neutrality in 1939. Despite his growing conviction that the United States' vital interests required opposition to both Japan and Germany, he could not do more than public opinion would permit. Thus in the fall of 1940, when Britain desperately needed escort ships for its Atlantic convoys, Roosevelt could only trade Churchill fifty obsolescent U.S. destroyers for ninety-nine-year U.S. leases on six British bases in the Western Hemisphere.

In the spring of 1941, polls showed that no more than one American in five favored entering the war. By then Britain had sold all its dollar holdings at a loss in order to pay for munitions. U.S. legislation stipulated that foreigners could buy arms in the United States only on a "cash-and-carry" basis. Roosevelt now persuaded congress to pass the Lend-Lease Act, empowering him to lend or lease the British whatever they needed. However, the act stipulated that U.S. ships must not enter combat zones. In August, Roosevelt and Churchill met at sea and promulgated the Atlantic Charter. This document set forth the kind of general principles Americans liked to affirm, including the right of self-determination. Churchill could only accept it, though he tried to insist to Roosevelt that the charter, which implicitly repudiated Britain's right to rule over other peoples, did not apply to the British Empire.

Thus step by step Roosevelt edged Americans toward war. As U.S. warships escorted convoys across the Atlantic, there were clashes, despite Hitler's orders, with German submarines. These encounters enabled Roosevelt to declare that the country was already virtually at war. Even after Pearl Harbor, however, he did not ask Congress to declare war on Germany. Hitler solved Roosevelt's dilemma by aligning himself with the Japanese, against whom Americans had been roused to fury. Vastly ignorant of the United States and contemptuous of its racially mixed society, Hitler saw no reason not to declare formally a war that had already begun in the Atlantic.

◀ ***Map 11.2 World War II: The Pacific Theater***

The Turning Points, 1942

Churchill immediately recognized the significance of the Pearl Harbor attack. From that moment he knew Britain would not lose the war. With the formation of the Grand Alliance, the tide of war began to turn in mid-to-late 1942. By the spring of 1943, the Axis had lost battles in Pacific jungles and North African deserts, in the snows of Russia and the storms of the North Atlantic.

The momentum of the Japanese seemed irresistible in early 1942. Their planes bombed northern Australia. Their fleet raided Ceylon. But in May 1942, in the Battle of the Coral Sea, the U.S. Navy parried the threat to Australia. A month later, a smaller U.S. force repelled the huge Japanese fleet sent to take Midway Island, only eleven hundred miles from Hawaii. In August, U.S. Marines landed on Guadalcanal in the Solomon Islands, a British possession occupied by the Japanese. Six months of fighting in the steamy, malarial jungle ended in an American victory. It was the first in the long-running battle that would lead from island to island to Japan itself.

In November, at El Alamein, less than one hundred miles from the Suez Canal, the British counterattacked and drove the Germans out of Egypt. Retreating westward, the Germans encountered the British and American troops that had landed in Operation Torch in French North Africa. Caught between these two fires, the Germans surrendered in Tunisia in May 1943. Meanwhile, enraged by the French failure to resist the landings, Hitler ordered the total occupation of France. This invasion shattered the illusion of the Vichy regime's independence. The French began to realize that the only independent French regime was the one de Gaulle soon installed in North Africa.

The war in the Soviet Union also reached a turning point in November 1942 with the savage house-to-house battle of Stalingrad. Hitler refused to allow any retreat. In three months he lost a half-million men. Thereafter the Soviet advance did not halt until it reached Berlin.

Despite these Allied successes, Churchill was still haunted through the spring of 1943 by the one German threat he really feared: the submarine campaign against ocean convoys. In the first years of the war the North Atlantic crossing demanded a quiet heroism of every merchant seaman. For fifteen days they battled through mountainous seas, dreading what they called "the hammer": a torpedo slamming into their ship to send it to the bottom in minutes. In the eighteen months after the fall of France, Britain lost a third of its prewar merchant tonnage. The British convoys dispatched through the Arctic to supply north Russian ports confirmed the Grand Alliance at a terrible cost in ships and lives. By late 1942, however, the Americans were building ships faster than the Germans could sink them. By deploying more escorts and wider-ranging aircraft, and by perfecting submarine detection by underwater radar, the British destroyed an unprecedented forty-one submarines in March 1943. A turning point had been reached on the Atlantic sealanes, too, allowing the Allies to bring the full weight of their home-front production against the Axis.

The Home Fronts

Even more than in World War I, the home front was a real fighting front in World War II. Not only were civilians much more subject to attack by enemy bombers, but victory or defeat depended largely on the governments' success in organizing their productive skills for the war effort. This was a war between economies as well as between armies. Churchill actually created a Ministry of Economic Warfare. Its responsibilities included organizing sabotage of the German-dominated European economies and denying Hitler vital raw materials by offering neutrals a better price for goods they would otherwise have sold to Germany.

Allied Mobilization

Victory in this war of economies was really decided, however, by the relative success of the two sides in mobilizing their home fronts. The Churchill all-party government, depending on a parliamentary majority, felt it could ask at least as much of its citizens as more authoritarian regimes imposed on theirs. The British National Service Act of 1941 put every adult from eighteen to fifty at the government's disposal, to be sent to work wherever he or she was needed. The government controlled prices and rationed such essentials as food and fuel. It paid part of the soaring costs of war by deducting compulsory savings from every paycheck. By 1945 it had allocated one-third of the British work force to war industry.

The Soviet government took equally drastic steps. Though the Five-Year Plans of the 1930s had begun locating industry farther from Russia's European border, German armies had seized one-third of the Soviet industrial plant by late 1941 and threatened another third. Stalin's response was to move some fifteen hundred entire factories eastward and to order the destruction of whatever had to be left behind. In 1942 he mobilized every Soviet citizen between sixteen and fifty-five. With 22 million men in uniform, more than any other combatant, the slogan "women to the tractors" came true. At the war's end, three-quarters of the Soviet Union's agricultural workers, and half of those working in war industries, were women. By 1943, despite invasion, these industries were turning out more tanks and planes than German factories were.

Hitler's European Empire

The mobilization of the German home front began late and was less thorough. Although Germany began the war woefully short of such essential weapons as ocean-going submarines, easy victories prompted Hitler actually to cut war production. Only at the end of 1941, when it became clear that Germany was in for a long war, did he order total mobilization. Such were the rivalries of the Nazi hierarchy, however, that production of some nonessential consumer goods continued to increase into 1944. Moreover, Hitler's views precluded drafting women, who were supposed instead to stay home and breed children for Germany. During World War II the German female labor force hardly increased at all (while in the United States the number of working women rose by one-third).

Foreigners from conquered Europe increasingly filled places at the machines that German women might have been assigned. By 1944, more than 7 million foreigners represented a fifth of the German work force. Most of them had been rounded up and brought to Germany virtually as slaves.

The need for labor was not what originally inspired the Nazis to shift huge numbers of people around Europe, however. From the moment of victory in 1940, they began to rearrange the ethnic map of the continent in accordance with their notions of racial hierarchy. The Nazi "New Order" decreed that "racial Germans" living elsewhere should be moved to Germany, where European industry was henceforth to be concentrated. The peoples of the rest of the continent were to be reduced to colonial dependency. The harshness of their fates would depend on how much "Nordic blood" the Nazis thought they had. The fortunate peoples of northern and western Europe, who supposedly had a measure of it, were subjected at first only to puppet governments like Quisling's and to systematic confiscation, through the payment of "occupation costs," of much of what they produced.

In Nazi eyes, non-Nordic peoples like the Poles and Russians were subhuman, fit only for enslavement. After erasing Poland from the map, the Nazis closed Polish schools and massacred the educated elite. They subjected the rest of the Polish population between the ages of eighteen and sixty to forced labor. Forced to wear a purple "P" on their clothing, Poles faced the death penalty for having sex with a German. As for the Soviet Union, Hitler declared his intention to "Germanize the country by the settlement of Germans and treat the natives as redskins," to be killed or herded onto reservations like American Indians.[4] Eighty percent of the Soviet prisoners taken by Germany died of overwork and starvation.

Historically, most empire builders have justified their conquests as the means of spreading some idea of general benefit to humankind. Nazi ideology is remarkably barren in this respect. The Nazi vision of the future depicted a Nazified, static world stretching from the Atlantic far into the Eurasian landmass. Thousand-mile expressways and oversized trains would connect the monumental fortresses from which the German racial masters would rule their enslaved inferiors. By implementing this vision as his armies advanced, Hitler made enemies even of ethnic minorities within the Soviet Union who had initially welcomed the Germans as liberators from Stalin. As the war began to go against the Nazis, Europe eventually became one large prison. Its restive populations made as small a contribution to the Nazi war effort as they dared.

Those carried off to the labor camps established by the SS or German industry could not choose how hard they worked. Nazi-occupied Europe did not only contain camps intended to work people to death, however. The Nazis designed some camps for the immediate extermination of minority groups they deemed unfit to live on any terms. Among these were Gypsies, Jehovah's Witnesses, homosexuals, and especially Europe's Jews.

The Holocaust

Long before the war, the Nazi Nuremberg Laws (1935) had deprived German Jews of their civil rights, and storm troopers had wrecked their businesses and places of worship (1938). But the war provided the opportunity for the "final solution" of what the Nazis called "the Jewish problem." After Poland's defeat, its 3 million Jews were sealed into walled urban ghettos. Special extermination units accompanied the German army into the Soviet Union. But their primitive massacres, in which thousands were shot and hastily buried dead or alive in mass graves, struck Heinrich Himmler, the head of the SS, as unnecessarily harrowing as well as inefficient.

Himmler called on modern technology to equip the extermination camps opened in 1941–1942 with a kind of production line of death, including specially designed gas chambers and crematoria. Into these camps the Nazis slowly emptied the Polish ghettos. They also deported Jews from the rest of Europe "to the east," never to return. So essential did the Nazis consider this task of extermination that they continued it even when Germany was on the brink of defeat. Sometimes they gave trainloads of deportees destined for the death camps the right of way over ammunition trains for their retreating armies.

Six million Jews perished in this Holocaust. The camp at Auschwitz probably established the killing record: a million people, not all Jews, in less than three years, twelve thousand in a single day. The rest of the world did little to hinder the slaughter. Poles did not come to the aid of the rebellion in the Warsaw Ghetto. The Allies did not bomb the death camps. Such indifference reinforced the Zionist argument that Jews could be safe only in a country of their own that they could defend themselves.

When the extent of these crimes became known after the war, some explained them as the result of a uniquely German sadism. Unfortunately, however, the underlying causes of these attempts to wipe out whole peoples arose from characteristics of human thinking not at all peculiar to the Germans of the 1940s. Human beings have always been too ready to deny the humanity of other people by stereotyping them; to believe that the problems of their own group could be solved by eliminating such a dehumanized enemy; and to excuse from moral responsibility those who are "just following orders."

To acknowledge that these common human traits helped make the Holocaust possible is not to deny its unique horror but to recognize the kinds of thinking that humanity has to unlearn if it is to escape future holocausts.

The Defeat of the Axis, 1943–1945

Italy was the first of the Axis Powers to fall. British forces had ousted the Italians from Ethiopia in 1941. The alliance with Germany that had sent 200,000 Italians to the Soviet front had never been popular. When British and U.S. forces crossed from North Africa to invade Sicily in July 1943, even many leading Fascists concluded that it was time for Italy to change sides. Within two weeks of the landing, the king ejected Mussolini from office and had him arrested.

When Italy surrendered to the Allies in September, Hitler's armies turned northern Italy into another German front line. German paratroopers rescued Mussolini from imprisonment and made him the head of a puppet state. Stubborn German resistance slowed the Allied advance up the Italian peninsula to a crawl. When the Germans finally surrendered in the spring of 1945, Italian anti-Fascist guerrillas executed Mussolini and hung his bullet-riddled body by the heels in a gas station as an object of public contempt.

Dreading another slaughter of British troops in France like that of World War I, Churchill had imposed his preference for attacking Italy rather than mounting the cross-channel invasion favored by U.S. military planners. Italy, he aid, was the "soft underbelly" of Hitler's Europe. In actuality the Italian campaign proved far from easy. Yet Stalin did not admit that fighting there amounted to a real "second front" that could reduce German pressure on the Soviet front by dividing German forces. Stalin's complaints help explain the compromises Churchill and Roosevelt made when they met him in Tehran, the Iranian capital, late in 1943. The location was symbolic of the Grand Alliance, for some American lend-lease supplies reached the Soviets through the Persian Gulf and the Trans-Iranian Railway.

At Tehran the "Big Three" recognized their need for each other's help. They therefore tended to put aside any issue that might divide them. Churchill and Roosevelt were keenly aware that Stalin commanded most of the soldiers actually fighting Germans. Having put him off in 1942, and again in 1943, they now gave him a firm date in 1944 for the cross-channel invasion of France. Roosevelt and Stalin rejected as a dangerous diversion Churchill's suggestion that the United States and Britain also attack another "underbelly" in the Balkans, so as to "join hands with" the Soviets. In return for the second front, Stalin pledged Soviet support for a postwar world organization to replace the League of Nations and a Soviet declaration of war against Japan soon after Hitler was defeated.

The liberation of Buchenwald concentration camp, 1945. *From the bare shelves on which they slept, starving slave laborers stare at the U.S. Army cameraman, hardly believing that freedom has come before death.* *Keystone Collection, London*

Stalin made it clear that he intended to keep the territories annexed by the Soviet Union in 1939. Though the Soviets had severed relations with the Polish government-in-exile in London, Churchill concurred with moving the Polish-Russian border westward and compensating Poland at Germany's expense. Roosevelt, characteristically mindful of the large Polish-American vote in the coming presidential election, preferred to avoid discussing territorial adjustments until the war was won. Like Woodrow Wilson, he envisioned a totally new postwar world order, in which the new United Nations would decide such questions. At Tehran. in fact, the president began to feel he had at least as much rapport with Stalin, who agreed with him that World war II should end European global dominance, as with Churchill, champion of the British Empire.

Thus the outlines of the postwar world remained largely undefined as Hitler found himself between the closing jaws of a gigantic vise in the summer of 1944. While the Soviets drove his armies out of their homeland, the Americans, British, and Canadians hit the beaches of western France on D-day, June 6. Operation Overlord was a technological and managerial feat as well as a military one. The Allies towed entire artificial harbors across the English Channel to provide ports for the landing of a million men in a month. Four pipelines laid on the seabed pumped fuel for the Allied advance across northern France.

In August, French and U.S. tanks reached Paris, where fighting had already begun between the forces of the underground Resistance movement and the retreating German garrison. General de Gaulle, the lonely exile of 1940, returned to be acclaimed as his country's liberator.

While Parisians rejoiced, the people of German cities had few illusions about the war's outcome by late 1944. When the Royal Air Force discovered early in the war that it could not hit precise targets such as particular factories, it adopted a policy of simply loosing its bombs indiscriminately on the populations below. In the summer of 1943, a week of incendiary raids on Hamburg had generated fire storms that killed fifty thousand and left a million homeless. The strategic effectiveness of this "saturation bombing" is doubtful. Postwar studies have shown that air raids did not even begin to slow German war production until the summer of 1944, when American "precision bombing" started. Even then, postwar polling revealed, only a bare majority of Germans would have favored surrender.

The last months of Hitler's Germany provide an eerie demonstration of the capacities of human determination—or madness. Hitler withdrew to an underground bunker in Berlin, from which he issued orders forbidding retreat to units that had already ceased to exist. To the end he hoped that his new secret weapons would save him. In addition to the world's first jet aircraft and robot flying bombs, these weapons included V-2s, missiles carrying one-ton warheads. Five hundred V-2s, crude prototypes of today's weapons, fell on London alone. Too few of them had been produced too late, however, to reverse the outcome of World War II.

Eventually Russian tanks overrode the elderly men and teenage boys Hitler had mobilized as a last line of defense and began shelling the ruins above his bunker. Only then did Hitler admit that the war was lost. On April 30, 1945, after marrying his mistress and writing a will blaming the Jews for his failure, he shot himself. She took poison. SS men burned their bodies in the courtyard above while the Russian shells continued to fall. Only then was the spell of this man, who had risen from obscurity to command the largest European empire ever known, finally broken. A week later, Germany surrendered.

Like Hitler, the Japanese warlords failed to mobilize their home front as effectively as the Allies had done. Just as the Nazis claimed that their conquests were building a united Europe, the Japanese asserted that they were establishing a "Great East Asian Co-Prosperity Sphere" and were reserving Asia for the Asians. These claims were belied by the cruelty of their occupying armies, however. Like the Germans, the Japanese people displayed great tenacity as defeat closed in on them.

In China the Japanese withstood the Nationalist armies of Chiang Kai-shek, despite heroic American efforts to arm him by airlifts over the Himalaya Mountains. But by the time of Germany's surrender, a British army including African and Indian troops was driving the Japanese from the Southeast Asian mainland. The Americans had begun the reconquest of the Philippines, and their bloody island-to-island campaign had won them air bases within easy striking distance of Japan itself. A single air raid by General Curtis Le May's B-29s on March 10, 1945, burned nearly half of Tokyo to the ground, killing or maiming 125,000 people.

Nevertheless the Allies dreaded the invasion of Japan. They expected suicidal resistance of the sort displayed by the kamikaze

Hiroshima, August 6, 1945. *Controversy continues over whether it was necessary to level whole cities with the world's first atomic weapons. Some historians have argued that the American decision to do so reflected a desire to end the war with Japan before the Soviets, entering it only in 1945, could claim a share in the victory.* *National Archives*

pilots, who deliberately crashed their planes into American warships. Considering the gloomy estimates of American casualties, Harry S Truman, who had become president at Roosevelt's death, unhesitatingly ordered the dropping of the first atomic bomb on Hiroshima on August 6, 1945. This single bomb, tiny in comparison with today's nuclear weapons, destroyed at least 100,000 people. The only other atomic bomb then in existence fell on Nagasaki three days later. In the meantime, the Soviets had hastened to declare war and invade Japanese-held Manchuria. On August 15, the Japanese people heard over the radio, for the first time ever, the voice of the emperor, announcing defeat. World War II was over.

The Revolutionary Impact of World War II

A World Divided into Three

The distribution of global power for most of the rest of the century was already taking shape in 1945. Hitler's defeat left Europe divided down the middle into blocs dominated by his two strongest enemies, the United States and the Soviet Union. In the next decade, Western Europeans would begin to recognize that recovery depended on European economic cooperation and political unity, not a vain attempt to re-establish global dominance. As former colonies won independence, a host of new nations emerged in Asia and Africa to form a Third World seeking to stay out of the superpower conflict that divided Europe.

The Yalta Conference and the Postwar World

Despite the Nazis' hopes, the Grand Alliance against them held together until they were defeated. Allies usually tend to diverge as soon as their common goal is in sight. Knowing this, and fearing a Soviet advance into the vacuum left by Germany's collapse, Churchill approached Stalin to propose a deal in southeastern Europe. The Soviets would be dominant in Bulgaria and Rumania, Nazi allies already invaded by Soviet armies. Britain would dominate in Greece. Each would have a half-interest in Hungary and Yugoslavia. Stalin seems to have been agreeable. He did not object when British troops crushed a communist attempt to seize power in Greece and imposed the monarchist government that had spent the war in London.

But after June 1944, for the first time, there were more American than British soldiers fighting Hitler. Churchill became the junior partner of the Western Allies. Henceforth it would be the Americans who set the tone in relations with the Soviets, and they contemplated no such deals. American military planners were preoccupied with the military objective of ending the war, not with seeking advantage for some postwar conflict between allies. They rejected as "political" Churchill's feeling that it would be desirable for the Western Allies' armies "to shake hands with the Russians as far east as possible" and even to beat them to Berlin.

The Big Three met for a second time at Yalta in the southern Soviet Union in February 1945. Once again the emerging differences among the Allies were papered over with ambiguous formulas. Roosevelt had reacted to Churchill's deal with Stalin as Woodrow Wilson had reacted to European power politics a generation earlier. He insisted that the Allies guarantee free postwar elections everywhere in Europe. In Poland elections were to be held by a new government that would somehow merge the Poles of the London government-in-exile into the pro-Soviet regime the Soviets recognized.

Stalin accepted these proposals but told a confidant, "Any freely elected government in eastern Europe would be anti-Soviet and that we cannot permit." He could not believe the Americans would not understand this, or that they intended the pledge of free elections everywhere as more than propaganda. In fact, U.S. foreign policy is often made by such a statement of principle, and Americans were outraged at Stalin's violations of it. From these differing perspectives eventually arose the East-West confrontation Churchill had tried to avoid.

Critics have sometimes accused the dying Roosevelt, who survived Yalta by only two months, of conceding too much to Stalin. Such criticism forgets the actual situation at the time of the Yalta conference. The war was not over. The Western Allies had yet to cross the Rhine, while the Soviets were already a hundred miles from Berlin. Expecting to need Soviet help in the final campaign against Japan, Roosevelt accepted Stalin's demands for Chinese territory. Expecting to withdraw U.S. troops from Europe as rapidly as they had left after World War I, Roosevelt secured whatever postwar commitments he could. Though he clearly overestimated his personal influence on Stalin, in early 1945 Roosevelt saw no reason to doubt

The Big Three at the Yalta Conference, February 1945. *Winston Churchill (left) and Stalin (right) flank President Franklin D. Roosevelt. Already, Churchill feared that Roosevelt had a "slender contact with life."* National Archives

his cooperation. Nor would American public opinion then have favored opposition to Stalin, for since 1941 Americans had been encouraged to see the Soviets as allies fighting the good fight.

In the end, as Churchill had expected, the realities of power, not declarations of principle, determined the division of the postwar world. For Stalin, the war before the German invasion of the Soviet Union had been a contest between equally dangerous capitalist powers. His country had narrowly escaped being defeated by one of them. Afterward, as a victor, he attempted to win control of as much territory as possible between the Soviet Union and the other capitalist powers. He expected the Americans to do the same. As Stalin said, "Everyone imposes his own system as far as his army can reach." And in fact until 1990—except in Germany, where the Americans withdrew westward some one hundred miles to the U.S. occupation zone agreed to at Yalta, and in Austria, from which the Soviets withdrew in 1955—the European frontier between the "free world" and the Soviet bloc ran where the respective armies stood at Hitler's defeat (Map 11.3).

Map 11.3 USSR Western Border Changes, 1914–1945 

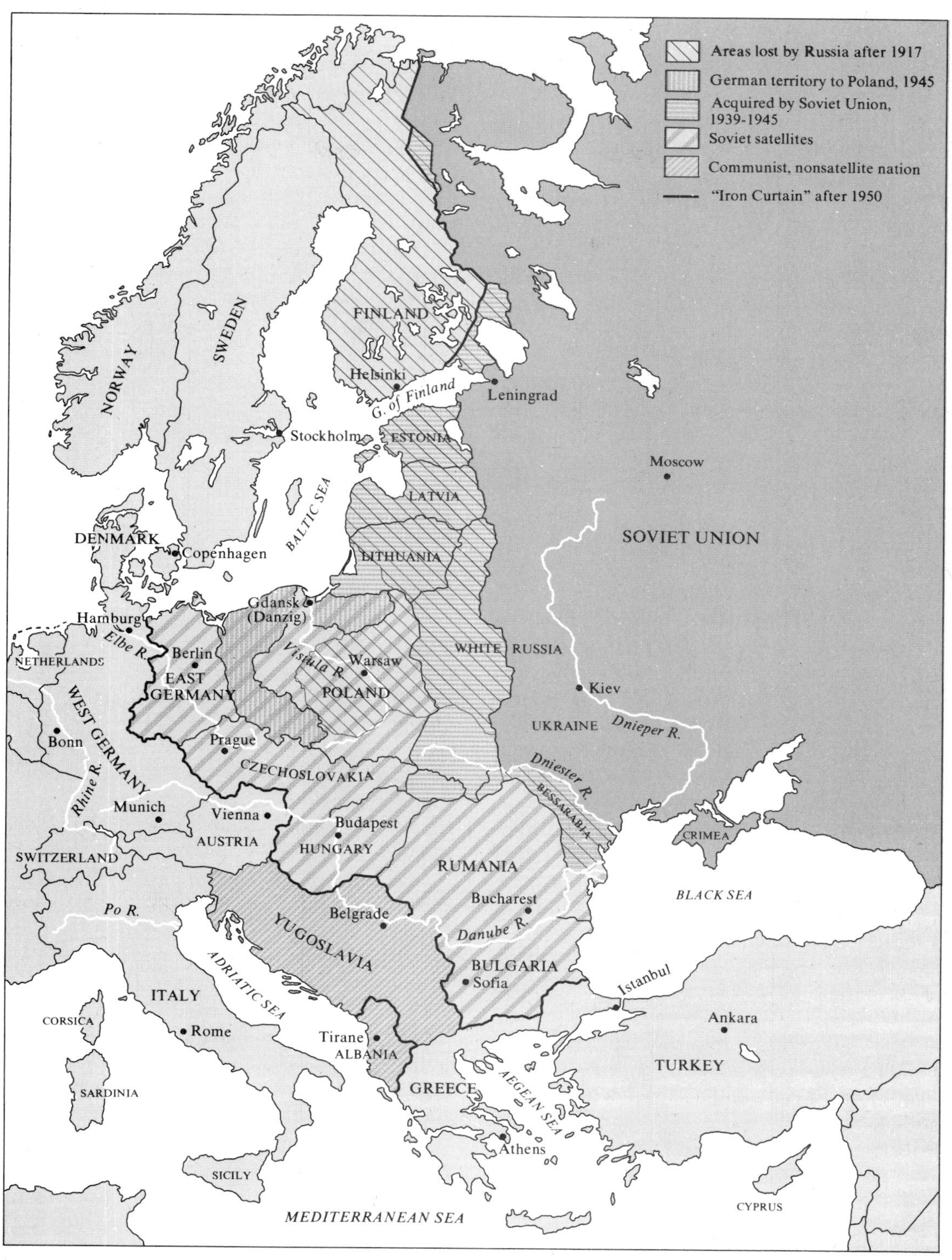

Areas lost by Russia after 1917
German territory to Poland, 1945
Acquired by Soviet Union, 1939-1945
Soviet satellites
Communist, nonsatellite nation
"Iron Curtain" after 1950
FINLAND
SWEDEN
NORWAY
Helsinki
G. of Finland
Leningrad
Stockholm
ESTONIA
Moscow
LATVIA
BALTIC SEA
DENMARK
Copenhagen
LITHUANIA
SOVIET UNION
Gdansk
(Danzig)
Hamburg
Elbe R.
Berlin
NETHERLANDS
EAST
GERMANY
Vistula R.
Warsaw
POLAND
WHITE RUSSIA
Kiev
WEST GERMANY
Bonn
Prague
UKRAINE
Dnieper R.
Dniester R.
BESSARABIA
CZECHOSLOVAKIA
Rhine R.
Munich
Vienna
Budapest
AUSTRIA
HUNGARY
CRIMEA
SWITZERLAND
RUMANIA
BLACK SEA
Bucharest
Po R.
Belgrade
YUGOSLAVIA
Danube R.
ADRIATIC SEA
BULGARIA
Sofia
Istanbul
ITALY
CORSICA
Rome
Tirane
ALBANIA
Ankara
TURKEY
SARDINIA
GREECE
AEGEAN SEA
Athens
SICILY
CYPRUS
MEDITERRANEAN SEA

The End of the European Empires

Even more than Europe's division into two blocs, the rapid dissolution of its colonial empires after 1945 revealed how World War II had ended European global dominance. In 1939, a quarter of the world's people, most of them nonwhite, lived under the British flag. They produced three-quarters of the world's gold; half of its rice, wool, and tin; and a third of its sugar, copper, and coal. France's overseas empire was twenty-six times larger than France itself, with three times the population. The Dutch ruled an empire with a population nine times larger than that of the Netherlands. Few of the colonial peoples enjoyed in 1939 even the limited self-government the British had conceded to India. Almost everywhere, however, a nationalist elite had emerged who had absorbed from their European masters the modern political ideal of a self-governing national state. World War II showed them that the Europeans could be beaten. In Asia especially, the Japanese not only drove the Europeans out but claimed to foster colonial nationalism—though they ultimately ruled these former colonies at least as harshly as the Europeans had. Moreover, the war left Europeans too exhausted for vigorous efforts to restore colonial rule. Wherever they attempted such a restoration, they encountered the opposition of both the Soviet Union and the United States.

Americans took seriously Article 3 of the Atlantic Charter, which proclaimed "the right of every people to choose the form of government under which it desires to live." As promised, they granted independence to their Philippine dependents in 1946, and they expected others to do likewise. Whether this attitude reflected the United States' own history or its colonies, as Americans often asserted, or its eagerness to penetrate more non-Western markets, as embittered Europeans complained, the effect was the same. In 1945 and 1946 U.S. agents encouraged Ho Chi Minh and other Indochinese nationalists to resist the reimposition of French rule after the Japanese departure. When the Dutch refused to recognize the independent Republic of Indonesia established in their former East Asian empire as the Japanese left, U.S. pressure through the United Nations forced them to abandon their military intervention. Over three hundred years of Dutch colonialism came to an end in 1949. The United States began to reverse its anti-colonial pressure only in the 1950s, when it began to perceive colonial nationalists as communist agents or dupes.

The Soviet Union also supported the non-Western drive for independence. Under this double pressure, Europeans gave up their empires more or less gracefully. The British habit of indirect rule simplified their surrender of formal power in Burma (1948), Malaya (1957), and much of sub-Saharan Africa (after 1957). The Commonwealth provided a kind of club within which former colonies could preserve a loose affiliation with Britain, though not all chose to join it. Thus the rich and gigantic empire of 1939 dwindled to a few bits and pieces by the 1970s.

After the debacle of 1940, the French found it harder to relinquish the overseas symbols of great-power status. France was almost the last European country to remain involved in colonial warfare. It fought for eight years (1946–1954) to hold Indochina, and another eight (1954–1962) to hold Algeria—all in vain.

The War and Postwar Society

In several respects, the end of World War II marked the beginning of the world we know today. Unlike the temporary controls of World War I, lasting changes in the relationship between government and the individual emerged from the experience of wartime government or, in German-occupied Europe, from social conflict between those who collaborated with the Nazis and those who resisted them. The war also did much to stimulate the technologies that now pervade our lives.

In much of Europe, World War II laid the foundations of the postwar welfare state. In Britain the wartime government had made great demands on citizens but had also assumed unprecedented responsibility for them. The population became accustomed to the provision of extensive social services—and to the high taxes needed to pay for them. When the Labour party defeated Churchill's Conservatives in the elections of July 1945, the new government moved rapidly to nationalize much of private industry and to implement such wartime proposals as a compulsory social security program and free secondary education.

On the continent, the ideas of the underground Resistance movements provided much of the impetus for postwar social change. Resistance originated with the lonely decisions of individuals that Nazism was intolerable and that they must oppose it somehow. Gradually they found others who felt the same way and began publishing clandestine newspapers, smuggling downed Allied airmen to safety, or transmitting intelligence to London. As Resistance movements grew with Germany's defeats, they inevitably became politicized. Because the regimes that collaborated with Hitler—like Pétain's Vichy government—were drawn from the prewar Right, the Resistance inclined to the ideas of the Left. This was true even of Catholic Resisters, who later founded Christian Democratic parties committed to programs of social reform.

In France, for example, General de Gaulle, like the leftist thinkers of the Resistance, was convinced that the defeat of 1940 reflected basic weaknesses of France's society and economy. The provisional government he headed until 1946 set out to transform both. It imposed government ownership of the big insurance companies and the coal, steel, and energy industries. It laid the foundations of the system that still sets goals for the French economy today: cooperative development of five-year plans by industry, labor, and government. And it greatly expanded the prewar welfare state. Thus one legacy of world War II was the idea that government has a comprehensive responsibility for the quality of its citizens' lives.

The War and Postwar Technology

The war was even more revolutionary in its acceleration of the pace of technological innovation. The Battle of Britain was an early clash in what Churchill called "the wizard war" (because it seemed magical to laymen)—German electronics experts devised a guiding beam for bombers, and British engineers found ways to deflect it. In this war of scientists the most formidable feat was the transformation of what was still, in 1939, only a concept of nuclear physics into the bomb dropped on Hiroshima in 1945. To turn its design into an actual weapon, the Manhattan Project constructed whole new factories employing 120,000 workers, including the first entirely automated plant in history. The total cost came to some $2 billion. Ever since, government-sponsored research has continued to demonstrate the possibilities of invention on demand, at vast cost.

Nuclear weaponry was only the most dramatic example of the technological breakthroughs stimulated by the needs of war. In 1940, the British invented *operations research,* the statistical study of war, a discipline that would profoundly influence postwar ideas of industrial management. In 1943 U.S. factories began to mass-produce the pesticide DDT and the antibiotic penicillin. Before long these two substances had fundamentally altered the conditions of human life. The application of DDT in Ceylon after the war, for example, reduced the death rate by half in one year by wiping out disease-bearing insects. Penicillin and the sulfonamides were the first of the wonder drugs that since 1945 have virtually eliminated infectious diseases in areas where the drugs are available.

Conclusion: The High Point of U.S. Power

Even in the United States, where no battles were fought, World War II had a revolutionary impact. After Pearl Harbor, formerly isolationist Americans threw themselves into the war effort with an enthusiasm that no war since 1945 has generated. U.S. industrial production quadrupled as assembly lines turned out over a quarter-million aircraft and vast quantities of other goods. Such feats demanded substantial relocations of population, as new factories opened in underindustrialized regions like the South and the Pacific Coast. Everywhere new opportunities drew rural people to the cities. The demand for labor led to Roosevelt's creation of the Fair Employment Practices Commission, the first federal agency charged with protecting minorities from discrimination.

By 1945, war-induced patterns of migration and economic growth had produced a society very different from the one Americans had known in 1941. The war effort carried over into peacetime, too, for the development of military technology had acquired a dynamic of its own. In 1945 the U.S. and Soviet military establishments raced to capture Hitler's missile designers. Those efforts marked the beginning of what has been called the warfare state, dedicated to developing new technologies of destruction. World War II had already hinted what a future war fought by such means might be like. Almost half of its 50 million dead were civilians (compared with only 5 percent during World War I). Many of these were victims of indiscriminate aerial bombings—a weapon that had seemed so terrible in imagination that many people in the 1930s believed that it never would be used or that it had made war itself unthinkable. World War II proved otherwise, and after 1945 the use of aerial bombing was taken for granted in all nations' defense planning.

The outcome of World War II suggested that future combatants in such a full-scale war would have to be as populous and industrially powerful as the United States, which then had more than 140 million people. Former great powers with populations of 40 to 50 million, like Britain and France, were already dwarfed. On this superpower scale, the only possible rival to the United States was the Soviet Union. A Soviet challenge seemed unlikely, however, for that country was exhausted and devastated. It had lost 20 million people, sixty times more than the United States had lost.

In the face of such Soviet weakness, the United States had probably reached in 1945 the high point of its twentieth-century power. So strong was the U.S. position that Americans redesigned the world's political and economic systems to their own specifications. The new United Nations, created to replace the League of Nations, set up its headquarters not in Europe, like the League, but in New York. Among the five permanent members of its Security Council, charged with keeping the peace, the United States could usually count on the votes of Britain, France, and China. Similarly the new International Monetary Fund, designed to balance international payments, and the World Bank, established to make loans to needy nations, conformed to the specifications of the U.S. delegation to the international financial conference held at Bretton Woods, New Hampshire, in 1944. Though ostensibly international, both institutions were actually subject to U.S. influence.

In many ways, then, the destiny of the world after 1945 seemed to be in American hands. World War II marked the climax of an incredibly swift U.S. ascent to world power. Until the 1890s, the United States had been seen as a second-rate power, not even accorded full ambassadorial representation by the great powers. Over the next half-century, it began to play a world political role corresponding to the fantastic growth of its economy. But the U.S. advance to world power had been interrupted by apparent retreats, like the return to isolationism after 1918. Today, when U.S. armed forces are stationed in more than a hundred countries around the world, it is hard to imagine the situation of 1940, when the Pentagon had not been built and the U.S. army was smaller than that of Belgium. It was World War II that marked the turning point to the global involvement Americans have learned to live with. For U.S. power did not long remain unchallenged. Only a few years after the war's end, the United States and the Soviet Union found themselves locked in Cold War confrontation.

Notes

1. Winston S. Churchill, *Their Finest Hour* (Boston: Houghton Mifflin, 1949), pp. 225–226.
2. Alan Bullock, *Hitler: A Study in Tyranny,* rev. ed. (New York: Harper & Row, 1964), p. 574.
3. Winston S. Churchill, *The Grand Alliance* (Boston: Houghton Mifflin, 1950), p. 370.
4. Peter Calvocoressi and Guy Wint, *Total War: Causes and Courses of the Second World War* (New York: Penguin Books, 1972), p. 212.

Suggestions for Further Reading

Bratzel, John F., and Leslie B. Rout, Jr. "Pearl Harbor, Microdots, and J. Edgar Hoover." *American Historical Review* (December 1982), pp. 1342–1351.

Browning, Christopher. *Ordinary Men: Reserve Police Battalion 101 and the Final Solution in Poland* (1991).

Calvocoressi, Peter, Guy Wint, and John Pritchard. *Total War: Causes and Course of the Second World War.* Rev. 2d ed. (1988).

Churchill, Winston S. *The Second World War.* 6 vols. (1986).

de Gaulle, Charles. *War Memoirs.* 3 vols. (1955).

Feis, Herbert. *Churchill, Roosevelt, Stalin* (1967).

Fourcade, Marie-Madeleine. *Noah's Ark: A Memoir of Struggle and Resistance* (1981).

Hersey, John. *Hiroshima* (1946).

Horne, Alistair. *To Lose a Battle: France 1940* (1979).

Hughes, Terry, and John Costello. *The Battle of the Atlantic* (1977).

Liddell Hart, Basil H. *History of the Second World War* (1980).

Prange, Gordon W. *At Dawn We Slept: The Untold Story of Pearl Harbor* (1981).

Rupp, Leila J. *Mobilizing Women for War: German and American Propaganda, 1939–1945* (1978).

Wright, Gordon. *The Ordeal of Total War* (1968).

CHAPTER 12

Emergence and Decline of Superpower Bipolarity

After the defeat of the Germans and the Japanese, the victors of World War II hoped that they had established peace for good. In one sense they were soon disappointed. Within five years the two superpower winners, the United States and the Soviet Union, were confronting one another in a Cold War that many feared would culminate in actual war. For over a decade in the 1950s, this bipolar conflict of the two superpowers seemed the dominant theme of international relations, defining the issues of every confrontation around the world. Thus the world held its breath in 1962 for fear that the superpowers' showdown over Cuba might escalate into nuclear war.

Looking back over the whole period since 1945 from the perspective of the 1990s, however, we can see that the confrontation of the superpowers was not the only factor at work in international relations, especially after 1962. Over the next thirty years, it became obvious that the authority of the superpowers over the two blocs into which they had divided much of the world was declining, as rival powers, whose strength derived more from economic achievement than from military might, emerged to challenge their authority.

The long standoff between the two nuclear superpowers does help to explain why the world has managed to live for nearly half a century since World War II without having to face World War III, whereas the interlude between the first and second world wars lasted barely twenty years. Neither superpower dared strike the other because the other's nuclear retaliation would have been so devastating. The cost to the economies and societies of both of sustaining this nuclear stalemate proved so debilitating, however, that by the

1990s the Soviet Union (as we shall see in Chapter 14) collapsed and disintegrated, while the supposed Cold War "victor," the United States, was beset (as Chapter 13 will show) by grave internal weaknesses undreamed-of by Americans in the heady days of triumph in 1945.

Thus we live today in a multipolar world, much more reminiscent of the pre–World War II world than of that of the Cold War. The two principal vanquished powers of 1945, a reunited Germany—dominating an increasingly united Europe—and Japan, have the economic potential to become as strong or even stronger than the United States, let alone what today we must refer to as the "former Soviet Union." This was an outcome not foreseen by those who waged the Cold War with such zest.

Interpreting Post-1945 International Relations

Publicly, the leaders of both superpowers asserted that their confrontation was between ways of life. The U.S. government declared, and most Americans believed, that confrontation with the Soviet Union was essential to the defense of political democracy and what is called the free-enterprise system. The Soviet government proclaimed, and most Soviet citizens believed, that confrontation with the United States was essential to the defense of revolutionary socialism.

Clearly the political and economic systems of the two superpowers were very different. And there is little doubt that one of them was more attractive than the other to most people. From 1961 to 1989, the Soviets maintained a barrier—the Berlin Wall—separating their part of the world from the rest. Its purpose, despite Soviet denials, was to keep people *in*. The United States, by contrast, considered legislation to strengthen its border with Mexico to keep people *out*.

Despite the genuine differences between the two systems, however, some aspects of the U.S.-Soviet confrontation suggest that it was not fundamentally driven by ideology. To counter Soviet influence, for example, the United States supported regimes around the world that had little more regard for freedom than a communist regime would. Nor did the Soviet Union consistently support communist regimes and movements. In the 1960s the two largest communist powers, the Soviet Union and China, became open enemies. In the same decade, the democracies of Western Europe were becoming increasingly impatient of U.S. direction.

What has really been at stake since 1945 is the world distribution of *power*. For much of the period, power was measured in purely military terms, by counting the gigantic arsenals of the two Cold War superpowers. Only recently have we begun to understand the lesson that centuries of history should have taught us: power ultimately derives from the strength of a nation's economy, which is sometimes weakened rather than strengthened by overarming.

The conflicting ideologies of the superpowers concealed the real nature of this contest for power, encouraging both sides to understand the aftermath of World War II by drawing analogies with the 1930s. As the wartime Grand Alliance dissolved in suspicion, American policymakers came to assume that the Soviet Union's aims, like Hitler's, were unlimited: the creation of a universal empire by conquest and communist revolutions. Soviet policymakers expected U.S. capitalism to envelop and try to destroy the homeland of communism.

Each side feared an ideological crusade by the other. But in practice neither superpower was willing to let ideological goals override its interests, defined by its power. The nonaligned nations of the world soon came to see the U.S.-Soviet confrontation as a power struggle, regardless of ideology. In 1955 at a conference in Bandung, Indonesia, many of these nations declared their unwillingness to line up with either superpower.

This perspective of the nonaligned Third World sometimes surprised Americans. Although isolationism was no longer a practical option after World War II, Americans were still significantly influenced by the idea that had lain at the heart of their earlier aloofness from international affairs: the sense that the United States was a uniquely superior society that might be defiled by contact with a more sordid world. This notion reinforced a strong impulse to improve the world and make it conform to the U.S. model. If the United States could no longer remain aloof from the world, then the world had to be made a safer place for U.S. ideals. Americans did not understand that other nations perceived these ideals as a smokescreen covering the use of U.S. power to promote U.S. interests.

The Soviets approached the postwar world in much the same spirit. They too tried to impose their ideals on their neighbors and on as much of the rest of the world as possible. Because both U.S. and Soviet policies were embodied in alliances, the world for a time came to resemble less the 1930s than the pre-1914 European world of armed alliances, confronting one another in successive crises.

During the periods of postwar international relations discussed in the next two sections of this chapter, from the end of World War II to Stalin's death in 1953 and from 1953 to the Cuban missile crisis of 1962, the dominant theme was the bipolar confrontation of the two giants, the United States and the USSR. This Cold War was an unequal contest, though the Americans, who dominated it, did not always see it that way. It pitted the United States, dominant in Latin America and Western Europe, against the Soviet Union, which controlled (beyond its own vast territories) only the band of adjacent lands overrun in World War II. The crises of the Cold War all occurred along this periphery of Soviet control—in Korea, in southeastern Europe, in Iran, in Berlin. In every case the Soviets' attempt to expand their perimeter was rebuffed, as was their probe of the U.S. perimeter in support of Cuba in 1962. The Soviets' strength was still so inferior that when President Kennedy gave them an ultimatum, they could only retreat. The Cuban missile crisis seemed to confirm American primacy in the world.

In the fourth section of this chapter, we shall see how the 1960s—a decade that did not truly end until 1973 with the withdrawal of U.S. combat troops from Vietnam—exposed the limits of the two giants' power. The Vietnam debacle shattered American self-confidence, appearing to prove that the United States could not defeat Third World revolutionaries determined to pull their country out of the U.S. orbit. Meanwhile, a prosperous Western Europe, spurred by a France once more led by General de Gaulle, increasingly challenged American dominance. Soviet power also seemed to be eroding in the 1960s. It was then that relations between the Soviet Union and China flamed into open hostility.

In the 1970s and the first half of the 1980s, as the fifth section will show, there were several dramatic reversals in the climate of superpower relations. With international politics evolving toward multipolarity as Western Europe and China asserted themselves, the United States and the Soviet Union at first seemed to have achieved *détente*—the word then employed to describe relaxation of tensions. With its economy weakened by a double effort to win in Vietnam and carry out social reform at home, and by the emergence of powerful competitors such as Japan, the United States was ready to come to terms with its perpetual antagonist. The Soviet Union, also in worsening economic shape, seemed ready to reciprocate. The fact that the superpowers were not so powerful as they had been facilitated some limited accommodation between them. But *détente* proved fragile. Within a few years relations soured again. Through most of President Reagan's first term there seemed little prospect of improvement. Indeed Americans tended to blame the Soviet Union for the defiance the United States increasingly encountered from small but resource-rich countries such as Iran, defiance that served as another sign of the world's evolution toward multipolarity.

Few people who attended the inauguration in 1981 of so staunch an anti-communist as Ronald Reagan could have imagined that the world's television audiences would see him strolling arm-in-arm through Moscow's Red Square with Soviet leader Mikhail Gorbachev as he neared the end of his second term in 1988. The sixth section of this chapter will show that the U.S.-Soviet accommodation symbolized by their Moscow embrace came too late for the purpose for which Gorbachev had attempted it: the economic and political revitalization of the USSR. Rather than reinforcing the USSR, Gorbachev's reforms proved the prelude to the collapse of the Soviet Union and its dissolution on December 25, 1991, into fifteen separate and independent republics. The administration of U.S. President George Bush, elected as Reagan's successor in 1988, could thus proclaim that U.S. steadfastness through nearly a half-century of Cold War had produced a victory and opened the way to a "New World Order" under American leadership. The economic realities of the 1990s discussed in the seventh section, however, make it clear that the "victory" was won at great cost to the United States and that the post–Cold War global configuration, far from being U.S. dominated, will be multipolar, with the United States not necessarily representing the strongest pole.

The Cold War to 1953

Allies in World War II, the United States and the Soviet Union did not become opponents overnight. The Cold War developed gradually between 1945 and 1950. There has been much controversy over who was to blame. Most historians now agree that the Cold War began as the Soviet Union, seeking to expand in accordance with historic Russian ambitions, aroused American fear that it would contest the emerging U.S.-dominated world system created by European and Japanese collapse. Each side reacted to successive challenges by taking new steps that it regarded as defensive but that appeared to the other as new threats. A dynamic of confrontation developed.

There were three stages in this process. During the first stage, which ran from Hitler's defeat to the spring of 1947, cooperation was curiously mixed with growing antagonism. Communists held seats in coalition governments in Western Europe, noncommunists in Eastern Europe. Expecting a permanent peace, the United States reduced the number of Americans in uniform from 12 million to only a million and a half. The Soviets also demobilized, but less completely. American soldiers handed over Soviet refugees in their jurisdiction to the Soviet authorities. As Truman and Stalin had agreed, the Soviets collected reparations from the other three occupation zones—American, British, and French—into which western Germany had been divided.

In the meantime, however, the Soviets sought to expand into areas that Russia had long coveted. They encouraged separatist movements in northwestern Iran and demanded a revision of the historic agreement by which Turkey controlled the passage to Russia's warm-water ports on the Black Sea. In the past, Britain had often pushed the Russians back when they attempted to encroach on these regions. Bankrupt postwar Britain, however, could no longer play this role.

In February 1947, the British indicated they could no longer afford to give aid to Turkey, or to the royalist government Churchill and British troops had installed in Greece, under attack from Communist guerrillas. Unwilling to allow what they interpreted as Soviet pressure in southeastern Europe to succeed, American policymakers took a step that marked a second stage in the development of the Cold War. On March 12, 1947, President Truman announced that the United States would aid the Greeks and Turks. It would be American policy, he declared, "to support free peoples who are resisting subjugation by armed minorities or by outside pressures."[1] He thus linked resistance to historic Russian ambition to ideological principles. In fact, however, the governments to which the United States extended protection were not necessarily very "free." This Truman Doctrine marked a major turning point in the history of American foreign policy. The U.S. president had offered an open-ended commitment to forestall revolution or aggression anywhere.

Prostrate Western Europe, where cooperation between Communists and the other parties in coalition governments broke down in the spring of 1947, seemed especially vulnerable. In June, Secretary of State George Marshall committed the United States to rebuilding the European economy. His offer of aid was extended to all the war-torn countries, including the Soviet Union. Americans, who saw the Marshall Plan as an act of spontaneous generosity, could not understand why the Soviets walked out of the Paris conference convened to implement it.

In fact, unsurprisingly, the Marshall Plan was designed as much in U.S. self-interest as for Europe's benefit. It required its recipients to accept U.S.-made goods, shielding the U.S. economy from a postwar slump, and to account to the U.S.-managed European Recovery Administration for aid expenditures. In effect the Marshall Plan tied the European market securely to the U.S. economy. It is not surprising that the Soviets rejected such subordination in a U.S.-dominated world economic system.

Integration into the U.S. economic orbit brought Western Europeans a rapid postwar recovery. By 1952, when Marshall Plan aid ended, European industrial production was a third higher than it had been before World War II.

Two separate European economies began to emerge: one oriented to the Atlantic, the other to the Soviet Union. Now Europe was truly divided by the "Iron Curtain" that Winston Churchill had described in 1946. In February 1948, a coup d'état in Czechoslovakia overthrew the last Eastern European coalition government and imposed a communist dictatorship. President Truman responded by reinstituting the American draft and encouraging the formation of the Brussels Pact, including Britain, France, and the "Benelux" countries (Belgium, the Netherlands, and Luxembourg). As the two blocs solidified, a key uncertainty was the fate of divided Germany.

Early in 1947, the Americans and British merged the economies of their two occupation zones. Clearly, it was only a matter of time before a western German state dependent on the United States emerged as a barrier to any further Soviet ambitions in Central Europe.

Even if they had no such ambitions, the growth of a resurgent Germany aligned with a hostile United States was a terrifying prospect for the Soviets. Stalin's countermove, in June 1948, was to cut off access to Berlin, which lay deep within the Soviet occupation zone of Germany. The ruined former capital, itself partitioned into zones, was to be used as a Soviet chip in the international poker game. But Truman raised the ante by airlifting all the needed supplies—including coal—into Berlin and by stationing bombers capable of carrying nuclear weapons at British airfields. Once again the

Soviets backed down, abandoning their Berlin blockade after a year. When the Federal Republic of West Germany was created in May 1949, the Soviets could only counter by establishing a communist-led German Democratic Republic in East Germany.

The U.S. strategy of containing the Soviet Union had not yet led to major American rearmament. The United States remained confident in its monopoly of the ultimate, nuclear weapon. When the Soviets exploded an atomic bomb in July 1949, a major reassessment was required. According to "NSC-68," a secret planning document prepared by the U.S. National Security Council in April 1950, the Soviet Union was a rampant aggressor bent on overrunnng all of Europe and Asia. To counter the threat, "NSC-68" declared, the United States must develop a thermonuclear bomb and European air bases from which the Strategic Air Command could deliver it. In Europe, U.S. troops should reinforce the North Atlantic Treaty Organization (NATO) formed to link the United States, Canada, Denmark, Norway, Iceland, Italy, and Portugal to the countries of the Brussels Pact (Map 12.1). Moreover, it would be necessary to rearm West Germany, despite the reluctance of Europeans whose countries had been ravaged by German armies. The implementation of "NSC-68" marks the third and final stage in the development of the Cold War. For the first time in its history, the United States began massive peacetime preparations for war, including the creation of the Central Intelligence Agency (CIA).

The sudden attack of North Korea on South Korea in June 1950 seemed to confirm the need for such preparations. Korea had been the object of imperial rivalries between Russia and Japan until the Japanese victory in the war of 1904–1905 placed it firmly under Japanese control. The defeat of the Japanese in 1945 left Korea divided between Soviet and American occupying armies. Each superpower established a client regime, north and south of the thirty-eighth parallel of latitude. U.S. Secretary of State Dean Acheson, however, had publicly excluded South Korea from the list of countries the United States was prepared to defend.

Thus emboldened, the North Koreans attacked. This seemed to be a clear case of aggression and an opportunity for the United Nations to demonstrate its ability to restore peace. Any one of the five permanent members of the UN Security Council could paralyze action by exercising a veto. At the time of the Korean attack, however, the Soviet representative was boycotting Security Council meetings to protest the UN's refusal to recognize the Chinese Communists in place of Chiang Kai-shek's regime. In the Soviets' absence, the United Nations prescribed collective action against aggression in Korea.

In fact, the so-called UN forces mustered to meet the North Korean attack were 50 percent American (and 40 percent South Korean). They were successful in containing the North Koreans' initial headlong advances and in pushing them back. Then the American UN commander, General Douglas MacArthur, became overconfident. He moved his forces close to the Chinese border while ostentatiously conferring with Chiang Kai-shek about his intervention in the war. Fearing an American attempt to reverse their revolution and restore Chiang, the Chinese rushed 200,000 "volunteers" into the Korean War. They soon pushed the UN forces back to the line where the conflict had begun. Forced to choose between this Korean standoff and the unknown risks of full-scale war with China, President Truman agreed in June 1951 to begin negotiations for a cease-fire, finally signed in June 1953.

This outcome of the Korean "police action"—after the loss of fifty-four thousand American lives—illustrated how frustratingly inconclusive peripheral bipolar conflicts could be. But the experience stimulated the Ameri-

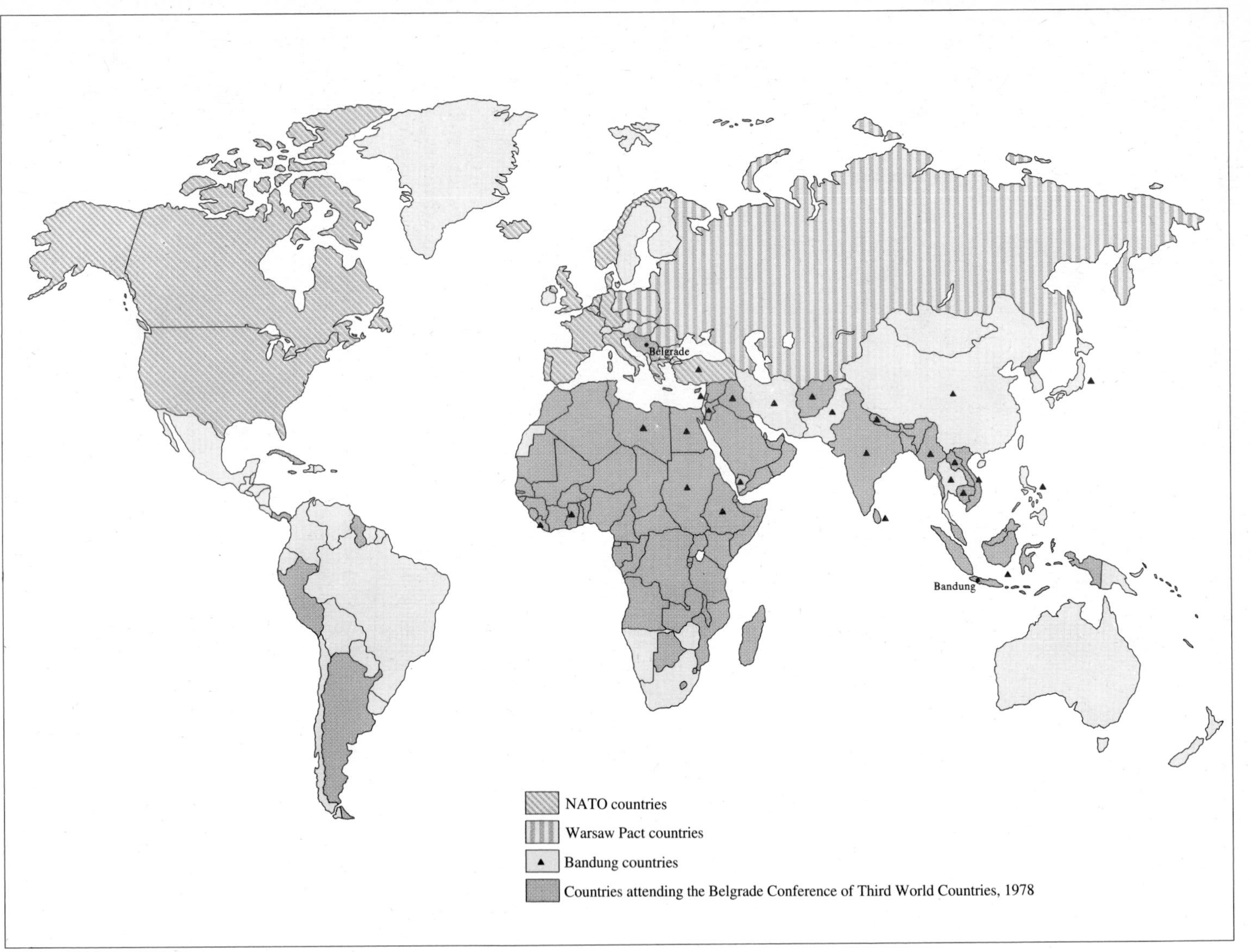
Belgrade
Bandung
NATO countries
Warsaw Pact countries
Bandung countries
Countries attending the Belgrade Conference of Third World Countries, 1978

can government to extend its guarantees wider still: to the Philippines, Australia, and New Zealand. During the 1950s, it gave a quarter of a billion dollars annually to Chiang Kai-shek's Taiwan, no small factor in that country's "economic miracle." The key to securing the Pacific was Japan, which, now, like Germany, changed rapidly from an American enemy into an American friend. In 1951–1952, the United States signed a peace treaty and withdrew its occupation troops. Many American servicemen remained in Japan, however. Japanese bases were a key link in the chain the United States had drawn around the Soviet Union from Norway through Greece and Turkey (added to NATO in 1952) to South Korea and Taiwan. Americans saw this strategy as containment or the defense of freedom—though strongman regimes like that of South Korea were hardly free. But to the Soviets it undoubtedly looked like encirclement. It would be up to Stalin's successors after his death in 1953 to find ways to break out.

The Containment of Khrushchev, 1953–1962

As we shall see in Chapter 14, the Soviet leaders who succeeded Stalin were anxious to reduce international tensions so as to reallocate arms spending for domestic purposes. It was not clear, however, how their conciliatory gestures would be received in Washington. President Eisenhower's secretary of state, John Foster Dulles, had come to office in 1953 arguing that the mere containment of the Soviets was not enough. Dulles professed to see international relations as a contest between good and evil, in which the Soviet rule over Eastern Europe should not go unchallenged. He did not, however, explain how the United States could drive the Soviets out of that region without going to war. Because Eisenhower was reluctant to unbalance the U.S. budget for a buildup of conventional forces, Dulles could only back up his aggressive language by threats of "massive [nuclear] retaliation" for any Soviet transgression. That threat became far less credible, however, when the Soviets exploded their hydrogen bomb in 1953, only nine months after the Americans detonated their first such weapon. For many years the United States retained an advantage in capabilities for delivering the fearsome new weapon. Nevertheless, the Soviet hydrogen bomb, rapidly evening up the arms race, was a vivid reminder that the two superpowers could not wish away each other's power.

The new Soviet leadership had to try to reach accommodation with the United States without alienating factions within the communist bloc that insisted the Americans were not to be trusted (the Chinese, for example). For this reason, Soviet policy alternated between concessions and intransigence through the 1950s. In 1955, for instance, the Soviets countered the entry of West Germany into NATO by forming the Warsaw Pact, an alliance of their Eastern European client states—but they also met with Western leaders in Geneva, in the first "summit conference" since 1945. Proposals at Geneva to de-escalate the nuclear arms race failed to overcome each side's suspicions that the other would cheat in any process of negotiated disarmament. Still, the discussions marked a departure from Cold War unconditional hostility. So did such Soviet concessions as withdrawal from Austria, on condition that it remain nonaligned.

Two simultaneous international crises in 1956 revealed that while the two superpowers

◀ ***Map 12.1 NATO, the Soviet Bloc, and the Third World***

Khrushchev visits an Iowa farm, 1959. *Recognizing his country's agricultural failures, the Soviet leader (left) hoped improved relations would enable him to borrow the techniques of U.S. agribusiness.* *Eliot Erwitt/Magnum*

might warily negotiate with each other, they would tolerate no independent initiatives from their allies or satellites. When Hungary rose in revolt against Soviet domination in October, the Soviets sent in armored columns to crush the uprising. Despite the encouragement the Hungarian rebels had received from CIA-financed radio stations such as Radio Free Europe, the United States could do nothing for them but take in some of the 200,000 who fled their native land. For all of Dulles's talk of "rolling back" Soviet rule, the United States would not intervene in a region tacitly conceded to lie within the Soviet sphere of influence.

The U.S. government in October 1956 brought pressure not against the Soviets but against its own allies—the British, French, and Israelis—when they provoked the other international crisis of that month (a godsend to the Soviets) by invading Egypt in retaliation for President Nasser's seizure of the Suez Canal. Nikita S. Khrushchev, who had emerged as the Soviet leader, threatened a nuclear war, but

Eisenhower's warnings to the U.S. allies were far more effective in ending the invasion. The future of the Arab world lay with Nasser-style Third World nationalism, U.S. policymakers decided, and not with a resurgence of European influence in the region. Thus nations on both side of the world's bipolar divide received sharp reminders in 1956 of their dependency—the Hungarians, of course, far more tragically than the British and French.

Meanwhile, relations between the two superpowers continued to oscillate between cordiality and confrontation. Khrushchev alternated blandishments and threats in his efforts to force the United States to recognize Soviet equality.

The Soviet Union and Berlin

A perennial bone of contention was the status of Germany and its capital. By surviving the siege of 1948, Berlin had become a symbol of freedom, a democratic and affluent island in a totalitarian and destitute sea. The official position of the West German government was that Germany should be reunified by free elections, with Berlin again becoming the capital. Official U.S. policy supported this scenario, though privately American policymakers, like those in Western Europe and the Soviet Union, were doubtless content to see Germany remain divided. Fearful of the power that West Germany alone contributed to the U.S.-led NATO alliance, the Soviets repeatedly tried to force the United States to recognize the permanent division of the country, including the Soviet domination of East Germany. Their lever once again was the vulnerability of isolated Berlin. Late in 1958 Khrushchev threatened unilaterally to end Berlin's privileged status as a free city within communist East Germany, a status which had provided an escape route for some 2 million fugitives. Encountering united Western resistance where perhaps he had hoped to expose disunity, he canceled this Berlin ultimatum in March 1959.

Confrontations of this sort alternated with attempts at communication. On a visit to the United States later that year, Khrushchev met with President Eisenhower at Camp David, Maryland. Those talks produced little except agreement for another summit meeting in Paris. The president and the premier made no progress on disarmament, though by now the Soviets had created a strategic bomber force (still far smaller than the U.S. Strategic Air Command) to deliver their nuclear weapons, and both nations were hard at work developing ballistic missiles. Khrushchev aborted the Paris summit meeting as soon as it convened, by revealing that the Soviets had shot down an American high-altitude U-2 spy plane over Soviet territory and by demanding an apology for the flight.

In June, 1961, this turn toward renewed confrontation was followed by an ultimatum to U.S. president John F. Kennedy. Within a year, Khrushchev declared, he would sign a peace treaty with East Germany and relinquish to the East Germans control over access to Berlin. A few months later he ordered the erection of a wall separating East and West Berlin to end the hemorrhage of Eastern European labor and talent from the Soviet empire. Kennedy's only response was to draft more young Americans into the army and send some of them to West Berlin. Forced to choose between acquiescence and war, the United States preferred to acquiesce.

The Cuban Missile Crisis

Though it solved a Soviet problem, the Berlin Wall was hardly a Soviet success. Presumably challenged by Soviet and Chinese hard-liners to achieve more successes in the continuing duel with the United States, Khrushchev took a step in 1962 that brought the world as close as it has yet come to nuclear war. He ordered the installation of Soviet missiles in Cuba.

The ultimate cause of the Cuban missile crisis was the Cuban revolution of January 1959, in which Fidel Castro overthrew the right-wing, U.S.-backed dictatorship of Fulgencio Batista. The United States reacted by virtually excluding sugar, Cuba's principal source of export income, from the American market and by denying Cuba most American goods. Castro retaliated by seizing control of Cuban economic assets—sugar mills, oil refineries, banks—that were largely American owned. In such a situation, Cuba and the Soviet Union inevitably drew together. Khrushchev saw opportunities to extend Soviet influence by helping developing countries. He had already promised aid to those seeking to escape dependency by fighting "wars of liberation." Castro had no alternative ally. By the end of 1960, the Soviet Union had agreed to buy half of Cuba's sugar crop and to provide Castro with the essentials the U.S. embargo denied him.

Unwilling to tolerate a Soviet client state ninety miles off U.S. shores, the Eisenhower administration ordered the CIA to develop a secret plan for overthrowing it. But the plan, executed in April 1961, proved a deeply humiliating fiasco for President Kennedy. Castro's forces easily killed or rounded up the fifteen hundred Cuban refugees the CIA landed at the Bay of Pigs. Contrary to Washington's expectations, the Cuban population did not rise up to welcome the invaders.

Castro's demands for Soviet protection against a renewed American attack undoubtedly prompted Khrushchev's decision to send missiles to Cuba. But he must also have had other motives for taking such a tremendous gamble. Soviet missiles in Cuba would put much of the United States at the same nuclear risk the Soviet Union already faced from American missiles in Turkey and Western Europe. They could be used as bargaining chips against a German settlement. Their emplacement would prove to Khrushchev's critics that he could get tough with the Americans.

In October 1962, when U.S. aerial reconnaissance revealed that launching sites were under construction in Cuba, a terrifying thirteen-day crisis began. Few voices in the U.S. administration called for negotiation; most favored some show of force. Rather than attacking the launching sites without warning, as some recommended, Kennedy chose to impose a "quarantine" on Cuba. That term was used because a naval blockade amounted to a declaration of war. In fact, however, the U.S. navy blockaded Cuba; it was prepared to stop and search approaching Soviet ships that might be carrying the missiles. As television news plotted the course of those ships, the world waited and wondered whether a clash on the high seas might lead to nuclear war. Kennedy himself is reported to have thought that the odds of war were at least one in three, and at worst even. The suspense ended only with the news that the Soviet ships were turning back.

Once again, and this time very publicly, Khrushchev had to back down. He paid for this humiliation in 1964 when his colleagues in the Politburo, the Soviet cabinet, fired him. Whatever credit he might have earned for ending the crisis was negated by the fact that he had provoked it. In exchange for his retreat he had received a tacit U.S. commitment not to invade Cuba and to remove American missiles (already obsolete) poised on the Soviet border in Turkey. But the Soviet Union had visibly failed in an attempt to project its power as close to American borders as U.S. power hemmed in its own frontiers.

The lessons of this hair-raising episode remain obscure. The Soviets concluded that they must never again be caught in such a position of inferiority and began constructing a navy and nuclear delivery systems that could challenge the Americans. In the United States, critics on the Left accused Kennedy of a strident, macho posturing that made the crisis worse, while those on the Right complained that the Castro regime survived unscathed. One thing was clear, however. The crisis proved that twentieth-century superpower leaders were ready to go to the brink of nuclear war to defend what they saw as their nations' vital interests.

Challenges to Bipolarity, 1962–1973

During the Cuban missile crisis, most of the world stood on the sidelines, at risk of destruction if the two superpowers clashed. This episode vividly illustrated the continuing danger for other nations of "annihilation without representation." That danger helps to explain the theme of the next decade of postwar international relations: the beginning of the breakdown of the bipolar world into a multipolar one. A resurgent Western Europe increasingly challenged U.S. leadership. At the same time, the U.S. assumption that Moscow orchestrated every move of world communism proved stunningly false as the Soviet Union and the People's Republic of China moved from mistrustful friendship to the verge of war.

First Steps Toward the Integration of Europe

The first steps toward Western European resurgence were taken while the continent was still rebuilding after the war. As the Cold War undercut the parties of the Left, power passed to Christian Democratic leaders. Their shared Catholic faith, transcending national loyalties, helped them to see that the European nations had become dwarfed and obsolete in a world of superpowers. Only by merging into a "United States of Europe" could Europeans regain even part of their former power. The first institutional embodiment of European integration was the European Coal and Steel Authority, established in April 1951. It merged the mines and steel mills of France, West Germany, Italy, and the Benelux countries. This proved to be only the first of many such supranational European organizations. In 1957 the same countries signed the Treaties of Rome, establishing the European Economic Community (EEC). Its members committed themselves to creating a "Common Market," eventually eliminating tariffs on one another's goods.

The Gaullist Challenge to U.S. Leadership

Though scornful of the federal model of European integration favored by the founders of the EEC, General de Gaulle, as president of France from 1958 to 1969, tried to make multipolarity a reality by compelling Western Europeans to abandon their dependency on the United States. He aimed to make a revived Europe, led by France, a power to reckon with in the world again. The Europe he had in mind extended from the Atlantic to the Urals (the Russian mountains that separate Europe from Asia), combining the two blocs created by the Cold War.

Western Europe's subordination to an American NATO commander, de Gaulle maintained, was frightening and unconvincing: frightening, because as the Cuban missile crisis showed, in a confrontation with the Soviet Union the United States would not consult its allies before acting; unconvincing, because as the Soviet Union developed its nuclear capability, it was no longer credible that the United States would risk destruction to save Europe from a Soviet attack. Therefore de Gaulle did all he could to foster an independent European defense system. He gave the highest priority to developing delivery systems for France's nuclear weapons, developed over U.S. objec-

Charles de Gaulle in 1965. *The French president votes in his village's town hall beneath his portrait as Free France's leader during World War II.* *Wide World Photos*

tions. Meanwhile he refused to allow the installation of NATO nuclear weapons on French soil, withdrew French forces from NATO command, and in 1966 ousted NATO from France. Similarly, when the British agreed in 1962 to replace their obsolete nuclear bombers with U.S. missiles, de Gaulle retaliated by vetoing Britain's application for membership in the EEC.

For a time, de Gaulle hoped the West Germans, unlike the British, would back his efforts for an independent Western Europe. He tried to persuade them to abandon their unrealistic, U.S.-backed insistence on a formula for German reunification that was unacceptable to the Soviet Union because it threatened the existence of East Germany. De Gaulle believed that a reduction of the German threat might persuade the Soviet Union, faced with a growing Chinese menace, to relax its grip on Eastern Europe. Then Europe's bipolar division might end, and the continent, from the Atlantic to the Urals, could return to world power.

In hopes of restoring European economic independence, de Gaulle attacked the international monetary system created under American auspices at Bretton Woods in 1944. Under this system, the dollar had become the world's principal means of exchange. De Gaulle argued that the dollar's privileged status enabled the United States to escape the discipline the world economy enforced on other currencies. The United States could ignore growing inflation and an ever-growing imbalance in the payments it exchanged with other countries. Its worldwide role protected the dollar from depreciating even when Americans spent more abroad than they earned. The endless outflow of dollars enabled U.S.-based multinational companies to buy heavily into the economies of other countries. Until the world monetary system could be revised, de Gaulle's remedy for France was to demand payments in gold, largely depleting the U.S. supply.

Many Americans denounced de Gaulle as an enemy. In fact, however, Gaullist foreign policy was only the most outspoken expression of a widespread European aspiration to break free of the post-1945 bipolar system. When the Soviets in 1968 crushed the attempt to create "communism with a human face" in Czechoslovakia, it appeared that de Gaulle's ambitious strategy of reuniting the continent had failed. But the Gaullist drive for European solutions to European problems, taken up by less abrasive leaders like Chancellor Willy Brandt of West Germany, would become a significant factor in the détente of the early 1970s.

Playing the China Card

In January 1964, de Gaulle's France extended diplomatic recognition to the People's Republic of China. To many Americans, this seemed another example of Gaullist unfriendliness. American policy was that "China" meant Chiang Kai-shek's refugee regime on Taiwan. De Gaulle, however, was bent on enlarging the number of players in the global power game, and recognizing China was one step in this process. Only in this way, he believed, could the world escape endless bipolar confrontations or the equally grim prospect of an agreement between the superpowers to rule the world, such as had occurred at Yalta in 1945.

By 1964, communist China was turning out not to be the obedient creature of Moscow once imagined. The Chinese had both ideological and practical reasons to complain of the Soviet Union. Mao Zedong was convinced that the Soviet Union was becoming a nonrevolutionary society closer in outlook to the capitalist nations than to China. At the same time, the Soviets, whose economic aid had always been meager, reneged on their promise to equip China with nuclear weapons. In 1960, as Sino-Soviet relations worsened, Khrushchev withdrew the Soviet technicians sent to facilitate Chinese development. By the mid-1960s, border clashes revealed the depth of hostility between the two communist giants. As de Gaulle saw, the West now had an opportunity to draw closer to a potentially powerful enemy of the Soviet Union, thus complicating Soviet calculations. Unfortunately, it would be nearly a decade before the United States could play this "China card" in the international game. For American leaders had become obsessed with victory on another Asian front—in Vietnam, where they mistakenly believed they were resisting Chinese expansion.

The American Misadventure in Vietnam

The total costs of the Vietnamese conflict, the United States' longest and most expensive war, are not easily reckoned. Over fifty-seven thousand Americans and hundreds of thousands of Vietnamese died. Total American expenses have been calculated at over a trillion dollars. Less tangibly, the lost war dealt a blow to Americans' self-confidence from which they began to rally only in the 1980s. The United States' obsession with Vietnam, and then its apparent renunciation of power when it withdrew, hastened the transformation of international relations to a multipolar system. Thus the Vietnam War must be regarded as a pivotal event. Certainly its impact has been far out of proportion to the size of this Southeast Asian country. The tragedy unfolded in four acts.

The first act, the end of French rule in Vietnam, involved the United States only tangentially. Vietnam had been part of the French empire at the beginning of World War II. The Japanese defeat of the colonial powers created a power vacuum at the war's end when Japan itself was defeated. Vietnamese nationalists seized the moment to reclaim independence. Their leader was Ho Chi Minh, who as a young emigrant to France in 1919 had vainly petitioned the Versailles Peace Conference for self-determination for his country. Disappointed by the indifference of Western leaders, he became a founding member of the French Communist party. The French had no intention of surrendering Vietnam to the Vietminh, the name given the movement Ho founded when he returned to his country in 1941. Negotiations between them ended in bloody clashes in 1946, the prelude to eight years of war.

American sympathies in this conflict shifted with events. U.S. undercover agents had cooperated with Ho's resistance to the Japanese. During the Cold War, however,

Vietnam, New Year's Day, 1966. *A U.S. paratrooper is pinned down by sniper fire while assaulting a "Viet Cong" stronghold. Caught in the middle, Vietnamese civilians wait for the shooting to end.* *Wide World Photos*

Americans began to perceive Ho as a creature of Moscow, rather than as a nationalist fighting for liberation. The French took advantage of this shift to enlist U.S. aid against Ho. By 1954 the United States was paying three-quarters of France's war costs, and three hundred advisers were in Vietnam. Though Vietnam's mineral wealth was sometimes cited as the reason for U.S. involvement, the real explanation seems to have been the *domino theory*. In this view the countries of Southeast Asia were like a row of dominoes standing on end: push one over and all the rest would immediately fall to communism.

This theory became critical when the Vietminh defeated the French at the Battle of Dien Bien Phu early in 1954. A new French cabinet indicated its intention to get out of Vietnam as swiftly as possible. An international conference in Geneva agreed to partition Vietnam temporarily, though it was to be reunited after free elections within two years.

These Geneva accords mark the beginning of the second act of the American drama in

Vietnam. Having refused to sign them, Washington felt free to disregard them. The promised elections, which all agreed would have given a majority to the Vietminh, were never held. Instead, as had happened elsewhere around the periphery dividing the spheres of the superpowers, two countries emerged. As it protected South Korea, the United States took under its protection the Republic of South Vietnam. Its president was Ngo Dinh Diem, a fervent anti-communist from the country's Catholic minority.

Diem's regime was corrupt, and its contempt for the country's Buddhist and peasant majorities soon provoked revolt. In 1960 a National Liberation Front (FLN in French) began guerilla operations in South Vietnam's jungles and villages. From the start, though the FLN claimed to be a multiparty, strictly southern movement, it received supplies and direction from Ho Chi Minh's North Vietnam.

This situation gave the Kennedy administration an opportunity to test its theory that guerrillas could be beaten by tactics of counterinsurgency, including programs to "win the hearts and minds" of a peasant populace by land reform and social change. By 1963, twelve thousand American advisers were in South Vietnam, helping Diem's army regroup peasants to prevent the FLN from living among them. However, the Diem regime's continued repression of Buddhists and other "enemies" made it impossible to claim that the United States was defending democracy in South Vietnam. Early in November, with U.S. encouragement, elements of the South Vietnamese army overthrew Diem.

The third act of the Vietnam tragedy began a few weeks later when Vice President Lyndon Johnson succeeded Kennedy. To understand why Johnson turned American involvement into a tragedy by vastly increasing the U.S. commitment to Vietnam, it is necessary to examine the perceptions of the policymakers who advised him.

In the context of twentieth-century history Ho Chi Minh is a familiar type. He is only one of many leaders who have mobilized mass movements against the European-dominated global configuration. Ho had warned the French that even if they killed ten of his men for every French soldier killed by the Vietminh, he still would win. He had.

U.S. policymakers, however, looked at the Vietnamese situation through a veil of American preconceptions. Americans knew, and cared to know, practically nothing of Vietnamese history, culture, or language. They had little understanding of how colonial rule had left societies throughout the developing world—not just Vietnam's—divided between small Europeanized and wealthy elites, made up of people like Diem, and an overwhelming majority of impoverished peasants who could be mobilized by champions of national independence and social change. Unable to recognize how this colonial legacy heightened the potential for revolution in Vietnam, Americans saw in the country a "cornerstone of the free world," a place to "stand up to" the Soviet Union and China. Before it became an American nightmare, Vietnam was an American fantasy—and the mightiest nation on earth was prepared to invest powerful energies in making the fantasy a reality. The policymakers who directed those energies wanted to make sure that events conformed to their preconceptions, because their careers and reputations were at stake. For such reasons many young men sometimes die.

Within a year of Johnson's 1964 pre-election promise not to expand the U.S. commitment, there were 200,000 American troops in Vietnam. When North Vietnamese patrol boats clashed in the Tonkin Gulf with U.S. warships, Johnson seized the occasion to force a resolution through the Senate giving him virtually unlimited powers to expand a war against the North Vietnamese without declaring it. Out of 100 Senators, only 2 voted against the resolution. While American infantrymen sweated through search-and-destroy missions in the South Vietnamese countryside, the U.S. Air Force dropped on Vietnam, North as well as South, nine times the tonnage of bombs dropped throughout the Pacific during World War II. This was massive support indeed for the dozen-odd mostly military governments that succeeded one another by plot and coup in the South Vietnamese capital, Saigon, between 1963 and 1965.

But it did not work. The North Vietnamese matched the Americans escalation for escalation, infiltrating regular troops into the South to back up the FLN. One of the many ironies of this terrible story is that both sides were obsessed with the "Munich analogy"—belief that surrender to aggression would mean never-ending subjection to it, as in 1938. American failure in Vietnam, Johnson and his advisers deeply believed, would expose the United States to a never-ending series of communist aggressions. The prime minister of North Vietnam, Pham Van Dong, declared in 1966, "Never Munich again, in whatever form." *He* meant that Vietnam had been cheated of total independence twice, in 1946 and 1954, and had no intention of negotiating anything away again.

In this contest of wills the turning point for Americans came with the FLN offensive during the Vietnamese month of Tet, in January 1968. The Tet offensive ended in military defeat for the FLN, but it was a psychological success. The nightly television news depicted an apparent American debacle. Coordinated FLN operations showed that not even the American Embassy in Saigon was safe from guerrilla attack. After Tet, influential figures in the administration joined campus protesters in doubting that victory could ever be achieved. Faced with these doubts, Lyndon Johnson declared he would not seek reelection.

The election of 1968 opened the final act of the drama: the slow facing up to the reality of defeat. The successful Republican candidate, Richard M. Nixon, knew the war could not be won. His "secret plan" for Vietnam turned out to consist of trying to cut U.S. losses by beginning withdrawal while trying to bomb the North Vietnamese into a settlement that would save American face. For four years negotiations dragged on in Paris. At last the United States agreed to essentially the same terms the North Vietnamese had held out for from the beginning: prompt U.S. withdrawal, with few effective guarantees for South Vietnam.

South Vietnam did not long survive the departure of the U.S. combat troops in 1973. Nixon's plan for "Vietnamization" of the war—preparing the South Vietnamese to defend themselves—proved illusory. In April 1975 the North Vietnamese army entered Saigon. U.S. helicopters lifted the last Americans out of the embassy compound, while Marines pried loose the clutching hands of desperate South Vietnamese supporters who wanted to flee too. It was a scene remarkably like that of the French departure from Vietnam twenty years earlier.

In 1975 most Americans probably considered the nation well out of Vietnam, even at such a price. With the passage of time, however, myths have begun to grow up, as often happens when a nation has suffered a defeat. One is almost reminiscent of the "stab-in-the-back" legend of post-1918 Germany in blaming defeat on civilian irresolution. It alleges that the Vietnam War was lost not by the army but by Washington's unwillingness to fight with sufficient determination. In crude terms, this view holds that "Next time, we should go in with everything we've got!"

As we have already seen, however, the lessons of history are not always clear. Certainly, hostility toward Washington by some Vietnam veterans is understandable. They neither caused the war nor failed in their duty—but after anguishing experiences, they returned to an indifferent or hostile home front. Moreover, the extension of North Vietnamese rule to the whole country since 1975 has belied the assurances of antiwar protesters that an FLN victory would bring freedom to South Vietnam. The unlucky South Vietnamese exchanged a regime of stark social inequality and fast-changing dictatorship under Diem and his successors for Soviet-style scarcities under the dictatorship of Ho Chi Minh's successors.

Had the United States gone all out for victory, some argue, none of this would have happened. But the implications of such a statement demand careful analysis. In pursuit of victory the United States extended the Vietnam War to the rest of Indochina, devastating once neutral Laos and Cambodia (Kampuchea). What further steps would have been involved in "going all out"? The United States could have gone to war with China, which was supplying the North Vietnamese (as was the Soviet Union). But none of the presidents who had to face the Vietnamese nightmare was willing to risk the American public's reaction to such steps. Far from favoring war with China, most Americans later welcomed improvement of Chinese-American relations. Meanwhile, once the Americans were gone, relations between Vietnam and China, traditional enemies, deteriorated into actual war in 1979.

If the risks of enlarging the war outweighed the possibilities of thereby winning it, could the United States have made a greater effort in Vietnam itself? This question cannot be answered without doing something American policymakers rarely did: understanding the mentality of their opponents and particularly their different understanding of *time.* To Americans of the television era, a year is a very long time, and three years of inconclusive fighting by large American forces in Vietnam proved insupportable by 1968. In the Vietnamese perspective, nearly a century of French colonialism had been a mere interlude; their history is one of a thousand years of resistance to outsiders, principally the Chinese. Even if the American forces had concentrated on defeating the North Vietnamese regular army instead of the FLN guerrillas, the resulting "victory" would probably not have been definitive. Vietnamese resistance would doubtless have continued, requiring an American occupying army. And Americans have shown little enthusiasm for commitments that would keep draftees indefinitely at risk. In the light of these considerations, the idea of victory in a place like Vietnam becomes elusive and problematical. Perhaps the best way of achieving victory would have been to follow the wise counsel of a senator who advised Johnson simply to announce that the United States had won—and then withdraw as quickly as possible.

Multipolar Détente Versus Renewed Confrontation, 1973–1984

After the Vietnam War, international relations were marked by an exploration of the possibilities and limits of diminished tension—détente—in a multipolar world. Through the mid-1970s, détente made it possible to set aside many of the festering issues of the Cold War. From the mid-1970s to the mid-1980s, however, Soviet-American relations took another sharp turn for the worse.

The Making of Détente

American diplomacy during the period of relative détente until 1976 was orchestrated by Secretary of State Henry Kissinger. Unlike many of his predecessors and successors in his office, Kissinger had a coherent world-view shaped by the European tradition of diplomatic *Realpolitik*—policy based on cold-blooded realism. Now that the revolutionary ardor of the Soviet Union and China had diminished, Kissinger believed, the United States could maneuver between them to secure its own interests and the balance of power. Though he too ritually denounced the Soviet Union on occasion, Kissinger did not see the world's future as the triumph of American right over communist wrong. Rather he envisioned an everlasting process of adjustment of interests among five centers of power: the United States, the Soviet Union, China, Western Europe, and Japan, now emerging as an economic superpower.

The most spectacular result of this idea was the reversal in Chinese-American relations. The process wound its way from secret negotiations, to the American table tennis team's visit to China, to a climax in a solemn state visit by President Nixon to China early in 1972. His televised toasts to Chinese leaders marked a dramatic contrast to the decades during which the United States had ignored the existence of the People's Republic. The new friendship of the two countries raised deep concern in the Soviet Union, which by the early 1970s was maintaining up to a quarter of its armed forces in the east against possible Chinese attack.

The Unites States and the Soviet Union in the World Economy

Partly because of Soviet concern about China, President Nixon was warmly received when he visited Moscow in May 1972, three months after his trip to Beijing. But many motives, both international and domestic, impelled the Soviets toward détente.

On the international plane, the Soviet Union had overcome the inferiority in nuclear weaponry so evident during the Cuban missile crisis. In the second half of the 1960s, it had more than tripled its land-based intercontinental ballistic missiles (ICBMs), its principal deterrent force. Each superpower now had enough nuclear warheads to destroy the other many times over. When President Nixon admitted there was no possibility that the United States could win a nuclear war, the Soviet Union could feel it had finally been accepted as an equal.

Domestically, however, Soviet society by the 1970s had weaknesses that could be addressed, if at all, only by achieving détente with the United States. The Soviet economy was in increasing trouble (see Chapter 14). The Cold War also imposed severe strains on the U.S. economy. On August 15, 1971, Nixon had reacted dramatically to the new combination of inflation and recession called *stagflation* and to the decline of the dollar. He ended the dollar's convertibility at fixed rates to gold or foreign currencies. Henceforth, currencies would "float," exchanged at whatever rate the markets thought best. By this unilateral action, the United States destroyed the Bretton Woods system on which it had insisted in 1944. By refusing to pay in gold, the United States was repudiating part of its debts by depreciating the dollar. Its ability to do so without provoking protest was a testimony to continuing American power. But its need to do so suggested that American power was no longer what it had been in 1944.

Thus, when Nixon met Leonid Brezhnev in Moscow in 1972, both leaders recognized their nations' limitations. Their meeting produced an agreement based on the Strategic Arms Limitation Talks (now known as SALT I) held over the previous three years. Both sides would retain the monstrous stockpiles of nuclear weapons they had already built, but future production of certain kinds of weapons would be limited. Modest though it was, this agreement was a sign of the "spirit of détente," which soon stimulated a large increase in trade between the Western and Soviet blocs.

Détente for Europeans

This increased flow of goods reflected the détente that had developed between the subordinate states in each of the superpowers' spheres of influence. While the United States was preoccupied in Vietnam, Europeans east and west had seized the initiative to begin melting down the Iron Curtain that divided their continent. The credit belongs primarily to West German chancellor Willy Brandt. His Socialist party wanted an *Ostpolitik,* an eastern policy that might lead to the reconciliation—perhaps even the eventual reunification—of the two Germanys. Brandt's first step was to calm Soviet fears of renewed German danger by signing a nonaggression treaty with the USSR in 1970. He also accepted Poland's western border with Germany. In 1972 the two Germanys acknowledged each other's legitimacy. Both were admitted to the United Nations the following year. Finally, in 1973 West Germany formally renounced the Munich Agreement of 1938 that had dismembered Czechoslovakia. Meanwhile, in 1971 the United States, the Soviet Union, Britain, and France had mutually recognized each other's rights, and those of East Germany, in Berlin. This period of détente climaxed in 1975 at the European Security Conference in Helsinki, Finland, where all the European countries, Eastern and Western, and the United States promised to honor each other's existing borders.

Critics of the Helsinki treaty contended that the East got considerably more out of it than the West. In return for Soviet promises to guarantee basic human rights, which soon proved valueless, the West acknowledged Stalin's expansion of the Soviet perimeter in Eastern Europe.

Yet, as de Gaulle had foreseen, the Soviet Union's rule in Eastern Europe had become so difficult that it found détente essential. Behind a façade of communist solidarity, the Soviets were trying to maintain Eastern Europe in a situation of dependency not unlike colonialism. Such a situation was wholly incongruous. Still developing itself, the USSR could not provide its satellites with capital. Meanwhile, some of the satellite states had reached a higher level of economic development than the Soviet Union. Thus, both the poor and the more affluent economies of Eastern Europe had economic reasons to complain of Soviet rule by the 1970s.

To the extent that détente offered an economic alternative to Soviet dependency, it was seized eagerly by the communist leadership of the various Eastern bloc countries. Moscow's tolerance of their growing indebtedness to Western banks suggested it had no better solution. As economic exchanges multiplied, the life of Eastern Europe was unavoidably altered. By the 1980s it was clear that its peoples, like those of Western Europe, desperately wanted to perpetuate détente. Their muted protests were a reminder to the Soviets that there were other voices to be heard in the Eastern bloc besides their own, that the world was moving from bipolarity to multipolarity.

The Carter Years: Détente Dissolved

The United States also found itself confronted with the realities of a multipolar world in the 1970s. Challenges arose from such unexpected sources as Iran, once a dependable U.S. client state. Meanwhile the American attitude toward the Soviet Union veered from ideological contempt to longing for accommodation, and back again.

President Jimmy Carter came into office in 1976 anxious to maintain détente. He left office with détente in shambles. Perhaps the rapid chill was inevitable, given the continuing rivalry of the superpowers. In October 1973, only a little more than a year after President

Nixon's visit to Moscow, the Soviet Union had threatened to send troops into the Middle East to intervene in the fourth Arab-Israeli war. Nixon responded by ordering U.S. forces on nuclear alert. Fortunately for the world, this incident did not prove to be the present-day equivalent to 1914's mobilization crisis. A countdown to nuclear war was not begun.

The Carter administration completed negotiations with the Soviets in 1979 for a second Strategic Arms Limitation Treaty (SALT II). Though this treaty was never ratified by Congress, both parties continued to abide by its provisions.

Despite these continuing contacts, Carter's foreign policy advisers convinced him that the Soviet Union was taking advantage of détente. They were alarmed by growing Soviet involvement in the rivalries among African independence movements. Except for their sponsorship of Cuba, the Soviets had not previously committed themselves in countries so far from their borders. American policymakers found it unacceptable that the Soviets should feel free to intervene on a global scale. In response, the Soviets asked why it was only the United States that had a right to support its friends in faraway places.

The Carter administration's greatest indignation, however, was reserved for the Soviet invasion of Afghanistan in December 1979. The situation in this undeveloped mountain nation bore certain ironic resemblances to that of Vietnam, with the very important difference that Afghanistan lies on the Soviet Union's southern border. A series of pro-Soviet governments had displaced the former nonaligned regime. Many Afghans held them in contempt. When fighting broke out, the Soviet puppet government could control the capital, the cities, and the main roads, but it could not control Muslim fundamentalist tribesmen in the hills, who had a proud historic tradition of warfare against all of Afghanistan's invaders. The Soviets were unable to master their resistance, despite extensive use of the kind of tactics—saturation bombing, helicopter gunships, napalm—employed unavailingly by the United States in Vietnam. There was little the United States could do for the Afghan rebels except secretly send them arms. But Carter took the initiative in several expressions of outrage, including stopping the sale of grain to the Soviets and boycotting the 1980 Moscow Olympics.

None of these measures had any effect on Soviet policy, but they did contribute to the end of détente and the renewal of bipolar confrontation. At the same time, however, the United States was discovering the power of the previously powerless—small countries rich in raw materials.

The OPEC Challenge and the Iranian Revolution

In 1973, when the Organization of Petroleum Exporting Countries (OPEC) embargoed the sale of oil to the West to protest its support for Israel, stocks on the New York Stock Exchange lost $100 billion in value in just six weeks. Even supposedly reliable U.S. allies among the oil producers, like the shah of Iran, were quite unapologetic about their new attitude. Oil prices quadrupled between 1973 and 1975.

Worse events followed in the oil-rich Persian Gulf. As we shall see in greater detail in Chapter 17, the shah's regime was overthrown in 1979 by a massive opposition front whose religious leadership regarded the United States as the "great Satan" of the world. After the shah fled to the United States, Iranian militants seized the American Embassy in Tehran in November, taking sixty Americans hostage. All of the United States' might could not help the hostages. For many months, television brought before Americans the humiliating spectacle of their fellow countrymen paraded before the cameras by enemies filled with the Third World's rage against superpower dominance.

President Carter was quite unfairly blamed for the hideous dilemma of a hostage situation—whether to sacrifice the hostages or give in. He succeeded in negotiating their release only minutes before Ronald Reagan was sworn in as president in January 1981.

Return to Confrontation

Reagan represented the right wing of the Republican party, which had been deeply suspicious of Kissinger's design for détente. During his first term, Soviet-American relations continued the deterioration begun during the Carter administration. By the end of his first term, experienced observers in Moscow declared that Soviet suspicions of the United States had become deeper than ever before, even under Stalin. Reagan ordered a record military buildup, which included preparation for the militarization of space. And he denounced the Soviet Union in language reminiscent of that of John Foster Dulles.

At the same time, the Reagan administration seemed keenly aware that while Americans liked a president who would "stand up to the Russians," they would be unsympathetic to belligerence that imposed sacrifices—such as the draft. Reagan preferred confrontational rhetoric to actual confrontation. U.S. Marines were sent to Lebanon on an ill-defined mission to show the flag. After a suicidal car-bomb attack by Islamic militants killed 243 Marines, the administration quickly withdrew the survivors. Critics claimed that the United States was signaling its unwillingness to maintain a presence in a region where its vital interests were at stake. In Latin America too, the Reagan administration held back from full commitment. The United States sent aid to the "Contra" rebels seeking to overthrow the revolutionary Sandinista government in Nicaragua, but no American troops.

When Reagan did send troops, it was to a place without strategic importance but also without risk. The U.S. invasion of October 1983 easily overthrew a new Marxist government that vainly aspired to change Grenada's typical Third World economic dependency on the export of cocoa, nutmeg, and bananas. Grenada provided just one more example of how the tragic and perhaps insoluble problem of Third World poverty could be perceived by U.S. policymakers as a challenge to the capitalist West by the communist East.

Reagan-Gorbachev Summitry

Many Americans, including President Reagan, interpreted the U.S. intervention in Grenada as a successful countermove, after years of failure, against the spread of communism and thus of Soviet influence in the Caribbean. Perhaps it was this "success," combined with the renewed American self-confidence produced by economic recovery and Reagan's military buildup, that prompted the president to announce in a speech on January 16, 1984, a far less confrontational approach to relations with the Soviet Union. Once he had denounced it as the "evil empire." Now he spoke of his hope of reaching an understanding with the Soviets, based on the common interests of the two superpowers, which included a reduction in nuclear armaments.

Reagan's offer of negotiations was gladly accepted by Mikhail Gorbachev when he became the Soviet leader early in 1985. In 1986, in Reykjavik, Iceland, they came close in their face-to-face conversations to envisioning the scrapping of all nuclear weapons, until the professional caution of their military advisers restrained their enthusiasm. Nonetheless, the first steps were taken toward elaborating a treaty to eliminate ground-based "intermediate nuclear forces" (the INF treaty). Though the treaty mandated the destruction of only a small portion of both sides' vast nuclear arsenals, it included the array of medium-range missiles the United States had only recently persuaded the often-reluctant Europeans to install on their own territories. The formal signing of this treaty, with its unprecedented provisions for on-site inspections by both sides to verify that the weapons were actually destroyed, was the principal achievement of another Reagan-Gorbachev summit held in Washington late in 1987.

No similar breakthrough on substantive issues marked the Moscow summit of the summer of 1988. Reagan would not sign Gorbachev's proposed joint pledge not to attempt to resolve any future superpower conflict by military means. His advisers felt that such a pledge would inhibit American shipments of arms to the anti-communist forces rebelling against the governments of Angola, Nicaragua, and Afghanistan. (Gorbachev had already begun withdrawing Soviet troops from Afghanistan, boldly cutting the losses of nearly a decade of futile Soviet intervention and leaving the Afghan communist government to fend for itself.) Despite the absence of substantive results, the world drew comfort from the spectacle of this friendly encounter in the Soviet capital.

How are we to explain this apparent thaw in nearly a half-century of Cold War, coming in the second term of the most outspokenly anti-communist U.S. president? Much of the explanation can be found in the respective visions of world realities held by the two men who brought it about. Gorbachev's most innovative pronouncement regarding foreign policy was his frank admission that the advent of nuclear weapons had invalidated all the old Marxist-Leninist ideas about the conflict of nations. In Lenin's time, a major war such as World War I had been a necessary precondition for the social revolution the Bolsheviks had made. Today, though, the prospect of nuclear war "called into question the very survival of the human race." In such a situation, to strive for military superiority was pointless.

Even more essential to explaining Gorbachev's foreign policy is the fact that, as we shall see in detail in Chapter 14, he saw his mission as the revitalization of the Soviet Union by a total renovation of its economy and institutions. Such a goal could be attained only if relaxation of tension with the United States enabled the Soviets to devote most of their resources to investing for domestic development, rather than arming for external confrontation.

By his frank admission that the Soviet Union needed to redirect its spending priorities, Gorbachev confirmed the diagnosis made by a number of increasingly influential historians about *both* the Unites States *and* the Soviet Union in the 1980s: they had fallen into the pattern, already established by Spain, France, and Britain over the last four hundred years, of empires in decline. Historically, according to this analysis, empires have entered into decline when they began diverting investment from the sources of domestic wealth that had originally made them strong to an ever-growing military machine intended to defend overextended foreign commitments. The result is what has been called "imperial overstretch"[2]—a vain quest for military security at the expense of renewing the foundations of economic power.

Gorbachev, who criticized his predecessor Leonid Brezhnev for failing to recognize that a nation cannot be powerful abroad if it is in domestic decline, seemed to share these historians' conclusions. Clearly President Reagan did not recognize, in approaching negotiations with the Soviets, any American "imperial overstretch"—though in light of the largest U.S. government and international trade deficits in history and the Wall Street crash of October 1987, the worst since 1929, many Americans did not agree that their economy was as robust as he believed. Consciousness of a need to reorient U.S. economic priorities does not explain Reagan's acceptance of a Cold War thaw. Perhaps the best explanation is the simplest: Reagan changed his mind. For all his ideological language, he proved, as did Gorbachev, to be basically a pragmatist. Recognizing that the advent of Gorbachev and his plans for reform marked a potentially historic turning point for the Soviet Union, Reagan was prepared to renounce his adamantly anti-Soviet stance and explore what negotiations could achieve.

The End of the Cold War

If Gorbachev hoped that by achieving accommodation with Reagan he could avert the disastrous consequences of "imperial overstretch" by reforming the Soviet economy, he was soon disappointed. The astonishingly rapid collapse of the Soviet bloc within six years of his coming to power in 1985 provides one more illustration of the historical generalization that no time is more dangerous for a decrepit authoritarian regime than when it attempts reform. As we shall see in detail in Chapter 14, Gorbachev recognized that he could not achieve economic change without granting a measure of independence to the Soviet satellites and a degree of political participation to Soviet citizens. But in doing so, he unleashed the pent-up demands for national freedom and democracy that had been growing for decades and raged far beyond his expectations or his ability to control them.

Ukrainians demonstrate for independence, 1991. *When some 90 percent voted in a referendum to secede from the Soviet Union, they not only doomed the Union but created Europe's fifth most populous country.* *Chris Niedenthal/© 1991 Time Pictures Syndicate*

The year after his triumphant Moscow summit with Reagan, 1989, began the most fundamental changes to the global configuration since 1945. The largest street demonstrations since 1953 in East Germany forced the tottering communist regime there to open the Berlin Wall in November. Once opened, it did not remain standing for long. For better or for worse for the world, Germany was effectively reunited when, in September 1990, representatives of its two former governments signed a treaty by which the Federal Republic in effect absorbed East Germany. Meanwhile, the other former Soviet satellites proclaimed their independence, so that by June 1991 both the Warsaw Pact and Comecon, the mechanisms for Soviet political and economic control of Eastern Europe, no longer had any function and dissolved themselves.

No more than in Eastern Europe could the genie of nationalism be forced back into the bottle within the Soviet Union itself. The new political institutions provided a forum in which one Soviet ethnic minority after another could express its frustration at continuing economic failure by demanding independence from Moscow. Under their secessionist pressure the Union of Soviet Socialist Republics simply broke apart into its constituent republics, no longer soviet or socialist. Soon no role was left for a central government. At the end of 1991, Gorbachev resigned as president of a Soviet Union that had ceased to exist, leaving behind a loose federation that awkwardly called itself the "Commonwealth of Independent States."

Such a stunning collapse of one of the antagonists naturally brought an end to the bipolar Cold War confrontation that had appeared to dominate international relations since 1945. Already in September 1991, President George Bush had ordered an end to the twenty-four-hour alerts in the underground silos where for a generation Air Force officers had awaited the order to launch nuclear Armageddon by dispatching U.S. missiles against Soviet targets. In February 1992, at yet another summit, Bush met not Gorbachev but Boris Yeltsin, president of the largest of the Soviet successor states, the Russian Republic. Together they formally proclaimed an end to the Cold War. The unequal terms on which it ended were reflected in the arms treaty the two signed in June. Both sides agreed substantially to reduce their nuclear arsenals; but while the Russians surrendered their land-based multiple-warhead missiles, the key to the former Soviet deterrent, the Americans retained their submarine-based warheads of the same type, the essential element of U.S. defenses. Desperate for American economic aid to prevent his famished country from sinking further into chaos, Yeltsin was in no position to insist on a better deal.

And so, some people claimed, the Cold War had ended with a complete U.S. victory. Or had it?

The Post–Cold War World System: U.S. Hegemony or "Geoeconomic Multipolarity"?

The Panama Invasion and the Persian Gulf War

The collapse of the United States' only military superpower rival naturally tended to embolden American leaders to assert U.S. power wherever necessary. President Bush's first such assertion came in a part of the world where the United States had always insisted on acting regardless of the USSR: Central America. In December 1989 he dispatched twenty-five thousand U.S. troops in Operation Just Cause to seize the dictator of Panama, General Manuel Noriega, a long-time U.S. ally and CIA informant now accused of complicity in the drug traffic that brought half of the world's narcotics to U.S. shores. U.S. helicopter gunships flattened Noriega's headquarters in the slums of the Panamanian capital at a cost of 26 U.S. and 314 Panamanian soldiers' lives. Between 202—the official U.S. count—and up to 4,000 Panamanian civilians, according to critics, also lost their lives. Few Americans were concerned that the United Nations General Assembly denounced the operation as a "flagrant violation of international law." With its large Third World majority, the Assembly was frequently critical of the United States. Noriega's eventual sentence by Miami court to forty years in prison seemed to Bush supporters to justify the operation, though within less than a year of his apprehension cocaine traffic through Panama had returned to pre–Just

Cause levels. Polls showed that most Panamanians welcomed Noriega's downfall. The new president who succeeded him breakfasted weekly with the U.S. ambassador to discuss the continuing problems of Panama, where trade unions were repressed, unemployment averaged 20 percent of the work force, and another 20 percent were underemployed.

Within a few months of December 1989, Panama vanished as completely from the U.S. front pages and evening news as Grenada had done after Reagan's invasion of 1983. U.S. intervention in Latin America, after all, is an old story and in this case seemed to most Americans to be amply justified by the triumph of bringing a vicious thug like Noriega to justice.

President Bush's next crusade against a thug—the Iraqi dictator Saddam Hussein—took American troops in far greater numbers much farther from home, raising a number of questions far less familiar than those of U.S.–Latin American relations. We shall leave to Chapter 17 a discussion of the significance of this Iraqi regime in the context of its region. Here our concern is the significance for the post–Cold War global configuration of the Persian Gulf war that resulted from Saddam's occupation of Kuwait in August 1990.

Saddam might be forgiven some surprise at the violent U.S. reaction to his invasion of his neighbor, for the Reagan and Bush administrations had given him substantial help in his long war against Iran, which Washington continued to regard as the major threat to Middle Eastern stability. Even after that war ended in 1988, Iraq received some $2 billion in U.S. aid, ostensibly to buy U.S. agricultural products, though some in Washington were aware that Saddam was diverting these funds to his ambitious arms program, which included both poison gas and nuclear weapons.

Even though the American public knew none of these facts, it was not easy for the Bush administration to portray the Iraqi-Kuwaiti conflict in the familiar terms of evil versus good with which U.S. foreign policy was so often discussed. Saddam's regime is a monstrously cruel dictatorship, but the Emirate of Kuwait was no democracy. Eighteen families, including that of the ruler, the emir, controlled 90 percent of the $100 billion in oil revenues Kuwait had invested in Western banks. Only a quarter of Kuwait's population were citizens, most of whom left work to ill-paid immigrants. Of the citizens, only sixty thousand males had the vote, which was of dubious value because the emir had suppressed his contentious parliament.

Nor was Saddam without genuine grievances against Kuwait. The border between it and Iraq had been imprecisely penciled in on a map by the British colonial administrator of the region in the 1920s and ran somewhere across an oilfield from which, Iraq claimed, Kuwait was surreptitiously siphoning oil. Worse, from Saddam's point of view, Kuwait was dumping all of its oil onto world markets at prices below those stipulated by OPEC (to which both countries belong) to curry favor with Western governments. Since Iraq too depended heavily on oil sales for foreign earnings, Saddam calculated that every dollar off the OPEC price cost his country $1 billion in income. Thus he had no lack of motives for overrunning his annoying little neighbor, especially since on the eve of the invasion the American ambassador, in a personal conference with him, raised no objections.

President Bush, however, soon decided that Saddam must be chastised as Noriega had been chastised. For the first time in forty years, since the beginning of the Korean War, the United States was able to mobilize the UN Security Council against an aggressor. Back in 1950, the Soviet Union had been boycotting the Council. Ever since, Cold War rivalry had paralyzed it: when the United States took one side of a dispute, the USSR usually took the other, both exercising their veto to protect their allies. Now, significantly, Gorbachev's faltering

USSR could only go along as the Council voted to dispatch a vast multinational army, largely composed of young Americans like the army in Korea, to the Persian Gulf. Their mission was, ostensibly, to reinforce the economic sanctions voted against Saddam to force him to end his occupation of Kuwait, though it now seems clear that Bush decided no later than November 1990, just after the U.S. elections, that only an attack on the Iraqi occupying army would force him out.

Bush argued a number of themes against critics of his policy. Sometimes he spoke, as U.S. leaders had done in the 1960s, of the "lessons" of the 1930s—that aggression must be resisted everywhere. He directly compared Saddam to Hitler, an apt comparison of character but not of power, since Iraq with its impoverished and passive population of 18 million was hardly even a regional equivalent of the Third Reich. Administration officials were more candid when they explained that what they were really defending in the Persian Gulf was "the American way of life," or even "jobs," both synonyms for cheap oil. By 1990 the United States had become dependent on foreign sources for half its supply, and notably on the relatively compliant monarchies of the region. (Unlike Japan, which had responded to the oil price shocks of the 1970s by planned reductions in per capita energy consumption, the United States during the Reagan years virtually abandoned the idea of conservation.)

When Saddam defied the UN deadline of January 15, 1991, to evacuate Kuwait, Bush, arguing that economic sanctions had failed, promptly ordered the long-planned attack. For six weeks the United States and allied air forces pounded both the Iraqi army in Kuwait and its essential facilities within Iraq. Mindful of how the American public had sickened of the Vietnam War after watching its destructiveness on television, the U.S. high command carefully filtered journalists' reporting of the bombing. It was described as "surgical," though postwar investigation revealed that the high-tech weaponry supposedly directed at military targets had taken a substantial toll of civilian lives. When the United States and its allies finally launched a ground attack on February 24, the war was over within a hundred hours. Outnumbered, abandoned by Saddam's fugitive commanders, the Iraqi army was simply massacred from the air as it stampeded home from Kuwait, suffering casualties perhaps a thousand times greater than the allies. U.S. combat casualties totaled 146, including 13 women and 35 killed by the misdirected "friendly fire" of their own comrades.

After such a lopsided victory, many Americans expected that the allied armies would push on to Baghdad, the Iraqi capital, and overthrow Saddam. But Bush decided otherwise. The cease-fire agreement ending the war required Iraq to complete its withdrawal from Kuwait and to surrender its chemical and nuclear weapons but not to change its government. In fact, by early 1992 most of the half-million Americans deployed in the Persian Gulf had gone home. Iraq, despite heavy damage to its infrastructure and the continuing pressure of embargo, was returning to something like normal life. Saddam seemed as firmly in control as ever. It seems likely that sober calculation had suggested to the Bush administration that if Saddam were overthrown, Iraq might collapse, altering the delicate Middle Eastern balance of power in favor of Iran, a country led by men who despite their long war with Saddam are at least as hostile to regimes like Kuwait's as he is.

The returning American victors of the Gulf War received heroes' welcomes. President Bush exulted that their success proved that the United States had at last "licked the Vietnam syndrome" of hesitating to commit forces overseas lest they become bogged down as they had in Southeast Asia. Some commentators even suggested that victory in the Persian Gulf signaled the beginning of a post–Cold War "New World Order" to be imposed by the United States through the now-pliable instrument of the Security Council.

Yet polls and journalists' interviews revealed that the mood of the American public was far from what might be expected after two victories like the collapse of the Soviet Union and the expulsion of Saddam from Kuwait. Perhaps this somber mood reflected realization that the defeat of the demoralized Iraqi army in a treeless desert might not be repeatable in more difficult terrain against a more determined foe, as it had proved unattainable in Vietnam. More likely, pessimism reflected Americans' growing recognition that military power exerted against the USSR and Iraq alike had yielded only hollow victories, for, as a widely current bitter joke had it, "The Cold War is over; it was won by the Japanese."

Hollow Victory in the Cold War

Though some American commentators gloated that the collapse of the Soviet Union had left only one superpower standing, there were almost as many to point out that the way the United States paid for the Gulf War revealed the real distribution of power in the new post–Cold War world system. Though the United States supplied the bulk of the troops for Operation Desert Storm against Saddam, it could muster only 10 percent of its $61 billion cost. The rest of the money had literally to be begged from U.S. "allies" like Germany and Japan, who offered no troops though they were far more dependent on Persian Gulf oil than was the United States. Burdened by a debt that had tripled in the 1980s, unbalancing a federal budget of which one-third went to pay for the nation's past, present, and future wars, the United States was also becoming a less effective competitor in the global marketplace. The vast military buildup of the Reagan years may indeed have finally convinced Gorbachev that the Soviet Union could not sustain the military confrontation of the Cold War. But while the United States was deploying the world's most sophisticated weapons, in the 1980s the already small American share of world exports of automobiles fell by 10 percent, of machine tools by 35 percent, and of semiconductors by 39 percent. Militarily, the United States might be the only remaining superpower. Economically—the term in which post–Cold War world power is increasingly being measured—the United States finds itself challenged, amid a host of emerging competitors around the world—above all by two superpowers: united Europe and Japan.

United Europe: Economic Superpower?

Since its foundation by France, West Germany, Italy, and the Benelux countries in 1957, the European Economic Community has doubled its membership from six countries to twelve, elaborated its institutions, and affirmed its intention ultimately to create a kind of United States of Europe. Between 1972 and 1985, Britain, Ireland, Denmark, Greece, Spain, and Portugal joined. In 1992, Sweden, despite a long tradition of isolation, applied for membership, and the EEC agreed to consider preliminary applications from three former Soviet satellites: Poland, Hungary, and Czechoslovakia. By the end of the century it seems likely that most if not all of the rest of the countries of the continent will have joined, vindicating General de Gaulle's vision of a "Europe united from the Atlantic to the Urals." Since 1979, a European parliament has met regularly in the French city of Strasbourg, though its powers are still overshadowed by those of the EEC bureaucracy with its headquarters in Brussels.

On January 1, 1993, all remaining obstacles to trade within the community were scheduled to be removed, eliminating the customs documents that European truckers have always had to carry and creating the largest consumer market in the world, one-third larger than the United States.

In December 1991, the leaders of the twelve member countries met in Maastricht, the Netherlands, and signed a treaty that, if unanimously ratified, will take Europe a momentous step farther toward economic unity by establishing a common currency, the ecu, to replace the long-familiar pounds and francs and marks. Though the Germans had hoped that the treaty would move Europe even closer to federation by expanding the authority of the Strasbourg parliament and creating a single European central bank, President François Mitterrand of France compared Maastricht's significance to that of the Treaty of Rome a generation earlier: "A great power is being born, one at least as strong commercially, industrially and financially as the U.S. and Japan."[3]

Some obstacles still remain to the emergence of Europe as one great power. In June 1992, referendums in two countries revealed that public opinion was still divided on Maastricht. The Irish voted in favor, but the Danes rejected the treaty by the narrowest of margins, blocking its implementation until they could be reconciled. (A later Danish vote ratified the treaty after it had been modified to meet Danish objections.) This initial Danish defeat suggested that many Europeans still had the kind of doubts the British had frequently expressed about submerging their historic national identities and institutions in a Europe to be ruled by the arbitrary decrees of Brussels bureaucrats. Moreover, though European federation was frequently defended as a means of limiting German power, there were clearly fears in the smaller countries that reunited Germany with its nearly 80 million people might not be so easily subordinated to a European federal government.

By 1992, indeed, jubilation over the reunification of Germany had given way to anxiety inside the country as well as outside. Unification gave the former East Germans freedom to vote in nationwide elections in December 1990, in which the former Communists won only 9 to 14 percent. But unification also meant the rapid destruction of the social and economic institutions under which East Germans had lived for forty years: the shutdown of unprofitable factories, the closing of free health clinics and day-care centers, huge increases in prices and rents. The East Germans were ill equipped for the challenges of life in a competitive society. Their schools had compelled them to learn Russian, not English. All who had been employed by the communist state, whether as judges or as bus drivers, were now politically suspect, uncertain of finding a new job. Small wonder that under such strains the suicide rate doubled in parts of former East Germany in 1990–1991.

Thus, of the several question marks about the future of a united Europe, one of the largest concerned Germany's future direction. Would it, as believers in German democracy insisted, blend quietly into a federated continent? Or would the economic strains of reunification, driving East Germans to despair and burdening resentful West Germans with the costs of modernizing the formerly communist regions, kindle a new wave of German nationalism bent not on European integration but on domination? Berlin is again to be the capital. Will its Brandenburg Gate, for forty years the site of a principal passage through the Wall, "Checkpoint Charlie," again be decorated, as before 1945, with the Prussian eagle and Iron Cross, symbols of a tradition of authoritarian militarism?

Even a democratic united Germany may prove more assertive in foreign policy than West Germany, which throughout the Cold War generally was content to follow a French lead within Europe, balanced by an acquiescence in U.S. domination of NATO. This was the price that had to be paid for protection from the Soviet threat. As that threat disappeared with reunification in the 1990s, however, the new Germany struck many observers as less enthusiastic about European federation and more inclined to unilateral foreign policies in keeping with its economic predominance on the continent. In 1991, for example, Germany insisted, despite French and American disapproval, on extending recognition to two of the republics that had seceded from Yugoslavia. This insistence seemed to some an ominous reminder of German domination of Southeast Europe under the Hapsburgs and under Hitler.

The Yugoslavian Tragedy: European Failure?

The tragedy of Yugoslavia's dissolution in civil war indeed provides more than one reminder of how strong nationalism can still be in a Europe groping toward multinational federation. Behind a façade of uniformity imposed by Marshal Tito's dictatorship, the bitter ethnic rivalries of the South Slavs, which had sparked European war in 1914, continued to smolder. If multiethnic Yugoslavia could not long survive Tito's death in 1980, we may wonder, how long will it take to build a multiethnic, but united Europe?

The two northern republics of Slovenia and Croatia were the first to secede in June 1991. These industrialized, Catholic republics felt more in common with the countries of the EEC than with the other nationalities, mostly agrarian and Orthodox or Muslim, of the rest of Yugoslavia. When ethnically and religiously mixed Bosnia also declared its independence in July 1992, however, its capital, Sarajevo, where the Hapsburg archduke was assassinated in 1914, again returned to the world's headlines. The cause once again was Serbian nationalism: the determination of Bosnian Serbs, backed by the Serbian-dominated former Yugoslav army, not to live under the rule of people of different ethnicity and religion, but instead to carve out from Bosnia a country of their own, ethnically "cleansed" of rival nationalities. To this end they laid merciless siege to Sarajevo, only the most dramatic act of an ethnic war of mutual annihilation. The piteous plight of over 2 million Yugoslav refugees aroused the world's sympathy. It was significant, however, of the still incomplete state of European unity that the EEC could find neither the means nor the will to intervene in this genocidal conflict on Europe's doorstep. The reluctance of European governments, as of the American government, to commit their troops to impose an ethnic truce in a region where centuries of Hapsburg rule and decades of Titoist domination had not achieved such a truce was understandable. Nevertheless, European inaction showed that Europe had a long way to go before it could be counted a superpower in the sense that the term was applied to the United States and the Soviet Union during the Cold War.

The doubts about European unity raised by continuing problems of national rivalry, uncertainty about Germany's role, and above all Europe's inability to bring military power to bear on a crisis like Yugoslavia's have led some American analysts to discount Europe's potential role in the post–Cold War world system. The first Pentagon plans for the "New World Order," revealed early in 1992, were based on the premise that the United States, as the only remaining superpower, must maintain sufficient armed forces, numbering over a million and a half, to discourage potential superpowers like Germany and Japan from developing nuclear weapons. The Pentagon's instincts still were for asserting U.S. world dominance. Only reluctantly did the military planners yield to public criticism to concede that the maintenance of world order was an international task. (Indeed, in 1991 the United Nations deployed some ten thousand troops on eight separate peacekeeping missions around the world. It seemed finally to be beginning to fulfill the purpose envisioned for it at its foundation, though it is still owed some $377 million in overdue payments by its members, notably the United States and the former Soviet Union.)

It is true that the reaction of many Third World nations to the collapse of the USSR has lent some credibility to the Pentagon vision of U.S. hegemony. In 1992 India, for example, after decades as a leading nonaligned nation, was eagerly realigning its foreign policy to emphasize close military cooperation with the United States. Moreover, it was reshaping its economy, abandoning the state socialism favored by Nehru for the "free-market" model preferred by the United States. Such a change demonstrates how the very notion of a "Third World" has become obsolete with the disappearance of the "second," Soviet world, leaving the poor nations little option but to reach accommodation, notably by the privatization of their economies, with a world economic system still apparently dominated by the United States.

And yet, as we have seen, the American public, perhaps wiser than the Pentagon's planners, has shown little jubilation at the United States' supposed Cold War victory. The reason is suggested by what a Nebraska farmer told a reporter asking him how he envisioned the nation's future: "It's not the military threat I worry about; I worry about the economics. . . . I don't think America is the world's savior anymore. We've got too many problems of our own and people just don't respect us the way they used to. It's the same way with the Russians, except they ran out of money first."[4]

Conclusion: From Geopolitics to "Geoeconomics"

From the days of the Truman Doctrine in 1947, U.S. leaders have measured the power relationships of the Cold War global configuration in *geopolitical* terms: how many nations, how well armed, stood on each side. In this last decade of the twentieth century, however, it is becoming increasingly clear that the distribution of power in the post–Cold War world system will be determined by *geoeconomic* competition: the share claimed by each economy in the global marketplace.

In this new geoeconomic world, the principal division is between the "Affluent North," including North America, Europe, and Japan, and the "Hungry South," comprising the rest of the world, including Latin America, Africa, and most of Asia. Between the rich North and the poor South the gap in standards of living has actually doubled since the 1960s. Today the North, with a quarter of the world's population, consumes 60 percent of its food and 70 percent of its energy. Parts of the South—still composed of countries whose economies rely on the export of raw materials, like the colonies of 1914—live in a state of pitiful geoeconomic weakness. Between 1983 and 1989, for example, countries of the South had to repay loans of over $240 billion extended to them by banks of the North and by the International Monetary Fund, at a time when prices of such typical southern exports as coffee, cocoa, and tin were falling by 50 percent. Given this desperate economic weakness, the countries of the South have little power despite repeated efforts to develop concerted action. To the extent that any consideration was given to the real and bitter grievances of the South in the past, it was because the rival superpowers competed for their allegiance. With the Cold War ended, the only remaining stimulus to concern for southern grievances is northern guilt at being rich in a world that is overwhelmingly poor. Since many in the North feel no such guilt, prospects for rescuing the countries of the South from their plight are meager.

The contest for geoeconomic power will therefore be limited to the nations of the developed North. Who is winning it? Today, the U.S. economy, with a GNP of over $5 trillion, is still almost twice as large as Japan's and more than three times as large as Germany's, the largest in Europe. American commentators who insist that the widespread perception of U.S. decline is mistaken rely for their reassurance on statistics of this kind. The U.S. share of world manufacturing fell from one-half in 1945 to less than one-third by 1980, they contend, because the recovery of the economies of Europe and Japan, deliberately fostered by the United States, naturally reduced the predominance the United States enjoyed at the end of World War II.

Yet it may not be the relative size of today's economies in the North, but the ways in which they are developing, that tell us most about the distribution of geoeconomic power as the twentieth century nears its end. In Europe, for example, it is not just Germany with which the United States will have to contend. Already in 1990, if the gross national products of the EEC countries were added to those of the other countries likely to join the community (Austria and the Scandinavian countries), Europe's total GNP exceeded that of the United States by over 20 percent.

The geoeconomic challenger of which Americans are most aware, however, is Japan. Long accustomed to regard the Japanese as subordinate Cold War allies, Americans in the 1990s discovered in Japanese economic expansion a threat to their future almost as grave as the one the USSR had posed during the Cold War. Shocking Japanese purchases of celebrated U.S. real estate like New York's Rockefeller Center reflected Japan's twenty-five-fold expansion of its net external assets in the 1980s. In 1980, Japanese banks controlled only 4 percent of the international market for loans. By 1989, they had more than doubled their overseas branches and had won 40 percent of that market, though this percentage fell to only 30 percent by mid-1992, as the government pulled money back to Japan.

Moreover, Japanese-American statistical comparisons of all sorts reflect a Japanese advantage in the 1990s. With a population less than half as large as that of the United States, the Japanese are regularly investing more in plant and equipment than Americans are. In 1991, in per capita expenditure on research and development, the key to future economic growth, Japan ranked third in the world and first among large industrial countries. The United States, if military research and development was subtracted from its total, ranked tenth and falling. More U.S. patents were awarded to each of three Japanese corporations—Toshiba, Mitsubishi, and Hitachi—than to any American firm. General Electric, which once regularly headed the list, ranked only sixth.

Such statistics, many commentators suggested, were the consequence of the United States Cold War "imperial overstretch." Even in 1989, with the USSR in visible decline, the United States spent $290 billion for military purposes compared to the Soviets' $119 billion and Japan's $39 billion. (This total nonetheless did make Japan the third-largest military spender, having increased the budget for its "self-defense forces" by 5 percent a year since the mid-1970s while also paying nearly half the cost of the sixty thousand troops the United States maintained in Japan to defend it.)

In the 1940s, the United States fought a Pacific war to destroy the "Great East Asian Co-Prosperity Sphere" the Japanese were attempting to establish through military conquest. Ironically, in the 1990s, the Japanese are re-creating by direct investment and the transfer of technology to less developed nations a far greater geoeconomic power over East Asia than they won by force of arms a half-century ago. Then, Japan invaded Malaysia to seize the rubber and tin that were its principal exports. Today, the Mitsubishi Corporation has helped Malaysia's drive to industrialize by providing the engineers and managers and one-third of the capital for the building of the first Malaysian automobile plant. The model it produces, the Proton Saga, not only is the preferred car of Malaysia but also is exported, notably to

Britain, where twenty thousand had been sold as of 1991.[5]

What is the significance for the balance of geoeconomic power of the fact that Japanese investment in Malaysia, seven times greater than the investment that the United States, which demands majority ownership, has provided, has also made Malaysia the world's leading manufacturer of room air conditioners? It can be argued that in today's globally interdependent economy of multinational corporations, it is irrelevant and anachronistic to measure national economies one against the other. After all, even Japan's national conviction that as a densely populated, resource-poor country it must "export or die" has not prevailed over the realities of global interdependence. The Japanese are now the world's third-largest importers, ranking not far, per capita, behind the United States. Though Americans complain continually about Japanese protection of their domestic market, the proportion of manufactured products imported to total imports into Japan has risen from under 25 percent in 1980 to over 60 percent in 1992.

History suggests, however, that humankind is inclined to see economic relationships as national conflicts even where there is interdependence, as between the British and German economies on the eve of World War I. The declining British saw German growth as a challenge to their primacy, while the ambitious Germans felt that the British lacked the will and talent to maintain it. Whether these sorts of perception will someday lead to renewed Japanese-U.S. armed conflict, as a few scholars have suggested, is doubtful. But the least we can say is that it is now clear that the Cold War bipolar world has given way to a new global configuration in which geoeconomic power is shared among Asian, European, and American poles, of which the American will not necessarily prove the strongest in the long run.

In 1990, U.S. per capita Gross Domestic Product (GDP), the earning power of each citizen, was $19,558, slightly behind Germany's $19,581 but well behind Japan's $23,190 (a difference of almost 20 percent). Polls in both the United States and Japan in 1991 revealed that a majority of Americans were pessimistic about their ability to compete with Japan while a majority of Japanese were convinced that the Americans, once much admired, were in visible decline.

Such comparisons suggest that Americans need to undertake today as fundamental a reconsideration of their country's policy priorities for the new world system of geoeconomic competition as they undertook at the beginning of the Cold War a half-century ago. In this new world, they may realize, to develop the kind of dazzlingly sophisticated weaponry that annihilated the armies of Saddam Hussein is no guarantee of national strength, which is rather to be found in better schools, more sensible investment priorities, a different attitude toward the distribution of economic rewards, and a less reckless consumption of nonrenewable resources. As they face this rethinking, Americans may even have something to learn from Japanese and European practices. Perhaps the widening gap between the U.S. and Japanese per capita GDPs, for example, reflects the fact that in Japan government is seen as the partner of business in planning for long-term economic growth while in the United States, especially since 1980, government has been seen as the principal obstacle to business' primary goal of short-term profits.

Whether the United States' political leaders will prove able to reorient the country's thinking toward a Japanese- or European-style "industrial policy" remains to be seen. Americans might be forgiven for feeling that they deserve a respite from such challenges after a half-century of Cold War. If history does offer any consistent lesson, however, it is that powerful nations seldom go for long unchallenged, economically as well as militarily.

Notes

1. Quoted in William R. Keylor, *The Twentieth-Century World: An International History* (New York: Oxford University Press, 1984), p. 272.
2. The term is Paul Kennedy's in his *The Rise and Fall of the Great Powers* (New York: Random House, 1987). For an overview of the historical "School of Decline," see Peter Schmeisser, "Taking Stock: Is America in Decline?" *New York Times Magazine,* April 17, 1988.
3. *New York Times,* December 12, 1991.
4. *New York Times,* March 11, 1990.
5. *New York Times,* March 6, 1991.

Suggestions for Further Reading

Beschloss, Michael R. *The Crisis Years: Kennedy and Khrushchev, 1960–1963* (1991).

Calleo, David P. *Beyond American Hegemony* (1987).

———. *The Imperious Economy* (1982).

Grosser, Alfred. *French Foreign Policy Under de Gaulle* (1967).

Kahler, Miles. "Rumors of War: The 1914 Analogy." *Foreign Affairs* (Winter 1980), pp. 374–396.

Keylor, William R. *The Twentieth-Century World: An International History,* 2nd ed. (1992).

Leffler, Melvyn P. *A Preponderance of Power: National Security, the Truman Administration and the Cold War* (1992).

Lewis, Gordon K. *Grenada: The Jewel Despoiled* (1987).

Luttwak, Edward N. *The Endangered American Dream* (1993).

MacDonald, Callum A. *Korea: The War Before Vietnam* (1987).

Wolff, Michael, Peter Rutten, and Alfred F. Bayas III. *Where We Stand: Can America Make It in the Global Race for Wealth, Health and Happiness?* (1992).

CHAPTER 13

Toward Postindustrial Society: The United States and Western Europe in the Postwar Decades

As we examine in this chapter the comparative internal histories of the United States and of the Western European democracies since the end of World War II, we will discover that a single fundamental issue has underlain most of the political debate in these countries over the half-century since 1945. That issue is, how much power and responsibility should be entrusted to the government of the guarantor state. This kind of government, foreshadowed in the 1930s by Roosevelt's New Deal, became the norm throughout the Western world after 1945 as people became convinced that governments were responsible for managing economies and societies to guarantee a decent standard of living for all citizens.

In Western Europe, as we have seen, this responsibility had long been championed by democratic Socialists. Indeed, the immediate postwar regimes of the Left, such as the Labour party in Britain, brought the guarantor state into being. To such democratic Socialists it seemed only natural, on the grounds that management in the public interest would be more generally beneficial than private management for individual profit, to extend the responsibilities of the state to include ownership of the basic means of industrial production. Thus British Labour "nationalized" Britain's coal mines, steel mills, and railways. Left-dominated governments on the continent took similar steps.

In the United States, no such substantial movement in favor of socialism has ever developed. Neither the New Deal nor subsequent governments advocated nationalizations or even the development of government-managed comprehensive health care. Nonetheless, American conservatives have continued regularly to denounce the "big government" created by the New Deal. American "liberals," by contrast, have insisted that reaching the goal of an equitable and livable society for all citizens requires an active role for government.

The vocabulary of U.S. politics today shows us that sixty years of argument since 1933 have not resolved this debate. People's judgments of the guarantor state, both in the United States and elsewhere, depend very largely on how its costs and benefits impinge on their own personal economic situations. The essence of the guarantor state is *redistribution:* from the taxes it collects it distributes payments of all sorts to support a variety of programs, from road construction to welfare. People tend to see the payments they collect as their just due and the payment that goes to someone else as a handout.

Given this human tendency, it is remarkable that through the 1950s and 1960s a kind of political consensus accepting the necessity of the guarantor state prevailed in the United States and throughout Western Europe. In the United States, only the most extreme conservatives advocated abolishing such essential pillars of the guarantor state as the Social Security system. Even in the 1960s, a decade of widespread challenge to existing beliefs and institutions, only a few radical students attacked the state as an oppressive institution. Many protesters in the United States—blacks and women, for example—actually sought to enlist the state on their side.

More recently, however, the postwar consensus in favor of the guarantor state has everywhere broken down. In the 1980s in the United States and in Britain, President Ronald Reagan and Prime Minister Margaret Thatcher built political careers by denouncing the guarantor state, though neither succeeded in demolishing it. Probably the essential explanation for the breakdown of postwar consensus is an economic one: while the 1950s and 1960s were decades of rapid economic growth worldwide, such levels of prosperity have never been regained since the economic crisis that followed the OPEC oil embargo of 1973. As long as economies continued to grow and living standards to rise, people were more tolerant of the idea that the guarantor state would redistribute some of the rewards of prosperity to others less fortunate. When, after 1973, there was less growth for everyone, people became less inclined to share it.

But it is not only the economic stagnation of the 1970s and 1980s that has changed the terms of the debate. Since consensus in its favor was at its highest, a whole set of momentous changes—changes summed up by the central themes of this book—have profoundly altered the economies and societies of the United States and Western Europe, undermining many of the assumptions by which the guarantor state was conceived.

The twentieth century's ever-growing global interdependence, for example, challenges the whole notion that a government can manage a nation's economy in isolation from the economies of the rest of the world. The most striking manifestation of economic interdependence has been the postwar proliferation of multinational corporations. As these corporations pursued profits around the world, they made national boundaries meaningless. As a consequence of this growing global integration, American workers and soon Europeans and Japanese found themselves competing for jobs in a worldwide labor pool that included the developing countries.

In such a global competition, there seemed relatively little a single guarantor state could do to protect its citizens from the hazards of lower wages and a declining standard of living, or even from unemployment.

The products of many multinational corporations, such as IBM (International Business Machines Corporation), reflect a second major theme of twentieth-century life: humankind's "triumph over nature." Since 1945 the process of self-compounding technological discovery that has characterized the Western world since the seventeenth century has dramatically accelerated. Change and its impact on the human environment have become so rapid that an influential book of the 1960s warned that humankind might soon come to suffer from "future shock"—an inability to adjust to the rate at which the future is overwhelming the present. Inventions that the New Deal generation only barely anticipated—television and the computer—profoundly reshaped the patterns of people's daily lives. A majority of Americans, Europeans, and Japanese, in fact, today probably feel more at home in the artificial electronic environment these machines have created than in the natural world of farms and fields their ancestors inhabited.

The kind of society created by these new technologies, first in the United States but soon after in Europe and Japan, is one the planners of the guarantor state as recently as 1945 could not have foreseen. It promises to be as different from the period between the mid-nineteenth and mid-twentieth centuries—when vast numbers worked, as in 1914 Berlin, at the machines of heavy industry—as that industrial era was from earlier centuries, when most people were farmers. In this new *postindustrial* society, a majority of people earn their living neither on the farm nor in the factory but in shops and offices, providing "services" that range from flipping fast-food hamburgers to processing the computerized data of large corporations.

Because nothing is more fundamental to society than the ways people earn their living, the advent of a postindustrial society has profoundly affected the patterns of relations between the races, the social classes, the generations, and the sexes. Because such changes are never easily accepted, they carried serious implications for politics. To the extent that the guarantor state both in the United States and in Europe tried to accommodate change by meeting some of the demands of such protesters as the young and women, it became the target of conservative backlash. Resentments grew deeper still with the downturn of the world economy after 1973. The general postwar assumption had been that by using the taxing and spending mechanisms Keynes had recommended, the guarantor state could "fine-tune" Western economies. But by the late 1970s it became clear that Keynesian management was not working. Blame for the unpredictable combination of rising inflation and rising unemployment was increasingly cast on governments. The resulting discontent provided a bonanza of votes in the 1970s for the conservative opponents of the guarantor state.

Thus, ironically, at the very moment that Western governments seemed to have become most responsive to democratic control, they were confronted with electorates increasingly mistrustful of government. The years since World War II have seen the climax of another central theme of the twentieth century: the mobilization of a mass electorate by democratic politics. When France, the last of the major democracies, gave women the vote in 1946, evolution toward the possibility of general electoral participation was almost complete. It only remained to extend the vote to eighteen-year-olds, as many countries did in the 1970s in response to youth revolts. With the collapse of the Spanish and Portuguese dictatorships, politics everywhere in the West seemed to have become democratic.

The troubling question that had already emerged in the 1950s and 1960s, however, was the extent to which these expanding political systems offered voters genuine alternatives. The principal differences between the parties that alternated in office seemed limited to details of how the guarantor state should manage the economy, and in whose interest. In no country did any significant party any longer advocate truly revolutionary change. The prevalence of protest—sometimes violent protest—in the 1960s suggested that many Americans, Europeans, and Japanese doubted whether their votes really counted for anything. In the emerging postindustrial global economy, dominated by huge government and multinational corporate bureaucracies, did the individual's choice make any difference?

In the depressed 1970s and 1980s, the most significant development has been the emergence of leaders and movements that challenged the postwar consensus by boldly denying the effectiveness of the guarantor state. On the Left in Europe the so-called Green parties warned that technological change was making the global environment uninhabitable. Only a return to local grassroots participation in vital decision making, they argued, could avert ecological disaster. Far more effectively on the Right, leaders such as Reagan in the United States and Thatcher in Britain offered some of the same criticisms. Rather than being the means of social improvements, they argued, governmental bureaucracies were the principal obstacles. This view came to be widely shared in the 1980s. Only the Socialist government of France's François Mitterrand, in 1981 and 1982, tried briefly to reassert the role of the guarantor state but the pressures of a global system being pushed in the opposite direction by Thatcher and Reagan soon forced him back into line.

Thus the bitter argument of the 1930s over the merits of a governmental role in managing the economy and improving the society, muted by the prosperity of the 1950s and 1960s, has broken out with renewed vigor—and the guarantor state's opponents seem to be prevailing. Yet the emergence of outspoken challenges to government has not inspired many voters with renewed trust in the democratic process. By their nonparticipation, potential voters seemed to be demonstrating their disbelief that in a modern postindustrial society decision making about public concerns is still within reach of the ordinary individual.

For a growing number of people today, the only discernible purpose of life in postindustrial society thus seems to be to make enough money to assure one's own personal well-being by the acquisition of the products of the new technologies. This retreat from public concerns to private individual self-preoccupation, however, leaves us with an unanswered question of values: if the guarantor state is discredited, and the individual is powerless, who will look after the general interest and take responsibility for society—now global society—as a whole?

In tracing these themes in postwar Western Europe, it is not necessary to chronicle the history of every country. Rather we shall cite examples, comparing Thatcher's Britain and Mitterand's France with the United States under Reagan. Dividing the history of the postwar Western world into five periods, each with a central theme, will also clarify our discussion.

The first period (from the early 1950s into the early 1960s) of *conservative political dominance* followed the short era of social reform immediately after World War II. Behind the appearance of immobility of the 1950s, however, accelerating technological and social change was fundamentally altering U.S. and Western European society.

The stresses of change burst out in protests that made the second period, the 1960s, *the decade of upheaval.* Some who protested—such as blacks in the United States—were demanding their share in newly affluent societies; others were challenging the notion that society's only goal should be affluence.

In the early 1970s, these combined revolts produced a third period of *backlash against the apparent collapse of authority.* Conservative values, however, could not cope with the economic slump that followed the rise in OPEC oil prices. The slowdown of the world economy brought global interdependency to the attention of the West in the most painful way. Europeans and even the Japanese discovered, as Americans already had, that their heavy industries could not compete with product turned out in developing countries with lower labor costs. As the withering of their traditional industries brought them into the postindustrial age, the peoples of the world restlessly voted governments, whether of the Left or the Right, out of power in rapid succession.

With the fundamental disarray of the world's economy masked in the 1980s by a partial recovery that benefited principally the United States, the theme of the fourth postwar period was *revulsion against the guarantor state.* But as even the U.S. economy sank into recession in the early 1990s under Reagan's successor, George Bush, a new period began. People no longer believed that the 1980s reassertion of classic nineteenth-century liberalism was an adequate response to the challenges of stagnant postindustrial societies. As even relatively affluent people began to face the consequences, such as massive layoffs, of global competition, they became increasingly disenchanted with all the old political slogans and turned to new leaders and movements who claimed to offer a better future. In the United States they flocked to the presidential candidacy of Ross Perot. In Europe, notably in France and Germany, they gave a growing proportion of their votes to parties whose language was disturbingly reminiscent of fascism. The fifth postwar period thus became one of a *quest for an alternative politics.*

The United States and Western Europe in the Cold War Era

To a considerable extent, bipolar confrontation with the Soviet Union shaped U.S. and Western European politics in the two decades following World War II. The momentum for postwar social reform died as the perceived necessity of resisting communism at home and abroad discredited the Left and brought moderate centrist or even right-wing governments to power by 1949 on the European continent and by 1952 in Britain and the United States. These governments, however, did not reverse the postwar expansion of the guarantor state.

In the United States the principal beneficiaries of this expansion were veterans. The GI Bill of Rights gave them educational grants, loans, and jobs. Although this was in reality a government reapportionment of income in their favor, an entire generation of Americans perceived it as a right.

Generosity to veterans did not mean that conservatives intended to leave the New Deal intact. The Taft-Hartley Law of 1947 prohibited some of the unions' most effective tactics. By upholding the anti-union right-to-work laws of the South, the law spurred the flight of industry from the unionized Northeast and Middle West to what would later be called the Sunbelt. Thus, the end of World War II, when a third of nonfarm labor was unionized, marked the high point of the union movement in U.S. history.

This law proved to be as far as U.S. conservatives could go in reversing the New Deal. Congressional actions in the second term of President Harry Truman, re-elected in 1948, suggested that most Americans did not want to see the New Deal extended, however. Truman's Fair Deal program called for the establishment of an American national health insurance system comparable to the systems that most other developed countries established after World War II. But a coalition of conservative Republicans and southern Democrats blocked enactment of Truman's proposals. Thus, though established programs of the guarantor state continued, Congress resisted their extension to other groups, such as the ailing poor.

The last years of the Truman administration were overshadowed by a crusade by Republican conservatives, led by Senator Joseph R. McCarthy of Wisconsin, to root supposed communists out of the U.S. government. Though he revealed hardly any such subversives, the climate of fear created by his hounding of persons with leftist associations lingered long after his Senate colleagues repudiated him. Henceforth, while the range of respectable political opinions in Western Europe continued to extend from socialists or even communists on the Left to conservatives on the Right, in the United States the comparable range was from moderate to conservative.

Republican nominee Dwight D. Eisenhower swept to victory in the presidential election of 1952. Under Eisenhower, as under Truman, the U.S. guarantor state grew slightly, rather than shrinking as Republicans hoped. Haunted by fear of runaway inflation, Eisenhower held it to a level of about 1 percent a year, maintaining the federal budget largely in balance. In his farewell address he warned, as only a former commander of Allied forces in Europe in World War II could, against the dangerous growth of the "military-industrial complex." The alliance of big business with the Pentagon, he declared, threatened not only war but economic ruin through uncontrollable inflation.

This prophetic warning was uncharacteristic of a president whose bland political style made the 1950s synonymous with political conformity. In Western Europe, similarly reassuring leaders from the past provided a sense of postwar continuity. In Britain the seventy-seven-year-old Churchill led the Conservatives back to power in 1951. They held it under his successors until 1964. The political life of the new Federal Republic of Germany was dominated until 1963 by "the old man," Chancellor Konrad Adenauer, leader of the centrist Christian Democratic party. In France, no such dominant figure emerged after de Gaulle withdrew in disgust from postwar politics in 1946. The postwar Fourth Republic was governed after 1947 by the kind of unstable and short-lived coalition cabinets of the Center and the Right that had dominated prewar political life. Their inability to deal with rebellion in Algeria brought de Gaulle back to power with a Fifth Republic in 1958.

Like President Eisenhower's administration, these European governments maintained, but did not greatly expand, the activities of the guarantor state. However, behind the appearance of political continuity, technological change in the 1950s was fundamentally altering Western societies.

The Acceleration of Change

A tremendous economic expansion followed World War II throughout the Western world, which increasingly included Japan. The U.S. gross national product (GNP) doubled between the end of the war and the early 1960s. Despite recessions, real wages (taking inflation into account) rose 20 percent during the eight years of Eisenhower's administration alone. Fully a third of American families had been living in poverty (by the official definition) in 1940, and over a quarter of them were still officially poor in 1950. By 1960, however, only about one American family in five was to be found below the poverty line.

Western Europe shared in the 1950s boom. By the end of the decade, the continent produced a quarter of the world's industrial goods, though even West Germany's "economic miracle"—a growth in industrial production of over 100 percent—was outstripped by Japanese expansion. Although their standards of living were still only half of U.S. levels, Europeans' pay envelopes reflected the boom. Real wages doubled in Europe between 1950 and 1966.

In the midst of growing affluence, the ways in which Americans and Europeans earned their living were changing. In the mid-1950s the number of U.S. nonfarm workers employed in blue-collar jobs dropped below the number of white-collar office workers for the first time. This was a momentous turning point. Once office workers began to outnumber workers in factories, commentators began to talk of the United States as a postindustrial society. U.S. industrial employment was not yet contracting. But jobs in the service sector—government, retailing, finance, insurance, health care—increased by over 200 percent between 1945 and 1970. The number of local government employees tripled.

Western European societies soon followed the United States into the postindustrial age. In the mid-1950s the farming, industrial, and service sectors of the French economy, for example, employed almost equal numbers of workers. By 1970 the postindustrial service sector, expanding much more rapidly than industrial jobs, employed almost half the French population.

Changing technology explains why industrial employment in the Western world had peaked by the 1970s. Until then, cheap energy made it advantageous for industry to replace workers with machines.

The Computer Revolution and the Knowledge Explosion

Machines replaced workers in complex tasks as well as in simple ones. In 1955, an American automobile plant opened in which the most highly skilled jobs were performed by automated machine tools without human intervention. This breakthrough reflected the increasing speed with which new knowledge found practical application. The very idea of the computer dated back only twenty years.

Of all the technological innovations of our century, the computer is probably the most revolutionary. In 1936, Alan Turing, a British mathematician, first sketched the concept of a machine that could almost instantly solve calculations that would take human beings a lifetime. Electronic technology and wartime need transformed this idea into actuality. During World War II, Turing was one of the British code-breakers who designed machines to uncover by high-speed computation the random settings of German ciphering machines.

The first programmable digital computers ultimately derived from these wartime machines. The invention of the transistor soon made possible the development of ever-greater calculating capacity in ever-smaller machines. In the 1950s, magnetic tapes began to replace the clumsy punched cards on which computer data were first stored. Computers proliferated at incredible speed, for advanced technology and the increasing number of human interrelationships vastly expanded the demand for calculations and detailed record-keeping. By the 1980s, worldwide computer capacity was doubling every two years, with over 5 million machines in use in the United States alone. IBM, a U.S.-based multinational corporation, continued to dominate production; as early as 1960 it was selling French-built equipment in over sixty countries.[1] By the 1980s, however, Japanese firms were planning to capture a third of the world market before the end of the decade. They already made most of the advanced computer memory chips.

People who have grown up with computers may find it difficult to imagine what life was like in the very recent past without them. In a sense the computer is simply one more machine with which human beings have harnessed nature to their purposes. This machine uses electrons moving in billionths of a second to manipulate numerical symbols. It is a kind of assembly line of information, producing conclusions in the way that the assembly lines of the 1920s produced automobiles.

In fact, however, the computer is a wholly new kind of machine. It produces not goods or energy like earlier machines, but information, the most important commodity in a postindustrial society. By the 1980s, half of the American work force was engaged in processing information of one sort or another. The more data computers produce, the more raw material they provide for processing to produce still more data. Thus the "knowledge explosion" continues in a self-perpetuating cycle.

The computer may have potential for harm as well as for good. Since the 1950s, critics have warned that its capacity to store information about every individual could reinforce bureaucratic control of human life. Not everyone believes that the computerized automation of whole factories (already accomplished in Japan and soon to be imitated in the United States) will create more jobs than are lost as workers are displaced by robots. Today, the ultimate impact of the computer remains to be seen. Some believe the personal computer will restore to the individual some of the creative autonomy of craftsmen. Others feel computers directly threaten jobs. In this gloomier scenario, the service sector of postindustrial society will provide a dwindling number of jobs to low-paid operators, performing repetitive tasks before a video terminal under conditions of discipline reminiscent of the industrial assembly line.

The computer has proved to be an essential tool in the postwar knowledge explosion. By 1960, the U.S. government was spending 10 percent of its budget on research, compared to less than 1 percent before World War II. Many scientists complained that far too large a share of research expenditures—three-quarters or more—went to military technology. Nevertheless, such government expenditures powerfully influenced the shape of society. The knowledge explosion helps to explain why so many people by 1960, not only in the United states, were doing different jobs and living in different places.

The Flight to the Suburbs

As more and more of the population moved into service-sector occupations such as computer programming, people moved inexorably from farm and city to the suburbs. Machine technology in agriculture made it possible to produce far greater yields with ever-fewer farmers. As agribusiness produced huge stocks of food, what had remained in 1945 of the distinctive rural life of the small farmer faded away. Only 9 percent of Americans still lived on farms in 1960, compared to 17.5 percent in 1945. By the 1980s, French and West German farmers made up equally small minorities of their populations.

The distribution of population within the metropolitan areas to which these formerly rural people were migrating reflected the dispersion that postindustrial employment made possible. The policies of the U.S. federal government accelerated flight to the suburbs in the 1950s. The Federal Highway Act of 1956, the most ambitious public works project ever attempted anywhere, revolutionized transportation. Fueled by an apparently limitless supply of cheap petroleum, automobile ownership tripled in the United States. By the early 1970s, there was almost one car for every two Americans. Unlike public transportation, the automobile conformed to Americans' longing for a private life. Since the suburban house fulfilled a similar aspiration, jobs and stores followed the new freeways to the new suburbs.

The landscape of the suburbia of the 1950s was semistandardized. An architecture of mass production produced neighborhoods that looked the same from one region of the country to another. Such sameness was reassuring to Americans who averaged a change of address every five years between 1945 and 1960. Postindustrial professional people engaged in research and development moved twice as often.

This apparent rootlessness of Americans and their willingness to conform to a single suburban lifestyle shocked Europeans. They were accustomed to a society where the ways of life of regions and social classes remained distinct. But by the 1960s, as global interdependency grew, the institutions of American suburbia were beginning to appear in Europe, too. The spread of fast-food chains and supermarkets provoked patriotic Europeans to decry the "Coca-colonization" of their societies by powerful U.S. corporations. Though U.S. multinationals did market their products aggressively in Europe, it was really the transformation of European societies that made such marketing possible. European firms were producing ten times as many automobiles for newly affluent consumers in the mid-1960s as they did in the late 1940s, for example. The resulting congestion of its ancient cities encouraged Europe's suburban sprawl. By 1980, half of France's nonrural population lived in suburbs developed after World War II. Like suburban Americans, suburban Europeans turned increasingly to the electronic entertainment provided by television.

Television: The Electronic World-View

Television has proved to be as momentous a postwar innovation as the computer. It has basically altered the way American viewers form their *cognitive maps,* their way of understanding reality. As the world increasingly becomes a single audience for the same programs, television may prove to have the same impact elsewhere.

In 1949 there were still only a million television sets in operation in the United States, though broadcasting had begun in 1941. By 1960 there were 46 million sets, watched for an average of five hours a day in 90 percent of American homes. As the mass audience grew, so did the U.S. networks' advertising sales—by a phenomenal 50 percent a year in the 1950s. To keep such a lucrative audience in front of their sets, television executives limited most programming to a predictable staple of quiz shows, comedies, and crime thrillers.

Such programming, endless commercials, and perhaps the very nature of the electronic medium itself have unquestionably affected the American consciousness. The average child has spent twice as much time in front of a television set as in the classroom. While growing up, most children watched some thirty thousand repetitive and frequently violent "electronic stories." The experience of television appeared far more direct to them than that of school. It gave the impression of mirroring reality, allowing people to "see for themselves."

In fact, television offers only a peculiar and partial view of the world. Studies have shown that people who watch television more than four hours a day—a third of all Americans—have a distorted view of the society in which they live. Heavy viewers, it has been found, made their judgments about social groups and issues on the basis of what they had seen on the screen, where until recently groups such as the elderly, blacks, and working women were seldom represented.

Television has broken down the barriers between politics and entertainment. It appeals to feelings, not thought, to the eye rather than the mind. In 1960, people who heard Richard M. Nixon and John F. Kennedy's presidential debate on the radio thought that Nixon had clearly worsted Kennedy on the issues. But the glamorous Kennedy, more skillfully made-up, projected a better image to those who watched television, and he won the election.

By the late 1960s, Americans were increasingly taking their political cues from television, rather than from the party leaders and influential opinion makers who had earlier guided them. Molding the politician's image—what he or she *appeared* to be—became crucial. In

Fast food in Paris. *Today, there are over a thousand fast-food outlets in Paris. The appearance of such multinational corporations as McDonald's in the capital of* haute cuisine *reveals how U.S. patterns of mass consumption are spreading throughout the developed world.* *David Moore/Black Star*

1984 the same advertising agency that had created the "Pepsi generation" designed television "spot" commercials for the re-election of President Reagan. It used the same technique: endless repetition of simple and emotionally appealing themes.

Television has also shaped the political thinking of Americans through its treatment of news. The percentage of prime-time programming devoted to public affairs has fallen by almost one-third since the late 1970s as the U.S. networks have increasingly come under the control of corporate managements more interested in profits than in loss-making documentaries about contemporary issues. Thus discussion of public events has been left largely to the nightly news programs. With only twenty-two minutes per night to convey what happened throughout the world, television news cannot devote much time to any happening, however complicated. It trumpets events—preferably visually striking confrontations such as battles or riots—as parts of an oversimplified saga. In political campaigns, this technique means a breathless day-by-day emphasis on who is ahead in the polls, rather than on any discussion of the issues. The interpretation of video events that television commentators supply often concentrates on exposing politicians as self-seeking bunglers. Television thus has confirmed many Americans' view of politics as a dirty business rather than as the mechanism for managing a complex society. In this way, television has contributed to the steady decline since 1960 in the number of Americans who vote for president.

Whether television will have the same overwhelming impact on other postindustrial societies as it has had in the United States remains to be seen. In 1980, there were 63 television sets for every 100 Americans, but only 33 for every 100 West Germans and 29 for every 100 persons in France.[2] But in 1984 even the Chinese had as many sets as Americans had owned in 1960, and the Chinese government was purchasing its first package of programs from CBS. On Wednesday nights in Shanghai, 70 percent of viewers watch a U.S. police thriller, interspersed with commercials for U.S. cigarettes and soap. "It's scary," declares one of its American producers, "because we're going to change the way these people act and feel and think."[3]

Today the television medium has clearly not realized the hopes of its early years. Culturally, television faithfully reflected growing global integration. It shrank the world to the dimensions of a "global village." But traffic within the "village" was virtually a one-way street. Twenty percent of British TV and 50 percent of French TV programming was imported, mainly from the United States. The number of people outside the United States who watched U.S.-made serials like *Dallas* far exceeded the number of Americans who could find on their TV screen a window into the lives of their fellow "global villagers" in Europe and the Third World. In fact, except in moments of international crisis, American television largely ignored other countries. In an interdependent world where human survival depends on greater public understanding of complex issues, television offered instead an escape into a world of illusory images.

The Challenge to Authority in the 1960s

Though television entertainment reinforced the escapism of the postindustrial suburban middle class, television news thrived on the dramatic images of protest in the 1960s. The first of the successive revolts that dominated the news of the 1960s came in the southern United States, as blacks protested its segregated society. Within a few years, television had shown young people throughout the world how to challenge authority by, for example, occupying a place and refusing to leave—the sit-in.

Protests against the Vietnam War reflected the growing integration of the Western world: a march on the Pentagon in Washington, D.C., in October 1967 occurred simultaneously with demonstrations in Amsterdam, Berlin, Oslo, Paris, Rome, and Tokyo.[4] Some of those who demonstrated were attacking not only the war but the technological, inhuman society that they blamed for the war's continuation. Thus challenged by Americans and faced with a no-win situation in Vietnam, President Lyndon B. Johnson had to abandon his ambitions to expand the guarantor state and did not run for re-election. In France the student and worker revolt of May 1968 so discredited General de Gaulle's government that he too had to retire within a year.

The Black Rebellion

Television images of policemen assaulting unresisting civil rights demonstrators brought home the conflict between American ideals and the realities of black life. Below the Mason-Dixon Line, the law segregated blacks from whites in their daily activities. Even getting a drink of water was segregated, with separate fountains for "White" and "Colored." Intimidation prevented any challenge to this system through the political process.

Blacks also faced discrimination outside the South. The postwar mechanization of agriculture in the southern states reduced employment there and accelerated northward migration. As whites moved out of the inner cities of the Northeast and the Middle West, blacks moved in. The nonwhite population of the Northeast rose by one-third in the 1940s and by a quarter again in the 1950s. Though northern laws did not often sanction segregation, blacks there faced effective exclusion from opportunities in housing and employment.

In the South the black revolt could be dated from December 1, 1955, when Mrs. Rosa Parks refused to give up her seat on a city bus in Montgomery, Alabama. (Mrs. Parks was already sitting in the "colored" rear section of the bus. The law required her to yield her seat to any white person who had none.)

Martin Luther King, Jr., a Baptist minister, began his rise to leadership of the civil rights movement by organizing a boycott of the bus system to bring economic pressure on segregation. King had been deeply impressed by Gandhi's success in compelling change in India by nonviolent resistance. The Southern Christian Leadership Conference, which King founded in 1958, helped spread this tactic throughout the South. The first southern sit-in occurred in 1960 when blacks refused to be ousted from a segregated lunch counter in Greensboro, North Carolina. Within two months, the movement had spread over nine southern states.

Media attention to these nonviolent demonstrators soon brought the weight of worldwide disapproval against southern segregationists. The Nobel committee in Sweden, for example, awarded its 1964 Peace Prize to Dr. King. By then, federal legislation was overruling the state statutes that provided the basis for southern segregation. King now turned his attention to the plight of blacks in the northern urban ghettos. Here it would not be enough to reassert political rights; the problem was to provide economic advantages for a minority. But such advantages, many white Americans believed, could come only at their own expense. As a result, King made little progress by 1968, the year he was assassinated.

Some blacks had always doubted that white America would yield to moral persuasion. As King's drive for economic equality stalled, more and more began to see their struggle as part of a worldwide conflict. They identified with the African nationalists then winning their independence from the white dominance of the European world-system. It was symbolic of this change that in 1966 the Student Nonviolent Coordinating Committee, founded in 1960 by whites and blacks to bring Gandhian pressure on southern segregation, expelled its white members and adopted the slogan "Black Power." Henceforth, "The Movement," as young people of the 1960s sometimes called their revolt, was divided.

The Rebellion of the Young

The movement that ended in racial separatism in 1966 had begun with a wave of youthful enthusiasm for interracial harmony. The three young men killed outside Philadelphia, Mississippi, on June 21, 1964, by a mob that included sheriff's deputies illustrate this idealism. Two were white New Yorkers, aged twenty and twenty-four, who had come south to help register blacks to vote. The third was a local black man of twenty-one. Their killers were never tried for murder. Some were convicted on federal charges of violating the dead men's civil rights. The worldwide youth rebellion of which the three were a part has many explanations. Among these, however, the young men's own reason—a dedication to equal rights that cost them their lives—should not be forgotten.

The principal theaters of the youth revolt were college campuses. At the University of California at Berkeley in the autumn of 1964, students protested the arrest of distributors of political literature. The student organizers of the Free Speech Movement argued that the academic environment could not be insulated from the emotional issues of race and war then dividing the country. Students challenged the administration by organizing campus sit-ins. For the next eight years, Berkeley students intermittently disrupted the usual academic routines. Calm returned only with the end of the Vietnam War and subsequent suspension of the draft.

This pattern of disruption was matched on many U.S. campuses. It reached a climax of horror in 1970 when nervous National Guardsmen opened fire on students demonstrating against the presence of the Reserve Officers' Training Corps (ROTC) at Kent State University in Ohio. Four young people were killed.

Campus unrest and even violence was not limited to the United states. Throughout the world, students copied the methods of their American counterparts to protest what they saw as U.S. racism at home and imperialism in Vietnam. Japanese students marched on U.S. naval bases and boycotted their classes to protest Japan's tacit support of the U.S. war effort. The German movement, Students for a Democratic Society (SDS), like the U.S. organization of the same name, insisted that in the age of the mass society, democracy had become a sham. Since no political party anywhere, not even socialists, questioned the quality of life under the capitalist guarantor state, the young could challenge the managerial elite who actually controlled postindustrial society only by demonstrating in the streets.

This revolt among European and Japanese students who did not risk, as American students did, being drafted for an overseas war baffled many observers. Conflict between generations, like conflict between the sexes and between social classes, has been a constant in history. But this young generation lived in the most prosperous societies the world had ever seen. Why should they rebel?

A partial explanation for the rebellion is that the large size of the "baby-boom" generation of the 1960s and its relative affluence made the usual generational conflict worse worldwide. When student protests began, American, Western European, and Japanese youth—in their late teens and on the verge of adulthood but not yet accepted by their societies as adults—were the most numerous age group in the population. This generation had grown up with higher expectations than its predecessors'. Before World War II, for example, only 15 percent of Americans between the ages of eighteen and twenty-one had gone to college. As it became evident that postindustrial society would require more complex skills to find a job, by 1960 one-third of the same U.S. age group was attending college. Many Western European societies too were approaching this proportion. This extension of adolescence into college years brought young people both benefits and liabilities.

The benefits often included continuing parental support. The price for that support was continued subordination to the older generation. Yet such dependency seemed unreasonable to young people raised in postindustrial suburban households in which both parents worked. In their absence, young people found role models within their own generation; they developed their own uniform—T-shirt and blue jeans—and their own music. Rock-and-roll began as a celebration of adolescent defiance of adult authority. The grandest rock concert of all brought nearly a half-million to Woodstock, New York, in August 1969. It was the celebration of a generation apart, aptly called "the Woodstock Nation." Whatever the justice of their protests, it is not surprising that many of this generation, reared in affluence and enforced conformity and identifying with each other and with generous ideals, should have risen in revolt.

Moreover, the Woodstock Nation extended throughout the world, and its members watched one another on television. Attacking a worldwide society they believed to be economically integrated by multinational corporations, some leaders of the youth rebellion hoped to generate a protest movement that was equally integrated globally.

Television helped to link the protest movements. The original nucleus of protest in France was provided by students at a suburban branch campus of the University of Paris who had been horrified by the daily spectacle of the carnage in Vietnam. But what fired the revolt of the French young was the changing nature of France's university system. In their ambition to move France into the postindustrial age, the technocrats of de Gaulle's government decreed a vast expansion of higher education. Like many American students, however, French students found the new campuses to be impersonal, bureaucratic, oppressive environments. Campus activists played on the general undergraduate feeling of powerlessness to provoke confrontations with university authorities.

Student occupation of the main campus of the University of Paris, the Sorbonne, in May 1968 provoked a crisis that paralyzed the whole economy. Following the students' lead, half of France's work force went on strike. The Gaullist government finally resolved the crisis only by decreeing an inflationary 10 percent wage hike. Thus pacified, the workers went back to work, leaving the students alone to face police repression. Nevertheless, the "events of May" had destroyed de Gaulle's credibility as the defender of law and order.

The French explained the youth revolt of 1968 much as Americans did campus unrest in the United States. Conservatives dismissed it as the misbehavior of a spoiled younger generation, which got out of hand only because the authorities were not firm enough at the outset. More tolerant commentators blamed

Protest at Berkeley. *A sheriff's deputy marches a struggling demonstrator off to jail from an anti-war picket line on the University of California campus, 1968.* Wide World Photos

the revolt on the stresses of adjusting the once-exclusive university system to a democratic mass society. New Left sympathizers discovered more basic causes. Scornful alike of Western technocratic capitalism and of Eastern bloc communism, these critics saw the French students as a vanguard of revolt against postindustrial society worldwide. The younger generation everywhere, in the New Left view, was resisting integration into a worldwide economy, refusing to become a new white-collar proletariat.

Understanding the youth revolts of the 1960s requires weighing the merits of all these explanations. Throughout the twentieth century, younger generations have oscillated between idealism and cynicism, as in the pre– and post–World War I eras. The generation coming to adulthood during the 1960s, buoyed by growing affluence and low unemployment, tended to take these blessings for granted. These young people questioned whether a comfortable lifestyle and a dull job were life's only goals. Assuming the economy would continue to prosper as it had in the last decade, they idealistically sought to assure that everyone would benefit from this growth, and set their expectations higher than any government could meet. Their increasingly shrill protests inevitably produced a backlash, but their rebellion forced the political retirement not only of Charles de Gaulle but also of Lyndon Baines Johnson.

The Postwar Welfare State in Europe and the United States

President Johnson aspired to make the United States a Great Society for all of its citizens. To many Americans, such a program seemed long overdue, since the country lagged far behind the powerful guarantor states of Western Europe in providing social services to its citizens. The so-called free-market economy that enabled West Germany to increase its share of world trade from 7 to 20 percent in the 1950s and 1960s, for example, was in reality based on capitalistic concentration and extensive government services. The three biggest German banks voted almost three-fourths of the shares in industrial corporations, providing economic planning in all but name. The government collected 10 percent of German GNP in social security taxes to provide a range of benefits far greater than those afforded by Bismarck's original welfare state.

Johnson's plans for his Great Society were more modest. The programs he pushed through Congress in 1965–1966 involved the federal government in improving the environment. Federal grants would support the cleansing of the nation's water supply, for example, and help rebuild its decaying mass transit systems. Medicare and Medicaid finally realized Truman's Fair Deal aspirations, giving elderly Americans some measure of security against dying untreated and penniless.

Johnson could see that even when guaranteed legal equality by the Civil Rights Act of 1964, blacks had no hope of becoming equal members of U.S. society so long as most of them were poor. He did not, however, propose a socialistic redistribution of income to remedy black poverty. In fact, the portion of U.S. income earned by the poorest 20 percent of the population remained constant at about 5 percent from the 1940s through the 1970s. Instead, the Great Society launched programs designed to rescue blacks from a "culture of poverty" similar, in the eyes of social planners, to that of the shantytowns of the Third World. The Equal Opportunity Act of 1964, for example, fostered such ventures as a Job Corps and community action programs to stimulate economic development in the ghettos.

In today's disillusioned atmosphere, it is fashionable to decry these programs as failures. Certainly they were inadequate to fulfill Johnson's grand goal of eliminating poverty. Critics pointed out that they provided opportunities for waste and corruption and filled ghetto dwellers with unrealistic hopes. Revolutions coincide with rising expectations. The wave of rioting and destruction that swept black areas of inner cities in the mid-1960s can partly be explained as the result of the misleading impression given by the Great Society that things were going to change.

By 1968 the ghettos seemed out of control, and Johnson, who was facing antagonism from several directions, declared he would not run for re-election. The young carried their protest against the Vietnam War to the streets outside the Democratic convention in Chicago. The majority of Americans who regarded these protesters as spoiled and unpatriotic had no love for Johnson either. To suburban Americans, he was responsible for handouts to rioting blacks. Nixon's victory in 1968 brought a Republican to the presidency, and the Great Society programs became the scapegoat for these ill-assorted discontents.

History in the long run may prove kinder to Johnson than public opinion was in 1968. He thought that the U.S. economy was strong enough to support both a huge military commitment abroad and a Great Society at home. Professional economists had assured him that there was no risk in running a federal budget deficit to reduce unemployment. As Johnson left office, however, it was already clear that this had not been good advice. As inflation increased, so did unemployment. This *stagflation*—rising prices in a stagnant economy—became the central economic problem of all the developed economies in the 1970s.

The Struggle in the 1970s to Re-establish Authority

The anger of many Americans and Western Europeans at governments' inability to revive the economy or to master the protest movements of the 1960s made the 1970s a decade of conservative backlash. The early 1970s also saw the climax of yet another revolt: women increasingly demanded that in the postindustrial era they should no longer be confined to the stereotyped roles of earlier times but should enjoy the same rights as men.

The Women's Liberation Movement

In the United States the most recent chapter of women's struggle for equality dates from the end of World War II. Veterans were demobilized and sought jobs that women had filled during wartime. Women were encouraged to be homemakers in order to reduce competition for work. An influential book derided feminism, women's demand for economic and social equality, as a "neurosis."

As so often happened in the 1950s, however, accelerating social change was quietly undermining such apparent certainties as the exclusively domestic role of women. To help support the suburban lifestyle, more and more women returned to work. In 1940, only 15 percent of American married women had been employed outside the home. By 1960, almost a third of them had jobs. As female employment grew, more women sought educational qualifications. The number of U.S. female college graduates doubled in the 1960s. It was largely among such women that the liberation movement found its members.

The federal government had not been energetic in prosecuting cases of alleged sex discrimination under the Civil Rights Act of 1964. This lethargy pushed the women's movement toward political mobilization. To liberate women from male domination, women's groups revived the demand for an Equal Rights Amendment (ERA) to the U.S. Constitution. To free women from economic dependency, they called for a national system of day care and the elimination of laws forbidding abortion. To

Women demand the right to an abortion, 1977. *Though the leading figure is costumed as an American comic-strip character, this march was in New Zealand.* Westra/Magnum

enforce such demands, groups such as the National Organization for Women (NOW) mounted a campaign to raise the consciousness of women and to turn their sexual solidarity into political power.

This political mobilization paid off. In the United States, federally imposed quotas required affirmative action by employers to ensure that women were sufficiently represented among their employees. (In Western Europe, the Economic Community monitored individual governments to see that women received the same pay as men for doing the same work.)

Under such government pressure, women penetrated in considerably greater numbers into professions once reserved for men. The percentage of U.S. lawyers who were women more than tripled during the 1970s, from 4 percent to 14 percent. The proportion of women doctors doubled, from 9 percent to 20 percent—a far cry from the 1930s, when most U.S. hospitals would not admit a female intern.

In France, to cite a European example, the proportion of women among the younger generation of doctors rose even higher, to over a third. This represented a remarkable change in a country where, until the mid-1960s, a woman had to obtain her husband's legal permission to open her own bank account or run her own business. In 1974 the French parliament legalized abortion, one year after a historic U.S. Supreme Court decision upheld this most controversial of women's rights. In the same year, President Giscard d'Estaing appointed Françoise Giroud as the first French cabinet minister for women's affairs.

As economic opportunities for women grew, their tolerance for a subordinate role in marriage declined. By the 1980s, one French marriage in six ended in divorce. The U.S. divorce rate was far higher: half of all marriages. Fully half of American women were single, compared to only a quarter of them in 1960. The kind of household that Americans had taken for granted only a generation earlier—father, dependent mother, two or more children—by the 1980s represented only 12 percent of U.S. households, and this proportion was still declining.

The acceleration of change in such a fundamental institution as the family naturally produced a backlash. In 1982 the ERA failed by a margin of three states to secure ratification. In the 1984 U.S. presidential campaign, the Republican party platform demanded that future federal judges be pledged to oppose abortion. European conservatives similarly attacked women's liberation as destructive of the social order. Faced with such adverse reactions, the women's movement seemed in retreat in the 1980s. A younger generation of women appeared to be taking the hard-won victories of women's liberation for granted.

Nevertheless, it seems unlikely that women in postindustrial societies will ever return to the state of domesticity that the 1950s took for granted. Economic necessity and educational inclination—half of France's university students today are women, for example—continue to attract women to careers. Such trends are viewed as intolerable by many people who grew up in a society with very different role models. In both the United States and Europe in the 1970s and 1980s, such people expressed their protest by voting for politicians who promised to restore traditional values.

Stagflation and the Search for Political Direction

Economic dissatisfaction, as well as nostalgic protest, dominated the politics of the 1970s. Political power changed hands with increasing rapidity in the United States and Europe as one government after another failed to grapple effectively with stagflation. The re-election of President Nixon in 1972 symbolized continuing backlash against the 1960s; he defeated Democratic Senator George S. McGovern, whose candidacy seemed to personify the revolt of blacks, youth, and women. Within two years Nixon resigned under threat of impeachment. Investigation of a burglary at the Democratic party's headquarters at the Watergate complex in Washington, D.C., and of the subsequent cover-up revealed a trail of complicity leading back to the president. In 1976, Democratic nominee Jimmy Carter profited from this scandal to defeat President Gerald R. Ford, who had succeeded Nixon. Carter promised to restore Americans' faith in their government. But by 1980, with inflation an annual rate of 13 percent and American hostages being held in Iran, the voters rejected Carter's presidency and elected former California governor Ronald Reagan.

In the 1980 presidential election, half the eligible voters chose not to cast their ballots. Such a turnout, despite the new political technology of computer-generated mailing lists and television commercials, was evidence of widespread skepticism that in a mass society, voting had any meaning. Polls revealed that as many as two-thirds of the U.S. electorate saw themselves as helpless victims of monied interest. In fact, campaign contributions to political action committees (PACs), formed to promote a single issue or special interest, increased tenfold in the 1970s. The temptations of these funds increased the voters' suspicion that politicians cast their ballots for the highest bidder.

In Western Europe, a far higher percentage of citizens continued to vote. Often, however, they voted to punish governments they judged to have failed to restore economic health, much as Americans had judged Ford and Carter. The British electorate voted the Conservatives into power again in 1970, out in 1974, and back in again, under Margaret Thatcher, in 1979. In and out of power, the British Labour party remained as divided as it had been during the Depression. In fact, its more moderate members finally seceded in protest, as they doubted that the program of radical social change, with which the party proposed to combat stagflation, was compatible with democratic politics.

Similar quarrels disrupted the German Social Democratic party, and the voters ousted it from power in 1982. Chancellor Willy Brandt's efforts to placate the young rebels of the 1960s by taking steps toward social change had angered middle-of-the-road voters. His successor in 1974, Helmut Schmidt, angered the Left by his indifference to the social costs of his deflationary economic policies. A significant number of young Germans turned away from the Social Democrats to the "Green" party, which championed many 1960s causes, including protecting the environment. In Sweden, Socialists had been in power for generations, but in 1976 the voters defeated them.

The reason for the voters' growing impatience in the 1970s lies in the worldwide economic crisis. Its differing impact on diverse social groups polarized politics. No longer did people believe, as they had in the 1950s and 1960s, that their economies would continue to grow indefinitely. Each social group within each nation had become preoccupied with casting its votes to defend its own threatened share in a stagnant, or even shrinking, global economy.

The crisis of stagflation spared no nation. Through most of the 1960s, Europeans had worried about "the American challenge." They feared that U.S.-based multinational corporations would buy up their basic industries while using superior technology to drive European companies out of world markets. This proved a groundless fear, for the economic troubles that appeared at the end of the Johnson presidency were symptomatic of a deeply troubled U.S. economy.

In some ways the developing crisis of U.S. industry had been foreshadowed by the fate of Britain after World War II. Despite their burden of debt, for a long while the British attempted to maintain the appearance of a great power—by having a nuclear deterrent, for example. At the same time, they provided the generous benefits of the guarantor state. Meanwhile, they failed to modernize industrial plants that were already becoming obsolete in 1945. The British share in production of the world's manufactured goods fell by half between 1960 and the mid-1970s. The growth of aggressive global competition, as well as British inefficiency, explains this outcome.

Overseas competition began to challenge U.S. industry in the 1950s. Japanese clothing sales in the U.S. retail market cost American textile workers 300,000 jobs. In the 1970s the United States increased its manufacturing output by a third, but employment in manufacturing grew by only 5 percent—testimony to the growing industrial applications of automation. But the products of many U.S. industries no longer dominated world markets. By 1970 the United States manufactured only one-fifth of the world's steel, for example, compared to nearly half of world production in 1950.

U.S. manufactured goods were at a disadvantage in world markets for interrelated reasons. From the mid-1960s onward, the rate of growth of U.S. productivity fell behind that of every other developed country except Britain. U.S. conservatives blamed wage inflation: paying people too much while expecting them to do too little. In fact, wages rose rapidly in the 1970s, though they lagged behind prices. Others blamed declining productivity on industrialists' reluctance to modernize existing U.S. plants. All too often, it was more profitable for multinational corporations to build new plants abroad where labor was cheaper. So prevalent did this trend become that by the 1980s, had the industrial output abroad of U.S.-based multinationals all been produced by a single country, that mythical country would have ranked third in the world, after the United States and Japan.

Some economists concluded that the U.S. economy had entered a period of crisis comparable to the Great Depression. Certainly the economy had some impressive achievements to its credit. It had found jobs—often service-sector jobs—for a labor force swollen by half by the baby-boom generation. The "entitlement" programs of the guarantor state—many, like Medicare and Social Security, distributed regardless of need—had improved the lives of the elderly, the disabled, and some of the poor. The costs of these programs, however, increased in the 1960s and 1970s from 5 percent to 11 percent of the U.S. GNP. Taxpayers, uncertain of their own prospects as the economy swung from recession to recovery and back again, blamed such costs for the decline of their own standard of living. Increasingly, they made the guarantor state and the recipients of its benefits the scapegoats for their fears and frustrations. Less and less was heard of the generous notion of the 1960s that society had a collective responsibility for its most vulnerable and least fortunate members.

By the 1980s, there existed two American societies: one was poor, urban, and mainly black; the other was relatively affluent, suburban, and mainly white. Increasingly their ways of life diverged. For those left behind in the shrinking central cities, the ups and downs of the economy hit much harder. At the depths of the recession of 1981–1982, for example, the unemployment rate hit 19 percent among laborers and 17 percent among factory workers, compared to only 3 percent for mainly suburban technical workers and professionals.

A growing number of those left behind in the cities had no job and no prospect of finding one. In 1960, almost three-quarters of black males had been either employed or seeking a job. By the early 1980s that proportion had declined to a little over one-half. The "black revolt" of the 1960s produced few economic gains. Largely because of federally enforced employment guidelines, some blacks joined the middle class. Overall, however, the gap between black and white family incomes has been steadily widening since the mid-1970s. Blacks' median income today is only a little over half that of whites.

Conservatives blamed this continuing gap on the mistaken generosity of the Great Society, which supposedly made it easier to collect government benefits than to work. Others thought the origins of black poverty were more complex. The kind of job that minimally skilled immigrants to U.S. cities had historically taken was rapidly vanishing, especially in the inner cities. The growing number of women in the work force took many of the low-paying jobs in the expanding service sector. The root cause of the desperate plight of most U.S. blacks was that postindustrial opportunity began deserting cities just as they moved in.

Visiting Europeans were often horrified by their glimpses of U.S. inner-city society. A stricken neighborhood like New York's South Bronx, for example,with its mile upon mile of abandoned buildings burned out by desperate landlords or tenants, reminded such visitors of the ruins of their continent in 1945.

Europe in the 1960s had no such army of the unemployed as occupied such U.S. neighborhoods. In fact, industrial northern Europe during the boom had to import labor from less-developed southern Europe and from such countries as Turkey and Algeria to do the jobs its own citizens did not want. Eighty percent of the workers on the Renault auto-assembly line in Paris, for example, were immigrants. But by the mid-1970s, European governments were attempting to induce or coerce such "guest-workers" to go home. Europe did not long celebrate its resistance to the American challenge: its own economies soon became mired in the same stagflation as the U.S. economy—and for many of the same reasons.

The rise in OPEC oil prices in 1973 hit Europe and Japan at least as hard as the United States. The postwar boom for all had been fueled by a raw material whose price had been nearly stationary. Its sudden rise was a heavy blow to the economies of countries like France and West Germany. After 1945, they had shifted from coal to oil as their prime energy source although they had little oil of their own. After 1973, Europe responded more effectively than the United States to the need to conserve oil. The European Economic Community actually reduced its petroleum imports by 4 percent, while the United States, whose own domestic supplies had equaled demand into the late 1960s, increased its imports by a third.

Nevertheless, the inflated cost of energy contributed to the spread of stagflation in Europe, as did other factors already familiar in the U.S. economy. The rate of growth of European productivity slowed. Average European hourly wages in manufacturing, which in 1960 had everywhere been less than half the U.S. rate, matched or even surpassed U.S. wages by 1980. Though most European governments centrally planned the growth of their economies, plans consistently emphasized the benefits of the guarantor state rather than reinvestment in plant modernization. European-based and even Japanese-based multinational companies began to locate new plants in places where taxes and wages were lower. Thus, steel made in Europe, for example, which had undercut U.S.-produced steel, was now undercut by steel produced in Brazil or India.

The effect of these developments on a country such as West Germany, where one in five jobs depended on exports, was devastating. As high energy costs slowed the whole economy and as German industry became increasingly uncompetitive, unemployment grew, particularly among the young. With higher unemployment, Germans could neither buy the products unsold on world markets themselves nor provide the investment to retool German plants. Meanwhile, tax revenues fell while government expenditures tended to inflate to relieve the hardships of a stagnant economy.

To a greater or lesser extent, this combination of problems beset all the economies of the developed world by the end of the 1970s. As individuals experienced the crisis in the form of high taxes and a living standard reduced by inflation, they tended to vote for politicians who promised to cut taxes and halt inflation by reducing the costs of the guarantor state. Moreover, as the growth of a postindustrial society changed the social composition of the electorate, a majority of voters everywhere had less and less sympathy with the unlucky poor who would be hardest hit by government cutbacks.

Americans and Europeans who managed to escape into the service sector as the number of industrial jobs dwindled lived in a milieu much more hostile to collective social action than that in which factory workers had lived.

The latter had often identified themselves as "us" (the union, often affiliated with the Left) against "them" (the management). Even so, one-half of the German and a third of the British working classes had usually voted for conservatives. Such a vote came even more naturally to postindustrial workers in the service sector, who tended to see themselves as individual middle-class competitors, not members of a group with shared goals. Though European unions have been more successful than U.S. unions at organizing service-sector workers, nowhere do unions today represent a force for change. Dwindling in numbers and political influence, all but a few concentrate on preserving the benefits of their aging membership.

Nor are the young any longer a force for change. Facing uncertain job prospects, they have little of the enthusiasm for collective action that characterized the 1960s generation. Their college studies did little to encourage young people to think about the problems of society as a whole. The number of U.S. students majoring in the humanities—subjects that taught critical thinking about general human problems—fell by 50 percent in the 1970s. The number of graduates in subjects like business that supposedly could ensure success in a constricted job market rose correspondingly. By 1988, an annual survey of the opinions of U.S. college freshmen found that a record 76 percent defined "being very well off financially" as an "essential" goal of their lives, compared to only 39 percent in 1970. Only two in five 1988 freshmen, by contrast, thought "developing a meaningful philosophy of life" was very important, compared to four out of five in the late 1960s. In Europe, where the unemployment rate among the young ranged over 20 percent by 1982, there was a similar preoccupation with acquiring marketable skills.

The faltering world economy of the 1970s thus produced an ethic of every person for himself or herself and each nation for itself. Politicians everywhere tinkered with economic solutions and, as they failed to work, were ousted by voters. Such traditional sources of alternative vision as the Left and the young seemed unable to provide a fresh dream while the world slid haplessly into the postindustrial future.

Continuing Problems and Old Slogans in the 1980s

Nations, however, cannot indefinitely muddle along in an atmosphere of political doubt. Eventually the voters will turn to leadership that promises a real change of direction. In 1979, after a "winter of discontent" during which the economy was virtually paralyzed by strikes of powerful unions, British voters returned the Conservatives to power under the leadership of Margaret Thatcher. In the fall of 1980 and the spring of 1981, the United States and France chose new presidents, Ronald Reagan and François Mitterand. Each promised, by diametrically opposed programs, to resolve his or her country's economic crisis. The limits of their success suggest that the problems of postindustrial society remain resistant to these most recent experiments in economic liberalism (which Americans call conservatism) and democratic socialism.

France Under Mitterand

The OPEC oil shock of 1973 marked the end of three decades of rapid French economic growth, during which the standard of living virtually doubled. Still remembered as a land of picturesque backwardness by those who had not see it since 1945, France by the 1970s had become the third producer of aerospace technology in the world, after the United States and the Soviet Union. Taking for granted that such dramatic modernization would continue, the government of President Giscard d'Estaing (1974–1981) failed to anticipate how quickly the industrial foundations of an economy could become outmoded in the postindustrial era. As in the United States and the rest of Western Europe, Giscard's government permitted wages and social services to increase at inflationary rates and at the same time failed to invest sufficiently in new technologies.

Thus when François Mitterand, who revived the French Socialist party after it had disbanded in 1969, succeeded Giscard as president in 1981, he inherited an economy already in decline. During his first year in office, he and his Socialist majority in parliament tried to combat stagflation by renewing economic growth. Like Léon Blum in 1936, they hoped to do this by ensuring a more equal distribution of wealth. Like Blum, Mitterand decreed wage hikes, reduced the workweek, and expanded paid vacations. He went further than Blum by nationalizing eleven large private companies and many of the banks that had escaped nationalization at the end of World War II. The Socialist hope was to stimulate the economy by expanding worker purchasing power and by confiscating for public investment the profits of large corporations. To finance compensation to these companies' former owners and to pay for enhanced guarantor-state benefits, the Mitterand government borrowed heavily abroad.

Within a year, the discouraging results of this program proved, as in 1936–1937, that in a globally interdependent economy, not even a major industrial power like France could single-handedly pursue the goals of democratic socialism. Inflation rose to an annual rate of 14 percent, yet unemployment remained unacceptably high due to the worldwide slump. Meanwhile, U.S. bankers, noting its growing debt, foreclosed further borrowing by France. By the spring of 1982, the policy of trying to stimulate growth by restoring full employment and redistributing economic rewards had clearly failed.

Mitterrand then completely reversed direction. His new program stressed cutting taxes and social expenditures. His government shut down unneeded capacity in loss-making nationalized industries such as steel and shipbuilding, though this cost many Socialist voters their jobs. By the fall of 1984, this new policy had brought France's inflation rate down to 6.5 percent. But over 9 percent of the French work force was unemployed, and among the young the rate was much higher. Conservatives denounced the original inflationary program. Mitterrand's own supporters were hurt and bewildered by his new program of harsh austerity, which made a Socialist government appear as uncaring as any other.

Thus the Socialists lost the parliamentary elections of March 1986. Though Mitterrand remained president, he had to accept as his prime minister the leader of the new conservative parliamentary majority, Jacques Chirac. Chirac hastened not only to reverse the nationalizations of 1981–1982 but also to sell off to private stockholders many of the government-owned corporations nationalized in the aftermath of World War II. Chirac thus added France to the long list of countries that "privatized" state-owned companies in the 1980s. Though new elections in 1988 returned a narrow Socialist majority, neither they nor Mitterrand promised any significant departure from Chirac's policies.

Thus, as in 1936–1937, when an experiment with democratic socialism ended in disillusionment, critics wondered what future the movement had. French voters for the Left—the working class, the poor, many of the young and idealistic—had danced in the streets when Mitterrand won in 1981. Within less than a year his had become a government like any other, paralyzed by what we have called "the dilemma of democratic socialism." Like Léon

Blum, Mitterrand had preferred to maintain democratic consensus rather than impose revolutionary economic change. But even his limited effort to revive the economy by Keynesian government spending had succumbed to the continuing stagnation of a world economy in which the obsolescence of French industry made it hard to compete. But if, in practice, democratic Socialists offered no alternative to the capitalistic system, and indeed joined its supporters in denouncing the costly inefficiency of the guarantor state, it was hard to see why anyone should vote for them instead of for conservatives such as Chirac—or Thatcher and Reagan.

Britain Under Thatcher

For Margaret Thatcher, the stagflation of the 1970s and the paralyzing strike wave of 1978–1979 were only the most recent symptoms of what Europeans had come to call the "British disease": the combination of amateurish education and management methods, of bitterly hostile relations between capital and labor, between rich and poor, that had reduced Britain from the world's leading economy in the nineteenth century to one of the less important European economies today. Thatcher took a narrower view of the causes of British decline. In her view decline was the result of the militant intransigence of the British labor movement in defending a wasteful guarantor state and the reluctance of the British upper classes, embodied in the Conservative party she now led, to crush that lower-class intransigence. Her own temperament inclined her, however, to the very opposite of the compromises that had characterized her predecessors. A fanatic believer in free-market economics, she was so sure of the rightness of her views that she relished pitiless confrontation with those she believed to be wrong. Not for nothing would she come to be called "the Iron Lady."

The general evolution of the global economy, as we have seen, might help her toward her goal of curing the British of what she called their "dependency culture" by smashing the guarantor state. Britain, like the other major democracies, was moving toward the postindustrial society. Manufacturing, still 70 percent unionized, was in decline while employment in the service sector, only 15 percent unionized, was growing. But Thatcher was unwilling to wait out that evolution. She set out to cripple the British unions. Her Conservative majority passed a variety of laws curtailing some of the unions' most effective tactics, including one law that compelled a majority of a union's membership to vote for a strike before one could be called—a potent incentive for division in unions where many members believed their leaders manipulated strikes for political purposes. Thatcher also broke strikes against government-owned companies like British Coal by simply refusing to meet strikers' demands. Coal miners' strikes had discredited earlier Conservative governments, as in 1974, by forcing them to give in. In 1984–1985 Thatcher refused to negotiate until she broke the strike; then, as the union had warned, she proceeded to close nearly seventy pits, throwing seventy thousand miners onto the already enormous unemployment rolls.

With British unemployment ranging up to 14 percent, it was now easier to break a strike: people lucky enough still to be working thought twice about losing the job they had. In such an atmosphere union membership naturally declined. After nine years of Thatcher, it had dwindled from over half to little over a third of the work force. Other measures were intended, at least in part, to further undermine working-class solidarity. The government sold off public housing at giveaway prices to tenants, for example, and offered shares in "privatized" former government-owned companies to the public. The number of British shareholders tripled from 1979 to 1988. These new working-class houseowners and stockholders were likely to join the third of union members who already voted Conservative, feeling that they now had more in common with the middle class than with their former "comrades."

Such have been the changes wrought since 1979 that observers of the country revived the theme of "the two Englands," a contrast first discerned in the grimmest days of early industrialization. One England was the prosperous south, especially the booming outer London suburbs, with their expanding network of motorways connecting the gleaming new headquarters of high-tech service enterprises. The other England consisted of two parts: the north (and Wales and Scotland), once the cradle of the British industrial revolution and now its tomb, a desolate landscape of abandoned factories and empty harbors; and the inner cities, mostly, as in the United States, crumbling ghettos where black and Asian minorities faced mass unemployment and racial hostility.

To many thoughtful people, including a substantial minority of the Conservative party, this growing polarization between the two Englands seemed to threaten future political stability. They noted, for example, that the once-great port of Liverpool, now impoverished and derelict with the collapse of British exports, elected a local government composed of militant Trotskyites*—a turn to extremism once unimaginable in British politics.

To Thatcher and like-minded people, however, the idea that the government should redistribute wealth from the winners in the south to losers such as Liverpool in the north was exactly what was wrong, not only with socialism but with the policies of all her postwar predecessors. Though she sometimes had to back off from tough initiatives when such misgivings reduced her parliamentary majority, she lost little of her near-revolutionary determination to turn Britain into a newly competitive nation, whatever the human cost. The hope of getting richer would motivate the rich; the despair of being poor would motivate the poor.

The pattern of taxation proposed in her budget in 1988 showed how she intended to redistribute the burden of the costs of government to achieve those ends. The budget called for a 20 percent cut for the wealthiest 5 percent of taxpayers, the lowest income tax rates since 1938, before the creation of the British guarantor state, and a general reduction in the property taxes of householders. To replace those taxes based on the value of property, everyone in the country, regardless of income, would pay a flat "community charge" assessed by local governments, thus adding some 15 million people, including the rapidly growing number living below the official poverty standard, to the tax rolls for the first time.

Public outrage at this "charge," when it was imposed in 1990, finally made Thatcher so unpopular that her own parliamentary Conservative majority turned against her. She had calculated that by forcing local governments, often controlled by the Labour party, to tax everyone at the same rate, she could destroy their power to spend for public purposes and thus to win elections. Widespread rioting and refusal to pay showed that the public blamed her for this regressive measure. Fearing for their own political futures, her colleagues forced her to resign at the end of the year.

The Labour party approached new general elections in April 1992 full of optimism. After thirteen years of Conservative rule, with Britain sunk in its worst recession since the Great Depression and an estimated 1 million homeless people living on the streets, Labour's expectation that the voters would opt for change

*See Chapter 14 for a discussion of Leon Trotsky and his followers.

is understandable. But it was a mistaken expectation: Labour won only 35 percent of the vote to the Conservatives' 42 percent—less than Labour's 38 percent in the 1979 election and a far cry from its 49 percent in 1951.

The explanation for this failure of the British Left may be of ominous significance for parties on the Left in all of the Western democracies in the 1990s. Labour had tried to improve its image by purging its radical Marxist wing and by downplaying its connection with Britain's dwindling unions. But Labour's program did call for increased government spending to improve the public services Thatcher had neglected, to be financed by raising the highest income tax bracket from 40 to 59 percent. This proposal did not trouble Labour's traditional supporters in the poverty-ridden North, where in some places two-thirds of young people under twenty-five could find no job. But Conservative warnings that Labour planned to drop a "tax bomb" alarmed not only the upper-middle and upper classes of the south, who would be hardest hit, but the rest of the suburban middle classes, who hoped someday to attain the highest tax bracket themselves. Despite Thatcher's unpopularity at the end of her reign, her economic policies, such as cutting taxes and selling public housing to private owners had paid political dividends. They had helped to create a narrow electoral majority that voted Conservative because it feared the taxes a Labour guarantor state would impose more than it feared the disinvestment in public services and the heightened tensions between social classes that Thatcherism had produced. Certainly John Major, the prime minister who succeeded Thatcher, was a less doctrinaire and condescending leader. He adroitly abandoned the hated "community charge," for example. But his comparatively benign personality does not explain the Conservative victory, which may signal that in 1990s postindustrial democracies, a majority of voters are sufficiently content to vote against the costs of the social democracy advocated by Labour. Thus history may eventually record, ironically, that the real victor of 1992 was Margaret Thatcher.

The United States Under Reagan

Like Thatcher, Ronald Reagan won office by campaigning against the excessive expenditures of the guarantor state. Reagan's policies once he was in office, however, were more reminiscent of the Keynesian idea of deficit financing than Republicans who had denounced the New Deal cared to admit. Reagan cut taxes, especially for corporations and the very wealthy. Despite this reduction in revenue, he also called for an enormous military buildup. This combination of policies vastly increased the federal budget deficit. The Reagan administration's first years seemed to confirm the inability of governments in the postindustrial era to restrain inflation (through raised interest rates) without substantial unemployment. The recession of 1981–1982 was the worst the United States had experienced since the Depression of the 1930s: up to 10 percent of Americans were unemployed.

The recovery that began at the end of 1982 carried Reagan to re-election in 1984. Many voted for him because they perceived his economic policies as being more successful than his predecessor's. Such a judgment depended on which of the twin evils of the 1970s, inflation or unemployment, the individual voter dreaded more. Consumer prices did rise less rapidly between 1980 and 1984 than they had risen between 1976 and 1980. But unemployment averaged 8.6 percent through the spring of 1984 under Reagan, compared to 6.4 percent in 1980 under Carter. By the election in the fall of 1984, about as many Americans were unemployed as when Reagan took office.

"Reaganomics" made some people "winners" and others "losers." Foreign, especially European, investors benefited, lending money at high rates to finance the U.S. deficit. Foreign workers suffered, for the European investment that might have expanded their own economies and relieved unemployment instead was flowing to the United States. The high interest rates that attracted such investment made the dollar so expensive that foreigners could not afford to buy U.S. products. These factors made those Americans who had to sell abroad—certain industries and most farmers—losers from Reaganomics.

On the other hand, the chief executive officers of large U.S. corporations were clearly winners: they voted themselves salary increases averaging 40 percent in 1983. But many employees of these companies were losers. Over a million manufacturing jobs were lost between 1979 and 1984. For the first time, white males composed less than half of the U.S. work force, outnumbered by lower-paid women. Of the new jobs created by the recovery, most were in the postindustrial service sector, which paid, on average, one-third less than industry.

Being comparatively well insulated against unemployment and benefiting from reduced inflation, members of the suburban middle class were marginal winners. Blacks and the poor in general were losers. More people lived in poverty in the 1980s than at any time since the inauguration of the Great Society programs, many of which the Reagan administration cut or discontinued.

This enumeration of winners and losers helps explain why so many Americans "voted their pocketbooks" in 1984. In the postindustrial United States, whether one was a winner or loser depended largely on how government, through taxation and domestic expenditure, redistributed economic rewards. In the election campaign of 1984, both candidates reassured middle-class voters by reaffirming their commitment to Social Security and Medicare, which consumed about one-third of federal expenditures.

In 1980 the Republican party had moved adroitly to exploit Americans' unhappiness with 1970s stagflation and the social changes of postindustrial society. Already the party of the nation's corporate leadership, it forged an alliance with groups opposed to such innovations as "abortion on demand." Outspending the Democrats five to one, the Republicans were able to set the tone of economic and social debate.

The legacy of the 1960s revolts had left the Democrats divided. Walter F. Mondale, their 1984 candidate, represented what was left of the New Deal coalition. But he had to fight off challenges from Gary Hart, who spoke for the party's affluent suburban wing, and from Jesse Jackson, who continued to represent the cause of Martin Luther King, Jr. Mondale chose a woman, U.S. Representative Geraldine M. Ferraro, as his vice-presidential running mate—a historic milestone. Whether his choice helped or hurt his candidacy is disputed.

Easily brushing aside such divided opposition, Reagan won re-election by a landslide and enjoyed continuing popularity through his second term. Since television news did not attempt to explain the complexities of economics, and Americans drew most of their information from television, relatively few were aware of the warnings of many economists that much was fundamentally amiss with his administration's management of the U.S. economy.

The direst warnings, however, seemed confirmed when on October 19, 1987, the New York Stock Exchange crashed, recording the worst single day's fall of share prices in its history. Though "Black Monday's" fall was not quite as bad as the two-day plunge of October 28 and 29, 1929, it was bad enough. In one day stocks lost almost a quarter of their value, at a cost to those who held them of over $400 billion. Within a few hours, moreover, instantaneous electronic communications carried the wave of panic selling to every stock market around the globe. For months after October 19, economists and a newly anxious public wondered whether, as in 1929, collapse on Wall Street would be the prelude to a global depression.

The root cause of the debacle was, as usual in such panics, that investors had suddenly lost confidence in the economic future, though the plunge was accelerated by a recent innovation of the electronic age: computers programmed to sell huge blocks of stock at a given signal. The loss of confidence stemmed from investors' belated recognition that the United States had insulated itself from the global "quiet depression" of the years since 1973 by a combination of policies that appeared to buoy its economy in the short run but might portend long-run disaster.

"Reaganomics"—the combination of tax cuts for the rich and vastly expanded military spending—created a huge hole in the federal budget that could be filled only by borrowing, issuing obligations that would have to be paid back with interest to their holders at home or abroad. By the time he left office Reagan had added more government debt—which the future would either have to pay or dishonor—than all previous U.S. presidents combined. Some critics charged that his administration had deliberately tripled the federal debt in order to make it impossible for his successors, already so deeply "in the hole," ever again to expand the programs of the guarantor state.

Much of this debt was owed to foreign investors. From 1948 to 1980, the balance between U.S. investments abroad and foreign investment in the United States had always been in U.S. favor, on average by $3 billion annually. In the 1980s this balance reversed: on average the United States obligated itself to pay $76 billion more annually to foreigners than it would collect from them. No longer the world's largest creditor, the United States became the world's largest debtor. Moreover, foreign investors were increasingly less willing to invest in U.S. paper obligations. They sought tangible U.S. property—land, buildings, corporations—in return for the money they poured into the U.S. economy.

At the same time it was thus mortgaging its future, concerned economists pointed out, the United States in the 1980s was neglecting to maintain and upgrade the economic plant that would have to generate the wealth to pay the debt off. While the wealthy bought luxury items such as "stretch" limousines, and Wall Street issued "junk bonds" of dubious worth to pay for the seizure by corporate "raiders" of valuable companies, the United States was investing less in capital equipment than any other industrialized nation except Britain, and less than Americans themselves had invested since World War II. They were putting less money aside than anyone else, saving at less than half the rate of the 1960s, a sure sign that they feared the return of high inflation. The United States spent less for civilian research and development than its rivals, so that by 1987 almost half of U.S. patents were awarded to foreigners, compared to a third in 1977. Above all, the United States continued to run a huge trade deficit, buying more abroad, especially oil, than it sold.

Not only U.S. private citizens and industry were failing to invest in the future. Government's priorities also were elsewhere. The Reagan administration fulfilled its electoral pledges to cut the costs of the guarantor state partly by such measures as closing a quarter of the offices at which the unemployed could seek compensation under a New Deal program. More damagingly, while claiming to return such responsibilities to the states, the Reagan administration spent on grants to education, health, urban renewal, and job training approximately half of what it spent on military aircraft. It rejected the idea that a nation's future well-being depends at least as much on the health of its schools and cities—which lost a quarter of their federal aid—as on its air force.

And yet the guarantor state did not fade away as promised. In 1988 the federal government actually had 150,000 *more* civilian employees than when Reagan took office, partly because such "entitlement" programs as Social Security and Medicare, supported by the middle classes who voted regularly as the poor did not, were not substantially trimmed. Subsidies to agriculture, which now meant primarily corporate agribusinesses, nearly tripled between 1981 and 1988.

In view of the mountain of debt piled up for the future to worry about, the Reagan years appear in retrospect as a kind of economic binge, with the grim awakening of the morning after postponed for his successor to face. Not everyone shared in the self-indulgences of the period, however. In actual purchasing power the incomes of the less wealthy 80 percent of U.S. families actually fell between 1977 and 1988. To keep up, both husband and wife in such families usually had to work and were still forced to resort to an unprecedented expansion of credit—"plastic"—to keep the boom in consumer goods going. Even so, for the first time since World War II, the percentage of Americans who could afford to own their own homes fell after 1980.

To those in this group who might have thought to enhance their earning power by striking, Reagan gave an unambiguous warning in 1981 by firing twelve thousand air traffic controllers who had illegally struck against the government. The 1980s saw many more such episodes of successful strikebreaking, so that by 1988 only 17 percent of the U.S. labor force was still unionized.

In reply to critics, Reagan's defenders retorted with some justification that if the guarantor state had not shrunk, it was because those who benefited from its programs had the ear of the Democratically controlled Congress. As for the economy, Reagan's defenders pointed proudly to the creation of over 14 million new U.S. jobs during the Reagan years, contrasting this achievement with the failure of Western Europe to create any. Indeed, the U.S. unemployment rate was under 6 percent in mid-1988, though Europeans argued that their rates were higher because their governments had actually cut spending rather than run Reagan-style deficits and that nine out of ten of new U.S. jobs were for "temporary" employees, earning few benefits and subject to instant dismissal whenever a recession struck.

Whoever eventually got the better of this argument, it is surprising that after such events as the crash of October 1987, Reagan lost little of his initial popularity even among those groups for whom his policies had created obvious disadvantages. Perhaps the explanation was that Americans now judged political contests not in the light of cold economic interest but rather on the basis of the "image" politicians projected. Reagan's experience as a film actor helped him project his jovial personality over television. But his popularity rested on more than appearances. The widespread belief in his effectiveness had reinvigorated a presidency tarnished by repeated disappointments.

Although Reagan described himself as a conservative, his greatest appeal was to those Americans for whom the transition to a postindustrial society represented a challenge rather than a disaster. To the relatively affluent suburban majority, many programs of the guarantor state now seemed increasingly irrelevant. They applauded his determination to dismantle a system of little personal benefit to them. They welcomed his message that, unhampered by government restraints, they could make the postindustrial age their personal success story, as earlier generations of Americans had made successes of the transition from rural to industrial America. This hope for the future was a welcome change from the political and economic pessimism of the 1970s. Moreover, Reagan's opposition to such innovations as legalized abortion seemed to suggest that the future could be won without abandoning the certainties of the past.

Conclusion: The 1990s Quest for an Alternative Politics

Though Reagan's combination of hope and nostalgia was especially well suited to American audiences, his government represented only the most prominent example of conservative resurgence in the 1980s. In much of the developed world, the dogma of the decade was the need to return to free enterprise, whatever the cost. Conservatives everywhere proclaimed that they had finally reversed the trend to government intervention in the world's economies begun during World War I and much heightened after World War II.

Conservatives' confidence could only be reinforced in the 1990s as they noted the continuous decline in France of Mitterrand's Socialist party. The Socialists' fall, like Labour's defeat in Britain, raised a serious question whether democratic socialism was not as doomed to extinction by the end of the century as Soviet communism had proved to be. Mitterrand's dilemma—of trying to improve the lot of the disadvantaged while simultaneously remaining politically respectable with the contented majority in French society—had long haunted parties of the democratic Left. Yet the Socialists' disastrous defeat in parliamentary elections in March 1993 suggested that democratic socialism as it had long been conceived had little relevance to the problems of the 1990s, which were really only the French case of the difficulties of postindustrial society. Socialism had developed since the late nineteenth century as a movement of hope for the working class of the industrial era. Just as much as capitalism, it had taken for granted the inevitability of economic growth, seeking only to distribute the products of growth more equitably. But for an economy where growth had slowed and industry was in decline, and for a society dominated by white-collar workers anxious to preserve what they had earned from the grasp of the state, Mitterrand seemed unable to find an answer very different from that of conservative governments elsewhere.

The conservative public mood of the 1980s had reminded many social critics of the complacent mood of the 1920s. Both were decades in which governments of the Left were, like Mitterrand's majority between 1981 and 1986, rare, short-lived, and disappointing. Conservative leaders like Calvin Coolidge in the 1920s and Reagan in the 1980s convinced their publics that the problems both of their own societies and of an increasingly interdependent world were best addressed by minimizing the role of government and leaving each individual and nation to pursue goals of enlightened selfishness, just as nineteenth-century European economic liberalism had prescribed. In this "culture of contentment,"[5] the prosperous—a majority of voters though a minority of the population—remained absorbed by the enjoyment of their own prosperity, while the less fortunate found little reason to stir from their habitual political indifference.

Yet the history of George Bush's presidency (1988–1992)—a story of a decline in popularity at least as great as Mitterrand's—showed that the complacent mood of the 1980s in the United States would not survive a worsening economy. The deepening recession of the 1990s, though statistically not as severe as the "Reagan recession" of 1981–1982, was alarmingly different in that it seemed to threaten the economic well-being of the "contented." As even middle-class Americans began to experience by 1992 some of the economic fears and political frustrations that Europeans had faced almost continuously since the 1970s, they began to react in similar ways, restlessly searching for an effective authority that would quiet their fears. The economic sluggishness of the 1970s had led to the triumphs in the 1980s of Mitterrand, Thatcher, and Reagan (and his heir-apparent, George Bush). But in the 1990s, economic hard times equally discredited the democratic socialism of Mitterand and the nineteenth-century liberalism of Reagan, Bush, and Thatcher. Anxious voters in all of the Western democracies seemed determined to turn to new leaders or movements that might grapple more effectively with worldwide recession. What these new leaders and movements stood for was not entirely clear—and perhaps not important. It was what they were *against*—politics as usual—that attracted both formerly contented and formerly apathetic citizens on both sides of the Atlantic.

In the United States, the demand for a new politics by voters equally mistrustful of Bush and his Democratic challenger, Bill Clinton, reflected a belated recognition of the long-term decline of the nation's economy even during the years of apparent Reagan prosperity—a decline accelerated by the stubbornly persistent recession that began in 1990. The root causes of the recession that devastated Bush's popularity could be found in the economic policies of his predecessor. Reagan's advisers had claimed that tax cuts for the wealthy would stimulate a wave of productive investment that would ultimately benefit all Americans. In fact it stimulated much unplanned waste, like the tax-advantaged construction of new downtown office space of which a fifth still stood vacant in the 1990s. Meanwhile, the money the U.S. government needed for its vast entitlement programs and for its military buildup was borrowed, mainly from foreign lenders. The revenues collected from the middle class and poorer payers onto whom the tax burden was shifted had increasingly to be committed to paying these lenders back, to servicing a government debt growing in the 1990s at the rate of $1 billion *a day,* rather than to making investments (in research or education, for example) that would strengthen the economy's productive capacity. At the same time the government's usual Keynesian weapon against recession—enhanced government spending to restart the economy—could not be used in the face of so intimidating a burden of debt.

Consumer purchases could not be expected to restart the economy because most consumers had little to spend. The rewards of the economic revival after the Reagan recession of the early 1980s had been very unequally shared. The 1980s in fact witnessed a growth in economic inequality unparalleled in U.S. history. By 1989 the wealthiest 1 percent of the population owned 37 percent of the nation's net worth, up from 31 percent in 1983. These fewer-than-a-million households owned more than the least wealthy 90 percent of the population, some 85 million families. Their holdings included half of the publicly owned stocks, three-fifths of the United States's business assets, and almost four-fifths of the bonds and trusts. Of course these wealthiest people lived a lifestyle very different from that of ordinary Americans. One economist characterized this different lifestyle as the "secession of the rich" from American society, as higher-income people withdrew to suburban strongholds protected from intrusion by an army of private security forces that well outnumbered the police.

Meanwhile, the vast majority of less fortunate Americans fared even worse in the 1980s than they had earlier. By the 1990s, many economists were reaching the sobering conclusion that the "American dream" of success through hard work from one generation to the next was becoming a less and less realistic prospect for most families. From the end of World War II through the early 1970s, American average family income had risen by over 100 percent. But from the 1970s to the 1990s

A Ford engine block plant in Chihuahua, Mexico. *To American readers the logo on the workers' shirts is familiar: the quality-control slogan suspended over the line, however, is in Spanish. These Mexicans earn less than twelve per cent of the wage of workers doing comparable work in Detroit.* *Mike Boroff/Texas Stock*

the gain was only 9 percent, and even this was achieved only by sending additional family members out to work. The purchasing power of single breadwinners actually shrank during this period. Part of the explanation for the failure of incomes to grow lies in the shift in postindustrial America of many millions from high-paying factory jobs to lower-paid service jobs. Yet it was not only the high school dropouts or graduates who filled many of these positions who faced dimmer job prospects in the 1980s. By the end of the decade, one in five college graduates was employed in a job in which college-level skills were neither required nor paid for.

It was not only the level of their wages that made so many Americans feel economically vulnerable. Almost 40 percent of working Americans were not covered by an employer-sponsored health-care program against the exploding costs of medical treatment, and the proportion covered by a pension plan fell from 50 percent in 1980 to 40 percent in the 1990s. This lack of coverage reflected the fact that businesses were relying increasingly on "temporary" workers—almost a quarter of the U.S. work force.

All these vulnerabilities help explain the apprehension a majority of Americans felt when the economy dipped into recession in 1990. In that year the foreign lenders whose investments had kept the U.S. economy afloat had more essential uses for their money: the Japanese to refloat their own now-troubled economy, the Germans to finance the reconstruction of the formerly communist sector of their country. Average Americans were in no position to take their place, for they were struggling to keep up with the bills by working longer hours, charging purchases that could not be deferred, or borrowing against the equity they held in their homes if they were fortunate enough to own one, as fewer and fewer were.

In this atmosphere of anxiety the familiar vicious cycle of an economic downturn quickly developed. As investment declined, earnings dwindled, and people consequently bought less. As consumption fell, businesses and even governments sought to cut costs by cutting payrolls. The chill of fear produced by these layoffs reduced business still further, forcing employers to further cuts, and so it went. In this climate industries that had already found themselves uncompetitive in the global marketplace concluded that they had no choices but to "downsize" or emigrate. General Motors, the world's largest business, "downsized." Losing half a billion dollars a month, the automaker, which had closed 19 factories since 1986, announced just before Christmas 1991 that it would close 21 of its remaining 125 plants and get rid of some 70,000 employees. Late in 1992, Smith-Corona, the last American typewriter manufacturer, decided to emigrate. It announced that it would close its one remaining U.S. plant, opened before World War I, and move to Mexico. It would lay off 875 of its remaining 1,300 employees, the last of the 4,400 people the factory had employed as recently as the 1970s. For this multinational company, half-owned by a British conglomerate and already making office machines in Malaysia and Singapore, the most immediate benefit of emigration would be an 80 percent cut in its wage costs. In its new location, it would become only one of some 1,800 U.S. or Japanese-owned factories just across the U.S. border, employing a half-million Mexicans at wages as low as 55 cents an hour to produce goods for the U.S. marketplace.

Such layoffs as those of General Motors and Smith-Corona seemed only good business to the companies' shareholders, since reduced costs eventually implied renewed dividends. However, unprecedented features of the recession of the 1990s alarmed many people who owned such shares. In earlier recessions, the loss of manufacturing jobs had been compensated for in part by the growth of employment in services. Now, however, the service sector was also cutting payrolls. In both manufacturing and services, moreover, businesses that were not particularly hard hit by recession were laying employees off, frankly admitting that they did not intend to rehire them when the recession ended. Worst of all, in this recession, in contrast to earlier ones, corporations were laying off blue-collar and white-collar workers in almost equal proportions. Managers, scientists, and engineers were no longer assured of a job: they constituted 40 percent of the employees laid off in 1991. Even firms versed in the new technologies that had once created jobs were now abolishing them. IBM, for example, having shed some 65,000 mainly white-collar employees between 1986 and 1991, planned to oust a further 20,000 in the 1990s.

Amid such economic contraction, the pay raises of college graduates—the managers and professionals who had best weathered the 1980s—fell below even the low rates of inflation prevailing after 1989. For the college graduates of 1991, job prospects were fewer than at any time since the early 1970s. Economic anxiety thus was no longer limited to the people on the lowest rungs of the economic ladder: the nearly 10 percent of Americans who had to supplement their incomes with food stamps, and blacks whose unemployment rate was double that of whites. (Almost one out of four male blacks, in his twenties was either in prison or on parole or probation in the 1990s, constituting a large proportion of a convict population that had become the largest criminal class, in relation to total population, in the world.)

Bush's defeat at the polls in November 1992 reflected the fact that his administration had recorded the worst economic scores of any presidency since World War II (though he and his supporters blamed this record on the Democratic Congress, with whom he had rarely agreed). In the 1990s U.S. economic growth slowed to rates comparable to those of the Depression—only half the rates of the 1960s. More people—11 percent of whites and 32 percent of blacks—met the official definition of poverty—a $14,000 income for a family of four—than at any time since Johnson had launched his Great Society programs in the mid-1960s.

It did not help Bush's image that he was perceived by many Americans as indifferent to the concerns that frightened them, basically as unconvinced as Hoover had been that government could do anything about the recession except wait for the economy to cycle back to prosperity. Reagan in 1980 and 1984, and Bush in 1988, had defeated Democratic challengers by firmly identifying with the moral and economic aims of the suburban middle class while depicting Democrats as so subservient to the inner-city poor that they encouraged crime. (One notorious Bush TV "spot" in 1988 depicted a prison with a kind of revolving door through which Bush's opponent was supposedly allowing vicious criminals like the rapist Willie Horton to go free.) Under better economic circumstances, a similar campaign in 1992 might have seemed certain to assure a Bush victory, for this was the first election during which a near-majority of the U.S. population—46 percent—lived in suburbs (compared to only 23 percent in 1950). Moreover, suburbanites were likelier to vote than the poor. In 1988, when 57 percent of Americans had voted, only a third of the unemployed went to the polls, compared to three-quarters of business executives and professionals.

In 1992, however, the best evidence that many even in such once "contented" groups were rejecting Bush was the startling support for the independent presidential campaign of Ross Perot. Perot was a self-made Texan, president of one of the world's largest producers of computer software. So large was his personal fortune that it was calculated that if he spent $100 million to get himself elected, it would cost him only $3 out of every $100 he had. Yet he was far from a typical leader of American industry. American industrial leadership with its "free-enterprise" slogans, he contended, had much to learn from the very different system of "organized capitalism" of Germany and Japan—a radical idea abhorrent to conventional conservatives like Bush, who preached that government involvement in the economy could only be harmful.

In 1992 Perot first disclosed such unorthodox ideas on television talk shows, where he also volunteered to be drafted for president. Once elected, he proposed to replace the deadlocked processes of the United States' eighteenth-century Constitution with the direct democracy that twentieth-century technology made possible: an "electronic town hall." After a televised debate, critical national decisions would be made by citizens casting votes by touch-tone telephone.

Perot actually won 19 percent of the vote in the presidential race of 1992, compared to 43 percent for the victor, Clinton. This outcome reflected the vast outpouring of volunteer support Perot's challenge to the conventional politics of the two-party system evoked. During the first three weeks of his candidacy, his office received a million phone calls offering support. Moreover, this support came not only from fellow computer tycoons and financiers but from hundreds of thousands of people of all backgrounds, all attracted by his unconventional mixture of conservative and liberal themes. The Perot phenomenon was additional compelling evidence of many Americans' deep concern that their economy had not just cyclically slowed but was sliding into decay, that future generations could not expect the higher standard of living earlier ones had taken for granted, and that the old political parties were equally incapable of stopping this decline.

The support for such an unusual savior as Perot was only the American example of worldwide frustration at economic stagnation and the fumbling inability of ordinary politicians of Left or Right to even address it, let alone fix it. In Europe, too, frustration was manifest, though in the absence of a potential savior, frustration was expressed there mainly by persecuting scapegoats, especially the growing numbers of poor non-Europeans whom the shrinking of the globe was bringing to the continent as refugees. In depressed eastern Germany, where the privatization or closing of former state-run and overstaffed enterprises had created unemployment rates ranging up to 40 percent, bands of youths hurling firebombs, shouting Nazi slogans like "Germany for the Germans" and raising their arms in the Hitler salute, battled police in the streets. They sought to torch the group homes in which refugees, who were entering Germany at the rate of at least a thousand a day, were temporarily housed. Significantly, these rioting youths were often cheered by the local populace, who blamed refugees subsidized by the government for their own economic misery (though the law prohibited refugees from working). The resentment directed at these wretched fugitives, some from as far away as tropical Africa, by youths and townsfolk alike was an expression of something deeper, akin to the feelings that drew many Americans to Perot: a conviction that they had been abandoned to economic despair by an uncaring democratic political system. So far in Germany no one movement has mobilized these angry masses, though, significantly, political parties whose leaders do not repudiate the Nazi past, as was once obligatory, now hold seats in three of the sixteen state legislatures. (Meanwhile, in France the far-right National Front almost matched the Socialist vote with a campaign that blamed African immigrants for the country's economic paralysis.)

These movements were a reminder that in Europe, with communism in collapse and socialism discredited, the alternative politics produced by frustration might take the form of a renewed fascism. The mayor of one German city whose people had applauded the anti-refugee rioters sadly warned his constituents, "This is how something began that ended at Auschwitz."[6] Of course such an analogy is much overdrawn. The triumph of fascism in the 1930s resulted from the fear generated by a far more devastated world economy than that of the 1990s. Still, Europeans and perhaps even Americans should remember, as the twentieth century nears its end, that some of its worst episodes began when people frustrated by the inability of traditional politics to fix the economy turned for salvation to men and movements they would in happier times have rejected as odd and marginal.

Notes

1. Richard J. Barnet, *The Alliance: America-Europe-Japan, Makers of the Postwar World* (New York: Simon and Schuster, 1983), p. 206.

2. J. Robert Wegs, *Europe Since 1945: A Concise History,* 2d ed. (New York: St. Martin's Press, 1984), p. 168.
3. *New York Times,* May 28, 1988.
4. Barnet, *The Alliance,* p. 274.
5. John Kenneth Galbraith, *The Culture of Contentment* (Boston: Houghton Mifflin, 1992).
6. *New York Times,* September 6, 1992.

Suggestions for Further Reading and Viewing

Books

Ardagh, John. *France Today* (1988).

Barnet, Richard J. *The Alliance: America-Europe-Japan, Makers of the Postwar World* (1983).

Bolter, J. David. *Turing's Man: Western Culture in the Computer Age* (1984).

Edsall, Thomas B. *The New Politics of Inequality* (1984).

Faludi, Susan. *Backlash: The Undeclared War Against Women* (1991).

Garreau, Joel. *The Nine Nations of North America* (1981).

Gilbert, James. *Another Chance: Postwar America 1945–1968* (1981).

Hacker, Andrew. *Two Nations: Black and White, Separate, Hostile, Unequal* (1992).

Jenkins, Peter. "Goodbye to All That." *New York Review of Books,* May 14, 1992.

Kavanagh, Dennis. *Thatcherism and British Politics: The End of Consensus?* 2d ed. (1990).

Lasch, Christopher. *The Culture of Narcissism: American Life in an Age of Diminishing Expectations* (1979).

Lukacs, John. *Outgrowing Democracy: A History of the United States in the Twentieth Century* (1986).

Priaulx, Allan, and Stanford J. Ungar. *The Almost Revolution: France 1968* (1969).

Ranney, Austin. *Channels of Power: The Impact of Television on American Politics* (1983).

Singer, Daniel. *Is Socialism Doomed? The Meaning of Mitterrand* (1988).

Toffler, Alvin. *Future Shock* (1971).

Wegs, J. Robert. *Europe Since 1945: A Concise History*. 2d ed. (1984).

Woloch, Nancy. *Women and the American Experience* (1984).

Films

American Dream (1990). An Oscar-winning documentary on the collapse of a strike in 1986.

Berkeley in the 1960s (1990). A documentary on the campus struggles of the Vietnam era.

CHAPTER 14

The Soviet Union and Eastern Europe from Stalin to Yeltsin

Readers of our account in Chapter 12 of the era of renewed bipolar confrontation in the first half of the 1980s might expect that the history of the Soviet bloc since the death of Stalin, to which we turn in this chapter, would bear little resemblance to the history of the Western world we examined in the last chapter. What could the history of the "evil empire" (as President Reagan once called it) possibly have in common with that of the democracies of Western Europe and North America? Were not the basic differences of these two kinds of society enough to explain their almost constant confrontation since they together defeated Hitler in 1945?

Of course there were fundamental differences in political institutions, social values, and economic systems between the two blocs. Stalin's quarter-century of dictatorship, from the late 1920s to his death in 1953, imposed on the USSR a system whose every feature flouted the values of the free society in which most Americans and Western Europeans believed. Moreover, he ruthlessly replicated that system in the Eastern European countries the Soviets overran in the war against Hitler: the German Democratic Republic, Poland, Hungary, Czechoslovakia, Romania, and Bulgaria. After Stalin, the central theme of the history of both the USSR and these satellites was the struggle of the post-Stalin Communist leadership to modify his system in order to make it more economically effective in an increasingly competitive global marketplace, without relinquishing political control. At the end of the 1980s, Soviet Communist Party General Secretary Mikhail Gorbachev and his colleagues, the leaders of the Eastern European "People's Democracies," were still wrestling with this Stalinist legacy.

If we ask *why* it was that Gorbachev and the Eastern Europeans felt compelled to try to reshape the Stalinist model of economics and politics, however, we discover that they were reacting to many of the same twentieth-century global trends—world interdependency, mass political mobilization, the dramatically accelerated and economically disruptive pace of technological change—that we have just seen at work in the West. Russian history before and under Stalin already reflected the impact of these global trends. The tsar's empire on the eve of World War I had curiously combined innovation and cultural conservatism. It was already the world's fifth-ranking industrial power, its city-dwelling intellectuals and revolutionaries aspiring to the most radical change. Yet in its rural villages, life still proceeded largely in accordance with the rhythms of culturally conservative societies elsewhere in the world. Stalin's collectivization of agriculture, as we saw in Chapter 4, forever smashed that tradition-bound rural society. When collectivization was accomplished, at a cost of millions of lives lost to deportation and famine, the orientation of Soviet society toward rapid change could no longer be doubted. Indeed, Stalin's USSR joyfully celebrated the triumph of human technology over nature: the image of a giant dam harnessing previously untamed waters to generate electricity was one of its favorite symbols.

Stalin's government made tremendous efforts to mobilize every Soviet citizen in the struggle for economic modernization. Not that it sought each citizen's free-willed assent; dissenters, in fact, faced exile to concentration camps or execution. Yet the contribution of every individual to the USSR's collective effort was essential to demonstrate to the world a new model of society. Nothing less could realize Stalin's goal of "socialism in one country," a society built on the principle of absolute economic equality and ultimately on true communism, the abolition of private property. This society was to be developed in isolation from the contaminating influences of the hostile capitalist world. Belief in socialism and Soviet patriotism thus became synonymous, a supreme Stalinist value to replace the discredited religious values of earlier centuries.

In its attempt to ignore global interdependency, Stalinism ran counter to one of the dominant realities of the twentieth century, though in its obsession with mass mobilization and with technological development it seemed at first to be very much in step with the times. As these trends continued after 1953, however, they revealed Stalin's legacy as less and less appropriate for resolving the problems of a modern and fully developed society like the USSR.

Growing global interdependency showed the Stalinist policy of enforced isolation of the Soviet bloc to be economically damaging, once the transfer of technology from one country to another became so critical to a nation's prosperity. Decades of continuous manipulative mass mobilization, affording every citizen a vote but no choice of candidates, produced widespread and corrosive cynicism and apathy. Growing technological sophistication undermined government control of ideas: by the 1980s anyone in the USSR could start an underground opposition newspaper by getting hold of a second-hand word processor and printer, increasingly common tools of the fully developed society to which most Soviets and Eastern Europeans—and their leaders—aspired. At the same time, such disasters as the accident at the Soviet nuclear reactor at Chernobyl in April 1986, which spread radioactive fallout halfway around the world, reminded the Marxist Soviets, like their Western adversaries, of the potential dangers that lurk in humankind's continuing technological triumphs. Marxism's quarrel had never been with economic development—only with the distribution of its benefits. But in the 1980s an increasingly vocal movement of "Red Greens" appeared, ready to question whether the economic benefits expected from such vast engineering projects as damming the Leningrad estuary truly outweighed the potential environmental damage.

Thus in Eastern as in Western industrial societies, a growing unease about the global future led many people to hope for more intelligent and innovative political leadership. To such people in Eastern Europe and the USSR, the stale official rhetoric of the Stalinist past seemed as irrelevant as the slogans of Reagan and Thatcher did to some in the West. In both the East and the West, conservatives clung all the more tenaciously to the political and economic principles of the past as they seemed more threatened by the proponents of change. Yet as the need for change became ever more acute, the Communist party's Politburo at last faced up to it in March 1985, naming Mikhail Gorbachev as the party's general secretary—the post Stalin had held. Gorbachev soon made clear that to achieve his goal of a humane and democratic though still socialist USSR, he was as determined to reject Stalin's legacy in domestic policy as he was willing, as we saw in Chapter 12, to reverse Stalin's foreign policy of implacable suspicion of the Western democracies.

As we shall see in the second section of this chapter, when Gorbachev looked to the immediate Soviet past for inspiration, he found few encouraging precedents. The first attempt to dismantle the Stalinist system, by Stalin's successor Nikita Khrushchev, ended in failure with his dismissal in 1964. By loosening the Soviet hold on the satellites, however, Khrushchev allowed their leaders, each in his own way, to begin reshaping his country's economic and even political system. We shall examine in the third section the contrasting cases of Hungary, Czechoslovakia, and Poland. Despite the spread of economic unorthodoxy among the satellites, in the USSR itself the years of Leonid Brezhnev's leadership, from the 1960s until his death in 1982, were an era of lost opportunities, stagnation, corruption, and disillusionment. As the fourth section will reveal, hardly anyone believed in Stalinist values anymore, but bureaucratic inertia kept much of the system in place while the Soviet economy drifted into ever-greater difficulties from the 1970s onward.

Gorbachev's attempts at economic and political reforms, we shall discover in the fifth section of this chapter, only accelerated the collapse of the Soviet Union—an event so stupendous that some historians think it marks the end of the twentieth century as 1914 marked its beginning. In the last two sections of this chapter, we shall see how the former satellites have fared since the collapse of communism, and how, after the dissolution of the Soviet Union, its largest remnant, the Russian Republic, has struggled, under the presidency of Boris Yeltsin, with political deadlock, economic chaos, social disintegration, and psychic demoralization.

Stalin's Legacy

Western visitors to the countries of the former Soviet Union are sometimes surprised by the nostalgia for the Stalinist years they encounter among some of their hosts. The explanation is surely pride in and identification with the Soviet achievement of modernization under Stalin. The USSR tripled its industrial work force between 1928 and 1940, on its way to becoming not the world's fifth industrial power but the second. Under the last of the tsars, only one Russian in four could read and write. By the beginning of World War II, four out of five were literate.

The governmental system that imposed such dramatic economic and cultural changes, however, was one that nobody who had personally experienced it would want to re-create.

Politically, Stalinism meant the personal dictatorship of one man who was held up as a model for virtual worship—a "cult of personality"—by a whole society. Pictures of the all-powerful, all-knowing Stalin loomed everywhere, the inspiration for the omnipresent portraits of "Big Brother" in George Orwell's novel *1984.* Economically, Stalinism meant what has been called the "command economy," in which central planners in Moscow ministries commanded from the managers of the government-owned factories ever-increasing quotas of heavy industrial goods produced with quantity, not quality, as the criterion of success. Socially, though the goal of the USSR at some unspecified future time was a society not divided into classes of differing wealth and privileges, Stalinism in practice meant a hierarchical society in which Communist party members enjoyed greater prestige and privileges than ordinary citizens and the people holding the top 3 percent of the jobs in the party, the *nomenklatura,* had the greatest prestige and privileges of all. Under Stalin, however, even these top party members lived in an atmosphere of constant fear for their lives, for culturally, Stalinism meant "thought control"—the prevention of disloyal thinking—by the imposition of mass terror. There was no one who did not need to fear the midnight knock of the secret police at the door, the prelude to arbitrary condemnation to death or years in a concentration camp. Even the most conservative estimates conclude that some half-million party members were executed in Stalin's Great Terror of 1934–1939, which also incarcerated nearly 4 million people under atrocious conditions in the camps.

Moreover, the Stalinist system strove to have Soviet citizens internalize the norms of obedience that the police and the camps enforced by sanctifying as heroes people who carried that obedience to extremes other societies might find inconceivable. For example, Stalin's propagandists glorified Pavlik Morozov, whose name was to be found in many Soviet textbooks, on schools and summer camps, on monuments, and even on a Moscow street. Son of a peasant but a loyal Young Pioneer (member of the Communist youth movement), thirteen-year-old Pavlik in 1932 denounced his father to the authorities for hiding part of his grain harvest from the government collectors. When his father's hoarding accomplices vengefully murdered Pavlik, he became a martyr to Stalinist morality, which put loyalty to the state higher than fidelity to one's own family. In Stalinist eyes, such a code was justified by the belief that the only hope for the future of humankind lay in the survival of the USSR, the homeland of revolution, in a uniformly hostile world. Thus any act that endangered Soviet survival, even the hoarding of grain, was a crime against the future of humanity, punishable without appeal.

As we saw in Chapter 4, historians still debate whether this terrifying system was the logical outgrowth of the kind of revolution Lenin and the Bolsheviks had made in 1917. The least that can be said is that Stalin could not have created this system without eliminating the opposition, both Left and Right, of most of his old Bolshevik colleagues. The left opposition was led by Leon Trotsky, the brilliant commander-in-chief of the Red Army during the civil wars that followed the revolution. Trotsky feared that if revolutionary momentum was lost, the movement would degenerate into bureaucratic dictatorship, as revolutions historically have often done. To keep up the momentum, he favored fomenting further revolution abroad and forcing through rapid industrialization at home by "squeezing" surplus capital from the peasants. A contrary view was held by the right opposition, led by Nikolai Bukharin. He had been the designer of the New Economic Policy (NEP) of 1921, which had returned small business and agriculture to private entrepreneurs. Bukharin believed the revolution's only hope lay in winning over

Russia's rural majority. He rejected the gospel of centralized economic planning, fearing that it would stifle the revolution under a cumbersome and oppressive planning apparatus.

Both men paid with their lives for their disagreement with Stalin, who first aligned himself with the Right to crush the Left, then turned on the Right. Trotsky was expelled from the USSR in 1929 and murdered, on Stalin's orders, in exile in 1940. In one of the most dramatic of the "show trials" of the Great Terror, Bukharin was framed as a Nazi spy and executed in 1938. His name, like Trotsky's, disappeared from the official histories of the revolution. Only after a half-century, under Gorbachev, was Bukharin posthumously exonerated. Only then did Gorbachev allow the truth about the Stalinist chapter of communist history to be publicly told—a truth so damning that the party did not long outlive its revelation.

Khrushchev and the Limits of Reform, 1953–1964

As long as Stalin was alive, even his closest associates of the Politburo—the dozen or so men delegated by the Central Committee of the Communist party of the USSR to direct the party and through it the nation—were not safe from the fates of Trotsky and Bukharin. Not surprisingly, when he died, they all agreed that no individual should ever again concentrate so much power in his own hands. Many of them were convinced that Stalin had made disastrous mistakes: in neglecting rural Russia, for example, or in failing to channel some of the gains of the growing Soviet economy into improving the standard of living of ordinary citizens, or in entrusting Soviet science to those whose chief qualification was ideological conformity rather than experimental brilliance. But their motive in vowing to prevent a future dictatorship was simpler than criticism of Stalin's policies. They wanted to end the terror that had hung over their own heads and over the heads of ordinary citizens. After 1953 the USSR always had a "collective leadership," a system of shared responsibility at the top, even when one individual such as Khrushchev or Gorbachev got most of the Western headlines.

On Stalin's death the supreme authority was officially vested in three top Politburo members, including Lavrenty P. Beria, chief of the secret police. Nikita S. Khrushchev (1894–1971), who assumed one of Stalin's old posts as general secretary of the Communist party, was not a member of this trio. Yet it was he who emerged within a few years as the dominant, though not dictatorial, leader of the USSR. The first to fall in the struggle for power was Beria, the dreaded living reminder of Stalinist terror. Arrested on behalf of his colleagues by the army (who could prevent his clinging to power with the armed backing of his police), he met the usual fate of Soviet political losers: execution. Beria's fall was followed by a general amnesty for political prisoners. Never again would the secret police be quite as powerful, though their prestige would rise again when Brezhnev consolidated his power after Khrushchev's fall. From 1953 to 1957 Khrushchev acquired more and more power until in the latter year his rivals tried to fire him. Mobilizing a fleet of military planes to fly members of the Central Committee to Moscow from all over the USSR, Khrushchev turned the tables on his opponents and won a crucial vote of confidence. He then proceeded to drive them from office, castigating them as an "anti-Party" group. Unlike Stalin, whose dual posts as first secretary of the Communist party and prime minister he now assumed, Khrushchev left his fallen enemies their lives.

Thus arrived at the summit of the Soviet hierarchy a former coal miner, still illiterate when he joined the party as a young man in

1918. Coarse, bullying, impetuous, he was nonetheless a true believer in the goals of Lenin's revolution, to which he owed everything. Though he had climbed the ranks by showing an unquestioning devotion to the party line under Stalin, he had already startled the world in 1956 by his speech to the Soviet Party Congress denouncing the crimes and errors of his former master. Now he hoped to rekindle faith in the goals of the Revolution after the years of Stalinist darkness. He knew that this would require basic changes in Soviet direction.

In domestic as in foreign policy, Khrushchev lashed out with initiatives of all sorts. Infuriated by the poor yields of Soviet agriculture, he frankly admitted that after over a generation of collective farming the USSR stabled fewer cattle than it had in 1917. To remedy such deficiencies he championed an ambitious program to plant new strains of hybrid corn on previously uncultivated land. To improve industrial productivity, and to scatter potential centers of bureaucratic resistance to his innovations, he launched the first of many Soviet attempts to decentralize economic decision making. A man of humble origins, Khrushchev was scandalized by the emergence under a supposedly socialist government of a new privileged class: fewer than half of Moscow's university students, he discovered, came from peasant or worker families. To restore equality of opportunity, his educational reforms abolished college entrance examinations and gave priority in admissions to young people applying from factories. He also insisted that the children of white-collar families, including party members, who made up the majority of students, should have experience on the factory floor.

Khrushchev seemed of mixed mind on the issue of allowing the Soviet people greater freedom of ideas. Perhaps because it helped discredit Stalin, he permitted the publication of Alexandr Solzhenitsyn's *One Day in the Life of Ivan Denisovich,* a searing depiction of life in a concentration camp. He also authorized the first exhibition of modern art the USSR had seen since Stalin imposed the style of Socialist Realism. On the other hand his regime closed half of the USSR's remaining churches, in line with the old Marxist idea that religion for the masses was like an addictive drug.

In 1961 the party's new program confidently predicted that the USSR would make the transition to "full Communism" and equal abundance for all by 1980. By that year, Khrushchev was fond of boasting, the USSR's gross national product would surpass that of the United States. All of his boasting was in vain, however, for most of his domestic schemes went just as awry as his bid to attain superpower nuclear parity by installing missiles in Cuba had done. After a bad harvest in 1963, he had to face the embarrassment of buying grain abroad to feed his people. Industrial decentralization seemed to produce only confusion. Educators and parents alike sabotaged his university reforms. His limited concessions to intellectual freedom frightened conservatives but failed to satisfy progressives. Meanwhile, Khrushchev's penchant for upheaval thwarted the career of many a party functionary: the membership of the Central Committee changed faster in the late 1950s than at any other time since Stalin's great purges. Even though he had named a majority among them, Khrushchev could not rally support as he had in 1957 when in 1964 the Politburo informed him he had "resigned." Ousted from power, he quickly faded from view, though at least one of his innovations survived: as he had not executed his opponents, they left him to die in peaceful retirement.

Khrushchev's chapter in Soviet history raised serious questions about the extent to which new leadership could transform the Soviet system. Khrushchev was a partial reformer, seeking to disarm the Stalinist mechanism of terror without bringing into question the rule of his party over Soviet society. Ironically, the frustration of his program suggests why Stalinists believed terror was essential to enforce change. No longer living in the same fear, the vast party bureaucracy—and all the other interest groups in Soviet society—simply opposed to Khrushchev's hasty initiatives the massive weight of their own inertia. The fact that they successfully thwarted him, however, did not lessen their resentment at his attempts to shake them up. Lacking, to his own credit, Stalin's means of coercion, Khrushchev might have succeeded in reform if he had been able to mobilize Soviet public opinion behind him. But such a genuine mobilization of enthusiasm may not be possible in a population so long unaccustomed to real political choices.

The Restive Satellites from the 1950s Through the 1980s

Among the many policies his colleagues alleged Khrushchev had bungled was his management of relations with the Eastern European satellite states. In fact, Khrushchev's "de-Stalinizing" policies toward Eastern Europe did launch the satellites toward a very different kind of communist society from the model Stalin had imposed on them after World War II. In this evolution, the way was led by Hungary, Poland, and for a tragically brief moment, Czechoslovakia. Despite important differences in pace and detail, developments in these countries followed a common pattern. After a bold assertion of national independence led by patriotic Communists was crushed by a Soviet invasion or the threat of one, the new and apparently servile leadership the Soviets installed then proceeded, cautiously and over many years, to diverge from Soviet orthodoxy in some of the ways the rebels they replaced had demanded. This progressive dilution of the full rigors of Communist rule made it easier at the end of the 1980s, when Gorbachev declared that each country could find its own "way to socialism" without the threat of Soviet invasion, for power to be transferred relatively peacefully to non-Communist governments.

Much of the explanation for Stalin's iron rule over Eastern Europe was to be found in his conflict with Marshal Tito, the Communist leader of Yugoslavia. Tito's guerrillas had come to dominate the Yugoslavians' resistance to the Nazi invaders and had freed their country from Hitler virtually without Soviet help—a very different situation from the rest of Eastern Europe. Standing on his own ground, Tito had no intention of submitting to Stalin's postwar direction. Enraged by Tito's repeated challenges to his authority, Stalin withdrew Soviet advisers, severed economic ties, and finally expelled Yugoslavia from the international Communist movement, the Comintern. By 1949, Tito was looking to the West to counterbalance Soviet hostility. Yugoslavia, which developed its own special brand of worker-managed economy, soon became not only the first unorthodox Communist nation but the first "nonaligned" one, setting an example of refusal to choose between East and West that many Third World nations would later follow. Such a spectacular defection was of course humiliating for the USSR. As part of his anti-Stalinist program, Khrushchev hastened to heal the breach with Tito, publicly admitting that each nation of Eastern Europe had the right to choose its own road to socialism. Such an admission sent a signal that Khrushchev did not intend, prompting others in Eastern Europe to seek comparable autonomy.

Hungary

The predictable anti-Soviet explosion came to Hungary in October 1956. Since 1949, Hungary

Hungarian Revolt, 1956. *Hungarian patriots crowd aboard a captured Soviet tank moving up to attack Soviet troops during the bloody street fighting in Budapest in 1956.* *Erich Lessing/Magnum Photos*

had been a typical People's Republic, ruled by men from whom Stalin knew he could expect slavish obedience. (Fearing the appearance of new Titos, Stalin had purged all the Eastern European Communist parties of anyone suspected of valuing patriotism more than loyalty to the USSR.) Symbolized by its hated secret police, this regime had begun the collectivization of agriculture and the rapid development of heavy industry geared to fulfilling Soviet needs. These new factories guaranteed full employment; but in this workers' state, as in the rest of the Soviet bloc, workers had no right to strike. In the drab society of the "command economy," obedience was imposed by the usual Stalinist method of mass terror.

In 1956 the vast patriotic resentment such a regime provoked was revealed when the secret police fired on a student-led protest demonstration. As in some of the great revolutions of the nineteenth century, the government's authority collapsed when the army, sent in to repress the rioters, instead took their side. A new multiparty government emerged, headed by Imre Nagy, a Communist but an outspoken anti-Stalinist. Briefly serving as prime minister after Stalin's death, he had released political prisoners, reversed the collectivization of agriculture, and sought to increase the availability of consumer goods until his Stalinist colleagues forced him out. Returning in 1956 as the leader of a national revolt, he requested the removal of the Soviet armed forces from Hungary. But his brand of nationalist communism was not enough by now to satisfy many of the rebels, who demanded an end to Communist rule and full national independence. Under their pressure, Nagy withdrew Hungary from the Warsaw Pact and appealed to the United Nations to defend Hungarian "neutrality." Rather than tolerate this bid for Hungarian independence, Khrushchev invaded with 150,000 troops and 2,500 tanks. After savage street fighting at a cost of thousands of lives, the Soviets reimposed the rule of a Communist presumed loyal to Moscow, János Kádár. His government condemned Imre Nagy to be hanged. The bloody lesson of 1956 was that the Soviets had the will and the power to crush any open challenge to their domination of Eastern Europe.

The task of the Communist leaders of the region, therefore, was to find means to provide some satisfactions to their unhappy peoples without provoking the Soviets to intervene. János Kádár, in the eyes of many Hungarians no more than a traitor and Soviet agent, nevertheless understood this need for national reconciliation. In a famous speech in 1962 he declared, "Those who are not against us are with us." In other words, his government would tolerate any attitude but overt opposition, a most un-Stalinist message. In 1968, when it launched a "New Economic Mechanism," his regime showed that it was prepared to be as unorthodox in economics as it was in politics. The new plan entrusted the cultivation of state-owned agricultural land to autonomous farmers' cooperatives. Their task, like that of Hungarian factory managers, was henceforth to earn a profit, not to fulfill a production quota. Though it retained control of banks, transportation, and heavy industry, the government sold off small service businesses to individual entrepreneurs. Moreover, it winked at the emergence of a huge "second" or "shadow" economy, an under-the-table labor market in which some 70 percent of Hungarians chose to work overtime for extra money, ignoring official norms of wages and hours. Taking advantage of international détente in the 1970s, Kádár also encouraged capitalist investment in Hungary, including the development of joint ventures with Western-based multinational corporations. By the 1980s, Budapest worker cooperatives were selling computer software in Western markets, to which Hungary sent half of its exports.

The combination of all these departures from Marxist orthodoxy produced a distinctive Hungarian economic system, jokingly called "goulash communism" or, more meaningfully, "consumer socialism." Under this system, the standard of living for the majority was higher than in the rest of Eastern Europe. By the 1980s, one Hungarian family in three owned a car, a thirtyfold increase since the 1960s. At the same time, however, social inequality was far greater in Hungary than in the rest of the Soviet bloc: the combined income of the wealthiest 5 percent of the population was eighty times greater than the combined income of the poorest 5 percent—an odd kind of socialism indeed. In 1987 the Hungarian government announced the establishment of Eastern Europe's first business management school, a joint U.S.-Hungarian venture whose language of instruction would be English.

The effect of relative economic success was to legitimate, to some degree, the government of Kádár, the "traitor" of 1956. In 1985 he felt confident enough of public support to pass a law requiring that there be two candidates for every seat in the 387-seat Hungarian parliament. Twenty-five non-Communists in fact were elected, hardly a threat to the regime. By the late 1980s, however, the partial consensus Kádár had created by such concessions was eroding. The economy lapsed into stagnation, prompting calls for further liberalization in imitation of Western economies. Gorbachev's regime promised not only more sweeping economic and political changes in the Soviet Union than Kádár had permitted in Hungary but also a relaxed Soviet grip that would enable Hungarians to restructure their government and economy as they chose. In this new atmosphere an elderly Stalinist like Kádár was an embarrassing reminder of the past: in May 1988 the Central Committee of the Hungarian Communist party ousted him in disgrace. A year later, the new leadership signaled its atonement for the repression of 1956 by ceremonially reburying Imre Nagy, Kádár's victim, who had long lain in an unmarked grave.

Such concessions came too late. In 1989, as the Berlin Wall fell and membership in the Hungarian Communist party dropped from 700,000 to 30,000, its leaders could only recognize that the game was up. They legalized rival political parties and called elections for March 1990. In these first free elections in Eastern Europe in more than four decades, the predictable winners among the twelve major parties in contention were those that promised to safeguard democracy and complete Hungary's long transition to a free-market economy. The 1990s would reveal, however, that in Hungary as in the other former satellites, not everyone would live happily ever after the fall of communism.

Czechoslovakia

The Czech challenge to Stalinism began early in 1968 when the leaders of the Communist party, in response to demands from intellectuals for greater freedom and from workers for better pay and job conditions, forced out the Stalinist first secretary. His successor, Alexander Dubček, promised extensive reforms, including a less centralized economy to allow more opportunity for individual initiative, a relaxation of censorship, and even a subordinate role for political parties other than the Communists.

Dubček intended no more—but also no less—than to create a "Czechoslovakian way to socialism," which he memorably described as "socialism with a human face." Unlike Nagy of Hungary in 1956, he would not be pushed into trying to withdraw his country from the Soviet bloc. But it made no difference. In the heady atmosphere of newly recovered freedom during the "Prague springtime," ideas far more threatening to Soviet control than his found voice. Fearing that Czechoslovakia would be "pushed off the road to socialism" whatever Dubček's intentions, the Soviets marched in a half-million Warsaw Pact troops. The suppression of "socialism with a human face" in Prague in 1968 was far less bloody than it had been in Budapest in 1956: fewer than a hundred lives were lost as the Czechs greeted the Soviet tanks only with passive resistance. By the spring of 1969, Dubček had disappeared from public life. He would not be heard from again until 1988, when he drew parallels between Gorbachev's reforms in the USSR and his own lost cause.

The regime of Dubček's successor, Gustav Husák, promptly resumed the drive for industrial production at all costs, despite ever-increasing, publicly unacknowledged evidence that the resulting pollution was doing irreparable harm to the environment. (One secret report warned that by the end of the century

60 percent of Czechoslovakia's forests would be beyond saving.) Only in the 1980s, when it felt the impact of a weakening world economy, did the Husák regime begin to talk, like its East European neighbors, about allowing the marketplace to determine production goals and prices. The question was whether this kind of tinkering with mechanics would suffice to revive the Czech economy in the absence of political and intellectual freedom, which Husák and his successors continued to reject. When student demonstrations reinforced by visiting Hungarians and Poles erupted in Prague in November 1989 on the anniversary of the repression of 1968, the police ruthlessly crushed them.

This last act of repression provoked the downfall of Czechoslovak communism. A small group of intellectuals grouped around the playwright Vaclav Havel, who had been bravely challenging the regime since 1977, formed a movement, Civic Forum, to lead continuing demonstrations by students and some workers. Though a majority of the population remained passive, the moribund Czechoslovak Communist party, knowing that it could expect no backing from Moscow, concluded that it had no choice but to bargain an end to the crisis. In December 1989 the Communists agreed to the formation of a coalition government including non-Communists. Havel, who had spent four years in Communist jails, became president of the Czechoslovak Republic. So relatively amicable and bloodless was this transition that it is remembered as the "Velvet Revolution." The 1990s would show, however, that Czechoslovakia's problems did not end with this negotiation of a Communist surrender.

Poland

History, religion, and the shape of its society combined to make Poland the most troublesome, as well as the largest, of the Soviet satellites. Polish history, which every Pole knew well, was largely a record of struggle against the German and Russian neighbors who divided Poland between themselves for over a century before World War I. Polish patriotism was nourished through such dark periods of history by a fervent Roman Catholicism: even under an officially atheistic regime, over 90 percent of the population was baptized into the Church. Polish rural society successfully resisted Stalinist collectivization, leaving a class of stubbornly independent peasants, unique in Eastern Europe, owning three-quarters of the land. Historic patriotism, backed by a powerful Catholic church, rooted not only among the third of the population who remained farmers but also among their sons and daughters who moved to the cities—all these spurred repeated and violent Polish resistance to the Soviet-imposed government. In 1956, large-scale rioting in protest against the hardships of life under the command economy brought to power Wladislaw Gomulka, a patriotic Communist imprisoned under Stalin for "nationalist deviationism." In a face-to-face confrontation, he forced Khrushchev to back down and consent to a liberalized Poland. Most of the few collective farms the previous Stalinist regime had managed to organize were dissolved. For a time Gomulka managed to contain Polish discontent. In 1970, however, workers enraged by his announcement of 30 percent rises in food prices went on strike, occupied their factories, and forced him from office. The new leader, Edward Gierek, came to apologize to the fifteen thousand workers at the Lenin shipyard in Gdańsk, leaders in the revolt, for the police gunfire that had cost some of their fellow shipbuilders their lives. Like Gomulka fourteen years earlier, Gierek announced a new economic policy.

The basic problem that Gierek in his turn now faced was that Polish investment had been channeled in the best Stalinist style into heavy industry, leaving few resources to be spent on modernizing agriculture to feed a rapidly growing population. Compounded by the monumental inefficiencies of a centrally managed distribution network, this policy made for scarce and expensive food. Thus consumer prices could be kept affordable to the ordinary wage earner only by maintaining government controls—in other words, by subsidizing consumers. Whenever the government ran short of money and tried to cut these subsidies by raising prices, as in 1970, there was an explosion of worker discontent.

Gierek's solution to this problem was to take advantage of the new international climate of détente to borrow heavily from Western banks. The loans would be used to make Polish industry competitive in world markets. Polish products, it was hoped, would earn enough to enable Poland to buy whatever it lacked, to raise living standards, and also to pay back the loans. A combination of factors doomed this attempt at a Polish version of consumer socialism. Agriculture still remained backward. Western loans, as in many of the Third World countries, seeped away into the hands of corrupt party bureaucrats, who used them to build hunting lodges and saunas. Meanwhile, the slump in international trade that followed the 1973 oil embargo hit the Polish economy, newly vulnerable to world economic trends, as hard as any in the West. In this situation the government could only keep on borrowing—Polish foreign debt increased 25-fold from 1970 to the mid 1980s—while raising prices and lowering living standards to try and pay off its foreign creditors.

In 1976 the now-familiar cycle of worker rioting followed by government promises to do better was repeated. But by August 1980, when the government announced new price increases, the workers' patience was exhausted. Meat consumption had fallen by 20 percent in four years. In a country that had been a net food exporter in the 1950s, much now had to be imported, and consumers stood in long lines to receive their meager monthly ration. This time, not satisfied with precipitating Gierek's fall, the striking Gdańsk shipyard workers demanded a concession no Soviet bloc government had yet granted: the right to form an independent trade union. They called their unique new movement "Solidarity." For fifteen months, under the leadership of a shipyard electrician, Lech Walesa, Solidarity grew into virtually a rival Polish government to the tottering Communist regime.

This was a far more formidable challenge to the Soviets' Eastern European rule than were the movements led by Nagy and Dubček. Over 200,000 Poles quit the Communist party, while 10 million, nearly a third of the population, joined the union movement. Uniting the discontent of intellectuals and peasants with that of workers, Solidarity forced more and more concessions from the government, which appeared to have lost control. The Soviets mobilized to invade but hesitated at the prospect of an occupation that would pin down at least 300,000 of their troops.

In the end it was the Polish army, at the orders of the new Communist party leader General Wojciech Jaruzelski, that temporarily ended Solidarity's hopes. In December 1981 he proclaimed martial law and jailed the movement's leaders, including Walesa. A year later he dissolved the union, forcing it underground, where it could no longer so effectively challenge the government. Meanwhile, Jaruzelski tried to re-establish authority by promising successive doses of economic liberalization along Hungarian lines, after a period of austerity had allowed Poland to begin to pay its huge foreign debt. In 1987 he held a referendum, inviting Poles to endorse these economic reforms, including annual price rises of 27 percent for the next three years, and his promises of greater political freedom. Fewer than half of the eligible voters cast affirmative ballots, one indication of the mistrust that continued to separate a majority of Poles from their government.

In the eyes of many Poles, Jaruzelski was like the Hungarian Kádár or the Slovak Husák—a mere Soviet stooge. In fact, his situation demanded a delicate balancing act, going as far as he dared to placate the Polish people but not so far as to risk for his country a Soviet invasion and for himself the fate of Imre Nagy or Alexander Dubček.

Under Gorbachev, however, such a Soviet invasion became much less likely. The continued deterioration of the Polish economy prompted another wave of strikes in 1988. Faced with this renewed evidence of the power of the banned trade union, and encouraged by Gorbachev, General Jaruzelski decided that since he could not destroy Solidarity, he must strike a deal with it if Poland was to survive. In the spring of 1989 he concluded a historic agreement with Lech Walesa to restore Solidarity's legal status and to hold free elections, though with 38 percent of the parliamentary seats "guaranteed" to Communists. This stratagem to preserve Communist control failed when many voters crossed off their ballots the names of Communist candidates running unopposed, and two small parties, long subordinate to the Communists, threw their support to Solidarity instead. Thus Jaruzelski had no option in September 1989 but to appoint a coalition cabinet with eleven of its twenty-three ministers belonging to Solidarity, while only four were Communists. Eastern Europe had reached a historic turning point: for the first time since the 1940s, the prime minister of a Soviet bloc country was an anti-Communist.

Stalin had once declared that trying to impose communism on Catholic Poland was like trying to saddle a cow. With the advent of one of Walesa's close associates as prime minister, more than forty years of attempts to communize Poland had proved completely futile. Yet it was not clear that the new regime, the fruit of compromise between Jaruzelski and Walesa, could solve Poland's problems.

The most obvious reason for the collapse of communism, in Poland as in the rest of Eastern Europe, was that after Gorbachev became the leader of the Soviet Union in 1985, the USSR was unwilling to back up these regimes with the threat of an invasion. That threat was all that had sustained these regimes, however, because communism had proved to be such an abject economic and political failure, despite the attempts of Eastern European leaders like Kádár in Hungary, Husák in Czechoslovakia, and Gierek and Jaruzelski in Poland to modify the Stalinist economic and political models imposed on these countries after 1945.

The Stalinist economic model, we have seen, derived from the Soviet example of the 1930s: its goal was to build a heavy industrial sector—steel mills, cement plants—to meet production quotas set by central planners. Since its products were not destined for competitive world markets, inefficiently high costs of production were not a prime concern. Workers' low wages were compensated for by job security, and in any case mattered less because the economy produced little beyond the barest necessities for consumers to buy.

Such a Stalinist model from the 1930s had enabled the Soviet economy to achieve growth rates of GNP above 5 percent through the 1960s. But as we have seen in earlier chapters, the postwar decades marked a profound shift throughout much of the developed world to postindustrial economies, which emphasized the provision of high-technology products like computers for an expanding and discriminating consumer market.

For the Soviet Union and its Eastern European satellites to have followed this worldwide trend would have required a complete reversal of Stalinist economic priorities. Bureaucratic planning of the Soviet sort would have had to give way to a climate in which entrepreneurial energy could flourish. A society whose censors tolerated only the Party line would have had to learn to permit the diffusion of the information that produced technological innovation. Even to modernize heavy industry would have required diverting scarce funds from their usual purposes of compensating for the inefficiencies of collectivized agriculture, subsidizing low consumer prices, and sustaining a costly military establishment. Such fundamental transformations proved beyond the capabilities of communist leadership, despite concessions by leaders like Kádár to deviations from the Stalinist model like "goulash communism." Thus the Soviet bloc faced the challenges of the 1970s and 1980s with economies still geared to the priorities of the 1930s.

Moreover, as fuel costs rose and falling birth rates reduced the supply of potential workers, Eastern bloc heavy industry lost two of the advantages—cheap energy and cheap labor—that had made it productive from the 1930s to the 1960s. After 1970 the rate of growth of Soviet GNP fell almost continuously—to 2.7 percent in the early 1980s. Thus most Eastern bloc economies were not only not renewing themselves but were even failing to do well what under Stalin they had done best.

Falling rates of growth of GNP reflected the low productivity of a sullen work force that remained alienated, despite some improvement in living standards since Stalin's day. The sour joke Soviet workers told about their communist bosses: "They pretend to pay us and we pretend to work" was a succinct summation of communist economic failure that found an echo throughout most of Eastern Europe.

The glaring contrast—obvious to any thoughtful person—between Communism's boasts that it had created a superior way of life and the realities of economic stagnation and consumer privation naturally produced widespread political disaffection. Police-state surveillance, periodically reinforced by Soviet invasions, made open opposition too dangerous. Most people throughout the Eastern bloc therefore resigned themselves to a hopeless political cynicism as long as the threat of Soviet repression loomed over them. When that threat disappeared after 1985, communism's record of economic failure and political disaffection doomed it to swift extinction in spite of the efforts of nationalist communists like Kádár and Husák to make it more palatable to their countrymen.

The Brezhnev Decades in the USSR: Transformation and Stagnation, 1964–1982

In the Soviet Union, the later years of the rule of Khrushchev's successor Leonid Brezhnev (1906–1982) witnessed a slide similar to that of the communist regimes of Eastern Europe from economic stagnation and political disaffection into crisis. Since Brezhnev did even less than his Eastern European colleagues to arrest the slide, his successors would be faced with a daunting task of economic and political renovation. His Soviet Union barely began the transition to a postindustrial society: five years after his death, for example, there were only 100,000 computers in the USSR, a total far smaller than the 5 million sold *annually* in the United States.[1]

It was probably inevitable that the stormy innovator Khrushchev would be succeeded as Soviet leader by a lethargic conservative like Brezhnev. Among the coalition of discontents that toppled Khrushchev in 1964 were both enthusiastic de-Stalinizers who found him too brash and Stalinists offended by his disparagement of the old leader. Not surprisingly they compromised on a successor who was bland and colorless enough to be acceptable to both groups. Brezhnev was too young to have known the Revolution. He belonged to the Communist generation that had made careers as party functionaries, climbing the bureaucratic ladder as a protégé of Khrushchev without incurring any of the animosity directed toward his mentor. Imposing and conventional, Brezhnev held on to power for nearly twenty years despite steadily failing health, combining Stalin's old post as general secretary of the party with the ceremonial leadership of the Soviet state at a time when he was often incapacitated.

He presided inertly over fundamental changes in Soviet life that brought the USSR in many ways much closer to the developed societies of the West than it had been in 1964. The population of Khrushchev's USSR had still been predominantly rural. In 1968, for the first time, more Soviet citizens lived in cities than in the countryside. (By the 1980s, two-thirds of the Soviet population lived in an urban environment; by the end of the century 80 percent will live there.) The chief stimulus of population movement to the cities continued to be industrial development. The Soviet boom of the Khrushchev years continued until the 1970s. For a time Japan was the USSR's only rival in annual rate of growth of GNP. The Soviets were simultaneously the world's leading producers of grain , of oil and iron ore, of steel (first surpassing the United States in 1971), and of chemical fertilizers. Continued economic growth made Brezhnev's early years a heady time for the USSR. Expanding their arms expenditures by an estimated 4 percent a year, the Soviets achieved nuclear parity with the United States and developed a navy designed to project their power around the world.

Growth seemed to provide the opportunity for the regime to satisfy the muted but unmistakable demands of the increasingly urban and sophisticated Soviet population for a higher standard of living. The Eighth Five Year Plan (1966–1970) was the first to stress the production of consumer goods. The results produced substantial changes in Soviet lifestyles. In Khrushchev's day, three out of five Soviet families had shared both bathroom and kitchen with at least one additional family. In a little over two decades the Soviets constructed some 50 million apartments. By the 1980s, three-quarters of Moscow families had one of their own, though it often sheltered three generations under one roof. Apartments were now likely to be furnished with the kinds of conveniences Western societies take for granted. In 1983, 83 percent of Soviet families had at least a black-and-white television set (which they watched for at least an hour and a half daily); 82 percent had refrigerators; and 58 percent had washing machines. But only one family in four had a car. In the late 1980s the USSR still had fewer telephones than France and fewer miles of improved road than Texas.

As in the West, the enjoyment of this standard of living required a large effort from wage earners. Not only did many male Soviet citizens work, as in the satellites, at illegal overtime jobs—the "second economy" has been estimated at 10 to 20 percent of Soviet GNP—but almost half of Soviet women were employed outside the home. The patterns of Soviet family life thus came to resemble what we have already observed in the postindustrial West. The birthrate continued to fall, most of all among the Slavic majority of the population. Already in 1970 it had fallen by half from the level of 1941. In the mid-1980s, two-thirds of Moscow's couples had only one child, and one Soviet marriage in three—in some places, one in two—ended in divorce.

Observers of the USSR had often predicted that as the patterns of Soviet society became more like those of the West, dominated by urban, skilled, increasingly white-collar couples, Stalinist-style censorship could not be perpetuated. Brezhnev agreed with his progressive colleagues that it was desirable to satisfy consumer demand; however, he shared with conservatives an abiding mistrust of unconventional ideas. Though he was far from reviving Stalin's imprisonment of millions, Brezhnev's years were marked by enough episodes of repression that it is not inappropriate to call his regime "neo-Stalinist." (Indeed, he put an immediate end to official criticism of Stalin.) The first political trial of dissenting intellectuals since Stalin's death occurred in 1966. Forbidden to accept the Nobel Prize for literature awarded him in 1970, Solzhenitsyn, not only the USSR's foremost novelist but one of its most vocal critics, was driven into exile in 1974. In the same year an impromptu open-air exhibition of modern art in Moscow was demolished by bulldozers.

These repeated reminders that critics still had something to fear reflected both Brezhnev's chief principle of government and the source of his support. Khrushchev had hoped, probably unrealistically, to revive mass revolutionary fervor. Brezhnev had no such illusions. The Soviet masses, he believed, needed "discipline" above all. This view was widely shared among the group from which he came, the bureaucratic oligarchy of top party officials who had controlled the USSR since Stalin's day.

They were a self-perpetuating elite. Soviet sociological research revealed that over a half-century of "socialism in one country" produced a society that offered fewer opportunities for social mobility than are found in some Western societies. Only 11 percent of Soviet young people went on from high school to college, a far lower proportion than in most of the Western democracies. The children of college-trained top party officials and factory managers were five times more likely than children from peasant or worker families to become officials and managers. They thus continued to enjoy their parents' privileges: chauffeured cars, special stores, private waiting rooms, passes that enabled them to go to the front of the long lines in which ordinary Soviets waited to buy scarce commodities.

The great danger of rule by this kind of elite is that the rulers, fearing no challenge, become concerned only with their own self-gratification, not with the general welfare. Around Brezhnev gathered an unscrupulous set of high officials who used their important connections to amass tremendous wealth, sometimes simply by embezzling public funds. Meanwhile, Brezhnev's fitful attempts to reshape the Soviet economy were stillborn. Though it was a Soviet economist who had worked out the ideas for the "goulash communism" that developed in the satellites, they remained a dead letter in his own country. Lacking incentives, Soviet sociologists discovered, workers in the USSR felt as powerless and manipulated as workers in capitalistic economies were supposed to feel. Ironically, in a society supposedly dedicated to developing the human capacity to share, the legacy of Brezhnev, the socialist leader with forty foreign limousines in his collection, was a general impulse to cynical self-gratification. "Wastefulness, irresponsibility, and an atmosphere of complete permissiveness intensified," declared the dissident historian Roy Medvedev. "The corruption which was rotting society became more open and brazen, [and] abuse of authority and embezzlement became the norm of life" under Brezhnev's "gerontocracy"[2]—the rule of old men.

In Brezhnev's second decade the Soviet economy went from dynamism to decline in the 1970s, and into crisis in the 1980s. Alarming evidence appeared in the statistics of rising infant mortality and declining longevity that the economy was no longer able to deliver such essential services as health care—that the quality of Soviet life was actually beginning to decline. The government's response was to publish fewer statistics. The "old men" would not face the problem. After Brezhnev finally died in 1982, the Politburo chose to replace him with two men in succession, aged sixty-eight and seventy-two respectively, who were both already mortally ill when they took office. Only in March 1985 did the old men of the Kremlin nerve themselves to elect to Stalin, Khrushchev, and Brezhnev's post of general secretary the youngest member of the Politburo, Mikhail Gorbachev.

From Gorbachev to Yeltsin: The Dissolution of the Soviet Union

Like Khrushchev, Gorbachev had risen from humble peasant origins to a brilliant career in the government hierarchy. Like Khrushchev, he wanted to rid Soviet society of the burden of its Stalinist history and to revive its flagging economy by a drastic reshaping of economic institutions. There were differences, however, between these two leaders that went deeper than appearances (though the elegant Gorbachev, suave master of the Western television cameras, marked a new stage in Soviet sophistication from the rumpled and belligerent Khrushchev). Gorbachev, an experienced civil servant, realized that the Soviet system as it had developed since Stalin's time was reaching a dead end, that the time for tinkering with partial economic reforms while treating Soviet citizens as passive spectators of their own national life had passed. Within a few years of taking power, he commanded the most sweeping array of economic and political changes the USSR had seen since 1917.

From the beginning, Gorbachev bluntly declared that the very future of the USSR was at stake. Though Stalin's industrialization had brought the USSR into the twentieth century, and his successors had given Soviet society some of the consumer benefits that industrialization had produced in the West, the country was no longer keeping up with the galloping pace of change. Unfavorable economic indicators—industrial productivity that lagged at half the American rate, an agricultural sector still employing almost a quarter of Soviet citizens (compared to 3 percent in the United States), declining growth rates, and food shortages—were merely symptoms of a basic failure to keep up with the technological innovations of the world marketplace.

Clearly the USSR's continuing relative isolation, with foreign trade only 5 percent of GNP, was cutting off an indispensable flow of innovation. But how, in a world market where the raw materials the USSR had to sell, like oil and natural gas, were depressed, could the Soviets earn the money to buy the technology they needed, when they also had to buy food periodically to supplement the inadequate yields of their backward agriculture sector? Certainly they could not count on selling many manufactured goods in an increasingly competitive world market as long as less than one-third of their products, by official admission, met international standards of quality. The problem was not only that Soviet factories, retooled in the 1950s and 1960s, were too antiquated to meet those standards. Workmanship was also poor, reflecting a work force with high rates of absenteeism, a rate of alcoholism three times what it had been in 1917, and a turnover of employees that in some plants amounted to 20 percent annually.

This combination of circumstances meant that the Soviet economy in the 1980s was caught in a vicious circle. With half of Soviet women already working and the birthrate rapidly falling to Western levels, the supply of cheap labor on which the USSR had long relied was dwindling. To improve productivity would require not only new technology but also greater incentives to a work force that wanted, but could not afford, sophisticated products of the consumer society such as automobiles and VCRs. But how could the USSR afford simultaneously to keep up in the arms race with the

United States, to retool its plants and improve its underdeveloped transportation network, to purchase technology overseas, and to allocate scarce resources to the production of more consumer goods? Greater investment and greater incentives—the production of more consumer goods that workers would work harder to earn—were essential to stimulate greater productivity; but while productivity remained low, the economy could not generate the resources for greater investment and more incentives.

To break this vicious circle, Gorbachev launched a veritable economic revolution he call *perestroika,* "restructuring." He insisted that it would not succeed, however, unless Soviet citizens learned to understand their relationship to the government in a new way. To foster this new understanding would require re-examining Soviet history and encouraging public discussion of controversial issues to an extent unprecedented since Lenin's time. His word for this whole process of discussion was *glasnost,* "openness."

Perestroika, approved by the party Central Committee in April 1987, undermined the Stalinist command economy. The role of the bloated planning bureaucracies in Moscow was much reduced. The manager and workers of each Soviet enterprise were henceforth responsible for its finances and could no longer depend on government subsidies to keep it going.

Likewise, consumers would have to pay the real costs of commodities: there would be no government subsidies to keep them low. One half of the service sector and 20 percent of consumer goods production would be entrusted to private enterprises; by the end of 1987, 13,000 new cooperatives and 300,000 family businesses had been created to meet this goal. In a substantial reversal of collectivization, 40 percent of agriculture was returned to individual cultivation—a predictable decision given that the small private plots permitted before *perestroika,* though representing only 3 percent of land farmed, produced a quarter of the Soviet crop and two-thirds of the potatoes and vegetables.

Gorbachev saw, however, that his new economic legislation would be unavailing until Soviet ways of thinking were changed. The only way to make the USSR a more productive society was to make it a more open society. As he declared in a historic speech on the seventieth anniversary of the Bolshevik Revolution: "In reorganizing our economic and political system it is our duty first of all to create a dependable and flexible mechanism for the genuine involvement of all the people."[3]

Involvement meant discussion: in the name of *glasnost* practically every subject once taboo in the USSR now came up for intensive discussion. Gorbachev himself set the tone in his speech by re-examining Soviet history. He stated unequivocally that Stalin's guilt in such episodes as the Great Terror and collectivization was "enormous and unforgivable." Bukharin, the architect of the NEP, which so closely resembled *perestroika,* now could be seen not as a traitor but as a prophet.

The leader's new "openness" set an example widely imitated. On Soviet television, citizens' panels peppered public officials with tough questions, and documentaries probed the damaging effects on Soviet society of the long, losing war in Afghanistan. Twenty million Soviet cinema goers saw a film that depicted Pavlik Morozov, the one-time boy hero of Stalinist propaganda, no longer as "a symbol of steadfastness and class-consciousness," as one critic observed, but rather as the culprit in the "legalized and romanticized betrayal"[4] of his own parent. Soviet environmentalists even imitated their Western counterparts by staging sit-ins to prevent the officially sanctioned destruction of historic buildings.

It is difficult for those accustomed to societies where frank discussions of controversial issues is taken for granted to imagine the stunning impact of this kind of "openness" on a society where public information, when official secrecy had permitted any, had always been given an official interpretation. Soviet intellectuals of course hailed the new freedom. The reaction of ordinary people was probably less wholehearted. For many older people who remembered his leadership during World War II, condemnation of Stalin cast doubt on a heroic past in which they took personal pride. Others found the open discussion in the once-muzzled Soviet press disquieting. To Soviet conservatives, it seemed another symptom of social decay, like the spread of drug abuse and the inexplicable fondness of the young for listening to clandestinely circulated tapes of rock music. Such people insisted that Russia had always needed a master—the tsar or Stalin. Freedom in Russia always led to anarchy, as during the early years of the revolution. Even Gorbachev had to admit publicly in the spring of 1988 that "there are people who think that everything is collapsing" as the old certainties came under challenge. Yet he pressed on.

Partly in order to make it harder to depose him, Gorbachev instigated a fundamental democratic reshaping of the USSR's political institutions. The new Soviet constitution established in 1988 called for elections in the spring of 1989 to a 2,250-member National Congress of People's Deputies. Though 750 of the seats in this new parliament were to be filled with candidates chosen by various organizations like the Communist party, the other 1,500 seats were left to the democratic choice of the voters—the first "free" election in Russia since 1917.

The results not only deeply humiliated the Communist party hierarchy but convinced even skeptical foreign observers that the possibility of making real choices had shaken the Soviet citizenry out of decades of apathy. Only 25 percent of the districts were uncontested—only a few more than the 20 percent of seats in the U.S. House of Representatives that went uncontested in 1988. Even in some uncontested districts, veteran Communist leaders critical of Gorbachev went down to defeat when voters crossed their names off their ballots, depriving them of the required minimum of half the ballots cast. Though nine out of ten of the candidates were Communist party members—no other party being legal—the contests often pitted a younger, reform-minded generation against an older one.

The political frenzy of the electoral period continued through the summer of 1989 as the proceedings of the new parliament were televised live to a record audience of 200 million stretching across the USSR's twelve time zones. Constantly clustered before their sets, Soviet viewers witnessed one unprecedented sight after another, including passionate criticism of the KGB, or secret police, and even acquiescence by its newly appointed leader to subjecting its operations to parliamentary scrutiny.

Already, however, there were signs that Gorbachev's incredibly bold historical gamble of trying to democratize the Soviet Union and liberalize its economy while still remaining faithful to the ideals of Lenin was doomed to failure. Gradually, it became evident that he could no longer control the forces of change he had unleashed. His efforts to do so brought him increasingly under a withering crossfire of criticism both from those Soviet citizens who felt his reforms did not go far enough and from those who believed they had already gone much too far.

It could have been predicted that with his loosening of Moscow's authority, the many ethnic minorities within the USSR—the world's largest country—would reassert the nationalism crushed in the civil wars of 1917–1921 and begin to demand autonomy or even outright independence. Thus Gorbachev found his rule challenged everywhere from the Baltic republics of Latvia, Lithuania, and Estonia (which had been independent from 1918 until Stalin seized them in 1940) all the way to the predominantly Muslim republics along the USSR's southern Asian frontier. Every concession he offered to meet their nationalistic demands led only to further demands for more concessions, until he was faced with the stark choice of watching the USSR disintegrate or of trying to keep many of its restive peoples within it by force.

However, it was less and less clear that such force could be found. What had held the USSR's more than a hundred ethnic groups together had been an internationalist ideology, communism, and an omnipresent institution that embodied it, the Communist party. Probably a majority of Soviet citizens both inside and outside the party had ceased, unlike Gorbachev himself, to believe in the promises of Lenin's revolution, but the party remained the backbone of the multi-national Soviet state. It was also the principal institutional obstacle to Gorbachev's reforms, however. To counter such resistance, he had launched the movement for *glasnost,* which discredited much of the party's past and present and had even allowed Soviet citizens to form and vote for other parties, even anti-Communist ones. Yet every blow he dealt to the obstructive party hierarchy not only damaged his own authority as its head, but also weakened the principal institution holding the multinational state together.

None of this might have mattered if *perestroika* had fulfilled its promise by improving the lives of the increasingly urbanized and educated majority of the Soviet population—people who compared their standard of living not with that of earlier generations but with the Western standard *glasnost* showed them on their television screens or on the trips now permitted outside the Soviet bloc. Instead, the Soviet command economy, always neglectful of consumers and already in rapid decline when Gorbachev took office, was plunged into chaos by *perestroika's* successive and sometimes contradictory plans for economic reform. Ironically, *glasnost* allowed ever louder and more indignant protests at its complete failure, which became undeniable in the spring of 1990. Meat and milk, salt and soap were all rationed; there were long lines for bread; and it became rare to find a pharmacy open, for the shelves were bare of medicines.

Gorbachev now found himself assailed on one side with demands for far more drastic economic reform and on the other side with protests from his party comrades that further upheaval risked provoking a national collapse. Such were these pressures that he appeared to be driven to one side, then to the other, though with his usual self-assurance he insisted that his path was down the middle of the road—a path that increasingly existed only in his own mind. Late in 1990, it appeared that he was leaning to the proponents of reaction. Though the Soviet economy had registered a negative growth rate of 6 percent, with a 17 percent deficit predicted for 1991, he backed away from a radical plan already announced for a 500-day transition to a market economy. In January 1991 he also acquiesced in a violent crackdown by Soviet troops in Lithuania, which had proclaimed its independence. This recourse to old-style Soviet repressive violence disgusted many believers in reform, who had once hailed Gorbachev but now concluded he was just another hypocritical *apparatchik.* Yet this lurch toward reaction did not reassure the growing anti-reform camp within the party, who were becoming convinced that if Gorbachev were not stopped, he would destroy the USSR.

By the late summer of 1991, Gorbachev seemed to have returned to the course of reform. He backed a treaty among the USSR's constituent republics that would share out among them much of the government authority wielded by Moscow. This prospect was too much for the old guard, who decided in August 1991 to snatch power back. Just a few days before the treaty was to be signed, the

Former states in the Union of Soviet Socialist Republics, which dissolved in 1991.
ARCTIC OCEAN
German reunification, 1990
Wall opened, Nov., 1989
Elections, 1989
Gorbachev in power, 1985–1991
Largest and most influential of the former Soviet republics after 1991
Broke into Czech Republic and Slovakia in 1993.
Communist regimes collapse, 1989
Dissolved into warring states
IRE.
U.K.
FRANCE
BELG.
NETH.
DEN.
NORWAY
SWEDEN
FINLAND
GERMANY
Berlin
SWITZ.
Prague
POLAND
LITHUANIA
Tallinn
ESTONIA
ITALY
AUS.
CZECH. REP.
Warsaw
Riga
SLOVENIA
CROATIA
Bratislava
SLOVAKIA
Vilnius
LATVIA
Minsk
BOSNIA-HERZE.
Budapest
HUNGARY
BELARUS
YUGOSLAVIA
UKRAINE
Moscow
ROMANIA
Kiev
MACE-DONIA
MOLDOVA
Bucharest
Kishinev
GR.
Sofia
BULGARIA
Barents Sea
RUSSIA
Sea of Okhotsk
Lake Baikal
Caspian Sea
KAZAKHSTAN
Aral Sea
GEORGIA
TURKEY
ARMENIA
AZERBAIJAN
LEB.
ISR.
SYRIA
JORDAN
IRAQ
UZBEKISTAN
TURKMENISTAN
KYRGYZSTAN
TAJIKISTAN
MONGOLIA
N. KOREA
S. KOREA
JAPAN
Sea of Japan
IRAN
KUW.
AFGHANISTAN
SAUDI ARABIA
QATAR
U.A.E.
OMAN
PAKISTAN
YEMEN
Arabian Sea
NEPAL
BHUT.
CHINA
0 400 800 Km.
0 400 800 Mi.
PACIFIC OCEAN

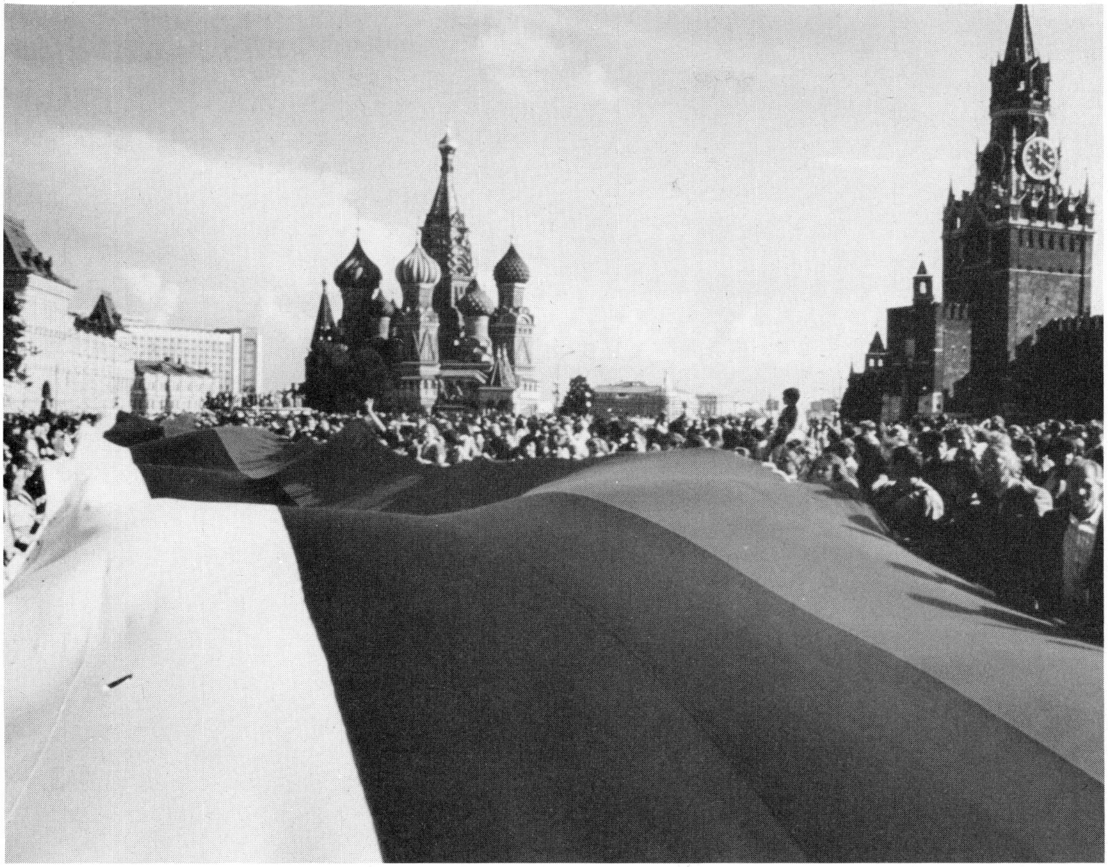

Anti-Communist demonstrators carry a huge prerevolutionary Russian flag into Red Square in Moscow. *Soon the flag would replace the Soviet flag flying from the tower of the Kremlin (right). Anthony Suau/© 1991 Black Star*

world learned with horror that a *coup d'état* had been executed in the capital of a nuclear superpower. An eight-man junta led by Gorbachev's own hand-picked vice president, prime minister, minister or the interior, and minister of defense announced that they had placed the vacationing Gorbachev on "medical leave" and concentrated all power in their own hands to save the country form disintegration.

Map 14.1 Changes in Eastern Europe since 1989

Fortunately, these plotters, perhaps believing they could oust Gorbachev as easily as his colleagues had ousted Khrushchev in 1964, had made only the sketchiest plans for their coup. Among other blunders, they failed to assure themselves of sufficient reliable troops to overcome the resistance inspired by Boris

Russian President Boris Yeltsin raises his fist in salute at the funeral of three young men killed in the defense of the Russian parliament during the attempted Communist coup in August 1991. *Georges Merillion/© 1991 Gamma-Liaison*

Yeltsin, the newly elected and popular head of the Russian Republic. Yeltsin dramatically mounted a tank outside the Russian parliament building to urge Moscow's citizens to resist the coup. Thousands of Muscovites did rally to defend the building from attack, while in St. Petersburg (as Leningrad had recently voted to rename itself) another gigantic rally called for resistance. It would be misleading to exaggerate the role of the Russian masses in blocking the coup: the provinces were largely indifferent to this latest turn in the distant capital's interminable and incomprehensible politics. Polls showed that as many Soviet citizens supported the coup, or were indifferent to it, as opposed it. But the show of resistance in Moscow and St. Petersburg was enough to discourage the ill-organized plotters. Within three days the coup collapsed. Its leaders fled or committed suicide. Yet the return of Gorbachev, released from house arrest, to his capital was not a triumphant one.

The effect of the botched coup was to complete the discrediting not only of the Communist party and of the Soviet Union, which the coup leaders were trying to hold together, but also of Mikhail Gorbachev, who in trying to save both had brought both to dissolution. Even the abortive threat of renewed control from Moscow persuaded the leaders of two of the largest republics, Ukraine and Byelorussia (Belarus) to follow the Baltic example by declaring their independence only a few days later. In the largest republic, Russia itself, President Yeltsin, whose leadership of resistance to the coup had made him a world figure overshadowing Gorbachev, suspended the Communist party and seized control of its assets.

Gorbachev, in fact, became little more than a spectator as the last act of the history of the Soviet Union was played out. Negotiating with the presidents of Ukraine and Belarus, Yeltsin cobbled together an ill-defined and loosely knit Commonwealth of Independent States to replace the Union. All but one of the fifteen former Soviet republics joined. Thus on January 1, 1992, the Communist hammer-and-sickle flag was hauled down from the towers of the Kremlin, to be replaced by the old Russian banner of the tsars. The Soviet Union ceased to exist, and Gorbachev, the heir of Lenin and Stalin as its president, left office and politics, probably forever.

He is, however, assured of a prominent place in the history books, though history's ultimate judgment upon him may well be mixed. For helping to end the Cold War, for lessening the shadow cast over humanity by the nuclear danger, and for attempting the transformation of a totalitarian state into a democracy, he is likely to be counted among the truly great figures of the twentieth century. Yet we should not forget that many citizens of the former Soviet Union remember him as the man whose advent, by destroying their party, their economic system, and eventually even their country, cast 280 million of his fellow citizens adrift into an unknown future.

Eastern Europe in the 1990s

The joyful mood that swept through Eastern Europe at the surrender under Gorbachev of Soviet dominance and Communist rule has proved very short-lived. Today many in the region contemplate the present with despair and the future with apprehension. While relatively few are nostalgic for the Communist era, the political and economic systems that have emerged since it ended evoke almost as little enthusiasm. Such an outcome sometimes surprises Western observers. Surely, they feel, once rid of the one-party state and the command economy, and of a society in which only the party privileged escaped the drab norms of an enforced equality, Eastern Europe could have been expected to prosper.

Such an expectation ignores the history of the region before and after Communist rule was imposed after World War II. Only Czechoslovakia had been a functioning democracy throughout the interwar period, and even its society had been so fragmented that governments were invariably based on multiparty coalitions. After the Communist collapse at the end of the 1980s, all of these countries saw a resurgence of multiple parties based on the ethnic and social divisions Communism had suppressed. Parliamentary government thus became a matter of ceaseless interparty squabbling. Some of these parties descended from some of the most sinister prewar movements. In Hungary, for example, teenagers cast adrift by the collapse of Communist youth organizations are being increasingly recruited to right-wing–backed "skinhead" movements. Their avowed objective is the restoration of Hungarian greatness by the abrogation of the 1920 treaty that put two-thirds of Hungary's prewar territory and one-third of ethnic Hungarians behind neighboring countries' borders. This is an objective shared by the largest of Hungary's many post-Communist parties. In a region historically wracked by savage ethnic hostilities, the resurgence of movements with such demands does not bode well for the political future.

The most important quarrel that divides the parties of the new Eastern European democracies is over how far and how fast to go in dismantling the command economies communism bequeathed. For all their oppressive drabness, these economies had swathed a majority of Eastern Europeans in a kind of economic and social protective cocoon. The wages they paid were not high by Western standards, but government subsidies kept the prices of necessities low. Services like medical and child care were provided free of charge.

After communism's collapse, however, its triumphant opponents insisted that Eastern Europe could ensure its future prosperity only by aligning its economies with the global free market. Indeed, the new democratic governments had little choice, because the International Monetary Fund, as a condition for lending these countries funds for development and for paying off their huge Western debts, imposed on them the same policies it demands from Third World countries. They were expected to privatize their few profitable industries and shut down the rest, to end price (but not wage) controls and consumer subsidies, and to balance their budgets even if doing so meant abolishing long-standing services like clinics and day-care centers. Moreover, these policies were to be implemented promptly, despite the fact that the whole global economy was sinking into deep recession in the early 1990s.

Even in Hungary, where "goulash communism" had long accustomed people to a substantial private sector, the imposition of the free market came as a shock. Though Hungary received over half of the disappointingly meager investment that Western nations were willing to make in post-Communist Eastern Europe, unemployment climbed to 9 percent by the spring of 1992 as outmoded and unprofitable factories closed and privatizing entrepreneurs trimmed padded payrolls.

In Czechoslovakia, regional disagreement over the speed with which such drastic economic reforms should be imposed actually broke the country in two. In the elections of June 1992, the Czech half of the country gave a plurality to a party headed by a dogmatic advocate of an immediate and complete shift to free enterprise. The Slovakian half, where industrial employment was already devastated by a two-thirds fall in exports to the former Soviet Union, voted for a Communist-backed advocate of a far more gradual transition. Unable to compromise, these two politicians agreed to dissolve Czechoslovakia on January 1, 1993. Rejected by the Slovaks in his bid for a new term as president, Vaclav Havel had already resigned in July 1992. Four years after the "Velvet Revolution," its most symbolic figure had been humiliated, his country had fallen apart, and in both of the country's remnants the public mood was one of dismay and frustration.

Poland attempted the swiftest and most sweeping shift to free enterprise in Eastern Europe. On January 1, 1990, under the inspiration of an American economist, Poland began a course of "economic shock therapy" intended to complete the transition to a free market within a year. To that end, the planners were willing to tolerate an unemployment rate of up to 50 percent for a few years as Poland halved its capacity for steel production and laid off 180,000 of its 300,000 coal miners. With the removal of price controls, the cost of electricity tripled in the first month of the plan's application, and by spring the cost of groceries had gone up 160 percent. Such economic hardship rapidly disillusioned the population with the Solidarity-backed government. In the elections of October 1991, only 40 percent of Poles exercised the right to vote that they had so recently recovered, though they had sixty-five different parties to choose among. Of those who did vote, fewer than one in five supported the parties that backed "shock therapy." A renamed Communist party came in second. During the summer of 1992, ironically, the Solidarity-backed government faced waves of strikes by the very workers whose earlier strikes had enabled Solidarity to unseat the Communists, but whose real wages had fallen by a third. Polls showed that Lech Walesa, now the president, had become less popular with his fellow citizens than General Jaruzelski.

Reacting at last to popular protest, the Polish parliament voted early in 1993 to halt the privatization of state-owned industries, though fewer than 20 percent of them had yet been sold off. But this did not solve the problem of what to do with them. Closing more of them would push unemployment beyond the already alarming official rate of 13.5 percent, but keeping these economic dinosaurs going, producing inefficiently for a glutted global marketplace, would require subsidizing them, thus contributing to an annual inflation rate of 40 percent while risking the wrath of the International Monetary Fund.

It is not surprising that faced with such choices many Eastern Europeans found the victory of democracy to be a hollow triumph. Not that everyone suffered as much from policies like "shock therapy" as redundant workers or elderly pensioners on fixed incomes did. As in the rest of Eastern Europe, Polish retail commerce was rapidly privatized: the number of private businesses doubled in 1991. Though few Poles could afford the kind of Western luxuries for sale in Warsaw's smart new shops, there were enough "new rich"—shrewd entrepreneurs, the leaders of the rapidly developing organized crime syndicates, former Communist managers quick-witted and well connected enough to retain control of privatized public enterprises—to keep them busy. Yet for many Eastern Europeans there is something profoundly wrong with this new democratic society in which the rich flaunt their Mercedes while throngs of the homeless camp out every night in railroad stations. Many long for a "third way" between the remembered oppression of communism and the pitiless rigors of capitalism. But with the guarantor state diminished by hard times even in Western Europe, there is little prospect of its reappearance either in Eastern Europe or in the fifteen lands of the former Soviet Union, where Yeltsin and others are struggling to create some kind of new economic and political order.

Conclusion: After Communism, What?

In hindsight, the collapse of Communism in Eastern Europe and even in the Soviet homeland might have been anticipated—though few experts foresaw it. The dominant trends of the twentieth century, the themes of this book, all pointed toward such an eventual collapse. Growing global interdependence meant that the Soviet bloc economies could not be kept isolated. As Stalinist-style economies failed, communism's worn-out slogans could no longer rationalize authoritarian mass mobilization. Almost as soon as Gorbachev relaxed control, the new technology of television, no longer censored, carried the tidings of reform from one country to the next, toppling Communist regimes like a row of dominoes until even the one in Moscow fell.

In their place, optimistic or naive Western observers expected the swift emergence of democratic political systems and market economies. We have already seen, however, that in Hungary, Czechoslovakia, and Poland (as in the rest of the Soviet bloc), this transition proved not to be so easy. What would happen in the republics of the former USSR and especially in by far the largest, the Russian Republic, where communism had been entrenched so much longer?

Part of the answer depended on the political skills his career had taught Russian president Yeltsin. After nearly a decade as the orthodox Communist political boss of a provincial city, Yeltsin in 1985 was named by Gorbachev to the key post of Moscow party secretary, where his earthy and unpretentious personal style won him widespread popularity among the ordinary Muscovites with whom he rode to work on the subway. In 1987, however, Gorbachev punished his outspoken criticism of the slow pace of reform by ousting him from office. The two became deadly enemies. Though only a narrow majority in the Communist-dominated Russian parliament elected Yeltsin president in May 1990, within two months he showed what he thought of the future of communism by ostentatiously quitting the party. In July 1991, he was re-elected president by popular vote, becoming the first popularly chosen leader in Russian history. To him, after the collapse of the August coup, fell the task of achieving for Russia alone what Gorbachev had failed to achieve for the USSR before it dissolved: the simultaneous creation of a democratic political system, a market economy, and a culture of civic cooperation. By the spring of 1993 it was not clear that Yeltsin had gotten much closer to those objectives than Gorbachev had.

On January 2, 1992, Yeltsin decreed the application to Russia of the kind of "economic shock therapy" American experts and the International Monetary Fund had persuaded Poland's government to adopt. Less than a year later, Muscovites were reciting an ironic riddle: "What has one year of capitalism achieved in Russia that seventy years of communism were unable to accomplish?" The answer was "It has made communism look good." The impact of a year of drastic reform on Russia's economy and society was indeed disastrous. Prices increased some 25-fold in 1992, pushing from 85 to 90 percent of the population below the official poverty line as people exhausted their savings. Russia's Gross Domestic Product fell by more than 20 percent during the year, and consumer spending fell at double the rate it had fallen in the United States during the first four years of the Great Depression. The despair of the population at the collapse of the economy was reflected in a birthrate that fell below the death rate for the first time since World War II.

It was undoubtedly Utopian to expect to transform in three or four years a country in which capitalism had long been reviled and in which entrepreneurial and banking skills were practically nonexistent. Indeed, what privatization of heavy industry did occur was largely the work of the former *nomenklatura*, ex-communist managers who simply stopped working their plants for the state and began working them for their own profit. The sight of economic authority continuing in the same hands only accentuated public disillusionment with reform. In December 1992, the angry Russian parliament withdrew Yeltsin's authority to rule by decree and forced him to dismiss the finance minister responsible for "shock therapy." Thus began a prolonged confrontation between president and legislature, with each blaming the other for the economic debacle. Indeed, there was plenty of blame to be shared under the 1977 Russian constitution, still in force though much amended since the Brezhnev era, which left the respective powers of president and parliament ill-defined. Yeltsin, for example, was unable to prevent the central bank from continuing to fuel inflation by subsidizing industries whose managers were often influential members of parliament. On the other hand, parliament contended that without subsidies the factories would close down, adding mass unemployment to the woes of a society that had long taken full employment for granted.

Having failed to muster the necessary votes to impeach Yeltsin for attempting to impose dictatorial rule, parliament could only grudgingly acquiesce in his appeal to the Russian people by a plebiscite on April 25, 1993. The answers the voters gave to the questions asked showed that among the two-thirds of those eligible who voted, Yeltsin was still far more popular than a parliament that dated back to the days of Communist rule. But the results also showed that Yeltsin was personally more popular than his economic program, while polls revealed that his popularity owed more to his supposed resemblance to strong leaders like the tsars or Stalin than to his attachment to democracy.

By the spring of 1993, indeed, the democratic idealism that appeared to have triumphed over communism in 1991 had faded badly. To many Russians, democracy seemed to have brought not only economic disaster but also higher rates of crime, corruption, and social inequality than even the Brezhnev years had witnessed. In Lithuania, where the battle for democracy had also been a battle for national liberation in 1991, post-Soviet economic developments proved so devastating that in the 1993 elections, the voters threw out the Lithuanian nationalists who had proclaimed independence and replaced them with former Communists pledged to slow down the transition to a market economy.

If a reversion to Communist rule was possible in a non-Russian state that had long chafed under Soviet domination, what may happen in Russia, where economic decline continues to be compounded by political deadlock even after the plebiscite of April 1993? Several scenarios of the Russian future can be imagined. Russia may traverse the agonies of economic transformation swiftly enough to make possible a real democratic revolution. Such a revolution would include formation of a grassroots democratic party, of the kind Yeltsin has not deigned to organize, to counter the new version of the outlawed Communists, still Russia's largest party. Though such a revolution has no precedents in Russian history, which records only the violent imposition of authoritarian rule, it is conceivable that Russian developments will thus converge with what may be a predominant twentieth-century current toward free-market democracies.

There are darker possible scenarios. One is the disintegration of the Russian Republic, which, like the Soviet Union before it, is actually a federation of some twenty different ethnic groups, encompassing almost ninety semi-autonomous regions and cities. As the power struggles have dragged on in Moscow, discrediting both Yeltsin and his critics in parliament, these many local governments have become accustomed to ignoring Moscow's decrees and exercising what little authority is left in a society where less than a third of the young men who receive draft notices actually report for induction.

An even more chilling scenario for the Russian future, from a Western point of view, is that of a successful *coup d'état* by conservative nationalists bent on restoring political authority, social stability, and Russian dominance to the lands of the former USSR. Its collapse has been a deep humiliation to Russian nationalists—now an established 15 to 25 percent of the population—who must endure the sight of Russia's only warm-water ports and 25 million ethnic Russians living under the "foreign rule" of newly independent non-Russian republics like Ukraine. An authoritarian regime pledged to righting these wrongs (by brandishing Russia's nuclear arsenal if necessary) may well appeal to the many Russians who believe that their country has always erred when it has followed Western models—whether Lenin's Marxism or Yeltsin's capitalism—instead of remaining faithful to its unique Slavic character. If the advent of such a quasi-fascist regime seems implausible, it may be pointed out that Russia in 1993 finds itself in much the same situation as Germany in 1918: its familiar political framework destroyed, its economy ravaged, many of its former citizens condemned to live "abroad," its pride humiliated by suspicion that government has fallen into the hands of agents of the national enemy.

A less dire scenario is that as a younger generation of Russians more attuned to the opportunities of the future than to the oppressive security of the past slowly accedes to political power, Russia will find its way to some form of responsible democracy and to a mixed economy combining entrepreneurial capitalism with the large role the state has always played throughout Russian history. In any case, it is clearly too early now to answer the question of what is finally to take the place of Soviet communism.

Notes

1. Paul Kennedy, *Preparing for the Twenty-First Century* (New York: Random House, 1993), p. 247.
2. Roy Medvedev, "Burying the Brezhnev Era's Cult of Stagnation," *New York Times,* April 17, 1987.
3. *New York Times,* November 11, 1987.
4. *New York Times,* March 20, 1988.

Suggestions for Further Reading

Bialer, Seweryn. *The Soviet Paradox: External Expansion, Internal Decline* (1986).

Garton Ash, Timothy. *The Magic Lantern: The Revolution of '89 Witnessed in Warsaw, Budapest, Berlin and Prague* (1990).

Gwertzman, Bernard, and Michael T. Kaufman, eds. *The Decline and Fall of the Soviet Empire* (1992).

Kaiser, Robert G. *Why Gorbachev Happened* (1992).

Kerblay, Basile. *Modern Soviet Society* (1983).

PART 5

Independence for the Developing Countries?

CHAPTER 15

Latin America: Mobilization and Development or Neocolonial Militarism?

Latin America's history since World War II includes two distinct economic and political periods and the start of a third. The trends toward industrialization and mass mobilization begun by the 1930s continued through the 1960s. The region then relapsed into economic neocolonialism and military authoritarianism. In another reversal of trend, elected civilian governments with market-oriented economic policies reappeared in the 1980s.

Living through these shifts, Latin Americans have had difficulty escaping political and economic subordination at either the national or—for most—the individual level. At the national level, subordination exists even in countries whose experience, through revolution, has seemed to differ most from that of their neighbors. An overview of the entire region, followed by closer looks at Argentina, Brazil, Mexico, and Cuba, will illustrate these points.

Continental Overview: The Shark and the Sardines

After 1945, many old Latin American problems persisted while new ones appeared. To make matters worse, the changing global distribution of power and wealth widened the gap between wealthy and poor countries. A survey of social, economic, and political problems suggests that the regressive trend, evident from the 1960s through the 1980s, stemmed in general from these facts, and the current turn toward democratization signals a new attempt to respond to these problems in the altered context of the post–Cold War era.

Mounting Social Pressures

Latin America today retains some of the worst of its old social problems: the hacienda system, debt peonage in a few places, abuse of native Americans (including elimination of whole tribes in Brazil and Guatemala), and discrimination against women. Only five Latin American countries—Ecuador, Brazil, Uruguay, Cuba, and El Salvador—gave women the vote before World War II. Argentina followed in 1947, Mexico in 1953, others even later.

Atop the old lack of social integration, new problems also appeared. Mass mobilizers discovered that the class structure of most Latin American societies had become more complex. The old pattern was made up of landlords and peasants, with rudimentary urban middle and working classes. But now many countries had a social structure more like that of industrial societies, in part because of rapid population growth.

Throughout the Third World—or the underdeveloped South, as it makes more sense to call it in the post–Cold War era—death rates began to decline in the 1930s, thanks to improvements in public health. Birthrates began to fall only later. A similar demographic transition occurred in nineteenth-century Europe, eventually leading to a new equilibrium between birth and death rates at lower levels. The South has yet to achieve equilibrium. Many poor Latin Americans—and Africans and Asians—still believe they have incentives to have large families. In the past, more hands meant more income, and numerous offspring were their parents' only security in old age, given high infant mortality. Now, death rates have declined, but birthrates have only partly adjusted to this decline. A population explosion has resulted.

In 1992, Latin America's population of 453 million was growing at a rate of 2.1 percent a year, down from about 2.5 percent in the 1970s. Different countries' 1992 growth rates ranged from Honduras's 3.2 to Uruguay's 0.8 percent. Overall, the world had become divided demographically between slow-growth regions with growth rates under 1.0 percent a year and fast-growth regions with rates exceeding 2.0 percent a year. The slow-growth regions were mostly affluent and in the North: Europe (western and eastern), North America, East Asia, Australia–New Zealand. The fast-growth regions were all poor and in the South, including Latin America. The problem of rapid population growth had dramatic effects on quality of life. For example, although Latin America had been the world's largest grain exporter in the 1930s, it had since become an importer. The amount of grain produced per capita in Latin America fell in the 1980s. Though falling, infant mortality rates in 1992 also told a shocking story: 11 per thousand live births in Cuba, 47 in Mexico, 69 in Brazil, 106 in Haiti, compared to 9 in the United States and 6 in Sweden. Illiteracy too was a problem. In both Brazil and Mexico, while the percentage of illiterates in the population declined, the actual number of illiterates grew for much of the post-1945 period because of rapid population growth.

Problems of population and living standards challenged Latin American societies on every level. They also challenged the United States, as the political controversy over illegal immigration made clear. The determination of Hispanics to escape the problems of their homelands has given the United States the fourth-largest Spanish-speaking population—22 million in 1990—of any country in the Western Hemisphere.

Economic change has channeled burgeoning Third World populations into the cities. Since about 1960, a wave of superurbanization has produced urban complexes in the Third World bigger than any in affluent countries. Usually focused on each country's single largest city, superurbanization overloads every urban facility and leaves the center ringed with shantytowns, known as *villas miserias* in Argentina. Mexico City grew from 8 million inhabitants in 1970 to perhaps 22 million in 1992 and was predicted to become the world's biggest city, with over 30 million, by 2025.

The Uncertain Course of Economic Development

The Latin American countries' economic and social problems are clearly inseparable. The national economies vary widely. Large and comparatively industrialized, Argentina, Brazil, and Mexico had exports valued respectively at $12, $27, and $31 billion in 1990, with manufactures accounting for about 40 percent of Argentina's and Mexico's exports and 56 percent of Brazil's. In contrast, the exports of the Central American countries (Panama, Costa Rica, Nicaragua, Honduras, El Salvador, and Guatemala) ranged between $0.4 and $1.5 billion in value in 1990, with agricultural products still accounting for 70 percent or more of each country's exports. That Latin American economies still have common problems, however, is apparent from regionwide debate over development strategies.

The debate focuses on two questions that all industrializing economies face: where the resources for industrialization will come from and how to use them. One answer is to extract resources from agriculture. Other sources are external: foreign investment or profits from foreign trade. Another possibility is to extract capital by holding down workers' wages. The success of any of these strategies depends in part on the strength of those who accumulate capital—industrialists, landlords, the state—in relation to those with whom they must deal at home and abroad. Another question is the goal of industrialization: what industries to create and for what market.

The larger Latin American countries, as noted in Chapter 8, began to answer these questions by the 1930s with a strategy aimed first at local production of formerly imported goods, then at heavy industry. The market for import substitution was by definition internal, and various devices, such as high import duties, were used to protect it. Governments exerted leadership by founding state enterprises or providing facilities, such as credit; and governments expanded in power and size as their economic role grew. Capital came from agriculture, to some extent. But only Mexico attempted any basic restructuring of agriculture, whose workings historically emphasized the landlords' dominance over the peasantry more than economic productivity. The usual failure to couple import substitution with agrarian reform undercut industrialization by restricting the productivity of agriculture, the size of the internal market, and the development of a skilled labor force.

Import-substitution industrialization predominated through the 1960s. But by then, the policy had reached its limits. After a first "easy" phase that satisfied domestic demand for simple consumer goods, import substitution meant moving into industries that required greater capital and more advanced technology, that produced proportionally fewer jobs, and that could produce efficiently only for large markets.

Rapid technological advance compounded these problems. It was one thing to conquer heavy industry symbolically by building a steel mill, another to become self-sufficient in machine tools or chemicals, not to mention advanced technologies like microelectronics. Without such self-sufficiency—something small economies could not aspire to—import substitution merely shifted the frontier of import dependency from the finished product to the machines or parts used to

Superurbanization and economic inequality. *This view of São Paulo, Brazil, shows the sharp contrast that these two forces create in contemporary Latin America.* *Maitre/Gamma-Liaison*

make it. Protectionist policies did not overcome these problems but merely led multinational firms to penetrate the protected economies by creating local subsidiaries.

The exhaustion of the import-substitution strategy became a major factor in opening a new period in the 1960s. The decades since have displayed two distinct approaches to economic development. The less common, socialist policy seeks development through radical structural change in society and economy, including agrarian reform and attempts to sever external dependency relations. Countries that attempted this approach include Castro's Cuba (1959 to the present), Chile under Allende (1970–1973), and Nicaragua after the Sandinista revolution (1979). Only in Cuba did this approach become established for the long term. Even Castro only changed the form of dependency, as Cuba's hardship after the collapse of its Soviet patron showed. Like most of the 180-odd countries in today's world, Cuba may simply lack the economic potential to rise above a subordinate place in the world.

The more common economic policy since 1960 has been neocolonial. In crude form, this recalls the old "liberal" view of Latin America as an agrarian region whose role was to export agricultural and mineral products and to import industrial ones. In the up-to-date view of finance technocrats, the policy seeks development largely through foreign investment, accepting the restrictions, including drastic squeezing of wages, that foreign investors and lenders like the International Monetary Fund (IMF) demand to secure their investment.*

Brazil's experience showed that this approach can produce gains. Brazil even became an exporter of advanced industrial products, but Brazil's growth proved uneven and worsened existing inequalities. In Brazil, as in other relatively industrialized countries, neocolonialism passed through two stages. Direct investment by multinational corporations characterized the first. Direct government borrowing from large international banks typified the second. The result of both phases was that foreign investment in Latin America, having fallen during the Depression, rose again sharply after 1960.

Both phases had important costs. Industrialization through direct foreign investment worsened balance-of-payments problems because money left the country to cover profits and royalties. The capital that multinational firms took out of Latin America probably exceeded their investments greatly. For example, Brazilian statistics record a total capital inflow for the period 1947–1960 of $1.8 billion but a total outflow of $3.5 billion. Latin American governments attempted to limit these outflows, but multinational firms defeated these efforts by working with the historically foreign-oriented local elites. In the military-dominated Argentina of the 1960s, for example, 143 retired military commanders held 177 positions in the largest and mostly foreign-controlled firms.

The foreign-debt approach to capital accumulation seemed to solve some of these problems but ultimately made them worse. Government borrowing brought capital into Latin American countries under the guise of national control and enabled the governments to enlarge their role as investors or lenders. Yet if direct investment by foreign firms required remittances abroad to cover profits and fees, government borrowing required larger foreign remittances to cover principle and interest.

Before the foreign-debt approach had gone far, global economic interdependency tightened abruptly as a result of the revolutionary oil price increases imposed by the Organization of Petroleum Exporting Countries (OPEC), which includes Venezuela, Nigeria, and Indonesia though most members are in the Middle East. The first increases almost quadrupled the price of oil on the world market, from $2.70 per barrel in 1973 to $9.76 in 1976. Further increases in 1979 led to a price of $33.47 per barrel in 1982.

No part of the world felt these price increases more than developing countries that had to import oil. By 1979, various factors—conservation, shifts to alternative energy sources, and recession—had reduced world oil consumption. Price drops followed in the 1980s. Then even oil-producing countries began to suffer—a fact suggesting that, despite their sudden wealth, they were not really different from other economies dependent on a single export commodity.

Partly because of double-digit U.S. interest rates provoked by the financial crisis of the early 1980s, Latin American foreign debt shot up, reaching $400 billion by 1990. Latin America transferred over $200 billion in payments to industrialized nations in the 1980s, and eco-

*The International Monetary Fund is a UN agency created to aid member states in temporary balance-of-payment difficulties. The IMF extends aid only to countries that draw up plans to eliminate their deficits. Among developing countries, the IMF is one of the most resented of international agencies. It is not hard to understand why: the IMF conditions its assistance on forcing poor countries to make the kind of choices between social spending and debt reduction that U.S. voters have generally refused to make.

nomic output per capita declined nearly 10 percent for the decade. In 1990, Brazil, Mexico, and Argentina—at $116, $97, and $61 billion, respectively—had the second-. third-, and fifth-largest foreign debts among the world's nations. Much of this debt had begun as "petrodollars," deposited by Middle Eastern oil states in Western banks and unwisely lent to Latin America.

The huge debt buildup suggests that the neocolonial development strategy had reached an impasse, as import substitution had by the 1960s. As of 1992, crisis symptoms for the region included a net outflow of funds for debt service, inflation at annual percentages in three or four digits in some countries, decline in real wages, and a near doubling in the percentage of households that could not provide for their basic needs, to 62 percent. How would Latin America develop economically if over half its households lacked the food and clothing needed for the adults to work effectively or for the children to learn in school?

Experts searched for economic policy alternatives. One widely used concept, in Latin America and the world over, was *privatization:* selling government-controlled companies to private interests. Brazil had over 400 government-owned companies; Mexico had over 1,100. Shifting these to the private sector, where survival depended on making a profit, might increase competition and productivity. Latin American statesmen also began to shift policy toward export-led growth and—in reaction to external changes such as European integration—to create free-trade agreements or common markets with other countries. From *Mercosur,* the "southern market" uniting Argentina, Brazil, Paraguay, and Uruguay, to the North American Free Trade Agreement (NAFTA) that would link Mexico to the United States and Canada, nearly enough such agreements have been proposed to blanket the hemisphere. The most daring such strategy, Mexico's commitment to NAFTA, has been interpreted as an attempted leap out of the underdeveloped South into the ranks of highly developed nations. How successful free-trade agreements will be, and how much they will do to reverse the erosion of most Latin Americans' living standards during the 1980s, remain to be seen.

Until such policy changes do produce significant benefits, the region's most painful economic policy choice will lie in deciding how to respond to the demands of international lending agencies. To restore Latin American nations' creditworthiness requires either politically intolerable sacrifices from consumers or higher export profits to cover debt repayment—as if debt-service obligations left capital to invest in promoting exports.

Underdevelopment has left Latin American nations the option of supporting social programs, investing for growth, or servicing their foreign debts, but not all three. The failure of international lenders like the IMF to recognize this dilemma spotlights the global need to restructure international economic relations so as not merely to demand that poor countries repay their debts but also to enhance their growth and their ability to pay (see Chapter 19).

Political Reflections of Socioeconomic Stress

Latin America's major post-1945 political developments followed from the region's social and economic history. Each of the three major economic policies—import substitution, socialism, and neocolonialism—was associated with a particular type of politics and with particular social groups. Since the 1930s, for example, the import-substitution strategy was associated with corporatist mass mobilizers, of whom Perón and Vargas still played leading roles after 1945.

Radical leftist policies appealed to frustrated nationalists and the disadvantaged.

Many radicals were communists, and a larger number held some ideas inspired by Marx, Mao, or Ché Guevara, who figures in the discussion on Cuba later in this chapter. Yet the communists were not united, and not all radicals were communists, as Roman Catholic political activism shows.

Radicals dominated the course of change in only a few places, chiefly Cuba. Cuba's efforts to export its revolution in the 1960s proved unsuccessful. However, the Cuban experience exerted a pervasive influence on Latin American politics. Leftists everywhere saw in it signs that revolution could succeed in Latin America despite U.S. opposition. Rightists took fright from Cuba's revolution, which toppled old elites and transformed socioeconomic relations in a way that earlier Latin American "revolutions" had not. Castro's triumph not only excited leftist hopes but also helped provoke rightist repression under the military dictatorships of the next quarter-century. Worsened economic conditions after 1973 played into military authoritarians' hands, confirming the secular radicals' eclipse.

Catholic activists remained at work, however, from El Salvador to Brazil, despite Pope John Paul II's demands to end political office-holding by priests and eliminate Marxism from religious thought. Religious thinkers also continued elaborating a theology of liberation, which demanded social justice and land reform and cast the church's lot with the poor. This new theology had a major impact, especially through the Christian Base Communities (known as "CEBs" in Spanish or Portuguese). CEBs are activist groups, led by clergy or trained lay delegates, who teach the poor that they, too, are made in God's image and should demand social change. By defining the common people as the church, CEBs invert the church's hierarchical authority system. Important mass mobilizers, they helped launch the Nicaraguan revolution. In Brazil, the growth of unions outside state control benefited from labor activists' experience in CEBs, even though CEBs as such took no part in the new unionization effort. Increasingly urbanized by the late 1980s, poor Latin Americans began to gravitate more toward Protestant Pentecostal sects. The fact remained that liberation theology had answered important needs.

Neocolonial authoritarianism, which became so conspicuous in the 1960s and 1970s, has clearly been associated with conservatives, especially military leaders. Not all Latin American military officers are conservative. But the shift to neocolonial policies coincided with the military installation of repressive regimes in Brazil, Chile, Bolivia, Uruguay, Paraguay, and Argentina. The only large Latin American country to escape military domination—for reasons that will merit further comment—was Mexico.

In the 1980s, the trend reversed. Elected civilian governments assumed power in most countries. Nowhere was democracy complete, however. In most places, the military retained extensive power or even a policy veto. Human rights remained in jeopardy. Soviet collapse tended to discredit the Left, and social reform lacked effective advocates.

Perhaps the key question was why narrow-based authoritarian regimes ever emerged in defiance of the global twentieth-century trend toward mass-oriented political systems. To explain this, some analysts focused on neocolonial economic policy, arguing that only a repressive government could restrain working-class demands, which populist leaders had mobilized, and impose the sacrifices needed to stabilize the economy and attract foreign investment. Others pointed to the impact of Cuba's revolution, which had incited leftist activism and rightist repression all over the region. Another explanation—not unrelated to the others—emphasized U.S.–Latin American relations.

U.S.–Latin American Relations, with a Chilean Example

At the end of World War II, U.S. influence in Latin America was at its highest point. The United States capitalized on its influence by persuading most Latin American governments to sever relations with the Soviet Union, ban local communist parties, accept a collective security agreement (the Rio Pact, 1947), and join the Organization of American States (1948). After the communist victory in China and the Korean War (1950–1953), the United States saw its struggle with communism as a global one. As a result, the United States concluded defense assistance agreements with ten Latin American nations during 1952–1954, with important results. Latin American military elites acquired U.S. equipment, far beyond what their governments could have bought them, and trained jointly with U.S. forces. Thus these elites became identified with the U.S. military and acquired greater prominence in their own countries than they would otherwise have possessed.

Under different U.S. presidents, policy toward Latin America shifted, but the military emphasis persisted. Truman (1945–1953) tried to balance the military policy with the Point Four Program, which offered technical assistance to developing countries. Eisenhower (1953–1961) mostly abandoned economic aid in favor of free enterprise. Faced with the Cuban revolution and Soviet penetration of the Western Hemisphere, Kennedy (1961–1963) shifted again, producing the Alliance for Progress. One part of it aimed at social and economic development. Latin American nations were to submit development plans covering topics such as agrarian and tax reforms, and the United States was to help finance the plans. Such development would help prevent more Cubas. But rapid development itself could create social stress that might lead to revolution. Working through the Alliance, the United States tried to prevent revolution through counterinsurgency, a policy that it also applied in Vietnam (see Chapter 12). The concept combined military and "civic action" in such fields as public works and health care and was to be carried out by military forces working to cement the people's loyalty to the existing governments.

Latin America may have seemed more promising for counterinsurgency than war-torn Vietnam, but the Alliance for Progress failed. Hindsight shows that it was unrealistic to expect freely elected Latin American governments to achieve economic growth and social reform at the same time. The Alliance's key economic assumption—that industrial development in Latin America could "take off" as it had earlier in Britain or the United States—erred because it ignored Latin America's dependency. Indeed, the Alliance reinforced dependency. Much of the aid took the form of loans, with requirements to spend the funds on U.S. goods. Also serious were the results of entrusting "civic action" to the military. Latin American officers felt it was insulting to ask soldiers to engage in manual labor like road building. The meaning they drew from the concept of counterinsurgency was that only military regimes could both push hard for economic development and control the stress it placed on workers and peasants. So viewed, the Alliance furthered the militarization of politics in the 1960s.

Kennedy's successor in Washington, Lyndon Johnson (1963–1969), abandoned the development side of the Alliance but not the military side. Reacting to events in Vietnam, the Nixon administration (1969–1974) declared that the United States could not keep peace all over the world; it shifted attention to regimes that could play the role of peacekeeper in their own regions—in Latin America, the military regimes. Despite the Carter focus (1977–1981) on human rights, no fundamental revision of the military emphasis appeared in U.S. policy before the late 1980s.

The Chilean experience of the 1970s provides the most memorable example of the military-oriented U.S. policy. Chile's economy had long been dominated by U.S. interests, especially in copper mining, and by a small local elite with interests in land, industry, and finance. As rapid population growth and urbanization began to strain Chilean society, it became clear that those interests could no longer control political mobilization. By the late 1950s, the country had acquired a range of political parties, from "Conservatives" and "Liberals" on the right to socialists and communists on the left. In the 1964 presidential election, the Right temporarily checked the radicalizing trend by joining with the left-moderate Christian Democrats to elect their candidate, Eduardo Frei, and beat the Left coalition's Salvador Allende.

Frei's presidency was not a success. He accepted aid under the Alliance for Progress and opened Chile increasingly to foreign investment, so deepening dependency. His attempts to define centrist policies on issues like land reform and nationalization provoked controversy. His Christian Democratic party competed with leftists to mobilize the populace, with sharp political polarization as the result. In the 1970 election, this polarization blocked formation of a broad coalition like the one that had won in 1964. Rightist, centrist, and leftist candidates ran. The leftist candidate, Salvador Allende, won, but with only 36 percent of the vote. The election went to the Congress, which approved Allende. A second Marxist government had come to power in Latin America, this one freely elected, but only by a narrow margin.

Allende's program called for a peaceful transition to socialism. Recalling European social democrats' failed hopes of the 1930s (see Chapter 5), this was a tall order for a narrowly elected Third World government that had to operate in the Western Hemisphere under U.S. scrutiny. Allende began by freezing prices and raising wages to redistribute income. He next sought complete nationalization of the copper companies. Nationalization then extended into other sectors, affecting both Chilean and foreign-owned firms. Allende also pushed ahead with land reform and by the end of 1972 had liquidated the large estates. In these measures, Allende tried to proceed by legal means, but left-wing radicals often forced his hand. Nationalization had soon gone so far that the government could not have compensated foreign firms if it had wanted to.

Opposition to Allende gradually mounted so as to block any peaceful transition to socialism. By late 1972, agricultural production and copper prices had fallen. Inflation was getting out of control. Radicals to Allende's left demanded faster change, while conservatives—who still controlled much of the media, the Congress, the bureaucracy, the military officer corps, and the church—organized actions such as a massive strike in the fall of 1972. The U.S. government and U.S. corporations with interests in Chile did everything possible to thwart Allende. The Nixon administration took steps to halt loans and private investment, and the CIA spent $8 million in three years—as later revealed in Senate testimony—to undermine the economy. Only to the Chilean military did U.S. aid continue. As the crisis mounted, Allende made concessions to his opponents but could not save the situation. In September 1973, military officers mounted a coup that left Allende dead and the Left crushed.

At the head of the new regime stood General Augusto Pinochet, an alumnus of the School of the Americas, founded by the U.S. Army to train Latin American officers. One of Latin America's most repressive and durable military regimes, Pinochet's survived long after civilian government resumed in Argentina (1983) and Brazil (1985). He could not have

"Widen the agrarian reform! The nation is stronger than the big landowners." *So proclaimed the banners of peasants and workers demonstrating for Allende shortly before his overthrow, September 1973.* *Ojeda/Magnum*

lasted so long if Allende's socialism had not frightened Chile's middle class into accepting from Pinochet even policies that undermined business and industry. He abolished political parties and suspended the constitution, with its guaranteed rights. Then he set out to reduce the state in size, shift government services into the private sector, establish a free-market economy, and ban the Left from politics. He turned economic policy over to technocrats who fulfilled the neocolonial program to the fullest. Import duties fell from 100 percent to 10 percent, depriving much Chilean industry of protection it needed to survive but—more important to Pinochet—attracting foreign investment and weakening the working class through job loss. To further undermine labor, unionization was limited to "factory unions," whose members all worked for the same firm. Privatization went so far that even schools and social security were privatized. Pinochet had the common rightist goal of shrinking the state. His purpose, however, was not greater freedom, for he also had the radically authoritarian goal of increasing the state's control by shrinking the society's potential for opposition even more. Pinochet sought to ensure his position through the constitution of 1980, which named him president until 1989 and empowered the armed service commanders to reappoint him after that.

What Allende could have achieved if he had not faced foreign intervention remains unclear: scholars debate the extent to which U.S. interference, internal opposition, or his own mistakes caused his fall. Pinochet, in contrast, had time to make his impact quite clear. His brutally conservative economic policies lowered inflation from 500 percent a year in 1973 to 20 or 30 percent a year in the mid-1980s, diversified exports until copper accounted for less than half of export value, privatized most of the 500 firms that the state had owned in 1973, and achieved economic growth of 7 percent a year in the late 1970s. But they also bankrupted much of agriculture and industry, worsened rural landlessness, and reduced workers' wages and social services. His efforts to destroy political parties and the labor movement never succeeded, and antigovernment protests resumed in 1983. Progressive church leaders embarrassed Pinochet by documenting his human rights abuses.

When he mistakenly gave them a chance, Chileans voted against Pinochet, electing a Christian Democrat, Patricio Aylwin, to the presidency in December 1989. Pinochet ceded the presidency in 1990 but was constitutionally entitled to remain army commander-in-chief until 1998. Under this odd arrangement, Chile resumed its unsure history as a democracy. Lessons remained to ponder about the impact of such rigidly conservative economic policies on a developing country and about the part U.S. policy had played in Chile's travails.

The Shark and the Sardines

Chile's experience illustrates not only problems of relations with the United States but also the other Latin American themes discussed in this overview. These problems began with the addition of runaway population growth and superurbanization to the old social inequalities. Such problems overtaxed the capabilities of governments that aimed at both political mobilization and economic development. By the 1960s, the characteristic economic strategy of these governments, based on import substitution, was exhausted. This fact, and the fears touched off by the Cuban revolution, then launched a trend toward military-authoritarian regimes. They pursued neocolonial economic policies more favorable to the foreign interests that supported them than to the local populace. Chile's experience was unusual in that the radical alternative briefly triumphed with Allende, between the Christian Democrat Frei and the military dictator Pinochet.

Pursuing the perceived interests of their nation, U.S. policymakers historically favored stability and a secure climate for investment and thus normally disregarded the political environment that Latin American rulers created for their citizens. In this way, U.S. policy contributed to the resurgence of militarism more than most U.S. citizens realized. Indeed, the average U.S citizen has little grasp of why former Guatemalan president Juan Arévalo (in office 1945–1950) described U.S.–Latin American relations in terms of "the shark and the sardines." Some Latin American countries are bigger than sardines, but U.S. leaders know what Arévalo meant.[1]

After the oil price increases of 1973 and 1979, economic pressures exposed the military regimes of Latin America to new difficulties. By the 1980s, it appeared that those regimes had not permanently thwarted the characteristic twentieth-century demands for mass political mobilization and economic development to benefit the people. To replace those regimes with more democratic ones would not be easy, considering how many parties and other institutions the military had destroyed. Partly because of the economic regressiveness of the military regimes, moreover, the continent still had no country that had risen to more than an intermediate position in the global pattern of economic relations, although Mexico stood poised to bid, through NAFTA, for economic integration with the United States and Canada.

Argentina: The Perils of Authoritarianism, with Charisma and Without

After 1945, Perón's influence gave a distinctive stamp to Argentine history. Even so, the country passed through the same phases noted elsewhere, starting with the relatively democratic, development-oriented regimes of Perón (1946–1955) and his Radical successors (1958–1966) and followed by a period of military authoritarianism. Throughout, several factors proved especially important. Perón was more effective at mobilizing the populace than at charting political and economic policy. The military not only had means to exert force but were politically assertive. Control of government firms that manufactured military supplies made them economically influential as well. Argentina suffered acutely from lack of political consensus. Peronists, middle-class Radicals, the military, the Left—all had splits and conflicts that made orderly political life difficult. But the most important problem was the economy. Despite progress in industry, almost all of Argentina's foreign exchange still came from agricultural exports, but Argentina's share of world trade was shrinking. By the early 1980s, the once "amazing Argentine" had become one more underdeveloped, unstable Latin American country.

Toward Democracy and Development?

Chapter 8 followed Perón's rise and his election to the presidency in 1946. As president, he aimed economically at industrialization through import substitution and politically at corporatist mobilization, which he set out to achieve by broadening his constituency into a labor-management-military alliance and redistributing income to his followers. To support industrialization, he enacted a Five-Year Plan and created a foreign trade organization, IAPI (Instituto Argentino de Promoción del Intercambio). IAPI was to monopolize the marketing of agricultural exports, and its profits were to go for industrialization. To reduce foreigners' economic role, Perón nationalized foreign-dominated enterprises, including railroads and the central bank, using wartime export earnings to compensate the owners. In 1947 he paid off the foreign debt. Perón's policies made Argentina almost self-sufficient in consumer goods by 1955, although there was still little heavy industry.

Perón's populism was strong, but his economic ideas were weak. They were inflationary: living costs at Buenos Aires rose some 700 percent from 1943 to 1955. Enlarged to provide new services, the government was one of the world's costliest. Despite his populism, the high taxes required to support the government were mostly indirect, hitting the poor hardest. By substituting bureaucratic inefficiencies for the spur of competition, nationalization also made firms less productive. As an intermediary between Argentine producers and world markets in which it lacked power to influence prices, IAPI could make a profit only by buying Argentina's grain and livestock at below-market prices, thus reducing incentives for Argentinians to produce and invest. Since

Argentina still relied on agricultural exports to earn foreign currency, Perón was killing the goose that laid the golden eggs.

For some time, most Argentines probably believed conditions were getting better. Industrialists and the urban middle class were pleased by patronage in the bureaucracy and the enlargement of the market for their goods as working-class living standards rose. The military liked industrialization and the salary increases and equipment they received. Given the vote in 1947 largely through the efforts of Eva Duarte Perón, women voted heavily for her husband. Thanks to the strong export market of the early postwar years, Perón was able to gratify labor with steady increases in purchasing power through 1949—another factor that helped diminish agricultural exports, because consumption grew at home. The flow of new benefits, such as improved health care, continued. Until her death in 1952, Eva Perón dispensed many of the benefits through her Eva Perón Foundation, becoming a cult figure as she received petitioners there.

Nationalism and populism on this scale are enough to explain the Peróns' lasting hold on Argentine affections. In 1949, Perón was able to secure a new constitution that embodied his principles and authorized presidential re-election to consecutive terms. Although military objections to the possibility of a female commander-in-chief blocked Eva's vice-presiden-

Juan and Eva Perón at his presidential inauguration in 1952. *To many Argentines, this charismatic pair symbolized the opening of an era of mass politics.* *UPI/Bettmann Newsphotos*

tial candidacy, Juan Perón easily won the much-manipulated election of 1952. Yet conditions were turning against him.

Populism without economic realism could not last. Income redistribution and expanded government spending depended on postwar boom conditions. After 1948, recession, bad harvests, and keener competition in export markets led to balance-of-payment deficits. Industrial output and real wages were falling by the early 1950s. Perón never coped successfully with this change, nor have his successors ever overcome the resulting combination of economic stagnation and political instability.

Perón's political alliance began to crumble, and he turned to erratic measures that led to his fall. Re-elected in 1952, he launched a new Five-Year Plan that departed from the first by calling for a two-year wage freeze and giving incentives to agriculture and foreign investment. As if to mask these changes, he tightened political discipline among his followers, became increasingly dictatorial (though he never eliminated all opposition), and emphasized the "Justicialist" ideology that he—not a profound thinker—had made up to explain his policies. Still, the complaints grew. In 1954, for unknown reasons, Perón attacked the Catholic church. Violent demonstrations resulted, the pope excommunicated him, and the military abandoned him. Facing a military conspiracy in September 1955, he fled without a fight. For the next eighteen years, Perón overshadowed Argentine politics from afar, while his followers, though divided, remained a major force inside the country.

After Perón's fall, the military took control directly. But they had no effective policy beyond the wish to root out Peronism. Their attempts to break the unions, end Perón's consumer subsidies, and deregulate the economy caused the exiled leader's popularity and that of his now-outlawed party to rise again. Politics became so fractious, and the economy so unstable, that the military soon decided to withdraw into the background and permit a return to electoral politics. The largest legal party was the Radicals, who had last ruled Argentina before the Depression. By promising to relegalize the outlawed Peronists in return for votes, Arturo Frondizi, the candidate of one of two Radical factions, won the 1958 election and became president.

Civilian presidents from the Radical party—actually not radical but middle-class moderates—governed Argentina for the next eight years. Their rule forms a second stage in the postwar trend toward mass political participation and economic development. As president, Frondizi's key problems were to cope with Perón's legacy of economic deterioration and political instability. Economically, Frondizi seemed ready to try anything to revive the economy—from a large initial wage increase for labor, to foreign borrowing, deals with foreign oil companies, and personnel cuts in the bureaucracy and state-owned firms. But his policies failed to reverse inflation and unemployment. Partly for this reason, Frondizi's political support eroded so much that thirty-five coup attempts occurred against his presidency. When he followed through on his deal with the Peronists and again allowed them to participate directly in elections, the armed forces overthrew him. Civilian government resumed indecisively under the rival Radical faction in 1963, but another military coup toppled it in 1966. The middle-class Radicals had again failed to rule Latin America's most middle-class country, and the problems stemming from Perón's combination of populism and economic unrealism persisted.

Neocolonial Militarism in Argentina

The new military government of 1966 dismantled the fragile institutions of Argentina's modern political life by closing Congress, suppressing political parties and the labor movement, purging the universities, and ruling through an alliance of military commanders, technocrats, and foreign investors. Its economic program featured a two-year wage freeze, elimination of all restrictions on profit remittances by foreign firms, and devaluation. Devaluation produced dramatic effects, making it harder for Argentine firms to import machinery or new technology and easier for foreign firms to buy them out. Foreign dominance of Argentine industry increased markedly.

Military rule could not make Argentines take such medicine quietly. In 1969, when troops fired on a labor demonstration in Córdoba, center of the automobile industry, the violence spread to other cities, opening a period of urban guerrilla activism. Numerous guerrilla groups emerged, such as the People's Revolutionary Army (ERP in Spanish) and the left-Peronist Montoneros. The revolutionary potential that some Argentine officers had mistakenly thought they saw in the masses in the 1940s was becoming a reality. Some radical movements were Marxist, but the roots of others lay in Perón's populism. His policies, and the military's reactions to them, had created the peril they were meant to thwart.

As violence grew—with attacks on government installations, kidnappings of foreign businessmen, the killing of a former president, and brutal retaliation by the government—Argentina drifted toward civil war. Military leaders finally struck a deal with the exiled Perón, hoping that his magic could still restore order. He returned to become president again, at age seventy-seven. This time, his wife, Isabel, was his vice president. They were elected in September 1973 with 62 percent of the vote.

From exile, Perón had made statements to encourage both Left and Right, for his one goal was to regain power. In office, he cracked down on the Left—the military commanders who let him return had not misjudged him. Perón died in 1974, and his wife succeeded him but was unable to control events. The crackdown on the Left intensified, as right-wing death squads, thought to be linked to one of her advisers, mounted a counterterror. When the economy went out of control, the army removed her from office in 1976, and military rule resumed. The generals who had seized power meant to change Argentine politics permanently. Their biggest problems were the Left and the economy.

The generals expanded the struggle with the Left into a "dirty war," in which both sides made fatal mistakes. The Left blundered from the start in bypassing mass mobilization and organization to launch military action against the regime. If leftists had first been able to win control of the labor movement from right-wing Peronists, for example, things might have ended differently. The regime's big mistake was to overreact, terrorizing the nation indiscriminately in order to quell guerrilla movements with perhaps ten thousand members. By the time the military won, ten thousand people—possibly several times more—had "disappeared," brutally tortured and in many cases pushed from helicopters to die in the sea. Many *desaparecidos* (those who have "disappeared") were university students or former students, middle class in background, whose interest in radical ideas was an understandable reaction to the neocolonial military regime that offered them so little. The desaparecidos' memory—first publicized by a movement that their mothers created—continues to haunt Argentine consciences.

Economically, the military rulers introduced predictable policies. Favoring the agrarian side of the economy rather than the industrial, they sold off state enterprises and tightened credit. Real interest rates rocketed to 20 to 40 percent. Workers' living standards plummeted. The industrial working class actually shrank by a quarter from 1975 to 1980. These brutal policies slowed inflation and produced a positive payments balance until the 1981 recession sent the economy reeling and added massive foreign debt to the military rulers' economic legacy.

In the spring of 1982, the troubled regime attempted the classic maneuver of rousing patriotic support through a popular war, fought over the Falkland Islands, or Malvinas, as they are known in Spanish. Located about three hundred miles off Argentina's coast, the islands were British ruled but claimed by Argentina. Argentina's defeat disgraced the military regime, which then had no choice but to step aside and call presidential elections for October 1983.

Again Toward Democracy and Development?

The winner, in an upset of the Peronist candidate, was Raúl Alfonsín, a Radical and human rights activist. His victory roused excitement in Argentina and abroad. For Latin America, it seemed to signal a new turn toward democracy and economic development in the national interest.

Alfonsín faced huge tasks. The "dirty war" had left a vast backlog of rights violations that he wanted to prosecute. In addition, the legacy of Perón's economic and political policies—combining state-dominated industry and a weakened agricultural sector with a highly politicized society—would have assured low economic growth and a high level of political conflict even without the foreign debt piled up under the military. To dismantle state corporatism and make the economy internationally competitive seemed urgent. Could this be done in a country edgy over the trials of military figures from the fallen regime, where Peronists remained a powerful political force and international lenders demanded austerity as a condition for debt rescheduling?

By the May 1989 presidential election, the economic situation had worsened to the point of food riots and looting. The Peronist candidate, Carlos Saúl Menem, won. Alfonsín dejectedly resigned before his term ended, and Peronists came to power for the first time without Perón himself. Forced by economic hardship to sacrifice ideology, Menem had to seek foreign investment, raise the efficiency of tax collection, privatize government enterprises, weaken unions, cut military spending, and even relax prosecution of rights violations under military rule. After shrinking by 25 percent in the 1980s, the economy did begin to grow again, by almost 9 percent a year in 1991 and 1992, the highest rate in Latin America. Yet policy makers worried that Argentina's performance in export markets was not strong enough to sustain these growth rates for the long term. At least Argentina was proving that economic restructuring was possible under democracy, without the brutal repression that backed economic reform in Pinochet's Chile.

Argentina's fifty-year slide into underdevelopment and instability spotlighted the difficulty of combining economic growth with social justice in a developing country. Perón's first presidency tested the possibilities of populist corporatism coupled with state-led industrialization. His military successors tested those of authoritarianism and economic neocolonialism. Alfonsín and Menem again faced the problem of achieving both democracy and development—with the complications added by their predecessors' mistakes. By 1993, the Menem administration seemed to have achieved a tentative success in this task, but it was not yet clear if the long downward trend had really ended.

Brazil: Political and Economic Vacillations

Events in Brazil after 1945 paralleled those in Argentina—but with significant differences. Here, too, the later years of the import-substitution phase were dominated first by a prewar populist leader, Getúlio Vargas (1951–1954), and then by two presidents who aimed, not very successfully, at nationalist economic development and political mobilization: Juscelino Kubitschek (1956–1961) and João Goulart (1961–1964). As in Argentina, the military was an important influence on the government and seized power completely in the mid-1960s. The Brazilian military also introduced neocolonial policies, although civilian rule resumed in 1985. Differences between the two countries included the existence of a sizable peasantry in Brazil. This fact prompted an attempt at political mobilization in the Brazilian countryside in the early 1960s. Another difference was Brazil's record in economic development, more successful than Argentina's in the 1970s, far less so by the early 1990s.

The Second Republic

The postwar part of Brazil's import-substitution phase coincided with its Second Republic (1946–1964). In reaction against Vargas's New State, the new constitution adopted in 1946 reduced the powers of the presidency, separated the three branches of government more effectively, and extended the vote to all but military enlisted men and illiterates (the latter still accounted for nearly 60 percent of the population). Several political parties formed in 1945 and helped to democratize the country over the next twenty years. Until 1950, the presidency remained in the hands of one of the generals who had overthrown Vargas in 1945. His neocolonial regime wasted on imported luxuries the foreign exchange accumulated during World War II. In the elections of 1950, Vargas ran for president with a program emphasizing industrialization. A coalition of labor, industry, and the middle class supported him.

Resuming the presidency at age sixty-eight, Vargas concentrated on the economy. Faced with deficits and inflation, he charted a middle-of-the-road policy that aimed to attract foreign investment but also had nationalist components. Vargas proposed to limit foreign companies' profit remittances and form a mixed public-private corporation, Petrobrás, to monopolize the petroleum industry. Like other middle-of-the-road programs, this one attracted opposition from both Left and Right—and from the United States.

As inflation and the foreign trade deficit continued to worsen, Vargas faced a cabinet crisis and other troubles in 1954. His finance minister tried to introduce a stabilization program, while his labor minister—the future president, João Goulart—demanded wage increases. Evidence of financial scandal also came to light. Then an attempt to assassinate an opposition journalist was traced to Vargas's security chief, though he had acted without Vargas's knowledge. The military demanded Vargas's resignation. His response was sensational: suicide.

Brazil's next elected president, Kubitschek, came to power in 1955 despite much maneuvering by military and political leaders. He committed the country to an inflationary development strategy summed up in his slogan "Fifty years' progress in five." From 1957 to 1961, the economy grew at the remarkable average annual rate of 7 percent. By the time Kubitschek left office in 1960, Brazil's heavy industry supplied half of the country's needs, from machine tools to mining equipment. By 1962, Brazil was the world's seventh-biggest auto manufacturer. There were also vast public works projects. New dams supplied electrical power. The most spectacular innovation was the new capital city in the interior, Brasília, built in three years at huge cost. The new capital, with the highway network leading to it, was meant to create a new sense of national unity.

Yet a reckoning had to come. Kubitschek's policies favored profits over wages, and he courted foreign capital by offering incentives not available to Brazilian enterprises. Foreign interests soon controlled half of Brazil's large corporations. The foreign debt shot up to $2.7 billion in 1961—a level that already required more than half of export earnings for debt service. Refusing demands to stabilize the economy, Kubitschek let inflation continue. As a result, the value of the currency, and Brazil's export earnings, fell drastically. Unrest spread through the country. In the northeast, Peasant Leagues formed, denounced by landowners as communist. Kubitschek's nationalist development strategy was proving no sounder than Perón's.

Kubitschek's successors faced crisis conditions. His immediate successor resigned after seven months. The next, Goulart, faced a congressional attempt to check his populism by amending the constitution to reduce his powers. Goulart regained full powers in 1963 but was less successful in economics. One ambiguous success was a law regulating foreign investment and restricting annual profit remittances to no more than 10 percent of the capital invested. The law almost halted foreign investment, creating a capital shortage that forced a return to Kubitschek's inflationary method of expanding the money supply. The currency collapsed again. Arguing that inflation and development went together, Goulart did nothing about this, and his moderate support began to evaporate.

Goulart responded to his difficulties by moving to the left. Unable to get Congress to pass a program for tax reform and expropriation of large estates, he presented more radical proposals: immediate expropriation of certain types of landholdings, periodic wage adjustments, votes for illiterates and enlisted men, legalization of the Communist party. He began to enact some of these measures by decree. His support of political activism in unaccustomed places—among the peasantry and in the enlisted ranks of the army—panicked moderates and conservatives. Civilian opponents of the regime called for military intervention. Finally, faced with rebellion in the enlisted ranks, the military commanders swung into action and forced Goulart to leave the country in April 1964. Having recently weathered Castro's rise and the Cuban missile crisis, the United States approved the coup in advance and sent a naval force to stand by off the Brazilian coast.

Goulart's policies were mistakes in many ways. He failed to tackle inflation and further politicized the military. Yet his was the only Brazilian government that has yet tried to complete political mobilization by carrying it into the countryside.

Brazil's Military Phase

Goulart's fall opened a twenty-year period of military rule. The 1964 coup ended the Second Republic, and a dictatorship took form under new constitutions in 1967 and 1969. All Brazilians could be deprived of their rights, as three former presidents were, and the generals replaced the old political parties with two new ones they created. Thereafter, the problems facing the military resembled those in Argentina: the Left, the economy, the demand to restore civilian rule.

Dissatisfaction with the new regime found expression throughout Brazilian culture, from popular songs to guerrilla attacks. By the late 1960s, moderates demanded a return to civilian government; the Left demanded social revolution. Student groups began to riot, and a Mothers' Union formed to protest the violent treatment the students received. Urban guerrillas began action on the far Left, government-linked death squads on the Right.

Brazil's military government soon mastered state terrorism sufficiently to offer itself as a model to other Latin American countries—such as Chile and Argentina—threatened by "subversion." Brazil's radical Left had suffered enough that it could no longer threaten the regime by 1973. Yet rights violations continued. Among the most vocal critics were activist churchmen, such as Archbishop Helder Câmara, in the arid northeast, one of the world's most impoverished and hunger-stricken places.

Economically, the most important feature of the military period was the so-called Brazilian miracle. Seeking to slow inflation and boost investment, the military governments pursued a blatantly foreign-oriented strategy. Foreign investment increased so much that foreigners completely controlled the tire and auto industries and were nearly as dominant in other industries. Though unbalanced, economic growth in Brazil averaged around 10 percent a year between 1969 and 1974. During this "miraculous" period, industrial products first surpassed coffee among Brazil's exports.

This change meant neither an end to dependency for Brazil nor anything miraculous for most Brazilians. Inequalities among social classes and regions of the country widened during these years. Brazil's income distribution became exceptionally unequal by Latin American, indeed by global, standards. As multinational corporations tightened their grip on the economy, their profit remittances often exceeded their investments in Brazil eight or ten times over. Agriculture, still dominated by inefficiently run estates, "modernized" by producing more for export and less for Brazil's soaring population—soybeans rather than black beans. Shortsighted attempts to develop the interior expanded into extensive cutting of the Amazon rain forest, producing lasting ecological damage for short-term economic gain.

The OPEC oil price increases destroyed Brazil's "miracle." The military government raised gasoline prices to reflect the 1973–1974 quadrupling of oil prices but let later price increases fall behind the inflation rate. They gambled that the increases were temporary and decided not to jeopardize future growth by further raising domestic oil prices. Economic growth continued in Brazil through 1978, but the major oil price hike in 1979 exposed the error in the government's strategy. Oil imports began to consume most of export earnings. Petrobrás stepped up exploration, and Brazil's oil production reached a half-million barrels a day by 1984. The shift to other forms of energy also progressed, and Brazil soon led the world in using alcohol derived from sugar cane as a fuel. Still, inflation slipped out of control, and the foreign debt soared, especially after interest rates in the United States rose to unprecedented heights in the early 1980s.

The results gravely threatened Brazil and the international banking system as well. Brazil's economic growth did continue, lopsidedly. The arms industry began exporting to such countries as Libya; the microcomputer industry became the world's third largest after the United States' and Japan's; and Brazil exported steel to the United States. Yet most Brazilians' fortunes had worsened. By the early 1980s, political and economic conditions turned against the military. Middle-class cooperation with the military waned, and pressures to return to civilian rule mounted.

The Return to Civilian Rule

In 1982, when Brazil held the first direct elections since 1965 for state governors, many opponents of the regime won. The victories strengthened the opposition, and the military began preparing for the election of a civilian president. This occurred in 1985, but the military retained enough power to make civilian control questionable. Generals held six cabinet posts, and the military controlled both its own nuclear program, separate from the civilian one, and the National Information Service, an intelligence agency with powers unequaled in democratic states. The new civilian president promised a new constitution, but he died three months after election, leaving fulfillment of the promise to his vice president and successor, José Sarney.

Despite talk of change, Sarney achieved little, though the military at least remained in the shadows. Inflation was back at 1500 percent in 1990, after a decade with almost no gain in production per capita. Brazil's industry had developed to the point that it could export jet planes to the United States, as well as steel. Yet Brazil had defaulted on interest payments to foreign banks in 1987 and stood second only to the United States in the size of its foreign debt. Supposedly to institutionalize civilian rule, a constituent assembly began drafting a new constitution. Yet corruption and threats of force poisoned the atmosphere, as Sarney and the military proved in 1988 by openly using treasury funds and coup threats to influence the terms of the new constitution.

Begun on that cynical note, the 1989 presidential campaign brought in the younger Fernando Collor de Mello. His campaign promises of honest, efficient government attracted voters but were soon forgotten. In 1992, a massive corruption scandal broke open. Collor resigned and was convicted in a senate impeachment trial. As Argentina recovered from the economic crisis of the 1980s, Brazil—distracted by scandal—had made no progress in reducing inflation, the foreign debt, the protectionism of the import-substitution era, the misery that ranked its northeast among the poorest places in the Americas, the unrivaled inequity of its income distribution, or the urban crime and violence that inequity provoked. Out of 151 million Brazilians, 65 million still could not feed or clothe themselves adequately. As the tense wait for the legislative and presidential election of October 1994 began, demands were even heard to restore military rule. Advanced in some fields of industry but not yet ready to face emerging geoeconomic realities, Brazil was perhaps still, as in colonial times, the land of the future.

Mexico Drifts Away from Its Revolution's Legacy

Mexico, too, moved through a series of phases—mass mobilization, then neocolonial authoritarianism followed by an opening to the world economy—with modifications that reflect its exceptional history before World War II. After a high point of reform under Lázaro Cárdenas, Mexico moved to the right, rather than to the left, though a populist reprise occurred in the late 1950s and early 1960s. Thereafter, the single dominant party remained more strongly institutionalized and broadly based than any other in Latin America. Because it had a degree of control over the military that other Latin American countries could only envy, the renewed rightward move toward authoritarianism and neocolonialism occurred under party auspices, without military rule. By the 1980s, Mexico's distinctive party-state combination remained more firmly established than the military regimes then reaching their ends in Argentina and Brazil, and Mexico had also become a major oil exporter. But rapid growth of oil exports had upset the balance among economic sectors, intensifying social stress and calling forth new challenges to the single-party system. As the 1990s opened, the party responded by not only tightening its grip on power but also extending its outward-oriented development policy into a high-stakes bid for free trade with the United States and Canada.

The Single-Party Regime

Mexico's relative political stability from 1940 until the 1990s was largely due to its system of one-party rule. As noted in Chapter 8, Cárdenas reorganized the official party along corporatist lines, with separate agrarian, labor, military, and "popular" (essentially middle-class) sectors. In this way he mobilized both workers and peasants but kept them separate. In 1945 the party was again reorganized as the Institutional Revolutionary party (PRI in Spanish), the name it still retains, with peasant, labor, and "popular" (middle-class) sectors.

Good organization enabled the one-party regime to endure. The party had firm control of both organized labor and the countryside. Party governance remained highly centralized in Mexico City. As usual in one-party systems, political interest focused more on nominations, an in-party matter, than on elections. Government and party interpenetrated each other so deeply that they became virtually indistinguishable. Because the state controlled many enterprises, the state-party symbiosis extended into the economy as well. The president had vast powers over this combine. For example, he originated the budget and most legislation, which the Congress merely rubber-stamped.

Opponents rightly accused the PRI of corruption, repression, and rigging elections. Indeed, the candidate with the most votes would win only if the government so allowed. Such methods helped the PRI maintain control, especially in rural areas with long histories of authoritarian rule. The PRI had also co-opted a broad range of opinion that might otherwise have fed opposition movements. It had inherited the rhetoric and symbolism of Mexico's revolution. Even opposition parties came under PRI patronage, once the government, responding to criticisms of one-party rule, began to guarantee them representation in the Chamber of Deputies. The Institutional Revolutionary party was not revolutionary, but it was institutionalized.

Emerging from party leadership ranks to head such a strong party-state apparatus, Mexico's recent presidents mostly did not have a profound impact as individuals, but there have been differences among them. Miguel Alemán (1946–1952), the PRI's first civilian candidate, reduced military expenditure to 7 percent of the budget, down from 30 percent in 1930 and 70 percent in 1917. Thus, Mexico escaped the military-dominated politics that still bedeviled most of Latin America. Adolfo López Mateos (1958–1964) came closest to the Alliance for Progress ideal. He revived land distribution by giving out more land than any president since Cárdenas. He also expanded social services, introduced profit sharing for workers, and began the system of assuring congressional representation to small parties.

The presidency of Gustavo Díaz Ordaz (1964–1970) began the shift back to the right then under way in other Latin American countries. The worst smirch on his record came in 1968, as the government prepared to host the Olympic Games—the first time a developing country got to show off its achievements in that way. Amid preparations for the games, antigovernment demonstrations began. As in other countries in the 1960s, students played a leading role, though up to 400,000 sympathizers would turn out to demonstrate with them. The government's response showed how much it had abandoned revolutionary populism. The climax came on October 2, when troops killed several hundred demonstrators and jailed two thousand. The Olympic Games went off without a hitch, and the guerrilla violence that followed was squelched by the early 1970s; but whatever else he did, Díaz Ordaz was remembered for the violence. Later presidents have never regained López Mateos's populist stance, and economic problems have preoccupied them increasingly.

Economic Issues to the Forefront

Stimulated by wartime demand for labor and raw materials in the United States, Mexico's economic growth remained rapid through the 1960s. By then, Mexico was nearly self-sufficient in consumer goods and was developing heavy industry. A major problem, until the mid-1950s, was inflation, especially for rural and urban workers, whose wages did not keep pace.

To deal with this problem, the government devalued the peso in 1954 and adopted a "hard-money" strategy. Mexico's ability to maintain a fixed exchange rate, while allowing unrestricted exchange of the peso against the U.S. dollar or other currencies, became a treasured symbol of development—one that few Third World countries could match. The 1954 devaluation made Mexican exports cheaper and Mexico itself cheaper for foreign tourists. Devaluation also stimulated foreign investment. In dollars of constant value, such investment in Mexico in 1940 was still only one-third what it had been in 1911. Although economic nationalism remained an official priority, the hard-money policy began a reversal of trend that vastly increased foreign—mostly U.S.—investment over the next twenty years, creating the usual problems about profit remittances. Eventually, Mexico tried to limit these dangers. The government borrowed in order to expand its role as investor and lender. It also limited foreign ownership to a 49 percent share of any company. These measures did not solve Mexico's economic problems, however. Government borrowing started Mexico's fantastic debt accumulation, and the limit on foreign ownership left many opportunities for elite Mexicans to cooperate with foreign interests, as they always had.

The 1954 hard-money strategy reduced inflation but led to new problems in the early 1960s. Mexico's population growth had begun to cause alarm in the late 1950s. Urbanization accelerated, partly because a mechanized "new hacienda" was emerging in the countryside. As in other Third World countries, many urban migrants could not find factory jobs and had to scratch out a living as bootblacks, street vendors, or the like. The government had long had programs to restrict the costs of goods and services to the poor. In the 1960s and 1970s, those programs had to be expanded. When population growth outstripped domestic food production and necessitated imports, the costs of the programs became prohibitive. This problem compounded the effects of rising oil prices. Inflation resumed, the 1954 exchange rate became untenable, and the government finally had to devalue the peso twice in one month in 1976.

Soon after, the world learned that Mexico was a major oil power. Discoveries raised its proven oil reserves to 49 billion barrels by 1984, ranking Mexico fourth in the world after Saudi Arabia, Kuwait, and the Soviet Union (with 169, 90, and 63 billion barrels, respectively, at that date). Iran's experience had shown that rapid growth of oil income could produce undesirable effects in a populous country with a complex economy. Mexico, which was not a member of OPEC, therefore set out to increase production only gradually. Even so, Mexico's petroleum earnings increased more than 25-fold from 1976 to 1981, when they reached $13 billion. Despite its intentions, Mexico did become dependent on oil exports.

The oil price slump after 1981 led to increased foreign borrowing that made Mexico one of the world's most indebted nations. Growth continued—but only spottily. Foreign firms kept opening assembly plants in Mexico to profit from low wage rates. Importing components and exporting finished products, mostly to the U.S. market, the plants shifted jobs to Mexican workers. Japan, too, used this method to penetrate the U.S. market. Japan was also eager for Mexican oil, since Mexico looked like a surer source than the Persian Gulf. Mexico's government searched for ways to reinvigorate the economy—for example, by selling state-owned companies. Yet overriding economic uncertainty could not be escaped. The Mexican stock market crashed in October 1987, shortly before the New York exchange did. In the aftermath, the Mexican government adopted a severe IMF-approved austerity program. It dropped the peso below 2,000 to the U.S. dollar, raised prices of subsidized goods and services, and installed wage and price controls. As part of the deal, Mexico also had to begin lowering its tariffs and promoting exports, abandoning its import-substitution policies. By the time of the 1988 presidential election, real wages had fallen 40 percent during the outgoing president's six-year term.

Reactions to this situation became clear in the election. Not surprisingly, victory went to the PRI candidate, Carlos Salinas de Gortari, who as budget and planning minister had initiated the 1980s austerity policy. For the first time, however, the PRI faced opposition from the Left and Right. The most exciting candidate was the leader of a breakaway PRI faction, Cuauhtémoc Cárdenas, Lázaro's son. Named for the last Aztec ruler (father Lázaro Cárdenas was proud of his mixed ancestry), Cuauhtémoc Cárdenas campaigned on a populist, nationalist platform, reasserting the revolutionary legacy against the PRI's rightward drift. Salinas won with only 50.3 percent of the vote, against Cárdenas's 31.1 percent. Considering the PRI history of winning in all races and the government's control of the vote-count, Cárdenas's followers thought him the victor, morally at least.

Once in power, Salinas took steps to adapt Mexico to changing geoeconomic realities, showing a conservative economist's biases as he did. Politically, he reformed the electoral law and the inner workings of PRI and made some concessions to the opposition on the right but not the left. Harassment of Cárdenas and his followers, and growing charges of torture and other human rights violations, raised questions about whether the reforms were supposed to make Mexico more democratic or merely tighten its existing system.

Economically, Salinas clearly aimed to reorient Mexico, at whatever cost to past policy. He lowered trade barriers, continued privatizing public enterprises, attacked the *ejido* (the communal land-tenure system sanctified in the 1917 constitution), allowed foreigners to own minority stakes in agricultural enterprises, and daringly proposed a free-trade agreement with the United States.

This proposal blossomed into the North American Free Trade Agreement among Mexico, the United States, and Canada. Initialed in October 1992, the treaty—if ratified—was not supposed to create a "common market" for the movement of workers, but it would eliminate most customs duties, entitle investors from each country to the same treatment as nationals in the other countries, ensure free exchange or transfer of currencies, and protect investors against expropriation.

Only the most publicized of many regional integration projects in Latin America, NAFTA excited all the hopes and fears awakened by the tightening of global integration in the 1990s. U.S. workers reacted with fear of losing more jobs and factories. Some Latin American analysts—echoing sentiments that Mexican revolutionaries of 1910 would have understood perfectly—argued that free-trade agreements generically furthered U.S. dominance in the region and that far from contributing to overall economic development in Mexico, the treaty would lead to further exploitation of the Mexican working class and further environmental degradation because of nonenforcement of Mexican environmental protection laws. Whatever the outcome, Salinas's Mexico did seem to stand at the opening of a new era.

Cuba: Social Revolution Without an End to Dependency

The small countries of Central America and the Caribbean (Map 15.1) have experienced many of the common Latin American problems—single-crop export economies, *caudillo* (strongman) politics, inability to resist outside powers—with special sharpness, without matching the developmental successes of their larger neighbors. Yet Cuba achieved Latin America's most successful social revolution to date. In the world of superpower bipolarity, Cuba's revolution showed that dependency could be altered, if not escaped. How solid was Cuba's achievement?

Whence the Cuban Revolution?

By the nineteenth century, Cuba had discovered its vocation as a producer of cane sugar and, secondarily, tobacco. A slave-based plantation economy grew up, and by 1860 Cuba produced almost one-third of the world's sugar.

Cuba's landowners did not rebel against Spanish rule in the 1810s and 1820s, when most of Latin America did. But Cubans of a half-century later resented Spanish domination and had economic ties to the United States more than to Spain. A first rebellion (1868–1878) ended without independence from Spain. Another rebellion broke out in 1895, and U.S. intervention forced Spain to concede Cuba's independence in 1898. Cuban revolutionaries opposed the U.S. role. What followed after "independence" showed why.

Cuba became independent under U.S. occupation. Americans intended to see that Cuban independence took a form favorable to U.S. interests. They seemed not to realize that their wishes might infringe on the "independence." The first U.S. act was to disband the rebel forces. Improvements in public works and sanitation followed—most notably, the elimination of yellow fever, made possible by a Cuban doctor's discovery that mosquitoes carry the disease. The United States encouraged Cubans to draft a new constitution (1901), then forced them to add the Platt amendment, which gave Washington extensive rights, whence the U.S. naval base at Guantánamo Bay. "Independent" Cuba was really a U.S. protectorate.

Economically, the protectorate meant an increase in U.S. investment, from $50 million in 1896 to $1.5 billion in 1929. Cuba was more than ever a colonial economy, vulnerable to variations in the size of the sugar harvest and its price. Export earnings in 1932, for example, were less than one-fifth 1924's earnings. During the Depression, U.S. investment, at least in sugar, began to decline, and by the late 1950s Cubans owned more than 60 percent of the industry, up from 22 percent in 1939. Cuba remained tied to the United States through special trade arrangements, however. From 1934 to 1960, a quota system gave Cuba a set share of the U.S. sugar market at prices above world market prices. In exchange, Cuba had to accept U.S. manufactures.

Cuba's dependence on the sugar industry had significant political and social effects. Just as the technology and capital requirements of sugar milling led to a concentration of ownership, the requirements of cane cultivation affected the Cuban people. Sugar cane is harvested annually but needs replanting only after five to twenty-five years. Laborers therefore get work during the three-month harvest season and have little or no work the rest of the year. Unable to buy or rent land because of the concentration of ownership, and often kept in place by debt servitude, the rural populace faced a bleak future.

Most rural Cubans were not typical peasants whose main goal was to acquire land but rather were workers whose main concern was wages, and they were in touch with their urban counterparts. By the 1930s, there was much migration between the countryside and urban slums. Partly because of improved public health, the population also grew rapidly, more than doubling between 1899 and 1931, to almost 4 million. By 1950, almost 40 percent of Cubans lived in cities, mostly in extreme poverty. Cuba's workers, rural and urban, were ready for political mobilization. Who would lead them?

As elsewhere in Latin America, the Depression provoked political change, but only briefly did this seem to answer the question just posed. The Depression led to the toppling of the brutal regime of Gerardo Machado (1925–1933). What emerged at his fall was an alliance of army sergeants, radical students, and Ramón Grau San Martín, who took over the civilian side of government.

At first, major change appeared to be under way. Grau proclaimed a socialist revolution and abrogated the Platt amendment. His government produced much social legislation—the eight-hour day, creation of a labor department, votes for women. But it antagonized Washington by suspending loan payments and seizing sugar mills. Then the United States encouraged Fulgencio Batista, one of the sergeants in the governing coalition, to overthrow Grau. Washington was ready to give up the Platt amendment by treaty in 1934 and was backing away from interventionism. But it had no hesitation in preferring a dictatorship that would collaborate with U.S. interests, to a democratic or populist regime that was eco-

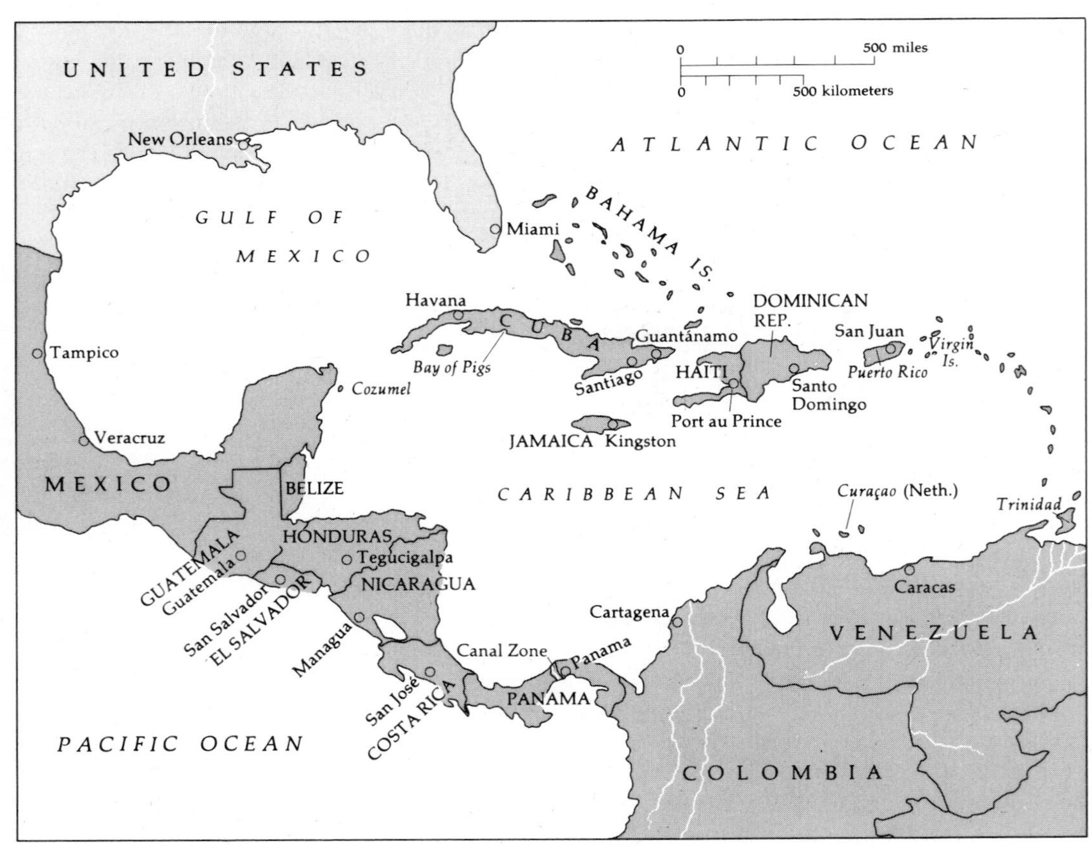

Map 15.1 The Contemporary Caribbean

nomically nationalistic—especially if it talked of socialism. If anything, backing away from interventionism heightened the U.S. "need" for cooperative strongmen such as Batista.

Batista dominated Cuban politics through 1958. Sometimes he was the president. Sometimes others were his puppet presidents. Throughout the period, corruption, violence, and popular disaffection marked political life.

Castro and the Revolution

Born in 1927, Fidel Castro grew up in the Batista era. While studying law, he became active in student politics. He mounted his first attack on the Batista regime on July 26, 1953, with an unsuccessful assault on a provincial army barracks. Fidel and his more radical brother, Raúl, survived but were sentenced to prison. Amnestied in 1955, Fidel fled to Mexico to plan a comeback. With him were Raúl and a young Argentine who would become one of the great martyrs of the revolutionary Left, Ernesto "Ché" Guevara. In December 1956, Fidel set sail with eighty-one others to land in Cuba. Barely a dozen—including Fidel, Raúl, and Ché—survived the landing, fleeing into the Sierra Maestra mountains to regroup their forces.

In the ensuing struggle, Batista proved to be his own worst enemy. His brutality alienated the people, while Castro's guerrillas, like the Chinese communists of the 1930s, had to learn how to operate among them without alienating them. When Batista mounted a "liquidation campaign" into the Sierra Maestra, his army performed disastrously, and he fled. Castro's rebels, about three thousand strong, entered Havana at the beginning of 1959.

It took two more years to consolidate the revolution and define its character. In 1959, an initial episode of collegial rule ended with Castro in sole charge. An agrarian reform law expropriated farmland holdings over a thousand acres and forbade foreigners to own agricultural land. Castro made two visits to the United States. He had not yet identified his regime with communism but presented himself as a reformer. Yet the land reform law and the accusations of Cuban refugees made it hard to win goodwill. U.S.-backed anti-Castro operations by Cuban refugees began almost immediately.

In 1960, several major changes helped define Cuba's course. First, when U.S.-owned oil refineries responded to a Cuban-Soviet agreement to trade sugar for crude oil by refusing to process the oil, Castro nationalized the refineries. The United States then embargoed U.S. exports to Cuba and suspended the sugar quota. Castro responded by nationalizing other U.S.-owned enterprises. He also began organizing an authoritarian mass-mobilizing regime based on the army, the militia, local citizen groups known as Committees for the Defense of the Revolution, and controls over the press and most other organizations. Finally, the regime introduced an egalitarian social and economic policy, freezing prices, increasing wages, and launching a literacy campaign that halved the already low illiteracy rate (25 percent) in one year. In response, the United States severed diplomatic relations and, through the CIA, supported an abortive invasion by Cuban exiles at the Bay of Pigs (April 1961). The Soviet attempt to exploit this failure by placing missiles on the island led to the Cuban missile crisis of 1962, which ended with withdrawal of the missiles and a tacit U.S. promise not to invade Cuba.

Meanwhile, in December 1961, Castro announced for the first time that he was a Marxist-Leninist. The statement proved epoch making for several reasons. It signaled a shift in Cuba's dependency, from the United States to the Soviet Union. The choice of the Soviet model also facilitated what Castro perhaps most wanted: consolidation of his personal dominance. For other Third World countries, finally, here was something new on the left.

Instead of the complex developmental processes of either Marxism-Leninism or Maoism, Castro had shown that one could overthrow a government, simply announce that one was a communist, and so—perhaps—transform one's country's position in the world. U.S. and local opposition made the pattern hard to repeat in Latin America. Farther afield, in Africa, it found a number of imitators.

With its Marxist character set, Cuba experimented through the 1960s to define its policies. A second agrarian reform law (1963) made state farms the dominant form of cultivation. By 1965, Castro had formed his revolutionary elite into a new Cuban Communist party. Meanwhile, debate raged over what to do about dependence on sugar. Ché Guevara dominated the debate at first with his Four-Year Plan for diversification and light industrialization, but its results fell short of target. The emphasis reverted to sugar, with Castro predicting that the 1970 harvest would reach a record 10 million tons.

Guevara then came out with an "idealist" strategy for reaching the new goal. His ideas recalled some of Mao Zedong's in China. Guevara argued for a clean break with capitalism, elimination of the market, and creation of a "new Cuban" whose heightened political consciousness would satisfy him or her with moral rather than material incentives. In this view, consolidating the revolution in Cuba also required promoting it elsewhere—whence the international guerrilla strategy that led Ché to his death in Bolivia in 1967. Not everyone agreed with Guevara. Some Cuban leaders advocated greater pragmatism, and the Soviet Union had little use for Guevara's claims to international revolutionary leadership. Castro began to back away from Ché's view in international affairs in 1968 but held to it in domestic policy until 1970, when the cane harvest reached 8.5 million tons—an all-time record but short of the announced goal of 10 million.

Facing the need for change, Castro made a dramatic speech, taking blame for the failure to meet the goal and offering to resign. The crowd shouted *no*. Castro stayed in power but changed policy. With the adoption of newer techniques of economic planning and the reintroduction of material incentives, economic growth rose to over 10 percent a year from 1971 to 1975.

Other measures of the 1970s showed a new concern to expand political participation in ways compatible with the regime's character. Castro broadened the social bases of the labor movement and Communist party. The party held its first congress in December 1975. The new constitution of 1976 set up a system of Assemblies of Popular Power, with the directly elected members of the municipal assemblies electing members of the provincial assemblies and the national assembly. Cubans still could not form political organizations at will, and many elections were not conducted by secret ballot. But opportunities for discussion of issues and political mobilization had increased. An official Cuban Women's Federation came into being, and a Family Code (1976) mandated equal division of household tasks—a departure from *machismo* but more on paper than in practice.

The policy shift of the 1970s affected international relations, as other Latin American nations resumed diplomatic relations with Cuba and demands to do so grew in the United States. The main obstacles, for U.S. officials, were human rights and Cuba's interventions in Africa and elsewhere in the Caribbean. An accord of December 1988 finally removed one troublesome issue by requiring Cuba to withdraw its troops from Angola, where Cuba had supported the Marxist government since 1975 against both U.S.-backed guerrillas and South African forces based in Namibia (see Chapter 16).

Cuba's was Latin America's most successful social revolution. However, its accomplishments depended on annual subsidies of \$3 to \$5 billion from the Soviet Union. In the late 1980s, over 80 percent of Cuba's foreign trade, both imports and exports, had also been with the Soviet bloc. Soviet collapse mortally threatened Castro, economically and ideologically. With the United States tightening its trade embargo and sugar prices in decline, Cuba's imports shrank by at least three-fourths between about 1989 and 1993, while the whole Cuban economy shrank by 50 percent. As oil imports shrank to the point where oxcarts replaced motor vehicles, Cubans watched their revolutionary gains erode.

In the limited room for maneuver that remained, Castro attempted to make adjustments and also maintained the high levels of repression that had long squelched dissent on the island (the fact that so many of his opponents fled the island had helped to keep him in power). Reforms were made to allow direct elections to the provincial and national Assemblies of Popular Power, remove atheism from the constitution, guarantee foreign investments against nationalization, and even add the thought of the nineteenth-century nationalist, José Martí, to that of Marx, Engels, and Lenin as guiding principles of the state—thus creating an escape hatch through which socialism might be sacrificed to national interest. In July 1993, Castro himself legalized the use of U.S. dollars in Cuba. Some Cubans thought this would launch a flood of remittances from relatives abroad and might even help to break the U.S. trade embargo. Others thought legalization of the dollar would only worsen hardships for those with no relatives abroad. In any event, the change suggested that Cuba was beginning an uncertain transition to its postrevolutionary era.

Castro and Gorbachev in Havana, 1991. *The end of Cuba's special relationship with the Soviet Union left Cuba more isolated than ever. How much longer could the aging Castro hold on?*
Kenneth Jarecke/© 1991 Contact Press Images

From the vantage point of the 1990s, Cuba's record looked bleak. Cuba had escaped dependency on the United States only at the cost of dependency on the Soviet Union. The fact that the world economy is capitalist overall had helped provoke Soviet collapse, and Cuba had to face the same fact. Still, most Cubans—the workers who had fared so badly before 1959—would remember the revolution as an improvement. Economic growth had not been impressive, but the distribution of available resources had become much more egalitarian. Illiteracy had almost vanished. The creation of a comprehensive school system had given many Cubans new power to shape their lives. The regime had done more for women than any other in Latin America. Over thirty years, improvements in public health had increased life expectancy from sixty-three to seventy-five years, and infant mortality had fallen by perhaps three-fourths. Dependent on Soviet subsidies and jeopardized by their withdrawal, these achievements far excelled Latin American norms. Allowed no dissent, Cuba's 11 million people would have to hope that the changes of the 1990s would not wipe out these gains.

Conclusion: Development or Disappointment?

In forty years following World War II, Latin America moved through two historical phases and into a third. Import-substitution industrialization and democratizing mass mobilization set the trend through the early 1960s. The weakness of Latin America's democratic institutions, the exhaustion of import substitution, the political stresses of the 1960s, and the military emphasis of U.S. policy then led to a turn toward military authoritarianism and economic neocolonialism. With the 1980s came a trend back toward civilian rule. Whether this would mean mass mobilization and economic development in the interest of the people was uncertain. Alternatively, the demands of the debt crisis might simply bring into the limelight the civilian technocrats who shaped the neocolonial economic programs of the military governments, in place of the generals.

The experiences of specific countries showed significant variations in the regional pattern. Some countries were too small to experience each developmental phase fully or, for that matter, to function effectively as nation-states. Cuba, for example, overturned old-fashioned caudillo rule only when it took a revolutionary turn to the left. Even then, Cuba could not escape dependency. Some larger states also introduced variations into the pattern of phases, while following it more fully. Mexico and Brazil became highly enough industrialized that they could be regarded as mid-size industrial powers. Mexico also became a major petroleum producer, although events of the 1980s showed that the ability to export large amounts of oil—one more mineral resource—neither cured dependency nor guaranteed political stability.

As the current rush to form free-trade agreements shows, no state escapes dependency on others in some sense. The crux of the Latin American nations' problems lies in coping with their growing populations' needs while trying to profit from participation in a capitalist world economy in which none of these nations holds a leading position. A long history of internal and external colonialism has helped shape this problem, but the rapid social and economic changes of the late twentieth century have made solving it more difficult than ever before. If Latin America's record has been this disappointing, have other parts of the developing world fared better?

Note

1. Juan-Jose Arévalo, *The Shark and the Sardines,* trans. June Cobb and Raúl Osegueda (New York: Stuart L. Stuart, 1961).

Suggestions for Further Reading

Books

Burns, E. Bradford. *A History of Brazil.* 2d ed. (1980).

De Jesus, Carolina Maria. *Child of the Dark* (1962).

Domínguez, Jorge I. *Cuba: Order and Revolution* (1978).

Guevara, Ché, *Guerrilla Warfare,* with an introduction and case studies by Brian Loveman and Thomas M. Davies, Jr. (1985).

Horowitz, Irving Louis, ed. *Cuban Communism.* 6th ed. (1987).

Keen, Benjamin, and Mark Wasserman. *A Short History of Latin America* (1988).

LaFeber, Walter. *Inevitable Revolutions: The United States in Central America* (1984).

Loveman, Brian. *Chile: The Legacy of Hispanic Capitalism.* 2d ed. (1988).

Meyer, Michael C., and William L. Sherman. *The Course of Mexican History.* 3d ed. (1987).

Puig, Manuel. *Kiss of the Spider Woman.* Translated by Thomas Colchie (1980).

Skidmore, Thomas E., and Peter H. Smith. *Modern Latin America.* 3d ed. (1992).

Waisman, Carlos. *Reversal of Development in Argentina* (1987).

Wiarda, Howard J., and Harvey F. Kline, eds. *Latin American Politics and Development* (1985).

Newsletters and Periodicals

Latin American Weekly Report.

Latin American Regional Reports.

CHAPTER 16

Sub-Saharan Africa: Development or Collapse?

Since World War II, sub-Saharan Africa has passed through two historical periods. The years from 1945 to 1960 were the twilight of colonialism. The years since 1960—the period this chapter emphasizes—have been ones of both formal independence and neocolonialism. The record of Africa's first thirty years of independence has proved disappointing for many reasons. Often the trouble stems from demographic and environmental problems that had only begun to become apparent in 1960. As we look first at Africa's experience overall and then more closely at the two countries with the continent's largest national economies, Nigeria and South Africa, we shall learn more about these problems.

Today as throughout their history, Africans display great creativity and resourcefulness. Sometimes the achievements are those of famous individuals, such as Desmond Tutu, Anglican bishop of Johannesburg and winner of the 1984 Nobel Peace Prize, or Wole Soyinka, Nigerian novelist and winner of the 1986 Nobel Prize for Literature. Sometimes the achievements are those of ordinary people working together, such as the thousands of Kenyan women's groups that formed the Greenbelt Movement to halt deforestation through tree planting and use of improved cookstoves, or the West African Naam movement that mobilizes local self-help traditions for soil and water conservation projects in the dry season. The greatest challenge facing Africa is to mobilize such energies on a large enough scale to achieve development and equity while also maintaining a viable relationship between human societies and their natural habitat. This is a key problem the world over, but Africa's poverty and hardship bring it into sharp focus.

Continental Overview: The Underdeveloped World par Excellence

Europeans took control of sub-Saharan Africa abruptly, at a time when European economies were the world's strongest. The costs of taking control in the nineteenth century were relatively low. By 1945, conditions had changed so much, and wartime experiences had so stimulated African nationalism, that colonial rule ended even more suddenly than it had begun. The largest colonial powers, Britain and France, prepared for the transition. Britain passed colonial development acts in 1940 and 1945; France provided larger amounts of aid after the war. Among smaller colonial powers, Belgium did not anticipate the end, and Portugal tried to hold on. Still, decolonization worked its way across the continent, leaving over fifty independent countries, most of which gained independence in the early 1960s (Map 16.1). Events soon proved how unprepared they were to face their demographic, economic, and political problems.

The Spread of Independence

The decolonization of sub-Saharan Africa began in 1956, when the Sudan, nominally under joint Anglo-Egyptian rule, won independence as a byproduct of the Egyptian revolution of 1952. The next countries to become independent were in West Africa, starting with Ghana (1957, formerly the Gold Coast) under the leadership of Kwame Nkrumah. Of Britain's other West African colonies, Nigeria became independent in 1960, Sierra Leone in 1961, and Gambia in 1965.

By then, French Africa also had won independence. France was preoccupied with colonial struggles in Indochina (1946–1954) and in Algeria (1954–1962). The political repercussions of the Algerian conflict led to the overthrow of France's Fourth Republic in 1958 and the advent of the Fifth. President de Gaulle then provided leadership for decolonization, eventually in Algeria (1962) and immediately in France's other colonies, to which he offered a range of options. Guinea, under Sékou Touré, chose immediate independence in 1958. By the early 1960s, fourteen former French colonies had become independent, most as republics within a new French community.

In the Belgian Congo (now Zaire), the Belgians failed to foresee that they could not hold on indefinitely. When the rise of nationalist opposition challenged their ability to resist, they abruptly granted the country independence on June 30, 1960. Civil war broke out immediately, as Katanga (now Shaba) Province, with its rich copper mines, attempted to secede. By the time order was restored, the country lay under the dictatorship of General Joseph Mobutu (president, 1965–) after one of many postindependence military takeovers.

White settler communities complicated movement toward independence in some eastern and southern African countries. In Kenya, where white settlers had taken much of the best land, the Kikuyu people were left with inadequate land to support them. This pressure produced the Mau Mau rebellion of 1952–1956, which the British repressed with thousands of Kenyan casualties. Still, Kenya, Tanganyika, and Uganda became independent under black rule in the early 1960s. The island nation of Zanzibar, becoming independent in 1963, joined Tanganyika on the mainland to form Tanzania in 1964. A key factor in the smooth transition to black rule was the care taken by leaders such as Kenya's Jomo Kenyatta and Tanzania's Julius Nyerere to reassure whites that the change would not hurt them.

Farther south, the British attempted to form a federation of Northern and Southern

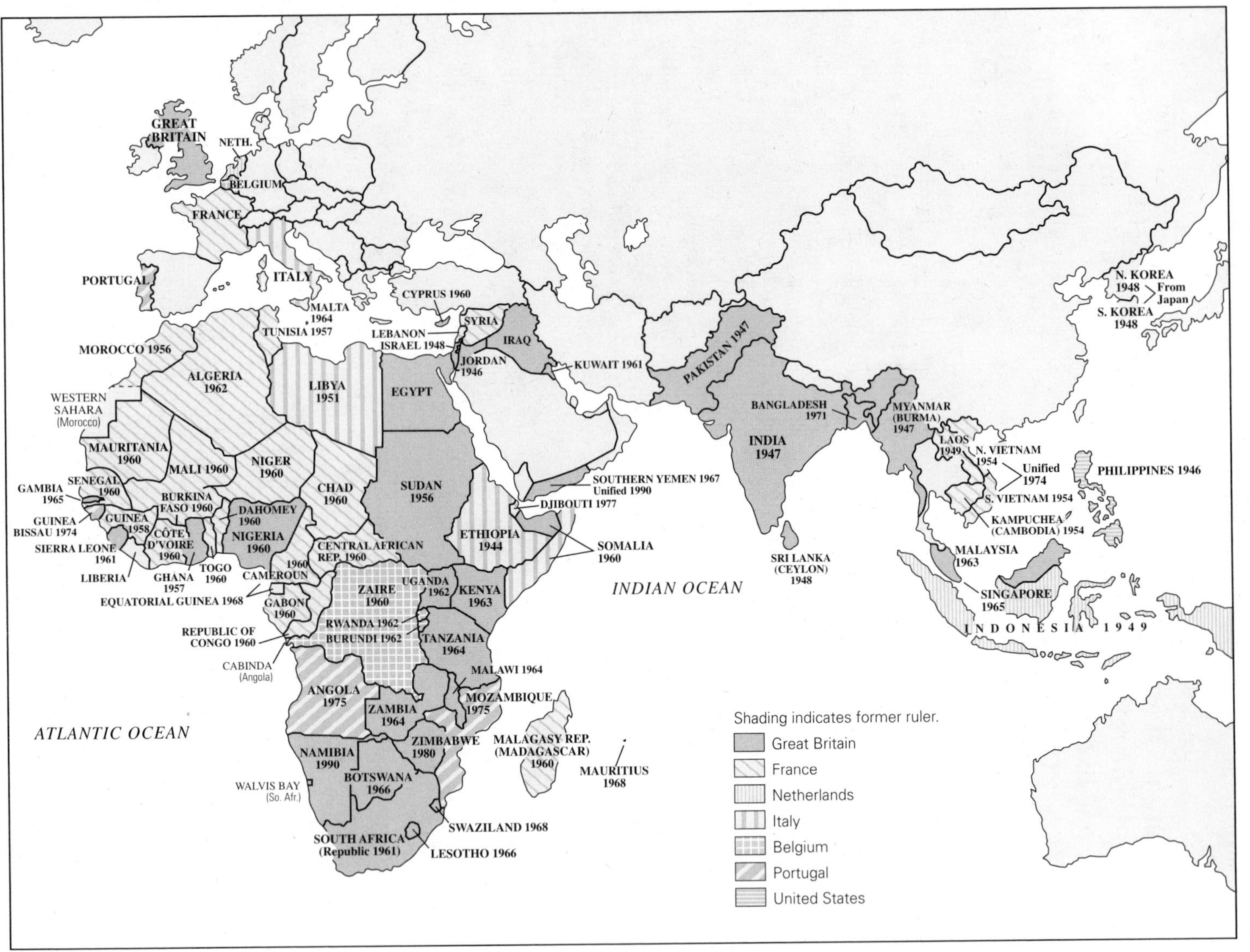

GREAT BRITAIN
NETH.
BELGIUM
FRANCE
PORTUGAL
ITALY
CYPRUS 1960
MALTA 1964
TUNISIA 1957
LEBANON
ISRAEL 1948
SYRIA
IRAQ
JORDAN 1946
KUWAIT 1961
MOROCCO 1956
ALGERIA 1962
LIBYA 1951
EGYPT
WESTERN SAHARA (Morocco)
MAURITANIA 1960
MALI 1960
NIGER 1960
CHAD 1960
SUDAN 1956
GAMBIA 1965
SENEGAL 1960
BURKINA FASO 1960
DAHOMEY 1960
GUINEA BISSAU 1974
GUINEA 1958
CÔTE D'VOIRE 1960
NIGERIA 1960
SIERRA LEONE 1961
LIBERIA
GHANA 1957
TOGO 1960
CAMEROUN 1960
CENTRAL AFRICAN REP. 1960
ETHIOPIA 1944
SOUTHERN YEMEN 1967
Unified 1990
DJIBOUTI 1977
SOMALIA 1960
EQUATORIAL GUINEA 1968
GABON 1960
ZAIRE 1960
UGANDA 1962
KENYA 1963
REPUBLIC OF CONGO 1960
RWANDA 1962
BURUNDI 1962
TANZANIA 1964
CABINDA (Angola)
MALAWI 1964
ANGOLA 1975
ZAMBIA 1964
MOZAMBIQUE 1975
ZIMBABWE 1980
MALAGASY REP. (MADAGASCAR) 1960
MAURITIUS 1968
NAMIBIA 1990
WALVIS BAY (So. Afr.)
BOTSWANA 1966
SWAZILAND 1968
SOUTH AFRICA (Republic 1961)
LESOTHO 1966
ATLANTIC OCEAN
INDIAN OCEAN
PAKISTAN 1947
BANGLADESH 1971
INDIA 1947
SRI LANKA (CEYLON) 1948
MYANMAR (BURMA) 1947
LAOS 1949
N. VIETNAM 1954
Unified 1974
S. VIETNAM 1954
KAMPUCHEA (CAMBODIA) 1954
MALAYSIA 1963
SINGAPORE 1965
INDONESIA 1949
PHILIPPINES 1946
N. KOREA 1948
From Japan
S. KOREA 1948
Shading indicates former ruler.
Great Britain
France
Netherlands
Italy
Belgium
Portugal
United States

Rhodesia and Nyasaland, whose economies were interdependent. By the early 1960s, the British had decided on independence on a basis of one person, one vote. This decision broke the federation, for the two Rhodesias' white minorities feared black domination. In 1964, Nyasaland became independent as Malawi and Northern Rhodesia—despite white opposition—became independent under black rule as Zambia. Southern Rhodesia—where whites formed 7 percent of the population, against 3 percent in Northern Rhodesia—followed a different course at first. The whites tried to preserve their dominance with a unilateral declaration of independence (1965). International opinion opposed the move, as did nationalist movements based among the Shona (Zimbabwe African Nationalist Union, ZANU) and the Ndebele peoples (Zimbabwe African People's Union, ZAPU). The white regime held out until 1980, when it too yielded. A black majority government, headed by ZANU leader Robert Mugabe, took power and Africanized the name of the country as Zimbabwe. Though a professed Marxist, Mugabe reassured whites, whose economic roles remained crucial, even as he began creating a one-party regime. After 1980, South Africa, with its exceptionally large white minority, remained the last holdout of settler rule.

Portugal's resistance delayed its colonies' independence. In Angola, where violent outbreaks began in 1961, the independence movement divided into several parties. Nationalist violence broke out in 1962 in Portuguese Guinea (now Guinea-Bissau), and in 1964 in Mozambique, where there was a single nationalist party (FRELIMO, Portuguese acronym for Mozambican Liberation Front). Fighting dragged on into the 1970s, draining Portugal's economy. Independence finally came in 1975 when an army mutiny overthrew Portugal's government. FRELIMO took over and set up a government in Mozambique.

Meanwhile, several parties vied for power in Angola, with support from outside powers. As a Soviet ally, Cuba supported Angola's Marxist government. The United States and South Africa supported the opposing UNITA (Union for the Total Independence of Angola) guerrillas. South Africa also still occupied Namibia in defiance of a UN Security Council resolution calling for Namibia's independence. In response, Angola supported the Namibian independence movement SWAPO (Southwest African People's Organization). In 1988 the intervening powers finally agreed on Cuban withdrawal from Angola, South African withdrawal from Namibia, and independence for Namibia by 1990.

As all of the continent but South Africa achieved independence under majority rule, a number of common problems stood out. Despite the artificiality of the colonial boundaries, they typically survived as national borders. Within them, national integration proved difficult to achieve. Because few African countries had ethnically homogeneous populations, political conflict among ethnic or kinship groups became extremely common, often with religious differences as a further complication.

Independence meant, too, that the nationalist leaders inherited their former rulers' administrative systems. Because this colonial apparatus was inadequately developed for governing independent nations, the new heads of state found themselves in charge of "weak" or "soft" states, with limited capacity to make and implement policy. The Somalia of the 1990s offers an extreme example of what can ensue from such a start. Moreover, political

Map 16.1 Political Independence in Africa and Asia. *The following countries became independent in stages: Egypt in 1922, 1936, 1954; Iraq in 1932, 1947; and Lebanon and Syria in 1941–1945.*

independence by itself did not mean a surrender of European economic interests. The heads of newly independent but weak states had to come to terms with international capitalism as best they could. Independent Africa's neocolonial dependency springs largely from this confrontation.

Yet despite the weakness of most African states, nationalist goals have so far remained more influential than those of regional or Pan-African integration. The Organization of African Unity (OAU) was set up in 1963, and many international African organizations have since emerged. At the continental level, the OAU has had some success in economic or social affairs, but frustrations such as its inability to end armed conflicts highlight the slow growth of African internationalism. Some of Kwame Nkrumah's experiences reveal reasons for such difficulties. After Ghana's independence, he turned his attention to Pan-Africanism. Other leaders, however, thought that he was trying to expand his small Ghanaian power base. Such suspicions kept regional and Pan-African integration from gaining greater momentum. Consequently, although most African countries lacked the potential to function effectively as such, nation-states remained Africa's key political entities.

Africa's Population Explosion

Population growth was probably the most fundamental problem the new states faced. Africa's population problems resembled those of Asia or Latin America but produced graver social and economic effects. Population data are unreliable for Africa, partly because census taking can raise political tensions if it shows that the balance among rival ethnic groups has changed. But available estimates indicate that Africa had about 224 million people in 1954 and about 654 million in 1992. Independent Africa's statesmen led populations that nearly tripled in the first thirty years of independence.

Africa's population growth raised many problems. One was large-scale migration, both from rural to urban areas and across national borders. By 1960 estimates, one-fourth of all wage laborers in sub-Saharan Africa had been born in a colony or country different from their current residence. Another problem was urban growth. In 1990, no sub-Saharan city was as big as Latin America's biggest, though estimates for Cairo (Egypt) ranged from 10 to 15 million people. But urban growth rates were quite high. Algiers (Algeria), Addis Ababa (Ethiopia), Ibadan and Lagos (both in Nigeria), and Cape Town, Durban, Soweto, and Johannesburg (all four in South Africa) each had over 1 million inhabitants. Abidjan (Ivory Coast) and Casablanca (Morocco) had over 2 million, and Kinshasa (Zaire) had over 3 million. At current growth rates, Africa will have twenty-five cities of over 5 million people by 2025, but Latin America will have only fifteen.

Africa's current rates of population growth and urbanization cannot go on, however. The ecological impact of such growth creates not only economic but also social and medical problems that will eventually restrain it. In the cities, sanitation and transportation facilities dating largely from the colonial period have been totally overwhelmed by urban migration. Urban or rural, the quality of life is poor by many indicators. In 1992 Africa combined the highest birthrate of any continent (43 per thousand) with the lowest life expectancy (52 years for males, 55 for females). The infant mortality rate was 99 per thousand in 1992, compared with 11 per thousand for Europe and 9 for North America.

Rapid growth means that much of Africa's populace is very young: 45 percent of Africans were under age fifteen in 1992. As a result, some of the most serious problems cluster around youth-related issues: inadequate schools, too few jobs for graduates, distinctive forms of political activism, crime, or violence. But the biggest demographic problem of extremely young populations is that so many members of them have yet to enter their reproductive years. Whatever efforts are made to stem population increase, such a young population will keep growing for decades unless other factors intervene.

In Africa in the 1990s, other factors are intervening. One of the most fearsome, acquired immune deficiency syndrome (AIDS), is more widespread in sub-Saharan Africa than in the world at large. It has mostly spread in Africa by heterosexual transmission. About 2.5 million Africans are thought to be infected with the AIDS virus, 1 million of these being in Uganda, 282,000 in Zaire, and 205,000 in Zambia. Some cities report one in five pregnant women infected with the virus. Barring unexpectedly rapid advances in prevention and therapy, AIDS will exert a serious negative effect on African populations. It is not the only obstacle to ongoing population growth in Africa.

Economic Development in Reverse?

Rapid population growth has produced major economic and ecological consequences. As late as 1970, Africa essentially fed itself. Ever since, per capita grain production has fallen at an average of about 1 percent a year. Over the same period, Africa's grain imports have roughly doubled. Between 1965 and 1990, sub-Saharan Africa increased its per capita gross national product (GNP) at an average rate of only 0.2 percent per year.* During the same quarter-century, GNP per person actually shrank in fifteen African countries. Africa has become the underdeveloped world par excellence.

Many factors depressed economic performance. Some were legacies of imperialism. National borders had been drawn by outsiders, whose interest in development did not go past resource extraction. Multinational firms continued this function for independent governments that often had no choice but to rely on them, especially at first. Decolonization, then, was more a political than an economic event. Economically as well as ethnically, most African countries lacked the makings of viable nations. Many were too small: in 1986, the total GNP of Africa's ten smallest nations was less than that of Luxembourg, one of Europe's smallest countries. After independence (1990), Namibia's national economy was no bigger than that of a midsize European town. Communication and transportation networks, too, still reflected colonial needs. Long after independence, telephone calls and letters to a neighboring country might still go through Paris and London. A major need is to create regional communication and transport links by cooperation among African states. For example, the Southern African Development Coordination Conference (SADCC, founded 1980), aimed to reduce nine countries' dependence on South Africa by creating regional railway, telecommunications, and electricity grids.

Other obstacles to development came from within the independent states and societies. For example, economic policies of colonial governments and their independent successors differed widely. Colonial regimes pursued limited goals with conservative financing, but independent states pursued ambitious developmental goals with deficit financing, often by expanding the state-run sector of the economy. Lack of qualified personnel to fill needed positions in government and the economy magnified the impact of the policy switch. Industry seldom went beyond

---

*A country's *gross national product* (GNP) is the total market value of all final goods and services produced in the country during a year, including income earned abroad by citizens of the country but excluding income earned inside the country by foreigners. *Gross domestic product* (GDP) is the same measure but without allowance for earnings paid abroad or received from abroad. Both concepts are ways of measuring a country's economic productivity. Only "final goods and services" are considered, because inclusion of intermediate products (like hides used to make shoes) would lead to double counting.

light import substitution. If not still foreign controlled, industry tended to be ineptly run in the public sector. All the while, forms of corruption rooted in the impact of kinship ties on politics—a subject discussed below—drained capital from productive use. Why else would the Paris magazine *Jeune Afrique* (*Young Africa*), aimed at French-speakers in this poor continent, carry advertisements for Mercedes-Benz automobiles and bulletproof vests? East Africa's Swahili-speakers satirized Mercedes-owners as if they were a distinct ethnic group, the "Wabenzi." Since only a few sub-Saharan countries—Angola, Gabon, Nigeria, Cameroon—had oil to export, the 1970s oil price rises also helped depress Africa's economic performance. In Nigeria, the oil boom's end in the 1980s caused similar hardship.

The black-ruled states' formal economic policies diverged widely—from the Ivory Coast's openness to foreign investment to Tanzania's self-reliance and village socialism. But none has yet overcome dependency and underdevelopment. One sign of this is the menacing scale assumed by foreign debt. By 1991, Africa's total external debt exceeded $264 billion—about one-fifth of the total debt of all developing countries. Individual countries' debts appeared small by Latin American—or U.S.—standards; yet together they absorbed 31 percent of Africa's export earnings, a critical matter for a continent dependent on commodity exports that had long declined in price relative to manufactures. Here more than in Latin America, the role of financial agencies like the IMF roused mounting criticism, for Africa's ability to pay would only decline without additional capital to invest in development.

Africa's agricultural problems were probably the hardest to solve. Some of these were inevitable—the savanna's aridity, the rain-forest soils' infertility. Tropical lands, which lack frosts to kill insect pests and tend to have either too much or too little rainfall, severely challenge agriculture. In 1988, for example, African countries from Ethiopia to Mauretania faced the worst locust plague in twenty-five years. Other agricultural problems amounted to policy mistakes, such as collectivization programs that reduced incentives to produce, or government marketing boards. Supposedly set up to aid in marketing export crops, the boards also extracted revenue by forcing farmers to sell below international market prices, thus, as in Perón's Argentina, undermining agriculture. But agriculture's worst problems arose from growing human pressures on fragile environments.

Sub-Saharan Africa has experienced several waves of drought and famine since the early 1970s. In the 1980s, starvation threatened almost half of Africa's countries. In the early 1990s, the worst drought in fifty years threatened 40 million people in eastern and southern Africa. At least in part, these droughts resulted from population growth. Increased cutting of firewood and overextension of cultivation have reduced moisture retention in the soil, accelerating runoff and soil erosion. These changes have disrupted climatic patterns that used to assure rainfall, leading to perhaps irreversible environmental degradation. Africa now produces less food per capita than it produced twenty years ago. Food donated from abroad may save lives but does nothing to solve the underlying problems.

Below, we shall consider Africa's two largest economies. Nigeria's $33.5 billion and South Africa's $91 billion in GNP accounted for 75 percent of sub-Saharan Africa's 1990 GNP of $166 billion. Here, to suggest the dimensions of Africa's problems more fully, we shall also consider Somalia, a less favored case.

Anarchy and mass starvation in Somalia gripped world attention in 1992. Somalia lies at the Horn of Africa, a landmass, vaguely horn-shaped, that projects into the Indian Ocean just south of where the Red Sea opens into it. Somalia and adjoining territories (Djibouti and Ethiopia's Ogaden Province) are home to the

Starvation victims await burial, Somalia, 1992. *The bodies are wrapped in sacks from food shipments that arrived too late for them.* *© 1992 Christopher Morris/Black Star*

Somali people, divided into numerous clans. Somalia is hot and arid, and many Somalis depend on camel nomadism for subsistence. Not surprisingly given the nearness of Islam's Arabian homeland, most Somalis are Muslims.

Nineteenth-century European rulers divided the Somali territories. The French took Djibouti, one of East Africa's best ports, and surrounding countryside; Djibouti finally became independent in 1977 as one of Africa's micro-nations. The British took the north side of the Horn (1884), the Italians took the south side (1889), and Ethiopia seized Ogaden Province (1890s). When the British and Italian colonies became independent in 1960, they merged to form the nation of Somalia.

Independent Somalia's history has been grim. A military coup soon toppled its civilian president, installing dictator Siad Barre (1969–1991). Hallmarks of his regime included rights violations, abuse of power, economic mismanagement, and failure in political institution building. At different stages in their policy toward Somalia and Ethiopia, both the United States and the Soviet Union, as well as various Arab regimes, supplied large amounts of weapons to Somalia. When rebels chased Barre from the capital, Mogadishu, no new government emerged. Instead, rival clan-based factions looted government armories and turned on one another. Civil war soon splintered the country. Common consumption of *qat* or *khat,* a mildly narcotic plant stimulant that makes trigger fingers itch, helped worsen the violence. Fighting had spread into Somalia's farming areas by March 1992. By then, two-thirds of Somalia's 6 million people faced starvation.

A food-importing country in the best of times, Somalia could not cope with mounting violence, devastation of its farmlands, and the worst drought in a half-century. By fall 1992, one-sixth of the country's population had fled to other countries. Despite massive international relief efforts, thousands of Somalis died each day, often because fighting prevented distribution of food.

The Somali crisis also tested what international action could do to alleviate such crises. To operate, relief agencies had to endure having part of their food supplies stolen or else pay for protection, which cost the International Red Cross nearly $50,000 a month. The United Nations sent in troops, but the lack of a government for them to cooperate with frustrated their humanitarian mission, raising serious questions about whether the UN should be empowered to respond more aggressively to local crises. Following a UN vote to authorize use of force, President George Bush sent in U.S. Marines in December 1992 to provide security for food distribution. Several other countries also sent troops for a short-term operation. Questioning whether temporary intervention could produce lasting improvement, experienced aid workers argued that the real need was for sustained humanitarian effort and a political settlement engineered to create institutions that the warlords could not subvert.

Media coverage to the contrary, Somalia's problems were unique only in degree. The same drought plagued much of Africa. The 1.3 million who have fled their homes in the Horn form only a fourth of Africa's refugee population. Clearly, no sub-Saharan economy—unless that of white-dominated, exploitative South Africa—has excelled the economies of Latin America in development. For most of them, food is the central problem. Is Africa's food problem only a warning of what will happen to the world if human beings do not find ways to limit the stress that their growing numbers impose on the natural environment? We shall return to this question in Chapter 19.

Political Evolution: Common Phases and Themes

Independent Africa's political development has been almost as problematic as its economic development. The new governments tended to pass through a common set of phases marked by certain themes: overcentralized and ineffective institutions, recurrent ideological preferences, ethnic tensions, and common problems in relations with the outside world.

In former British colonies, the political phases commonly began with an independent government headed by a prime minister responsible to the legislature. As in Britain, if the prime minister could not muster a parliamentary majority on a key vote, the government fell

Political mobilization of Africa's women. *Song and costume alike express support for Zimbabwe's Robert Mugabe. David Harrison/BBC*

from office. These countries generally became independent as members of the British Commonwealth.

Most countries that began with a prime minister soon changed to a government headed by a president. Former French colonies began their independent life with this phase. The advantages of this system were that the president's tenure in office did not depend on the ability to command a parliamentary majority and that the constitution could define presidential powers extremely broadly, even more so than in the United States. Blazing the trail into this second phase, Ghana adopted a new constitution (1960) that gave the president vast powers over the budget and lawmaking. Nkrumah created a virtual presidential dictatorship, soon widely imitated elsewhere.

The next phase, in countries that had more than one party to start with, was to abolish all parties other than the one in power. Nkrumah did this in 1964 by making his Convention People's party the sole legal one. Most other African countries followed suit. We shall offer an explanation of this practice in discussing the impact of regionalism and ethnicity on politics.

In the fourth phase in postindependence politics, a military dictatorship replaced the civilian presidency. In some countries, as in Ghana after the military overthrew Nkrumah in 1966, power shifted back and forth between military and civilians several times. However, the general trend was toward military rule. The number of military governments rose from two in 1963 to twenty-four in 1984. Several factors reinforced this trend. Colonial rule was imposed by force and often carried out by military officers. Independent Africa's coup makers were European-trained officers. They had little difficulty seizing control of a weakly institutionalized government that lacked a strong tradition of military subordination to civilian authority.

Access to power politicized the military elites more and more. Over time, the coups tended to be the work of younger men of lower rank overturning generals or colonels. The younger men were less likely than earlier military interventionists to shed their uniforms after taking over or to promise a return to civilian rule. Lieutenant Jerry Rawlings, in his early thirties, led two successful coups in Ghana in 1979 and 1981. Before reaching the age of thirty, Sergeant Samuel K. Doe led the 1980 coup that overthrew Africa's oldest republican government, that of Liberia.

By 1990, however, the fading of the Cold War and the growth of European integration seemed to produce a dramatic shift of trend, much as in Latin America. New demands began to be heard for civilian rule, multiparty democracy, human rights, greater equality for women, and sustainable development. Outside pressures stimulated these demands. For example, France tied its aid to democratization and development from 1990 on, and U.S. president Clinton sent similar messages in his contacts with African leaders. Africans who backed these demands were also increasingly numerous and insistent, even though heads of state were not always readily responsive.

One notable feature of the change was the proliferation of international organizations, ranging from the Organization of African Unity, to the Economic Community of West Africa (ECOWAS), the Inter-African Union of Human Rights, or the biennial Franco-African summits, which in 1992 brought together heads of state or government from twenty-three African countries and France. Increasingly, too, emphasis was on economic integration, as in the West African Monetary Union (UMOA in French), whose member states retain a common currency linked to the French franc, or the Southern African Development Coordination Council (SADCC), whose member states are now trying to turn it into a common market called the Southern African Development Community (SADC).

In each phase—parliamentary government, presidential republic, one-party dictatorship, military rule, and democratization—most governments showed only limited political or administrative capacity. Scarcely unique to Africa, this trait of underdevelopment manifested itself in many ways. Governments proved unable or unwilling to conduct impartial elections or accurate censuses, to implement effective family planning or agricultural development programs, or to adopt more than rudimentary forms of revenue collection, such as the compulsory marketing boards that served essentially to tax exports. In most African countries, the excessive size of the public sector and the lavish perquisites it inherited from colonial days both reflected and compounded governmental inefficiency. On the positive side, it is worth noting that few African regimes have been as repressive as some found on other continents. Only a couple of other African regimes—like that of Jean Bedel Bokassa in the Central African Republic—have rivaled the violence of Uganda's Idi Amin, who killed over a hundred thousand Ugandans before his fall in 1979.

As independence spread, African leaders propounded official ideologies to justify their rule. Many of these were socialist in one of two senses.

The first was an African populist socialism that had little to do with Marx. Instead it reflected the desire for a program of mass mobilization and development, a program expressly suited for Africa. Formative influences on populist socialism included the communalistic heritage of African societies, Pan-Africanism, and the idealization of African identity (*négritude*) by writers such as Aimé Césaire, a French-speaking West Indian of African ancestry, and Léopold Senghor, president of Senegal (1960–1980) and an internationally known French-language poet. Their notion of *négritude* had counterparts in Nkrumah's idea of "African personality" and in a widespread concern for authenticity that led, for example, to many name changes. The Congo became Zaire, Leopoldville became Kinshasa, and Joseph-Désiré Mobutu became Mobotu Sese Seko. Sometimes dismissed as "tinsel modernization," such Africanization was a needed adjustment to a new order, much as the reevaluation of blackness in the United States was an adaptation to the conditions created by the civil rights movement. Julius Nyerere of Tanzania developed one of the most widely admired populist socialisms with his concept of *ujamaa,* or kinship communalism. Tanzania took populism seriously, by trying to redirect education away from the elitism of the colonial system, for example, and by stressing agrarian change. The attempt to create village cooperatives was not highly successful, partly for reasons beyond Nyerere's control (like the agricultural crisis conditions of the 1970s); but such recognition that development depended on structural change in the rural sector has been all too rare in developing countries.

Largely inspired by Cuban example, the other type of African socialism has been called Afro-Marxism. Contrary to Marxist-Leninist assumptions, revolution came first in Cuba, and then Castro announced that he was a Marxist-Leninist and used this identification to alter Cuba's external dependency ties. Starting in Congo-Brazzaville in 1968–1969, a similar phenomenon appeared in Africa, as ruling military groups simply announced the advent of "Marxism" in a number of countries: Somalia (1970), Benin (1974), Madagascar and Ethiopia (1975–1976), Mozambique and Angola (1977).

Afro-Marxist regimes were Marxist-Leninist mostly in trying—like Cuba—to use this identification to reshape external dependency relations. They also took a Leninist view of the party as an elite vanguard, in contrast to the populist-socialist regimes' mass movements. Otherwise, most Afro-Marxist regimes pursued few Marxist policies. Except for Ethiopia, most steered clear of agricultural collectivization. Otherwise, Afro-Marxist regimes typically created a state-controlled sector and nationalized foreign interests regarded as vestiges of colonialism. But almost all of them tried to attract Western investment. Angola depended on Gulf Oil, a dominant firm in the international oil industry, for almost all its government revenue and foreign exchange and used Cuban troops to guard Gulf's operations. In Zimbabwe, the Marxism of the Mugabe regime did not keep it from trying to reassure an economically vital white minority or collaborating in some ways with South Africa.

The scant economic rewards of pro-Soviet policies took most of the Marxism out of Afro-Marxism, even before the Soviet Union fell apart. In the long run, Afro-Marxists could not escape the capitalist nature of the world economy anymore than could Cuba or the Soviet Union. Today, Africans scan their past for indigenous bases for—not socialism—but democracy.

One way or the other, pre-existing sociopolitical patterns did as much to govern African political behavior as did ideology. The political parties and movements that grew up in the various countries before independence were mostly regional in scope, rather than national, and represented one or a few, but not all, of the peoples living in the country. The hasty organization of postindependence political life according to imported models meant giving power to one of these parties, or perhaps to a coalition, and casting the others in the role of opposition. We shall see how this worked out in Nigeria, but there are many other examples.

Liberal democracies assume that all citizens are equal as voters—one person, one vote—and that the political parties succeed each other in office. The parties differ on policy and political philosophy but are all loyal to the political system, so that those out of office form a "loyal opposition." But what happens if voters' and parties' primary loyalty is not to the nation and its constitution but to their own ethnic groups, clans, or regions? Then there can be no loyal opposition, and the political victory of any party means that a single sectional interest has captured the entire government. Somalia's anarchy offers an extreme example of what can follow. In Zimbabwe, a less acute case, the importance of ethnic identifications helps explain why Robert Mugabe's ZANU government, based among the Shona people, was at times more lenient to the whites than to Joshua Nkomo's ZAPU movement: ZAPU represents the Ndebele minority, who are potential rivals, as the whites no longer are, for control of the country. In countries like Zimbabwe that have two main ethnic groups, some Africa experts think that a single-party regime actually serves a useful purpose if it includes members of both groups. Zimbabwe acquired a single party in 1987, at the cost of expanding government services, so that Nkomo followers could receive patronage plums without Mugabe followers losing theirs. In Kenya the merger of two parties into one enabled Daniel Arap Moi, of the former minority party, to become president.

Yet more than ethnic tension lies behind the intolerance of opposition. Many Africans have pointed out that in kinship societies, decision making was historically by discussion among the elders. The goal was to reach consensus, after which no one would be allowed to oppose the group decision. Discussion progressively worked out disagreement, until the decision could be regarded as unanimous. In the past, this kind of decision making was not unique to Africa but characterized kinship societies in many places, including rural prerevolutionary Russia and the Middle East. Analysts cite this tradition of decision making as a reason for intolerance of political opposition today. In Africa, such thinking goes so far that the secret ballot, seen in the United States as a vital safeguard of democracy, may be seen as "un-African." Kenyans now vote by "queuing" or "open voting": voters line up behind the picture of their candidate. If elections by secret ballot had been marred by corruption and violence, would this method be less manipulable?

In Africa, again as in many parts of the world, kinship and ethnicity also help shape certain forms of political corruption. Indeed, behavior that appears corrupt to outsiders may not seem so to Africans. Historically, kinship societies typically held much property in common, and a major leadership function was to distribute the group's wealth among its members. Such leaders headed great households, supporting many dependents, dispensing much hospitality, and seldom distinguishing between personal and public property.

Given this outlook, postindependence politics turned into a contest among parties based in specific regions or ethnic groups to control the whole country and parcel out its benefits as if they were those of the group's ancestral lands. Politicians saw no distinction between public funds and personal compensation. At best, it would take time for behavior to adjust to a situation that called for new standards. Meanwhile, politics degenerated into runaway patronage, misuse of public funds, and manipulation of political power for private enrichment. For example, after a Nigerian military coup of 1983, it was reported that an official of the fallen government had a house in England with a gold bathtub appraised at $5 million. The fact that the story was believed, whether true or not, gives an idea of the stakes of the political game in one African country. To make matters worse, as Nigerian novelist Chinua Achebe pointed out in his novel *A Man of the People* (1966), anyone who attacked corrupt leaders would be suspected of wanting to take power and follow their example.

The best way for Africa's states to move beyond local loyalties to national integration remains unclear. So far, ethnic and local interests prevail, so much that startled British visitors have sometimes heard people say they wish "the Queen would come back." The success of the current push for democratization and integration among African nations will depend on producing tangible solutions to these problems.

Africa and Outside Powers

No single outside power has as much influence in independent Africa as the United States has in Latin America. However, a survey of African affairs would be incomplete without a look at international relations.

Both Britain and France tried to maintain connections with former colonies. Britain did so through the Commonwealth of Nations. After de Gaulle's French Community (1958) dissolved in 1961, France relied on cooperation agreements and succeeded, more than Britain did, in retaining functions it had performed before 1960. After France joined the European Economic Community (EEC), France's former colonies' special economic relations with it were extended into analogous relations with the entire EEC. France remains the largest aid donor to sub-Saharan Africa, and its Franco-African summits bring together high-level delegations from many states. Such ties have helped make the postcolonial era one of neocolonialism. Britain has retained former positions less well than France, but they can still be imposing. In 1980, about half the $25 billion in foreign investment in South Africa was British.

Superpower rivalries also had an impact. Seeing the African independence movements of the 1950s and 1960s as a chance to advance its influence, the Soviet Union provided some of them with arms and military assistance. More intense Soviet involvement followed the rise of Afro-Marxist regimes in places like Ethiopia, Angola, and Mozambique. But in the long run, Africa had low priority in Soviet policy. African populist-socialist leaders either dissatisfied the Soviets ideologically or became dissatisfied with Soviet aid. The USSR served as Africa's chief source of weapons, for which it demanded payment in hard currency. By the 1980s, however, African leaders no longer found the Soviet system credible as a model of development. Racial discrimination against African students in the USSR created added resentment. Unpleasant experiences with "socialist imperalists" helped prepare African leaders for a change of policies in the 1990s.

If Soviet interest in Africa developed tardily and thinly, U.S. policy at first went little beyond advocating an end to colonialism. After independence, the United States still assumed that the former colonial powers would be those most active in African affairs. Gradually, however, the United States became more forward in pursuing certain interests: ensuring access to minerals and a stable investment environment, preventing the Soviets from acquiring strategic advantages in Africa, and protecting the shipping lanes around the Cape of Good Hope so as to ensure oil imports. Gradually, too, the United States took more interest in some of Africa's trouble spots—for example, joining in British efforts of the late 1970s to achieve a settlement in Rhodesia or propping up the Mobutu regime in Zaire in order to ensure access to the country's minerals. Consistently, however, the United States gave less aid to sub-Saharan Africa than to the Middle East or Asia—and usually less than to Latin

America. In the long run, the thorniest policy problem was to define a policy toward South Africa that could both satisfy U.S. business interests and show Africans that the United States opposed *apartheid* (racial separation) with more than words.

By reinforcing incentives for economic and political liberalization and integration, the end of the Cold War marked a turning point in Africa's international, as well as its domestic, politics. We have noted some aspects of this change and shall see others in the discussions of Nigeria and South Africa that form the rest of this chapter.

Nigeria: Independence plus Oil Dependency

Home to one in six sub-Saharan Africans, Nigeria is Africa's most populous country and potentially one of its wealthiest. Yet it shares such of its neighbors' problems as ethnic factionalism and military rule. Nigeria's experience shows what obstacles even an oil-rich nation may face in political and economic development.

Rise and Fall of the First Republic

By the end of World War II, several rival nationalist movements had emerged in Nigeria, and experiences of the war years had raised political expectations. The British had not yet taken additional steps to broaden political participation, however, and they had only begun to emphasize social and economic development. After the war, change accelerated on all fronts.

The economy quickened dramatically. From 1947 to 1958, government revenue rose from 14 million British pounds to 58 million, while the amount of money in circulation rose from 23 million to 55 million pounds. Over the same period, exports tripled, from 44 to 136 million British pounds in value, while imports quintupled, from 33 to 167 million. The shift from a positive to a negative foreign trade balance worried economists but was associated with rapid growth of investment. The basis of the economy remained colonial exports, 85 percent agricultural and the rest mineral. Government marketing boards bought and marketed the agricultural goods, and industrialization was only starting. But the government made efforts at diversification, including oil exploration. Small-scale oil exports began by 1960.

These economic changes affected Nigerians profoundly. In particular, the growth of the economy and the approach of independence increased the need for educated Nigerians. The colonial government expanded education greatly, especially at the secondary level. Many Nigerians received scholarships to study abroad, and in 1948 the University College of Ibadan opened. Still, the numbers of graduates remained far short of the need. Education became a political issue, too, for many nationalists preferred to emphasize universal lower-level education, even at the cost of limiting expansion at higher levels. And the spread of education had economic effects. Rural youngsters with primary schooling, especially boys, no longer wanted to work on farms as their parents did. Instead they flocked to the cities seeking jobs as clerks and thus launching the superurbanization of Lagos.

Amid these economic and social changes, preparations for independence advanced. Nigeria received new constitutions in 1947, 1951, and 1954. The result was a federal system of government, headed by a prime minister, with an elected federal legislature and three self-governing regions: Northern, Eastern, and Western (Map 16.2). With modifications, the 1954 constitution remained in force until 1966. Meanwhile, important new issues emerged.

The most troublesome point was ethnic and regional tension. The three regions were

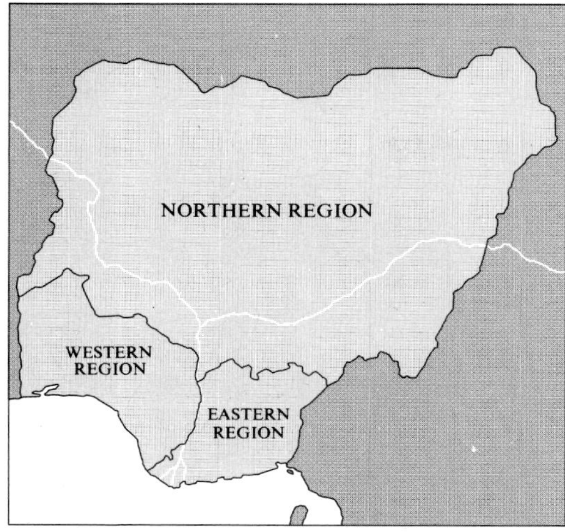

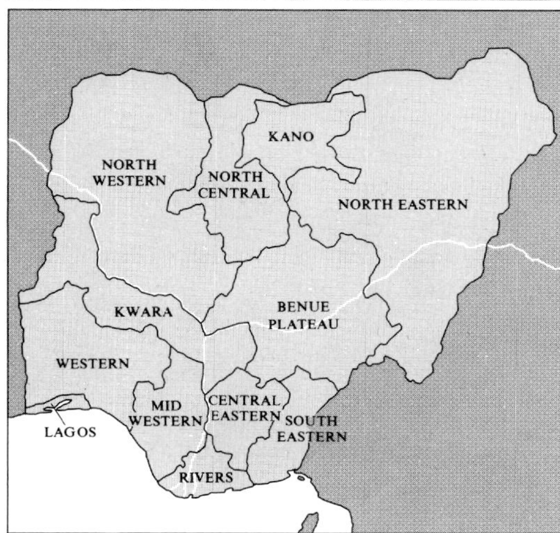

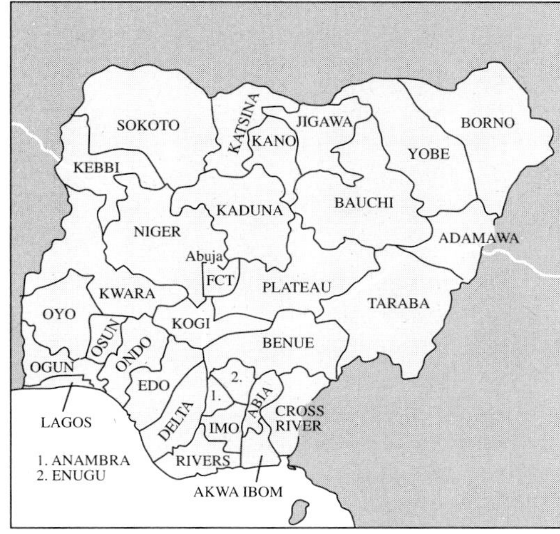

dominated by the Hausa-Fulani (Northern), Yoruba (Western), and Ibo peoples (Eastern). The Northern Region was larger and more populous than the other two combined. Before long, the strongest national movement, the National Council of Nigeria and the Cameroons (NCNC), broke apart into ethnically based parties. Founded in 1944 by the Ibo leader Nnamdi Azikiwe, the NCNC initially had Yoruba and Ibo support, but relations between the two groups soon became strained. The northern Muslims also formed a political organization. They feared that southerners, who had been quicker to seek Western education, would gain political dominance after independence. Soon there were three regional parties based on specific ethnic groups: the Northern Peoples Congress (NPC, Hausa-Fulani), the Action Group (AG) in the Yoruba West, and the NCNC. The NCNC was basically an Ibo party centered in the East, though the presence of many Ibo migrants in other parts of the country gave it followers elsewhere and made its outlook less regional than the other parties'. Small ethnic groups began to demand increases in the number of regions so that they could acquire local dominance.

Despite such problems, Nigeria moved toward independence more by negotiation than by violence. The first federal general election (1954) produced a coalition government combining the Northern Peoples Congress and the National Council of Nigeria and the Cameroons. The NPC leader in the House, Abubakar Tafawa Balewa, a northern Muslim from a small ethnic group, became the first federal prime minister. The three regions became self-governing between 1957 and 1959, and the country became independent in 1960

Map 16.2 Nigeria's Three Regions (1960), Nineteen States (1976), and Thirty States (1991).

under a government headed by Balewa. Azikiwe assumed the mostly ceremonial role of governor-general, or president, after the change to a republic in 1963.

Nigeria's parliamentary government lasted only until January 1966 before falling to a military coup. Until then, Nigeria never abandoned multiparty for single-party rule. In that, Nigeria differed from many African nations. Yet by 1966, several factors had discredited the republic. One factor was most politicians' corruption and lack of concern for their constituents in a time of rising prices and widening income inequality. The government also failed to respect constitutional requirements, especially in high-handed acts directed at the Western region and the Western-based Action Group, then an opposition party. A third problem was regional imbalance. This became a chronic problem, affecting even census taking, which Nigeria's combination of a multiethnic society and a federal political system made a very touchy issue. After the last preindependence census in 1952–1953, Nigeria's next three censuses produced results that were contested or officially disavowed. Problems like these pushed Nigeria toward chaos.

From the Biafran Civil War Through the Oil Boom—and Bust

After the overthrow of Nigeria's First Republic in January 1966, civilian rule was not restored for thirteen years. Two military coups occurred early in 1966, largely Ibo backed. A new constitution, rushed through after the second coup, abolished the three regions, creating a unitary rather than a federal state. By now, Nigerians had noticed the prominence of Ibo among the coup makers—but not among the victims. Further, Nigerians saw the abolition of federalism as an attempt to gain power for the Ibo, who had a larger educated elite and were more widely dispersed nationally than other ethnic groups.

July 1966 therefore witnessed a third coup, which installed a government under a northern officer from a small ethnic group, Lieutenant-Colonel Yakubu Gowon. Discussion of return to civilian rule continued. But massacres of the Ibo also occurred. The Eastern Region refused to recognize the Gowon government, thousands of Ibo began returning from other parts of the country, and secession seemed likely. In May 1967, Gowon tried to defuse the issue by dividing Nigeria into twelve states, in place of the former regions, so appealing to the interests of small ethnic groups in the East as elsewhere. Three days later the Eastern Region declared its independence as the Republic of Biafra. This was a major challenge: most of Nigeria's oil was in the East, though not in Ibo territory proper.

In the ensuing civil war, Biafrans, supported by multinational oil companies, succeeded at first. Nigerian forces soon turned the tide, however, reducing Biafran resistance village by village. The war roused much outside interest, partly because the Biafran government claimed, and overseas sympathizers believed, that the Nigerian forces intended genocide. When the Biafrans capitulated in January 1970, the Gowon regime responded with a magnanimous call for reconciliation, and the former rebels were reintegrated into the nation in much that spirit.

With the civil war past, Nigeria entered a new period of opportunity, though military rule proved hard to end. Even the war years brought some gains. The new states became established relatively smoothly, and the wartime foreign exchange shortage stimulated import substitution. By the early 1970s, Nigeria was becoming self-sufficient in consumer goods such as textiles, footwear, beverages, and soap. Foreign automobile firms had opened assembly plants in the country, and

The Biafran Civil War, 1967–1970. *An officer of the Nigerian army issues instructions through an interpreter to the chief of a captured Ibo village.* *Bruno Barbey/Magnum Photos*

the government was pressuring them to use Nigerian-made parts. As elsewhere in Africa, "indigenization" decrees were used to force sale of foreign-owned firms, wholly or partly, to Nigerians.

What drove economic change, however, was Nigeria's emergence as a major oil exporter. The value of Nigeria's exports increased fortyfold between 1960 and 1980. At the start of that period, agricultural goods and tin represented 84 percent of exports. By its end, their share had fallen to 3 percent, and petroleum had shot from 3 to 96 percent of exports.

Such changes predictably created economic and social stress. Agricultural exports declined not only proportionally but also in absolute amount, largely because the agricultural marketing boards deprived producers of incentives to produce. This was one cause of the labor shift out of agriculture. But the petroleum sector could not absorb all the available workers. It produced too few jobs—perhaps only twenty thousand by 1980. Rapid urbanization also meant the need to reorient agriculture from export crops to foodstuffs for domestic consumers. Neither the declining rural population nor the government responded to this need effectively.

The major growth of Nigeria's oil exports coincided almost exactly with the price rises engineered by OPEC, which Nigeria joined in 1971. But the Gowon government failed to use its gains wisely. Since oil revenue went to the central government, increasing its power in relation to the states, the key problem was its incapacity to manage and redistribute the benefits. The growth of oil revenue seriously overstrained the country's supply of qualified technical and managerial talent. The fact that many Nigerians still lack running water, modern sewerage, or even a regular fuel supply indicates the grave consequences of this problem.

Leadership was clearly part of Nigeria's problem. After the Biafran war, Nigerians expected a return to civilian rule. Instead, Gowon announced that the change would take six more years, during which he would implement a nine-point program, including a development plan, a census, and organization of national political parties. Gowon's increasingly inept military regime had little success with all this. The 1973 census became the third since 1962 to yield politically unacceptable results. As dissatisfaction grew, Gowon kept postponing civilian rule until he fell to another military coup in 1975.

The new regime, led from 1975 to 1979 by Major General Olusegun Obasanjo, made a strong start. It set a date—October 1, 1979—to restore civilian rule and called for preparatory steps, such as deciding whether to create new states and drafting a new constitution. By 1976, the number of states had grown to nineteen. Along U.S. lines, the new constitution prescribed a popularly elected president, a bicameral federal legislature, and elected state governors and assemblies. A federal commission was to monitor formation of truly national, not regional, parties. Of some fifty attempts, only five new parties passed commission scrutiny. In 1979, the country's 48 million voters elected Shehu Shagari of the Northern-based National party of Nigeria (NPN) as president of Nigeria's Second Republic.

Shagari began with important assets. The U.S.-style presidency and federal system strengthened the central government in relation to the states, as did oil revenues. Other problems remained unsolved, however. The new parties still proved too responsive to regional interests. Shagari's NPN was little more than a Northern party that agreed to rotate people from other parts of the country in leadership positions. To heighten the problem, the tendency toward single-party dominance, familiar all across Africa since the 1960s, now asserted itself in Nigeria too. When Shagari won re-election in 1983, voting patterns showed blatant manipulation: the list of voters turned out to contain 65 million names, even though Nigerians old enough to vote were probably not two-thirds that numerous.

Economic problems worsened the political ones. Annual oil earnings peaked at $25 billion in 1981 but fell to a fraction of that in the late 1980s, while the foreign debt rose to $25 billion. Austerity measures had to be imposed as early as 1982, especially because Nigeria had lost agricultural self-sufficiency and had to import basics like sugar and rice.

The Second Republic fell to a military coup in 1983, followed by another in 1985. However, the problems that had caused the Second Republic's fall persisted, forcing President Ibrahim Babangida's military government to adopt a two-part economic and political program in 1987.

Economically, Babangida's "structural adjustment program" devalued the currency, cutting imports by raising their cost, and abolished commodity marketing boards so as to restore agricultural producers' incentives.

Plans were made to privatize government firms and raise subsidized prices of consumer goods. Five years later, critics blamed the president for neglecting the economy to concentrate on his failed political reforms. Nigeria's economic readjustment had been thwarted by political corruption, the costs of joint West African intervention in Liberia, where a civil war was going on, and the unmanageable foreign debt of $30 billion.

Recalling the 1970s, Babangida's political program provided for a five-year, phased return to civilian rule. New parties were to be formed, excluding old politicians, and a new constitution drafted. In 1991, the number of states was raised to thirty, and the capital was moved from the coastal supermetropolis, Lagos, to the centrally located Abuja. By not collecting the religious or ethnic data that had made earlier attempts controversial, the government finally managed to carry out a census in 1991. It yielded a total of 89 million, nearly 20 million less than earlier estimates, inflated by ethnic and regional interests' attempts to claim more of federal resources. Election irregularities continued, however, and Babangida repeatedly promised to quit office without doing so. In June 1993, after the results of a reputedly free and fair presidential election had been set aside, apparently because the military's preferred candidate had not won, widespread riots and protests broke out.

Having known civilian rule for less than ten of over thirty years since independence, Nigerians who protested the quashing of the June 1993 elections showed the strength of their desire for democracy. To last, a democratically elected government would need the ability to inspire Nigerians to move beyond the political cynicism and the ethnic and religious particularism that were so deeply imprinted on their history. Such a government would need a greater capacity to define and implement policy. Perhaps the most basic need, however, would be to remedy the fact that the average Nigerian's real income—oil or no oil—is probably lower today than in the 1960s.

South Africa: Inequality, Exploitation, Isolation

Until 1948, South Africa's history had been that of two struggles—one between the British and the Afrikaners for political power, the other between whites and Africans for control of the land. The introduction of the apartheid policy in 1948 under the Afrikaner-dominated Nationalist party, which ruled the country continuously into the 1990s, marked the victory of the whites, especially the Afrikaners. With the old dual struggle settled, South Africa embarked on a period of prolonged economic growth, but its political system became more exclusionary than ever. The result was a new struggle that pitted Africans vying for political as well as economic power against the institutional bastions of white minority rule. Not until the 1990s, after white rule had collapsed everywhere else in Africa, did South Africa's isolation and bizarre internal contradictions force it, too, to risk change in the direction of racial equality and democratization.

White Domination, Economic and Political

Into the 1980s, growth and inequality became more than ever the dominant traits of South Africa's economy. Minerals remained basic to its prosperity. South Africa ranked first in the world in reserves of gold, platinum, chrome, manganese, and vanadium. The country ranked second in reserves of diamonds, and between third and eighth in antimony, asbestos, coal, lead, nickel, phosphate, silver, titanium, and perhaps uranium. The land produced a sizable agricultural surplus for export, although millions remained malnourished in the black reserves. By 1965 the country had become virtually self-sufficient in heavy industry, and manufactured goods accounted for 40 percent of exports. As before World War II, the state controlled key industries, particularly in energy, one field where South Africa had resource shortages. With no known petroleum resources, the government founded SASOL (South African Coal, Oil and Gas Corporation) in the 1950s to manufacture oil from coal. After the Iranian revolution of 1979 deprived South Africa of its one regular source of oil, efforts began to expand SASOL's production. South Africa also developed nuclear power and began exploring for offshore petroleum.

Another resource essential for South Africa's economic growth was nonwhite labor, exploited through bad working conditions and grossly unequal pay. In 1984, the average salary for whites was almost four times that for Africans. African living standards were especially bad in the black "homelands," which reserved 13 percent of the land for over 70 percent of the population (Map 16.3). But South Africa's exploitation of blacks did not stop at its borders. The mines had long employed migrants from as far north as Zambia. This practice increases the supply, and lowers the price, of black labor in South Africa. It also helps ensure South Africa's dominance over neighboring countries.

Exploitative but resource-rich, the South African economy grew at an average annual rate of nearly 7 percent from 1910 to 1974, an astonishing record. The OPEC oil price increases and other factors then caused a crisis. When the United States stopped buying and selling gold at a fixed $35 per ounce in 1971, however, the world price soared, reaching an all-time high of $875 an ounce in January 1980. Despite wide subsequent fluctuations, gold price increases of such an order for a time helped pull South Africa back out of recession. But drought and commodity price declines caused a new downturn by 1983. From 1984 on, the costs of virtual black rebellion at home and trade sanctions abroad—South Africa's coal exports fell by 40 percent in the first half of 1987—created new pressures that left South Africa scrambling for solutions. The government privatized even such key state firms as SASOL, the oil-from-coal concern, and planned to create new indirect taxes so as to raise revenue from those too poor to pay income tax. Meanwhile, growing labor militancy highlighted the contradiction inherent in trying to separate economically interdependent races, especially in a complex economy where growth required placing nonwhites in more and better jobs.

In politics, South Africa remained formally a parliamentary democracy. Yet changes over time greatly eroded resemblances to the original British model. From 1948 into the early 1990s, for example, the Afrikaner-dominated National party always controlled the government. Single-party rule signaled the Afrikaners' political triumph over the English-speaking South Africans. In 1961, when the country declared itself a republic and severed ties with the British Commonwealth, British influence further diminished.

The character and policies of selected prime ministers reinforced this trend. With the Nationalist party victory in 1948, Prime Minister D. F. Malan (1948–1954) formed the first government to consist of Afrikaners only. Its legislation systematized racial separation (apartheid). The consistency of the governments from then on derived not just from the party but from a larger complex of Afrikaner interest groups. The most important was the Afrikaner Broederbond (Brotherhood,

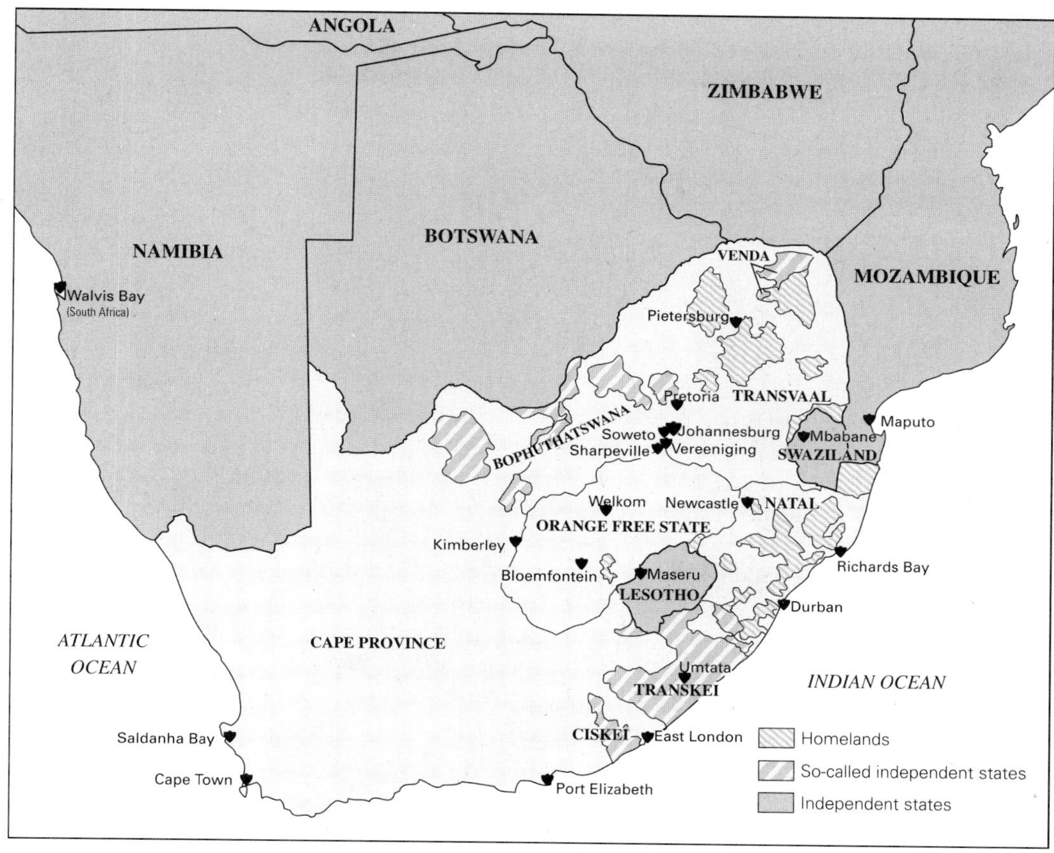

Map 16.3 South Africa, with the Homelands and Surrounding States

founded 1918). All prime ministers since 1948, and virtually all Afrikaners in public life, have been members of this secret society, whose members largely formulated the apartheid idea. The triumph of such interests meant a shift from British-style restraint toward Afrikaner authoritarianism—a shift facilitated by English-speaking South Africans' belief in white supremacy, though not always in Afrikaner methods.

Prime Minister Hendrik Verwoerd (1958–1966) reflected this shift. A former Nazi sympathizer, he fulfilled the Afrikaner dream of a republic without links to Britain. At the same time his policy of separate development aimed at transforming the native reserves into homelands that would become "independent," theoretically quite separate from the white republic.

The first prime minister to react significantly to the collapse of white rule in neighboring countries was P. W. Botha (1978–1984). But his new constitution (1984) still made only limited political concessions to coloreds (persons of mixed race) and Asians—and none at all to Africans. By then, such limited concessions were clearly inadequate responses to the forces they were meant to contain.

Apartheid in Action

Over time, South African racial policy became minutely regulated and rigidified. The bases for apartheid long predated 1948. For example, the Native Land Act of 1913 created the Native Reserves, the Native Urban Areas Act of 1923 segregated black residents of towns, and the Native Representation Act of 1936 removed Africans from the common voter rolls in Cape Province. From 1948 on, discriminatory laws proliferated rapidly.

By 1960 they had transformed South Africa more than ever into a racially based caste society. The purpose was to separate racial categories—white, colored, Asian, African—in every way possible and to deny political participation to the non-white categories, all three of which are known in South Africa as "black." Apartheid was to ensure white minority control by "dividing and ruling" and by maximizing inequality. Africans were not even supposed to reside permanently except in small parts of the country set aside for their various ethnic groups, whose differences were emphasized to fragment the African majority. Africans were to go elsewhere only as temporary migrant workers. They had to carry passes, so that their movements could be controlled, and they could hold only jobs not reserved for whites. First set up for the mining industry, the system assumed that migrant workers were bachelors who did not need a "family" wage. Wages were further depressed by bringing in workers from other countries, as noted. Since jobs for Africans—including industrial and domestic jobs, as well as those in mining—were mostly remote from the places where they were supposed to reside, the impact of such labor conditions on African family life was drastic, through either long-term family separation or extremely long daily commuting times, in addition to inadequate pay. In fact, because most jobs for Africans are in cities, it proved impossible for the government to make them all live in rural reserves. The main response to this was the creation of segregated "townships," like Soweto, in which Africans who worked in the cities had to live, far from their jobs.

Bad working and living conditions indicate the dehumanizing intent of apartheid but do not show how far it went. Under the Promotion of Self Government Act (1959), the many native reserves were consolidated into ten tribal homelands, or *bantustans*. The consolidation was only administrative, for the homelands still consisted of scattered pieces of land. Still, Prime Minister Verwoerd, mastermind of the policy, argued that just as whites could find fulfillment only in a state they controlled, "separate development" was the key to fulfillment for each African ethnic group. The ultimate fulfillment was to be the homelands' "independence," which would provide the excuse to deprive homeland residents of South African citizenship.

In 1976, South Africa began giving "independence" to some homelands. No other nation recognized them as independent nations, however, and some ethnic groups refused to accept this status. Set aside for the Ndebele, an ethnic group that historically had no home in South Africa, the "homeland" KwaNdebele was in fact a dumping ground for ethnically mixed elements ejected from the cities under the pass system. Nowhere did the government's concern for ethnic fulfillment extend to economic development or good government. In fact, part of the government's strategy was to bring ruthless people to power within the impoverished homelands, then watch the residents divide into warring bands as henchmen, or opponents, of their government-backed "leaders."

As the homeland policy developed, segregation and inequality worsened in countless other ways. Not only was education segregated at all levels, but the requirement that African children be educated in their various ethnic languages for the first eight years played up ethnic differences and left the children unprepared for secondary or higher education in English or Afrikaans. Other laws were designed to protect racial barriers by prohibiting mixed marriages (1949) and interracial sex outside marriage (1957), or by requiring people over sixteen to carry an identity card specifying their race (1950). The Suppression of Communism Act (1950) defined communism as practically any attempt to change the status quo. What whites lacked in numbers, they attempted to make up through socioeconomic advantage, control of the state, and unrestrained use of the state's coercive power.

As prime minister (1978–1984) and then president (1984–1989), P. W. Botha reacted to the erosion of white power elsewhere in Africa by readjusting foreign and domestic policy. In addition to neighboring countries' economic dependency, long since effected by employing migrant miners, Botha sought to achieve a regional dominance not unlike that of the United States over Central America. For this purpose, South Africa fought its opponents on neighboring states' territory and supported movements hostile to unfriendly regimes in those states. For example, South Africa invaded Angola repeatedly after 1975 and supported an opposition movement, UNITA, against the Cuban-backed Angolan government. To undermine the Afro-Marxist government of neighboring Mozambique, South Africa also supported the so-called Mozambican National Resistance Movement (RENAMO in Portuguese), in origin not a nationalist movement but a mercenary force that ravaged the country until an internationally brokered ceasefire in 1992. Diplomatically, Botha sought agreements that would keep opponents of the regime, particularly the African National Congress, from operating out of neighboring countries. Namibia, controlled by South Africa since the end of World War I, remained a special case. In 1988, as earlier noted, South Africa agreed to Namibia's independence as part of a U.S.-mediated attempt to end the Angolan civil war. The apparent motive was to spare South Africa's white minority the costs and casualties of military intervention. One measure of the independence intended for Namibia was that South Africa intended to retain sovereign control over Walvis Bay, Namibia's only deepwater port.

Internally, Botha made certain concessions to nonwhites. For the African majority, concessions were mostly limited to the field of labor relations. African and mixed labor unions received official recognition (1979). As the need for skilled African labor grew, Botha also gave Africans some recognition as permanent residents of urban areas by letting them buy their own houses—but not the land—in the townships. Since the 1960s, a system of local councils had existed in nonwhite areas. Yet administering and policing the townships remained insoluble problems, for institutionalizing these services would mean admitting what the homeland policy denied: that Africans' urban presence was legitimate.

The two other nonwhite communities, the coloreds and Asians, represented about 9 and 3 percent, respectively, of the estimated 1988 population of 35 million, compared to about 15 and 73 percent for whites and Africans. Botha's 1984 constitution made political concessions to the two smaller groups. Alongside the white House of Assembly, it created a smaller Colored House of Representatives, and an even smaller Asian House. The constitution replaced the prime minister with an executive president, elected by a white electoral college, and a President's Council with members elected by the three houses of parliament as well as appointed members. If any of the representative bodies attempted to obstruct a policy, the president could refer it to this council. The official reason for not making such concessions to Africans was that they had political institutions in the homelands.

The new constitution, another step away from British parliamentarism, made only a guarded attempt at political mobilization of the two minorities that stood between whites and Africans. Offering the African majority nothing, the 1984 constitution opened a new phase in their resistance to white domination.

In the long run, the African majority's response to these maneuvers would be the most important one, but it was not the only consequence Botha had to consider. The 1984 constitution and African opposition to it raised international awareness of South African racism to new levels, symbolized by the economic sanctions that European and North American governments imposed on South Africa and by mounting demands for multinational firms to disinvest from South Africa and stop doing business there. Inside South Africa, controversy racked the white minority. Ultrarightists assailed the Botha government for making concessions to nonwhites. More moderate elements, including business people concerned about international sanctions and about how the systematic impoverishment of three-quarters of the population under apartheid limited the market for consumer goods, advocated further change. Some analysts argued that apartheid's costs would kill it, if nothing else did. Aside from the costs of military intervention abroad and repression at home, the 1984 constitution increased the number of cabinet members and members of parliament many times over, while civil service payrolls grew to one-third of government spending. Such issues are worth keeping in mind as we examine black African opposition to apartheid and prospects for change in the 1990s.

African Responses to Apartheid

Black South Africans' radicalization was already beginning during World War II. In the African National Congress (ANC), younger intellectuals, such as Oliver Tambo and Nelson Mandela, grew dissatisfied with older leaders and formed a new pressure group, the ANC Youth League. They won control of the ANC in 1949 and pushed through a program of strikes, civil disobedience, and noncooperation. During the 1950s, the ANC still emphasized civil disobedience campaigns in collaboration with Indian, colored, and liberal white organizations. This phase culminated at a Congress of the People that adopted the Freedom Charter (1955). Asserting that South Africa's people, black and white, were "equal, countrymen and brothers," and would work together for democratic change, the charter remains the official ANC ideology.

Reactions to the Congress of the People opened a new phase in the history of the African opposition. The government responded by passing more repressive laws and arresting 156 people, including leaders of the congress. They were charged with conspiring to overthrow the state and replace it with a communist one. All the defendants were later released, but not until 1961 in some cases.

Meanwhile, African activists began to differ about nonviolence and cooperation with other racial groups. One group wanted a purely African movement that would use any means to ensure majority rule. It broke from the ANC and formed the Pan-Africanist Congress (PAC) in 1959. Seeking to retain leadership, the ANC planned a civil disobedience campaign against the pass system for late March 1960. But the PAC launched a similar campaign a few days earlier. At Sharpeville, near Johannesburg, the police shot at the demonstrators, killing 67 and wounding almost 200. When demonstrations ensued, the government mobilized the armed forces, outlawed both ANC and PAC, and jailed some 18,000 Africans, with much violence. With both ANC and PAC forced underground, even men like Tambo and Mandela concluded that nonviolence—after the response it got at the Sharpeville massacre—would not work for their movement.

The ANC then organized an underground group, *Umkhonto we Sizwe* (Spear of the Nation), which carried out its first act of sabotage in December 1961. The group's first commander, Nelson Mandela, was captured in 1962 and given a life sentence. Repeatedly offered freedom if he would renounce violence, Mandela steadfastly refused and thus became South Africa's most revered leader. By 1963, all ANC leaders but Tambo, who had gone abroad to found an exile branch, had been captured. For the remainder of the 1960s, the government managed to repress other anti-regime organizations as well.

When black activism resurfaced inside the country, it focused at first on issues arising from segregation in education. Under the influence of the U.S civil rights movement, a black consciousness movement emerged to challenge the white liberals' idea of integrating blacks into white society. The movement's slogan became "Black man, you're on your own." The government began cracking down in 1973. In 1976 the attempt to impose Afrikaans as a language of instruction in the Soweto schools brought out thousands of children to demonstrate. When the police shot a student, protests swept the land. The government response left 575 dead, of whom only 5 were white and 134 were younger than eighteen. Ruthless repression led many activists to join ANC forces abroad. Inside South Africa, anti-regime organizations continued to form, such as the Soweto Civic Association and the Azanian People's Organization (AZAPO). Defiance spread among all three subordinate castes.

In the period between the Soweto uprising and the 1984 constitution, the struggle proceeded both inside and outside South Africa. Inside, Africans had some leaders who still emphasized nonviolence, such as Desmond Tutu, Anglican bishop of Johannesburg and winner of the 1984 Nobel Peace Prize. Among resistance groups, the most important event inside the country in this period was the creation of the United Democratic Front (UDF, 1983), an umbrella organization that combined hundreds of groups with some 1.5 million members. The UDF shared the ANC commitment to interracial collaboration and was therefore opposed by groups like PAC and AZAPO, which reject white participation.

Externally, the exile branch of the ANC remained the main opposition force after Soweto. In the early 1980s, it conducted military operations from foreign bases, bombing South Africa's main oil-from-coal plant (1980), a new nuclear plant (1982), and South African air force headquarters (1983). As at Sharpeville in 1960, the government responded disproportionately to such acts.

The ANC's actions paled, however, compared to the violence inside South Africa after September 1984. Sparked both by attempts to increase rents on government-owned township houses and by the new constitution, disturbances occurred all over the country in a way that made them harder to control than earlier, localized incidents. From abroad, the ANC had long called for making the townships ungovernable. This now happened in townships and homelands alike, but the ANC—like Nelson Mandela—was only the symbol of resistance, not its organizer. Africans, and eventually other nonwhites, challenged every aspect of repression. In the townships, Africans who had collaborated with the authorities by assuming leadership roles or, still worse, by serving as police informers faced summary execution by the "necklace"—an old tire placed around the neck, filled with gasoline, and set afire. Where competing political groups faced one another, violence became especially common, all the more when criminals took advantage of disorder to mask their own acts. Such was the "black-on-black" vio-

Nelson Mandela addresses a crowd of a hundred thousand people in Soweto, February 1990, shortly after his release from prison. *The African National Congress elected Mandela its president in 1991.* *AP/Wide World Photos*

lence that the government cynically publicized, as if its kind of "law and order" had nothing to do with what was happening. In the homelands, conflict raged between the corrupt and repressive government-backed leaders and their henchmen, on the one hand, and the young "comrades" who opposed them, on the other. There, too, the "necklace" became familiar. Even children took part in resistance through school boycotts organized by activist groups. The resistance asserted itself economically, not only through rent strikes, which cost the government hundreds of millions of dollars, but also through boycotts of white businesses and through actions like the mineworkers' strike of August 1987, which caused over $50 million in production losses to the country's largest gold-mining company.

Faced with such problems, the government declared a state of emergency (June 1986), detained tens of thousands of people without even allowing their names to be published, and banned all political activity by the UDF, African labor organizations, and other groups.

Toward Majority Rule?

As South Africa approached mass political mobilization of a sort incompatible with survival of the existing order, signs of readiness for accommodation began to appear. Facing political and medical problems, P. W. Botha resigned from the presidency in August 1989. In 1990, his successor, F. W. de Klerk, lifted the ban on the ANC and—needing someone of stature to negotiate with—freed Nelson Mandela from prison. At this, the UDF disbanded and urged its affiliates to support the ANC.

These events launched a still-unfinished South African restructuring that depended on the two leaders' ability to work together and maintain their positions as leaders of the country's whites and blacks. With militant whites to de Klerk's right and many forces at work among the African population—the most conspicuous being the Inkatha Freedom party, whose agenda combined Zulu ethnic reassertion and economic ideas to the right of the ANC's—success was not assured. De Klerk's government abolished apartheid in 1991; in compensation, foreign governments began lifting the sanctions they had imposed. Having announced suspension of the armed struggle in 1990, the ANC held a national conference in July 1991. Electing Mandela its president and bringing members of a younger generation into other leadership positions, the conference looked like a step toward turning the ANC into a political party. The government agreed with the ANC—and Inkatha—to open negotiations for a new constitution, and the Convention for a Democratic South Africa (CODESA) began meeting in December 1991. In March 1992, nearly 70 percent of the white electorate voted to end minority rule. Optimists predicted the formation within months of a multiracial interim government.

Progress was not so swift, however. Racial violence, abuses, and insubordination among government security forces, disclosures of corruption in homeland administration, and a deteriorating economy weakened de Klerk's position. The ANC had to contend with internal scandals, continuing violence in homelands and townships, and opposition from both the Left and Inkatha. Yet by February 1993, the government and the ANC had agreed that white rule would end in April 1994 with the election of a new parliament, which would serve for five years and write a new constitution. A further agreement negotiated in September 1993 provided for the creation of a transitional council, including black representatives, to serve as a check on the government during the period leading up to the election. Black South Africans would get to vote in the 1994 election, and minority parties—which would thenceforth include the Nationalist party—would be eligible to participate in the interim government of the next five years. At last South Africa had come this close to achieving majority rule without sacrificing the multiracial ideal of the ANC's 1955 Freedom Charter.

Conclusion: Change Without Development?

Africa was the last of the continents to be integrated into the European-dominated global pattern of the pre-1914 era and the last to be formally decolonized. Mostly becoming independent in the 1960s, just as the Third World population explosion was emerging as a policy problem that could no longer be ignored, Africa's nations remained impoverished despite their natural resources, disunited, plagued by corruption, and politically unable to resist military authoritarianism. The oil-related stresses of the 1970s and 1980s seriously affected all African countries, including the few that had oil to export. By the late 1980s, the same pressures for democratization were at work in Africa as in Latin America. Caught between foreign debt and the ecological and socioeconomic consequences of the demographic explosion, however, African nations had difficulty responding to the new trend.

The post-1945 period has been one of extensive change but little positive development, as Africans themselves have admitted. The two largest sub-Saharan economies both illustrate this point: Nigeria with its inability so far to use its oil income for balanced development, South Africa with its still-unfinished political transition and its barely begun economic transition to greater equity for the black majority. Famine-stricken and anarchical, Somalia illustrates the same point more starkly. No region has displayed the problems of underdevelopment more acutely than sub-Saharan Africa. Africans will need all the creativity and resourcefulness that so fills their history to redress this situation. Africa's plight must also concern the outside world as it contemplates the future of humanity.

Note

1. Leonard Thompson and Andrew Prior, *South African Politics* (New Haven: Yale University Press, 1982), pp. 17, 131, 166–167, 170.

Suggestions for Further Reading

Books

Achebe, Chinua. *A Man of the People* (1966).

Crowder, Michael. *The Story of Nigeria* (1978).

Curtin, Philip, Steven Feierman, Leonard Thompson, and Jan Vansina. *African History* (1978).

Fieldhouse, D. K. *Black Africa, 1945–80: Economic Decolonization and Arrested Development* (1986).

Hull, Richard W. *Southern Africa: Civilizations in Turmoil* (1981).

Kirk-Greene, Anthony, and Douglas Rimmer. *Nigeria Since 1970: A Political and Economic Outline* (1981).

Lodge, Tom, Bill Nasson, Steven Mufson, Khehla Shubane, and Nokwanda Sithole, et al. *All, Here, and Now: Black Politics in South Africa in the 1980s* (1991).

Mazrui, Ali. *The Africans: A Triple Heritage* (1986).

Schrire, Robert. *Adapt or Die: The End of White Politics in South Africa* (1991).

Thompson, Leonard. *A History of South Africa* (1990).

World Bank. *World Development Report: Development and the Environment* (1992).

Newspapers and Periodicals

Africa Report.

Africa Research Bulletin.

Jeune Afrique (*Young Africa,* French-language weekly published in Paris).

CHAPTER 17

Asian Resurgence

After 1945, the Third World's most dynamic efforts at national development occurred in Asia. The Middle East became both a major arena of conflict and the center for transformation of the oil industry. Soviet collapse effectively enlarged the Middle East by freeing six historically Muslim republics to reassert their ties with it. India, with one-seventh of the world's population, became the largest democracy and achieved significant economic growth, despite much inequity. China, with one-fifth of the world's people, emerged from one of history's most drastic revolutions and embarked on an economic transformation of epic scale. Japan, all but destroyed in World War II, re-emerged as the world's second-largest national economy, effectively a part of "the West." Some experts foresee an East Asian economic complex able to excel Western Europe and perhaps the United States.

These Asian superlatives imply this chapter's agenda. A brief overview opens the discussion; as noted in Chapter 10, Asia's exceptional diversity requires greater selectivity than in our overviews of Africa and Latin America. This chapter's following sections look at the Middle East and North Africa, an Asian-centered region whose population approximates that of the United States; then at the world's two most populous nations, one democratic (India) and one communist (China); and finally at the economic prodigy, Japan.

Long home to the world's most brilliant civilizations, Asia has produced the greatest contemporary challenges to Western dominance. The conclusion of Chapter 10 compared major Asian countries in order to identify factors governing their success in adapting to twentieth-century conditions of tightening global integration, accelerating change, and mass mobilization. After 1945, similar factors again proved critical: success in mastering new ideas; consensus about national identity and the organization of political life; responsiveness to the demands of mass mobilization (in terms of both politics and social justice); and development of economic growth strategies capable of meeting the people's needs and bettering the country's economic place in the world. The countries that performed best by these criteria are the ones that have done most to rectify the imbalance among civilizations that European expansionism had created.

Asia: From Decolonization to Reassertion

Chapter 10 began with an account of the Asian civilizations' development and the patterns of interaction that linked them to the rest of the world. The rest of that chapter, and other parts of this book, threw light on Asia's integration into, and efforts to break free from, the web of European global dominance. Here, to prepare for discussion of specific countries since 1945, basic points significant for all Asia merit notice: decolonization, population trends, economic development, and cultural reintegration.

Decolonization

Weakened by World War I and the Depression, challenged by Asian nationalism and economic development efforts, Western dominance collapsed in Asia in the 1940s and 1950s except for outposts such as Britain's Hong Kong. Decolonization began during World War II. Japan seized many European colonies: French Indochina (now Vietnam, Cambodia, and Laos), Burma, Malaya, the Dutch East Indies (now Indonesia), and other Pacific islands; as well as the U.S.-controlled Philippines. Japan also took control of much territory—Manchuria, parts of China—that had not been under direct European control. After 1945, former colonial powers' attempts to regain control of some countries, such as Indochina and the Dutch East Indies, proved short-lived. The Philippines gained independence in 1946. In the Middle East and North Africa, decolonization began during the war. France held Morocco until 1956, Tunisia until 1957, and Algeria until 1962, but lost Syria and Lebanon between 1941 and 1946. The British gave up Jordan, Iraq, and Palestine by 1948 and Egypt by 1954. In 1947 they lost Burma, India, and Pakistan (including East Pakistan, which became independent as Bangladesh in 1971). Map 16.1 shows Asian as well as African independence dates.

As the wartime U.S.-British-Soviet alliance broke up, it seemed for a time that Stalin's effort to create a defensive perimeter for the Soviet Union in east and southeast Europe would extend across mainland Asia as well. Turkey and Iran (like Greece in southeast Europe) managed to resist Soviet pressure only with U.S. support. In East Asia, while Japan remained under U.S. occupation (1945–1952), Mao's Communists triumphed in mainland China, creating the People's Republic of China in 1949; Chiang Kai-shek's Nationalists withdrew to the island of Taiwan and set up the rival Republic of China. Like Germany, Korea and Indochina were divided between communist and noncommunist regimes. Outsiders would take a long time to grasp that Chinese and Vietnamese communists were strong nationalists, not Soviet puppets. The later Soviet invasion of Afghanistan (1979–1989) looked like a throwback to Soviet policy of these years.

Except in China, Indochina, and North Korea, however, Asian nationalisms mostly kept a distance from Marxism. In reaction to the Cold War view of the world as divided between the "Free World" (the United States and Western Europe) and the "Communist Bloc," India, especially, took a leading role in promoting nonalignment, or solidarity within the "Third World" of Asian, African, and Latin American nations, whose interests differed from both superpowers'.

Population Growth and Superurbanization

Decolonization meant formal political independence but, as ever in the Third World, not necessarily an end to dependency. The postcolonial regimes' prime need was economic development or, for Japan, reconstruction. The question was how to attain that goal while also facing the problems, starting with explosive population growth and even faster urbanization, that blocked its achievement elsewhere in the developing world.

Statistics show that most, but significantly not all, of Asia has failed to solve these common population problems. The Middle East's three most populous countries—Turkey, Egypt, and Iran—had populations of 28, 26, and 21 million, respectively, in 1960; they had 59, 56, and 60 million in 1992. Turkey and Egypt each had more than doubled in population since 1960; Iran had nearly tripled. India's population growth rate began to exceed the developed countries' in 1941, when India had 319 million people. The figures for India (no longer including Pakistan or Bangladesh) rose to 435 million in 1960 and 883 million in 1992. What is now Pakistan (West Pakistan from 1947 to 1971) rose from about 25 million in 1947 to 122 million in 1992. Between 1947 and 1992, the population of Bangladesh (what had been East Pakistan from 1947 until independence in 1971) grew from about 50 million people to 111 million. Bangladesh is the most populous of the world's poorest countries, with some two thousand people per square mile.

To the east, China's population rose from 600 million in 1947 to 1.2 billion in 1992. China's increase rate—now 1.3 percent yearly, closer to the rates of affluent lands—shows how an authoritarian government can use pressure to slow population growth. Japan's population, which rose from 72 million in 1945 to 124 million in 1992, has fallen to a truly low growth rate: 0.3 percent. Southeast Asia includes others of the most populous nations. Indonesia rose from an estimated 77.2 million in 1955 to 185 million in 1992, becoming the fourth most populous nation. In 1992, both Vietnam (70 million) and the Philippines (64 million) were more populous than any West European country but Germany (80 million).

As in other developing countries, the largest cities grew faster than the nations they belonged to. For example, between 1930 and 1990, while Turkey, Iran, and Egypt's national populations increased 3.5 to 4.3 times over, Istanbul's metropolitan population increased nearly tenfold, from 700,000 to 6.7 million; Tehran's increased twelvefold, from half a million to 6 million; and Cairo's may have increased thirteenfold, from 1.2 million to 15 million.

Projected into the future, such rates of growth would produce almost unimaginable supermetropolises all over Asia. By 2025, Istanbul and Tehran would both reach 15 to 20 million; Cairo would hit 20 to 30 million. China's Beijing and Shanghai, Indonesia's Jakarta, Pakistan's Karachi, and India's Bombay, Delhi, and Calcutta would grow from 7 to 13 million inhabitants apiece in 1990 to between 20 and 30 million in 2025. Metropolitan Tokyo, already at 17 million in 1984, would grow more slowly, to 20 million. One of the few traits Japan still shares with poor countries (and some other affluent ones) is its biggest city's dominance compared to the nation's other cities—a problem that has inspired many plans for decentralization but little progress.

For countries attempting rapid development, numbers alone do not reveal all the problems of extremely rapid population growth. How can a struggling economy provide schools, health care, and jobs for such a population? How can such a society train the high-quality scientific, technical, managerial, and administrative personnel it needs for development? Asian societies that have not lowered their population growth rates have had little success in meeting such needs.

Strategies for Economic Revitalization

Asian societies' economic development strategies have varied widely but display common traits, which also appear in other developing regions. What distinguishes Asia is the success that some of its nations have achieved.

Many states followed the common Third World assumption that the state must lead in economic development. In the Middle East, a major constituent of the Arab socialism of the 1950s and 1960s (like African populist socialism, a populist nationalism with few debts to Marx) was centralized planning and the nationalization of much of the economy. India also assigned the state a key economic role; Mao's China did so even more. In Asia, too, it seemed natural for countries with underdeveloped private sectors to rely on government initiative to industrialize. Facing the poor results, however, Asia joined the global retreat from state-dominated economies in the 1980s.

Agriculture, meanwhile, presented familiar questions of whether growth could be achieved by technical means or whether it would require structural change in rural society and land tenure. India combined the former approach with limited land redistribution; China followed the latter. One measure of the results is that India's daily per capita calorie supply rose only from 2,021 in 1965 to 2,229 in 1989, while China's rose from 1,929 to 2,639. Countries in which 70 percent of the population lives in the countryside, as in India and China, cannot develop by ignoring the rural majority's need for employment and subsistence.

Another theme has been reliance on natural resources for development. This was notably true of the oil economies concentrated in the Middle East. In the 1970s they acquired a threatening degree of leverage over the world's developed industrial economies. Close scrutiny shows, however, that the oil boom was another colonial export boom, differing only in scale from those experienced by other raw-material-exporting economies in commodities ranging from cotton to diamonds. In the Middle East as elsewhere, the oil boom hardly provided its beneficiaries with a sure route to diversified economic development.

The most successful development strategy—but also the most difficult, given the competitiveness it requires—proved to be export-oriented industrialization, as represented by Japan and later by Taiwan and South Korea. Often admired as examples of free enterprise, all these countries have political and economic features that differ from Western norms in ways that need to be recognized. Long ruled by authoritarian regimes, South Korea and Taiwan offered less to admire politically than economically. In the 1980s, Turkey also began to command recognition as an Asian country that had both developed into a multiparty democracy and had made the transition from import substitution to export-led growth. However, Japan achieved unmatched success, becoming so dominant as an exporter that international pressure forced it, from 1985 on, to revalue its currency and enlarge its imports.

Cultural Reintegration

Underlying Asian societies' drives for independence and development was a push for cultural decolonization, or—stated positively—cultural reintegration. Since 1945, characteristic ideological preferences in the Middle East have shifted from the early nationalists' liberalism, to the populist Arab socialism of Egypt's Gamal Abdel Nasser and his contemporaries, to resurgent Islam. As they escaped from political and economic dependence, Muslims seemed to assume that politics still had to follow an imported model—whence Arab socialism—and only gradually realized that they might do better, as religious activists had always argued, to turn to the value system that was authentically theirs: Islam.

India's democracy also underwent distinct shifts, from Nehru's liberal democratic socialism, to his daughter Indira Gandhi's authoritarianism, and perhaps back toward a liberalism further from classic British models under her son Rajiv Gandhi. Tensions between the Hindu majority and the Sikhs, one of India's many religious minorities, that culminated in Indira Gandhi's assassination, and still more the Hindu-Muslim violence of the 1990s, prove the resurgence of religious politics in India, too, where democracy now appears in jeopardy.

In East Asia, Mao's thought always had a strong nationalist dimension, and policy under Deng Xiaoping, in retreating from Mao's excesses, not only moved further away from Marxism-Leninism but also showed greater tolerance for traditional Chinese culture. In Japan, finally, not only has the country's economic development gained from traditional Japanese traits and work habits, but historical worldviews have reasserted themselves in a revival of Japanese nationalism. Prime Minister Yasuhiro Nakasone (1983–1988) expressed this in ways foreigners sometimes found alarming, such as a speech praising Japan as a "monoracial state," or a controversial official visit to the Yasukuni shrine, where Japan's war dead are worshipped. Japan's extremely rapid development has left as one of its costs a lingering identity crisis expressed in wavering between imitation of the West and virulent insistence on Japanese uniqueness.

Renewed interest in traditional belief systems had become a global phenomenon by the 1970s. In the former colonial lands, this renewal follows upon political, economic, and finally cultural decompression from the stresses of European dominance. Nowhere has this phenomenon been more marked than in Asia, especially in those societies that are most directly heirs of the greatest Asian civilizations of the past. An examination of selected countries in the Middle East, South Asia, and East Asia will illustrate this point.

The Middle East and North Africa: The Struggle for Unity and Development

The World War I peace settlement introduced a new degree of political fragmentation into this region, as we saw in Chapter 10. This fact contradicted the historical tendency of the Middle East—as of the other major Asian civilizational centers—toward unification in one or a few large states. For Muslims, Islam has reinforced this tendency by emphasizing that the unity of the faithful should be a political and not just a spiritual reality.

Fragmentation into numerous states has greatly complicated modern Middle Eastern and North African history (Map 17.1). Even more than sub-Saharan Africa, this region displays a tension between the "hardening" of state structures—some of them created by imperialism—and larger, integrative concepts. While struggling with state formation, Middle Eastern peoples have had to sort out inherited concepts of organization—kinship, ethnicity, and religion—and recently acquired concepts of nationalism and secular political ideologies,

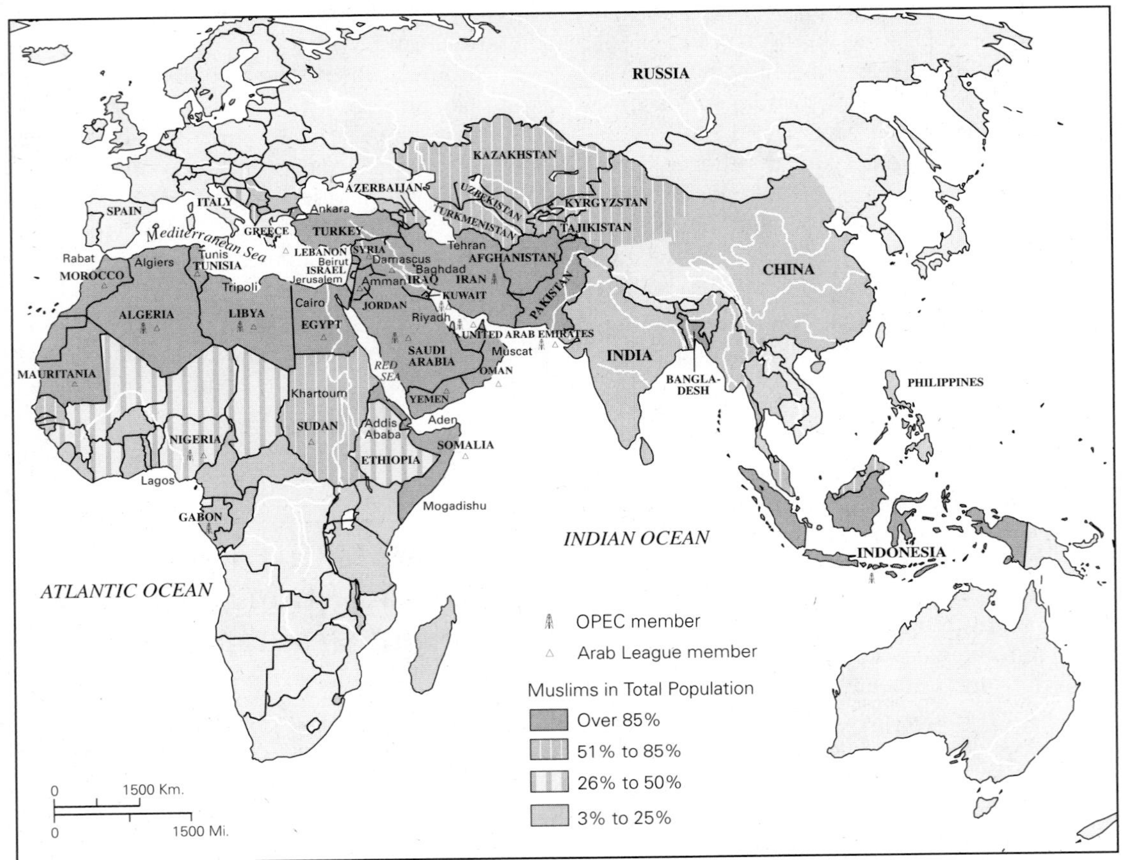

Map 17.1 The Islamic World

and then have had to try to reach consensus about relationships among these ideas.

It has proved difficult to solve these problems while also achieving goals of political mobilization and economic growth. Material constraints and outside pressures have added to the difficulty. Into the early postwar years, for example, Turkey maintained its political independence and pursued its policies of national development. The Turks of Turkey shared cultural and historical ties with other Turkic peoples (a larger category including speakers of all languages related to Turkish); but the fact that most of these peoples lived in Soviet Central Asian republics made it impossible to develop close relations with them prior to the Soviet collapse. Iran, too, shared cultural ties with peoples in adjacent lands, but its political life also remained focused on Iran, which had been a center of empire before it became a modern nation.

In contrast, many Arab countries were still under British or French rule at the end of World War II. As soon as most of them had gained independence, they began to think in terms of Arab unity—Pan-Arabism—an idea usually coupled with "socialism" to produce a populist nationalism. After Israel had decisively defeated the partisans of Arab unity in the Six-Day War of 1967, however, and especially after the petroleum revolution of 1973 had supplied new wealth to use in pursuit of larger aspirations, emphasis shifted from Arab unity to Islamic unity. This goal could be pursued through many forms of international action—aid programs, diplomatic collaboration, Islamic summits—as well as through reform or revolution in specific countries. Sanctioned by tradition, the call to Islamic unity had potential appeal—not just to Arabs—but to Muslims everywhere, from West Africa to Soviet Central Asia and the Philippines. The outside world tends to identify this re-emphasis on Islam only with its most violent manifestations—from the Iranian revolution of 1979 to the bombing of New York's World Trade Center in 1993. In fact, most Muslims are no more violent than other people, and the radical fringe is weakened by majority opposition and internal disunity.

Because it played a major part, both in the shift of emphasis from local nationalism to Pan-Arabism to Islamic unity, and in the world economy, the transformation of the petroleum industry is important to understand. In post-1945 Asian economic history, the OPEC oil boom of the 1970s is second in importance only to Japan's growth. Yet the situations of Japan and the OPEC countries, most of which are in the Middle East, were quite different. Japan developed one of the leading industrial economies, whereas the oil-exporting countries experienced a huge export boom based on one commodity. In the Middle East, the results were not equitably distributed, for some countries—including two of the most populous, Egypt and Turkey—were not major oil producers. Because oil is a nonrenewable resource, even the exporting countries' future depended on how long the high income continued and how well it was invested for development.

The earlier history of the Middle East's oil industry throws added light on the OPEC experience. International firms, acting under concessions from local governments, had exported Middle Eastern oil since before World War I. At first, demand for the oil was low, and the host governments received only about 25 cents per barrel in royalties. Significant change came after World War II. The Marshall Plan for European reconstruction assumed the availability of cheap Middle Eastern oil, and that gave the oil states potential leverage over the oil companies. The oil states won agreements for equal profit sharing in the early postwar years. Iran made the first attempt at nationalization in 1951. It failed, partly because the producing countries were unorganized and failed to support Iran. The companies continued to dominate the industry, and the major Western economies' oil consumption continued to grow rapidly.

In 1960, Iraq, Saudi Arabia, Iran, Kuwait, and Venezuela—then the one major Latin America producer—formed the Organization of Petroleum Exporting Countries (OPEC) as a means for joint action to improve prices. By 1973, the cartel's membership grew to include Algeria, Libya, Qatar, the United Arab Emirates, Ecuador, Gabon, Nigeria, and Indonesia; and Libya, Iraq, and Iran had successfully nationalized their oil industries.

The Arab-Israeli war of 1973 brought bigger gains—in fact, the biggest change in economic relations between the Middle East and the outside world in the five hundred years since the voyages of exploration. The war governed the timing, but the underlying causes were OPEC's determination to control production and pricing and the fact that U.S. oil consumption was growing while U.S. production had begun to decline. Imports accounted for 36 percent of U.S. oil consumption in 1973, 48 percent in 1977. With Europe heavily dependent on OPEC oil and Japan almost totally so, growing U.S. dependency gave OPEC the leverage to raise prices unilaterally. Angered by Israel's retention of territories occupied in 1967 and by U.S. aid to Israel in the 1973 war, the Arab oil states also cut production and embargoed nations friendly to Israel.

The five-month-long embargo, the quadrupling of prices in 1973–1974, and another doubling or more caused by the 1979 Iranian revolution jolted the world economy, creating an unprecedented new flow of wealth. OPEC's combined oil revenues rose from $22.5 billion in 1973 to $272 billion in 1980.

By then, rising prices had caused global oil consumption to fall. Soon prices fell, too. Plunged into the worst recession since 1929, the industrial nations grew serious in the 1970s about conserving energy, developing non-OPEC oil sources (such as Mexico and Alaska's North Slope), and—to a degree—shifting to other forms of energy (see Chapter 19). Today it seems clear that because oil is a depletable, nonrenewable resource, scarcity and high prices will in time return. But it is not clear that OPEC will again control supplies and prices as it did in the 1970s. Today, the Middle Eastern oil exporters' future looks no surer than their oilless neighbors'. As in Mexico and Nigeria, Iran's experience proved that oil cannot ensure stability or development.

The waning of the oil boom provides a good point for comparing the post-1945 experiences of several Middle Eastern countries. We shall consider Turkey, a successful developing country economically and politically; Iran, a major oil exporter and the scene of an Islamic revolution; Iraq, a case of development gone wrong; and Israel, the Jewish state and a major factor in recent Middle Eastern history. The remainder of the chapter will then consider selected countries in South and East Asia.

Turkey: Democratization and Development

Before the OPEC era, economists commonly cited Turkey as the Middle Eastern country with best all-round potential for economic development. It had little petroleum but otherwise had a better resource endowment than any of its neighbors. The oil boom silenced these arguments and shifted interest to the oil-exporting countries. By then, Turkey's pro-Western orientation—it had become a member of NATO in 1952 and an associate member of the European Economic Community (EEC) in 1964—also seemed to distance it from other Middle Eastern countries, despite its manifold ties to the region. In the 1980s, however, when the end of the oil boom revealed the oil exporters' vulnerability, Turkey's advantages reappeared as it moved beyond import substitution to export-oriented industrialization and began to exert greater influence in the region.

Turkey's experience during World War II helped define the starting points for its postwar development. Learning from the mistake that the Ottoman Empire had made in entering World War I, Turkey remained neutral. It thus escaped the costs of warfare and possible defeat yet had to pay the price of full mobilization to defend its neutrality in case of need. With the drafting of large numbers of men and the requisitioning of agricultural animals, GDP declined nearly 40 percent during the war years. Unwise economic policies, ranging from forced sale of agricultural goods at low prices to a capital levy that discriminated against minorities, worsened the situation. However, Turkey managed to accumulate foreign exchange; and certain commercial and agricultural interests profited from wartime inflation and commodity shortages.

Turkey came through the war still under the presidency of Atatürk's deputy and successor, Ismet Inönü, and still with only one party, the Republican People's party (RPP; see Chapter 10). Atatürk had strongly believed in liberal democracy, however. The social and economic effects of the war had created new demands for liberalization, and Inönü responded in 1946 by authorizing the organization of new parties. The chief beneficiary of this change was an alliance of urban businessmen and landowners, enriched by the war, who formed the Democrat party (DP) and defeated the RPP in the 1950 elections. For an opposition party to win power from the ruling party in a developing country was almost unheard-of, and the event was widely hailed as a triumph for democracy.

Developments in foreign policy reinforced this trend. Immediately after World War II, Turkey had faced Soviet demands for territory in the east and for concessions concerning passage through the straits that flow from the Black Sea past Istanbul to the Aegean Sea. Turkey had resisted these demands alone at first and then, from 1947–1948 on, with U.S. aid. Turkey's pro-Western policy orientation was consolidated with its participation in the Korean War and its admission to NATO in 1952.

Led by Adnan Menderes as prime minister and party leader, the DP ruled Turkey for a decade (1950–1960). It did not chart a radically new course. Politics was dominated by the unfamiliarity of the multiparty system and by the Democrats' tense reactions to their RPP opponents, especially the prestigious Inönü. With rapid population growth and even faster urbanization, the combination of business and agrarian interests that had created the DP proved effective in making government more responsive to the voters and establishing closer links between Ankara and the towns and villages. The fact that the DP relaxed some of Atatürk's secularizing policies appealed to conservative rural voters, although the Democrats did not fundamentally abandon secularism.

In economics, too, the Democrats shifted emphases more than they changed policy. The DP favored private enterprise, agriculture, and consumers but did little to reduce the role of the state sector. Although the country was officially committed to import-substitution industrialization, some of the most important changes occurred in agriculture. Until the late 1950s, the supply of land still exceeded demand in Turkey. The RPP had used a 1946 land reform law mainly to distribute state land and divide communal pastures. Menderes continued this process, but increasingly, growth in agriculture depended on productivity gains, chiefly caused by the introduction of tractors. Even smallholders who could not afford tractors benefited by striking crop-sharing deals with tractor owners. As rural-to-urban migration accelerated, land distribution and mechanization boosted productivity to compensate for the population shift.

Benefiting at first from foreign exchange reserves built up during World War II and from boom conditions during the Korean War, the DP opted for consumer-oriented policies, including liberalization of imports, that sparked inflation. The DP remained popular at the polls through the 1954 election. By the 1957 election, however, inflation and DP intolerance of opposition had eroded the party's support. Menderes's problems worsened when growing foreign debt forced him to accept a World Bank stabilization program in 1958. Inflation had hit salaried officials and the military especially hard. Trained to view themselves as guardians of the republic and seeing Inönü—their revered former leader—reviled as head of the RPP, a group of military commanders overthrew the Menderes regime in a coup on May 27, 1960.

Political scientists regard Turkey's 1960 coup as differing significantly from most military coups discussed in this book. Unlike poorly institutionalized postcolonial regimes where military intervention in politics reflects lack of consensus about governmental norms, the Turkish republic was a strongly consolidated state, heir to the centuries-old tradition of the Ottoman Empire. Identifying with Atatürk, the charismatic leader of the national independence struggle who had taken care to set aside his uniform and reappear in civilian dress as the republic's first president, Turkey's career officers were steeped in democratic principles—including civilian control of the military—which their experience in NATO had reinforced. However, Atatürk had entrusted the defense of the republic to the military. When military commanders thought civilian government had broken down, they would act to correct its course. This happened in 1960 and on two later occasions.

The 1960 coup makers quickly showed that they did not mean to rule indefinitely. They not only banned all political parties but also appointed a group of professors to write a new constitution. The 1924 constitution had served in the past but did not provide the checks and balances needed for new conditions. The 1961 constitution expanded the role of the judiciary, added a second house to the legislature (the Senate, as a check on the Grand National Assembly), slightly strengthened the presidency, and guaranteed many individual and collective freedoms, giving autonomy to the universities and the media and—for the first time—giving unions the right to strike. This constitution provided the basis for the return to civilian rule under Turkey's Second Republic (1961–1980).

Later experience showed that although the 1961 constitution solved some problems, it opened the way for others to emerge. During the 1960s, demographic growth—especially the fact that much of the population was very young—gave mass political mobilization new meanings in Turkey. Relatively good economic conditions presumably made these political problems less severe than they might otherwise have been. With economic planning entrusted to a State Planning Organization created in 1960, GDP grew at an annual average rate of 6.4 percent, more than enough to keep up with population growth. From 1962 on, the migration of Turkish workers to Germany also provided a new source of hard currency through the homeward flow of their remittances. Even so, Turkey had its share of the worldwide youth radicalism of the 1960s. Turkey still had two major parties: the RPP, now repositioning itself as a "left-of-center" social democratic party, and the Justice party (JP), successor of the now-abolished Democrats. The two governed together in coalition until 1965, after which the JP, led by Süleyman Demirel, governed for the rest of the decade.

Turkey's political problems came not from the big parties in the center but from the widening of the political spectrum to include new parties and groups not committed to the constitution or to parliamentary politics. By the end of the 1960s, the far Right had divided into a secular ultra-nationalist National Action party and a religious National Order (later National Salvation) party, and the Left had produced a Confederation of Revolutionary Workers' Unions and a Turkish Workers' party. Leftist and rightist groups also formed among university students. Much of the political extremism expressed reactions to rapid social and economic change, reactions that could be much more freely expressed under the 1961 constitution. The situation became especially dangerous when violence broke out in the universities, where the 1961 constitution prevented the police from responding effectively.

Mounting violence led the military high command to intervene again in March 1971. This time, they did not suspend the constitution or civilian politics, but they installed a series of new governments and forced them to take their advice. The Workers' party was abolished, the constitution was amended to limit freedoms, and martial law was declared in some provinces. Having attempted to correct the course of political development, the army withdrew again from politics in 1973.

During the rest of the 1970s, however, Turkey's political problems grew worse, partly because the economic situation deteriorated badly. The effects of the oil price increases were compounded by declines in remittances from the half-million Turkish workers in Europe, where economic activity had also slowed. By 1978, the foreign debt had grown alarmingly, and Turkey had had to accept an IMF stabilization program. The 1979 oil price increase caused further economic contraction, and inflation reached double digits.

Under such conditions, Turkish politics became even less stable than in the 1960s, again because of political activism on the extremes. Throughout the decade, a large majority of Turks voted for one or the other of the large center parties, the center-left RPP or the center-right JP. Most governments, however, combined one of these parties with smaller, extreme parties. This pattern magnified the influence of the smaller parties, to which the large parties had to make concessions. Politics became polarized. Worse than that, ministers tried to "colonize" the ministries they headed by filling them with officials who shared their politics. The spread of this problem into the police forces gravely jeopardized their ability to keep order.

Threats to law and order also became more serious than they had been in the 1960s. The late 1970s witnessed violence among students and workers, between the country's Shii minority and its Sunni majority, and between the Kurds of southeastern Turkey and the Turkish armed forces. Prominent figures were assassinated. Islamic revivalism created tensions throughout Turkish society, especially angering those, like the military, most committed to Atatürk's tradition of secularism. Emboldened by the Iranian revolution of 1979, the National Salvation party even called for the restoration of Islamic law.

Concluding that the parties and government institutions could not cope with this situation, the military intervened for the third time (September 1980), acting more decisively than in 1971 and receiving wide public support. They mounted security operations to halt political violence. They retained an economic stabilization program that the last precoup government had launched under the direction of Turgut Özal, head of the State Planning Organization. Including such IMF trademarks as devaluation, increases in subsidized prices, cutbacks in the public sector, and restrictions on wages and labor activism, this program also had a truly far-reaching objective: to replace the protectionist import-substitution policy pursued since Atatürk with a promarket orientation. The generals intended to restore democracy, but only under a new constitution designed to correct problems that had grown out of the constitution of 1961; they also disbanded the old parties and banned many politicians from politics.

The constitution drawn up for Turkey's Third Republic provided for a strong president who could appoint the prime minister, dismiss parliament, and declare a state of emergency. It restored a single-chamber parliament on the ground that Turkey did not need bicameralism; limited the rights granted in 1961, chiefly by forbidding their use to undermine the established order; and—to limit small parties' influence—denied parliamentary representation to any party receiving under 10 percent of the vote. When elections were held with all new parties in 1983, the winner was neither of the two parties the military preferred but the Motherland party (MP) headed by Turgut Özal, the technocrat responsible for the new economic program. It had restored growth in per capita GDP and—quite remarkably—achieved double-digit growth in exports.

Continuing in this vein, Turkey, which had pioneered in import-substitution and public sector expansion in the 1930s, became one of the most successful developing countries in shifting to export-led growth in the 1980s. The

Tansu Çiller (pron. CHILL-lehr) of Turkey, the first woman prime minister of an Islamic Middle Eastern country (June 1993). *She symbolizes change but faces difficult economic and social policy problems. ABC Ajansi/Gamma Liaison*

policy produced losers, especially workers, as well as gainers. It also failed in some respects—for example, by doing little to shrink either the public sector or inflation. Yet the magnitude of change becomes apparent from the fact that although agricultural and mineral products had made up more than 90 percent of Turkey's exports in the early 1960s, by 1990 manufactures accounted for over 75 percent. Between those dates, moreover, the dollar value of Turkey's exports had grown thirty times over, to about $12 billion, and their destinations had become more diverse. During the Iran-Iraq War, in particular, Turkey profited by trading with both its warring neighbors.

Prime Minister Özal dominated Turkish politics through the 1980s, securing election as president in 1989. With time, however, criticism mounted and support declined. After the ban on old politicians ended in 1987, a set of new parties reappeared, much like the old ones. Ending Özal's power, though he remained president, the October 1991 elections led to the formation of a coalition government under Süleyman Demirel of the True Path Party (a remake of the old JP).

At Özal's death in 1993, Demirel succeeded him as president, and Tansu Çiller, former minister of state for economics, succeeded Demirel as prime minister. With her, Turkey became the first Islamic Middle Eastern country to appoint a woman prime minister.

By that time, Turkey more nearly combined democracy and development than any other Islamic Middle Eastern country. Economically, double-digit inflation persisted, privatization languished, and external debt had grown to nearly $50 billion. Yet GDP had still grown at nearly 6 percent in 1992. One tangible symbol of Turkey's development was the Southeast Anatolia Project (GAP in Turkish, Anatolia being the Asian part of Turkey). Taking advantage of the fact that Turkey was the only Middle Eastern country with surplus water resources, the project aimed to develop the irrigation and hydropower potential of one of the country's poorest regions by building numerous dams and power plants on the Tigris and Euphrates Rivers, both of which rise in southeastern Turkey (see Map 10.2). All Turkish-built, the GAP Project demonstrated the expertise of Turkey's engineers. Ongoing diplomacy will be required to resolve water disputes with the downstream states, Syria and Iraq. Yet the project was intended not only to promote development in southeastern Turkey but also to ensure the country a major role in an era when scarcity will make "hydropolitics" at least as important for the Middle East as "petropolitics."

The country's most acute recent problem has been its Kurdish minority of 12 million, of whom half still live in the southeast, where the GAP project has been built, and half have moved westward, integrating into Turkish society. (Mostly Sunni Muslims who speak a language related to Persian, Kurds also live in adjoining parts of Iran, Iraq, and Syria). In southeastern Turkey, the Kurdish Workers Party (PKK in Kurdish) launched a separatist rebellion in 1984. The Iran-Iraq War, in which Turkey fulfilled its NATO responsibilities, at first threatened to worsen the Kurdish problem, as hundreds of thousands of Iraqi Kurds fled into Turkey. However, the outcome may have provided a way to settle the issue instead. Turkey and the Iraqi Kurdish leaders, whom the Marxist PKK condemn as "feudal," found common interests in stabilizing northern Iraq and cooperating against the PKK. Soviet collapse also helped, inclining Syria to improve its relations with Turkey by denying the PKK its base in Lebanon's Syrian-controlled Biqa' valley. (However, concerns about the effects of the GAP project on their water supply also give the Syrians motives to support the PKK as a way to put pressure on Turkey.) By early 1993, the PKK was ready for a ceasefire, but lack of agreement on the terms led to renewed fighting. Many Turkish Kurds would prefer life in a democratic Turkey to further bloodshed for the sake of a united Kurdistan, a PKK dream that Iraq, Iran, Syria, and Turkey would all oppose.

The international ramifications of the Kurdish issue offer one sign of a major growth in Turkey's regional standing since the Soviet collapse. Having applied for full membership in the EEC in 1987, albeit with low expectations of admission, Turkey has preserved its links with the West but also pursued foreign policy initiatives in other directions. Turkey has become the key player in an effort to create a Black Sea Economic Cooperation Region that will include a number of Balkan and formerly Soviet states. With Iran and Pakistan, it belongs to an Economic Cooperation Organization that the predominantly Muslim post-Soviet republics have also joined. What these organizations will amount to remains unclear, but Turkey indisputably has major affinities with five formerly Soviet republics—Azerbaijan, Kazakhstan, Kyrgyzstan, Turkmenistan, and Uzbekistan—whose peoples speak Turkic languages. Other countries also vie for influence in these new states; yet linguistic affinity enables Turkey to do things others cannot, from extending the range of its electronic media, to bringing thousands of Central Asian students to study in Turkey, to holding Turkic Summit meetings.

Turkey's growth in international influence adds another dimension to the country's recent development. Imperfect as its record remains in both democracy and development, Turkey now holds first place in the Islamic Middle East as a "newly industrializing country" and one of the developing world's rare examples of a functioning multiparty democracy.

Iran in Revolution: Turban Against Crown and Necktie

For much of the postwar period, Iran remained an authoritarian monarchy. Few such regimes survived elsewhere. But Iran's government seemed stable largely because of its oil wealth. The revolution of 1979 revealed a mortal antagonism between Iranian Islam and the secular-national monarchy, however. Alarmists saw the shah's fall as the start of a wave of revolution in the Islamic world. Part of a widespread Islamic resurgence, Iran's revolution was too rooted in Iranian conditions to be easily exported. However, it raises important questions for the comparative study of revolution.

When the British and Soviets occupied Iran in 1941 to use it as an Allied supply route to the USSR, Reza Shah (r. 1925–1941) abdicated in favor of his son, Muhammad Reza (r. 1941–1979). It was a long time before the new shah built up the power he wielded later. First, Iran had to wait out World War II and—with luck and U.S. help—evade Soviet efforts to divide the country and gain access to Iranian oil. Then, since Iran was formally a parliamentary monarchy under the constitution of 1906 and politicians had seized the initiative after Reza Shah's abdication, the young shah had to regain political initiative from parliament. The opportunity arose out of a parliament-led effort to nationalize the oil industry, which the Anglo-Iranian Oil Company (AIOC) controlled.

To the British and their U.S. allies, the crisis offered a choice like many faced in U.S.–Latin American relations. Nationalization was highly popular in Iran and made its champion, Prime Minister Muhammad Mosaddeq, a hero. Britain and the United States might have chosen to foster democracy in Iran by seeking accommodation, though at some cost to their economic interests. Or they could defend those interests and attack the parliamentary government that challenged them. Britain and the United States chose the latter course. Iranians never forgot the CIA-backed coup that toppled Mosaddeq in 1953.

The Western powers then helped the shah form the strong pro-Western regime they preferred. AIOC (later British Petroleum, BP) and other foreign oil interests worked out a new agreement. One new prop for the monarchy was the Plan Organization. It was to take charge of economic development, although its taste for vast projects, the privileges it gave foreigners, and corruption kept the agency from doing much for Iranians. Economically, oil revenues—from $34 million in 1954 to $358 million in 1960—kept the shah afloat. He also increased his security apparatus, which included both the U.S.-equipped military and the secret police, known by the Persian acronym SAVAK. Developed with aid from the CIA and the Israeli intelligence agency Mossad, SAVAK targeted Iranians who opposed the shah. Its abuses helped provoke the revolution of 1979. But the shah used the carrot as well as the stick: he made the government services an enormous patronage machine ultimately including over 300,000 civil servants and 400,000 military.

Pro-Western foreign policy, government-controlled economic growth, the security forces, patronage—these were the supports of the throne. For most Iranians, the shah allowed no political participation. The parliament survived, but the government manipulated elections, chose all candidates, and reorganized "parties" at will. Pushed by U.S. president John F. Kennedy's administration to consolidate the people's loyalties, the shah enacted a "Shah-People Revolution," including land reform, women's suffrage, and a literacy campaign. Because the parliament, many of whose members were large landowners, opposed these policies, the shah suspended parliament in 1961 and ruled by decree. The religious leadership also opposed the shah, objecting not so much to specific policies as to the secularism and dictatorial character of the regime. The shah exiled his sharpest religious critic, Ayatollah Ruhollah Khomeini, in 1964.

The outcome of land reform told a lot about the shah's goals. The first phase (1962–1963) bore some of the Kennedy imprint that appeared in the Latin American Alliance for Progress. In this phase, landlords who owned more than one "village" had to sell their land to the state for resale to their sharecroppers. Later phases, truer to the shah's outlook, asserted central government authority more strongly in the villages, preserved landlords' rights, and shifted emphasis to capitalist mechanization of agriculture rather than land reform. Ultimately, 92 percent of Iran's sharecroppers received some land. But wage laborers, a large part of the rural population, got none. Even those who got land ended up more dependent on the central government. In the past they could blame the landlords for their problems. Now they blamed the shah.

For years, oil wealth hid the failures of the Shah-People Revolution, at least from foreigners. Iran, the most populous Middle Eastern oil state, took the lead in quadrupling oil prices in 1973. Its oil revenues shot up from $5 billion in 1973–1974 to $20 billion in 1975–1976, staying at that level until the revolution. Iran's population doubled in twenty years, reaching 41 million by 1982, but real GNP increased more than tenfold between 1963 and 1978.

For most Iranians this growth was destructive. Agriculture represented 27 percent of GNP in 1963 but only 9 percent in 1978, while the contribution of manufacturing remained constant at 13 percent. Rural Iran was in a decline, for which industrial growth did not compensate. Only government services and the petroleum sector grew. The latter accounted for one-third to one-half of GNP through most of the 1970s but employed less than 1 percent of labor. Such unbalanced growth had high human costs. People poured into the ill-equipped cities—Tehran, for example, had no modern sewers. Iran's income distribution was one of the world's most unequal. Conspicuous consumption and corruption flourished in high places, while the majority struggled with high inflation. How could they express their grievances?

Since 1925, the Pahlevi shahs had modernized Iran in many ways but denied mass political participation by attacking other power centers in the society, including liberal democrats such as Mosaddeq, the radical Left, and even the religious leadership. Power became so concentrated in the shah's hands that the only way to change government policy was to overthow him.

The only "political" force strong enough to lead a revolution was the religious leadership, the only organized group of national scope. While Turkey was developing national political parties, the shah thwarted that kind of development in Iran. But he could not get rid of the religious functionaries, who numbered about ninety thousand in 1979 and lived in every city and town, though in few villages. These men were custodians of the belief system that offered hope and comfort to Iranians in a way that the shah's secular nationalism could not.

The fact that Iran was the only country officially committed to the Shii branch of Islam, as opposed to the majority Sunni branch, proved highly significant. Shii concepts of authority, as developed in Iran, make it very hard to justify a state that does not conform to strict Shii ideals. In a radical departure from historical norms, Ayatollah Khomeini pushed the argument to the limit by insisting that the religious leaders should seize executive power. His demand gained force from the fact that Iranian Shiism emphasized the ordinary believer's duty to defer to the most senior experts in Islamic law, known by the title *ayatollah*. Unable to win over the religious leaders, the shah had attacked them. But they were Iran's mass mobilizers, not he.

What launched Iran's revolution was socioeconomic stress coupled with the shah's wavering in reaction to criticism—by U.S. president Jimmy Carter among others—of his rights violations. The wavering between concession and repression led to a series of bloody riots. All political forces—religious conservatives, liberal democrats, leftists both secular and Islamic—united, and the shah's support vanished. With millions of people shouting "Death to the Shah" and "Death to America," mass political mobilization became a fact. The shah fled in January 1979. Khomeini returned from exile on February 1.

How successful has Iran's revolution been? Chapter 4 argued that in a society marked by socioeconomic inequity, revolution must

Political mobilization and the revolution against western-style modernity converge in Khomeini's Iran. *Weapons training for women clad in the enveloping black chador.* Gaumy/Magnum

change more than politics. It must so alter social and economic relations as to redistribute power and wealth. The most profound revolutions restructure culture as well. For a dependent country, successful revolution means breaking external dependency relations. Achieving such goals requires decisive leadership, a coherent ideology, and a well-organized movement.

Iran's revolution meets these criteria more fully than any other since Cuba's. The comparison of conservative, Islamic Iran with communist Cuba may seem paradoxical. Chapter 6 pointed out, however, that fascists of the 1930s thought of themselves as revolutionaries from the Right. One insightful analysis of Iran's revolution compares it to fascism in that sense. Perhaps, then, Cuba and Iran were equally revolutionary, despite their radically different ideologies. The Cuban comparison is also relevant on one more point: a revolution may improve conditions for most of a nation but still not produce high levels of development.

In Iran, the united front that toppled the shah did not long survive. By 1983, Khomeini and associates had suppressed the Left, neutralized the liberals, and silenced dissident religious leaders. To consolidate its power, the regime built new institutions and Islamicized old ones. It purged thousands of the shah's officials. The constitution of 1979 provided for a parliament and president but subordinated them to a senior expert in Islamic religious law (or, in certain circumstances, a council of experts). The regime organized its followers into an Islamic Republican party, which monopolized parliament. The regime created institutions to mobilize the populace—and to establish totalitarian control. Suspicion of military forces patronized by the shah led to creation of a Revolutionary Guard, which soon rivaled the regular military. Islamic courts enforced religious law. Khomeini attached special importance to the prayer leaders of the larger mosques, where Muslims congregate for the Friday noon prayer followed by a sermon. No one knew better than he how to exploit these sermons for political effect. By 1983 he had organized the prayer leaders under a national agency. By 1987 they had taken over political mobilization so fully that the Islamic Republican party was abolished: religion had reabsorbed politics.

Nor did Khomeini neglect morals and thought control. A Ministry of Islamic Guidance took charge of propaganda. Islamic societies appeared in all important organizations to ensure conformity. Vigilante groups did likewise in the streets. For example, the Sisters of Zaynab stalked women violating the Islamic dress code. Education underwent strict Islamization. Religious functionaries assigned to military units saw to their Islamic indoctrination. Internal intelligence organizations, more fearful than the shah's SAVAK, reappeared. Thus political revolution shaded into social and cultural upheaval. Many Iranians approved, agreeing with Khomeini that secularism and westernization had been a sickness.

Had Iran experienced social revolution—a basic reallocation of wealth and power, usually signaled by violent class conflict? If so, it was not in terms Marx would recognize: the classes that had won and lost were defined in cultural, more than economic, terms. To state things in symbolic terms Iranians understood, the "turbans" had toppled the "crown" and the "neckties."

Iran's uneven economic record shows how much its Islamic revolution differed from commonly cited models of social revolution: the French, Russian, or Chinese cases of 1789, 1917, and 1949. Despite the shah's failed land reform in the 1960s, and the spontaneous land seizures that began after his fall, the regime wavered on land reform. In 1986 the parliament finally passed a law ratifying land seizures prior to a date in 1981. This was hardly a radical act, especially for a government that blamed the shah for Iran's loss of agricultural self-sufficiency and still faced rising food imports.

Nor have business and industry prospered. The government controlled 80 percent or more of the economy through the 1980s. By 1989, inflation was out of control, and high officials admitted that expanding the state's economic role had been a mistake. With population growth of almost 4 percent a year, the country still suffered many ills of the 1970s: low productivity, inflation, rapid rural-urban migration, unemployment, and housing shortages. Perhaps Khomeini failed even more than Castro in economic development.

Where Khomeini excelled Castro was in cultural revolution, noted above, and in severing external dependency ties. Iran quickly made clear its determination to break external bonds—for example, with the detention of the U.S. embassy hostages (1979–1981). Iran's economic problems partly result from this determination. The government paid off its international debt. To balance the budget, it cut spending betwen 1979 and 1983 by 18 percent of GDP, far more than the IMF would have demanded from a debtor country. To Khomeini, the Iran-Iraq War (1980–1988), launched by Iraq, was a war of the worlds, pitting secular Arab socialism against Iran and Islam. Both were oil states, but Iran's population was three times Iraq's and should seemingly have prevailed, especially given Khomeini's use of the Shii mystique of martyrdom to incite young Iranians to suicidal bravery. In 1988, however, Khomeini accepted a UN ceasefire. Scrupling at nothing, not even chemical weapons, Iraq had held its own.

Khomeini's international goal was not just to defeat Iraq or defy the U.S. and Soviet "great satans" but to export Iran's revolution. Differences of doctrine in fact confined the exportability of his ideas to Shii minorities in other Islamic countries with weak or favorably inclined governments (mainly Lebanon or Syria). Until his death in 1989, however, Khomeini exhorted Iranians to endure every hardship to establish a universal Islamic state.

The mass display of grief at Khomeini's funeral, as hundreds of thousands struggled to touch his shrouded body, expressed both his hold on the masses and the insecurity Iran faced without him. Leadership passed to his associates among the religious elite with little apparent disorder. Since that time, however, two major tendencies have competed in Iran's politics. The moderate trend, identified with President Ali-Akbar Hashemi-Rafsanjani, favored freeing the economy, inviting foreign investment, luring back highly educated Iranians who had fled the revolution, and normalizing relations with other countries. The radical trend, identified with Khomeini's successor as Iran's top religious authority, Ayatollah Ali Khamenei, favored a centrally controlled economy and rigorously Islamic domestic and foreign policies. Through the April 1992 parliamentary election, the moderates appeared to be gaining ground. Thereafter, the radicals regained the ascendancy, and international anxiety grew with reports of Iran's attempts to gain nuclear weapons technologies and its support for radical Muslims elsewhere.

One problem with the radicals' ambitions was that they ignored critical economic needs: millions of unemployed Iranians, millions of Afghan and Iraqi-Kurdish refugees in Iran, runaway inflation, and falling national income. That many Iranians were alienated from the revolution became clear from accusations of corruption among the religious authorities, urban riots targeting such bastions of their control as the Islamic Propaganda Organization, and the weak turnout for the June 1993 presidential election, in which Rafsanjani won reelection but not a strong mandate. As with other revolutions examined in this book, the radicals' fervor could not exempt Iran from the need for realism, both in economic policy and in relations with a world where not everyone shared the same ideology.

Iraq's Struggle to Consolidate a Weak State

After World War I, when the European powers at the Paris Peace Conference carved up the defeated Ottoman Empire, they combined three of its provinces into a country and called it Iraq. Under the League of Nations, Iraq was placed under British mandate. In keeping with the idea of preparing the country for independence, the British set up a monarchy, bringing in a prince of the Hashimi dynasty, which still rules in Jordan, and making him king of Iraq as Faysal I.

Like most African states, and like the other Middle Eastern countries that Europeans carved out of the Ottoman Empire (specifically, Syria, Lebanon, Jordan, and Palestine), Iraq started with all the problems of a "weak state" created by imperialism. Large empires had once been centered in Iraq, but the last of them had fallen over five hundred years before. The new king was an outsider. His British overlords were even more so. The country had ill-defined borders, which threw together populations that lacked cohesion.

Iraq had never been a nation before. Some 55 percent of its population were Shii Arabs, found especially in the south. Another 20 percent were Sunni Arabs, mostly in the center and center-north. About 20 percent were Kurds. There were also small minorities of Jews, Christians, Turks, Persians, and others. What could hold such a population together?

Made independent in name in 1932, Iraq's monarchy survived until 1958. It tried to appeal to the people by promoting two competing claims to loyalty—Iraqi nationalism and Pan-Arabism—that have remained central to Iraqi political life. Yet over time, the regime faced problems with which it could not cope. These began with defeat in the 1948 war with Israel, the event that led to the emergence of radical regimes in Egypt and Syria. The monarchy's problems worsened in 1955 when Iraq joined an alliance, the Baghdad Pact, that included Turkey, Iran, Pakistan, and Britain. The next year, when Britain, France, and Israel mounted a surprise attack on Egypt in hopes of toppling the regime of Gamal Abdel Nasser (1952–1970), who was then emerging as the champion of Arab socialism, Iraq was left stranded as the only Arab state allied with the imperialists. Having survived the attack, Nasser subjected Iraq to a Pan-Arab propaganda blast. Other Arab states turned against Iraq. Many Iraqis also turned against the monarchy, which fell to a bloody military coup in 1958.

The 1958 coup opened a decade of military rule that featured more than ten coups or attempted coups and ongoing civil war with the Kurds. The officers who carried out the coup had no large political movement behind them, and they failed to consolidate new government institutions. Amid the instability, elements of the Ba'th party, which would later rule Iraq, briefly held power (1963–1964). President Abd al-Karim Qasim (1958–1963) at least shifted social and economic policy significantly. Attacking the landowning class that had supported the monarchy, he enacted a land reform that limited the size of landholdings and divided all land above the limits among the peasants. Qasim pursued industrialization, with limited results. He attacked foreign control of the Iraqi oil industry, a process that culminated in its nationalization in 1972. Finally, he improved women's lives through secularist legal reforms that limited polygamy and equalized women's inheritance rights.

As in other Arab countries, defeat in the 1967 war against Israel discredited the military regime. This set the stage for the 1968 coup that installed the Ba'th party, by then reorganized under the leadership of General Ahmad Hasan al-Bakr and his deputy, Saddam Husayn, who displaced the general and took over the top position in 1979.

In time, Saddam Husayn produced solutions in excess to the problems of the "weak state." He turned Iraq into a totalitarian machine that left no Iraqi safe and antagonized other countries to the point of bringing Iraq into mortal danger. An examination of the Ba'th party and ideology, the regime's socioeconomic policy, and its use of violence will show how this happened.

Originating in Syria in the 1940s, the Ba'th party developed the most influential Pan-Arab ideology. Ba'th thought combines an emotionally intense emphasis on Arab unity, a non-Marxist "Arab socialism" largely inspired by the Soviet example of rapid development, the idea of the elite vanguard party, and a Fascist-style emphasis on the Leader. These ideas were supposed to spark the "renaissance" (*ba'th* in Arabic) from which the party took its name. With the ideas went a multilayered cell organization, with all power concentrated at the top. The Iraqi branch of the Ba'th ultimately applied these concepts more thoroughly than the Syrian, with which the Iraqi branch has long been at odds.

Saddam Husayn took these ideas and institutions and—much as Stalin did with Soviet communism—twisted them into a system of one-man dominance. Under Saddam, the party remained small, with only 25,000 full members out of Iraq's 1984 population of 14 million. But the party had many grades of membership, and the total of its hangers-on amounted to 1.5 million. Because most of them worked for the state, party and government practically became the same thing. Largely because of the state's control of Iraq's oil revenues, the Ba'th state grew exceptionally large compared to the rest of society. As of 1980, civilian and military government personnel were estimated at roughly half the urban labor force in a population that was two-thirds urban. The state had practically absorbed Iraqi society, and the state was controlled by one man, surrounded by an elaborate personality cult and the network of relatives and cronies through which he operated.

Not everything about Ba'thist Iraq was bad, especially compared to conservative neighboring states. Iraq used its oil revenues not only to benefit public and private enterprise but also to create a welfare society. The nationalization of the Iraqi petroleum industry (1972), followed by the oil price increases of the 1970s, increased the government's resources—and also its power—far beyond those of earlier regimes. Urbanization progressed rapidly, and many migrants found employment in the state sector. The fact that oil alone remained the nation's chief export raised questions about Iraq's future prosperity, but the small size of the population (18.2 million in 1992) in relation to oil income, which peaked at $26 billion in 1980, meant that the benefits could be widely felt while they lasted.

Many Iraqis did feel those benefits. The expansion of education made a majority of Iraqis literate for the first time. The position of women improved with better access to education and employment, improved health care, and reforms in family law. Women in Saudi Arabia, who were still forbidden to drive or to hold most jobs, had reason to envy their Iraqi sisters. Iraq's middle and lower classes, especially in the cities, generally profited from improvements in education, public health, electrification, transport, housing, and industrialization. Boosted by oil revenue, Iraq's version of Stalinist forced-draft development raised living standards even while stripping Iraqis of political and human rights.

The extent to which Saddam's Iraq relied on violence was high by any standard. The factors that make Iraq exceptionally violent spring partly from Saddam Husayn's personality. They also reflect the fact that the Ba'th, once in power, used staged acts of mass violence to bring Iraqis into complicity with the new regime, while also giving them a first taste of something that could later be turned against them. China's Communists did the same thing after coming to power in 1949; Iraq's Ba'th had more incentive to do this because it had come to power without revolution. The way Saddam Husayn uses force, especially military force, also probably reflects the fact that he—unlike many Middle Eastern rulers and despite the uniform he often wears—rose to power through the party and has no military experience. In fact, controlling the Iraqi military was initially a problem for the Ba'th (Syria's Ba'th party failed in this and was taken over by military officers).

The pervasive violence of Saddam's Iraq expresses itself in characteristic forms, including purges and mass executions. Coming to power in a coup a year after the Arab-Israeli war of June 1967 had discredited Arab governments in general, the Ba'th blamed the tiny remnant of the Jewish community for Iraq's defeat, exposed a fabricated "plot" with mostly Jewish villains, tried and condemned the accused, and hanged them in a Baghdad square. Hundreds of thousands of Iraqis were brought in to revile the dangling corpses while listening to inflammatory speeches. In 1979, less public purges solemnized Saddam Husayn's displacement of Bakr as president. By then, party control over the military had been consolidated, and differences were emerging over how to respond to the Iranian revolution.

Saddam purged Bakr and then staged an extraordinary meeting of the Revolutionary Command Council (RCC), where some ministers were forced to "confess" (their families were being held hostage). Then Saddam ordered the other ministers to form firing squads and execute those who had confessed. With this ghoulish twist, Saddam assured the survivors' complicity in his own bloody rise.

Ordinary Iraqis were not exempt from such methods. The Ba'th regime has three secret police agencies, each independent from the others: State Internal Security, Military Intelligence, and Party Intelligence. All of them primarily target Iraqi citizens, who have no individual rights. The state sponsors mass organizations for youth, women, and workers. The youth organizations start the political mobilization of Iraqis very young, breaching the security of the family as they do so: children are encouraged to inform on their parents. Until the Iran-Iraq War, the army, too, faced almost no opponents but dissident Iraqis, especially the Kurds in the north. In addition, the party militia serves as a military reserve and tool for politically molding its members. Finally, the fact that the regime totally controls the flow of information and forbids all foreign publications creates a climate of psycho-cultural violence in which communication and indoctrination become the same thing.

Although the instruments of state violence could be turned against anyone, their main targets within Iraq were groups that did not fit into the Ba'th system, notably the Shii majority and the Kurds. The regime carried out mass deportations of Kurds and Shiis, dumping hundreds of thousands of Iraq's Arab Shiis at the Iranian border and relocating the Kurds to arid places in the south where they could not survive.

Once Saddam had assured his hold on power, the regime also turned its violence outward. Many reasons have been offered for his attack on Khomeini's Iran, from historical tensions along the ethnic frontier between the Arab and the Iranian zones of the Middle East, to the incompatibility of Saddam's secularism with Khomeini's Islam. The best clue to Saddam's motivation may lie in the name he gave the operation, *Qadisiyyat Saddam,* Saddam's Qadisiyya. In the original battle of Qadisiyya (A.D. 635), the forces of the early Islamic community (which was then also an Arab community) had conquered Iran, bringing it into the Islamic fold for the first time.

If Saddam had thought he could win a similarly quick and decisive victory against a country that had three times the population of Iraq and half again as much oil, he must have overestimated the disruption caused by Iran's revolution. Khomeini understood early Islamic history better than Saddam did and, once the latter had begun to fire missiles at Iranian towns, exploited the symbols most meaningful to Iran's Shiis, motivating vast numbers of them to face martyrdom in human wave attacks on Iraqi positions. (Identifying as Arabs and not finding Iran's religious radicalism attractive, Iraqi Shiis—who provided most of the enlisted men in Iraq's army—supported Iraq in the war.) In the long run, fears roused by the Iranian revolution led the Arab governments and the United States primarily to support Iraq. Discouragement over this fact—and over Saddam's willingness to use poison gas against Iranians and any who helped them, as the Kurds of northern Iraq did—finally led Khomeini to end the war by accepting a cease-fire in 1988.

Iraq emerged from the war much damaged yet with the government's military capabilities greatly expanded. The army had more than quintupled, to about 1 million men. Iraq clearly had acquired the means from U.S. and European firms to produce chemical weapons and was attempting to develop nuclear ones as well. Saddam's biggest problem was that falling prices and wartime disruption had depressed Iraq's petroleum revenues to only about $10 billion a year during the war. He tried various maneuvers, including privatizing state enterprises, to compensate. But what he needed was higher oil prices. Early in 1990, he tried to get other Gulf rulers to lower production so as to push up the price. When that failed, he revived claims to part of Kuwait. On August 2, 1990, he occupied Kuwait and began to plunder it.

Surprised, the international community responded first by freezing Iraq's assets and closing its oil pipelines running through Saudi Arabia and Turkey. The United States secured Saudi permission to station troops in Saudi Arabia, then urged other nations—including several Arab states—to join the coalition. In the new climate of East-West cooperation created by the end of the Cold War, the UN Security Council became a key arena for responding to the crisis. The council passed numerous resolutions, including ones that demanded immediate Iraqi withdrawal, imposed economic sanctions, and authorized coalition forces to use force if Iraq did not withdraw by January 15, 1991.

Even more than the Iran-Iraq War had, the outcome illustrated the costs of a system in which one man with no military training made all decisions. Far from trying to defuse the crisis, Saddam rhetorically connected his annexation of Kuwait to Israel's retention of territories occupied in 1967 and argued that the solution to the Kuwait crisis hinged on a solution for the Arab-Israeli crisis. Moreover, when the United States and its allies began hostilities on January 15, 1991, with air raids against Baghdad, Iraq retaliated with missile attacks against both Israel and Saudi Arabia. None of this could diminish the coalition forces' technical superiority, especially after the early bombing raids destroyed Iraq's command, control, and communications systems and damaged its nuclear and chemical weapons facilities. The ground operations that began on February 24 progressed so fast that not only Kuwait but also southern Iraq were taken within one hundred hours.

Before the war, Saddam Husayn's totalitarian system had more than compensated, it seemed, for Iraq's historical lack of cohesion. Defeat weakened this system and exposed its brittleness but also revealed a lack of viable alternatives. Two years later, Saddam Husayn's reconsolidated regime survived in Baghdad, despite unprecedented UN restrictions.

Before the war ended, as U.S. president Bush called for Iraqis to overthrow Saddam Husayn, uprisings began among both the Shii Arabs in the south and the Kurds in the north. As the Shiis learned to their cost, Western powers proved more responsive to the Kurds, partly because of greater familiarity with the Kurdish problem, partly because of U.S. fear that successful resistance among Iraq's Arab Shiis would serve Iranian ends. For over a year, Saddam was left to do as he wished in the south. In the north, however, U.S. and other troops were sent to help Iraqi Kurdish refugees, of whom several hundred thousand fled to Turkey and a million to Iran. Returning under protection of a "no-fly" zone that the allies proclaimed in April 1991 north of the thirty-sixth parallel of latitude, and with U.S. and other foreign troops on the ground, the Kurds attempted to rebuild, iron out differences among their many political movements, and organize an autonomous "federated state" within Iraq.

Meanwhile, Shii rebels in the south had to fend for themselves. The United States, Britain, and France did not establish a no-fly zone south of the thirty-second parallel until August 1992. By then, Saddam's forces had bombed Shii villages with napalm. After the battle at the Shii holy city of Karbala, its two mosques were restored but left standing alone, everything nearby having been bulldozed.

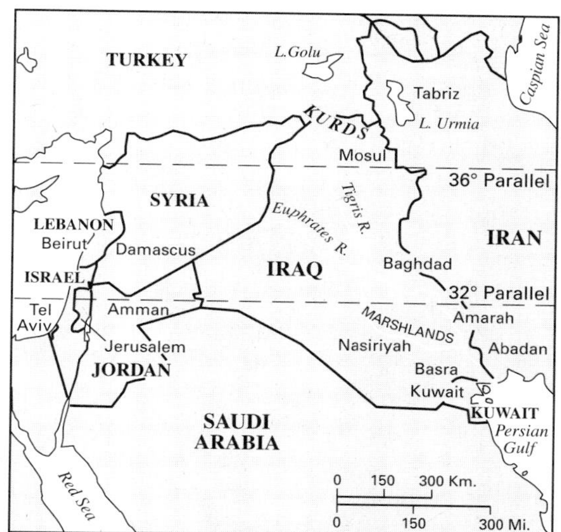

Map 17.2 Iraq. *The "no-fly" zone to protect Iraq's Kurds is north of the 36th parallel. The "no-fly" zone for Iraq's Shiis is south of the 32nd parallel.*

Without foreign ground troops, the no-fly zone alone could not protect Shiis from Saddam's repression.

In central Iraq, too, between the thirty-second and thirty-sixth parallels, the still-defiant government faced externally imposed restrictions. UN resolution 687 had provided for a permanent ceasefire and progressive lifting of sanctions on certain conditions, among them that Iraq's nuclear, chemical, and biological weapons, and its ballistic missiles with ranges exceeding 150 kilometers be destroyed. The UN commission set up to eliminate these weapons met repeated resistance. U.S. reconnaissance flights over central Iraq provided another focus of contention. Because of the slow progress in eliminating major weapons programs, the trade sanctions remained in effect long after the war had ended. For the average Iraqi, essential foodstuffs could be had only at vastly inflated prices. Because the government's modern health-care system depended totally on imported medicines, health conditions deteriorated radically. The UN Security Council passed special resolutions to allow Iraq to sell limited amounts of crude oil, with the proceeds to be used to pay for food and medicine, war reparations, and UN expenses. Criticizing these terms as interference in domestic affairs, Iraqi officials—who had privileged access to scarce goods—refused to cooperate, leaving fellow Iraqis—including children—to suffer the consequences.

What could ordinary Iraqis do about their situation? Having little sympathy for the Kuwaitis, fearing that Saddam's fall would produce some other strongman, and believing that the West really wanted that outcome, many Iraqis seemed resigned to their situation. Those who were not left the country, if they could. Political activists in exile labored to unite their factions into an Iraqi National Council that could offer a pluralist, democratic, free-market alternative to the Saddam regime. But they were still far from taking power in Baghdad.

As radicals regained the ascendant in Iran next door, Iraqis—and the world—needed a way to move beyond the aftermath of the Gulf War. Meanwhile, Saddam's battered regime hung on, a warning of what could result from trying to compensate for the noncohesion of an artificially created state by concentrating all power in the central government. Across the Middle East, voices were being raised to demand multiparty democracy and economic freedom. Saddam Husayn offered the most glaring illustration of the need for such a change.

Israel and Its Search for Security

The Zionist movement that created the State of Israel is unique in the history of nationalism. The movement claimed the ancient homeland of the Jewish people yet emerged outside that country among Jewish communities scattered across nineteenth-century Europe. At the time, the land the Zionists claimed had long-established inhabitants who saw it as rightfully theirs and developed their own nationalist movement as Palestinians, opposing Zionism. These facts help explain the resultant conflict over nationalist goals. The interference of outside powers complicated things much more.

After World War II, the British faced urgent demands for large-scale immigration of European Jews to Palestine. Sensing that they could not accept these demands and preserve influence in the Arab world, the British announced in 1947 that they would turn their mandate over to the United Nations, which adopted a complex partition plan (Map 17.3). Civil war broke out between Jews and Arabs, with atrocities by both sides, and refugees began fleeing to other Arab lands.

When the British withdrew on May 14, 1948, the Zionist leaders proclaimed the independence of the State of Israel. The proclamation announced the new state's openness to Jewish immigrants from all the world and the equality of all citizens without regard to religion, race, or sex. The proclamation offered peace to neighboring states and called on Arabs inside Israel to participate as equal citizens in developing the state. Fulfilling all parts of this vision would not be easy.

Several Arab states—Egypt, Jordan, Lebanon, Iraq, and Syria—responded by invading Israel. With the Holocaust fresh in mind, and with a small territory and few forces, Israelis saw the conflict as a life-or-death struggle against a much larger foe. In fact, most Arab states were not yet fully independent, they lacked unity of command, and they did not field as many soldiers as the Israelis. For the Arabs, the conflict, the first test of a dawning era of independence, ended as "the disaster." Israel won but got only UN-mediated armistices, without peace treaties or diplomatic recognition from neighboring states. For the first time since antiquity, however, the country had a Jewish majority: Israel then had 650,000 Jews and 165,000 Arabs. About 750,000 Arabs had fled, mostly to the refugee life that fueled later Palestinian militancy.

Within Israel, the years from 1948 to 1977 form a single period of Labor party (Mapai) rule. Founded by a 1929 merger of socialist groups, the party resembled European social democratic parties. Its leaders were mostly eastern Europeans who had immigrated to Palestine before World War I. The party dominated Israel's great labor federation, the Histadrut, and had close ties to an important type of collective agricultural settlement, the *kibbutz*. Kibbutz members played key roles in agriculture and politics, though they represented only 5 percent of the population in 1948 and less since.

The Labor leaders' European origins and socialist ideas set the tone for the new state, but its population quickly changed. Mass immigration doubled the Jewish population in three years, first with European survivors of the war, then with Jews from Islamic lands where the new Arab-Israeli conflict was destroying the historical pattern of intercommunal accommodation. After 1951, immigration diminished but continued in smaller waves. Every Jew's right of migration (*aliya*) to Israel was a basic Zionist principle.

Questions arose about relations among Jews, as well as between Jews and Arabs. By 1951, Jews of African or Asian origin represented a third of Israel's Jewish population, and their rate of increase was almost twice that of the Europeans. The Europeans who dominated the Labor party—people like David Ben-Gurion and Golda Meir—had only so much time to assimilate later immigrants, it seemed, or Israel would become "orientalized." When the Labor party fell in 1977, this seemed to be happening.

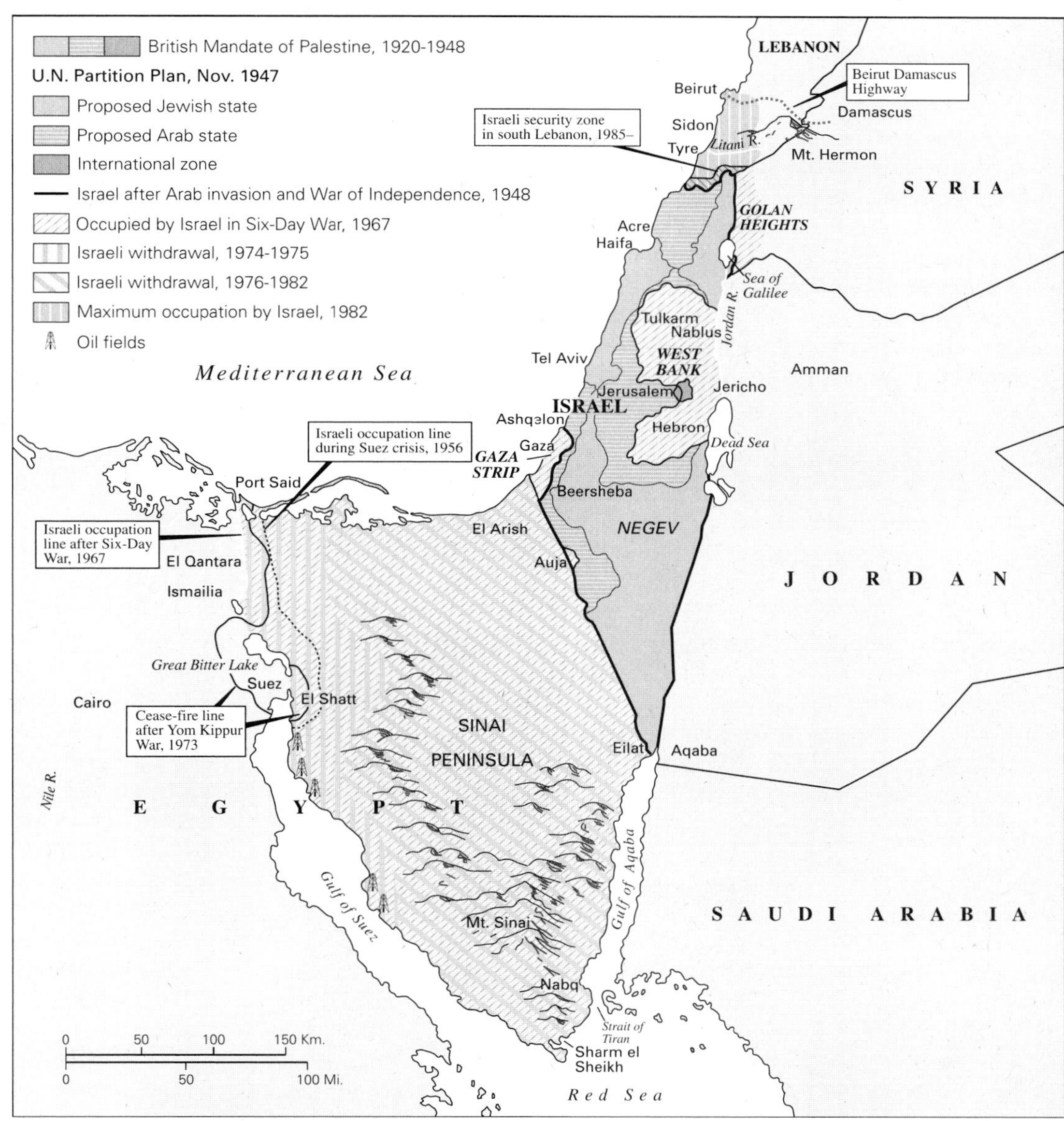

Map 17.3 Israel and its Neighbors

A key Zionist goal had always been economic: to create a self-sustaining Jewish community that could become a viable state. After 1948, massive immigration demanded economic development on an expanded scale. Development began slowly yet made great progress through the 1970s. Israel faced huge obstacles to growth. It had little water and few other natural resources. Zionist goals required high welfare spending to attract and retain immigrants. The Arab countries boycotted Israel economically, and the lack of real peace kept defense spending high. By 1967, Israel and its Arab neighbors devoted more of their GNP to defense (11 percent in Israel) than any other countries except the Soviet Union.

Israel's development also benefited, however, from exceptional positive factors. For its citizens, the "upbuilding of Israel" was a life-or-death matter. They brought to the country high educational levels and technical skills. Israel's educational institutions became better, its irrigated countryside greener, and its industry more advanced than those of surrounding countries. Israel enjoyed high investment levels. From 1950 through 1973, annual capital investment equaled an average of 25 percent of GNP—a rate rarely matched elsewhere. Most of the capital came from U.S. aid or loans, German reparations, support from Jews abroad, or funds that immigrants brought with them. By 1973, Israel had received $18 billion from such sources. The economy had an exceptionally large service sector, and the diamond-cutting and arms industries were unusually prominent. For its first quarter-century, Israel achieved an average annual growth rate of 10 percent, fractionally higher than Japan's.

In politics, strong consensus about defense, and Labor party control of the government through 1977, created a superficial appearance of simplicity. In fact, the political system was complex. Among twenty or more parties, three clusters were especially important. On the left was a group ranging from social democratic to Marxist, dominated by the Labor party. On the right stood a group of staunchly nationalist parties, the best known being the Freedom (Herut) party, headed by Menachem Begin. It took a militant stand on territorial unification of the historical land of Israel. Although Labor would gladly have accepted diplomatic recognition from the Arabs within the 1949 armistice lines, Herut continued to call for a "Greater Israel" including the Kingdom of Jordan as well as the West Bank (biblical Judea and Samaria). The third major group consisted of religious parties that aimed to make Israel a state run according to Jewish law. Because no party ever commanded a majority, Israel always had coalition governments. Until the 1980s, the religious parties were the favored coalition partners, largely because they would exchange votes on other issues for support on the religious issues they cared about.

In many ways, the high point of Labor's twenty-nine years in power was the victory in the Six-Day War of 1967, which gave Israel control of Sinai, the Golan Heights, the Gaza Strip, the West Bank, and the Old City of Jerusalem. The victory strengthened Israel strategically, tripling the amount of land under its control but shortening its land boundaries by 25 percent. The war also generated enough support from abroad to touch off an economic boom that lasted into the early 1970s. The Arabs still refused to conclude a peace treaty that recognized Israel's right to exist as a state, however. Later, the realization came that such bitter defeat could not induce Arab states to make concessions. But Israel did not grasp this lesson immediately, and the triumphal mood of 1967 prepared the way for the surprise of October 1973.

The foremost question to emerge out of the 1967 war was that of the occupied territories. Sinai meant relatively little to most Israelis. The Golan Heights seemed vital for security. The West Bank meant more, at least to rightists and religious conservatives to whom this was ancient Judea and Samaria. Old Jerusalem meant most of all. The Labor leadership at first seemed willing to trade territory for peace. But the territorial issue soon eroded Israel's consensus about defense. Some Israelis thought it in Israel's interest to trade territory for diplomatic recognition. To hold territories with a large Arab majority could create a demographic danger, given the high Arab birthrate. Other Israelis rejected this argument, holding that the occupied territories provided a buffer that should be consolidated by Jewish settlement, especially in places identified with biblical Israel. This view worked its way into policy in the 1970s. Many Israelis became used to a new status quo in which Arabs from the territories seized in 1967 would never participate fully in Israeli life, whatever their numbers, because they had not been granted citizenship. Still, some Israelis protested that retaining the territories on such a basis would make Israel another South Africa.

Meanwhile, Palestinians in the occupied territories and surrounding states grew in militancy. After the 1967 war, Palestinian activists in exile concluded they would have to regain their homeland by their own efforts, not await help from Arab governments. The most important Palestinian organization was al-Fatah (Movement for the Liberation of Palestine), headed by Yasir Arafat, who also became the leader in 1968 of the Palestine Liberation Organization (PLO), the Palestinian umbrella organization. Though sympathizing with the Palestinians, Arab governments could not allow guerrillas to operate from bases in their territory without provoking Israeli retaliation. After 1971, Lebanon—least resolute of the Arab states because of its religiously fragmented society—was the only country adjoining Israel in which Palestinians could operate at all freely. Their increased activism was probably the strongest expression of the global wave of guerrilla violence in the late 1960s. Israelis saw Palestinians' efforts to regain their homeland as terrorism and viewed Israel's larger-scaled retaliatory attacks as legitimate self-defense.

With Palestinian militancy as a backdrop, the October War of 1973 marked the beginning of the end of unbroken Labor rule. The success of the Arabs' surprise attack raised questions about Israeli military intelligence and preparedness. An official investigation led to the resignation of Prime Minister Golda Meir and Defense Minister Moshe Dayan. The next Labor government, under Yitzhak Rabin, was tainted by scandal. Economic woes included defense spending that stayed above 30 percent of GNP after the war, high inflation, and swelling foreign debt. The OPEC shock also weakened diplomatic support for Israel. The UN and more than a hundred nations recognized the PLO. Inside Israel, Jews of Afro-Asian origin became a majority of the Jewish population in the 1970s. They remembered past inequalities and identified more readily with Begin's simply stated Greater Israel ideology than with Labor party theory.

The May 1977 election consequently opened a new period. The winner was the Likud (Unity) bloc, formed around Ariel Sharon, hero of the 1973 war. The bloc included Begin's Herut party, and he became prime minister.

Begin emphasized the greater Israel theme. In an effort at peacemaking initiated by Egyptian President Anwar al-Sadat and mediated by U.S. President Jimmy Carter, Begin joined in concluding the Camp David Accords of September 1978 and the Egyptian-Israeli treaty of March 1979, Israel's first peace treaty with any Arab state. These agreements led to the return of Sinai to Egypt, an economic and strategic concession that did not detract from the Greater Israel idea. As for the West Bank, Begin agreed at Camp David to negotiate autonomy for its inhabitants. But he went on to develop an autonomy plan that offered Arabs no more than they already had: Israeli military control and sovereignty and continued freedom for Israelis to settle there. The founding of settlements did continue. By 1982 the state had acquired control of more than half the land on the West Bank and was making it available for construction of planned communities. Soon, so many Israelis would own property there that it might become politically unthinkable to return the region to Arab control.

The position of Arabs in the occupied territories deteriorated, but the greatest blow to the Palestinians came in Lebanon. The Israelis invaded south Lebanon in 1978 with twenty thousand troops. In June 1982, Israel again invaded, pushing all the way to Beirut. Defense Minister Sharon appears to have convinced his government that the invasion would not only protect northern Israel from guerrilla incidents but also thwart militancy in the occupied territories by smashing the PLO center in Beirut. In fact, Arafat and many PLO activists were forced out of Lebanon in August 1982. A rebellion within al-Fatah challenged him again a year later.

The invasion of Lebanon inflicted grave blows on the Palestinians, but also handed Israel its first defeat. It took Israel three years to disengage from Lebanon. Israel suffered many casualties, and some soldiers refused orders to serve. More upsetting were the massacres in September 1982 that the militia of the Maronite Christian Phalange perpetrated in two Palestinian refugee camps in West Beirut, an area under Israeli military control.[1] Israeli commanders claimed not to have known that hundreds of civilians were being massacred, but many Israelis, with long memories of the Holocaust, reacted with revulsion. An official inquiry censured the responsible parties, including Begin and Sharon. Meanwhile, concentrating on his territorial policy, Begin had neglected hard economic issues. Aggravated by the settlement policy and the Lebanese invasion, the inflation rate reached triple digits in 1984.

Begin withdrew from politics in 1983, and the next general election, in 1984, reflected Israel's problems. Neither Labor nor Likud emerged with enough votes to form a coalition. The result was a national unity government combining the two, with Labor's Shimon Peres as prime minister for two years, followed by Likud's Yitzhak Shamir for two years. The government withdrew from Lebanon in 1985, unable to leave behind anything to secure Israeli interests, other than a shallow border zone manned by the Israeli-backed South Lebanon army. The withdrawal helped stabilize Israel's economy, but a new stage in Palestinian resistance soon jeopardized this gain.

What Palestinians call the *intifada* (the "throwing off" of Israeli rule) began in December 1987 when a traffic accident provoked riots, first in the Gaza Strip, then in the West Bank. The uprising produced many casualties, mostly Palestinian. More significantly, it opened a new era in Palestinian nationalism. Now, Palestinians living under Israeli rule took the initiative. They created an underground Unified National Command (UNC). Linked to the PLO outside, the UNC combined representatives of various Palestinian and Islamic movements in the territories. Israeli security could not root out the UNC. It kept itself invisible, except for the directives it published. If one of its members was captured, the movement that member represented simply appointed a replacement. The uprising included a broad range of actions: stones thrown at Israeli security forces; barricades in the streets; mass resignations by Palestinian policemen; demonstrations by men, women, and children; boycotts of Israeli goods; refusal to pay taxes; strikes, especially by Palestinians working inside Israel; and school closings. A major goal was to create an alternative infrastructure with its own schools, medical services, and even intifada gardens. The UNC having forbidden use of firearms, the intifada remained predominantly nonviolent for several years. Israeli security forces faced the nerve-racking task of policing an occupied country where, as often as not, the stonethrowers were not guerrillas but schoolgirls.

The uprising was not enough to win Palestinian independence, but it led to important changes. For Palestinians, it meant political mobilization more thorough than any yet seen in Arab lands. For Israel's economy, which had profited from the occupation by $1 billion a year, the uprising turned that profit into loss. Like the Lebanese invasion, the uprising prompted some Israelis to refuse military service. It also affected Israel's election of November 1988, which produced another stalemate between Likud and Labor and another National Unity government, headed by Yitzhak Shamir.

The uprising profoundly affected international relations. In November 1988, the Palestine National Council (the Palestinians' parliament in exile, an agency of the PLO) reacted symbolically to the uprising by declaring an independent Palestinian state in the West Bank and Gaza. In December 1988, Yasir Arafat, addressing the United Nations in Geneva, condemned terrorism and called on Israel to join in peace talks. In a startling turnaround, the 1988 U.S. State Department Report on Human Rights accused Israel of human rights violations, noting that the first year of the uprising had left 366 Palestinians dead and over 20,000 wounded or injured by the Israeli Defense Forces and that thousands of Arabs had been held in administrative detention without trial. The United States, accepting that the PLO had renounced terrorism and recognized Israel's right to exist, also agreed to negotiations with the PLO. By then, large sectors of U.S. Jewish—and Israeli—opinion were prepared to support this move, even if the Shamir government was not.

The Likud-Labor coalition government broke down over this issue in 1990. Labor failed to form a new coalition, and the next government was a coalition of Likud and the far Right. By then, however, the world was changing in ways that made the apparent Likud consolidation deceptive. The end of the Cold War implicitly lessened Israel's strategic importance as a U.S. ally in the Middle East—a trend dramatized in the Gulf War when a number of Arab states became U.S. allies but Israel remained nonbelligerent. The migration of hundreds of thousands of Soviet Jews to Israel in some ways seemed likely to strengthen Israeli conservatives' resistance to compromise, first of all by altering the Arab-Israeli demographic balance. However, the Likud government had to face the costs of absorbing these immigrants, on top of other expenses, including its costly settlement building in the occupied territories. The attempt to secure additional U.S. assistance for immigrant absorption provoked an unprecedented decline in U.S.-Israeli relations, with the Bush administration refusing to grant the added assistance as long as the settlements continued.

The end of the Cold War and the Gulf War also affected the intifada in several major ways. Because the PLO supported Iraq in the conflict, Iraqi defeat wiped out a large part of the Palestinians' financial support. The Arab states of the Gulf, which had been major donors to the PLO, cut off their aid, so forcing the PLO to reduce its operations and the support it had given to many institutions in the occupied territories. In addition, the many Palestinian exiles who had worked in Kuwait or other Gulf states before the war suddenly became unwelcome; their loss of jobs and income reduced remittances to the occupied territories by three fourths. At the same time, the collapse of communism in eastern Europe deprived the Palestinians of a major source of foreign support and created a new political situation where Arab governments, which before had all given at least verbal support to the Palestinian cause, now began trying to reposition themselves in relation to the United States. These factors helped produce a decline of the intifada as it had been known and a deterioration of conditions in the territories. The arsenal of techniques that the Israelis developed for controlling the uprising—including mass arrests and deportations—furthered this trend and

Dr. Hanan Ashrawi, a leading Palestinian representative in the peace talks that began in Madrid in 1991. *No one has done more to humanize the image that the Palestinians present to the world than this literature professor from the Israeli-occupied West Bank.* *Ricki Rosen/SABA*

caused Palestinian resentment of the occupation to grow greater than ever.

At the same time, however, U.S. cooperation with a number of Arab states in the Gulf War provided the impetus for a new effort to settle the Arab-Israeli conflict through a series of conferences, starting at Madrid in October 1991. Because it had supported Iraq, the PLO was excluded from direct participation in the negotiations, and Palestinian representatives were chosen directly from the occupied territories, one of them being Dr. Hanan Ashrawi. She, in particular, succeeded in presenting the Palestinian cause in a humane, reasonable way that compared favorably both with the PLO leadership and with Likud militancy.

With the appropriateness of Likud policy challenged both by the need to negotiate and the costs of absorbing Soviet immigrants while continuing to build settlements in the occupied territories, Israel's 1992 election produced the biggest upset since that of 1977. Many Israelis blamed the Greater Israel idea for the mounting Palestinian violence. Support for Likud among Israelis of Afro-Asian origin weakened because of a feeling that Arab-Israeli peace would improve economic conditions. Russian immigrants, whom analysts had expected to support Likud out of anti-socialist bias, voted for Labor to punish Likud for not providing them with housing and jobs. Fast becoming Israel's largest ethnic subgroup, the secular-minded Russians also threatened the religious parties' power. The result was a defeat for Likud and a new coalition led by the Labor party with Yitzhak Rabin as prime minister.

Labor's return to power produced major consequences. Rabin did not stop settlement in the territories, but he did stop building new settlements, while continuing work on existing ones. This change sufficed to regain for Rabin the U.S. financial support for immigrant absorption that had been denied to Shamir. Rabin had long supported relinquishing part of the occupied territories, while retaining points of strategic significance. The negotiations begun at Madrid had made so little progress, however, that the Palestinians had begun to oppose both them and the West Bank leaders who participated in them.

Violence mounted, both in the territories and inside Israel, a major factor being the growth of the militant Islamic movements, Hamas and Islamic Jihad, both backed financially by Muslims abroad. Rabin responded in December 1992 by trying to expel 415 suspected activists into Lebanon, which refused to accept them, and by closing the territories in March 1993. The closure made it impossible for most of the 120,000 Palestinians who had worked inside Israel to get to their jobs and practically denied Palestinians access to their cultural and economic center in East Jerusalem, which Israelis class as Israeli territory. For Palestinians, the closure meant further economic disruption and the breakdown of law and order. For Israelis, it demonstrated both Rabin's commitment to security and the possibility of separating Israel from the territories. On the far Right, advocates of the settlements threatened violent resistance if the government withdrew from the West Bank and Gaza, but their attempts to rally political support drew little response.

Rabin had argued that agreement with the Palestinians was the key to peace with the Arab states, and in 1993 events moved dramatically in that direction. The Israelis' major incentive for new initiatives was to strengthen the secular nationalists of the PLO, as opposed to Islamic activists like Hamas, who opposed negotiation. After months of negotiation, the PLO recognized Israel's right to exist and renounced violence; Israel reciprocated by recognizing the PLO as the Palestinians' representative. This exchange opened the way for Israeli Prime Minister Yitzhak Rabin and PLO Chairman Yasir Arafat to meet at the White House in Washington in September 1993 for the conclusion of a historic Israeli-PLO peace accord. It provides for a five-year period of limited Palestinian autonomy, starting in the Gaza Strip and the West Bank town of Jericho. The agreement calls for withdrawal of Israeli security forces, Palestinian responsibility for municipal administration and police, Israeli protection for remaining Israeli settlers, joint Israeli-Palestinian cooperation for economic development in the Gaza Strip and West Bank, and further negotiations within three years for a permanent agreement.

The 1993 accord marks the most promising change in international relations since the end of the Cold War; yet much stands between it and real peace between Arabs and Israelis. The accord has to be ratified. Israel and the PLO have to succeed in defusing radical opposition to it. Adding the new PLO agreement to its treaty with Egypt, Israel still has to make peace with its other Arab neighbors, Syria, Lebanon, and Jordan (an agreement laying the bases for further negotiations with Jordan was concluded immediately after the accord with the PLO). Negotiations for a permanent peace between Israel and the Palestinians must solve difficult problems sidestepped in the 1993 accord, especially the status of East Jerusalem, the Old City, which both sides claim. Ultimately most challenging is the fact that what nationalist movements like the PLO have historically sought is not administrative autonomy but the full independence and sovereignty of the nation-state.

After a breakthrough as astonishing as the Rabin-Arafat handshake at the White House in 1993, however, creative solutions might be found for even these problems. Some analysts have long argued that the real solution to the Arab-Israeli conflict is not land but economic development. Probably nothing could do more than Arab-Israeli peace to enable the Middle East to participate more fully in the resurgence of the major Asian centers of civilization.

India: Development Amid Underdevelopment

To leave the Middle East and look toward South and East Asia requires expanding the scale of analysis to accommodate the world's most populous nations. India is the second most populous, with 883 million of the world's 5.4 billion people in 1992, surpassed only by the People's Republic of China, with 1.2 billion. Both countries are historical centers of empire, with strong governmental traditions.

Both have changed greatly since 1945. Yet the two also differ sharply. India is the world's largest democracy, shaped without revolution. Its dominant Hindu tradition has shown a marked capacity to absorb new ideas. China is the largest communist state, created by revolution. Its historically dominant Confucian tradition strongly resisted assimilation of alien ideas. India's democracy, coexisting with the Hindu caste system and tremendous linguistic and religious diversities, tolerates inequalities that China does not. But India has developed remarkably in some ways, with less loss of life than in communist China. Recent strains have moved India away from democracy, while China has begun to liberalize economically, though not to weaken its political authoritarianism. Less egalitarian than China, India combines traits of both development and underdevelopment. An examination of India's history during the premierships of Jawaharlal Nehru (1947–1964), his daughter Indira Gandhi (1966–1977, 1980–1984), her son Rajiv Gandhi (1984–1991), and his successors will throw light on this paradoxical record.

India Under Nehru

The evolutionary character of Indian nationalism (see Chapters 4 and 10) found expression in the Congress party's character as mostly a coalition of elites: merchants, professionals, and landowners. To gain influence at the grassroots, members used traditional relationships based on caste, clientage, or kinship to mobilize support. With partial exceptions—chiefly Mahatma Gandhi's attempts to improve Untouchables' and women's status—the party accommodated, rather than transformed, traditional social relations. Yet economic development formed a major goal, particularly for Nehru and other left-wing reformist socialists. The key question was whether the party could combine development with its accommodative approach to political mobilization.

In the way of the accommodative approach stood huge obstacles to social integration, even after the 1947 partition had created a separate Muslim state, Pakistan, with territories in both west and east (Bengal). Some 10 million people had fled, suffering a million fatalities, in trying to get to the "right" side of the partition lines. Separatist violence also occurred among the religious and linguistic minorities, such as the Sikhs of the Punjab and the speakers of Dravidian languages in the south. Not all the 570 princely states wanted to accept the control of the nation in which their territories lay. India used force to establish control over some and fought Pakistan over Kashmir, which was partitioned. Finally, socioeconomic inequalities, reinforced by caste, remained stark. The average Indian was one of the most ill-fed, disease-ridden people on earth, with a life expectancy of only thirty-two years. The population had reached 360 million by 1950 and was increasing by 5 or 6 million a year, more than offsetting gains in food production.

With Nehru (1889–1964) as prime minister, India began organizing its national life. It had some political assets few newly independent nations could match: a respected parliament; a political party with a national organization and quality leadership; and professional, nonpoliticized military and civil services. Over half the articles of the 1950 constitution came from the 1935 Government of India Act, a familiar source. Federalism helped accommodate India's social complexity through power sharing between central and state governments. The constitution also proclaimed equality and abolished untouchability—on paper. Memories of religious conflict strengthened initial consensus in favor of secularism and social democracy. Compared to Pakistan's military politics, India's enduring, though imperfect, democracy shows how much more it inherited from pre-1947 state-building efforts in the subcontinent.

Nehru retained power for life. One weakness of India's democracy was, in fact, the

Congress party's preponderance and the personalization of leadership within it, from Mahatma Gandhi on. Most other parties were not national but represented linguistic or religious minorities. Nehru also acted as foreign minister, building an international reputation as an advocate of nonalignment. Along with India's size, especially as compared to its South Asian neighbors, nonalignment helped India emerge from dependency much more than most Third World countries could.

The Nehru government tackled India's developmental problems with a mixture of reformist socialism, Gandhian idealization of village society, and tolerance for private enterprise. World War II had stimulated industrialization. At least after the disastrous Bengal famine of 1943, the British had also pushed agricultural development. Nehru attempted to build on this base through centralized planning and state control of major industry. He introduced five-year plans for 1951–1956, 1956–1961, and 1961–1966. Benefiting from foreign aid, the plans produced modest results.

In agriculture, land reform eliminated some abuses, such as large-scale absentee landlordism. Landowners wielded enough influence that only part of the land was distributed, and the reform did little for the landless quarter of India's rural households. But the reform made another third of them into "bullock capitalists," so called after their draft animals; with 2.5 to 15 acres each, these small farmers held over half of India's farmland by 1972. The government also promoted technical modernization of agriculture and mobilized villagers politically to participate in development through over 200,000 elected local councils (*panchayats*). Community Development and Rural Extension Programs helped villagers reclaim land, dig wells, and obtain fertilizers or improved seed.

The later 1960s brought major gains in food production thanks to a strategy known as the Green Revolution, requiring improved seed, irrigation, and heavy use of chemical fertilizer. The strategy was costly; it was vulnerable to increases in the cost of petroleum, needed to make fertilizer; and inadequate water supplies excluded use of the new seed in many places. The Green Revolution thus accentuated rural inequality, setting up divergent trends in the politicization of "bullock capitalists," who could afford the new techniques, and poor peasants, who could not. From the 1970s on, the government faced serious political problems for this reason.

The Nehru years saw notable gains in industry, too. In the 1960s, import substitution neared completion, thanks to high protectionism. The push for self-sufficiency, even where India could not produce efficiently, proved costly, yet—like nonalignment—helped reduce dependency. Nehru's socialism shaped India's economy by making government a third economic "actor," along with labor and capital. The private sector included huge industrial empires but lacked autonomy, thanks to government regulation and the low prestige of entrepreneurship. To cite one indicator of uneven development, by 1966 India produced 7 million tons of steel but—too underdeveloped to use it—exported much of it to Japan. India's industrialization suffered from the Third World problem that only a small percentage of the populace had enough income to buy many industrial products. Yet in India, even that small percentage amounted to a market the size of France.

Major thrusts of social reform under Nehru included women's rights and education. The constitution gave women the vote. By the late 1950s almost half of the eligible women did vote. Laws on marriage and inheritance revolutionized women's social status—on paper. Some elite women took part in public life, but tokenism prevailed for both women and Dalits (former Untouchables). Most Indian women were too uneducated or isolated to take advantage of the laws. Indian women's hardships led to one of the highest rates of female suicide in the world. Inequities permeated education, too. Higher education expanded greatly under Nehru, especially in technical fields—a fact significant for India's economic future. Simultaneously, literacy rose, but no higher than 28 percent in 1961 for the whole population—and barely half that for women.

India Under Indira Gandhi

Nehru's death in 1964 opened a succession struggle between the right and left wings of the Congress party. The Left's leader, Indira Gandhi (no relation to Mahatma Gandhi) emerged in 1966 as the winner, partly because party leaders thought they could manage her. They were wrong.

Over the next three years, voter support for the Congress party, especially its right wing, eroded. But Mrs. Gandhi became a popular leader; and when Congress tried to "expel" her in 1969, she split the party. Most members followed her into the new Congress-R, or Requisition, party and the left-wing coalition that she built around it.

Prime Minister Gandhi faced serious challenges, both in development policy and in holding together such a complex country; yet development continued with some significant results. The fourth and fifth five-year plans (1969–1974, 1974–1979) produced important gains, although rising prices for oil and grain imports increased India's trade deficits. Land reform initiatives failed, but the Green Revolution brought production of food grains to 100 million tons in 1968–1969. By then, the average Indian's daily food consumption had passed 2,100 calories, and life expectancy had reached fifty-one years. The government invested increasingly in family-planning programs, although gains in life expectancy offset the program's impact on total population during the 1970s. Industry reached the point where, by 1975–1976, it produced half of India's exports. Mrs. Gandhi's increasingly socialist emphasis led to bank nationalizations and greater government controls over private business. An underground nuclear test in 1974 and the introduction of satellite television transmission later in the decade showed what India's scientists and engineers could do.

Mrs. Gandhi's political dominance grew through most of the 1970s. In the 1971 general election, her branch of the Congress party won two-thirds of the seats in the lower legislative house, while the Congress Opposition won only a handful. When Bangladesh broke away from Pakistan in 1971 to form a separate state, the crisis that followed also redounded to her credit. India supported the seceders and won the ensuing war with Pakistan. Pakistan's breakup into two nations increased India's regional dominance. The Sino-Soviet split and the long-standing India-Pakistan hostility also helped move Mrs. Gandhi's regime further to the left. By the early 1970s, Pakistan and the United States were cultivating China, while India and the Soviet Union had become allies.

Victory against Pakistan gave Mrs. Gandhi momentum to carry through more socializing measures, but economic stress created new challenges to her power from 1973 on. Students and workers demonstrated to protest inflation and party corruption. By 1975, a broad coalition of anti-Congress parties, the People's Front (Janata Morcha), had formed, and anti-government violence was occurring. Mrs. Gandhi soon found herself in court facing charges of campaign abuses.

She retaliated in June 1975 by arresting her leading opponents and declaring a state of emergency. She proclaimed a Twenty-Point Program, including social and economic promises significant for the rural poor. Some observers thought the emergency provided the strong rule needed to restrain corruption and slow inflation. But such benefits, felt temporarily in the cities, did not extend to the countryside.

India was suffering from domination not by a single party but by a single person, Mrs. Gandhi. Her son Sanjay (1947–1980) also emerged in this period as a powerful figure and her presumed successor. He was largely responsible for the abuse of the population policy that led, during the emergency, to the involuntary sterilization of millions of Indian men, mostly from lower castes. When Mrs. Gandhi terminated the emergency and called for general elections in 1977, India's 200 million voters showed what they thought of corruption and nepotism by ending thirty years of Congress party rule and giving a parliamentary majority to the Janata opposition.

Under Prime Minister Morarji Desai, the Janata government (1977–1980) proved but an interlude, marked by economic destabilization and unrest. Mrs. Gandhi won re-election to parliament within a year. When the Janata government briefly jailed her, she became a martyr. The 1980 general election gave her party, now known as Congress-I (for Indira), a two-thirds majority in the lower house and swept her back into office as prime minister.

During her second premiership (1980–1984), India's combination of problems and achievements became more paradoxical than ever. Although the population had doubled since 1947 to more than 700 million, India achieved self-sufficiency in food grains in 1978. It was a precarious achievement. Aside from whether Indian production could keep up with population growth, this was the self-sufficiency of limited demand. Poverty still doomed one-third of the population to chronic hunger, and agricultural modernization depended on strategies beyond the means of most rural Indians. Moreover, exploitation of the land could not intensify forever without causing environmental degradation. After tripling between 1965 and 1985, India's grain harvest did level out. By then, the geographic unevenness of agricultural development had raised political tensions, too. The Punjab, where wheat production had tripled in the 1960s, happened to be the center of the Sikhs, a discontented religious minority (2 percent of the population).

Achievements in industry and technology presented a similar paradox. Partly because of its educational elitism, India in the 1980s was home to the world's third-largest scientific community and to half the world's illiterates. India sent up its first communications satellite with an Indian-made launch vehicle in 1980 and opened its first microelectronics plant to produce silicon chips in 1984. Enthusiasts predicted that India might become a colossus of industry and technology, but critics worried about government controls on the economy. From 1960 to 1980, the public sector share of GDP had risen from 10 to 21 percent, a growth bound to depress future productivity.

Politically, Mrs. Gandhi faced severe tests. Increasingly, Indians demanded political power and better lives. Women and Dalits campaigned more militantly against their worsening lots. The world learned with horror that many Indian women mysteriously die in kitchen fires, freeing their husbands to remarry and gain a new dowry. (South Asia is the only major world region where men's life expectancy normally exceeds women's.) Prosperity emboldened "bullock capitalists," who belonged to the "backward classes" (lower castes), to demand better access for their children to schools and to occupations historically monopolized by higher castes. Tensions in outlying provinces raised fears of secessions like that of Bangladesh. In 1983, the government was severely criticized for its handling of Muslim-Hindu violence in the state of Assam—the worst communal violence since 1947. In June 1984, facing a Sikh autonomy movement in the Punjab, the government sent troops into the main Sikh temple at Amritsar.

Having described her father as "a saint" lacking "the necessary ruthlessness" for politics, Mrs. Gandhi tried to show that she was tough. Nehru had coached his ministers in democratic norms and insisted on nonpolitical professionalism among officials. Throwing such caution to the winds, she risked politicizing the army by using it to police or administer strife-torn regions. She politicized the civil service by demanding personal loyalty, openly disdained parliament, crowded out rivals from her own Congress-I party, and bribed opposition leaders to desert their parties. In opposition-controlled states, she declared "president's rule" so that she could replace elected state officials with rule from New Delhi. Challenged by her people's mounting political demands, Mrs. Gandhi did much to undermine India's democracy, until Sikh assassins felled her in October 1984, a few months after she had sent troops into the Sikhs' Golden Temple at Amritsar.

India's Democracy in Danger

The dynastic theme in South Asian politics reasserted itself as her son, Rajiv Gandhi, succeeded her. He attracted initial support by showing understanding of the need for power sharing and consultation. In 1985, he concluded an agreement with moderate Sikhs, one of several cases where he conciliated groups his mother had antagonized. A figure with whom India's technocratic and managerial elites could identify, he represented a growing sentiment that the state's economic role had become a source of inefficiency, rather than a key to development. With time, however, many Indians decided that he had betrayed these hopes. The middle class thought economic liberalization had not gone far enough. Peasants resented unfulfilled pledges to end corruption in the villages. Indeed, political corruption seemed to reach right to the top: accusations that Gandhi had taken huge bribes from a Swedish arms firm led to his defeat in the 1989 elections. Two years later, while campaigning to make a comeback, he encountered his mother's fate—assassination—at the hands of militant Tamils, who dominate the southern state of Tamil Nadu and also live as a minority in Sri Lanka, where Indian intervention in a civil war between Tamil separatists and the dominant Sinhalese had caused much bitterness.

With the Nehru dynasty at an end, the Congress party government of Prime Minister P. V. Narasimha Rao (1991–) has faced mounting challenges, partly as a result of India's ongoing economic development. Annual growth in GDP, having averaged 3.6 percent from 1965 to 1980, accelerated to 5.3 percent between 1980 and 1990. The results were felt widely enough that the urban middle class grew to over 100 million people by 1990. During the 1980s, food consumption grew at a rate almost twice that of population growth, and production of consumer goods grew even faster. India's financial metropolis, Bombay, became a boom town where—many Indians thought—differences of caste and religion no longer mattered: only ability did. The India of spinning wheels and hand looms was fast fading away. The government and many of the two-hundred-odd state enterprises were near default, however. Prime Minister Narasimha Rao responded in 1991 by redirecting economic policy toward privatization, greater freedom of enterprise from bureaucratic interference, and openness to foreign investment.

Segments of the population that stood to benefit hailed the change, but India's economic inequity and cultural complexity multiplied the grievances of those whose prospects were less sure. India's democratic institutions and the Congress party had been in decline since Indira Gandhi's abuse of them. Political corruption remained a major issue, and commitment to the secularist synthesis that state and party represented was wearing thin. In the 1990s, the government faced new challenges not only among minorities and in outlying provinces but also among the Hindu majority. In the northwest, separatist revolt continued among the Muslims of Kashmir, a territory that had been divided between India and Pakistan and over which they had fought two wars. In the northeast, insurgency movements among the indigenous peoples of Assam targeted that state's often foreign-controlled tea plantations. All over the country, migrants from backward zones had crowded into places of greater economic opportunity, especially the cities, bringing people of different cultures and religions together in new ways. Indian Muslims' migration to work in Middle Eastern oil-exporting states, and returning migrants' visible prosperity, had heightened jealousy of the country's 100 million Muslims. Hindu backlash against changes that so often called attention to minorities was perhaps inevitable. What resulted took the form of religious activism of the type then typical around the world.

The political party that expressed this phenomenon was the Bharatiya Janata (Indian People's) party (BJP, founded 1982), but it was only one of a group of movements of different types, the oldest being a Hindu revivalist movement, the National Volunteer Corps (founded 1925). These movements appeal both to many newly prosperous Hindus and to those who feel left behind by the changes occurring around them. The movements feed off the belief that every concession made to non-Hindus for the sake of maintaining India's cohesion amounts to discrimination against the Hindu majority. A salient feature of Hindu militancy has been to highlight a single strand from Hinduism, a religion with many different forms, by emphasizing devotion to Rama, who was originally the hero of the epic *Ramayana* but is regarded in some parts of India as a divinity. Devotees' belief that Rama was born in the town of Ayodhya, on a site where Muslim conquerors later built a mosque, focused militant energies on demands to demolish this mosque—a violation of the constitution—and replace it with a temple to Rama. When militants destroyed the mosque in December 1992, a wave of violence swept India, causing thousands of deaths. Soon after, even Bombay—India's combined New York and Hollywood—endured both an anti-Muslim pogrom, which a local militant group, Shiva's Army (Shiv Sena), fomented with police complicity, and a series of mysterious blasts in the financial district.

Those—mostly in the elites—who still cared about pluralism and democracy had cause for anxiety. In parliament, the Congress party lacked a majority and depended on support, where secularism was concerned, from both the Left and the regional parties uncomfortable with the BJP. It had not yet become a truly national party, but electoral support for it was growing. The BJP's politics were ill suited to serve many Hindus' needs. Its vision of a Hindu nation meant less to most Indians than loyalties of region, caste, or language. Long on chauvinistic ideas about foreign policy and the revision of schoolbooks to reveal Hindu greatness, the party's high-caste leaders showed less concern about most Indians' depressed condition. States where non-BJP politicians from backward castes had gained power and kept policy focused on social and economic needs had experienced fewer cases of communal violence.

Perhaps, as some Indian analysts hoped, the BJP would prove a self-limiting threat. If so, the country would still need more effective leadership than the Narasimha Rao government was providing. In the 1990s, the manifold tensions within the country seemed to prove anew two of the major lessons of Indian history: that Hinduism alone cannot hold India together, and that the nation's welfare requires improving the lot of the impoverished majority.

China Under the Communists

In number of people affected and depth of political, socioeconomic, and cultural change, China since 1945 has undergone perhaps the greatest revolution in history. To an exceptional degree, this revolution bears the mark of

Mao Zedong (Mao Tse-tung, 1893–1976), but his was never the only influence. In a sense, events since 1945 only continued the crisis touched off at the beginning of this century by the collapse of China's two-thousand-year-old synthesis of imperial state and Confucian culture. The crisis was not easy to end.

In the long run, Mao proved more successful in making a revolution than in building a state. Since the Communist triumph in the civil war of 1946–1949, the People's Republic of China (PRC) has evolved through four phases: first, revolution under Communist rule (1949–1953); then the "socialist transformation" (1953–1961), which runs through the Great Leap Forward; next the "second revolution" (1962–1976), which climaxed in the Great Proletarian Cultural Revolution; and finally, the post-Mao period of economic liberalization and "market socialism." Through these phases, the PRC has gone far toward creating a mass-mobilizing authoritarian state that is economically egalitarian and development-oriented. The human costs have been high, however; and if the future of India's democracy is in doubt today, that of China's socialist regime is more so.

The First Phase of Communist Rule, 1949–1953

The second common front between Chiang Kai-shek's Guomindang (GMD) and the Chinese Communist party (CCP), formed in 1937, officially united China against the Japanese invaders. Inwardly, however, China remained divided by competition between its two nationalist movements. At war's end, the United States, hoping to see China emerge as a great power under the Nationalists, mediated an agreement between GMD and CCP. The agreement collapsed, and China lapsed into civil war in 1946. The GMD at first had many advantages, including larger forces (3 million fighters initially) and more foreign aid. But the Communists had a disciplined party, politically indoctrinated military forces (1 million strong), command of guerrilla tactics, and commitment to mobilize the peasantry. Defeated on the mainland in 1949, Chiang and his supporters retired to Taiwan, which remained under GMD rule as the Republic of China. The CCP, with a 1947 membership of 2.7 million, had won control of a nation of almost 600 million people.

The period from the proclamation of the People's Republic in 1949 to 1953 formed a consolidation phase. Mao believed that China must have a "democratic revolution" before its "socialist revolution." In this New Democracy phase, a common-front coalition including noncommunists would embody the "people's democratic dictatorship." Private property would survive at first. Already, however, the CCP was restructuring Chinese life. It developed a triple organizational base of party, army, and government. The party controlled policy making and had a hierarchical organization, from the Central Committee under Mao down to the village level. To mobilize the populace, the regime created mass organizations, often with scores of millions of members, for such groups as youth, women, and peasant members of agricultural cooperatives.

Economically, the Communists had to cope with the damage done by years of war. The first task was to restore infrastructure and control inflation. To bring about land reform, cadres (party workers) then went into the villages, arousing the villagers to stage public "trials" of the landlords and redistribute their land. The Communists repeatedly used such procedures to mobilize the people for specific objectives. Tens of millions of families acquired land for the first time and became swept up in acts of collective violence that cost millions of lives. In fact, private landownership did not last long; the organization of cooperatives began almost immediately, and full collectivization followed. Unlike Brazil or India, China restructured rural society as it modernized agriculture.

Social and cultural reform began with attacks on the family system idealized in Confucian thought. The marriage law of 1950 equalized marriage and property rights for men and women. Though still emphasizing the family unit in many ways, the Communists encouraged children to denounce their parents as enemies of the revolution, rather than obey them blindly. Amid the patriotic fervor of the Korean War (1951–1953), denunciation of neighbors and relatives crescendoed into a reign of terror. The Communists insisted that literature and art serve political ends. They also widely employed thought-reform techniques—called "brainwashing" in Chinese slang—originally used to discipline the party. Individuals were drawn into a group, exposed to Mao's thought, and excited with a sense of belonging. Intense psychological pressure then created a fear of rejection and humiliation that led them to submit to indoctrination, repudiating old ideas and loyalties for Mao's new orthodoxy.

Industrialization was a major economic goal. China's foreign economic relations had previously focused on Japan, Europe, and the United States. After 1950, the Communists turned toward the USSR and tried to industrialize along Soviet lines, with Soviet technical assistance and loans, which had to be repaid by exporting raw materials. The strategy worked poorly. China's economy was less developed in 1950 than the USSR's had been at the start of its first five-year plan in 1928, and China's resources differed greatly.

The Socialist Transformation, 1953–1961

Like Stalin, Mao concluded that the resources for industrialization must come from agriculture and that collectivization was the way to extract them. The CCP ordered the formation of agricultural producers' cooperatives in 1953 and full collectives in 1955. Farm families gave up their shares in the cooperatives and became wage laborers, though they retained small plots for their own use. By 1957, Chinese agriculture had been reorganized into about 800,000 collectives, averaging from 600 to 700 people each.

As collectivization progressed, the government began to nationalize business and industry. The first five-year plan (1953–1957) projected heavy industrialization, with much slower growth in agriculture and consumer goods. Under the plan, China's industrial growth became the fastest in Asia.

By 1956, however, collectivization had run into trouble because of peasant reluctance, lack of qualified cadres, and ideological disagreement within the Central Committee. Mao—ever the enthusiast for revolution—was unhappy at backtracking. Anxious to mobilize China's mostly Western-educated intellectuals and improve party discipline, he called for freer criticism of party and government under the classical phrase "Let a hundred flowers bloom."

At first intellectuals did not respond, but after repeated prompting, they loosed an unexpected torrent of criticism, which the government cut off in 1957 with an "anti-rightist" purge. Many intellectuals and cadres were subjected to "downward transfer" to the villages to end their "separation from the masses" and to boost agricultural output. The experience exposed important tensions among the leaders—over the value of "mental" versus "manual" labor and of "expertise" as opposed to "redness" (ideological commitment).

Mao's solution to agricultural productivity problems expressed his revolutionary romanticism. China must mobilize the people's energies for a Great Leap Forward in industry and agriculture. Industrialization must be decentralized and combined with agriculture by merging the collectives into communes of twenty-thousand people or more. Private plots and most other personal possessions would be taken away. Commune members would be organized into production brigades and teams that would work twenty-eight days a month. Children would be cared for in day nurseries, so that women could work full-time. Nothing better symbolized the Leap than the "battle for steel," the attempt to decentralize steel production in thousands of improvised furnaces scattered about the country.

Mao's approach to building communism proved too long on redness and too short on expertise. The people could not stand the pace. For peasants used to performing all the tasks on small holdings, labor in production brigades—performing a single task over a large, unfamiliar area—proved extremely difficult. The decentralization of industry also backfired. Most products of the "battle for steel" were unusable. Many furnaces dissolved in the rain. In fact, the Leap plunged China into depression. The Leap's impact on agriculture caused an estimated 16 to 30 million additional deaths (2 to 4 percent of the population) between 1958 and 1960. Eventually, the 24,000 large communes were subdivided into 74,000 smaller ones.

China's leaders disagreed as never before about how to combine social and economic development. Senior functionaries more practical-minded than Mao—notably Liu Shaoqi (Liu Shao-ch'i), first vice chairman of the Central Committee and Mao's chosen successor, and Deng Xiaoping (Teng Hsiao-p'ing), party general secretary—eased Mao out as chairman of the People's Republic, although he remained party chairman. Gradually, too, they shifted policy, restoring private peasant plots in 1962.

The Second Revolution, 1962-1976

Liu and Deng thought the time had come for organization and expertise, but Mao thought the party needed to change, either from within or by external force. He tried the first approach in 1962 with a Socialist Education Movement, under which many cadres, teachers, and students were transferred downward to work among the peasants. Mao blamed the disappointing results on sabotage by people like Liu.

By 1965, Mao was ready to try changing the party from without. He launched the Great Proletarian Cultural Revolution to destroy the "four olds" (ideology, thought, customs, and habits) and complete the "transition from socialism to communism." Mao used the media to attack supporters of Liu and Deng. He relied on the army, which had undergone intense indoctrination under Marshal Lin Biao (Lin Piao), defense minister since 1959. Mao also mobilized youth, forming groups of teenagers into Red Guards—at least 13 million of them by 1966. Mao charged them to "bomb the headquarters" of Liu and Deng. Armed with the little red books of quotations from Chairman Mao Zedong, the Red Guards bypassed the party and its Youth League to launch a reign of terror across the land. Probably because of Mao's age and infirmity, his wife, Jiang Qing (Chiang Ch'ing), rose to a controlling position in the arts, media, and education. Attacked as "capitalist roaders" (advocates of moving China onto a capitalist road to development), Liu and Deng were toppled, and Lin Biao became first vice chairman of the Central Committee and heir-apparent to Mao.

The Cultural Revolution created for young Chinese some of the excitement that the Long March of 1935 had given their elders. The youth of other countries also noticed: Chairman Mao's mobilization of young people to attack China's political and intellectual leaders helped inspire the global student activism of the late 1960s. In fact, the Red Guards included various interests: children of peasants, who felt they had been denied a fair chance for advancement; children of party functionaries, who sought to preserve their advantages; children of former landlords, who joined in attacking government offices in hopes of destroying records of their families' past. Soon, the Red

Guards were fighting each other as much as the "four olds." By 1967, even Mao thought it was time to use the army to restrain the Guards. As millions of students followed party cadres in "downward transfer" to the communes, the shock troops of the Cultural Revolution suffered the same fate as its enemies.

The Cultural Revolution continued into Mao's last years, producing immense disruption despite some positive gains. Higher education was in disorder for a decade. Purging "proletarian culture" of foreign and traditional Chinese influences, Jiang Qing persecuted many artists and writers. On the other hand, Mao's effort to close the urban-rural gap led to major improvements in public health. China trained 1.6 million paramedics, or "barefoot doctors," and over 3 million health workers between 1966 and the late 1970s. Remarkably, too, economic growth continued despite the turmoil. GNP in 1970 was 40 percent higher than in 1965.

By 1969, efforts were under way to rebuild the party. Policy changes also occurred, such as the normalization of relations with the United States in the 1970s. Deng Xiaoping re-emerged in 1973. But confusion lingered at the top. For example, Mao tried to ease out Marshal Lin Biao, whose status as heir-apparent contradicted the principle of party control of the military. According to the official account of what followed, Lin attempted a military coup in 1971 but failed and perished while trying to escape to the Soviet Union. A new purge followed to discredit Lin. Jiang Qing and her associates—later derided as the Gang of Four—tried to continue the Cultural Revolution. She also aimed to become her husband's political heir.

Economic Liberalization

Mao died in 1976, shortly after Zhou Enlai (Chou En-lai, PRC premier since 1949). In the succession struggle, an opposing coalition first toppled the Gang of Four. Then a shakeout followed among coalition members. The Cultural Revolution officially ended in 1977. By 1980–1981, party vice chairman Deng Xiaoping had become China's most important leader. Already in his late seventies, Deng had survived the Long March, opposed the Great Leap, and endured disgrace under the Cultural Revolution and the Gang of Four.

With long memories of his hectic past, Deng faced the tasks of institutionalizing the Communist regime so as to ensure an end to China's decades-long crisis of authority, charting a new course for economic development and restoring the party unity shattered by the Cultural Revolution. Deng set about his tasks with the practical-mindedness that had made Mao distrust him. In many ways, Deng seemed successful, especially to the outside world. Then, in the spring of 1989, the bloody outcome of student demonstrations in Beijing exposed deep contradictions among his policies.

Signs of a new era had appeared by 1980–1981, in the last phases of the power struggle that brought Deng to power. The Mao personality cult gave way to criticism of Mao, and the Gang of Four was tried on charges stemming from the Cultural Revolution. Jiang Qing's claim that she acted only on Mao's orders turned her case into a virtual trial of her late husband. Yet the Deng regime could not totally repudiate Mao. He had been both the Lenin and the Stalin of China's revolution: his "policy errors" of 1957–1976 might be repudiated, but an ideal image of him had to be saved to legitimate the regime. Henceforth, Deng and the party would interpret "Marxism–Leninism–Mao Zedong Thought" and restrain "leftist extremists."

Deng's key problem was the same one that faced reformers in other socialist countries in the 1980s. He masterminded economic reforms aimed at retaining the essential controls of a command economy while also allowing small private businesses to re-emerge and reopening

Map 17.4 South and East Asia, 1990s

China to foreign investment. To gain new technology, China expanded its foreign trade, especially with Japan. Dismantling the communes made the shift toward a market economy clearest in the countryside. To feed the people and raise capital for development, Deng offered peasants incentives, including the right to farm specific tracts of land under contract. Such stimuli, along with adoption of new technology, increased China's grain production by nearly half between 1976 and 1984. When most countries no longer could, the world's most populous nation still fed itself, increasing food supplies per person by one-third during the 1980s.

In China as in other socialist countries, however, economic liberalization raised expectations of political and cultural liberalization, which occurred only to a limited extent. For example, while dissidents still faced trouble, ordinary people could busy themselves with nonpolitical pursuits under Deng, as they could not under Mao. Deng rehabilitated mental labor, citing the need for scientists and technicians. The universities resumed operating, but China's secondary and university-level schools could still accommodate only a fourth of all applicants. Cultural life became freer. Even Confucianism, attacked under Mao, again enjoyed official interest.

Deng had seemed to favor democratization at times on his way to power, but anyone who thought he truly favored it was in for a shock. Deng might use market forces to boost production. As Marx wrote, society must pass through a capitalist stage before achieving socialism; China had skipped that stage and might need something of it. If Deng was a "capitalist roader" to that extent, however, his goals remained socialist. As he stated to party leaders in 1986: "Without leadership by the Communist Party and without socialism, there is no future for China. . . . Bourgeois liberalization means rejection of the Party's leadership; there would be nothing to unite our one billion people, and the Party itself would lose all power."[2]

During the 1980s, foreigners, and many Chinese, lost sight of this point. Economic and cultural change gave various social groups a sense of empowerment—peasants, business people, students, intellectuals. Deng had not restructured politics to give them channels for real participation, but he had also not restored the party's authority as wielded before the Cultural Revolution. Deng's lack of interest in ideology demoralized party members, many of whom had no expertise aside from "redness." With Deng telling the public—as part of economic liberalization—that "getting rich is glorious," officials and party functionaries began using their power to enrich themselves. Party and government sank into corruption and ineffectiveness. Startling results followed. For example, revenues fell as Chinese bent on getting rich ceased to pay taxes. A generational cleavage opened as the young lost interest in the party. The party became divided between "conservatives," authoritarians who opposed liberalization, and "liberals," some of whom preached a "new authoritarianism," arguing that China would develop faster with a

The student demonstrators' Goddess of Liberty under the gaze of Chairman Mao, Tienanmen Square, Beijing, 1989. *Political mobilization advanced beyond government control, until tanks and troops invaded the square on the night of June 3–4.* Wide World Photos

strongly centralized government like Taiwan's or South Korea's!

With the gap between economic liberalization and political decay as backdrop, the seventieth anniversary of the May Fourth Movement (see Chapter 10) set the stage for confrontation in the spring of 1989. The 1919 movement had marked a milestone in the politicization of young Chinese and in the rise of nationalism. The regime made plans for commemoration, omitting one of the original slogans: "democracy." Students made their own plans, resulting in protracted mass demonstrations in Beijing's Tienanmen Square and similar demonstrations elsewhere, supported by many nonstudents. Faced with student hunger-strikers who said they would rather die than live without democracy, the government hesitated. On May 20, however, troops were called into Beijing, and martial law was declared. Zhao Ziyang, leading "liberal" and Deng's heir-apparent, was stripped of power, and "conservative" premier Li Peng presided over what followed. The troops opened fire on June 4, massacring hundreds, perhaps thousands. Thousands were arrested; some were summarily executed.

Four years later, Communist control had collapsed almost everywhere else, but China still seemed to be advancing along the path it had followed before Tienanmen. In 1993, the aged Deng sought to ensure continuity by having his concept of the "socialist market economy" written into the constitution and giving top leadership positions to a number of men from a slightly younger generation, most notably Jiang Zemin, who became state president (he already controlled the party and the military). The Chinese were looking forward to regaining control of Hong Kong in 1997, where the British were making belated efforts to introduce democratic reforms before surrendering power.

China's economy was booming more than ever, with growth above 12 percent for 1992. Government control of the economy had slipped so much that only 7 percent of industrial production would be subject to central planning in 1993. Foreign investment was flooding into the country, especially its port cities: $6.6 billion in the first three quarters of 1992 alone. Foreign firms had liked China as a low-cost, high-quality production site in the 1980s; rising incomes now made them see it also as the world's largest consumer market. Stated in terms of purchasing power (the purchasing power parity, or PPP, method of calculation, as opposed to the commonly used exchange-rate method), China's 1991 GDP amounted to $1.66 trillion and ranked third in the world. The PPP figures were controversial (see Chapter 20). Moreover, GDP per person, at $1450 by the PPP method (or only $370 by the exchange-rate method), showed that most Chinese were far from rich. Rapid growth in fact was creating new inequalities between the port cities and the rural interior. Yet if current growth rates continued by 2010 China would regain the status it enjoyed for most of its pre-modern history as the world's largest economy.

How long could such growth continue where political and economic systems developed on such divergent paths? Comparing India and China highlights this question. China under either Mao or Deng was less free than India and could not match Indian science and technology. Yet China developed further and faster and did a better job of equalizing access to the benefits of growth, thus excelling India in combining development and social justice in a poor country. Politically, while India's governments abused democratic institutions and endangered their future, Deng undermined China's socialist institutions even more. Sweeping away the wreckage of those institutions will be the task of the generation who had their baptism of fire at Tienanmen Square in 1989.

Japan: Re-emergence and Pre-eminence

When U.S. atomic bombs fell on Japan in 1945, its phenomenal rise seemed all undone. The war left 2 million Japanese dead, 40 percent of Japan's urban areas destroyed, industry smashed, and agriculture in decline. But Japan rose again to become a major world power. The postwar U.S. occupation played a part in this revival, but the Japanese people's qualities were more important. Japan stood third in the world in GNP by 1970. By 1985, Japan had outstripped the Soviet Union and stood second in GNP only to the United States. In a country 10 percent smaller than California, having no significant natural resources and a population of 124 million in 1992, such an achievement justifiably excited global admiration.

Reconstruction Under U.S. Occupation

Japan's reconstruction began under the nominally Allied, but in fact U.S., occupation. Many changes made then produced lasting benefits, partly because they coincided with a new Japanese consensus for reconstruction, democratization, and demilitarization. Political reform began with the prosecution of top war leaders. The emperor renounced the divine status that had been attributed to him, and a new constitution went into effect in 1947. It transferred sovereignty from the emperor to the people, renounced war "forever," transformed the government into a British-style cabinet system, and guaranteed fundamental human rights. Further reforms mandated equality for women, extended the number of years of compulsory schooling, and tried to make higher education less elitist.

Like the U.S. New Deal, the occupation gave many Japanese a bigger stake in Japan's postwar order. One important reform was to break up the zaibatsu firms that dominated the prewar economy. Some old company names survived, but business and industry assumed new organizational forms. The occupation authorities brought labor legislation up to international standards and encouraged unionization, regarding it as part of democracy.

In the countryside, land reform virtually eliminated absentee landlords and reduced the proportion of tenant-operated farms to under 10 percent. The average farm size was henceforth only 2.5 acres. Yet the reform created a more egalitarian rural society, and technical improvements eventually made the small farms highly efficient. Together with land reform, tax reform gave Japan one of the world's most equitable income distributions—an important factor in assuring the demand needed to stimulate economic recovery.

After the occupation ended in 1952, Japan continued to depend on the United States for aid and defense. A bilateral security pact provided for U.S. bases in Japan, and most Japanese remained opposed to large-scale rearmament. Low military spending became a factor in Japan's economic growth.

The Emergence of an Economic Superpower

As Japan entered its postoccupation era, economic change became—even more clearly than in other countries—the driving force in its development. Prime Minister Shigeru Yoshida (1946–1947, 1948–1954) adopted policies designed to promote Japan's rebuilding. Later known as the Yoshida doctrine, these policies guided Japan's development for the next forty years. Key points included limiting military spending, following the U.S. lead on issues of security and international relations, favoring producers rather than consumers, and promoting exports. With ambitious targets set under these policies, Japan's real economic growth, net of inflation, averaged nearly 10 percent a year until the 1970s. At the time, only Israel was growing faster, by a fraction of a point.

The global growth of the first postwar quarter-century probably benefited Japan more than it did any other country. Growth became a virtual religion. The Japanese took great pride in international recognitions of Japan's re-emergence, from the 1964 Tokyo Olympics to the Nobel prizes won by Japanese scientists. By the end of the 1960s, Japan had begun to run trade surpluses, and its productive capacity had become almost as great as all the rest of Asia's.

Dependent on imports for most foodstuffs and for almost all energy and raw materials, Japan suffered several shocks in the 1970s but responded well to them. Tensions had mounted in U.S.-Japanese relations since the late 1950s, as Japanese exports to the United States grew in volume while U.S. exporters had difficulty gaining access to Japanese markets. Facing serious balance-of-payments problems, partly because of the Vietnam War, the United States placed a 10 percent surcharge on imports in 1971 and suspended the convertibility of the dollar into gold. A U.S. embargo on soybean exports in 1973 further antagonized the Japanese, who depend on soybeans for protein. The United States also surprised the Japanese by announcing that President Nixon would visit the People's Republic of China. The Japanese had been led to expect consultation before such a reversal of U.S. policy toward China.

The oil shock that followed the Arab-Israeli war of October 1973 hit Japan harder. Dependent on imported petroleum for nearly three-fourths of its energy, Japan was more threatened than any other country by the oil crisis. The short-term effects of higher oil prices included negative trade balances and inflation. Average GNP growth fell to 5 percent per year for the 1970s.

The Japanese responded creatively to this new phase in their economic development. They searched for alternative sources of energy. They began to move away from heavy industries like steel and shipbuilding, which had eclipsed the light industries of the early postwar years, toward a new generation of "knowledge industries." These required less energy, less labor, and fewer raw materials and took advantage of Japan's high levels of skill and technology. Another reason for the change was that other East Asian economies, such as Taiwan and South Korea, were developing heavy industry and resented Japanese domination of their markets. The most important goal, however, was to move beyond importing and refining technologies developed elsewhere and to pioneer new technologies that Japan could export to earn royalties. Quadrupling the funding of research and development, Japan became a technology exporter by 1980. In all, Japan probably adjusted more successfully than any other developed country to the new era of scarcity. Evidencing its successful adaptation, Japan's trade surplus mounted annually from $5 billion in 1981 to $86 billion in 1986, of which over $50 billion came from trade with the United States.

Under international pressure to readjust such imbalances, Japan revalued the yen in 1985. Revaluation challenged Japan as had the shocks of the 1970s, but its responses opened a new growth period. The yen more than doubled against the U.S. dollar, from 240 in 1985 nearly to 100 in 1993, raising the price of Japanese goods in foreign markets but cheapening imports for Japan. By making foreign assets cheaper, the high yen made it easier for Japanese to invest abroad. They invested $21.7 billion in the United States in 1988 alone. For Japan's economic policy, revaluation implied a growth strategy aimed more at domestic rather than at foreign markets. Austere domestic living standards needed to rise. More foreign consumer goods needed to be allowed into the country—although the intricacies of Japan's market structures made that easier to say than

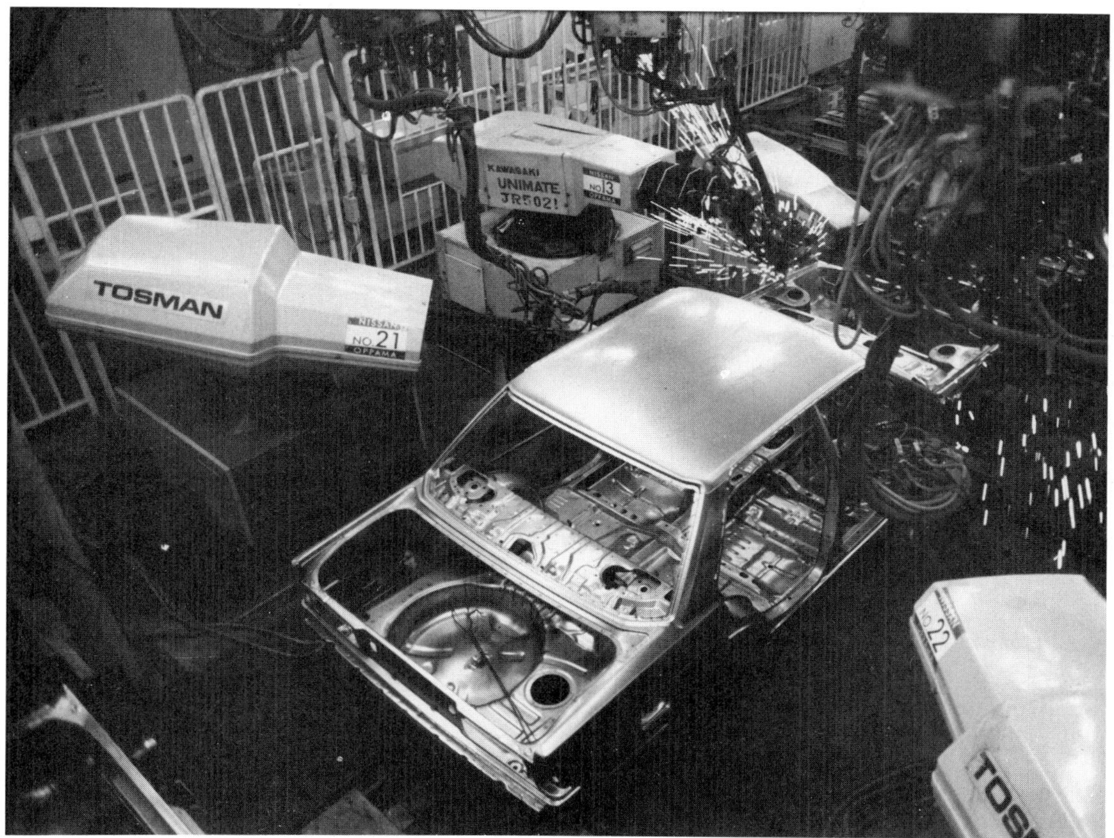

Robots on a Japanese auto assembly line. *In the 1980s, some plants were so highly automated that workers only tended the robots. However, over-emphasis on automation has been found to increase costs more than productivity.* *© Richard Kalvar/Magnum Photos*

do. With Japanese wages as high as U.S. or West German ones, revaluation required shifting some types of production to foreign labor markets. Japan, too, began to experience the industrial "hollowing out" that U.S. industry went through with the shift from heavy industry to services. Japanese firms, however, cut costs so rigorously that Japan's exports began to increase in value again within a few years.

The late 1980s turned into a booming "bubble economy," which burst when the Tokyo stock market collapsed late in 1989, losing nearly $2 trillion (almost half of total market value) by 1993. Scandals linking major brokerage houses and the Ministry of Finance to Japan's crime families (*yakuza*) worsened matters by shaking investor confidence. Land prices plunged. The crisis spread to Japan's banks, requiring the Bank of Japan to provide unaccustomed support for troubled institutions. Manufacturers faced plunging sales and urgent need to cut costs before they could profit from new investments made during the "bubble" years. Despite the tradition of lifetime employment in major corporations, layoffs and plant closings began. After over two decades of growth, even auto production fell after 1989, and Japanese auto sales in the U.S. market contracted in 1992.

These events ended a boom and helped provoke major political change but did not signify any major economic decline. Japan's economy was still the world's second largest. Japan's worldwide trade surplus reached $133 billion in 1992, of which its surplus with the United States accounted for $45 billion. The trillions of dollars invested during the boom in research and new plants would ensure long-term advantage. Japan's problems were those of a dominant economy in a tightly integrated world. More than any other, Japan's had become a global economy, dependent worldwide for raw materials and markets. In ruins fifty years before, Japan had outperformed other highly developed economies.

Major Factors in Japan's Success

How had Japan done this? Many factors played a part. Land reform and income equalization during the occupation helped by stimulating agriculture and raising internal demand. So did limiting defense spending to 1 percent of GNP—a rate that still gives Japan the third-largest defense budget in the world. But some of the most important factors lie in the realm of business and government-business relations.

Commercial organization made a major difference in Japan's growth. In place of the old zaibatsu firms, each a complex of interests dominating a single industry and controlled by a holding company, large-scale organizations known as *keiretsu,* or "business groups," emerged by the 1960s. These grouped firms in different industries around a large bank or industrial firm. In the absence of anti-trust laws, the business groups could be extremely large. A key part of the group, the general trading company, conducted the group's foreign trade. Bigger than most U.S. export-import firms, the trading companies benefited from economies of scale and maintained large expert staffs. Because the business groups tended to raise capital internally rather than by selling shares, they were freer than U.S. firms to reinvest profits instead of paying high dividends. Having interests in different industries also made it easier for the business groups to shift investment from fields where growth had slowed to others with better prospects.

Japanese labor relations, too, contributed to business success. Unions were typically company unions, less militant than other industrial countries' industrywide unions. Japanese corporations were less top-heavy than U.S. firms, less likely to segregate managers from workers, and keener on team spirit and corporate loyalty, qualities deep-rooted in Japanese society.

Government has played a major role in Japan's economic development, though government has been smaller than in other industrial countries. In 1980, government officials formed only 1.7 percent of Japan's working population, against 2.3 percent in the United States. Government revenues were also low; 22 percent of GNP in Japan in 1977; against 30 percent in the United States and 38 percent in West Germany. Partly because spending for defense and welfare was low, more of Japan's budget went for purposes that strengthened the economy, such as public works.

Fiscal conservatism enabled the government to maintain balanced budgets through 1966. After that, expanded welfare spending without offsetting tax increases produced an internal debt of $425 billion by 1983, roughly 60 percent as much debt per capita as in the United States at the time. An important consequence of conservative government finance was that Japan maintained a high savings rate: from 25 to 33 percent of GNP through the mid-1970s and still 19 percent in 1988 (in 1990, savings per household averaged $71,016 in

Japan, compared to a U.S. rate of $28,125). Inducements to save included both low welfare spending and—until the tax reform of 1988—tax exemption for interest on postal savings accounts.

Special government agencies, particularly the Ministry of International Trade and Industry (MITI), played a key role in economic development. MITI provides leadership in targeting specific industries for development and in phasing out others where Japan has lost its competitive edge. MITI collaborates with the large business groups, preserving the principle of competition by bringing different firms together to work on any given project.

A distinctive approach to research and development undergirds MITI-industry collaboration. Japan's funding for scientific research began to reach the level of other developed countries' only in the late 1960s. This was especially true of basic research, which tackles new problems for the advancement of science without immediate regard to practical applications or profits. Basic research does more to advance science and industry in the long run, but applied research can produce huge economic benefits. Japan historically emphasized applied research more than basic. Recently, reacting to criticism of its export surpluses and its history of exploiting others' discoveries, Japan has placed new emphasis on basic research. The founding of several cities for scientific research, starting with Tsukuba Science City, symbolized this thrust. Some key features of Japanese research did not change, however. Military priorities dominated U.S. research, but Japan's remained consumer-oriented, and the private sector provided more of the research funding—81 percent in 1985.

By the late 1980s, Japan's success had created new challenges for organizations like MITI. MITI's capacity to lead had eroded, once the largest Japanese corporations had research budgets larger than its, and the corporations had become less willing to share their research findings. MITI responded by concentrating more on basic research.

Japan's industry-government collaboration will continue to face challenges, but the comparative historical significance of this relationship remains clear. Japan's collaborative pattern differed radically from communist economies, which eliminated competition for profits. It differed too from common Western ideas of free enterprise in that government helped chart the course of growth, rather than leaving the economy to itself or intervening only to regulate it. The results spoke loudly in Japan's favor.

Japanese Society and Economic Growth

Japan's postwar resurgence depended above all on its people, the country's one abundant resource. After the war, the Japanese faced daunting problems—food shortages, runaway inflation, unemployment, repatriation of 6 million Japanese from overseas, and a baby boom (1946–1948). But the same qualities that underlay Japan's earlier rise helped open an era of rapid growth.

With growth, certain social traits persisted. These included strong family ties and a sense of group solidarity recalling that of village life. Many Japanese assumed their commitment to their employers was for life, although in fact only a third of Japan's workers worked in large firms that guaranteed career-long employment. Tradition also affected the lives of Japanese women, despite legal equality. Until recently, most who worked when young withdrew into family life after marriage. An emphasis on education was another tradition that helped ensure Japan a highly qualified labor force. Examination pressures produced occasional student violence against teachers or even suicide; yet these remained less common than other types of youth-related problems familiar in the United States. Finally, while

Masako Owada, Harvard-educated Foreign Ministry official, became crownprincess upon her marriage to Prince Naruhito, 1993. *Images of her in modern and traditional dress symbolize debate about women's roles in Japan. Kaku Kurita/Gamma Waison (left); Noboru Hashimoto/SYGMA (right)*

other Asian societies were losing their traditional arts and crafts, the Japanese retained many of theirs—rich sources of distinctive design and workmanship.

In time, kimonos and scroll paintings became affordable luxuries for people among whom, by the 1960s, 80 to 90 percent saw themselves as middle class. Japanese men aspired to the image of the white-collar "salary man" employed by a large corporation. Population growth fell to about 1 percent per year by the 1970s, before declining to 0.3 percent by 1992. Low growth created a labor shortage. Despite an ethnocentric reluctance to import workers, several hundred thousand foreign workers had reportedly entered Japan by the early 1990s. Rising wages and scarce workers provided reasons to emphasize the knowledge industries, automation, and robotics.

Meanwhile, urbanization progressed. The rural population fell to 8 percent of the total in 1989, down from 50 percent in the 1940s. Many rural Japanese combined work in town with agriculture. As the cities grew, the largest grew fastest. The population of greater Tokyo reached 8 million in the 1960s and 17 million by 1984, when it was the world's largest city.

The reduction in Japan's birthrate occurred voluntarily, reflecting the shift in attitudes that has accompanied urbanization and the rise of the middle class the world over. People came to prefer having only a few children so that family resources could be concentrated on their education and placement in society. With this shift in attitude, the proportion of students receiving higher education rose between 1965 and 1989 from 13 to 31 percent.

Rapid social change had its troublesome side effects. Severely crowded—half the population lived in 2 percent of the land area—Japanese remained poorly housed by European or U.S. standards. Yet housing costs were far higher in relation to income than in the United States or Europe. In the late 1980s, Japanese land prices were up to 75 times higher than U.S. prices. As in Third World supermetropolises, many workers spent as much as four hours a day commuting. Park lands and public facilities of all types were scarce, and industrial pollution was a familiar problem.

Urbanization and other factors took their toll on the extended family. By the 1980s, nuclear families (not including grandparents) accounted for 60 percent of Japan's 36 million households. But the need for family support remained strong, particularly because public spending on welfare was low. (At 1980 rates, deductions from workers' wages for income tax and social security added up to 32 percent of GNP in Japan, compared with 38 percent in the United States, 51 percent in West Germany, and 64 percent in Sweden.) Many workers had company health and retirement plans. National health insurance was instituted in 1961. The government expanded benefits by deficit financing, however. Demographic trends threatened the stability of the benefit program because the percentage of the population aged sixty-five or over was growing faster than in the United States, Britain, France, or West Germany.

Rapid change and the increasing isolation of the individual produced displays of alienation especially among the young. Leftist university students attracted international attention in 1960 with their demonstrations—in which many other Japanese joined—against ratification of the new U.S.-Japanese security treaty. In 1968, student violence flared again, primarily directed against the poorly financed universities. A radical fringe group, the Japanese Red Army, remained active in international terrorism into the 1970s.

Today, prosperity plays a key role in creating social change and sometimes tension. Today's salary men work less compulsively, display less organizational loyalty, and demand more leisure than did their fathers. Perhaps that helps explain why the U.S. products that succeed best in Japan seem to be those of mass consumerism—fast food, casual clothing, films, theme parks. Boom conditions created much new wealth but also a new readiness to criticize inequity. This change had important implications for gender relations. Partly because of high housing costs, 51 percent of married women held jobs by 1987. The labor shortage contributed to this trend, as did changing educational levels and attitudes. With these changes came reports of young women who refused to marry, rather than conform to most men's traditional expectations of their wives, and of older women who divorced their husbands rather than face postretirement life together—an uncertain prospect after decades when the husband was almost never at home. Old values will surely help shape Japan's answers to future challenges, yet rapid change is also creating a Japanese version of the postindustrial society.

Political Consensus: Rise and Decline

For almost forty years, Japan's economic growth sustained an extraordinary political consensus. Post-war Japan produced many political movements, but by the mid-1950s, these had sorted out into what has been called a one-and-a-half party system. From its coalescence in 1955 until the election of July 1993, the Liberal Democratic party (LDP) dominated every government. The next-largest party, the Japan Socialist party (JSP) polled fewer votes, and Japan did not have a leftist prime minister again after 1948.

Japan is a constitutional monarchy with a government headed by a prime minister. Within the British-style outlines of this system, distinctively Japanese realities prevail. We have already noted the policy framework that became known as the Yoshida doctrine: an export-oriented industrial policy favorable to producers rather than consumers and low military spending under the U.S. security umbrella. What really ruled Japan was not so much the government as a combination of interests that Japanese called the "iron triangle." At one corner stood big business, which supported the LDP by giving money and mobilizing employee votes. At the second corner stood the LDP, which influenced business by awarding contracts or stalling legislation on topics that businessmen disliked, such as product liability. At the third corner stood the bureaucracy, which regulated business. Bureaucratic interference in the economy was very extensive, but vaguely worded laws gave regulators discretion to do favors for firms that backed the LDP. Carefully controlled markets also helped to limit competition by foreign firms inside Japan and thus to support the widespread prosperity that gave most Japanese a stake in this system. Leadership and decision making came not so much from the government as from within the triangle, and the prime ministers tended to produce much less individual impact than did heads of other powerful governments.

In time the LDP yielded to the temptations of power, and eventually it had to pay for its misdeeds. In April 1989, during the "bubble economy," a scandal over political contributions toppled Prime Minister Noboru Takeshita. In the July 1989 elections, the LDP met its first electoral defeat, as the JSP, then led by Takako Doi, the first woman to head a Japanese political party, won control of the upper house of parliament. Over the next two years, the JSP challenge faded, and the LDP remained in power. The scandals continued, however, climaxing in 1992–1993 with revelations that Shin Kanemaru, head of patronage for the largest LDP faction, had taken money from a firm with mob ties and had over $50 million stashed in his home and office.

Ordinary Japanese were stunned to learn that corruption had reached such extremes. The Kanemaru revelations provoked an outcry, followed by splits in the LDP. In the election of July 1993, the LDP met defeat and, although it retained the most parliamentary seats of any single party, lost control of the government for the first time since 1955. The new government, formed under Prime Minister Morihiro Hosokawa, was a coalition of conservatives and socialists, who had joined forces to defeat the LDP. How long such a coalition could hold onto power was unclear, but its advent looked like a turning point. A younger generation had come to power. Women assumed three cabinet posts, more than ever before, and Takako Doi became speaker of the lower house of parliament. Policy debate became more open and more contentious. Most important, members of the new cabinet wanted to change every aspect of the old LDP system—the Yoshida doctrine and the "iron triangle." From one faction or another came proposals to apologize to other Asian countries for World War II, review constitutional limits on Japan's joining collective security arrangements, deregulate the economy, open Japan's rice market, and end corporate political donations. Many of Japan's internationally oriented business interests supported these proposals.

Economically, Japan has adapted to the new age of global interdependence more fully than any other country has, but the quality of its political leadership has so far hindered Japan's adjustment to this new age outside the realm of economic competition. In this paradox may lie the greatest challenge confronting Japan's new leaders.

Conclusion: India, China, Turkey, and Japan Compared

In the post-1945 world of tightening integration, accelerating change, and ongoing mass mobilization, Asian societies made the Third World's strongest bids for independence and reassertion. Their success depended on much the same factors that governed the success of prewar independence struggles: mastering new ideas, especially in science and technology; reaching consensus about national identity and the organization of political life; responding to demands for mass participation (in terms of both politics and social justice); and formulating economic growth strategies to meet the people's needs and better the country's place in the world. As we conclude our survey of major Asian countries, we can substantiate these observations by comparing the two most populous nations, India and China, and two others that have better combined democracy and development, Turkey and Japan.

India has achieved many gains but still has not overcome its structural problems of poverty and inequality. The loss of life accompanying the 1947 partition into Muslim and Hindu states convinced many Indians that the state should be secular—a principle that today's Hindu militants seem bent on changing. A long pre-1947 history of strong state institutions helped give India's government the institutional "hardness" that many Third World states lack, even though the Nehru-Gandhi dynasty, especially under Indira Gandhi, recalled older authoritarian models at odds with democracy. Mrs. Gandhi's authoritarianism resembled other Third World examples, as she strove to control the mass politicization caused by socioeconomic change and the widening social inequality created by the Green Revolution. India's size and dominance in South Asia relieved it from many consequences of its developmental shortcomings and many problems of external dependency. As its acute contrasts of illiteracy and technological expertise show, India today belongs partly to both North and South. Yet India can never gain a place among the world's most developed nations without resolving its social inequities and politically accommodating its ethnic and religious diversity.

From 1949 to 1989, China appeared to have replaced dependency and chaos with strong government under an authoritarian mass-mobilizing regime. China could not rival Japan, or even India, in science and technology. Yet at the grassroots level, the PRC made real improvements for its 1.2 billion citizens, even prior to the economic liberalization under Deng Xiaoping. The demonstrations and reprisals of 1989 again showed that the commitment to social and economic welfare was not matched by concern for democratic politics. Economic liberalization had awakened demands for political change that will outlive

Deng, especially given the resumption of rapid economic development in the 1990s. The fall of communism throughout eastern Europe underscores the futility of trying to maximize economic growth without accommodating rising expectations for political change. If China resolves this problem and continues its growth, it will become the world's largest national economy and one of the most important nations of the twenty-first century.

Smaller in scale but more successful to date in balancing economic and political development, Turkey has realized the ideal of multiparty democracy more fully than any other Islamic country and has also made the transition to export-oriented growth. Its combination of agricultural self-sufficiency, an export-oriented industrial economy, and surplus water resources now gives Turkey advantages that no other country in its region enjoys. In terms of GDP per person, Turkey has outstripped both India and China in economic development. Moreover, the collapse of Soviet rule in Turkic Central Asia implies new possibilities for Turkey as a regional power. Its combination of democracy and development ranks Turkey as the Islamic Middle East's leading country and as one of the more successful anywhere in Asia.

Unmatched in the world, Japan's performance since 1945 recapitulates its prewar rise, except that militarism has given way to peace, democracy, and pursuit of external dominance by economic rather than military means. With an exceptionally well-educated and industrious populace, Japan seems to have excelled all other nations in formulating effective economic policy. Japan's progress from postwar reconstruction, through the heavy-industry and "knowledge industry" phases, to the current high-yen phase, illustrates this point. Japan's mastery of science and technology—together with the consumer-oriented rather than military thrust of research and development—has made a vital difference in this economic resurgence. Though not without its implied vulnerabilities, as the fall of the LDP illustrates, Japan's economic leadership remains a reality of global significance.

Since 1975, U.S. trade across the Pacific has exceeded U.S. trade across the Atlantic in value. Not only Japan but also the "four little dragons"—Taiwan, South Korea, Hong Kong, and Singapore—have played important parts in this change (see Chapter 20). The People's Republic of China seems to be on the verge of doing likewise on a vast scale. Japan has fulfilled Asian dreams of regaining a powerful place in the world, and other Asian economies may soon do so as well, as the oil producers briefly did in the 1970s. The "Pacific rim" has become as important in world affairs as the "Atlantic rim" was for the preceding five hundred years. Few changes tell more about how integration patterns have changed and tightened in today's interdependent world.

Notes

1. Ze'ev Schiff and Ehud Ya'ari, *Israel's Lebanon War* (New York: Simon and Schuster, 1984), pp. 250–285.
2. Quoted in the *Wall Street Journal,* June 16, 1989, p. A4.

Suggestions for Further Reading

Middle East and North Africa

Arjomand, Said. *The Turban for the Crown: The Islamic Revolution in Iran* (1988).

Bakhash, Shaul. *The Reign of the Ayatollahs: Iran and the Islamic Revolution*. Rev. ed. (1990).

Hansen, Bent. *The Political Economy of Poverty, Equity, and Growth: Egypt and Turkey* (1991).

Horowitz, Dan, and Moshe Lissak. *Trouble in Utopia: The Overburdened Polity of Israel* (1989).

Hourani, Albert. *A History of the Arab Peoples* (1991).

Hunter, F. Robert. *The Palestinian Uprising: A War by Other Means*. Rev. ed. (1993).

Hunter, Shireen T. *Iran After Khomeini* (1992).

Keddie, Nikki. *Roots of Revolution: An Interpretive History of Modern Iran* (1981).

Lustick, Ian. *For the Land and the Lord: Jewish Fundamentalism in Israel* (1988).

The Middle East. 7th ed. (1991; published by Congressional Quarterly Inc.).

Middle East International (London).

Middle East Report (New York).

Richards, Alan, and John Waterbury. *A Political Economy of the Middle East: State, Class, and Economic Development* (1990).

Rivlin, Paul. *The Israeli Economy* (1992).

al-Shaykh, Hanan. *Women of Sand and Myrrh*. Translated by Catherine Cobham (1989).

Smith, Charles D. *Palestine and the Arab-Israeli Conflict*. 2d ed. (1992).

Yapp, M. E. *The Near East Since the First World War* (1991).

India

Brass, Paul R. *The Politics of India Since Independence*. Vol. 4, pt. 1, of *The New Cambridge History of India* (1990).

Frankel, Francine R. *India's Political Economy, 1847–1977* (1977).

Lal, Deepak. *The Hindu Equilibrium*. Vol. I of *Cultural Stability and Economic Stagnation: India, c. 1500 BC–AD 1980* (1988).

Rudolph, Lloyd I., and Suzanne H. Rudolph. *In Pursuit of Lakshmi: The Political Economy of the Indian State* (1987).

Wolpert, Stanley. *A New History of India*. 3d ed. (1989).

China

Fairbank, John K., Edwin O. Reischauer, and Albert M. Craig. *East Asia: Tradition and Transformation*. Rev. ed. (1989).

Far East Economic Review (Hong Kong).

Meisner, Maurice. *Mao's China and After: A History of the People's Republic* (1986).

Schram, Stuart. *The Thought of Mao Tse-tung* (1989).

Tisdell, Clement. *Economic Development in the Context of China* (1993).

Japan

Hane, Mikiso. *Modern Japan: A Historical Survey*. 2d ed. (1992).

Iwao, Sumiko, *The Japanese Woman: Traditional Image and Changing Reality* (1993).

Hofheinz, Roy, Jr., and Kent Calder. *The Eastasia Edge* (1982).

Ito, Takatoshi. *The Japanese Economy* (1992).

Look Japan (Tokyo).

Reischauer, Edwin O. *Japan: The Story of a Nation*. 3d ed. (1981).

PART 6

The World Today

CHAPTER 18

Urbanization North and South: A Contemporary Photographic Essay

In Chapter 2 we visited a European capital and a colonial village, symbols of the two poles of human experience in the European-dominated world of 1914. Now we shall make similar visits to places that symbolize the diversity of the world's experience today.

Dramatic change in the political map of the world since 1914 has replaced the European empires with over 180 supposedly sovereign nations. Economically, however, the world is still divided into two parts. The highly developed countries that own 90 percent of the world's industry, situated mainly in the Northern hemisphere (Canada, the United States, Europe, parts of the former Soviet Union, Japan, Australia, and New Zealand), earn three-quarters of the world's income, though they are inhabited by only a quarter of the world's population. The rest of the world, mainly in the Southern hemisphere, is made up of still-developing countries. To reflect today's realities, this photographic essay will visit representative environments of both North and South.

Both these environments are giant cities of the kind sometimes called supermetropolises or megalopolises. The modern processes of urbanization that had already given Europe cities like Berlin and North America cities like Chicago have since swept the world. By the year 2000, twenty-one of the world's cities will have populations of over 10 million, eighteen of them in the poor countries of the South. Cairo vividly illustrates the problems of these megalopolises, as this chapter will reveal. Because the United States exerts vast influence over both the developed and the developing world, however, we shall visit a U.S. city first.

We have chosen Los Angeles as a symbol of the most recent accomplishments and problems of the developed world.

Los Angeles: Modern Megalopolis

Like Berlin on the eve of World War I, Los Angeles—"LA"—has been transfigured by explosive growth in less than two generations. Because of the city's importance as a staging point for the Pacific campaigns of World War II, federal government expeditures in LA increased fiftyfold between 1940 and 1945. In the postwar years, this impetus made Los Angeles, like Berlin, a center of innovation—producer of the new technologies of the knowledge explosion.

Like Berlin's, Los Angeles' society is made of layers sharply differentiated by wealth. Because of its sprawling geography (Map 18.1) shaped by the automobile, rich and poor meet far less often than did their counterparts in 1914 Berlin.

Although in many respects Berlin embodied the Western love of change, it also harked back to the traditions of the Prussian past. But Los Angeles, critics have charged, has been so obsessed with the present and the future that it has regarded the past with contempt. Idealizing progress through technological innovation, LA until recently demolished most of its few historic buildings. The city's architecture reflects continual and uncontrolled improvisation, partly because LA lacks Berlin's effective city government. The Los Angeles city charter, dating from the beginning of the century, was deliberately designed to keep all authority weak, in keeping with a basic American mistrust of government power. Tasks assumed by the municipality in Berlin were left to the individual in LA. Only recently, for example, has Los Angeles outlawed the individual backyard incinerators in which its citizens burned their rubbish as they pleased, regardless of pollution.

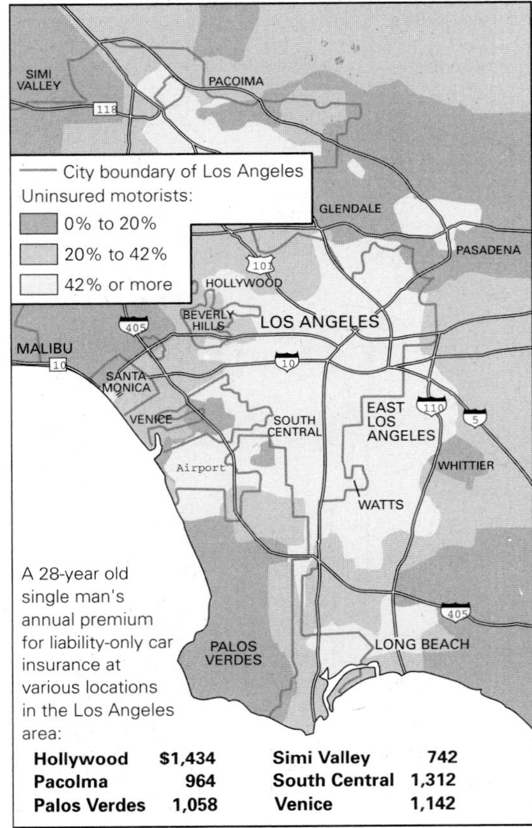

Map 18.1 LA: Same City, Different Worlds. *There is a higher percentage of uninsured motorists in inner-city neighborhoods like South Central because incomes there are lower, while insurance premiums are higher. Source: Insurance Busters; Statistical Analysis Bureau, California Department of Insurance. Used with permission.*

The political ideal of LA is radically different from the socialism of most 1914 Berliners. Mass mobilization in LA has produced a political outlook that stresses the rights of the individual over those of the community. This idealization of individualism, some critics contend, compounds the psychological stresses of a population composed of uprooted strangers. A large number of cults invented by spiritual entrepreneurs prey on the loneliness of newcomers to LA.

Other observers consider the array of LA religious experiences a virtue—an illustration of the city's vibrant variety—rather than a drawback. Like Berlin in 1914, LA today has a controversial reputation. The restless, impermanent quality of its life seems exhilarating to some, disturbing to others. In the boom years of the 1950s and 1960s, LA came to symbolize the future to Americans. Its changing fortunes from the 1970s through the 1990s symbolize the crucial dilemmas of the developed world at the end of the twentieth century.

Technology and the LA Economy

In 1992, Los Angeles with a population of 11.9 million, was the seventh-largest metropolitan area in the world, surpassed only by Tokyo-Yokohama (the world's largest) and New York in the developed North and by Mexico City, São Paulo (Brazil), Shanghai, and Bombay in the developing South. Los Angeles is a creation of twentieth-century technology. It was no small achievement to build a supermetropolis in a sunny but otherwise inhospitable environment where the accessibility of beaches and mountains is counterbalanced by the near-absence of usable water. LA's prodigious growth between 1900 and 1940 (1,600 percent) would have been impossible without the construction of a 233-mile-long aqueduct, 53 miles of it in tunnel, to bring water from the mountains to the arid plain on which the city lies.

But it was the technology of the post-1945 knowledge explosion that made LA a megalopolis. The decades of Cold War boom transformed it from a remote provincial city into a center of the world economy. Jet aircraft shrank to a few hours the distance between the U.S. West Coast and the eastern power centers. In the years of bipolar confrontation, the armaments race flooded the Southern California aeronautical industry with orders. Filling the aerospace needs of the warfare state, from ten to twelve thousand firms—some with famous names, such as Hughes Aircraft, Litton Industries, and Ramo-Wooldridge—helped make LA the United States' second industrial center. LA also became the home of half of the Americans employed in the film and television industries.

A Society of Immigrants

As employment opportunities beckoned, newcomers from the Northeast and Midwest flocked to LA, overwhelming any feeble efforts to create an orderly plan for the development of the mushrooming region. Because of the dispersion of its population, critics derided Los Angeles as "a collection of suburbs in search of a city," lacking the central amenities (first-class orchestras, theaters, and museums, for example) typical of close-knit, long-established communities with elite traditions of culture. The massive invasion of newcomers, coinciding with the nationwide American flight to the suburbs, did little to change this situation. Angelenos (as LA's inhabitants are called) wanted to be their own landlords and chauffeurs. These preferences precluded the kind of high-density, vertical development characteristic of the older great cities of the Western world such as Berlin and New York. For a time in the 1960s when it was welcoming a thousand newcomers a day, Los Angeles had the highest growth rate of any city in the developed world. Ranchers and orange-growers of the region, watching land prices increase by a third in a year, sold off their holdings, which were instantly transformed into sprawling subdivisions of standardized houses. At one point, 260 acres of Southern California land were being "urbanized" every day, providing LA

A Los Angeles suburb in the 1990s. *Such limitless development was undertaken on the assumption that southern California's economic potential for growth was unbounded—an assumption some economists now question.* *© 1991 John Humble*

with the highest proportion of privately owned, single-family dwellings in the world.

During the boom years, LA confirmed its reputation as a new and distinctive kind of twentieth-century urban landscape. Stretching seventy miles from one end to the other, reaching into five counties, and including some eighty other municipalities around the central city, Greater Los Angeles had a population density only a quarter that of cities like New York, which had developed in the era of the pedestrian and the street railway. LA was the city that taught Americans how to live much of their life in their automobiles. Its most eye-catching constructions were not the ornamental buildings on which earlier cities had prided themselves but the arteries of transportation: the freeways. Until environmentalists got it

Rush hour on an LA freeway. *The stalled traffic reflects a paradox. LA was built to accommodate vehicles that allowed drivers freedom to go wherever they liked in high-speed privacy, unlike public transportation. The result of these individual choices when everyone is using the same route, however, is chaos. By 1980 the average speed on LA freeways had dropped to 37 miles per hour; it was projected to drop to 17 miles per hour by the end of the century.* *Earl Young/ Robert Harding Picture Library*

changed in 1965, the law required that these giant ribbons of concrete be built by "the most direct route." In the process, the homes of approximately a quarter-million people were destroyed—a striking testimony to the relative value of mobility and permanence in LA.

The choice of the name *freeway* was not accidental. The central value of the LA lifestyle was individual satisfaction through material consumption of the products of technology, with a minimum of social organization and control. The freeway was conceived as the high road to this goal, an ideal toward which mass societies of the developed world had been steadily moving in the twentieth century.

Angelenos might travel fifty or sixty miles to work over the freeway, shaving or dictating letters or listening to an inspirational tape as they drove. They moved at the level of the rooftops, unaware of communities of fellow Angelenos whose conditions and backgrounds were utterly different from their own. Neither necessity nor any ethic inherent in the nature of LA compelled an interest in these communities. Many freeway travelers had other concerns. Often they were absorbed in white-collar, high-technology jobs requiring expertise of which they were proud—for example, perfecting an inertial guidance system for jet fighters. Or they might work for the RAND Corporation, the Air Force–financed think tank that employed physical and social scientists to prepare Cold War strategies. From this exacting postindustrial work, these Angelenos returned home to a subdivision full of people quite like themselves. In the evening they watched standardized mass entertainment on television, including crime thrillers—most of them made in LA and even set there, so that the obligatory car chase hurtled through LA's characteristic landscape. On weekends Angelenos entertained friends at cookouts at the backyard barbecue pit or attached their boat or skis to the car for a trip to the beach or the mountains.

Critics from an older tradition often satirized this pleasant lifestyle, along with LA's propensity for religious cults and oddly shaped restaurants. Though the economic center of the United States was rapidly moving westward toward them, many Angelenos reacted to such criticism with the defensiveness of Middle Americans faced with East Coast snobbery. A great majority of white, non-Hispanic Angelenos *were* transplanted Midwesterners, drawn by the double lure of perpetual sunshine and opportunity.

Politics: Home Base of Nixon and Reagan

The fact that so many found opportunity in LA explains much about the region's politics. White middle-class Angelenos tended to be fervent believers in individualism and "free enterprise," attributing their own success to these systems of social and economic organization. They were suspicious of government, especially the federal government—even though in the 1960s a third of LA's employment was sustained directly by federal dollars and much more of it indirectly. Most Angelenos did not see any analogies between the defense contracts that gave them jobs and the government's welfare subsidies to the poor. They supported politicians who set the American agenda by championing a stronger military and repudiating the domestic generosity of the New Deal guarantor state. Two such politicians became president of the United States. Richard Nixon grew up in the suburbs of Los Angeles. Ronald Reagan, whose roots were in small-town Illinois, took the earliest steps of his political career in the Hollywood movie industry before becoming a conservative spokesman as the host of television programs sponsored by General Electric.

The careers of these self-made men were larger-than-life versions of typical LA success stories. The Los Angeles of the boom years during the 1950s and 1960s marked the fulfillment of the American dream. Since the foundation of their country, Americans had been pushing ever westward in search of more privacy, more elbow room, more success, and more money. By 1900 the frontier was closed—the Pacific had been reached. Yet in their suburban houses and automobiles, Angelenos of the boom years could still believe that despite the interdependent organization of postindustrial society, they were as independent as nineteenth-century frontiersmen.

Watts, 1965

Black Angelenos had not shared in this fulfillment of the American dream. On a hot summer night in August 1965, white police officers arrested a black motorist in the heart of Watts, the vast ghetto that stretches south from the center of LA. The resulting confrontation eventually escalated into a six-day riot, quelled only by sending in nearly 14,000 troops. The death toll rose to 34, most of them poor and black, an indication that the rioters were not as well armed as those who repressed them. The 1,000

Watts riots, 1965. *Police officers and national guardsmen prepare to search suspected looters for weapons and stolen merchandise during the Watts riots of 1965.* Los Angeles Times *photo*

injured included 136 firemen hurt while battling some 600 separate blazes, sometimes under sniper attack. Two hundred buildings were totally destroyed, for a total property loss of over $40 million.

The riots of 1965 provoked a short-lived interest in sociological analysis of Watts, until then just another of those anonymous communities beside the freeways. LA's blacks lived in bungalows on palm-decorated streets, but Watts was as much a ghetto as New York's South Bronx. Studies found that LA had a higher degree of racial segregation than any other American city except Chicago and Cleveland. The twenty-one-year-old driver whose arrest had touched off the riot was typical of thousands of young people in Watts. Born in Oklahoma, a high school dropout, he worked part-time at a gas station. (He had held only one full-time job, for five months at the age of nineteen.) Though many blacks, like whites, had migrated to LA in search of opportunities, they were frequently disappointed. In Watts, half the children came from broken homes, and half the population lived on public assistance. In a city with the highest per capita automobile ownership in the world, relatively few people in Watts owned cars, though the nearest jobs (like the nearest hospital) were ten miles away.

The riots of 1965 marked a turning point in the history of LA by drawing attention to some consequences of uneven growth. Similarly, as the 1970s forced Americans to recognize that the world had only a finite supply of natural resources, the energy-intensive, freewheeling LA lifestyle lost some of its appeal. Californians consumed an average of 533 gallons of gas annually (compared with 349 for New Yorkers). LA was the most extreme example of a way of life in which Americans, 6 percent of the world's population, consumed a third of its resources. Many people in the 1970s began to see LA as a warning rather than as a promise for the future.

Frontier of the Developing South in the 1980s

The 1980s brought startling demographic changes to LA. The city became the United States' open door to the developing South, not only Latin America but the entire Pacific rim of Asian nations. Today, it is the place that provides the most striking evidence of the impact of tightening global integration on U.S. life.

In 1984, Los Angeles, the heart of a sprawling supermetropolis, became the second-largest U.S. city. Demographers calculated that the gain of 150,000 people, which enabled LA to exceed Chicago's population, would not have occurred without the massive Hispanic and Asian influx. In fact, without these new arrivals the city proper would have lost 200,000 people, as white Angelenos, like their middle-class counterparts elsewhere, continued their flight to the suburbs. The 1970s saw an increase of one-third in the population of Orange County, a bastion of political conservatism southeast of LA, where average household income was $43,000, compared with $15,000 in the city and $19,000 in the suburbs as a whole. Court-enforced busing of children, intended to diminish racial segregation in the city's schools, actually had the opposite effect as white Angelenos moved beyond its reach to suburban school districts.

Whites represented only 21 percent of the city's population in the early 1980s, down from 54 percent in the early 1960s. Newcomers of Hispanic and Asian origin took their places and spread out into Los Angeles County as well. In 1960, only one in nine county residents was Hispanic, and Asians represented less than 1 percent of the total. By the 1980s the county was nearly one-third Hispanic and 10 percent Asian. White Angelenos were a minority like everyone else. Since blacks constituted almost 20 percent of the population, LA could be called the first Third World city in the United States, because a majority of its population was of African, Asian, or Latin American descent.

By eliminating quotas based on country of origin, President Johnson's Great Society legislation of 1965 reopened to immigrants the gates that Americans had closed in the 1920s. The new Angelenos came from everywhere in Asia and Latin America. The Iranian contingent grew from 20,000 in 1970 to 200,000 in 1983, the Korean from 9,000 to 150,000. These and many other newcomers, in the tradition of nineteenth-century immigrants of European stock, were fleeing political disorder or misrule in their homelands. Angelenos from El Salvador, fewer than 2,000 in 1970, by the mid-1980s numbered up to 350,000. Their eagerness to pay smugglers as much as $4,000 to move their families across the border to live ten to a room in an LA apartment was understandable. In El Salvador, a country plagued by landlessness, rapid population growth, and civil war, inflation ranged up to 30 percent, unemployment up to 50 percent, and wages for those fortunate enough to find work were a sixth or a tenth of wages paid for menial jobs in Southern California.

Other sizable LA ethnic communities included Armenians, Filipinos, and Arab Americans, each numbering over 100,000. At Hollywood High School, which in the 1950s enrolled the children of movie stars, 70 percent

Bilingual culture, LA. *A mural painted by street artists on a wall in a Hispanic neighborhood proclaims a demand for Hispanic power. The legend in Spanish reads, "Bilingual and bicultural education is a right, not a privilege."* *© Carl Ganter/Contact Press Photos*

of the students by the 1980s were immigrants who spoke 32 different languages. Only two-thirds of them had some command of English.

Mexicans made up the largest contingent of newcomers. Ironically, they could be said to be resettling their own country, for LA had been part of Mexico until seized by the U.S. army in 1846. Four-fifths of LA's Hispanic population, over 2 million people, are of Mexican origin. Their numbers reflect the fact that LA lies not far north of the world's longest and most easily traversed border between the developed North and the developing South. In 1983, with Mexican unemployment officially estimated at 36 percent—and in reality perhaps higher—U.S. authorities arrested a half-million immigrants who had illegally crossed the sixty-six-mile-long border between San Diego County and Mexico. Most illegal immigrants, of course, were not apprehended. Their arrival put considerable strain on LA's social services. Ten percent of the babies born in Los Angeles County were the children of illegal aliens, mostly Mexican. In 1984, almost two-thirds of the kindergartners in the Los Angeles school district were Spanish-speakers, many with little command of English.

Like education, employment for this tide of newcomers represents a critical problem. Like the rest of the United States, LA has shifted rapidly into the postindustrial age. Despite its image as a city of unusual occupations like moviemaking, LA at the end of World War II had a substantial industrial base, including nine automobile plants turning out 650,000 cars annually. By the 1980s, LA's share of smokestack America had waned, leaving only one automobile plant struggling to stay open. Even the aerospace industry slumped, with the rest of the U.S. economy, in the 1970s.

LA is the principal broker of the United States' rapidly growing Pacific trade, which today outstrips trans-Atlantic trade. This growing business may compensate for the decline of industry. Yet even LA's remarkable assortment of some hundred colleges and universities may not be enough to train unskilled immigrants for postindustrial occupations. Angelenos were increasingly unwilling to spend for such community purposes as education. Proposition 13, passed by the voters in 1978 in the first of many revolts by middle-class and corporate taxpayers nationwide, so limited California tax rates that it was no longer possible to continue the generous policy of providing free higher education for all.

Indeed, Angelenos recently seem to have lost some of the exuberant confidence in unlimited growth that has characterized their twentieth-century history. In the 1980s they showed a new willingness to recognize that constraints might have to be imposed on urban sprawl, even at the cost of legislating limits to the hitherto sacred rights of property owners. Conservatives joined with environmentalists late in 1986, for example, in voting for a public referendum that cut in half the floor space permitted in new commercial buildings. Many suburbs imposed moratoriums on new apartment construction. Stiff new standards required industry to improve LA's air quality—the worst in the nation, with ozone levels three times higher than federal standards allow.

Even in affluent Orange County, where population increased tenfold since 1950, and where outer suburbs—in a trend visible everywhere in the postindustrial world—have come to rival old center cities in their concentration of high-rise offices and hotels, the outlook changed. In June 1988 the voters there rejected only by the narrowest of margins a legislative ban on any further private development if unaccompanied by corresponding investment in roads and the provision of public services. Critics charged that by proposing such bans the affluent were attempting for their own convenience to prevent the new generation of aspiring immigrants to LA from benefiting as they had from growth.

South Central, 1992

Whether growth would ever regain the pace of the boom years became increasingly doubtful as LA's economy was devastated by the recession of the 1990s. The region had already lost 200,000 jobs between 1978 and 1989. From mid-1990 to the end of 1992 an additional 800,000 were lost as the end of the Cold War reduced orders in the vital military and aerospace industries. California's unemployment rate rose from 5 to 10 percent, the highest among the industrial states. (Unemployment among minority youth ranged up to 50 percent.) Economic stagnation meant that fewer taxes could be collected and local governments had less money to spend on such essential services as schools: already in 1990 California had dropped to forty-eighth among the fifty states in expenditures per pupil.

It is against the background of economic decline and societal deterioration that the LA riots of April–May 1992—the worst American civil disorders of the twentieth century—must be understood. They began with an incident similar to the one that had triggered the Watts riots twenty-seven years earlier, though this

LA riots, 1992. *Neighborhood people loot a grocery at the corner of Vermont Avenue and Martin Luther King Boulevard in South Central Los Angeles during the riots of 1992.* © *1992 Gary Moss*

new eruption of violence in LA differed in several significant ways from its predecessor.

On the night of March 3, 1991, a group of LA police officers savagely beat and kicked an intoxicated black motorist, Rodney King, after stopping his speeding car. Unknown to them, a neighbor videotaped the entire incident. The tape, endlessly replayed first on local and later on national television, showed King being struck 61 times in 81 seconds. It was therefore widely expected, when four of the policemen were put on trial, that they would be convicted of brutality. Instead, the nearly all-white jury in the middle-class suburb to which the trial had been transferred brought in a verdict of acquittal in late April 1992.

When news of the verdict reached South Central, an impoverished inner-city neighborhood not far from Watts, it was greeted with an explosion of rage that lasted nearly a week and spread well beyond South Central. Night after night, Americans watched their television sets, transfixed by images of the skyline of their second-largest city lighted by the flames of hundreds of buildings burning out of control, or of Korean merchants, pistols in hand, defending their little convenience stores against mobs of rioters bent on setting them afire.

When it was all over, 58 people, including 27 blacks, 17 Hispanics, and 11 whites were dead, 2,300 were injured, almost 17,000 had been arrested for looting or arson, and $1 billion worth of property had been destroyed. As in 1965, though firemen were severely injured, none of the dead was a soldier or policeman: again, these were better armed than the rioters. But there were some striking and ominous differences between Watts 1965 and South Central. The 1992 rioters did not limit themselves to burning their own neighborhoods but ranged well into Hollywood. Fearful suburbanites mounted nightly guard, arms in hand, over their homes, dreading rumored attacks by the Crips and Bloods, LA's notorious drug-dealing ghetto gangs. Meanwhile, some white motorists who blundered into South Central were dragged from their vehicles and beaten as savagely as Rodney King had been.

After the Watts riots, a federal investigative commission chaired by Governor Otto Kerner of Illinois had warned that the lesson of those disorders was that the United States was on its way to becoming two separate but unequal nations—one black, one white. Analysis of what happened in South Central showed that this basic division of the 1960s had been blurred by the huge surge of Hispanic immigration, much of it illegal, into LA's inner city. Of those arrested in 1992 within the city limits, the 38 percent who were black were outnumbered by the 51 percent who were Hispanic, mainly recent arrivals.

In 1992, there were clearly still "two nations" in LA, one still mainly white, relatively affluent, and suburban, but the other composed not only of blacks but of Hispanics, two groups that compete for the dwindling number of low-skilled and low-paying jobs still to be found. (The unfortunate Koreans, many immigrants themselves, were resented and envied as exploiters of ghetto poverty and were caught between the two nations. The rioters demolished 90 percent of their little stores.)

In 1992, there was much less national soul-searching after a cataclysmic riot than there had been after Watts. President Bush and Democratic presidential candidate Bill Clinton briefly toured the ruins of South Central, but neither made any real commitment of federal help to rebuild them. In a time of recession, the government's deficit was too large, and tax revenues were too scarce, for such extravagances. The rebuilding of the devastated parts of LA was left largely to private initiative, which by mid-1993 had accomplished little. Although 60 percent of Hollywood's damaged buildings had been reconstructed, in South Central fewer than a third were being rebuilt. The nation's interest and sympathy had moved elsewhere even more swiftly than in 1965.

Yet the Los Angeles riots of 1992 are a reminder that the realities of the developing South—overpopulation, unemployment, poverty, dependency—that seem remote to most Americans are to be found right on their doorstep. Most of LA's recent immigrants have revived the dream of success of earlier immigrants who became middle-class Americans. Having escaped from places like rural El Salvador, some will doubtless eventually raise a family and make a success in business. Nevertheless, a thoughtful visitor to LA today must wonder how long and under what conditions the developed North can remain an island of plenty in a sea of poverty. In areas of LA where Asian and Hispanic immigrants have settled, the sights and sounds of other cultures suggest a supermetropolis of the developing South. One could almost be nineteen hundred miles away in Mexico City—or even in Cairo.

Cairo: The Urbanization of Poverty

The village was the representative environment in the colonial world of 1914, but the distinctive environment of the poor countries today is the megalopolis. From Mexico to

South Africa to the Philippines, social and economic pressures have pulled so many people to the cities that the world is nearing a point where a majority of its population will be urban. Descendants of many people who lived in the Egyptian village of Dinshawai in 1906 today live in Cairo. Their experiences have distinctively Egyptian facets but also other facets seen throughout the developing countries.

Cairo, a Megalopolis of the South

By Middle Eastern standards, Cairo is not an old city. It is barely over a thousand years old, although it has grown to incorporate earlier settlements. Only recently has Cairo become a supermetropolis. When the British occupied Egypt in 1882, Cairo's population was only about 400,000. With twentieth-century improvements in public health and the migration from the countryside, growth became rapid. By 1920, the city's population had reached 800,000; by 1950, 2.3 million; by 1960, 3.5 million. The 1986 census total was 9.7 million, but estimates as high as 15 million are common.

By the 1960s, Cairo's population density had reportedly risen as high as 250,000 people per square mile in some areas. Much housing in poorer neighborhoods had only three or four stories, and Cairo—like other cities in poor countries—had few of the parks and open spaces that grace Paris or Washington. In some neighborhoods, living quarters with as little as 1.4 square yards per person were reported. Some Cairenes already lived in the world of "standing room only." Some did not occupy any space at all permanently but rented a nook for only part of the day.

Cairo's many neighborhoods and districts fall into four general categories (Map 18.2).[1] Districts of the same type are not necessarily located together. The oldest are medieval (or older). These include the central districts on the site where Cairo proper was founded, together with several originally separate settlements: the southern district of Old Cairo, or Fustat, which goes back at least to Roman times, and the former villages of Bulaq and Gizah. The medieval districts include Cairo's greatest architectural monuments, its old-fashioned bazaar, and many poor peoples' homes. Some live in buildings built during the Middle Ages. But much of the housing is newer, and more is being built.

Another type of district is the Western or European-style quarters of the nineteenth century. The most important such district, on the east bank of the Nile, forms the city's center. The present riverbank was developed only in the nineteenth century, as drainage work and the building of embankments made new land available. On the east bank, near Liberation Square, are many of today's government buildings, embassies, luxury hotels, and international businesses. Especially elegant is the area just south of Liberation Square known as Garden City, with its winding streets, European-style apartment houses, and opulent villas. The development of the islands in the Nile, Rawdah and Gazirah, and of the river's west bank began as an extension of the nineteenth-century European district on the east side of the Nile. Recurrent attempts to imitate European, especially Parisian, urban-design concepts justify the name Western for the nineteenth-century districts. The echoes of Paris have been overwhelmed, however, by the modern city's poverty and congestion.

Outward from the center and especially northward toward the Nile Delta is the modern or twentieth-century part of Cairo. Here are many of the most prosperous districts. Ayn Shams, also known as Heliopolis, is noted for its luxurious private houses and apartments. Farther out, the buildings become taller, bigger, more ultra-modern. On the west bank of the Nile, areas like al-Muhandisin show a similar pattern of growth to the north and west. The architecture is no longer distinctive, as in

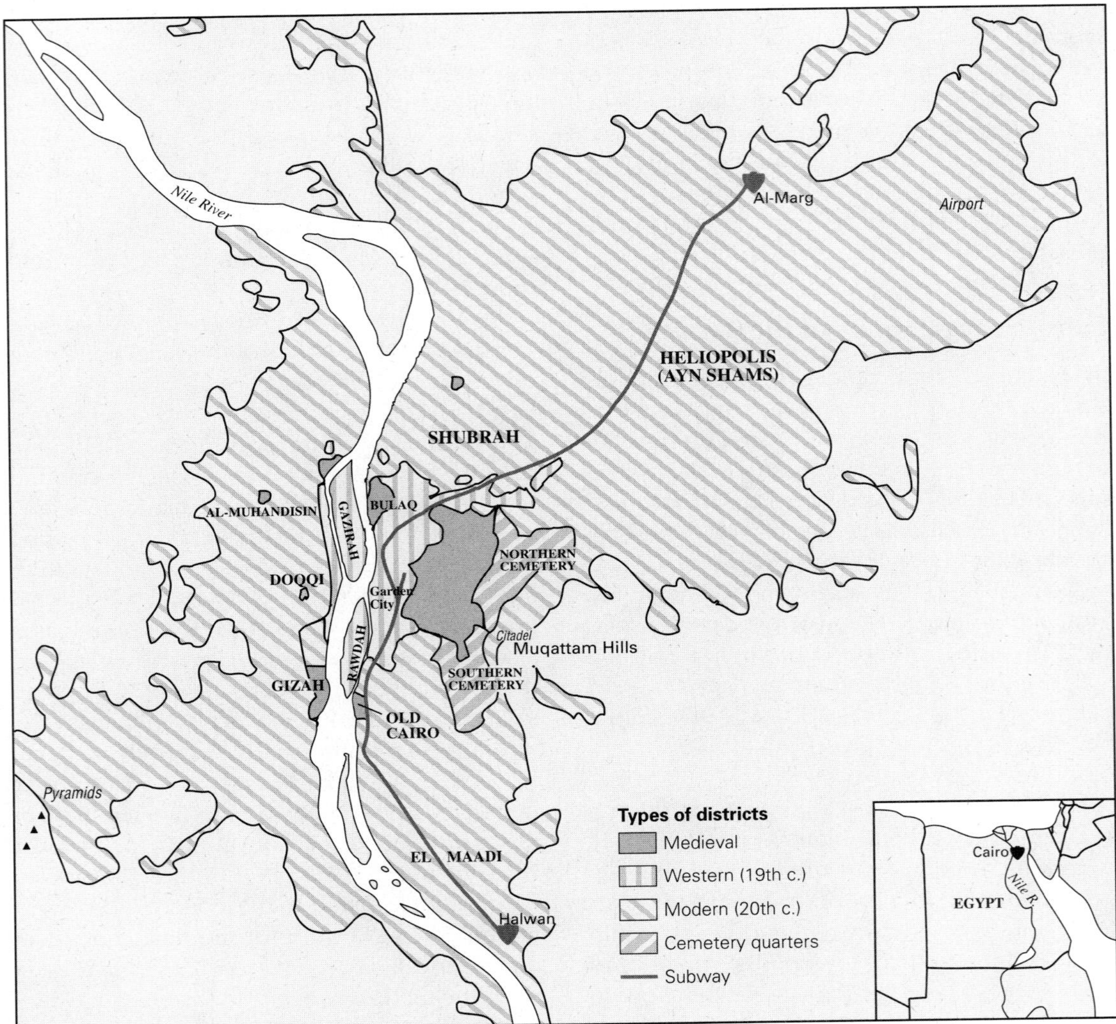

Map 18.2 Contemporary Cairo

the medieval or the Paris-inspired sections, but rather is the generic modern of today's developing countries. The city has grown so fast in the twentieth century that one occasionally finds former villages, with their narrow lanes and mud-brick houses, engulfed in the urban tide.

Few Cairenes can afford to live in places like Garden City or Ayn Shams. In recent years, many could not find a place even in the shabby medieval quarters. Their solution to the housing problem created Cairo's distinctive variant of the shantytowns found around other cities in poor countries.

Between the eastern edge of the city and the Muqattam Hills lie large cemeteries, where fine mosques and tombs built by past rulers rise among contemporary Cairo families' burial places. The simpler burial places consist of lots enclosed by a wall the height of a one-story house, with a gate opening onto the street. Inside is a courtyard with one or two rooms or a shed for shelter from the sun. Burials occur in the courtyard or in an underground vault. Suggesting the influence of ancient Egyptian attitudes toward death, the finest tombs resemble houses, with resident caretakers, reception rooms for mourners, and separate crypts for men and women, so that even the dead obey Islamic norms of gender segregation.

In recent years, poor migrants began to move into the cemeteries as squatters. As the city grew more crowded, the silent streets lined with walls and gates must have made the cemeteries look like uninhabited neighborhoods. Gradually, new construction began to go up. Today, the Qait Bay Cemetery includes multistory apartment buildings, a garage for auto repair, and a workshop making cafe tables—to name a few of the buildings. In places, new construction has obscured all traces of the cemetery.

The first settlers in the cemeteries lived without utilities, but the authorities gradually responded to the "urbanization" of these areas. Today, Qait Bay has schools, electricity, some kind of water supply, and a police station. Still, urban services, inadequate throughout Cairo, are not good here. Puddles of standing water—it might be sewage—extend the width of a busy lane. Living among burial places inevitably suggests health risks. But the cemetery quarters are more pleasant and less crowded than Cairo's slums.

Life in the cemeteries, as in the shantytowns of other supermetropolises in poor countries, is depressing in many ways. Yet it illustrates the determination of the human spirit. A visit to the Qait Bay cemetery quarter early on a June evening revealed an irresistible gaiety about the place. Because it was Ramadan, pious Muslims were obliged to fast from sunup to sundown each day. From the top of the minaret of the mosque-mausoleum

Yellow Lane, a side street in medieval Cairo, 1983. *A woman wears the robe* (milayah) *that urban women in general used to wear in public to conceal their persons and clothing.* C. V. Findley

of Sultan Qait Bay, an observer could sense the holiday mood that emerged as the heat faded and the sixteen-hour fast neared its end.* Clothes, drying on tombstones, flapped in the breeze. There was laughter and animated conversation in the streets. A woman tended goats and chickens on the roof of a four-story apartment house. Other rooftops displayed similar attempts to re-create the village environment high above the cemetery's lanes. Children were flying kites. From an upper window of a seven-story apartment house, two boys lowered a basket on a rope, yelled their mother's order to the grocer below, and hauled the basket up after he had filled it. Lights, strung between the minarets of mosques for the festive month, flickered on. And everyone listened for the signal that the time had come to begin the evening meal.

Social Fabric of the City

The social world of Cairo today differs greatly from the kinship society of the village as seen in Dinshawai in Chapter 2. Although individual neighborhoods may preserve a village-like cohesiveness, the city throbs with diversity. Cairo is Egypt's focus of urban migration and exerts an international attraction as the Arab world's leading metropolis. As a result, the city's populace varies widely in speech, dress, and color. Cairo has an astonishing range of religious institutions: the Muslim majority's countless mosques and shrines, many Coptic churches and fewer churches for many other Christian sects, and a few synagogues, though most Jews had left Egypt by 1956.

Unskilled villagers, driven to Cairo by economic pressure, have tremendous difficulty adapting to the congested and noisy city, where much of the populace now displays stress-related symptoms. But village and city are alike in rapid population growth. The Nile Delta's towns and villages, like Cairo, all seem to be doubling and tripling in size, gobbling up scarce cultivable land. In place of the mud brick of earlier times, the new buildings are framed and floored in reinforced concrete and walled in baked brick covered with stucco. In Cairo, a combination of outdated rent-control laws and unsafe building practices means that most housing is substandard or even dangerous.

Cairo society contrasts with that of the village in the marked differences between the poor and the middle class. In the village, extended kinship ties are more likely to bridge economic inequality among people of different incomes. In Cairo, such connections less often persist. In the city, upward mobility is possible in principle, and religious values encourage equality among Muslims. Yet inequality remains hard to overcome.

The gap between urban classes shows in many ways. Cairo's poor often still dress like villagers, whereas the middle class wear either Western dress or the distinctive new "Islamic dress." Members of the middle class differ from the poor in education and often in the value they attach to it. Partly for this reason, there are class differences in speech. In their leisure activities, the poor are more likely to maintain gender segregation: the women visit each other at home, and the men congregate in teahouses. The affluent enjoy a wider range of amusements, often in mixed company. Perhaps the greatest class-related differences are in values. Middle-class Cairenes, for example, are more willing to see women

*Ramadan is the ninth month of the Islamic religious calendar—a lunar calendar with twelve months that average 29.5 days each, rather than a solar calendar (like the commonly used Gregorian calendar). There is no fixed relation between months in the Islamic calendar and the seasons. Each year, Ramadan begins eleven days earlier than in the previous solar year. As a result, the sunup-to-sundown fast varies in length over the years, being much shorter in winter than in summer.

Qait Bay Cemetery in Cairo looking toward Muqattam Hills. *Characteristic family mausoleums, with plaques over the doors naming the families to whom they belong. The sign advertises a driver training center housed in the corner mausoleum.* *C. V. Findley*

work outside the home, but the poor often still see this as disgraceful, even though unavoidable.

Urbanization has exposed Egyptians to an environment more complex than the village, but few of them have experienced individual liberation or the mobilization into social movements that occurs readily in affluent parts of LA. The broadest-based social movements are probably religious associations (*gama'at*) that unite Muslims for many purposes, mostly benign (founding mosques, schools, or clinics) but sometimes radical, as we shall see. Social mobilization tends to vary with income levels in a way recalling the contrast between Beverly Hills and Watts. In affluent Cairo families, women and men go to university; enter professions, business, or government; and join a variety of political, social, or cultural movements. Paradoxically, studies of political leaders suggest that the affluent excel the poor in maintaining extended kinship ties after moving to the city; such ties probably help these people become political leaders.[2] Ever since a few patrician ladies flung aside their veils to join in nationalist agitation after World War I, moreover, affluent women have led in feminism. Today such women hold high positions in

A crowded street in Cairo. *The contrast between the village dress of the man in the foreground and the Western style dress of the man behind him is a common expression of the city's diversity.* *Sam Doherty/Gamma-Liaison*

telecommunications, tourism, education, the arts, medicine, even politics.

The poor face much less satisfactory conditions. They are likely to live as nuclear, rather than extended, families with six or more children crowded into a tiny apartment, which may lack running water, electricity, or both. "You could faint in there and not fall over," Cairenes say of such housing. Other relatives may live in the city, but they can rely on one another much less than they could in the village. Although crumbling under pressure, social discipline still remains stronger than in poor neighborhoods of U.S. cities. A visitor who would not feel safe in Watts could walk through Bulaq without fear, at least if careful not to offend conservative Islamic values. Women, especially, should not appear in public with more than their face and hands showing and preferably should be accompanied by a male relative. For a poor Cairo woman, the main cost of these norms is that her sphere of acquaintance (all female, except for relatives) and her range of movement tend to be restricted to her immediate neighborhood, where she and her family are known.

Perhaps the harshest effect of poverty is to hinder fulfillment of idealized sex roles among those who still value most the traditional, highly differentiated role concepts. The poor commonly think of the father as the breadwinner, who should not only provide but also show his love for his wife and daughters by gifts of gold jewelry. The wife should be a homemaker and mother. She and her daughters should lead irreproachable lives that will maintain the family honor. Custom and religion add other requirements: offering hospitality to friends and visitors; providing for the feast at the end of Ramadan, when gifts of new clothing should be given; and arranging the exchanges of property that should accompany a marriage. Inability to meet these norms exposes one's inadequacies. Poverty thus makes it impossible for men and women to fulfill their expectations of themselves.

Economic Life of the City

An unskilled migrant from Dinshawai faces bleak prospects in Cairo. A man can look for low-level factory or construction work. Many find marginal subsistence as street vendors. Men and women take jobs as domestic servants. Their income barely covers their families' routine expenses, and nothing is left for needs created by illness, the children's schooling, or special occasions.

Even education will not necessarily enable a young person to escape from poverty, given the effects of Nasser's populist socialist policies. In 1963 the government decreed open admission to the universities; the following year, it guaranteed employment to every university graduate. Drastic overloading of both universities and government services ensued. Academic standards sagged, and government payrolls swelled to include one in ten of Egypt's 56 million people. The results include extreme underemployment among officials and low salaries, so that most—despite their degrees—cannot earn enough to support themselves. Many hold two jobs. In the 1970s, the booming economies of the Arab oil-exporting countries began to slow migration to Cairo by attracting both laborers and university graduates to them instead. Iraq's attack on Kuwait and the Gulf War forced nearly a million Egyptians to return home in 1991.

Cairo's economy today shows the effects of not only superurbanization but also government policy shifts since the 1952 revolution. Survivors of the landowning elite that dominated Egypt before 1952 still occupy shuttered mansions in Garden City or Zamalek. Many Cairenes lived through Nasser's socializing reforms that peaked in the early 1960s. The 1970s brought an attempted "opening" to the West, frustrated by foreign investors' limited interest and by riots that forced the govern-

The Cairo subway opened in 1987, the first in Africa and the Arab world. *Most Cairenes, however, find the government-subsidized fare too high.*
Wide World Photos

ment to back down from attempts to reduce costly consumer subsidies. Since Egypt joined the allies in the 1991 Gulf War, foreign aid and the affluent nations' agreement to write off nearly half of Egypt's $50 billion foreign debt have provided new impetus for structural reforms designed to privatize state enterprises, which still account for over half of industrial production, and shift to a market economy. Now even the Nasser-era land reform and rent-control laws are to be phased out.

These policy changes have created dangers for those who could not adjust but opportunities for the agile. Even under Nasser, the well connected prospered in politics, administration, the professions, and some fields of business and industry, often by serving as subcontractors for state enterprises. As in other countries with weak business and industry but rapid urban growth, many investors favored urban real estate and construction. In recent years, Cairo's housing shortage became so acute that young couples who were unable to find apartments began to marry secretly, defying the strong tradition of family control over marriage. Greedy landlords' efforts to create housing by violating building codes and adding stories to existing buildings regularly led to structural collapse and loss of life. Cairo's October 1992 earthquake measured 5.9 on the Richter scale, as did Los Angeles's 1987 quake. Los Angeles's death toll was only eight; but Cairo's was six hundred, with thousands of families left homeless, largely because buildings collapsed.

The Islamic resurgence also affected the city's economic life with the advent of Islamic investment companies, which profess to operate according to Islamic principles—for example, they pay no interest but do pay dividends. Some such companies became huge conglomerates, but some proved to be no more than pyramid schemes. When the largest Islamic investment company collapsed in October 1988, 135,000 Egyptians lost about $1 billion. Such figures testify to Egyptians' readiness to invest in Islamic firms. The government's failure to regulate these companies, like its inability to maintain safety standards in construction, suggests the limits of its control over the economy.

Many of Cairo's economic problems result from superurbanization. Most Cairenes are too poor to have cars, yet the city's traffic jams never end. Burning low-grade gasoline and subject to no emissions controls, the cars and buses emit exhaust that blends with the black smoke from garbage incinerated on the city's outskirts and with airborne dust from the desert, covering the city with a thick pall. Cairo's growth has totally overwhelmed its road, bus, water, sewerage, telephone, and postal systems. Mostly foreign financed, major public works projects began in the 1980s to equip the city with new sewer and water lines, a fiber-optic telephone network, parking garages, freeways, and a subway. A twenty-six-mile north-south subway line has been completed, and plans have been made not only to build a second line but to build the trains for it in Egypt. Yet most Cairenes find the subway fares too high, and the city's U.S.-style garages and freeways tell more about where the money to build them came from than about Cairene lifestyles.

Political Mobilization Without Participation?

Politically, Cairo is the Arab world's most important city. The Arab League headquarters building on Liberation Square symbolizes this fact. The Egyptian state's role in Cairo's life finds expression in many government agencies, such as an immense administrative complex also on Liberation Square. For most Cairenes, however, political mobilization remains as imperfect as Egypt's economic development. Despite experiments in mass political organization, Gamal Abdel Nasser was a char-

Islamic militants on trial, April 1992. *Brandishing religious books and showing contempt for the court, followers of Shaykh Umar Abd al-Rahman stand trial. Seven of the forty-nine defendents were condemned and hanged.*
© Frederic Neema/SYGMA

ismatic but "pharaonic" leader, more eager for the citizens' cheers than for their ballots. The political liberalization of the 1970s produced a number of political parties, but all were middle class and lacked wide followings. Despite changes in name, what is now the National Democratic party has been in power since 1952.

Poor Cairenes have turned out in mass at moments of crisis to demonstrate support for, or opposition to, their leaders of the day. Most of the time, however, they have looked on politics with cynicism and apathy. In December 1990, most opposition parties boycotted the parliamentary elections, and low voter turnout signaled Egyptians' lack of faith in President Husni Mubarak's promises of democratization.

By the 1980s, alienation had found its outlet mainly in Islamic activist movements. In Cairo as throughout the Islamic world, the activists came from the laboring and lower middle classes. Many were migrants from village Egypt or migrants' children who had studied for professions like engineering only to find no prospect but a dead-end government

Official propaganda against Islamic militancy. *Two pedestrians pass a Cairo sign attacking extremist violence. "Islam is not to blame for them," says the sign in Arabic. The stereotypical terrorist carries a sack of loot labeled, "Killing is permitted! Theft is permitted! Tourism is forbidden!"* *Barry Iverson/© 1991 Time Pictures Syndicate*

job. Unlike most of Egypt's Islamic associations, the most extreme movements were ready to commit violence against the secular state or, in the 1990s, against tourists, precisely because the government counted on the $3 billion a year that tourism added to the Egyptian economy. Some militants were "Afghans"—that is, they had gone to Afghanistan to fight the Soviets and were now returning with military experience—and automatic weapons. Cairo's status as the leading Arab city made it predictable that such people would make a mark there. In a world where foreign tourists cruised up the Nile in pharaonic luxury past villages in which soaring population growth and shrinking livelihoods provoked radicalism and conflict, perhaps it was also not surprisng if some militants extended their operations to the tourists' homelands, as the World Trade Center bombing in New York in 1993 suggests they did. Nor was it surprising, perhaps, that the exiled Egyptian Shaykh Umar Abd al-Rahman, with whom the Trade Center bombers were associated, was the spiritual leader of Egypt's Islamic Group (*al-Gama'ah al-Islamiyyah*), which seeks to overthrow the existing government and replace it with an Islamic state.

Despite the radicals' violence, most Egyptians did not think they had the capacity to topple the government. Most of Egypt's Islamic activists were not terrorists, and most Egyptians—over 90 percent of whom are Muslims—were probably not activists or militants at all. Egyptian human rights groups did feel, however, that the government's repression of its radical Islamic opposition had done much to turn the latter into the threat it had become. The chief victims of human rights violations had become the chief perpetrators.

Cairo as a Center of Intellectual and Spiritual Life

Culturally and spiritually, Cairo stands at the far end of a continuum from villages like Dinshawai. Villages and country towns were the historical centers of popular religion and folk culture. The religious scholars' strict Islam and the learned literary culture were urban products, though city and village each displayed some of the other's traits. The contrast to the village is particularly marked in the case of Cairo, for it is the leading cultural center of the entire Arab world, stretching from the Atlantic shores of North Africa to Arabia and Iraq. Cairo's influence as a center of Islamic religious learning stretches farther—to the utmost limits of the Islamic world.

Evidences of Cairo's cultural pre-eminence abound. The city houses the al-Azhar mosque university, historically one of the greatest centers of Islamic studies. Cairo was one of the first centers of Arabic journalism. Since the 1950s, it has become a center of the electronic media. Cairo has been home to a large share of the great Arab thinkers and writers. Some were Cairo natives, some were drawn from Egypt's villages, and many came from other Arab lands. In modern times, Cairo's literary culture has become largely secularized, adding an Islamic-secular tension to the historical popular-learned tension. Even Naguib Mahfouz, who won the 1988 Nobel Prize for Literature for a lifetime of writing about the city, has lately been attacked—along with other artists—as an "enemy of Islam."

The Islamic religious life of the great city displays much of the mixture of elements found in a delta village eighty years earlier, but with greater emphasis on strict Islam. The steady influx of villagers does help to perpetuate forms of popular religion close to folk tradition. The healing ceremonies of the zar cult, discussed in Chapter 2, have their urban practitioners and followers even now. Though they have been attacked by both secular-minded modernizers and advocates of strict Islam, the saint cults and mystical orders also live on in the contemporary city, though less so than in the past. Closer to strict Islam, the devotion of Cairenes to the Prophet Muhammad and his immediate family is a hallmark of the city's religious life, as shown by the prominence of shrines dedicated to members of the Prophet's family. Finally, the strict Islam of the religious scholars and activists has become increasingly influential in recent years.

The exponents of the strict Islam of Qur'an and religious law are a diverse group. Their influence has varied greatly over the last century, and major conflicts have raged among them. For many years, Western expansion eroded their influence, though some people always looked to Islam for a way to overcome the Western threat. For such people, part of the problem was that pure Islam had become mired in the mysticism evident in Dinshawai at the start of this century. From the late nineteenth century on, religious activists taught that God meant for Muslims to flourish in this world and the next and that a return to strict Islam and a revitalization of religious thought to address the needs of a new age would help liberate Muslims from foreign domination. In the post-1945 era of independence, especially after the 1970s oil revolution, experience seemed to confirm these arguments, and Islamic revivalism grew more influential in Cairo and across the Islamic world.

As Islamic activism extended its scope, leadership passed out of the hands of "established" religious leaders found in institutions like al-Azhar. Instead, Islamic activism became the kind of mass phenomenon that politics—at least the government's kind of politics—had not produced. Incidents involving Islamic militants, from the assassination of President Anwar al-Sadat in 1981 to attacks on tourists in the 1990s, illustrate this point. On Cairo streets, the many people whose conservative dress advertises their Islamic commitment give quieter evidence of this change: bearded men, and women whose clothing leaves only their faces and hands visible.

The situation of the women especially merits note. Some are daughters or granddaughters of women who cast off an older style of Islamic dress in the interest of achieving greater independence. Today's young women begin at a level of independence their mothers had to fight for, and they seek to combine these gains with a renewed expression of their Islamic identity. Nothing could be more typical of contemporary developing countries than the desire to combine the advantages of modernity with inherited values.

Conclusion: Contrasts in Urbanization

While it was difficult in 1914 to imagine environments more dissimilar than a great European capital and a colonial village, comparison of Los Angeles and Cairo shows more resemblances between contemporary supermetropolises of the developed North and developing South. Both Los Angeles and Cairo are products of growth processes of national and international scope. Both cities are socially highly differentiated. Los Angeles has a greater variety of ethnic groups, many of them recent migrants from the South, and both cities display marked socioeconomic inequalities. Both cities are major political centers, though their characteristic forms of political mobilization are different. Cairo offers Cairenes fewer channels for effective political participation than LA offers Angelenos, but South Central residents and poor Cairenes probably have much the same feeling about the responsiveness of their political systems. Culturally, both cities exert an international influence. The contrast between the two environments in religion and secularism, which was so marked in Chapter 2, seems less striking in the 1990s. Los Angeles and Cairo differ most in their economic life, although even here they are perhaps closer together than were Berlin and Dinshawai. Both cities suffer from overcrowding and pollution, but LA's problems are those of a postindustrial society, and Cairo's may be those of worsening underdevelopment. Our visits to these two great cities suggest that tightening global integration has narrowed differences between dominant and dependent societies in the late twentieth century.

Notes

1. Based on Janet Abu-Lughod, *Cairo: 1001 Years of the City Victorious* (Princeton: Princeton University Press, 1971), pp. 171–180.
2. Robert Springborg, *Family, Power, and Politics in Egypt: Sayed Bey Marei—His Clan, Clients, and Cohorts* (Philadelphia: University of Pennsylvania Press, 1982).

Suggestions for Further Reading

Los Angeles

Cohen, Jerry, and William S. Murphy. *Burn, Baby, Burn: The Watts Riot* (1966).

Davis, Mike. *City of Quartz: Excavating the Future in Los Angeles* (1992).

Reid, David, ed. *Sex, Death and God in L.A.* (1992).

Rieff, David. *Los Angeles: Capital of the Third World* (1992).

Cairo

Abu-Lughod, Janet. *Cairo: 1001 Years of the City Victorious* (1971).

Rugh, Andrea. *Coping with Poverty in a Cairo Community* (1979).

Shorter, Frederic. *Cairo's Leap Forward: People, Households, and Dwelling Space*. Cairo Papers in Social Science, vol. 12, monograph 1 (Spring 1989).

Springborg, Robert. *Mubarak's Egypt: Fragmentation of the Political Order* (1989).

Theroux, Peter. "Cairo—Clamourous Heart of Egypt," *National Geographic* (April 1993), pp. 38–69.

Waterbury, John. *The Egypt of Nasser and Sadat: The Political Economy of Two Regimes* (1983).

CHAPTER 19

A World of Interdependence amid Scarcity

The comparison of Los Angeles and Cairo in Chapter 18 illustrates this book's themes: global interdependence amid scarcity; confrontation among cultures in an age of accelerating change; the mass society, democratic or authoritarian; and technology's mixed blessings. It is time to examine these themes more systematically, as illustrated by the most pressing contemporary problems. This chapter examines issues of population; food, energy, and environment; economic development; and science and security, with emphasis on nuclear and other weapons of mass destruction. Chapter 20 will offer a look toward the twenty-first century. The issues raised in these final chapters all converge on the question of whether the human community can make the world a safe, secure, and equitable place for its offspring.

Nothing better symbolizes the urgency of this task than the UN Conference on Environment and Development convened in Rio de Janeiro in June 1992. By bringing together top-level representatives from 178 nations, this Earth Summit became the largest meeting of world leaders in history. The summit produced two treaties and several nonbinding statements of consensus. The biodiversity treaty aimed to protect endangered species, and the global warming treaty called for curbing emissions of carbon dioxide and other gases conducive to atmospheric warming. Under a conservative president, George Bush, who was then running for re-election, the United States refused to sign the first treaty and insisted that the second not set targets for reducing carbon dioxide emissions. The consensus documents consisted of a Declaration on Environment and

Development that emphasized the connection between economic development and environmental protection; "Agenda 21," an 800-page blueprint for environmental protection and environmentally sound development; and a Statement on Forest Principles that called on nations to assess and minimize the impact of development projects on their forests. The summit disappointed environmentalists because of the toothlessness of the documents and U.S. opposition to the treaties. Diplomats reacted more favorably, noting that the documents offered starting points for further elaboration and that the summit signified global recognition of environmental protection as an international issue on a par with economic development and national security.

This linkage among environment, development, and security forms the unifying theme of this chapter. On balance, the urgency of these issues argues for a more incisive approach than that taken at the Earth Summit.

Population: The Demographic Transition?

Discussion of global interdependence amid scarcity logically begins with *demography,* the study of population. This idea is not new. In his *Essay on Population* (1798), Thomas Malthus pointed out that although humanity's means of subsistence could grow only by arithmetic increments, unchecked population growth would compound itself in a geometric progression. Strictly speaking, arithmetic progression means addition of a fixed factor ($2 + 2 = 4$, $4 + 2 = 6$, $6 + 2 = 8$). Geometric progression means multiplication by a fixed factor ($2 \times 2 = 4$, $4 \times 2 = 8$, $8 \times 2 = 16$), the result being a much faster increase.

Malthus's idea that unchecked population growth would outstrip increases in food supply has never been forgotten. Yet for a long time, exceptional increases in food supplies, resulting from the opening of new continents and improvements in agricultural yield, postponed the reckoning he predicted. Today, no more continents remain to be opened, world population is six times higher than in Malthus's day, and technology's new benefits seldom come without undesirable side effects. Malthus's logic again haunts us. As much of the world sinks deeper into poverty, population growth is a major problem.

On a scale unmatched in history, the twentieth-century population explosion illustrates the geometric growth Malthus dreaded. In 1500, world population was about 600 million and was growing slowly. Birth and death rates were both high and roughly in equilibrium. Plague, famine, or war periodically wiped out any growth. The population began to rise in the eighteenth century. In nineteenth-century Europe, the economic growth of the Industrial Revolution led to declines first in the death rate, then in the birthrate. Because the drop in deaths preceded that in births, population grew rapidly as the rates fell. Growth did not slow until the two rates regained equilibrium at a lower level. Western Europe's experience—this shift from high to low birth and death rates, with rapid population growth during the shift—became the classic case of what demographers call the *demographic transition.* The transition coincided with the rise of Europe's urban middle class, who typically wanted smaller families than their peasant grandparents had had.

During this century, public health improved the world over, raising life expectancy and lowering death rates; but poor nations' living standards did not rise greatly, and their birthrates remained high. In most places, gender bias compounded this problem both by making women dependent on children for social status and economic security and by limiting women's access to adequate education

Young Dubliners react to legalization of condom dispensing machines in Ireland, 1993. *An overwhelmingly Catholic and historically conservative country reacts to demands for social change in the AIDS era.* *Eamonn Farrell/* © *1993* The New York Times

and health care. The worst conditions are found in sub-Saharan Africa and South Asia, where women suffer from high rates of reproductive-tract infections, most often give birth without trained medical assistance, and face risks of maternal death up to a hundred times higher than women face in developed countries. Numerous African countries still have birth rates of 50 per thousand, compared to 20 in China, and 10 in Japan.

By 1987 a wide gap had opened between countries with low rates of population increase and countries with high rates. The low-growth countries, mostly affluent and all in the Northern Hemisphere, included 2.3 billion people with a collective annual increase rate of 0.8 percent. The rate for Western Europe had virtually fallen to zero. The high-growth countries, all poor and mostly in the Southern Hemisphere, included 2.6 billion people with a collective growth rate of 2.5 percent a year—three times the rate for the slow-growth countries. By 1992, population increase rates were beginning to fall in

Indian health worker demonstrates the intrauterine device (IUD) to fellow village women. *Population control in poor countries depends on improving women's knowledge and status. Used by a hundred million women worldwide, current IUDs are safer than earlier models but still carry risks of pelvic inflammatory disease.* *© Baldev/SYGMA*

many developing countries. Yet with few exceptions, mostly in Latin America or East Asia, the gap between high- and low-growth regions—the latter now including all Europe—persisted. World population was still increasing by 92 million people a year, 71 million of them born in the South. Since China, increasing at a rate of 1.3 percent, belonged to the slow-growth group but was not an affluent country, over 90 percent of each year's added population was being born in poor countries. Current projections indicate that global population, at 5.4 billion in 1992, will not stabilize until 2150, when it will surpass 11 billion.

Can earth support such populations? Low lying, vulnerable to flooding and cyclones, and mostly made up of one of the world's largest river deltas, Bangladesh packs almost half the population of the United States into roughly the land area of Wisconsin. Is such congestion a picture of the world's future? Or what about Africa, which in the 1970s became the first region of such size to experience a decade-long peacetime decline in income per person since 1929?

Before world population could double again and "stabilize" at 11 billion, the obstacles Malthus identified—famine, pestilence, and war—will again push death rates past birthrates for a time, causing the pattern that demographers call *dismal peaks.* The AIDS epidemic that began in the 1980s may go down in history as such an event; it is the first uncontrolled, global disease scourge since the post–World War I influenza epidemic. Other threats have emerged in its wake in the form of new strains of diseases like tuberculosis, staphylococcus, and gonorrhea. The advent of antibiotics virtually eliminated old forms of these diseases—until new strains resistant to these wonder drugs, which have been overused and misused, began to appear. The cost and difficulty of coping with these new threats will severely tax even the affluent countries' health-care services.

The pressure of human numbers on natural resources could eventually cause an *ecological transition.*[1] That is, if growing populations consume natural resources faster than they are replaced, the point could be reached where vital life-support systems collapse. Death rates would rise and remain high. Birth and death rates would regain equilibrium, if at all, only when population readjusted to a level where human demands on natural resources did not exceed sustainable rates of consumption.

If humankind does not complete its demographic transition, it risks the obverse: the ecological transition. China has dramatically lowered its birthrate, but only through harsh policies that few other developing countries could implement. Elsewhere some societies' efforts to improve the welfare of the poor, especially women, have reduced family size, even without strong gains in income. Most poor countries now at least have family-planning programs. Birthrates that are declining but still high reflect the results. Still, by UN estimates, to keep the world from exceeding a population of 6 billion in 1999, annual investment in developing countries' family-planning programs will have to triple, to $9 billion. Escaping the ecological transition will be a vast endeavor, all the more because environmental and resource issues must also be taken into account.

Food, Energy, and Climate: The Ecological Transition?

Preventing the ecological transition depends on the *sustainability* of a given population in a finite world. "A sustainable society is one that shapes its economic and social systems so that natural resources and life-support systems are maintained."[2] Achieving such a balance is not a simple task. The sustainable yield of a given fishery or forest, for example, is not a fixed quantity but fluctuates with changing conditions and must be continually reassessed. Yet whatever the difficulties of assessing sustainability, the oil crisis that ended a quarter-century of rapid growth in 1973, Africa's recent famines, and growing evidence of global warming show how vital it is to undertake the task. A full assessment would have to embrace all facets of the relationship between population and resources. By way of example, we shall consider the questions of food, energy, and climate.

Food for the Billions?

Some discussions of the food problem attempt to isolate it from population and resource questions. Such presentations make the world food problem look like one of distribution, rather than one of supply. In this view, the needed response to Africa's famines appears to be more efficient redistribution of agricultural surpluses from regions like North America. In fact, such measures provide only short-term relief and leave Africa's demographic and agricultural problems of sustainability untouched.

The historical record yields a better measure of food problems. These focus on grains. Directly consumed, grains provide half of world caloric intake; indirectly consumed in the form of eggs, milk, and meat from grain-fed poultry and livestock, they provide much of the rest.

Until the late 1930s, Western Europe was the only major world region not self-sufficient in grain, and Latin America was the largest grain exporter. After 1945, faster population growth reduced the number of grain exporters, although U.S. and Canadian exports mounted sharply because of improved productivity. By the 1970s, only a handful of countries could be counted on to export grain: the United States, Canada, Australia, Argentina, and France. In the 1980s, the United States and Canada still produced the vast bulk of world cereal exports, but Western Europe—an economically advanced region with stable population and high price supports—also became a grain exporter for the first time in two hundred years. Since the early 1980s, very high farm subsidies in the European Community, the spread of technical improvements, and the abandonment of collectivization in formerly communist countries have increased global grain production by about 15 percent. However, this growth masks important problems of sustainability.

An assessment of sustainability in agriculture requires examining limits on productivity. Globally, as Table 19.1 shows, rates of growth in both production of food and use of agricultural resources have begun to decline. After growing almost 3 percent a year from 1950 to 1984, grain production rose less than 1 percent a year from 1984 to 1992. In soybeans, the leading protein crop, the decline started earlier, in 1980, and was proportionately greater. Because of the use of both grain and soybeans as feed, slowed growth in their production helps explain slower growth in meat production after 1986.

World grain production per person rose nearly 40 percent between 1950 and 1984 but has since fallen nearly 1 percent a year. Most

Table 19.1 *Growth in Food Production and Use of Agricultural Resources*

	Rapid-Growth Period		Slow-Growth Period	
	Years	Annual Rate (%)	Years	Annual Rate (%)
Leading food commodities				
Grain production	1950–84	+2.9	1984–92	+0.7
Soybean production	1950–80	+5.1	1980–92	+2.2
Meat production	1950–86	+3.4	1986–92	+2.0
Principal agricultural resources				
Grainland area	1950–81	+0.7	1981–92	–0.5
Irrigated area	1950–78	+2.8	1978–92	+1.2
Fertilizer use	1950–84	+6.7	1984–92	+0.7

Source: Adapted from Lester Brown et al., *State of the World, 1993: A Worldwatch Institute Report on Progress Toward a Sustainable Society* (New York: Norton, 1993), p. 11.

of the drop has been in poor countries. Leading causes of slower growth are limits on critical inputs—land, irrigation, and fertilizer—and environmental degradation.

The cropland used to grow grain grew by about 24 percent from 1950 to 1981 but then declined slightly from 1981 to 1992. As some countries added new cropland, others lost it through degradation or use for other purposes. Little prospect remains to increase world cropland area. Growth in population has also outstripped growth in irrigation. For the world as a whole, irrigated area per person grew nearly a third from 1950 to 1978 but shrank by 6 percent a year after 1978. The shrinkage reflects unsustainable irrigation practices, such as neglect of drainage, which lowers fertility in arid countries by causing mineral salts to accumulate on the surface of fields, or depletion of "fossil" groundwater sources, such as the United States' Ogallala aquifer, that cannot be renewed because water from the earth's surface no longer reaches them. Today serious water scarcity threatens perhaps a quarter of the world's nations. To cite the worst irrigation disaster, Soviet diversion of water for irrigation from the rivers that flow into the Aral Sea, located between Kazakhstan and Uzbekistan, caused that sea to lose two-thirds of its volume. The wind now picks up millions of tons of salt a year from the former sea bottom and deposits it on farmland downwind.

Experience shows that chemical fertilizers cannot compensate indefinitely for limits on the supply of land and water. Fertilizer adds chiefly nitrogen, phosphate, and potash to the soil; but fertility also depends on trace minerals, organic matter, and nitrogen-fixing bacteria. Through the 1970s, agriculturally advanced countries could raise yields by adding more fertilizer, but gains slowed thereafter. World food production suffered further when the shift from subsidized to market prices in the former Soviet Union lowered fertilizer use by 23 percent between 1988 and 1991. Poor countries that have not benefited fully from chemical fertilizers could still raise their yields by this means, but international lenders now also pressure poor countries that subsidize fertilizer use to cease doing so in order to lower government spending and repay their debts more quickly. The eventual limits on productivity gains and, in some countries, economic constraints on fertilizer use short of those limits thus threaten the world's ability to feed added billions of people.

Mounting damage from environmental degradation compounds these problems. As exploitation intensifies, the world's cropland loses an estimated 24 billion tons of topsoil each year—a loss that fertilizers alone cannot offset. In different ways, land degradation occurs in rich and poor countries alike. As noted in Chapter 16, excessive cultivation, grazing, and woodcutting, plus overstrained water supplies, have been major factors in Africa's recent famines. Elsewhere, too, farmers have extended cultivation into marginal lands, raising short-term yields but creating long-term risks of soil degradation. In mountainous regions from Japan to the Andes, extending cultivation depended historically on laborious terracing. In recent years, growing food needs have led to cultivation of improperly terraced slopes. Erosion and landslides have been the result. In less difficult environments, other dangers have arisen from neglect of sound cultivation practices. U.S. farmers have increasingly planted their lands in crops like corn or soybeans, relying on fertilizers to replace the nitrogen once supplied by periodic planting of legumes even though research has shown that the new practice may increase erosion. Meanwhile, the expansion of cultivation has increased wind erosion in many places.

Deforestation worsens soil and water-control problems. In South Asia, deforestation has lowered water retention on Himalayan slopes and worsened downstream floods, like the one that covered two-thirds of Bangladesh for six weeks in 1988. Tropical rain forests, home to most of the earth's living species, have already been cut back by nearly half and are still being cut by 1 percent a year. Because most nutrients in rain-forest ecosystems are stored in the vegetation, felling the trees exposes soils that cannot sustain cultivation for more than a few years before turning into wasteland. Tropical deforestation also worsens atmospheric concentrations of carbon dioxide by eliminating trees that convert that gas into oxygen. In developed countries, acid rain from industrial pollution kills temperate-zone forests and further worsens air quality.

Air pollution takes an added toll on crop production, estimated in the United States at 5 to 10 percent of production, or between $3.5 and $7 billion per year. In more polluted environments—especially the formerly communist countries of Eastern Europe—the damage is proportionately greater. Stratospheric ozone loss further lowers productivity by increasing exposure to ultraviolet radiation, which interferes with photosynthesis and stunts plant growth.

Available knowledge can theoretically correct many of these problems. For example, nonchemical means of soil enrichment—such as nitrogen-fixation methods based on the algae that grow in flooded rice paddies or on the acacia trees that grow in Africa's Sahel region—could be studied and revived. Biotechnology can also probably develop crop strains that require less land and water. The question is whether such remedies can keep food production abreast of population growth and the environmental stress that accompanies it.

Energy, Nonrenewable and Renewable

OPEC may have done the world a favor, for the price shocks of the 1970s may have driven home an awareness that the world has only a finite amount of oil. For the quarter-century preceding the 1973 embargo, the price of oil had been kept low, and world oil consumption had more than quintupled, to 20 billion barrels in 1973. Petroleum and related products had become the basis for much of the world's transportation, heating, and electric-power generation. Because they were produced in huge quantity, byproducts of the refining process had become the basic raw material for much of the chemical industry, even where other materials could have served as well. Plastics, synthetic fibers, and even fertilizers were manufactured from petroleum derivatives.

One measure of oil dependency is how many barrels of oil it takes to produce $1,000 of world GNP. With GNP reckoned in 1980 dollars, that figure stood as low as 1.33 barrels in 1950, then peaked at 2.27 in 1973 before beginning an irregular fall that again brought the figure below 2.0 in 1981. During the third quarter of the century, then, the world consumed ever-larger amounts of oil and relied on oil for more uses. Of course, there were gross regional disparities. In 1973, for example, producing $1,000 of GNP required only 1.04 barrels of oil in China, as compared to 5.11 barrels in the United States. An oil exporter, the Soviet command economy used energy even more wastefully than the United States, though with less benefit to the average citizen.

People could not go on forever using a nonrenewable resource without regard to the risk of depletion. The high consumption levels of the developed economies and the concentration of much of the world's oil resources in a handful of culturally similar Middle Eastern states made OPEC possible. Conservation, the shift to alternative forms of energy, and global recession then lowered world oil consumption from 1979 on. In 1980, oil prices also began to fall, bottoming below $20 per barrel in 1986, the lowest price since 1975.

Oil prices began to rise again in 1986, and by 1989 demand had almost regained its his-

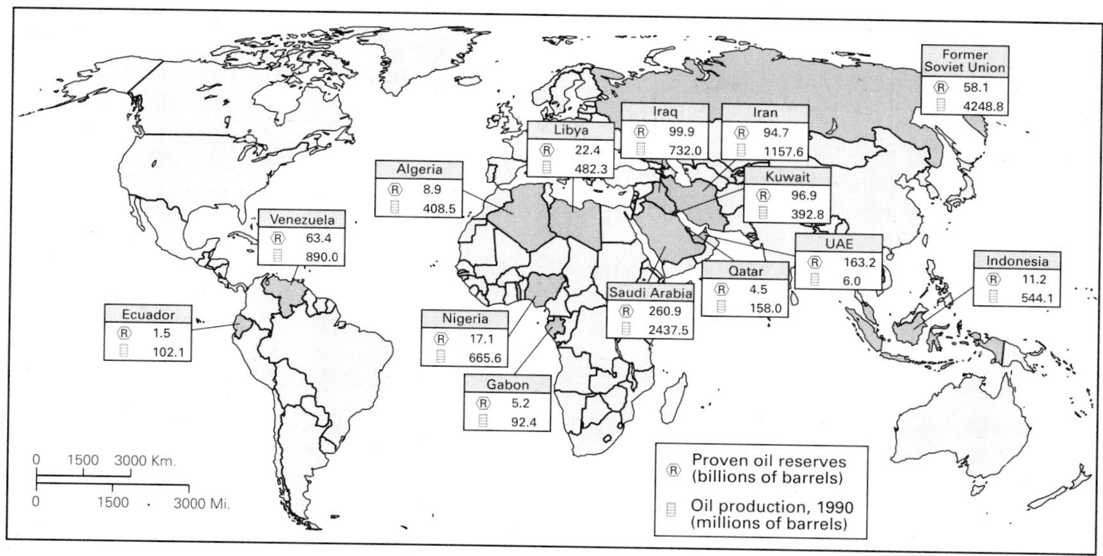

***Map 19.1* OPEC Oil Resources, 1990: Current production and proven reserves.** *The former Soviet Union was not an OPEC member, but was the world's largest producer.*

toric peak of a decade before; but the oil crisis was not over. At 1983 production levels, world proven oil reserves would be depleted in 37 years, and oil deposits extractable by more costly techniques would last another 114 years. As other regions depleted their reserves, the Middle East's dominance as the major supplier would grow. That region had produced 22 percent of the world's oil in 1986 but held 57 percent of world proven reserves. With declining oil output elsewhere—the United States, Europe's North Sea, the former Soviet Union—the outlook was for the Middle East's share of the world oil market to near 40 percent by the year 2000 and for scarcity conditions like those of the 1970s to return. The crisis following Iraq's invasion of Kuwait had already briefly pushed the price of oil above $40 per barrel in October 1990. In terms of oil scarcity, the main difference between the 1990s and the 1970s would likely be that efficiency gains by developed economies, coupled with increased consumption in developing countries, would shift the impact of the crisis more than before onto oilless developing countries. At any rate, the age of cheap, abundant oil was over.

What future energy alternatives lie before us? A common reaction in the 1970s was to point to coal and nuclear energy. The world has enough coal to last for centuries at present rates of consumption (although coal, too, is a nonrenewable resource). But the role of coal burning in air pollution and acid rain has become too familiar an issue in North America and Europe. Moreover, the burning of soft coal (lignite) has given Eastern Europe some of the highest sulfur dioxide levels in the world. Today, China is almost unique in relying on coal to power its rapid economic development.

Nuclear power's disadvantages have been highlighted both by costs higher than those for other forms of electric power and by the nuclear plant disasters at Three Mile Island (Pennsylvania, 1979) and—far worse—Chernobyl (Soviet Ukraine, 1986). In the 1990s, countries that had nuclear power plants kept on using them, but only Japan remained committed to building more such plants. As France earlier had done, Japan tackled the difficult and dangerous challenge of building and operating fast breeder reactors (FBRs), which, by producing more plutonium than they consume, are supposed to give Japan the domestic energy source it otherwise lacks. Japan's prototype FBR, "Monju," named after the Buddhist divinity of wisdom, has already cost over $5 billion, and commercialization of electricity from Japan's FBRs is not expected before 2030. On such terms, it is hard to believe that even Japan can long afford nuclear power.

What will solve the world's energy problems will be not some quick technological fix but rather greater energy efficiency in the short run and development of nonpolluting, preferably renewable, energy sources for the long run. To date, the largest efficiency gains have come from using energy less wastefully. Between 1973 and 1993, efficiency gains reduced the energy required to produce a dollar of GNP by 30 to 50 percent for North America, Europe, and Japan. If the United States had not improved efficiency beyond 1973 levels, its energy costs for 1990 would have been $160 billion greater than they were; and the United States is hardly the most efficient of the industrialized countries in minimizing energy costs. In the mid-1980s, the United States paid 10 percent of GNP for energy; Japan paid only 4 percent.

Further efficiency gains are clearly possible. Home appliances, heating, cooling, and lighting systems are all undergoing refinements that enable them to operate, in some cases, at fractions of the energy formerly required. For example, an 18-watt screw-in fluorescent bulb produces as much light as a 75-watt incandescent bulb and lasts ten times longer, more than repaying a higher purchase price. In formerly communist countries of Eastern Europe and in less developed countries, where available technologies are typically less energy-efficient than in the most advanced countries, up-to-date improvements can save even more energy. Distinctive needs of developing countries also cannot be overlooked. Such countries still depend on wood and plant products (biomass) for 35 percent of their energy needs. Possible improvements in biomass utilization, already introduced in some places, include using gas turbines to generate electricity from sugar-mill wastes, substituting charcoal and improved ceramic stoves for cooking over open wood fires, or planting degraded land with fast-growing trees.

Some of the most important gains in efficient energy use must come in transportation. The urban fuel efficiency of new passenger cars sold in the United States almost doubled, reducing U.S. gasoline use by 20 billion gallons a year between 1973 and 1985. Further gains will come through use of lightweight materials (alloy metals, high-grade plastics, ceramics), replacement of the gearbox with a continuously variable transmission, or microelectronics that regulate engine and transmission operation. By 1987, several cars already in production averaged over 50 miles per gallon on the road or even in urban driving; a Toyota prototype diesel averaged 98. Large gains in both energy conservation and pollution control can still be made by raising automobiles produced in Eastern Europe and developing countries to comparable standards. Ultimately, however, transportation must rely less on oil and probably less on automobiles. Signs of what may come are apparent in growing use of motor vehicles powered with natural gas, increasing efforts to develop viable electric or solar-powered vehicles, renewed interest in rail transport, and efforts to equip major cities—from Los Angeles to Cairo—with subways.

Long-term energy solutions require not only conservation but also shifting to renewable, nonpolluting energy sources. For some years after the oil shocks of the 1970s, it was not clear how best to choose among the many possibilities for experimentation. By the early 1990s, however, outlines of optimal strategies were coming into view.

One aspect of these strategies will be diversification. Instead of concentrating on coal and oil as in the past, future societies will seek to satisfy their energy needs by a wide variety of renewable and environmentally sound means, including sunlight and other energy sources that derive from it. Such societies will generate electricity from hydropower, wind power, biomass conversion, or geothermal or solar energy. California, for example, already leads in producing electricity from geothermal energy, wind-powered generators, and solar-thermal power plants. The market for photovoltaic cells, which convert sunlight into electricity, had grown to $500 million by 1992 and will grow much larger as costs for the cells come down. The main limitation on these diverse and mostly solar energy sources is that most of them operate intermittently, generating power that serves many uses but is hard to store and cannot provide a steady, basic power source for widespread use.

Optimal energy strategies for the future must thus also rely on certain basic energy sources for steady operation. Natural gas will fill this role for a transitional period of several decades, after which hydrogen will predictably become the fuel of choice.

Although natural gas is neither renewable nor completely nonpolluting, it is important because it produces much less pollution than oil or coal and has recently been found in far larger quantities than had previously been known. As late as the 1970s, the geology of natural gas had not been well studied, and most available information was a byproduct of searching for oil. The realization that natural gas often occurs apart from petroleum led to important finds around the world and higher estimates of reserves. U.S. reserves, sufficient for sixty years of use at current rates, are only 5 percent of the world total. Natural-gas extraction poses some risk of environmental damage, and its use cannot eliminate global warming (discussed below). Because substituting gas for oil and coal will significantly reduce carbon emissions, however, use of gas to power vehicles or generate electricity will be a prominent part of the transition to energy sustainability. An emerging technology that is expected to assume a major role in generating electricity is the fuel cell, an electrochemical engine that, without combustion, converts hydrogen (derived from natural gas or methanol) into electricity.

Ultimately, depletion or need to eliminate carbon emissions will require phasing out natural gas. As a new basic fuel, hydrogen gas will then come to the fore. Consisting of a single atom, hydrogen can be produced by passing an electric current through water (electrolysis). Hydrogen produces almost no air pollution when burned, can be distributed through pipelines, and can be substituted for most other energy sources. Further technical improvements will be needed to make hydrogen cost-competitive with natural gas or to adapt it for vehicular use. However, the German government has already launched a combined government-industry hydrogen program, and German and Japanese automakers are at work on prototype hydrogen-powered vehicles. In a hydrogen-based energy economy, fuel cells will retain the central role in electrical generation.

The transition to energy sustainability will create opportunities for societies that can negotiate it successfully and probably also hardships for others, especially the oil-exporting countries, that have vested interests in older ways. In any event, optimal strategies for the energy transition include a transitional period of expanded natural-gas usage, followed by a solar-hydrogen economy—a label applicable in two senses. The basic fuel for the new energy economy will be hydrogen, produced electrolytically, often with electricity derived directly or indirectly from the sun. In that sense, the system will be based on solar hydrogen. Additionally, electricity will be generated from a diversity of renewable sources, also mostly solar in origin. With solar power and hydrogen as its two primary energy sources, the new energy economy will achieve the goals of renewability, freedom from pollution, and sustainability. The urgency of achieving such an energy economy becomes clear from the evidence on climate change.

Climatic Change

In sharpening public awareness of ecological problems that result from population growth, 1988 was the pivotal year when the "greenhouse effect" became front-page news. The term refers to what happens when the atmospheric concentration of certain gases, especially carbon dioxide, increases. The carbon dioxide absorbs infrared radiation from the sun, gradually warming the lower atmosphere. Years of record-breaking heat occurred almost steadily in the 1980s. In 1988, a year of severe heat and drought, the world also learned that the stratospheric ozone layer, which protects life on earth from harmful ultraviolet radiation, was thinning not just in polar regions—a fact discovered several years earlier—but globally. In the early 1990s, the depletion rate was found to be twice as fast as previously thought. Mechanisms of climate change are still not well known, and there had been controversy about whether human-induced increases in atmospheric pollution would cause temperatures to rise or fall. Increasingly, the experts predicted warming.

The evidence indicated that the greenhouse effect was indeed a global problem. Since 1970, less developed countries, housing three-fourths of world population, have almost tripled their energy consumption, while industrial countries increased their energy usage by only a fifth. Tripling consumption produced much higher pollution levels, especially with the proliferation of automobiles and the usual lack of emissions controls. As a result, some cities in developing countries now have average concentrations of sulfur dioxide or suspended particulate matter—two major forms of atmospheric pollution—ten times as high as in the cities of affluent countries. *Ecological colonialism,* found where multinational corporations relocate hazardous industries, such as asbestos or pesticides, to poorer countries or where some such countries keep environmental regulations lax to attract investment, aggravates these problems. Accelerated by short-sighted development policy in some poor countries, deforestation also worsens air pollution. The cutting of the Amazon rain forest, for example, not only endangers unknown numbers of plant and animal species, many of which may produce substances of medicinal or other value, but also adds to atmospheric carbon dioxide and disrupts the hydrologic cycle (the circulation of water between earth and atmosphere through evaporation and rainfall).

The collapse of communist rule, however, revealed that the worst pollution was in Eastern Europe. Having been much less efficient than the United States or Japan in energy usage, East European economies produced some of the highest pollution levels ever recorded. In the Soviet Union, the health costs of pollution were estimated at $330 billion for 1987, or 11 percent of GDP. Not surprisingly, environmentalist "green" movements proliferated in Eastern Europe in the 1980s and became political parties upon the end of communism.

Among the greenhouse gases, the chief pollutant is carbon dioxide, produced mostly by fossil-fuel combustion, secondarily by deforestation (decaying or burning plant matter releases carbon; live plants convert carbon

July 1993: Severe heat and climatic stress in the United States. *Boys sought relief in a Baltimore fountain from severe heat blanketing the east coast, while the Mississippi basin struggled with record-breaking floods.* *Michael Lutzky/© 1993* The Baltimore Sun

dioxide into oxygen). Over the past century, atmospheric carbon dioxide has risen from 274 to 354 parts per million. As of 1989, carbon emissions amounted to one ton a year for each human being on earth. Other greenhouse gases include methane, from waste disposal and agriculture, and nitrous oxides, from fertilizers, industry, and motor vehicles. Chlorofluorocarbons (CFCs) and halons present a special challenge. At their height, CFCs were widely used in cleaning processes and cooling systems and as a blowing agent in aerosol cans and in the making of insulating foams. Halons are used in fire extinguishers. CFCs release chlorine, and halons release bromine; both chemicals rise into the stratosphere and react to break down ozone (oxygen's three-atom form).

The effects of these greenhouse gases make global warming a serious danger. Rapid warming would threaten biological diversity because many plants and animals would not be able to survive change in their habitats. Warming would also raise the danger of sea-level rise. Low-lying countries like Bangladesh, the Maldives (consisting of 1,190 islands with no point above two meters), and the Netherlands would be mortally threatened, as would the world's major coastal cities.

Ozone depletion poses still other dangers. Ozone is harmful at ground level, where it forms the prime constituent of smog, hindering plant growth and lung functions. Stratospheric ozone, however, is vital: it is the only gas that prevents harmful ultraviolet radiation (especially UV-B wavelengths) from reaching earth's surface. Ozone depletion makes exposure to the sun more dangerous. Increased exposure to ultraviolet radiation will increase the incidence of skin cancer and cataracts and may depress the human immune system, so increasing the incidence of disease in general. UV-B exposure also lowers crop yields and kills tiny marine organisms vital to the ocean food chain.

Experts now project that atmospheric concentrations of heat-trapping gases will double over the next fifty years, largely because of carbon emissions. At that rate, global temperatures will rise between 0.2 and 0.5 degrees Celsius per decade for a century, with far-reaching effects on sea levels, weather, and endangered species. The momentum of climate change is already too great to stop. The rate of change cannot even be slowed without reducing use of fossil fuels and, especially, of CFCs. Because the atmosphere cannot discriminate where pollutants come from, only intense international cooperation can produce results. The Montreal Protocol on Substances That Deplete the Ozone Layer (1987) provided a model for further initiatives. As more alarming evidence came in, other multinational agreements followed, prescribing a halt to CFC production after 1995. Probably none of this would have meant much if major corporations, after initially fighting efforts to restrict CFCs, had not begun to shift position with the discovery of profitable substitutes. As a result, global CFC production fell 46 percent from 1988 to 1991. Changing corporate policy and the growth of *environmental diplomacy* express a new concept of what affects financial and national interests in today's interdependent world.

A report issued in 1992 by the U.S. National Academy of Sciences and the Royal Society of London began: "If current predictions of population growth prove accurate and patterns of human activity on the planet remain unchanged, science and technology may not be able to prevent either irreversible degradation of the environment or continued poverty for much of the world."[3] This judiciously worded statement warns anew of the danger of the ecological transition—a radical collapse in humankind's ability to sustain itself with remaining resources. To avoid the dangers cited, human activity will need to change in many ways. Many have been suggested, and steps have been taken to implement some. Environmental diplomacy—as in the ozone agreements or the 1992 Earth Summit—is one high-priority way to tackle these problems. Environmentalists and some economists argue, too, that conventional methods of measuring productivity must be revised to take account of depreciation, not only in plant and equipment but also in resources and environment. By this argument, statistics like GNP or GDP, which measure production only, should be replaced with an Index of Sustainable Economic Welfare (ISEW), which also factors in costs of resource depletion. Governments can target sustainability in many ways, from effective family-planning programs, to "green" taxes levied on polluters, to mobilizing the public. The search for ways to save resources and reduce the emission of greenhouse gases makes demands not only on science and technology but also on industry and business. After prolonged opposition from the business world, public demand, government policy, and opportunities to profit by bringing new processes and products to market—from recycled paper goods to fuel cells—have begun to make environmental priorities into a positive force in what some environmentalists hail as a new industrial revolution. Such massive changes will be needed in a world where the security of nations depends increasingly on the maintenance of a sustainable balance between humankind and the habitat on which it must depend.

Alternative Strategies for Economic Development

In the 1980s, GNP per person declined in forty-nine of the world's countries, and about 3 billion people—over half of humanity—still lived at the margin of subsistence in poor countries. Thinking about population and resources thus necessarily raises questions about economic development and patterns of global economic integration. This section briefly surveys economic development strategies, North and South, and major issues in international economic integration. The prime focus for discussion is global inequity in the distribution of population and income, shown in Maps 19.2 and 19.3, and possible ways to promote sustainable development in a world of such disparities.

Developmental Strategies in the North

The world's leading national economies developed according to three general economic strategies; the fall of communism in Eastern Europe has discredited one of them. Especially given growing public awareness of the need for sustainable development, however, economic development strategies must not be considered solely at the national level.

What existed in Eastern Europe was not Marx's vision of communism—a utopia never yet realized—but state-dominated economies long regarded as less successful variants of the major capitalist economies. All pursued the same goals of growth through industry and technology. What made Soviet state-socialism—it could as well be called state-capitalism—less efficient was basically that the state controlled investment and prevented the operation of market forces, which make economic survival dependent on productivity and profit. In addition, the system prioritized heavy industry and military goals at the expense of consumers. Through the 1960s, the centrally controlled Soviet economy remained relatively competitive with other industrial economies. However, once the capitalist countries began to move beyond heavy industry and concentrate more on consumer-oriented, knowledge-intensive industries—electronics, communications, or pharmaceuticals—the Soviet Union was unable to follow suit. In particular, advances in computing and telecommunications threatened the very idea of state control over the economy and the flow of ideas. With time, the Soviet economic system became less and less viable and more vulnerable to the costs of its own historical inefficiencies in use of labor, raw materials, and especially energy. The consequences not only proved fatal to communism in the Soviet Union and Eastern Europe but also gave pause to developing countries that had opted for socialist-inspired ideologies or government-led approaches to economic development.

The strategy that launched the industrialization of countries like the United States, Britain, and France, in contrast, was the free-enterprise philosophy of nineteenth-century liberal economics. Over time, these na-

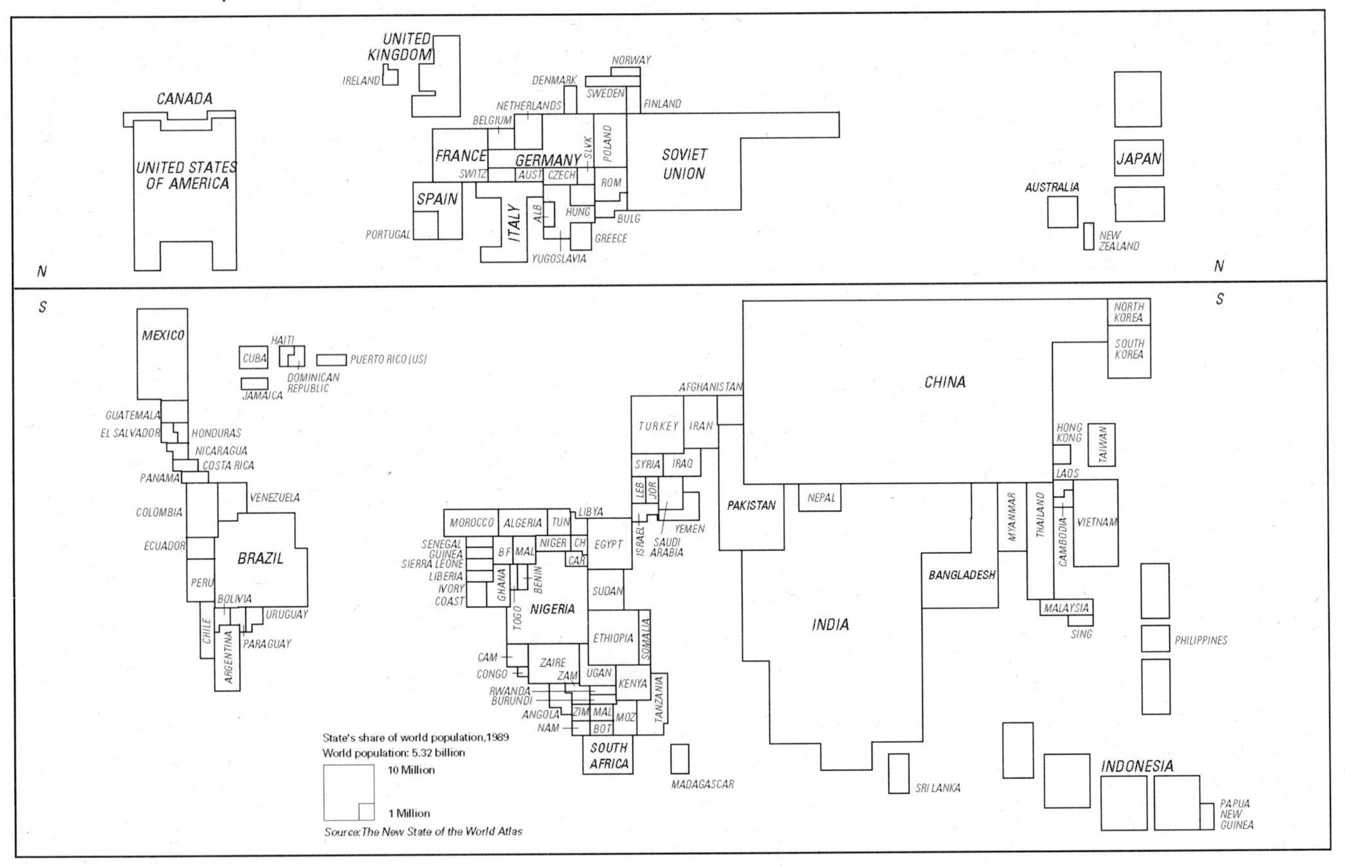

Maps 19.2 and 19.3 Alternative Maps of the World, by Population and National Income. *The North produces the bulk of the world's income. The South is home to populations whose economic problems multiply with high birthrates. Source: From* The New State of the World Atlas, *4th edition, by Michael Kidron and Ronald Segal, maps copyright © 1991 Swanson Publishing Limited. Reprinted by permission of Simon and Schuster, Inc.*

NATIONAL INCOME, 1989 (CALCULATED IN EXCHANGE RATE TERMS)

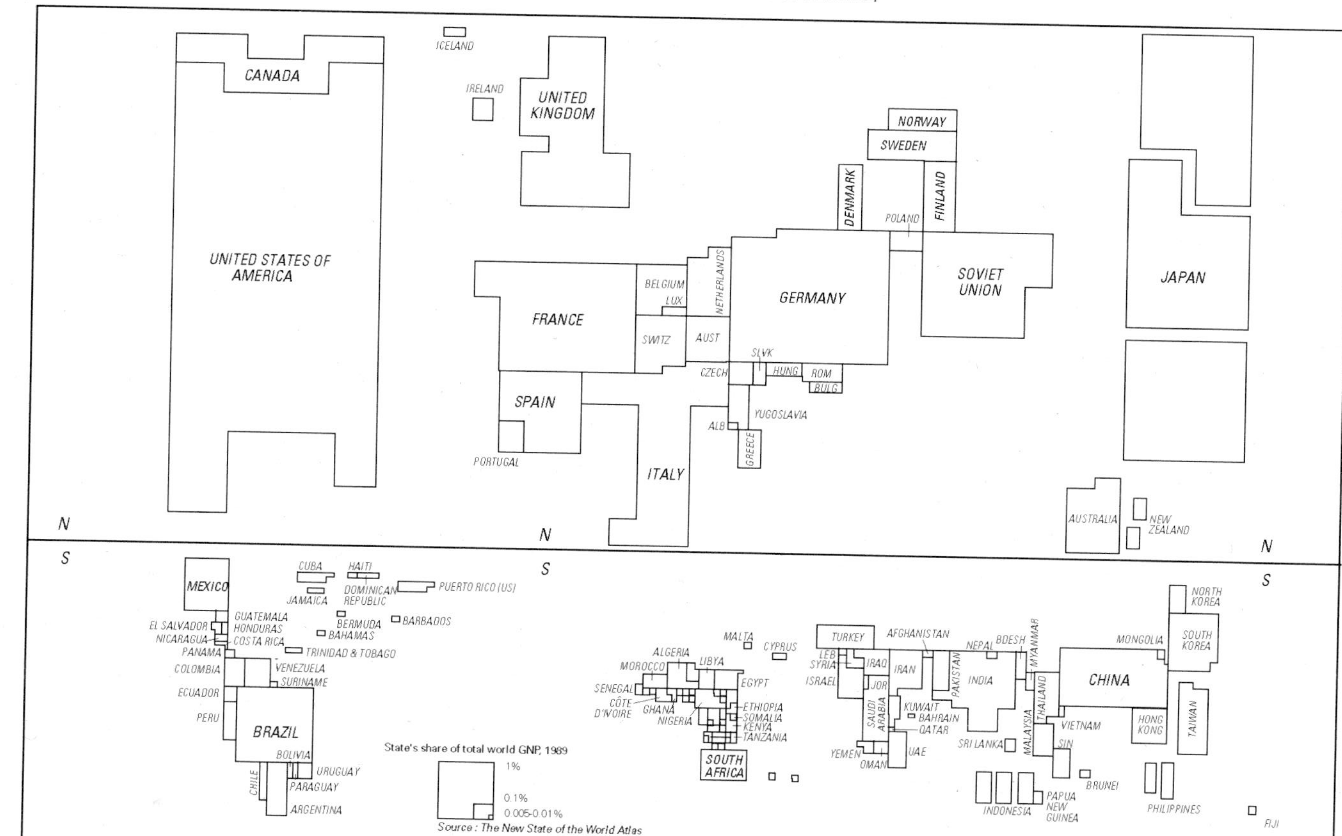

On a map based on GNP computed in terms of purchasing power rather than exchange rates, many affluent countries would become somewhat smaller, and many developing countries would become larger. China would become several times larger. In GNP per person, however, the countries of the North are more affluent in either exchange-rate or purchasing-power terms.

tions created various social safeguards, such as those pioneered in Germany in the late nineteenth century, developed in the United States with the New Deal, and widely applied in Europe after World War II. By the 1980s, all these economies displayed problems symptomatic of postindustrial societies: obsolescence of industrial plant, falling productivity, high unemployment, inability to compete with imports from Japan or developing countries, demands for protection against imports, high government welfare expenditures, threatening deficits, and environmental deterioration. Social tensions, like those underlying the Los Angeles riots discussed in Chapter 18, and high welfare expenditures show that many people find it impossible to rise out of povery, even in affluent countries. Largely because of a long history of racial injustice, the United States suffers greater socioeconomic inequity than most West European countries or Japan. The share of national income going to the poorest one-fifth of the population amounts to only 5 percent in the United States, compared to 7 percent in Germany and 9 percent in Japan.

In the 1980s, U.S. and British responses to these problems suggested a desire to return to an earlier era of free enterprise. Britain's privatization of formerly nationalized industries seemed even to inspire global emulation. However, the acceptance of the guarantor state, even by conservatives, had grown too great to permit fundamental retreat, as the uproar provoked by any suggestion of reducing U.S. Social Security benefits made clear. Protectionism was not the answer either. It had brought international trade to a standstill during the 1929 Depression. By the 1980s, one of every six U.S. industrial jobs depended on exports to the Third World, and debt repayment by Brazil or Mexico hinged on their earning foreign currency by exporting. The 1992 U.S. presidential campaign featured suggestions that the next administration develop an industrial policy for long-term technological innovation, but no such policy had emerged by mid-1993. At $3 trillion, the national debt was bound to constrain U.S. policy options in this respect, as in others.

As of the 1980s, the most successful development strategy among highly developed nations was Japan's hybrid approach. In some respects, such as conservative financial policy and low welfare spending, Japan was closer than any European or North American economy to the liberal-capitalist tradition of the nineteenth century. In economics as in politics, however, the inner workings of the Japanese system were distinctively Japanese. Chapter 17 has noted the producer-oriented business policy, the reliance on the U.S. security umbrella, and the "iron triangle" of business, bureaucracy, and party that dominated Japan during the decades of rule by the Liberal Democratic Party. In this context, the history of collaboration between the Ministry of International Trade and Industry (MITI) and the major business groups has been especially important. This government-industry symbiosis emerged organically from Japan's modern development—the first signs had appeared during the Meiji period. This made it unlikely that other countries could simply copy Japan's approach. Indeed, some of them were still stronger than Japan in important areas, such as basic science. Some U.S. corporations that had experimented with Japanese management techniques had found them frustrating because of cultural differences and had developed other alternatives.

Still, Japan's example offered much to challenge U.S. policy makers. Democrats traditionally thought of government's role as regulating the economy, whereas Republicans demanded a decrease in government's economic role. Both were used to the argument that military-oriented research and development benefited the entire economy. Japan had created an alternate model of government leadership in economic development. Moreover, Japan's low military spending had directed research and development spending toward consumer products, which generally cost far less to develop than advanced military technologies. The one affluent nation most dependent on others for raw materials and markets, Japan had proved most dynamic economically and had emerged the real winner of the superpower arms race—by staying out of it.

As the United States and other countries attempt to develop industrial policies, Japan continues to lead. MITI and industry are now developing a hundred-year plan ("New Earth 21") for ecological sustainability, and the government has set up a new research institute to focus on environmental technologies. Japan's continuing commitment to nuclear power challenges this planning effort, as does recent instability in politics and in investment markets. The immense resources of Japan's "high-yen" economy and the vast investment they have made possible suggest that Japan's economic leadership will continue for some time, however. Not only that, but even as some Japanese private fortunes have grown to become the world's largest, Japan has retained one of the most equitable income distributions of any highly developed country, thus combining equity with one of the highest per capita income levels in the world.

Development strategies can readily be contrasted at the national level, but economic performance, even in centrally controlled economies, depends on the contributions of countless groups and individuals. Never has this fact been more important than in the transition from Cold War priorities to those of sustainable development. We have already noted signs of an increasingly positive response from the business world to environmental issues. However, most such changes would never have occurred without initiatives from the public. Recognizing the role of popular initiative thus becomes an essential complement to our discussion of economic development strategies.

Among many examples, Germany's Green party and the proliferation of similar movements in Eastern Europe show how environmentalism can become a means of political mobilization. In a number of affluent countries, consumer-oriented organizations also actively support "green" priorities. Examples range from the International Organization of Consumers' Unions, which has member organizations and affiliates in over sixty countries, to Japan's Seikatsu Club, which began as a housewives' purchasing cooperative and has become a large marketer and producer of foods and household goods. Related phenomena include the publishing of guidebooks that rate companies and products in terms of social and environmental responsibility, such as those published by the Council on Economic Priorities in the United States and Britain's bestselling *Green Consumer Guide* (1988). A number of countries now also have "eco-labeling" systems, such as Germany's Blue Angel label, which evaluate products in environmental terms. Such examples remind us how the statistics that economists discuss mask the actions and decisions of concerned individuals.

Developmental Strategies in the South

Since developing countries' national economies are more exposed to external pressures than are the North's, it is more difficult to think in terms of national development strategies for the South. Still, looking at these economies at the national level is a good way to begin. That is how poor countries' policy makers have to start as they confront their limited options. The choices they make not only affect their fellow citizens but also produce wider consequences. For example, the $170 billion that developing countries spent in 1988 on defense could have accomplished a great deal if invested instead in sustainable development. That individuals and communities make important economic choices in developing countries is, however, also clear from the emergence of grassroots movements analogous to those in wealthier countries.

A classic economic argument states that each economy should maximize its comparative advantage by concentrating on production processes in which its efficiency, relative to other producers, is greatest. In the 1980s, conservative economists repeated this counsel to Third World governments. In crudest form, the argument meant continued reliance on exports of agricultural products and minerals. The argument points toward industrialization primarily in the sense that a poor country can exploit its comparative advantage in low wage rates to develop labor-intensive industries. For most small countries, however, the comparative-advantage argument will continue to mean neocolonial dependence, given their limited resources and capabilities. Not only that, but increasing the volume of raw-material exports tends to drive down their prices, which have in fact declined for years in relation to the prices of manufactured goods that poor countries have to import.

Social issues also bear on economic development. Failure to restructure a historically inequitable agrarian economy hinders economic development. The severe inequalities still found in India and much of Latin America limit the productivity of the agricultural sector and its ability to provide capital for investment, qualified workers for industry, or a market for industrial products. Because their country had abundant land and a comparatively open rural society—with the great exception of slavery and subsequent discrimination against African Americans—Americans tend to underestimate such problems. They tend to see the universal key to agricultural development in the technical improvements that increased U.S. productivity. In many poor countries, however, trying to develop agriculture by technical means without changing its social bases cannot produce balanced development. Especially in countries with little industry, still-large rural populations need effective ways to make a living in the countryside.

Of course, the leaders of most developing nations are beneficiaries of the very social order that needs changing. The most inequitable income distributions in the world are found not in wealthy capitalist countries but in developing countries. One of the worst examples is Brazil, where the poorest fifth of the population receives only 2 percent of national income, compared to 9 percent in Japan—a gap further magnified by the fact that Japan's national income is several times larger than Brazil's. Such inequity as Brazil's helps explain why fundamental change in social structure has usually required social revolution, as in the USSR, China, and Cuba. Yet successful social revolutions are rare, and those that occur do not always produce economic development, even when they do achieve social justice.

Can a developing country bring about the needed changes in social structure without the violence of revolution? Japan underwent its social restructuring in two stages. First—and not without some violence—the Meiji Restoration (1868) eliminated the privileged warrior class. Later land reform, introduced under U.S. occupation after World War II, almost eliminated absentee landlordism and tenant farming. Then, war and defeat, not revolution, provided the impetus for social restructuring. But other countries cannot readily copy Japan's experiences. Even in some that carried out agrarian reform—as Egypt did under Gamal Abdel Nasser (1952–1970)—population growth has outstripped the gains, leading to superurbanization and loss of self-sufficiency in food. The lack of easy solutions to agrarian social problems again spotlights the linkages among issues of population, resources, and sustainable development.

Whatever their record on agrarian social change, developing countries' policy makers have characteristically been keen to industrialize, initially through import substitution behind high protective barriers. In the 1930s, runaway protectionism and the collapse of international trade created exceptional opportunities to pursue this strategy. In countries where rural society had not been appropriately restructured, that fact exerted an ongoing drag on industrialization. Everywhere, it meant drastic changes: growth in scale of enterprise, mechanization, development of linkages between new industries and other enterprises that supplied their needs or used their products, diffusion of new skills, infrastructural improvements in energy, transportation, and communication. By the 1960s, most developing countries had developed a fair measure of manufacturing, at least for the local market.

Ultimately, import-substitution industrialization reaches limits, as it did in Latin America. To develop further, a developing country facing these limits needs to shift to an export orientation. Because other countries also want to export, such an orientation implies moving away from protectionism toward free trade. But it is dangerous for a small developing country to try to compete unprotected in international trade with the world's greatest economies. To a degree, such a country can exploit its comparative advantage in cheap labor by developing labor-intensive export industries. This advantage may prove short-lived, however. Either development will lead to rising wage demands, as happened in Japan, or the advantage will pass to multinational corporations that move in to exploit it, as many U.S. corporations have done by locating plants in Mexico or the Caribbean. In the long run, the most fruitful export strategy for a developing country is to identify specific product lines in which it can compete and for which it can become internationally known. Often, the shortest route to this goal is to acquire a competitive position in processing goods previously exported as raw materials. If more countries followed this route, many petroleum products—from motor oil to fertilizers—might eventually be marked "made in Saudi Arabia," and premium brands of cocoa would be "made in the Ivory Coast." At best, the transition to export-led growth is a painful one, accompanied by political tension and worsened economic inequality.

Such an export strategy is also bound to be difficult for very small countries. They can probably succeed, if at all, only by performing unique combinations of functions. Switzerland's historic specialization in banking and watchmaking perhaps offers the best model for this kind of development. Hong Kong and Singapore hold analogous positions in Asia, with their own combinations of service industries, trade, and manufacturing.

Countries that cannot develop distinctive and competitive export lines or a unique service role are probably doomed to dependent status in the world economy, barring a major restructuring of international economic relations. The developing world's industrial success stories are rare and—as in Brazil—often less impressive if politics and social development are taken into account. Then, too, some countries experience economic decline, rather than development, whether at Argentina's relatively high level or at the very margins of survival, as in parts of Africa.

A key difference between today's world and that of a century ago is that the affluent countries no longer monopolize manufacturing. Two centuries after England began to dominate global markets by exporting machine-made cotton textiles, affluent countries import textiles and other low-technology manufactures from the developing world, systematically relocating many of their own fac-

Kenyan women working in their tree nursery in Isiolo town, 300 kilometers north of Nairobi. *A grassroots effort to improve supplies of fuel, reverse environmental degradation, and provide new opportunities for village women.* *Peter Williams/Photo Oikoumene, World Council of Churches*

tories to low-wage countries with lax environmental regulations. With rare exceptions, such as the cluster of high technology firms at the Indian city of Bangalore, the persistent inequality in the global availability of advanced technologies suggests, however, that Third World industrialization has not eliminated but has merely shifted the frontier between rich and poor nations.

This survey of development policies at the governmental level is mostly bleak, but that does not mean that individuals and local groups have no chances to pursue their own interests. Today, grassroots movements seem to offer the best route to the basic social change that most poor countries' governments have neglected. Instead of the monumental dams and factories favored by governments and international lending agencies, often at great harm to local communities and ecosystems, these movements organize the poor to meet their own socioeconomic needs, usually with results far more conducive to sustainable development.

Many grassroots movements have emerged in South Asia and seem to show Gandhi's influence. For example, India's Swadhyaya ("study of the self"), a religious movement, sponsors social and economic projects, such as farms and orchards worked by volunteers, the proceeds being distributed to the needy or used to expand the program. The Working Women's Forum, organized and led by working women of India's Tamil Nadu state, provides such services as small loans, job training, health care, family planning, political action, and—to break down caste barriers—mass intercaste weddings. In Sri Lanka's SSM (Sarvodaya Shramadana Movement), specially trained young people work with their fellow villagers to carry out programs in housing, irrigation, rural industry, health, and other fields. Bangladesh's Grameen Bank makes small loans to the landless poor—especially women—who join local support groups, use the loans to create self-employment opportunities, and become bank shareholders.

Africa, too, has produced such grassroots movements as the Naam movement, founded in Burkina Faso in 1966 to mobilize a traditional kind of village young people's group to undertake local development projects. Out of the Naam movement grew the Association for Self-Help During the Dry Season in the Savannah and the Sahel, which has spread to nine West African countries and aims to provide credit and relieve underemployment during the dry season. In Kenya, Wangari Maathai, chair of the National Council of Women, organized the Greenbelt Movement to plant trees, improve the supply of firewood, rehabilitate the land, create jobs, and improve opportunities for women. She aims to expand this organization into a Pan-African Green Belt Movement.

Such movements fall far short of setting the overall direction for most poor countries' development strategies. Together with their counterparts in wealthy countries, however, they have an important role to play in development and in transforming patterns of international cooperation.

International Economic Integration

A critical question about the institutions and processes that bind the world together is whether they reinforce or diminish inequalities among nations and peoples. To date, the evidence indicates that they reinforce inequality, although there are exceptions to note.

Multinational corporations, the key agents of international economic integration, have been much criticized for reinforcing developmental inequalities. The sales of the largest firms, such as Exxon, exceed the GNP of 90 percent of the world's nations. Such corporations transfer capital from South to North, where almost all of them are based. They reinforce a "vertical" division of labor that assigns unskilled work to the South. Most of these jobs are deemed "women's work," not because of their content, but because the corporations' desire for docile labor interacts with the host societies' patriarchal norms to identify young women as ideal short-term workers, cheaply replaced when family responsibilities reclaim them. Most highly skilled jobs go to males, either citizens of affluent nations, or educated men from poor countries, who may be employed in their home countries at low wages or may migrate to the wealthy countries, becoming part of the international "brain drain." Many Third World factories merely assemble parts prepared by more highly skilled workers in the company's home country. In industries such as oil, multinational corporations rely on capital-intensive and technologically advanced processes that split developing countries' economies into sectors of low and high productivity, as happened in Nigeria and Iran, with too few jobs in the high-productivity sector to relieve local unemployment. These firms also import their advanced technologies. In countries that lack high levels of technological sophistication, what is commonly called *technology transfer* usually retards or blocks development of technology or research skills. In cases of "ecological colonialism," the transferred technologies export environmental hazards no longer tolerated in the corporation's home country. Many corporations produce items the host population does not need or cannot afford, like tobacco products or luxury hotels. Foreign investment has positive potentials for poor countries' development, but host governments mostly lack the expertise to protect their interests in dealing with the corporate giants, while the corporations have little trouble recruiting members of local elites with interests in maximizing inequality.

With change in the world economy, new models of corporate organization may emerge; firms may become more truly globalized and begin to change this picture. To date, however, multinational corporations have compounded international inequity more than diminished it.

Similar criticisms apply to the international financial institutions set up after World War II to prevent recurrence of the crisis conditions of the Depression. As Latin American experience shows (see Chapter 15), the International Monetary Fund applies conservative economic principles, requiring governments with balance-of-payment deficits to sacrifice full employment and growth in an effort to repay their loans quickly. Moreover, under its typical "stand-by arrangements," the IMF applies conditions to each country's access to its line of credit, and the conditions become stricter for each installment. A typical "stabilization program" requires liberalization of imports and foreign exchange, devaluation, tightening of credit, reduction in real wages, and openness to foreign investment. The programs call for increasing exports and abolishing the consumer subsidies that largely make up the Third World version of the guarantor state.

Such policies have attracted so much criticism that even IMF officials can no longer ignore the problem. The stabilization programs, intended as short-term economic correctives, produce lasting social consequences. The programs protect the interests of a poor country's foreign creditors, without considering the country's long-term developmental needs. Urging all countries to increase exports also risks flooding the market and lowering the prices of the exported goods. Moreover, all nations presumably desire a positive foreign trade balance, but obviously not all can achieve it at once.

Comparable problems surround the International Bank for Reconstruction and Development, known as the World Bank. For example, it played a major role in Chile by cutting off aid to the Allende government (1971–1973) and then restoring aid, at a 50 percent higher level, to the Pinochet regime. The impact on Chile has been noted in Chapter 15. Of late, the World Bank has been criticized for backing grand-scale, showcase projects, especially dams, like the thirty dams planned for India's Narmada River. Rulers of developing countries tend to value such projects for prestige reasons. Yet implementing the Narmada scheme will require the flooding of large tracts of land, including badly needed forests, and involuntarily resettling 200,000 people, for whom little provision has been made. World Bank energy projects have been criticized not only for their human impact but also for emphasizing expanded power production and neglecting questions of efficient energy use. The World Bank has begun trying to reorient its policies and has announced policy goals for sustainable development. It and the IMF have also announced that they will work with borrowing countries to reduce military spending, but further effort will be required to silence critics.

The end of the Cold War has aggravated the tensions surrounding all questions of international development assistance, because affluent countries and international institutions like the IMF and World Bank have begun to divide their resources between Eastern Europe and the developing world. The fact that Eastern Europe needs assistance not only for conventional development goals but also for cleaning up its extreme environmental pollution and for destroying weapons that recent arms control agreements require to be destroyed greatly magnifies the drain on resources.

Many proposals have been made to bring North-South economic relations into line with the requirements of sustainable development, and some measures have been taken. One starting point would be to restructure the IMF and World Bank, so as to increase loan funds and redesign IMF stabilization programs to serve less the interest of affluent creditors and more the debtor countries' needs for sustainable development, thus improving their ability to repay. Another often-heard demand is to increase international aid to 0.7 percent of donor nations' GNP—a target achieved as of 1992 only by the Netherlands, Denmark, Norway, and Sweden. Critics point out, however, that conventional forms of aid reinforce dependency and underdevelopment, either through requirements that the money be spent on products from the donor country or through misappropriation and corruption in the receiving country. In contrast, aid directed to specific development programs, especially those of grassroots organizations, more readily escapes these pitfalls.

Another theme in thinking about North-South relations has been to foster the development of regional cooperative organizations among developing countries. Many such countries have entrenched dependency relationships with affluent countries but only weak ties with their neighbors. With Europe's slow progress toward unity and the widely felt repercussions of the end of the Cold War, regional integration projects have proliferated. Enough such organizations have been proposed to cover the map of the Americas, Africa, and much of Asia. The larger organizations especially, such as the Islamic Conference Organization, have difficulty maintaining unity or focus. However, the potential exists for significant gains through infrastructural linkages among neighboring countries, expanded regional markets, or cooperation in the processing and marketing of commodity exports.

In a world where most nations can no longer feed their people, China's ongoing ability to feed one-fifth of humankind in a country only slightly bigger than the United States points to food sufficiency as another target for both national policy and international economic relations. Relevant policy goals include national and regional programs to improve food supplies, prevent further environmental degradation, or work to stabilize export prices through international agreements. Working at the regional and global, as well as the national, level to enhance food security requires coping with such related problems as increasing energy supplies, starting with the biomass on which many poor societies rely for fuel, stabilizing population, and—prerequisite for that—improving the status of women, whose economic contributions are persistently undervalued because so much of women's work goes unpaid. On the research front, the kind of effort invested in developing improved varieties of wheat and rice should be extended to improving crops like millet, sorghum, and manioc, tropical Africa's principal crops. A related issue in North-South economic relations and environmental diplomacy could lead to significant change in existing patterns of technology transfer, in which multinational corporations' claims about patent protection figure prominently. Poor countries have begun to argue that if a firm profits by developing new products from genetic materials obtained from such countries, as pharmaceutical and seed companies often do, then the nation of origin should receive compensation, preferably including access to the new technology.

Realizing any tangible realignment in international economic relations requires locating and organizing the needed financial and human resources. Reducing military spending is the obvious way to start in finding funds, although shifting patterns of global militarization (discussed below) may make such gains difficult to realize. In dollars of 1990 value, global military spending since 1945 has amounted to $30 trillion. Although it may have peaked, global military spending continued at an estimated rate of $1 trillion per year in 1990. With the end of the Cold War and the ongoing shift from a military-oriented idea of national security to a sustainability-oriented concept of global security, scope certainly exists to redirect some of this spending to developmental goals.

Organizationally, national governments and the large organizations they create and work through, like the IMF and World Bank, will continue to play large roles in international economic relations, especially if needed changes are made in the way some of these institutions operate. Multinational corporations, too, will continue to be a fact of life. Pressure from shareholders and consumers, of the sort directed in recent years against corporations doing business in South Africa, could help produce constructive change in such firms. Growing emphasis in industry on energy-efficiency and environmentally sustainable production—a shift that some environmentalists argue is now in progress—may also help to impell this kind of change.

Voluntary associations and grassroots groups can also do much to establish new types of links between rich and poor societies. For example, alternative trading organizations seek to counteract inequalities in international trade by working at both ends of the production and marketing chain to assist producers in poor countries—often villagers or indigenous peoples—in marketing their products internationally. Some of these organizations, found from Finland to New Zealand, have multi-million-dollar turnovers. Specifically addressing the needs of indigenous peoples, Survival International tries to help them preserve the environments on which they depend for their livelihood. Many analogous organizations have goals that are not primarily economic or environmental yet help to improve the quality of life. Examples include Amnesty International, which attempts to expose and counteract human rights abuses around the world, and Denmark's International Rehabilitation and Research Center for Torture Victims. Compared to government agencies or multinational corporations, such organizations are small and weakly financed. Their advantage is precisely that they accomplish more with less. Not enough to change the world by themselves, they nonetheless create alternative mechanisms to work for sustainable development.

Science and Security: 160 Million Chernobyls

Perhaps the only force of greater consequence for the twentieth-century world than explosive population growth is the development of science and technology to a point where human beings—once pitifully unable to protect themselves from natural forces—have acquired the ability to degrade or even destroy the world. Like so much else today, these two phenomena are interdependent, for the tripling of world population in a century would not have been possible without great advances in medical science and public health. Paradoxically, in the same century when health-care professionals finally learned how to heal more people than they lost, specialists in other scientific and technical fields developed the means to destroy humankind and the earth.

Advances in health care are not the only ones in paradoxical contrast to the destructive potentials of modern science and technology. So much in their development has been beneficial, in fact, that it is difficult to single out the greatest recent advances. In terms of profound social consequences, the invention of oral contraceptives in 1960 played a revolutionary part in giving women control of their reproductive capacity. In basic science, the most revolutionary event since 1945 was probably James Watson and Francis Crick's 1953 discovery of the double-helix structure of deoxyribonucleic acid (DNA), the substance that transmits the genetic information of living cells. Their work opened the fields of molecular biology and genetic engineering. In terms of change in the way people live and work, perhaps no advance has produced greater impact than computers. Not only did the computer industry revolutionize information processing at all levels from preschool to advanced research; it also symbolically opened a new phase in the development of industrial—more exactly, postindustrial—societies. The combination of computers with other technologies has yielded such phenomena as electronic mail—networks that can transmit computer-generated data instantaneously around the world. Next in prospect is multimedia, the intermeshing of computer, telephone, and television in a global network that promises to revolutionize how people entertain themselves and do business. An outstanding feature of these innovations, which increase the ready availability of information the world over, is their democratizing impact.

Scientific and technological advance, however, has been a two-edged sword. When it becomes dangerous, the problem is not only its inherent potentials but also the way people use them. Sometimes, harm is done unintentionally. Chlorofluorocarbons, for example, were introduced without awareness of their danger to the ozone layer. At other times, the harm is intentional. This is true above all of the military uses of technology. Historically, potential military applications of new technologies have always found users. Nothing has illustrated this more decisively than the advent of the nuclear age.

The questions surrounding the uses of science and technology extend far beyond the realm of nuclear weapons, as many of the environmental issues discussed in this chapter illustrate. However, nuclear and other weapons of mass destruction merit special consideration, not only because of their extreme destructive potential but also because of their centrality to concepts of security, even as these change in the post–Cold War era. For this reason, the following discussion will focus on these weapons systems.

A thorough discussion of weapons of mass destruction must range across many topics, including the characteristics and destructive impact of the weapons, modes of deployment, tactics and strategy, the lack of effective defense against nuclear attack, arms control, and *proliferation* (the spread of such weapons to powers that do not already have them). Moreover, a thorough discussion of weapons of mass destruction must consider not only nuclear weapons but also chemical weapons, biological and toxin weapons, and ballistic missiles, which can be used to deliver warheads of any of the preceding types, as well as conventional explosives.

Because the United States and Soviet Union possessed over 95 percent of the 55,000 nuclear warheads then in existence—enough to create a nuclear blast 160 million times more powerful than the 1986 Chernobyl disaster—discussions of nuclear weapons and related issues long tended to focus heavily, often exclusively, on the two superpowers and the possibility of large-scale nuclear war. This approach dangerously neglected proliferation and the non-nuclear weapons systems, which poor countries can acquire much more readily than they can nuclear warheads. The end of the Cold War makes it essential to redress this imbalance. We shall therefore focus on the major issues for the 1990s: global militarization, progress in arms control at what used to be the superpower level, and proliferation and arms control worldwide.

Global Militarization

Today's world has undergone a dramatic militarization. Before World War II, military spending absorbed less than 1 percent of gross world product. In 1986, the figure stood around 6 percent. Between 1973 and 1986, world military spending rose from $474 billion to $825 billion. After 1980, U.S. debates about the federal deficit drew attention to the size of defense spending, which usually amounted to 6 percent of GNP as long as the Cold War continued. The Soviet Union presented a starker picture of an economy drained by military spending—11.5 percent of GNP in 1984—among other problems. The paradox of a USSR that was strong militarily but weak economically went far to explain Gorbachev's efforts to reorient domestic and international policy (see Chapter 14).

U.S.-Soviet rivalry lay at the heart of increased military spending, but it was a global phenomenon with great costs for developing countries. The United States and the Soviet Union stood first and third among the world's nations ranked by GNP. When poor countries devote as large a percentage of GNP to military spending as did the United States or Soviet Union, the developmental costs are far more severe. As of 1990, poorer countries that spent more of their GNP on the military than the long-standing U.S. rate of 6 percent included Syria, Jordan, Israel, Pakistan, Zimbabwe, and no doubt others for which statistics are not available. In contrast, Western European nations spend smaller percentages than the United States. Japan's low military spending, still barely over 1 percent of GNP, helps explain its economic dynamism.

Far from reversing the trend toward global militarization, the end of the Cold War may have strengthened it. Arms exports have declined in value from their peak in the mid-1980s, but only because of temporarily worsened economic conditions. The availability of arms for sale has increased. A major contributing factor is the economic difficulties of the post-Soviet republics and their willingness to sell their most advanced weapons to earn hard currency. Especially in the Middle East and East Asia, buyers are not lacking. In 1992, for example, Russia's largest purchasers were China, Syria, and Iran. However, the post-Soviet republics' willingness to sell is only one part of the problem. Sales by U.S. firms are actually greater, accounting for more than half the world arms market. At $1.4 billion in 1992, Israel's defense exports were smaller but had virtually held their own in a year when sales were down overall. Nor do arms merchants' moral scruples appear to have improved. The Johannesburg *Weekly Mail* reported on November 8, 1991, that arms firms in the United States, Japan, Australia, Brazil, and eight West European nations had violated the UN embargo on arms sales to South Africa. In October 1991, a Pennsylvania firm was charged with supplying South Africa with arms that were then made available to Iraq and used against U.S. forces in the Gulf War.

Experts have long argued that military preparedness is the key to national security. During the Cold War, commentators on superpower military policy commonly maintained that nuclear preparedness was essential to deter nuclear attack: "deterrence" was held to be the best defense. However, the historical association between the buildup of arms and the eventual outbreak of war is very strong. Now that the end of the Cold War has at last made possible a shift of policy emphasis at what used to be the superpower level, what has been accomplished in arms control, and what needs to be done in response to ongoing global militarization?

Arms Control in the Cold War Context

The need to control the spread of nuclear weapons was realized quite early. By the 1980s, numerous control agreements of limited scope were negotiated. Multilateral agreements prohibited deployment of nuclear weapons in the Antarctic, on the sea bed, in Latin America, in the South Pacific, and in outer space. The Nuclear Nonproliferation Treaty (1968) prohibited signatory states that did not have nuclear weapons from acquiring them. As of 1993, over 150 governments had adhered to the treaty—not enough to keep nuclear proliferation from being a very big problem, especially in the case of post-Soviet republics that still held parts of the Soviet nuclear arsenal. One of the most important multilateral agreements was the Limited Test Ban Treaty (1963), prohibiting nuclear testing in the atmosphere, in space, and under water. Only underground testing remained possible. This treaty is also significant as an instance of government response to popular pressure, roused by fears of nuclear fallout from atmospheric testing.

The United States and the Soviet Union also reached several important bilateral agreements. Among these are the Hot Line Agreement (1963), establishing radio (later satellite) links between the superpowers for emergency communications, and the SALT I (Strategic Arms Limitation Talks) agreements (1972). SALT I restricted numbers of intercontinental ballistic missiles (ICBMs) and submarine-launched ballistic missiles (SLBMs) for five years and limited deployment of anti-ballistic missiles (ABMs) by each superpower to two sites, a limit lowered to one in 1976. For nuclear warheads, ICBMs and SLBMs are two out of the three delivery systems of intercontinental range, the third being long-range bombers. The low limit on anti-ballistic or defensive missiles reflected the then-prevailing view that an anti-missile defense system would not be effective under attack.

Two more recent bilateral agreements were not ratified by the U.S. Senate. The first, the Threshold Nuclear Test-Ban Treaty (1974), was intended to limit even underground tests to nuclear devices with yields of less than 150 kilotons (equivalent to the explosive force of 150,000 tons of TNT). The SALT II Treaty (1979) would have placed carefully defined limits on strategic weapons and limited some technologies, such as multiple independently targetable re-entry vehicles (MIRVs). MIRVs, which enable a single attack missile to carry a number of warheads aimed at different targets, had been developed precisely as a way to overwhelm anti-missile defenses. Although the Senate did not approve the SALT II Treaty—because of reservations about specific provisions and such other issues of the day as the Soviet invasion of Afghanistan—the terms of the agreement were observed in practice.

For several years after SALT II, the net momentum ran against arms control. In June 1982, the Soviet Union did take the important step of declaring that it would not be the first to use nuclear weapons. But the United States refused to take the same step, on the grounds that NATO plans for defending Europe required the threat of first use of "theater" nuclear weapons—that is, weapons of intermediate (less than intercontinental) range. The idea of a ballistic missile defense also resurfaced in 1983 under the Reagan administration in a form known officially as the Strategic Defense Initiative (SDI) but popularly referred to as the "Star Wars" defense. Instead of relying on defensive missiles, SDI would rely on particle beams and lasers to destroy attacking missiles. In a time of unprecedented federal deficit, questions about its costs and workability under combat conditions made SDI highly controversial. Opponents argued that the plan violated the 1972 Anti-Ballistic Missile Treaty and that the Soviets would see SDI as an escalation of the arms race and invest in counter measures, such as depressed-trajectory (cruise) missiles. SDI was cut back under the Bush administration and survived, as of 1993, only in the reduced form of the Ballistic Missile Defense Organization. It was supposed to provide the United States with a ground-based defensive system to counter incoming missiles, not in midflight but in an earlier phase of their trajectory, before they could fall on U.S. territory.

What eclipsed SDI was not so much cost and technical difficulty as political developments that opened the way for dramatic progress in arms control in the mid-1980s (see Chapter 12). The first major breakthrough was the Intermediate Nuclear Forces (INF) Treaty (1988).

Under the INF Treaty, the superpowers agreed—for the first time since invention of the atomic bomb—on mutual reductions in their nuclear arsenals. The treaty eliminated both intermediate-range (600–3,400 miles) and shorter-range (300–600 miles) land-based missiles, prescribing procedures for destroying the missiles and their launchers. The treaty would apply wherever in the world the missiles were based but was especially significant for Europe, where such missiles were heavily deployed. One of the most essential features of the treaty was its provisions for monitoring, which included not only satellite surveillance but also new on-site inspections. Under the treaty, the United States and Soviet Union were to destroy 2,695 missiles and 2,096 nuclear warheads.

Although a milestone, the INF Treaty was only a beginning. The question of reducing the superpowers' conventional forces needed to be faced, as did that of chemical and biological warfare. Most critical was the fact that the INF Treaty represented less than a 4 percent reduction in the superpowers' combined stock of 55,000 nuclear warheads. Within another five years, negotiations on these topics had been undertaken and in most cases concluded.

In reducing conventional forces in Europe, Gorbachev announced unilateral cuts in 1988–1989, and President Bush countered with his own proposals for reductions. The upshot was the Conventional Forces in Europe Treaty (CFE, 1990). In perhaps the most radical arms cuts in European history, this placed equal limits on the military equipment of the forces of NATO and the Warsaw Pact, from the Atlantic to the Urals. Because the Warsaw Pact's forces had been much larger, its cuts were far more extensive than NATO's. With the breakup of the Warsaw Pact (1991), the former member states distributed the cuts among themselves.

Chemical weapons were a less pressing issue in superpower defense policy than they are in the field of proliferation control. Yet the Soviet Union had had a much larger chemical weapons program than the United States, which, having ceased to produce chemical weapons in 1969, had consequently resumed production in 1987. Partly because of the use of poison gas in World War I, efforts to control chemical weapons have had a comparatively long history. During the Cold War, the United States had worked with its allies to limit international traffic in chemical weapons agents, a difficult undertaking because many of the chemicals also have legitimate uses. Under a U.S.-Soviet agreement of 1990, the two states undertook to cease producing chemical weapons and to reduce their arsenals, with further reductions to follow when a global ban went into force. Such an agreement, the Chemical Weapons Convention (CWC), was negotiated and opened for signatures in 1993. At that point a Biological and Toxin Weapons Convention (BTCW) was still under negotiation.*

After the unratified SALT II Treaty, work on the most important goal—reducing the superpowers' strategic (long-range) nuclear arsenals—resumed in the 1980s at the Strategic Arms Reductions Talks (START) in Geneva. The result was two treaties: START I (1991) and START II (1993). START I called for cuts by one-third in nuclear warheads on U.S. and Soviet missiles. START II prescribed cuts by two-thirds in U.S. and Russian strategic nuclear arsenals by the year 2003. Ultimately, each side's nuclear warheads would be reduced to between 3,000 and 3,500 in number. Because the START treaties place ceilings on numbers of weapons, rather than banning them as the INF Treaty did, they present complex verification problems and will require more on-site inspections.

The breakup of the Soviet Union further complicates implementation of the START treaties in at least two ways. One is the Soviet successor states' need for outside assistance to cover the costs of weapons destruction. U.S. government agencies have committed billions of dollars to pay for weapons destruction or to buy the highly enriched uranium removed from the dismantled warheads. Total costs for weapons destruction will ultimately run much higher. The other problem arises from the fact that Soviet nuclear weapons are now divided among four republics: Russia, Ukraine, Belarus, and Kazakhstan. This fact raises thorny issues pertaining to the Nuclear Nonproliferation Treaty (NPT, 1968), to which both the United States and the Soviet Union had subscribed, and the START treaties. All but Ukraine have ratified START I and signed or promised to sign the nonproliferation treaty. Unless all four republics ratify both START I and the NPT, START I cannot take effect. In that case, Moscow and Washington are not expected to ratify START II.

Fearful of possible future aggression by Russia, which will remain a nuclear power under the START treaties, many Ukrainians are less reluctant to ratify START I than to sign the NPT and so commit themselves to become a non-nuclear state on the borders of the much larger Russian Republic. While the Ukraine understandably delays, large numbers of nuclear warheads still stored there go without the periodic servicing required to prevent accidents or unintentional detonation. Ukrainian reluctance illustrates both the complications that Soviet collapse introduced into arms control problems and the resentments provoked by arms control agreements based on the idea that some countries may possess weapons of mass destruction but others may not.

Since 1985, then, arms control efforts have accelerated in an unprecedented way. However, the breakup of the Soviet Union and the end of the Cold War have destroyed the framework within which the major agreements were negotiated. Efforts to control or eliminate nuclear and other weapons of mass destruction must henceforth proceed in the broader global setting.

Proliferation and Arms Control Worldwide

The idea of proliferation is a byproduct of the historical development of nuclear weapons from a U.S. monopoly to an attribute of a relatively small number of powers, among which the United States and Soviet Union had by far the largest arsenals. An example of Cold War thinking, the concept of proliferation im-

*Chemical weapons poison their victims; biological weapons infect them; toxins are poisons derived from living organisms.

plicitly accepts the same idea of nuclear haves and have-nots that has worried the Ukrainians. This implication will be questioned increasingly in the post–Cold War era. Logically, the only satisfactory answer is disarmament, the elimination by all countries of the weapons in question. However, the practical difficulties of achieving disarmament suggest that limiting the spread of dangerous weapons may be one worthwhile step toward that goal.

The end of the Cold War has increased the danger that weapons of mass destruction will spread to nations that do not already have them or even to terrorist groups. Assessing the problem requires surveying not only nuclear weapons but also chemical and biological weapons (sometimes called "the poor nations' nuclear weapons") and ballistic missiles, which can be used to deliver nuclear, chemical, biological, or conventional payloads.

As of 1993, the countries that possessed nuclear weapons were the United States, Russia, Ukraine, Belarus, Kazakhstan, Britain, France, and China. Countries believed to possess nuclear weapons or to be able to assemble them quickly were Israel, Pakistan, and India. South Africa, long listed in this category, announced in 1993 that it had destroyed its nuclear weapons and eliminated its nuclear weapons program. Countries thought to be seeking nuclear weapons were Libya, Iran, Iraq, and North Korea. Argentina and Brazil had been in that category but had placed restraints on their nuclear programs. Some reports indicated that Iran was trying to assemble nuclear weapons from parts provided by formerly Soviet Muslim republics. Since Iraq's defeat in the Gulf War, UN efforts, under Security Council Resolution 687, to eliminate Iraq's weapons of mass destruction have made that country the scene of an unprecedented experiment in arms control—a goal normally pursued by diplomatic negotiation. For proliferation control, the major lesson of the Iraqi case is that a country with a limited technological base can initiate a major nuclear weapons program and largely conceal it from international scrutiny.

Large-scale use of chemical weapons has not occurred since World War I, but new concern about them emerged in the 1980s. Although only the Soviet Union, the United States, and France had possessed chemical weapons for many years, some twenty countries—including Iraq, Iran, Libya, Egypt, Syria, Israel, Indonesia, Thailand, Vietnam, North Korea, and Taiwan—are suspected of having chemical weapons programs. Iraq used chemical weapons during the Iran-Iraq War; the use of chemical and biological weapons by Iraq was also a threat during the Gulf War. Compared to nuclear weapons, chemical weapons are much easier and cheaper to produce, and their production and storage are much harder to detect. Historically used only when one party to a conflict has them, chemical weapons cause high casualty rates that can decisively affect the outcome of a conflict, as in the Iran-Iraq War.

The list of diseases whose pathogens can be used for biological warfare is long; genetic engineering could be used to make it longer. Biological agents can be highly effective in much smaller quantities than chemical agents. However, it takes longer for them to work their course, and it is difficult to ensure that users do not infect themselves. Partly for such reasons, historical evidence of the use of biological weapons in warfare is sketchier than evidence on chemical weapons. As of 1988, however, at least ten nations were thought to have or be developing biological weapons, among them Iraq and the Soviet Union.

A versatile delivery system for any of these weapons, ballistic missiles travel several times as fast as aircraft and are not subject to pilot error. For a long time there was no effective defense against missile attack, although one effective antimissile defense system, the Patriot, was introduced in the Gulf War in January

1991. Because the technology required to develop ballistic missiles and satellite launch vehicles is the same, a government can easily hide a weapons-oriented missile program as a peaceful one. For all these reasons, the spread of ballistic missiles is a major facet of global militarization. Cruise missiles—essentially pilotless aircraft that can be used to deliver warheads—make proliferation even harder to control. Small aircraft, particularly jets, make quite adequate cruise missiles. Given the Global Positioning System (GPS), consisting of twenty-four satellites that emit signals for navigation, a cruise missile equipped with a low-cost GPS receiver can strike within feet of its target, compared to accuracy of a half-mile for the Scud missiles fired by Iraq during the Gulf War. When the GPS became fully operational in 1992, it ended what had been the technologically advanced countries' monopoly on accurate navigation.

Exporters of missile technology have included China, the former Soviet Union (and now Russia), Israel, Brazil, India, North Korea, Sweden, and Argentina. Other countries that have at least deployed ballistic missiles include Algeria, Libya, South Africa, Iran, Iraq, Syria, Egypt, Saudi Arabia, Yemen, Pakistan, South Korea, and Taiwan. Most countries seek intermediate-range missiles (those with ranges of 600 to 3,400 miles); some are thought to be developing long-range, intercontinental missiles. The fact that the list of exporters includes several countries that are not major industrial powers suggests that missile technologies will continue to spread.

The extensive weapons programs that came to light in Iraq, and more recent intelligence reports that North Korea is also close to developing nuclear weapons, clearly illustrate the urgency of efforts to control proliferation in the 1990s. Real safety from weapons of mass destruction requires not just preventing their spread but rather eliminating them completely or at least reducing them to the lowest achievable levels. Where does the world stand in these tasks?

Without question, the ending of the Cold War has helped in a number of respects. First and foremost, proliferation control, which the superpower confrontation had eclipsed for decades, has come front and center among arms issues. Largely because of the momentum that developed as the Cold War ended, enough arms control treaties have been concluded that the emphasis in arms control is now shifting from negotiation to implementation. For purposes of controlling global proliferation, the most important agreements are not the INF and START treaties, which loomed so large in the Cold War context, though the nuclear arms cuts they call for represent major steps toward reducing the immense gaps between nuclear haves and have-nots. Rather, proliferation control depends, or will depend, on the Nuclear Nonproliferation Treaty (NPT, 1968) in the case of nuclear weapons, the Chemical Weapons Convention (CWC, 1993), the Biological and Toxin Weapons Convention (BTWC, still under negotiation), and the Missile Technology Control Regime (MTCR, 1987), which is not a treaty but an agreement among highly developed nations to try to halt the spread of ballistic missile technologies. None of these has been adhered to by all the world's nations. But the NPT and CWC both had been signed by 150 nations as of 1993; foreseeably, the same nations will sign the BTWC when it is opened for signatures.

The emerging system of treaties needs further strengthening. Implementation of the START treaties must still be assured. The NPT will expire in 1995 and should be renewed and strengthened. The MTCR should be replaced with a binding treaty comparable to the others. Nations that have not signed should be encouraged to sign these agreements. Some additional agreements, such as a comprehensive test ban, would further strengthen the system. Additional treaties at the regional level could also help persuade signatory governments to spend less on weapons and more on sustainable development. Nowhere is this more true than in the Middle East. However, a treaty framework is at last emerging within which the world community can act to broaden the scope of compliance.

Between signing a treaty and verifying compliance, a gulf looms. For a long time, experts warned that many forms of proliferation control would be exceedingly difficult. Controlling the export of dual-use items—such as chemicals that could be used either for legitimate purposes or for making chemical weapons, or missile technologies that could be used either to launch satellites or to wage war—would be especially difficult. Yet recent events have set precedents that show how much can be accomplished in arms control with sufficient commitment and resources. To verify compliance, U.S.-Soviet agreements, starting with the INF Treaty, prescribed both satellite surveillance and on-site inspections. The terms imposed on Iraq after the Gulf War effectively internationalized the system of intrusive inspections, making the UN the enforcer—a valuable precedent for an era in which the main threats to global peace are likely to be regional conflicts. The International Atomic Energy Agency's unprecedented censure of North Korea in 1993 for noncompliance with the NPT provides another example of how the international community can raise the costs of proliferation. In this case the censure was followed by threats of UN sanctions and—as a positive inducement—offers of U.S. aid on condition that offending weapons programs be phased back. Experts now also believe that verification of treaty-compliance will be possible, even in fields like chemical or biological weapons, if arms control agreements include two requirements. One is on-site inspection. The other is prior declaration by each state of its activities in the treaty-regulated field. The declarations provide a base line against which the inspectors can verify compliance.

The point of these and other measures is that the framework of arms control agreements provides only the beginning of a web of restraints that raise the costs of noncompliance and may deter other states from violating the treaties. It remains far from clear that the international community will always be willing to commit the level of resources to restraining violators that it committed in Iraq. The task of reducing global militarization will surely remain difficult, dangerous, and costly. In a world that has learned how to destroy itself but still has trouble finding the resources to support sustainable development, however, the incentives to reduce investment in weapons of mass destruction are not far to seek.

Conclusion: Self-Destruction or Sustainability?

Are the world's peoples moving in any conscious, concerted way toward creation of a rationally structured global order? World history always displays a global pattern of interrelatedness, changing over time. When stresses build to an intolerable level, they produce the kind of global crises—two vast wars and a crushing depression—that destroyed the world of 1914. The twentieth century is unique only in that runaway growth in population, on one hand, and in science and technology, on the other, has raised unprecedented questions about the sustainability and the potential for self-destruction of the world's societies.

Today awareness of problems and alternatives is not lacking. Massive evidence shows the need to complete the demographic transition if the world is not to succumb to the ecological transition. Concern about human-induced climatic change spotlights the urgency of solving myriad problems of food production, resource depletion, and environmental degradation on which the sustainability of life depends. Televised images of hunger, disease, and death in poor or wartorn countries, broadcast into the homes of the affluent at dinnertime, mock middle-class comfort as insistently as peasant want devalued aristocratic luxury in prerevolutionary France or Russia. Facts and figures—now instantly available in volume thanks to electronic data processing and communications networks—warn all who pay heed about global militarization and the colossal displacement of attention that equates "security" with national defense rather than with global sustainability. The world is tightly integrated but not yet so reordered as to maximize productivity and equity for all.

All these problems have solutions—or at least strategies for coping. Ways exist to slow population growth, move toward regional sustainability in food and energy, slow human-induced climate change, stimulate economic development, harness development plans to the needs of the people they affect, and control weapons of mass destruction. But can the world's peoples implement these strategies without first coming to see themselves primarily as members of a global community, rather than of particular villages or nations? Must they not see themselves, too, as parts of the natural order, rather than as its overlords? If they cannot respond to their common interests, the risk is that the world of interdependence amid scarcity will lurch toward a new configuration, shaped perhaps by weapons of mass destruction, perhaps by ecological catastrophe.

Individuals ask what difference they can make in the face of such problems. Only despair counsels a negative answer. Twentieth-century history is full of instances where individuals made a difference: national independence struggles, the women's movement, movements for civil and human rights, grassroots groups working for development in poor countries, and the anti-nuclear and environmental movements. In the mass society, history belongs less than ever to the powerful few.

Notes

1. Lester R. Brown et al., *State of the World, 1987: A Worldwatch Institute Report on Progress Toward a Sustainable Society* (New York: Norton, 1987), pp. 26–27.
2. Brown et al., *State of the World, 1984,* p. 2.
3. Quoted in Brown et al., *State of the World, 1993,* p. 3.

Suggestions for Further Reading

Bailey, Kathleen C. *Doomsday Weapons in the Hands of Many: The Arms Control Challenge of the '90s* (1991).

Brown, Lester R., et al. *State of the World: A Worldwatch Institute Report on Progress Toward a Sustainable Society* (1984–1993, published annually).

Brown, Lester R., et al. *Vital Signs, 1992: The Trends That Are Shaping Our Future* (1992).

Crow, Ben, Mary Thorpe, et al. *Survival and Change in the Third World* (1988).

Ekins, Paul. *A New World Order: Grassroots Movements for Global Change* (1992).

International Monetary Fund, *World Economic Outlook* (May 1993).

Kidron, Michael, and Ronald Segal. *The New State of the World Atlas.* 4th ed. (1991).

Reitsma, H. A., and J. M. G. Kleinpenning. *The Third World in Perspective* (1989).

Reynolds, Lloyd G. *Economic Growth in the Third World: An Introduction* (1986).

Schell, Jonathan. *The Abolition* (1984).

———. *The Fate of the Earth* (1982).

Schroeer, Dietrich. *Science, Technology, and the Nuclear Arms Race* (1984).

World Bank. *World Development Reports* (1984–1993, published annually).

CHAPTER 20

Toward the Twenty-First Century

As the twentieth century draws to a close, what inferences can we draw, not just about the contemporary problems of environment, development, and security discussed in Chapter 19, but about the overall shape of the world in the near future? Predicting the future is hazardous, especially for those who try to look far ahead. However, it is not unreasonable to ask what existing conditions and trends imply for the near future. This chapter concludes our survey of a century of unprecedented change by asking that question. We shall examine the evidence under four headings reflecting the themes of this book: tightening global integration; the disequilibrium among cultures as they react to this tightening; the future of the mass-oriented society; and nature, technology, and the mass society in an interdependent world.

Toward a New Pattern of Global Integration

In the longer perspective of world history, the twentieth century will likely be remembered as a time when one pattern of global integration collapsed after almost five centuries of development and was replaced, after a transitional period, with a new and different pattern. What collapsed was the European-dominated pattern that began with the voyages of Columbus and da Gama and ended in the triple crisis of 1914–1945. The transitional period that followed was the interlude of superpower polarity: the Cold War. The global pattern now forming differs in two key respects: geoeconomic competition has eclipsed the geopolitical rivalry of the Cold War, and the number of power centers is increasing. The pre-1914 world had essentially one major power center, Europe (although the great powers within that center competed with each other for hegemony, and new, non-European powers—especially the United States—were contending for recognition). The world of 1945–1991 had two predominant power centers, the United States and Soviet Union, which rivaled each other for hegemony; with time, the United States was challenged by growing European integration and Japanese expansion, and the Soviet Union was challenged by China. The world of the year 2000 will have at least three regional power centers located in Europe, North America, and East Asia. Whether the Soviet successor states can achieve enough political and economic stability to figure as a fourth power center remains to be seen. Whether any of these regional groupings can achieve hegemony within this new world of geoeconomic competition is an open question: the world of interdependence amid scarcity may differ from the old European-dominated pattern in having multiple centers of power and productivity, no one of which will clearly dominate the rest.

The global pattern of integration cannot be understood solely in terms of its concentrations of power and wealth, however. Indeed, a number of other features of the emerging pattern are also becoming clear and demanding recognition.

Global Integration Versus Local Disintegration

One of the most persistent trends of the twentieth century has been the tightening of global integration in one way after another—from the globalized impact of war and depression, to the multiplication of international and global economic ties, to the obliteration of differences in time and space by advanced electronic communications. As this tightening has progressed, however, the nation-state has paradoxically remained the sovereign political entity, answerable to no higher power; and the number of nation-states has roughly quadrupled, until this particular form of political organization covers practically the whole inhabited earth.

The incessant reproduction of the nation-state model suggests that it may have been applied in environments where it does not fit well. Indeed, many of the new nation-states are not cohesive or viable. Often their problems are economic. Africa is now home to over fifty nation-states (including several nearby island nations). Chapter 16 noted the severity of their socioeconomic problems and the bleak prospects that many of them face, as illustrated by the Somali crisis of the early 1990s.

Often, too, the outward form of the state masks an inner lack of the ethnic cohesion implied in the concept. Because most nation-states are in fact multiethnic, the overarching trend toward interdependence and global integration has at times sharpened local ethnic or religious conflict and, in acute cases, has led to political disintegration. Notable cases are the Soviet Union and Yugoslavia, multinational states that had been held together by authoritarian regimes. When that central power loosened, each fell apart into smaller would-be nation-states in potential or actual conflict with their neighbors and in search of ties with larger regional groupings that could compensate for the new states' small size and limited resources. It was as if the growing global trend toward integration made it less risky for small ethnic groups—such as the Baltic nationalities or the Slovenes and Croats—to go it alone and possibly later join some other large group, like the European Community, on their own terms.

It has been argued that the challenges to the nation-state as a form of political organization signify a reassertion of historically deeper-rooted differences of culture and civilization.

Such a reassertion of civilizational solidarities and differences may well figure as a major force in the world of the foreseeable future. As a divisive force, it may help explain the breakup of the Soviet Union or Yugoslavia or the controversy surrounding Hindu revivalism in India. As a unifying force, it helps explain phenomena as diverse as the drive for European unity, the Islamic resurgence, or the rapid development of a group of Asian countries that share Confucian culture. Against the backdrop of twentieth-century world history, it seems unlikely, however, that this reassertion of cultural identities will occur in isolation from other major political and economic forces.

What Is Happening to the North-South Gap?

As the new world pattern of tightened integration and multiple power centers takes shape, one of the most important questions concerns the gap between the technologically advanced North and the less developed South.

During the late twentieth century, the evidence indicates that as the world became more tightly integrated, the gap between the affluent and the impoverished widened. Especially between 1945 and 1973, the world economy grew very rapidly, but the results of this growth were very unevenly distributed among the world's nations. As of 1990, GNP per person stood at or below $1,000 in some 50 countries. In contrast, GNP per person had reached $21,790 in the United States, $25,430 in Japan, and $32,680 in Switzerland. Not only had incomes fallen in 49 countries during the 1980s; but over the entire quarter-century between 1965 and 1990, GNP per person had shrunk in at least 23 nations, all in Africa and Latin America. In all the industrialized, high-income countries, in contrast, production per person had grown over the same period. Of course, there were major developmental differences among both developing and developed countries; we shall say more about these below. Multinational corporations and the development of a globally integrated financial market, operating around the clock with transaction volume of $1 trillion per day, had played a major part in creating and widening the North-South gap. As of 1990, over $40 billion per year flowed from the poorer to the wealthy countries.

The statistics that economists have conventionally used on GNP per person, including the figures just quoted, are open to objection on a number of fronts. They are affected by distortions in the monetary exchange rates in terms of which they are computed. A better way to measure incomes, now coming into wide use, is in terms of purchasing power. Other statistical refinements have also been proposed. The human development index (HDI) devised by the UN Human Development Program, takes account not only of incomes, but also of health and education. By the HDI, Costa Rica outranks Kuwait, and Cuba outranks Saudi Arabia—rankings radically different from those based solely on GNP per person, however it is computed. Yet another refinement, the Index of Sustainable Economic Welfare (ISEW), deducts measurements of resource depletion from those of economic production, costs ignored by other measures of economic output.

As alternative statistics accumulate for enough years and enough countries to permit broadly based comparisons, changes in perceptions of the world's economic inequalities will result. Production figures calculated in terms of purchasing power parity (PPP), as opposed to exchange rates, have lately attracted much attention, partly because the rankings of the world's largest national economies come out differently. This is true above all for China. In 1991, it had only the tenth-largest economy in the world by the exchange rate method of calculation but had the third-largest by the PPP method.

The shift from the exchange-rate method to the PPP method of calculation also affects perceptions of the overall developmental gap. For example, by the exchange rate method, the industrialized economies of Western Europe, North America, and Japan accounted for nearly 73 percent of world GDP at the end of the 1980s, and the developing countries accounted for only 18 percent. Calculated by the PPP method, the gap shifts to 54 percent for the same industrial economies compared to 34 percent for the developing ones.[1]

The shift in methods of calculation thus narrows the assessment of the development gap but does not make the gap disappear. One way to verify this is to compare statistics on economic production with those on population. Even by the PPP method, income per person in China in 1991 was less than one-tenth as much as income per person in Japan. China's huge population made its economy one of the world's largest, but most Chinese were still poor. Considering that the population of the developing countries accounts for nearly 75 percent of world population, while Western Europe, North America, and Japan account for only about 15 percent of world population, the economic gap between affluent and poor societies looms disproportionately large, whether the poor countries' share of world GDP is 18 percent or 34 percent.

This gap in development will thus predictably remain a key global issue. Especially because the gap has widened in recent decades, it is likely to give rise to some of the greatest challenges of the twenty-first century.

Industrialization of the South As noted in Chapter 19, a conspicuous difference between today's North-South gap and the 1914 gap between great powers and colonies is that the wealthier and more powerful states no longer monopolize industrial production. This is one sense in which the North-South gap is changing and will predictably continue to do so, with consequences both for developing and for industrialized countries. For developing countries aspiring to improve their position in the world, the highest economic goal will be to master the high-technology, high-value forms of production that will enable them to compete successfully in export markets. South Korea and Taiwan have begun to do this. Some other countries that have not yet achieved high overall levels of development or income certainly have firms that can perform at high international standards; this is notably true of India, with its technology center at Bangalore or its booming business center at Bombay.

The fact remains that international business is dominated by large multinational firms, six hundred of which accounted in the 1980s for half of the world's industrial output. Some developing countries—including South Korea, Malaysia, Turkey, Brazil, or Argentina—now have their own multinational firms. Yet as of 1989, three-quarters of all multinational firms were headquartered in the United States, Japan, Britain, France, or Germany. Many critiques have been levied against these corporations for reinforcing global inequalities in development and income (see Chapter 19). Today, some of them are becoming so globalized that they are beginning to loose their national identifications. This does not yet mean, however, that these firms have become forces for reducing the development gap, or that most developing countries will not continue to have difficulty defending their interests in dealings with firms that have more resources than they do.

Looking at the industrialization of the South from the viewpoint of societies in the North raises another important point. The relocation of much of basic manufacturing to poorer countries has—as many residents of former U.S. factory towns can tell—practically wiped out certain types of industry in the highly developed countries. The result is sometimes referred to as the "hollowing out" of their economies. What remains is an economy that may have a strong high-technology sector and will surely have an enlarged service sector. But much of old-fashioned industry—clothing, other light consumer goods, metallurgy—is gone, and people who formerly held factory jobs in those fields are either unemployed or have found lower-paid jobs, mainly in the service sector.

The implications for global interdependence are not far to seek. The United States faced World War II, for example, self-sufficient in most vital resources and productive enough industrially to satisfy its own needs and some of its allies' as well. If the United States faced a crisis of such magnitude in the future, dependent on imports for many manufactured goods as well as raw materials, and deeply in debt to foreigners, its independence of action would be far more limited. Even without a crisis of that magnitude, leading figures in the still-dynamic U.S. computer industry point out that the country has lost so much of its basic manufacturing capacity that their ability to produce new products in the United States is seriously affected.

For an era of geoeconomic competition, the implication is that the widening gap between affluence and poverty does nothing to lessen global interdependence. On the contrary, the very idea of "national economies" is losing its meaning. Each decision to relocate a factory to a cheaper labor market confirms the perception that the real market is a global one characterized by a stark developmental gap.

Migration The people of poor countries have not been slow to draw their own conclusions from the combination of an increasingly interdependent world and a widening North-South income gap. Continuing a practice that has done more to shape world history over the ages than has the modern phenomenon of the nation-state, they migrate in growing numbers in the hope of improving their prospects. Most of this migration is still the rural-to-urban migration within countries that has created supermetropolises like Cairo and Mexico City and is expected to make a majority of the world's population urban by the year 2000. Affluent countries—especially Germany since its reunification—also have important internal migration patterns. However, more and more of the migration crosses national borders. The UN now estimates that at least 100 million people, or 2 percent of the world's population, live outside the countries where they were born, but mostly still in the South. Of the 100 million, 17 million are refugees, fleeing war or persecution, and additional millions flee environmental degradation, drought, or famine. Most migrants, however, are economically motivated. In fact, the economic hardship of many poor countries has blurred the distinction between refugees fleeing persecution and economic migrants fleeing starvation. Historically, many migrants moved only temporarily, but more and more migrants move to stay. Totaling \$66 billion in 1989, the sums that migrants remitted to relatives in their countries of origin were second only to the oil industry as an item in international trade and far exceeded that year's foreign aid payments (\$46 billion). Increasingly, too, the migrants are women, often traveling alone. Generally destined for wage discrimination and perhaps other abuses, they remain more reliable than males in sending money to relatives at home.

With no frontiers left for them to open, the flood of migrants has become one of the most pressing policy concerns for the affluent nations. As of 1990, foreigners made up 3.3 percent of the population in Great Britain, 6.4 percent in France, 8.2 percent in the former West Germany, 8.5 percent in the United States, and 16.3 percent in Switzerland. In all cases, the figure was higher than it had been five years earlier. Even Japan—economically

Migrants from Morocco head for Spain by motorboat. *At the Strait of Gibraltar, only ten miles separate Africa from Europe. People come from as far away as China or the Philippines to attempt the dangerous crossing.* *José Luis Moreno*/El País, *Madrid*

the most internationally oriented of the wealthy countries, but socially the most insular and the most insistent on maintaining its ethnic homogeneity—had 280,000 foreigners who had overstayed their visas in 1992, up from 20,500 only three years earlier. Plagued by neo-Nazi violence against foreigners, Germany in 1993 abandoned the liberal asylum policy that it had maintained for over forty years. France did the same. Even the United States, which had prided itself on being a land of immigrants, began to turn away boatloads of illegal immigrants from China.

Experts warned, however, that legal barriers to immigration could not withstand the pressure of such great human need. Migrants would come illegally if they could not come legally. The only real solution would be sustainable development in the South and a narrowing of the North-South gap. Like the growing industrialization of the poorer countries, then, migration from South to North spotlights the contradiction between the widened income gap and today's global interdependence. In the twenty-first century, the outlook is that this gap will be narrowed through either development in the South or migration that batters down whatever defenses the affluent attempt to build around themselves.

Geoeconomic Competition Among Multiple Power Centers

During the five centuries of European world domination, the great European powers constantly contended among themselves for pre-eminence. Several powers held this position in succession, the last and most successful being Great Britain, the most powerful state of the nineteenth century. In the very different circumstances that followed World War II, the United States appeared so pre-eminent for the next quarter century that enthusiasts talked about the start of an "American century." The record of world history shows, however, that hegemony is at best a cyclical phenomenon and never lasts. Britain's proved unusually long: there really was a "British century." That of the United States was comparatively brief.

History also shows that the world does not have to have a hegemonic power at all. Before the European voyages of exploration tied the entire world together into a European-controlled network, a series of thirteenth-century trade networks had tied together most of Afro-Eurasia into a "world" of hemispheric scope, but no single power or trade network had dominated more than its own region. Many observers think that the world of the twenty-first century may resemble this multicentered pattern rather than the more recent pattern of European domination. One of the resemblances may be, in fact, that East Asia will resume its historical prominence as the most productive economic region. A survey of potential power centers will help us better appreciate the possibilities for such a multicentered pattern of global integration. How well equipped is each of them for global economic competition? We shall consider the former Soviet bloc, Europe, North America, and East Asia.

The Old Second World: Cooperation or Conflict? The former Soviet Union's potential in natural resources for geoeconomic competition is enormous. Covering a sixth of the earth's surface, the former USSR contains as much farmland as the United States and Canada combined. It is also rich in minerals. In the early years of the Soviet command economy, such riches raised the USSR to second place among the world economies. But, as we saw in Chapter 14, the communist regime could not survive the triple breakdown of political legitimacy, economic and social effectiveness, and ethnic cooperation that developed in the 1970s and 1980s. After the disintegration of the USSR, the dominant power of the Cold War "Second World," into fifteen loosely federated republics in 1991, the economic prospects for all of the republics seem dim at least for the foreseeable future. The prospects for the former eastern European satellites appear almost as bleak.

The former satellites are pinning their hopes for the economic future on their applications for admission to the European Community. It seems likely, however, that even after their admission, their communist legacy of outmoded plant, inadequate infrastructure, and ecological devastation will retard their ability to compete in the global marketplace for some time.

In the former Soviet Union, none of the conflicts that led to its collapse has been resolved. Within Russia itself, a political battle continues between President Boris Yeltsin and the Russian parliament. The hardships associated with the attempt to convert to a market economy continue to discourage many Russians to the point that polls reveal growing nostalgia for the former regime. Beyond the new frontiers of the Russian Republic, multiple wars rage. Some of these pit ethnic minorities within one of the successor republics, aided by their cousins from outside, against the dominant ethnic group. Such is the case of the struggle between Armenians and Azerbaijanis for control of part of the Azerbaijan Republic. Elsewhere, as in Tadjikistan, rival factions respectively championing communism and Islam are in contention. Nor do these wars exhaust the possibilities of conflict, for the collapse of the USSR left 25 million ethnic Russians living outside Russia, potential victims of ethnic discrimination for which they would seek remedies in Russian military power. Indeed, elements of the former Red Army have already been involved in some of these conflicts, and the commanders of other units are selling their most sophisticated arms to the highest bidder.

In the midst of so many conflicts, achieving a rate of economic development that would make the nations of the former USSR effective competitors in the global marketplace will be virtually impossible. Ironically, the most hopeful sign for the economic future may be the partial reconstitution of the former USSR by some of the same people who ran parts of it until the collapse of 1991. Eleven of the fifteen successor republics are now led by men who acquired their political experience in communist governments but who proclaim themselves to be economic reformers. Despite their professed nationalism, such men know that cooperation among the republics is essential to the economic future of all of them. Thus in July 1993 the leaders of Russia, Belarus, and Ukraine agreed to establish a customs union of the three Slavic republics, economically reuniting 70 percent of the population of the former USSR. The twenty-first century may be far advanced, however, before this partially reconstituted USSR becomes a geoeconomic contender, for there are grave problems to surmount. For example, several republics are dependent for substantial proportions of their energy on nuclear reactors as inherently unsafe as the one that produced a catastrophe at Chernobyl in 1986.

Progress and Pitfalls on the Road to European Integration The signing of the Maastricht treaty in December 1991, we saw in Chapter 12, seemed to herald a new chapter in Europe's progress toward the goal that champions of European unity had imagined since the 1950s: a political and economic union, a United States of Europe of a size to rival the United States of America in geoeconomic competition. The events of 1992 and 1993, however, revealed that there were pitfalls on the road to a Europe sharing the same currency and even the same government.

It had long been obvious that some nations were less favorable than others to a tightly integrated union. Much of British opinion, for example, remains hostile to the prospect of conforming to the dictates of European Economic Community (EEC) bureaucrats in Brussels on such touchy subjects as agricultural subsidies, or the rights of labor unions, or the minimum wage. Similar concerns about EEC infringement of national sovereignty led Danish voters in June 1992 to refuse to ratify the treaty. They reversed their verdict only when the other nations of the EEC conceded that Denmark could opt out of Maastricht's requirements for a common European citizenship, police force, and defense policy.

In September 1992 the French ratified the treaty by the same narrow margin (51 to 49 percent) by which the Danes originally rejected it. Analyses of how the French voted proved that fault lines of disagreement over the merits of European integration ran not only between nations but within them. Most of rural France and many regions hard hit by recession and industrial decline voted against Maastricht. The tiny margin of victory came from the cities (Paris voted over 62 percent in favor). Clearly France's farmers and unemployed industrial workers feared that the changes integration brought could only hurt them, while managers and professional people welcomed such changes as advantageous.

The fact that different French social groups voted differently on Maastricht showed that after almost thirty-five years of progress toward integration, people still thought of European unity in terms of economic calculation—whether it would help them or hurt them—rather than as a focus for political idealism. To most people, "Europe" still meant a marketplace—whether tempting or frightening—rather than a common home.

With the populations so ambivalent, progress toward fulfilling the goals of Maastricht has been halting. In September 1992, for example, Britain and Italy, to defend their currencies against speculators, withdrew them from the system of fixed exchange rates by which members of the EEC were supposed to abide. Their insistence on going their own economic way led many observers to wonder whether the goal of a common European currency managed by a common central bank would be achieved by the year 2000, if at all. The last day of 1992 did bring the long-anticipated shutdown of frontier customs offices, but Britain, Ireland, and Denmark still required visitors from other countries of the EEC to display a passport.

Further economic difficulties for the EEC loomed ahead. It had already proved difficult to integrate the German economy with the economies of Greece and Portugal, where per capita GNP was three or four times smaller. It would take even longer for Poland, Hungary, the Czech Republic, Slovakia, Slovenia, Romania, and Bulgaria to meet the stringent requirement of a functioning market economy that the EEC set as a condition for acting positively on their applications for membership.

Today, then, the prospects for the emergence of a united Europe as a fully effective global competitor are still somewhat clouded. Even though a number of Europe's national economies are themselves among the world's largest, geoeconomic logic urges the continent's integration. It is not certain, however, that such logic will invariably prevail over the powerful forces of nationalistic sentiment. Logic supports the decision of Volvo and Renault to merge into a single car maker. But it will probably be far into the twenty-first century, if ever, before the Swedes and the French perceive themselves as above all Europeans.

USA, the Last Superpower? Because historians can no better foretell the future than anyone else can, it may be true, as some critics contend, that people who are dubious about the United States' position in the global configuration of the next century are merely "declinists," unwilling to acknowledge that the nation will long remain the world's only superpower. In this optimistic view, inherent U.S. strength will enable the nation to overcome the late-twentieth-century problems that most Americans acknowledge: the burden of debt, social tensions, failures of basic institutions such as the schools, the apparent inability of even middle-class young people to attain the level of affluence of their parents' generation. In this view the recession of the early 1990s is merely one more downswing of the economic cycle, not a warning of the kinds of disappointments that the twenty-first century reserves for Americans.

It is undeniable, however, that as we approach the year 2000 the U.S. position vis-à-vis the rest of the developed world is quite different from what it was at midcentury. Then, the U.S. economy was in the midst of unparalleled growth, spurred by a manufacturing sector perfected in the newest technologies. That sector's skilled employees, led by the world's best-funded research scientists, saw their standard of living steadily rising. As the U.S. gross domestic product continued to grow at annual rates of at least 4 percent through the

1960s, U.S. resources seemed adequate to fund an improving society, defend American interests militarily around the world, and still avoid going into debt. Indeed as late as 1970, when GDP growth began falling far below 4 percent annually, U.S. economic output still exceeded the outputs of both Europe and Japan combined, though both had by then fully recovered from the ravages of World War II.

Today, however, the U.S. position relative to these two rivals is very different. By the late 1980s U.S. economic output was equal only to about two-thirds of their combined totals. Among eight key industries, ranging from the low technology of textiles to the high technology of semiconductors and computers, the U.S. balance of trade with Europe and Japan was favorable only in commercial aircraft and chemicals.[2]

Growing consciousness among Americans that if their country's economic direction were not changed, the United States might not prove an effective competitor in the twenty-first century global marketplace helps to explain why the Democratic candidate, Bill Clinton, won the presidential election of November 1992 with 43 percent of the vote and why independent candidate Ross Perot received an astonishing 19 percent. Both Clinton and Perot campaigned for fundamental changes in the nation's economic direction; President Bush's message that nothing was wrong was not persuasive.

Six months into the Clinton presidency, however, in the summer of 1993, many of the new economic initiatives that Clinton had campaigned for were yet to be enacted.

It is too early to tell whether these innovations will be indefinitely thwarted, but to some historians, Clinton's early frustrations came as no surprise. The United States, they contended, was trying to prepare for the twenty-first century with a constitution better suited to the eighteenth century, when it was written. Its emphasis on the separation of executive and legislative power serves far better to block than to foster change. Congress's procedures offer virtually unlimited possibilities to vested interests to reduce or eliminate such change.

In addition to these institutional obstacles to American economic renovation, there are instinctual obstacles. American instincts in favor of complete free enterprise managed by local choices run counter to the hints of government-business cooperation found in the Clinton program. Americans instinctively have considered their tax burden—though it is the lightest in the developed world—outrageous, and suggestions of raising taxes (as might have to be done to pay off the debt and renovate the economy) they consider unconscionable, though polls in the 1990s found this feeling less strong than it had been.

The continuing influence of such instincts has led some historians to wonder whether, despite the anxieties that brought Clinton to the White House in 1993, Americans will really be willing to face up to the kind of changes needed to prevent the gradual decline of their economy from accelerating as the next century begins. These historians recall that a century before the 1990s, farsighted British analysts had anticipated *their* country's decline, warning that it could be averted only by substantial changes in Britain's fiscal, educational, industrial, social, and investment policies. But their warnings had gone unheeded. Such changes, imitating the policies that foreigners had found successful, would have seemed disruptive and uncongenial in a society like late-nineteenth-century Britain, which believed that it was uniquely qualified to set an example for the world. And so Britain, still the world's workshop and banker in 1990, dwindled into relative economic insignificance long before 2000. Only time will tell whether this analogy drawn between Britain at the beginning of this century and the United States at the beginning of the next will prove wildly farfetched or grimly prophetic.

Defenders of the idea that the United States has not exhausted its capacity for economic innovation in the 1990s can point to one bold new idea from the otherwise conventional Bush administration: the North American Free Trade Agreement (NAFTA). Endorsed, after some modifications, by the Clinton administration, NAFTA envisions the creation over a decade beginning on January 1, 1994 of the world's largest free trade zone, in which all the tariffs separating the economies of 256 million Americans, 27 million Canadians, and 94 million Mexicans would be eliminated. Clearly conceived as a response to the challenge to North American economies represented by the European Economic Community, NAFTA by late summer of 1993 had already been ratified by the Canadian parliament and was expected to pass the Mexican parliament easily. Yet NAFTA faced uncertain prospects in the U.S. Congress.

Supporters of NAFTA in all three countries were attracted by the same basic argument that defenders of the European Economic Community have always made: a nation's economy can only grow if its ability to export its products grows with the removal of obstacles like foreign tariffs. Moreover, American proponents argued that NAFTA imposed sufficiently strict standards on Mexican environmental and labor laws to keep U.S. businesses from moving across the border in quest of laxer regulation and less costly payrolls. At the same time, American NAFTA partisans argued, a more prosperous Mexican economy buoyed by enhanced exports to the United States would raise living standards there enough that Mexicans would no longer be tempted to seek a better life by illegal immigration into the United States.

For Mexican President Carlos Salinas de Gortari, NAFTA was the capstone of a policy of drastic economic innovation intended to lift Mexico out of the less developed South. However, Mexican critics of NAFTA, while less vocal than its U.S. opponents, accused Salinas of surrendering Mexican economic independence. They argued that the treaty would lead to further exploitation of Mexican workers, environmental degradation, and greater U.S. dominance. There was evidence to support such views. The Ford plant at Hermosillo, Mexico, ranked fifth in product quality among forty-six North American auto plants. However, workers at Hermosillo earned only $2.38 an hour, compared to $17.50 per hour paid to auto workers near Detroit. Such a wage differential explained Ross Perot's prediction that ratification of NAFTA would produce a "giant sucking sound" as American jobs were drawn south of the border. American consumers would not find the lower prices on cars produced in Mexico any lower. Living in a country where GDP per person was only a small fraction of that in the United States, most Mexicans would be unable to afford a new car.

According to this pessimistic scenario, NAFTA's effect would be to shrink the U.S. middle class through job loss without enlarging the Mexican middle class, since Mexico—despite its promises—would continue to restrict labor's rights to strike and bargain collectively. NAFTA would thus level the North American standard of living down, rather than up as its supporters contended.

Such fears were sufficiently widespread that in 1993 NAFTA's passage through the U.S. Congress remained doubtful. To some of its critics, the NAFTA idea was a hasty attempt to catch up with the EEC by lashing together economies and societies that had far less in common than those of Europe. Whether that criticism is sound or not, it is clear as we approach the twenty-first century that powerful pressures exist for regional economic integration along the lines of the EEC or NAFTA, though it is still unclear how cohesive these emerging economic blocs will become.

East Asia and the Chinese Challenge East Asia's economic development in recent decades has been dominated by Japan's extraordinary growth, with the four little "dragons" or "tigers"—Taiwan, South Korea, Hong Kong, and Singapore—in supporting roles as the world's most successful "newly industrializing countries" (NICs to economists). Although they differ in many ways among themselves, these five entities share important traits that help explain their development. Significantly, these shared traits reflect China's cultural influence in East Asian history. This fact spotlights how anomalous it would be, by historical standards, for East Asia to become one of the world's dominant power centers without China playing a leading role in it. And in fact, China's economic growth rate in the early 1990s has accelerated dramatically.

Because Chapter 17 has already emphasized Japan's and, to a lesser degree, China's economic development, it will suffice to complete the picture by presenting evidence here on the four smaller economies and the overall picture for the region. Although a number of other nearby countries—including Thailand, Malaysia, and Indonesia—also achieved rapid growth in the 1980s, Japan, China, and the little "dragons" command special interest because of cultural affinity as well as economic performance.

Japan has emerged out of economic underdevelopment twice, once before World War II and once since. The little "dragons" have become the most successful of the developing economies in recent decades, with average annual growth rates for the 1980s ranging from Korea's 9.7 percent to Singapore's 6.4 percent. Incomes per person have reached levels that place Hong Kong and Singapore in the lower ranks of the "high income countries" in World Bank Statistics. Although experts consider China's statistics less reliable, China claims average growth by 9.5 percent for the 1980s.

These six economies are different in many ways. China is the world's most populous country, whereas Singapore and Hong Kong are essentially city-states (still legally a British colony until 1997, Hong Kong is officially not a "state" at all). Still, all six share several traits that contribute to their economic dynamism.

Foremost among these shared traits is a strong emphasis, shaped by Confucian tradition, on education. The benefits of this emphasis include literacy rates above 90 percent and enrollment rates (for both secondary and higher education) that are generally comparable to European rates and are far higher than typical enrollment rates in other parts of Asia, Latin America, or especially Africa. A second common feature of these six economies is high savings rates. The Japanese are famous for saving much of their income. As of 1987, however, Taiwanese and Koreans had even higher savings rates of 39 and 37 percent, respectively, compared to Japan's 32 percent or the U.S. rate of 13 percent. Carefully fostered by government policy, these high savings rates pile up capital that can be loaned at low interest to support new enterprises. A third shared trait is a tradition of strong political institutions that may infringe democracy, as the military regimes of South Korea and Taiwan did, but also foster and support economic growth. Finally, while many developing countries still focused on import substitution, the East Asian economies strongly committed themselves to export-led growth. Japan's trade surpluses with the United States are well known. Less well known is that China's U.S. trade also has a surplus, which increased from $3.4 billion in 1987 to $18.3 billion in 1992. Hong Kong's and Taiwan's trade surpluses with the United States declined over the same period, mainly because their manufacturers began shifting production into China in order to take advantage of cheaper labor costs.

East Asia's emergence as the center of the world economy has been predicted for more than a decade. During that time, Japan has become the world's second-largest national economy. Calculated in terms of purchasing power rather than exchange rates, as the International Monetary Fund began to do in 1993, China's output emerges as the world's third largest, following the United States and Japan. On such a basis, East Asia's combined economic power already makes it globally eminent, if not pre-eminent.

Reflection shows, however, that East Asia's prospects of dominating the world economy are no more sure than those of any other region. The gap between Japan's economic performance and the quality of its political leadership has become only too clear from the fall of the Liberal Democratic party. However vibrant China appears economically, it has never resolved the political contradictions dramatized at Tienanmen Square in 1989. Most significantly, however, East Asia is not all one. Many Asian countries are highly uneasy with Japan's aspirations to regional leadership. Chinese leaders seem focused not on East Asia but on China as an aspiring superpower. Historical norms from any period before the 1800s would suggest, in fact, that if East Asia is to have a dominant power, it should logically be not Japan but China. East Asia will predictably be a major center of economic power and productivity in the twenty-first century, but not without its own problems to solve.

The South: Prospects for Development and Regional Integration

Just as the affluent nations of the world are not all alike, the same is true of the developing nations. Chapters 15, 16, and 17 have already noted the deterioration of economic conditions in much of Africa, the mid-range economic performance of Latin America, and the much stronger performance of parts of Asia. Today, some countries appear to be emerging out of underdevelopment. Others clearly are doing less well, and some are losing ground in a way that leads observers to speak of the Third World and the Fourth. It has been argued, in fact, that the gap among developing countries' growth rates has grown even wider than the overall North-South gap.

Emerging out of Underdevelopment? In addition to the rapidly growing countries in East Asia, a number of other countries have also begun to emerge out of underdevelopment in recent decades. The list begins with the four "little dragons," and has continued with Indonesia, Thailand, Malaysia, Turkey, and perhaps Mexico. During the period from 1965 to 1990, when the average annual rate of growth per person for all the high-income countries (those with GNP per person of $9,500 or higher in 1990) stood at 2.4 percent, all of these rapidly developing countries achieved higher average growth rates, ranging from Turkey's 2.6 percent to South Korea's 7.1 percent. Especially significant for these countries was growth in exports and in the percentage of exports that consisted of manufactures. In manufactures as a percentage of total exports, some of these fast-growing economies had matched or exceeded the average level for the high-income economies by 1990.

Predictably, rapid economic growth did not occur without favorable social and political conditions. All of these countries had high and rising literacy rates. Rates of school enrollment had risen sharply, in some cases matching those of the wealthiest nations. A few countries—South Korea, Singapore, Hong Kong, Malaysia—had virtually eliminated the gender gap in enrollments, at least through the secondary level. The food supply was generally not a problem. In most instances the daily calorie supply per person ranged between 2,800 and 3,300 in 1989, compared to an average of 3,400 for the high-income economies. Politically these countries varied considerably, but their success in development seemed to correlate with a well-established, uncontested sense of collective identity, continuity of leadership, government policy supportive of economic growth, and administrative capacity to implement policy effectively.

The Third World—and the Fourth? Further down in the rankings of developing countries, performance becomes less consistent in terms of the criteria just discussed. For example, the oil-exporting countries tend to rank highly in GNP per person in some cases but poorly in the development of manufactures or some social and political criteria. Saudi Arabia, in particular, has nearly exhausted its financial reserves and now faces credit problems. The mid-ranking countries include many of those most noted for persistence in protectionist import substitution, like India, or for overdevelopment of the public sector, like Argentina or Brazil.

At the bottom, finally, come countries with serious shortcomings on most of the points where places like Taiwan stand out. Many of these poorest countries are in Africa, but not all. For example, in 1990, the lowest third, roughly, of the world's countries as ranked by GNP per person included Nepal, Bhutan, Laos, Bangladesh, India, China, Pakistan, Sri Lanka, and the Maldive Islands in Asia, as well as Haiti, Honduras, and Guyana in Latin America. Probably belonging to the same list, although income figures were missing for them, were several other Asian nations: Afghanistan, Cambodia, Myanmar, and Vietnam. During the quarter century from 1965 to 1990, many of the poorest countries actually declined in GNP per person. Average annual rates of decline exceeded 2 percent in the cases of Zaire and Uganda. Some of these countries' exports in 1990 were worth less than $100 million (compared to South Korea's $65 billion), and some of these poorest countries' exports actually declined between 1965 and 1990.

Social indicators told a similar tale. In most of the poorest countries—with exceptions such as China and Vietnam—a majority of the population was still illiterate in 1990. Female illiteracy rates commonly exceeded those of males by 10 to 15 percentage points, and these reported rates may understate reality. At the end of the 1980s, school enrollment rates were often below 50 percent, especially for females. In some countries, this was still true even at the primary level. The low enrollment rates told nothing, moreover, of the limits on funding, equipment, and teacher training, which further widened the educational gap between Burkina Faso, for example, and South Korea. Available food supplies averaging less than 2,000 calories per day per person could still be found in a number of countries, although the average for the poorest countries was close to 2,300—or to 2,500 if India and China are included in this group. Politically, the ranks of the poorest included countries as ill fortuned as Somalia and Haiti.

The vast gulf that separates the rising and sinking stars among developing countries explains why the two extremes have at times been spoken of as the Third World—and the Fourth. What is most troubling about the disparity is that the gap was not always so wide. For several years prior to 1960, for example, the growth rates of Zaire, the Sudan, and Ghana reportedly exceeded South Korea's. A key task for the twenty-first century will be to try to reverse existing trends toward widening inequality among nations so that the 3 billion people who live in the world's poorest countries can also share in the benefits of sustainable development. The task will embrace everything from reversing environmental degradation to peacemaking to international agreements to ease the burden of international debt on the poorest of the poor.

Regional Integration in the South For much the same reasons that regional integration has appealed to many Europeans, projects of a similar kind have lately commanded increased attention all across the developing world. The end of the Cold War reinforced this trend by suddenly withdrawing the divisive option, which a number of countries in Africa and the Middle East had taken, of following a pro-Soviet as opposed to pro-Western foreign policy. Suddenly, the models projected by the world's developed and powerful nations became much more consistent, with free trade and common markets as prominent themes. The impact of these themes on Latin America and Africa well illustrates the trend toward regional integration in the developing world.

Many, though not all, of the regional groupings among developing nations were economically oriented. Practically the entire Western Hemisphere would be covered by free-trade agreements that are now in various states of negotiation. NAFTA is supposed to combine the United States, Mexico, and Canada; G-3 (the Group of Three) is to include Colombia, Mexico, and Venezuela; Caricom (the Caribbean Community) combines thirteen small nations; CACM (the Central American Common Market) brings together Costa Rica, El Salvador, Guatemala, Honduras, Nicaragua, and Panama; the Andean Pact includes Bolivia, Colombia, Ecuador, Peru, and Venezuela; and Mercosur (the Common Market of the South) covers Argentina, Brazil, Paraguay, and Uruguay. Some advocates see the vision of a hemispheric free-trade association—perhaps an expanded NAFTA—shimmering in the background.

Africa's organizations of regional and continental scope may be more varied in purpose and scale, but they have formed by the dozens in the period since independence. In addition to the Organization of African Unity, often-noted examples include the Economic Community of West Africa (ECOWAS) and the Southern African Development Coordination Council (SADCC), both mentioned in Chapter 16. In open imitation of the EEC, African states attending the 1991 OAU summit drew up a treaty to create an African Economic Community by the year 2025 and began to collect signatures. How much optimism Africa's economic deterioration can leave among the advocates of this ambitious project is unclear; yet it demonstrates the global extent of the reactions to the prospect of European integration.

Economists and policy advocates have long argued the need for "South-South" cooperation through organizations in which developing nations would collaborate to solve their common developmental needs. Although the regional integration projects now under discussion in the developing countries address this goal, most of them are more plan than substance so far. What they can accomplish is something that the next century will have to reveal. In any event, the drive for regional integration is clearly an existing trend, driven by the sense that integration can help solve common developmental problems.

If this perception is sound at the regional level, would it not also be so at the global level? In particular, what implications does the drive for integration have for the United Nations?

Organizing Global Integration: Prospects for the United Nations

As we saw in Chapter 11, the victors of World War II hoped to make a permanent peace by establishing the United Nations. All of the world's nations that joined found seats in the UN General Assembly—a first step, believers in the centuries-old dream of a federated world hoped, toward global political integration. By reserving the permanent seats on the UN's powerful Security Council to themselves, the United States, the Soviet Union, Britain, France, and China intended to keep the world's peace by perpetuating their wartime alliance. The history of the United Nations over the next forty-five years disappointed both the believers in global federalism and the exponents of great-power cooperation. As more and more Third World nations took seats in the Assembly, it became a sounding board for their resentment of the policies of the wealthier nations, especially the United States. Meanwhile, the Cold War largely paralyzed the Security Council, as the United States and the Soviet Union vetoed resolutions it passed against their respective clients.

The end of the Cold War, however, marked a turning point for the United Nations, though its future configuration and direction still remain to be determined. Germany and Japan now demand permanent Council seats, in recognition of their economic might. But even if they are added, permanent seats will still be monopolized (except for China's) by the developed nations of North America, Europe, and East Asia. To redress the balance, critics argue, why should India, Brazil, and Nigeria not have permanent seats?

The UN's proper future role is as controversial as the future composition of the Security Council. Once it was no longer paralyzed by superpower deadlock, the United Nations undertook as many operations in defense of peace from 1989 to 1993 as it had attempted in the previous forty years. In the summer of 1993 over eighty thousand soldiers from many nations, all wearing the same blue UN helmets, were deployed around the world on more than a dozen such missions. Moreover, the aims of these missions were bolder than they used to be. For most of its history, UN forces have been "peacekeepers," preserving a cease-fire between hostile armies by their presence between them. Today, however, UN missions have also become "peacemakers," overseeing the honesty of elections in Angola or Cambodia or actually attacking the stronghold of a "warlord" blamed for the deaths of UN soldiers who had been overseeing food distribution to the starving people of Somalia.

Observers of the United Nations disagree not only on whether the UN has adequate means for this kind of aggressive operation but also on whether it should attempt them at all. The United Nations depends for funding on the contributions of its principal members, who are currently $1.2 billion behind in their payments (the United States owes over $300 million). The UN depends for its soldiers on contingents provided on a mission-to-mission basis by its members. Despite their blue helmets, these forces ultimately take their orders from their governments back home, not from the UN commander on the spot. Governments are often reluctant to risk the lives of their troops by allowing them to become embroiled in an ongoing war. Under such restricted rules of engagement, the 22,500 UN "peacekeepers" in Bosnia in 1993 were unable to keep the peace of civilians living near the encampments, let alone impose a peace between Bosnia's warring ethnic groups.

Because the United Nations lacks a reliable army of its own, its peacekeeping missions too often appear belated and ineffectual, like the one in Bosnia. To some critics, this appearance of weakness is an argument not to overtax the United Nations by assigning it missions beyond its means, such as protecting ethnic minorities in civil wars or reconstructing government authority in countries where it has disintegrated. To other critics, the UN's weakness urges the creation of a substantial permanent UN army. This solution is contested by small nations that fear such an army might intervene on their territories, as well as by great powers, which prefer to do their intervening themselves.

Amid such arguments, the United Nations is still far from being the guarantor of world peace its founders envisioned in 1945, though its usefulness has grown. It remains to the new century to define its nature and functions more clearly.

Disequilibrium Among Cultures: Reactions to Tightening Global Integration

Throughout this book we have been considering the impact on twentieth-century world history of the disequilibrium of cultures described in Chapter 1 and depicted in Chapter 2. Berliners of 1900, we suggested, had little in common with the villagers of Dinshawai.

By the 1960s, some thoughtful analysts were suggesting that the bombardment of people's attention by the new electronic mass media would efface such cultural imbalances. As people around the world became acclimated to a new universal culture by watching the same television programs and listening to the same music, their habits of thought and patterns of behavior would begin to converge. The world of 1900, sharply differentiated between its Berlins and its Dinshawais, would be transformed by the year 2000 into a "global village" where everyone lived on familiar terms with everyone else. In this section we shall evaluate the extent to which this prediction had come true by the 1990s.

What Became of the Global Village? Elements of a Common Global Culture

For an observant world traveler there is plenty of visual evidence of what appears to be a common global culture. McDonald's golden arches, for example, send the same signal to hungry people in Moscow and Beijing as they do in San Diego. Essentially the same Disneyland, created by the same company, is to be found now outside Paris, outside Tokyo, and outside Los Angeles: Mickey Mouse has become a universally recognized symbol.

Our experience on a more personal level of the electronic communications revolution of recent years can remind us of how we now live in a "global village." Today many of us matter-of-factly switch on our computers to read our "electronic mail," then tap out on our keyboard a reply that will be sent instantaneously to our fellow "villager," someone we may never have seen, sitting at another keyboard halfway round the world. We seldom reflect how inconceivable this now-routine activity would have seemed to people living only a few decades ago.

Undeniably technological change has moved humankind some distance toward a common global culture. Yet people are also *resisting* this global cultural homogenization, battling to reassert their own cultural values and traditions against its onslaught. Sometimes resistance to the encroachment of a common global culture takes the form of a reassertion of religious values; sometimes it takes the form of conflict over national identity and the organization of political life. We shall consider examples of both types.

Religious Revivalism

Considering that the world's religions have produced movements of renewal throughout history, the revival movements active around the world today have ample precedent. Even so, the late twentieth century stands out as a time when religious revival movements are on the upsurge all over the world. Each of these movements is articulated in terms of the belief system from which it springs; yet all have common traits. All the movements react against global homogenization and secularization. Far from demanding a return to the past, they assert an alternative vision of the modern world in which their own values will reign supreme and the technical details of modern life will be reordered—some accepted, some rejected—according to those values. Especially in less developed countries, the revivalist movements vigorously counterattack the encroachment of the outside world. Even more vigorous are the attacks that some movements launch against public figures in their own societies who should be among the faithful but have compromised with the outside world and not lived up to the standards that the movements uphold.

In the United States, not only are there numerous fundamentalist movements, but the religious right is becoming increasingly active in politics. One strategy is to contest seats in school board elections, in the interest of enforcing conservative standards on what is read and taught in the schools. Another strategy is to oppose abortion rights, an issue that has grown into a flashpoint in the sometimes violent clash between traditional moral and ethical values on the one hand and changing possibilities in medicine and social policy on the other.

In the former Soviet Union, the collapse of communism came as a major vindication for Russian Orthodoxy. Its magnificent liturgy offers ordinary Russians perhaps the only beautiful, uplifting experience for which most of them can hope. Competition from Protestant evangelical movements seeking converts has provoked a reaction in the form of a law to prohibit unlicensed religious movements in the Russian Republic—a reaction that combines religious and nationalist motives.

In India, too, as noted in Chapter 17, a Hindu revivalist movement, based on a new interpretation of one strand out of an extremely diverse religious tradition, has mobilized resentment against the country's religious minorities, especially the largest minority, the Muslims. With its political side organized as the Bharatiya Janata party, Hindu revivalism now jeopardizes the element of secularism and compromise in Indian politics and, thus, the survival of Indian democracy.

In Latin America, where the predominant Roman Catholic church had a long history of close identification with the ruling elites, alternative movements have appeared. Promoted by progressive Catholic leaders in the 1970s, liberation theology—sometimes described as a tropical blend of Marxism and Christianity—called for social justice and land reform. More recently, the increasingly urbanized poor have found their needs better answered by Protestant Pentecostal churches, often housed in storefronts in shanty towns. In thirty years, Latin American Protestants have tripled, rising to 12 percent, or 51 million, of the region's population. Religious change has not stopped there. For example, followers of the Afro-Brazilian Candomblé religion, once an outlaw cult, have successfully fought for official recognition and have won a court case against trivialized use of their sacred images to promote tourism.

Nowhere has religious revivalism caught the world's attention more powerfully, however, than in the Islamic world. There, the Iranian revolution of 1979 provoked exaggerated fears—and hopes in some quarters—that revolution was about to sweep through Islamic societies everywhere from West Africa to Southeast Asia. In fact, militant Islamic movements, not all of them compatible with one another, played significant roles in several important conflicts—for example, in Afghanistan following the Soviet invasion (1979), and in Lebanon's civil war. In Egypt, Islamic militants assassinated President Anwar al-Sadat (1981) and have since re-emerged, threatening the regime of President Husni Mubarak and even extending their operations into the United States with the bombing of New York's World Trade Center in 1993.

Readily inflating news items like these into a biased image of Islam, the outside world ignores the fact that most of the world's billion Muslims are no more violent than other people. Average Muslims, however, may feel quite as much of a need as do Brazilian Protestants, Orthodox Russians, or even U.S. fundamentalists to change the world as they find it. Islamic revivalists may have more in common with America's Protestant fundamentalists, for example, than either side would like to admit. A comparison would disclose differences of degree, some of them reflecting the varied stresses to which different societies are subject, others reflecting differing degrees of government tolerance for dissent. But similarities would also stand out. A number of U.S. fundamentalist groups resemble Islamic militant groups in having originated as offshoots of more moderate religious movements that were readier to live with the existing sociopolitical order. Religious activists on both sides share a readiness to identify only people like themselves as Christians or Muslims and to exclude a majority of their fellow citizens from those categories, no matter how those excluded might identify themselves. American fundamentalists and Islamic revivalists both share ambitions to change existing political conditions. In this case the similarity is surprising, for religion and politics have always been regarded as inseparable in Islam, a view very different from the biblical injunction to render unto God what is God's and unto Caesar what is Caesar's. If, as recent events in Egypt would suggest, Islamic radicals are more ready to use violence, perhaps it is because they confront governments that are more ready to repress them with violence; they also articulate the less developed countries' grievances against global inequity. But some potential for violence exists in both settings—powerful proof of the deep-seated human impulse to correct perceived cultural imbalances in terms of deeply held beliefs.

Nationalism and Political Consensus

Revived religious faith is not the only system of beliefs that has proved strongly resistant to global cultural homogenization. Nationalism—belief in the uniqueness and superiority of one's own ethnic group—also grips the imagination of many people who, in the 1990s, might be expected to be more tolerant of other groups because of their shared enthusiasm for the same modes of expression spread worldwide by electronic media. To illustrate this point, we may begin by looking at the messages sung by certain rock groups in Germany and Eastern Europe.

At first glance the universal appeal of rock to the world's young might seem a clear demonstration of global cultural homogenization. Rock concerts do not appear to differ much from one continent to the next. Everywhere there are the same flashing strobe lights, the same clouds of fog generated by dry ice, the same pounding, amplified beat of drums and electric guitars. But the *words* shouted by the German band called Destructive Force to their punk heavy-metal hit "Strength for Germany" are more uncommon: they end with the old Nazi slogan "Germany, wake up!" In fact the lyrics sung by this and other bands openly express the kind of racist German nationalism that has inspired so many attacks in the 1990s by mobs of right-wing youth on Turks and other foreigners living in Germany. The Hungarian band that calls itself Gypsy Destroyers Guard Regiment is even more explicitly genocidal: "The flame-thrower is the only weapon/With which I can triumph/Exterminate the Gypsies/Whether child, woman, or man."[3]

Of course only a minority of East European rock bands sing such songs (though another neo-Nazi group, Bad Uncles, had a hit that rose to number five on the charts). But the point to be noted is how bands like these have adapted rock to express some very old ideas.

This kind of adaptation would surprise some of the first analysts of global culture, who insisted that in the new world of electronic communication "the medium is the message." They meant that what mattered at a rock concert was just the audience's experience of joyful earfuls of sound, but nothing more. Concerts of groups like Destructive Force suggest, however, that the new electronic media can be used to reaffirm an old belief—German or Hungarian racist nationalism—that challenges the very idea of a shared global culture.

Similar points emerged even more starkly from the war that ravaged the former Yugoslavian republic of Bosnia and Hercegovina in the early 1990s. What but inflamed nationalist hostility, it might seem, could cause the relentless cruelty—the mass rape and "ethnic cleansing"—that characterized the conflict? A closer look suggests, however, that the differences of nationality apparent on the surface were not the main issue. They aligned with deeper differences of culture and religion; but these, too, were only pretexts. The critical issue was probably the loss of consensus among closely related ethnic groups about how to organize political life in what had been the Socialist Federal Republic of Yugoslavia.

Yugoslavia, the land of the South Slavs, only achieved unification in 1918. It was home to six South Slavic nationalities: the Bosnian Muslims, Croats, Macedonians, Montenegrins, Serbs, and Slovenes. These six closely related ethnic groups have differences in religion and culture. The Croats and Slovenes are Roman Catholic; the Macedonians, Montenegrins, and Serbs are Eastern Orthodox; and the Bosnian Muslims are descendants of Slavs who converted to Islam. Despite their differences, all six groups have much in common. Their languages are closely related, although the alphabets they use vary according to historic religious ties. Croats and Slovenes write in Latin letters, as most Bosnian Muslims also now do; Macedonians, Montenegrins, and Serbs write in Cyrillic letters. A unity movement developed among the South Slav peoples in the early 1800s, and a deliberate decision was made in the 1830s to develop a common literary language, Serbo-Croatian, in addition to which Slovenian and Macedonian remained distinct languages.

The creation of a unified monarchy in 1918, with the Serbian dynasty as its ruling house, was a major victory for the unity movement. However, tensions developed among the nationalities. In particular, Croats and Slovenes felt that Serbs wielded too much power. During World War II, fighting both between rival resistance movements, one Communist and one supporting the exiled king, and between Yugoslavs and the Axis occupation forces gave the country a foretaste of intercommunal conflict such as it has experienced in the 1990s. The Communist resistance, led by Josip Broz Tito came out on top, abolished the monarchy in 1945, and created a federal republic. The federal system combined six republics: Bosnia and Hercegovina, Croatia, Macedonia, Montenegro, Serbia, and Slovenia. In addition, Serbia included two autonomous provinces, Vojvodina and Kosovo.

Under Tito (d. 1980), Yugoslavia succeeded both in keeping its distance from the Soviet Union and in holding together; yet economic and political pressures mounted with time. From the late 1970s on, the economy declined, and developmental gaps among the country's regions gave rise to protests. In the late 1980s, demands for a multiparty political system also mounted. In January 1990, the Communist Party voted to give up its monopoly of power. Communists, now called Socialists, won majorities in Serbia and Montenegro. However, non-Communists won parliamentary majorities in all other republics. With these differences of party went different visions about the future of Yugoslavia. Slovenes and Croats at first favored federalism, democracy, and a market economy, but Serbs wanted central rule from Belgrade and a managed economy.

Frustration over these conflicting goals, coupled with the lure of Europe's long-anticipated economic union in 1992, then led Slovenes and Croats to opt for secession, so beginning Yugoslavia's disintegration (noted in Chapter 12). Many Slovenes and Croats had long felt that the national government drained away too much of their income and hoped, once independent, to find a more congenial home in the EEC. Slovenes voted for independence in June 1991 with the slogan "Europe now." In July 1991, the Serbs tried by force to keep Slovenia from seceding. Failing in this, the Serbian forces moved into Croatia, ravaging and "ethnically cleansing" much of it in the second half of 1991. UN troops were originally sent in to monitor the war zone in Croatia. Armed conflict between the Serbs and other nationalities proved grossly unequal because the Serbs both retained control of the Yugoslav army and persuaded the UN to embargo arms sales to the former Yugoslav republics, a decision that made it impossible for the other Yugoslav successor states to defend themselves adequately.

Things worsened when Bosnia and Hercegovina voted for independence in February 1992. Like a smaller version of Yugoslavia, Bosnia was home to several nationalities, none of which formed a majority. Croats made up 17 percent of the population; Serbs (who had boycotted the independence vote) made up 31 percent but controlled a large part of the countryside; and Bosnia's Muslim Slavs made up 44 percent. Fighting started in April, with the Serbian-controlled Yugoslav army attacking the new state. After the army pulled out under UN pressure, the Bosnian Serbs continued fighting with support from Serbia. At first, both Muslims and Croats fought against the Serbs. Once UN mediators produced plans to divide Bosnia into three ethnic components, however, the conflict degenerated into a three-cornered struggle for territory. Residents of the global village now had their nightly look at televised coverage of war and atrocity, especially at the destruction of Sarajevo, a cosmopolitan European city which, if it had witnessed the assassination of an Austrian archduke by a Bosnian Serbian nationalist in 1914—the event that provoked World War I—had since become enough of a showplace to host the Winter Olympic Games successfully in 1984. Could such a breakdown happen anywhere?

What did the carnage in Bosnia mean? Was it a civil war, as was often said? Was it a Serbian war of aggression, as the way it began indicates? Was it a demonstration to nationalists elsewhere, as thoughtful analysts feared, that they, too, could get away with "ethnic cleansing" without the world community doing anything effective to stop it?

Part of the difficulty of understanding the conflict arose from the way the global village's technological gadgetry could be used to manipulate presentation of the issues. Serbia's government-run media, in particular, systematically used biased and propagandistic terms to refer to the other nationalities. Referring to the same television footage that the rest of the world saw as the killing of Muslim villagers in Bosnia, Serbian announcers said that it showed the killing of Bosnian Serbs by Muslims. Especially deplorable are attempts to identify Bosnia's Muslims with Islamic radicals in places like Iran. Bosnia's Muslims are just as much South Slavs as any of the country's other nationalities (in Yugoslavia, the Muslims were recognized in the 1974 constitution as a national group). The fact that the Bosnian Muslims' ancestors converted to Islam, rather than Catholicism or Orthodox Christianity, does not make them Islamic radicals. In the towns, especially, Bosnian Muslims tend to be cosmopolitan and secular in outlook. At home in a Bosnia where the various nationalities historically coexisted in peace and even intermarried, Bosnian Muslims now find themselves fighting to save a multi-ethnic, multicultural Yugoslav society that has been all but destroyed by the Serbs' demand for a greater Serbia and the Croats' and Slovenes' decision to seek integration with Western Europe.

To refer back to the European rock singers mentioned earlier, Yugoslavia's disintegration shows what unbridled indulgence in that kind of ethnic rhetoric can lead to. Of course, Yugoslavia would not have come to its present pass if the political consensus that its unity movement historically represented had not collapsed. Earlier chapters of this book have frequently noted how much a nation's development depends on basic consensus about the definition of national identity and the organization of political life. Yugoslavia today shows how vulnerable such a consensus can become when circumstances change as radically as they did at the end of the Cold War.

However much a shared global culture grows in the twenty-first century, especially in the realm of technology and material culture, the world will thus not become a global village. At times, people will strive to reassert their religious values in an effort to master the forces of change. At other times, the accumulation of stresses on national communities and their political systems will probably continue to produce breakdowns like those of the Soviet Union or Yugoslavia. Perhaps the ultimate question in a highly interdependent world is whether men and women of the future, as they resist the homogenization of the global village, will remember that they all have common interests as human beings and that members of all ethnic and religious communities must somehow learn to live in a world where not everyone is like themselves.

The Future of the Mass-oriented Society

At the beginning of the twentieth century, more of the earth's people were governed by rulers claiming a divine or an inherited mandate, like the emperor of Japan, than were ruled by governments responsive to the will of the people. As we near the end of the century, by contrast, almost all of the world's governments are "mass oriented." Governments everywhere claim to derive their authority in some way from the mass of the people. As we have seen throughout this book, mass-oriented governments can take different forms. In the United States we are most familiar with constitutional, representative democracy based on regular votes by the mass electorate. But the twentieth century has also provided many examples of authoritarian mass-oriented regimes, in which the vast power of leaders like Hitler or Stalin was supposed to be validated by the masses' enthusiasm for their leadership.

Just as Marx once argued that history would come to an end with the defeat of the middle class by the proletariat, some American political analysts concluded in the 1990s, after the collapse of communism, that history is coming to an end with the triumph throughout most of the world of American-style free enterprise and representative democracy. In the following sections we shall test the validity of this assumption by looking at the future of the mass-oriented society in the Western democracies, in the former Soviet bloc, and in some of the nations of the South.

Disillusionment and Alternative Forms of Mass Mobilization in the Democracies

As we noted in Chapter 13, the economic stagnation of the last two decades has provoked growing impatience among voters even in the long-established representative democracies with the ineffectiveness of the traditional political parties. As we near the end of the century, are there any signs that in the next century voter discontent may strengthen some alternative kind of mass movement—perhaps even an authoritarian one—to the parties that have habitually alternated in power?

In 1993, the answer seems to be no, at least partly because the traditional parties have made the message of outsider-challengers their own. In Germany, neither of the two formal neo-Nazi parties attracted enough voters in the 1990 national elections to win any parliamentary seats, though in 1993 one of them got nearly 11 percent of the vote in a local election. In France, on the far Right, the National Front likewise won no seats in the spring elections of 1993. These election results confirm that in both Germany and France, movements of authoritarian mass mobilization have won a core of voters but have been unable to expand it, partly because the traditional conservative parties in both countries took up these movements' principal theme of hostility to continued foreign immigration.

In the United States, the principal challenger to the established political party has been Ross Perot's United We Stand movement, which only a few critics have compared to an authoritarian mass movement. Perot himself would certainly repudiate any such characterization. His support, like the support for the European movements, is holding steady but not growing, no doubt because since the 1992 election both Republicans and Democrats have focused their economic attention, virtually to the exclusion of other concerns, on how best to reduce the federal deficit—the issue with which Perot won one voter in five.

If systems of democratic government do not seem to be under serious challenge in major Western democracies today, the explanation lies not only in the major parties' preemption of extremist demands. At a deeper level, the strength of these countries' democratic political systems stems from the long tradition of political pluralism in Europe and North America, even if this tradition has not always prevailed without lapse. After the twentieth century's epic struggles with fascism and communism, perhaps these are regions where pluralist democracy can be expected to prevail in the twentieth-century. How confidently can the same be expected of other parts of the world?

Collapse of Communism: Advent of Democracy?

We have already seen in the concluding sections of Chapter 14 how inauspicious for the growth of the kind of democracy that Americans would recognize the 1990s have proved in the former Soviet bloc. In the former satellites, the growth of multiple parties reflecting differing ethnic and social groups threatens to produce a democracy of deadlock, and mass-oriented movements of the authoritarian Right have reappeared just as they did after World War I. In the Russian part of the former Soviet Union, three-quarters of a century of communist rule following centuries of tsarist absolutism have clearly taught many people a political passivity they may never unlearn. One-third did not vote in the crucial plebiscite of April 1993—not a high figure by contemporary U.S. standards but disappointing in a nation where democratic freedoms were so new.

Part of the explanation is undoubtedly to be found in the hardships of the attempted transition to a market economy, which have been so severe that polls now show that a third of Russian young people wish they could emigrate. This is not to deny that the new freedoms have opened a period of giddy enthusiasm for some Russians. Intellectuals have created thousands of new magazines, many turned out on copy machines once rare in the secretive Soviet Union. A class of young entrepreneurs whom Americans might call "yuppies" has emerged to wheel and deal in the high finance of the shift to private enterprise.

Yet thoughtful observers of the Russian scene have concluded that a majority of Russians regard the word *democracy* as being a synonym for *capitalism,* by which they understand a society in which people are exclusively out for themselves. Perhaps this was inevitable. Because communism had preached that the indivdual's only responsibility was to work for the good of all, its antidote could only be a spirit of unlimited individualism. Such a spirit, however, does not necessarily facilitate the development of the kind of institutions with which a pluralistic democracy best functions. Thus there are many factions maneuvering for advantage in Russian political life, but there are no recognizable parties in the Western sense, though democracy works best when voters make common cause with their representatives for a shared goal.

Many analysts of the Russian scene therefore wonder whether the country may not revert to some authoritarian form of the mass-oriented society. Such fears may be premature. Still governed by aging men who made their careers under communism, Russia is living through a period of transition. Only in the next century, when a younger generation that did not grow up with the command economy and the one-party state comes to power, shall we see whether Russia will join in a universal movement toward American-style representative democracy. In Russia as elsewhere, history is far from over.

The Outlook for Democracy in the Developing Countries

However much the collapse of communism may have raised the hopes of leaders in Western capitals, both modern history and prior tradition limit the prospects for pluralist democracy in most developing countries. Some exceptions have been noted in earlier chapters. We have noted Turkey's reorientation toward the West, and India's now shaky status as the world's largest democracy. We have also noted the general post-Cold War growth of interest in democracy and market economies, as well as some of the obstacles in its way: the deeply entrenched influence of Iberian absolutism and military elitism in Latin America, the ethnic particularism and militarization that beset African politics, and the tradition of centralized, authoritarian states in the major centers of Asian civilization.

Perhaps nowhere is the outlook more discouraging than in Africa. A 1983 survey of some fifty countries in or off the shores of Africa classified only seven as multiparty democracies, including two tiny island nations, Seychelles and Mauritius. More than thirty countries, in contrast, lived under some form of authoritarian rule. Thirteen of these gave token recognition to the principle of mass participation by permitting a single party. But an additional nineteen were under military or "despotic" rule.

A similar survey of Africa published in 1991 revealed that little had changed. In thirty-five countries, the population had little or no political voice. Eleven of these still lived under dictatorial or military rule, although twenty-four permitted a single political party to provide an appearance of legitimacy through rigged or token elections. Only three of the nations classified as multiparty democracies in 1983—Botswana, Senegal, and Zimbabwe—were similarly classified in 1991.[4]

Will such conditions always prevail? The end of the Cold War, which had enabled Third World dictators to deflect international censure by aligning themselves with one of the superpowers, has certainly brought pressures for change. In Africa, Western nations and Africans themselves have shown a new concern to

Democratization in Nigeria? *Before opening the polls, election officials show waiting voters that the ballot box is empty, Lagos, June 1993. The military government's refusal to accept the election results led to widespread disturbances.* *Agence Press France*

promote democracy. In a 1990 conference with leaders of its former colonies, France, provider of the most foreign aid to Africa, explicitly linked its aid to democratization. The Pan-African Conference on Democracy and Transition in Africa, held in Dakar in 1992, celebrated the advent of multiparty democracy in four countries, though more than forty had yet to begin that transition. To encourage movement toward multiparty rule, the conference established as two of its goals the creation of a communications network among all of Africa's political parties and the formation of an international observer group to monitor changes to majority rule. On a continent where Amnesty International had found human rights violations in all but two countries in 1990, the transition to democracy, if it occurs, will stretch far into the next century.

Obviously a critical question is how much desire for democracy actually exists in most developing countries. Attended by representatives of 160 countries and over two thousand nongovernmental organizations, the UN

Conference on Human Rights, held in Vienna in June 1993, yielded vivid insights into this issue. The conference touched off bitter controversy between "universalist" and "relativist" interpretations of rights issues. The universalist view is that human rights are the same everywhere—are "universal." Humanity must not be divided into blocs with unequal access to these rights. The "relativist" view is that the rights of the individual depend on his or her culture—are "relative" to the culture—and that attempting to prescribe a universal standard in human rights amounts to asserting moralistic domination of some cultures over others.

The universalist camp included the developed countries of North America and western Europe; women's groups, which presented petitions with 200,000 signatures from all over the world; and human rights activists from many developing countries, most of whom had suffered rights violations themselves. The relativist bloc, led by China, Indonesia, Malaysia, Myanmar, Pakistan, Iraq, Iran, and Syria, had asserted in its Bangkok Declaration of April 1993 that rights depend on regional, cultural, and religious factors. Integral to relativist thinking is the idea that a society has the right to defend the rights of the collectivity over those of the individual and that economic development takes primacy over human rights. Relativists further attacked the way affluent countries sought to condition development aid on democratization and rights reforms: was not development itself a human right? The relativists also accused countries like the United States of applying a double standard—for example, by forcing Iraq to withdraw from Kuwait while doing nothing to stop Serbian aggression against Bosnian Muslims. Universalists could retort that none of the relativists had shown how torture, assassination, or other rights abuses had actually benefited their countries either culturally or developmentally. Nor had relativist governments explained away the risks their own citizens took to organize and oppose them as rights activists.

If the fall of communism signified a victory for liberalism, both politically and economically, the North-South rights gap suggests that developing societies respond more readily to the new emphasis on the market economy than to that on democratization. Like the North-South development gap, the rights gap spotlighted at Vienna promises to remain an acute issue of the next century, with far-reaching implications for the future development of the mass society. Major gains in democratization and human rights are likely to come only slowly in the developing world.

Conclusion: Nature, Technology, and Mass Society in an Interdependent World

As the dawn of the twenty-first century approaches, thoughtful people around the world have a sense of limits quite different from the self-confidence that prevailed in the affluent societies of Europe and North America before 1914. The twentieth century has witnessed many of the greatest advances in human history, especially in science and technology, but it has also witnessed, especially in World War II, the greatest destruction that human communities have ever wrought on themselves or the world they live in. Partly because of advances in medical science, human populations have tripled, but this very fact has strained the natural environment and created risks of ecological collapse. During the first half of this century, a pattern of global integration that was highly inequitable to most of the world was destroyed. Another pattern, in which centers of wealth and power will at least be more numerous and dispersed, may now be emerging. Yet with few exceptions, the gap between wealthier and poorer societies, and even that among poorer societies, has widened.

As the twenty-first century dawns, the greatest challenge facing humankind will be to balance productivity, sustainability, and equity. Human societies' potential to create, to explore, to fulfill their higher potentials has always depended on how well they could provide their basic requirements for survival. However, the issues explored in Chapter 19—population growth, the increased demands it places on environment and resources, and the power of modern technology—have given this task new urgency. How well will humanity make the choices on which its future survival and welfare depends?

In the emerging world of multiple centers of power and wealth, this question has implications for all societies and cultures. Controversy will surely continue over demographic and ecological issues, as the 1992 UN Conference on Environment and Development (the Rio Conference) showed. It has been said, in fact, that as a flashpoint for political polarization, green issues have replaced the red threats of the Cold War years. Amid the controversy, some basic questions are likely to present themselves. Will the easy sacrifices that many people now willingly make for environmental reasons—things like setting aside used aluminum, glass, and paper for recycling—prove sufficient to preserve the earth for later generations? Or will harder choices have to be made and lower standards of living perhaps accepted? If so, what kinds of social and political conflict may result, and how will they be managed? Can scientists and engineers successfully direct the development of technology away from the military priorities of the recent past toward new goals that are not only consumer-oriented but also environmentally sound? For example, will the benign vista of a future solar-hydrogen energy economy relying on fuel cells materialize (see Chapter 19), or will genetic engineering produce breakthroughs to relieve world hunger, without producing unintended, harmful side effects analogous to those that destroyed optimism about nuclear energy?

Additional questions are likely to be raised—in some cases already are raised—from developing societies. In a world whose present polluted state is mostly to blame on the high consumption of its industrialized societies, why should developing countries invest scarce resources in pollution abatement or worry about individual rights as opposed to pushing for development by the shortest route? Why should Brazil, for example, refrain from cutting down its rain forest or worry about endangered species to please environmentalists in affluent countries? Did not North Americans long ago wreak analogous kinds of environmental havoc to develop their countries? Did not Europeans act similarly in the Middle Ages? Why, members of some such societies may also ask, should they adhere to the Nuclear Nonproliferation Treaty, rather than try to acquire nuclear and other weapons of mass destruction? Would a developing country's interests not gain more respectful attention if it could back them up with force, as great powers historically did?

The way men and women of the coming century respond to questions they all face will depend in part on the ideas and values that influence them as they think about those questions. Logically, to solve global problems, people will need a global outlook. However, the revivalist movements now stirring in many parts of the world as people of different societies struggle for cultural reintegration and reassertion show that globalist ideas and outlooks will be far from the only ones influencing public debate as the twenty-first century opens. This confrontation between global needs and the demands of specific cultures and traditions is likely to define the sharpest conflicts of the new century.

Presumably, humankind's success in solving its problems of productivity, sustainability, and equity will depend on its ability to rise above parochial interests, or at least to draw on the traditions of different societies as a source of diversity and alternate inspiration rather than conflict. Will sufficient numbers of men and women be able to recognize the interests and needs they all share? Will they find ways to narrow, rather than widen, the developmental gaps among the world's societies? Will they learn to join in nurturing a common sense of symbiosis with nature? If so, then the diversity of their cultural traditions can become a source of inspiration, rather than of the kind of conflict seen in Somalia or Yugoslavia in the 1990s. Like the biological diversity that ecologists try to defend against the ravages of deforestation and environmental degradation, this cultural diversity offers a range of resources that people need to conserve and learn to use wisely as the global community faces the challenges of the twenty-first century.

Notes

1. International Monetary Fund, *World Economic Outlook,* May 1993, p. 117, Table 33.
2. Paul Kennedy, *Preparing for the Twenty-first Century* (New York: Random House, 1993), p. 300.
3. Quoted in *The New York Times,* December 2, 1992.
4. Michael Kidron and Ronald Segal, *The New State of the World Atlas* (London: Heinemann, 1984), map 23; Michael Kidron and Ronald Segal, *The New State of the World Atlas,* 4th ed. (New York: Simon and Schuster, 1991), pp. 60–61.

Suggestions for Further Reading

Brzezinski, Zbigniew. *Out of Control: Global Turmoil on the Eve of the 21st Century* (1993).

Huntington, Samuel P. "The Clash of Civilizations?" *Foreign Affairs* (June 1993), pp. 22–49.

International Monetary Fund. *World Economic Outlook* (May 1993).

Kennedy, Paul. *Preparing for the Twenty-first Century* (1993).

Lukacs, John. *The End of the Twentieth Century and the End of the Modern Age* (1993).

Snow, Donald M. *The Shape of the Future: The Post–Cold War World* (1991).

World Bank. *World Development Reports* (1984–1993, published annually).

Index